Mass Media and Society

Edited by
Alan Wells
Central Michigan University

Lexington Books
D.C. Heath and Company/Lexington, Massachusetts/Toronto

For Rebecca Leigh Wells

Library of Congress Cataloging-in-Publication Data

Mass media and society.

Includes index.
Bibliography: p.
1. Mass media—Social aspects—United States.
2. Mass media—United States.   I. Wells, Alan,
1940–
HM258.M26578   1987   302.2'34   85-46050
ISBN 0-669-13010-9 (alk. paper)

Published simultaneously in Canada
Printed in the United States of America
Paperbound International Standard Book Number: 0-669-13010-9
Library of Congress Catalog Card Number: 85-46050

The paper used in this publication meets the minimum requirements of American National Standard for Information Sciences—Permanence of Paper for Printed Library Materials, ANSI Z39.48-1984. ∞™

87 88 89 90 91   8 7 6 5 4 3 2 1

Contents

Preface

Today's mass media are more pervasive than ever before, in the rich
countries of the world and in the poor. The transistor radio is common deep in Africa, Asia, and Latin America, and a radio or tape
player accompanies Western youth wherever they go. Communications satellites circle the globe, and more spectacular technologies are probably just
around the corner. The modern era is a media age.

The last few years have seen a growth of interest in how the media work,
how they affect our daily lives, and how the public might ensure the fulfillment of the media's staggering potential. In the United States, critics on both
the Left and the Right have expressed alarm over the growing political impact
of television and the press, the management of news, and the effects of the
media on our quality of life. Perhaps as never before, mass communication
is a public issue, one that demands the fullest understanding of the mass
media industries and their effect on society. In selecting material for *Mass
Media and Society*, I have kept this need for critical understanding in mind.

This book is designed to serve as a basic text for general liberal arts
courses in mass communications offered by social science, broadcasting, ra-
dio-TV-film, journalism, and communications departments in two- and four-
year colleges. As in the earlier editions, the emphasis is on factual or controversial issues rather than complicated technical articles. Because of the rapidly changing nature of the subject, only one reading has been retained from
the third edition. Some critics may find the book insufficiently scientific, but
most students and instructors, I believe, will prefer the new edition.

About half the material in this edition was written especially for this
book by a highly talented group of media scholars and teachers. The remaining articles were chosen from previously published works for their insight,
creativity, interest, and sometimes humor. Their work represents what I consider the best by academic, media, and freelance writers on the media.

In summary, the book is aimed at a nonspecialist but intelligent public,
which wants to understand the impact of the media on society. I hope that
the book is topical but not faddish; readable yet serious and important. Al-

though this book is not designed for advanced media students and researchers, it should offer them a convenient source of nontechnical work by media teachers and practitioners and suggest an approach to the study of mass media that takes into account the organizational structure of the media industries. Present or future communications insiders, creative artists, and public-service-oriented media personnel may find in this book much that is familiar, as well as much to trouble and inspire them.

The book begins with an overview of the mass media and the way in which they affect our lives, followed by a detailed examination of the media industries in the United States as complex organizations with their own inner dynamics and interests. Despite claims that freedom of thought, artistic values, and public service motives prevail, it is shown that the press, radio, the recording industry, television, and film are organized and consequently operated as private corporate businesses within the context of the U.S. economy as a whole. The media corporations are interlocked with each other and with other corporations. They are seldom autonomous and competing voices, nor is their primary concern the public interest.

The next topic is advertising and public relations: who runs it, how, and with what results. Advertising is a crucially important adjunct to American mass media. Because other sources of finance have not been firmly established, newspapers, magazines, radio, and television have had to rely almost entirely on advertising revenue. This inevitably means that those who desire to promote cultural and educational content must compromise their goals, for the primary task of these media is to sell goods to the public. If they fail, they cannot survive.

The later chapters deal specifically with the content and effects of the mass media. Chapter 8 examines the news content of the media. The authors offer differing views on the credibility of the news, evaluations of bias, and prescriptions for better reporting. Chapter 9 looks at the relationship between the media and politics and the law. The last two chapters are devoted to the issues of sex and violence in the media and the treatment of women and minorities.

No single collection of readings could do justice to the task of examining fully the relation between the mass media and society. The subject is too vast and complex. But these readings, augmented by additional material and references in the chapter introductions, should provide leads for continued study and a deeper understanding of the media. Perhaps the best sources to use to keep abreast of media developments are the numerous trade magazines and four journals: *Journalism Quarterly,* the *Columbia Journalism Review,* the *Washington Journalism Review,* and the *Journal of Communication.*

I hope that these selections, written by perceptive and creative women and men, will make readers more sensitive to the media that engulf us all. We must become, and remain, an informed and aroused public, for nothing less will make the media serve the public interest.

I would like to acknowledge the encouragement and guidance of my former colleague Thomas Ktsanes in the crucial formative stage of this book and the efforts of my students who helped gauge the value of this and much discarded material. William Rivers provided early encouragement and valuable criticism.

The fourth edition has benefited from the advice of reviewers of the second, third, and this edition. My thanks also to Mike Weber of St. Martin's Press and Bruce Katz of Lexington Books for their support of this project. Grace Maxbauer and my daughters, Erica, Danette, and Rebecca, have provided the love that any veteran of midlife crises knows is indispensable. Finally, I thank the other authors in this book for sending their promised articles to me on time or permitting me to reprint their previously published work. As a brief look at the contents will show, it is more their book than mine.

About the Editor

Alan Wells is professor of sociology at Central Michigan University. He holds M.A. and Ph.D. degrees in sociology from Washington University in Saint Louis. He has served on the faculties of Tulane University and the University of Rhode Island. His other edited books include *Mass Communications: A World View* and *Contemporary Sociological Theories*, and he is author of *Picture Tube Imperialism?* and numerous articles on sociology and mass media.

1
Mass Media: An Overview

Introduction

During the last two centuries, many changes have taken place in Western societies, changes that many social scientists claim have produced a qualitatively unique form of organization, often referred to as *mass society*. With the democratic revolutions in America and France at the end of the eighteenth century, men—and later men and women—came to be viewed increasingly as political equals. The Industrial Revolution of the nineteenth century completed the pulverization of the old aristocratic order in Europe and the nascent one in the United States. Although industrialization shattered the economic basis of the old middle class, advanced industry did not lead to a simple division of society into impoverished workers and rich owners as Karl Marx had predicted. Because industrial society required a wide range of skills, class divisions were no longer clearly discernible. A job could not provide concrete social identity, for one was no longer simply an aristocrat or a peasant, a capitalist or proletarian. The nation or the state became the primary source of self-identification. In this sense, society became more of a mass.

Industrialization also gave rise to the explosive growth of cities, and cheap transportation between them facilitated the establishment of national markets. Regional differences became less significant, and the new urbanites, with their standardized, mass-produced possessions and uniform environment, became more like their fellow citizens than ever before. Society is characterized by bigness, standardization, sheer concentration of numbers, and formal equality of individuals. The mass media are a product of this mass society, and they in turn produce a standard product for their audiences. It is often argued that the development of mass society leads to a homogenization of culture—the arts, values, and overall life-style of the population—which is in part due to the media's impact. Proponents of this view point out that the media constantly need material for their mass audiences. To fill pages and airwaves, they borrow and popularize work meant for more refined tastes.

(A record album entitled *Beethoven's Greatest Hits* comes readily to mind.) Artists themselves are tempted by the lucrative popular market, and artistic standards are undermined. The criteria of excellence becomes: "If it sells, it's good."

Of course, uniformity of culture is a matter of degree, since no audience is entirely homogeneous, and distinct social groups still exist. Ethnic groups, youth, and college-educated "highbrows," for example, often support their own specialized media.

Survey research carried out by Bradley Greenberg and Brenda Dervin indicates that we must modify our views on the pervasiveness of the general mass media.[1] It shows that the amount of media exposure, as well as the tastes of the poor, are in many ways more nearly homogeneous than those of the general population. The poor watch more television and choose the most popular programs, and they are less open to such specialized media as magazines and newspapers. Since the media habits of the black and white poor do not vary much, the pattern of varied taste and exposure has been attributed more to class characteristics, such as income levels and occupations, than to race. But throughout the classes, the long-run historical trend seems to be toward increasing cultural uniformity.

Herbert Schiller has examined the uses of the media in industrial societies.[2] Commercial "messages" and the increasing use of advertising skills in political management, he claims, make them a form of mind management. He skillfully ties in this theme with social and cultural changes taking place in the rich nations. Ben Bagdikian also warns of the dangers of the media system in the United States.[3] Growing concentration of ownership, along with the commercial nature, of the media may mean that real public debate of issues is being stifled.[4]

Today's mass media—radio and records, television, film, and the press—constitute an important part of the modern environment. This communications web, which has been aptly called the *noosphere*, serves as a background for many activities. Like the rest of our environment, we often take it for granted or, alternatively, blame it for all our ills. In this book, we attempt to avoid these extremes by taking the media seriously, without assuming that everything can be explained by their effects. This does not mean that we want to remain impartial, if impartiality means accepting the mass media as socially innocuous phenomena. Far from it. The readings in this book reflect the view that the operation of the media in the United States is far from satisfactory. Our purpose is to remain critical while avoiding blanket condemnations.

Modern mass media are contemporary phenomena and are still changing rapidly. In the West, people under the age of forty are fully attuned to television; their parents grew up with radio, and their surviving grandparents may still marvel at the novelty of the broadcast voice. In much of the rest of the world, this media revolution is being telescoped into a single generation, and the entire globe may be on the threshold of new media breakthroughs in the age of satellites and advanced electronics. For these reasons, the study of the media, and of their impact on society, must be continually updated.

The American public probably spends more time occupied with the mass media than with any other single activity, including gainful employment, which itself is often accompanied by the sounds of music. Even college students, when they accurately log their media exposure, average around six hours of media contact per day, more time than most spend in the classroom. Social psychologists tell us that experiences shape character, so the media must be an integral component in the development of the self. If we are to understand society and the individuals who comprise it, we must understand the part played by the media, a major although often neglected part of our environment.

In this chapter, we first examine the history of the media and future technologies. The following readings look at the communication process and media ethics, topics useful to take into account before studying specific media and issues.

The first reading, by Geoffrey Pace, gives a short history of mass media in the United States. He first traces the growth of the press from colonial times to the penny press, yellow journalism, and the increasing professionalism of today. Magazines have a parallel history in the early years. By the beginning of this century, though, the top magazines had national circulations. In the 1930s, the picture magazines, *Post, Look,* and *Life,* were very popular. Since the television age, however, magazines have aimed more at specialized interests. Books also aim primarily for limited rather than mass audiences.

Pace next surveys the nonprint media, first film and then the electronic media, radio and television. Radio interests developed the first networks and then dominated television.

Bruce Klopfenstein picks up from Pace in the next reading, which focuses on these new technologies and their potential impact. Although technologies do not revolutionize the media overnight, he argues, they are "part of the evolution of the media." He first explains digital and analog technology, a key to many probable changes. He then deals with radio, where AM stereo is a new component along with subsidiary communications authority (SCA) and satellite and cable FM service. Audio is changing rapidly with the digital compact disc. Television's changes include high definition television, multichannel sound, cable, direct broadcast satellites, television receive-only (TVRO) satellite antennas, and home video. New technologies are also making more accurate measurement of television audiences possible. The print media, in turn, may be changed by teletext, videotex, and the optical disk. All these technologies, however, will be adopted only if there is a need for the services and people are willing to pay for them.

The next reading takes a closer look at communications satellites. Jon Powell notes that global satellite communication is well established today and will likely continue to grow. He first discusses the physical dimensions of the technology, the difference between active and passive satellites, and types of transmission. He then describes the operational dimensions, the organizations that run this form of communication—ITU, Comsat, Intelsat, and others. Next he turns to social and sociopolitical perspectives and concludes with speculation about future trends. Although not without dangers, this new technology promises to bring the peoples of the world together.

In one of the classics of media studies, Wilbur Schramm outlines the basic chain of communication. Information held by the sender is coded; that is, an idea is put into words, print, or film. This message is then sent out as a signal. If it is received by an audience, it may be decoded and reinterpreted as an idea. Only then is the information received. A break can occur at every link in this chain: the intended meaning may not be conveyed in the coding process, the signal may be faulty and hence not received, the decoder may infer meanings other than those intended, and, finally, the message may be rejected by the receiver. Schramm outlines the conditions under which such breakdowns can be avoided. In mass communications, the sender is an organization, while the receivers are individuals. Unlike face-to-face communication, there is no real feedback enabling the receiver to become the sender, and the communicator has no immediate cues to indicate whether the message has been received as intended.

In Schramm's communication scheme, the sender must sift the information before coding a message. The sender selects from all the information available only those elements that he or she wants to convey. Newspaper and television news editors will probably rely on a wire service for their information. The content of the wire is a product of several editorial stages. Field reporters are selective in what they report; regional and national wire editors decide which incoming news items to pass on. Any person who serves this editing and condemning function may be called a *gatekeeper*. David M. White examined in detail the way one of these people, a newspaper wire editor, went about the task.[5] Decisions were highly subjective; that is, they reflected the editor's own values and prejudices rather than those of the audience or the intrinsic newsworthiness of the items selected. This subjectivity no doubt affects all gatekeepers to a degree.

At the other end of the communication chain, mass media messages often do not go directly to the target audience. Instead there is what has been termed a two-step flow of information. The message transmitted by the mass media is picked up by opinion leaders who pass it on to the mass population. This idea has generated considerable interest among communication researchers. Irving L. Allen, for example, has shown that knowledge of public affairs was greater for those in his sample who talked about the news than for those who silently absorbed it from the media.[6] Apparently interpersonal contacts reinforce mass-directed messages. Other researchers, however, set out to test the two-step flow hypothesis and were less convinced.[7]

People today may well be turning more and more to the media rather than to other individuals, not only for technical information but for general news of political and social issues as well. The media, then, appear to have a more direct effect on us than ever before.

In the last reading, Deni Elliott provides a general discussion of mass media ethics. While most journalists learn the prevailing ethical standards on the job, overall ethics come both from the larger culture and personal values, as well as the legal proscriptions on the media.[8] What are current professional ethical standards, and can they, or should they, be improved?

Notes

1. Bradley Greenberg and Brenda Dervin, "Mass Communication among the Urban Poor," *Public Opinion Quarterly* (Summer 1970): 224–235.

2. Herbert Schiller, "Mind Management: Mass Media in the Advanced Industrial State," *Quarterly Review of Economics and Business* (Spring 1971): 39–52.

3. Ben H. Bagdikian, "The U.S. Media: Supermarket or Assembly Line," *Journal of Communication* (Summer 1985): 97–109.

4. For a recent account of media mergers, see Karen Rothmyer, "Hot Properties: The Media," *Columbia Journalism Review* (November–December 1985): 38–43.

5. David M. White, "The 'Gate Keeper': A Case Study in the Selection of News," *Journalism Quarterly* (Fall 1950): 383–390. This classic study brought the term first coined by psychologist Kurt Lewin to the attention of media researchers. Several have researched the topic further. See, for example, Abraham Z. Bass, "Refining the 'Gate Keeper' Concept," *Journalism Quarterly* (Spring 1969): 69–72.

6. Irving L. Allen, "Social Relations and the Two-Step Flow: A Defense of the Tradition," *Journalism Quarterly* (Autumn 1969): 492–498.

7. See, for example, Verling C. Troldahl, "A Field Test of a Modified 'Two-Step Flow of Communication' Model," *Public Opinion Quarterly* (Winter 1966): 609–623; and Bradley S. Greenberg, "Person-Model, Communication in the Diffusion of News Events," *Journalism Quarterly* (Autumn 1964): 489–494. See also Charles R. Wright and Muriel Cantor, "The Opinion Seeker and Avoider: Steps beyond the 'Opinion Leader Concept,'" *Pacific Sociological Review* (Spring 1967): 33–43.

8. See also Fred F. Endres, "Influences on the Ethical Socialization of U.S. Newspaper Journalists," *Newspaper Research Journal* (Spring 1985): 47–56.

THE ORIGINS OF MASS MEDIA IN THE UNITED STATES

Geoffrey L. Pace

Geoffrey L. Pace has spent the major portion of his career in media and marketing. Since 1984, he has been teaching on the faculty of the broadcast division of the Communication Arts and Science Department of Western Illinois University. He obtained his BFA at Ohio University and his M.A. in mass communications at Brigham Young University, and he is pursuing a doctorate in journalism at Southern Illinois University.

Newspapers

Although printing was practiced in Mexico as early as 1539, it was not important in the British Colonies until the revolutionary era. The first newspaper, called *Publick Occurrences Both Foreign and Domestick,* lasted only one issue. Published in 1690, it was a response by the Colonists to what they perceived as mounting British interference in their affairs. In it, the printer attacked many important people, including Indians friendly to the British government and British notables (DeFleur and Dennis 1985, pp. 38–41). This was perhaps the first underground press in the country.

A few years later in 1704, John Campbell began publication of the *Boston News Letter.* Because he was a representative of the government, the paper was above ground and taxpayer supported. It was dull but safe reading. Fifteen years later, the *Boston Gazette,* a literary improvement, was produced by William Booker. Its printer was Benjamin Franklin's older brother, James. In 1721, James became publisher himself and put out a crusading newspaper, the *Courant.* It took on so many public issues that the older Franklin was jailed for his bumptiousness. Benjamin, using the pen name Silence Dogood, continued in the tradition of his brother. After a couple of years, he too fled Boston, settling in Philadelphia where he took over the *Pennsylvania Gazette* (DeFleur and Dennis 1985, p. 42).

The Colonial publications, while politically important in fomenting revolution, were sporadic and unavailable to the mass population. In the early years of the Republic, the press was more a partisan than a commercial venture. The first daily newspaper, the *Pennsylvania Evening Post and Advertiser,* founded in 1783, was thus designed for politically engaged readers. The introduction of the mass production steam press in the late 1820s produced the first true mass medium in the United States. It provided the average reader with access to a newspaper for a penny—hence the term *penny press.* Soon publishers were aiming at the less sophisticated part of the literate public.

In 1833, Benjamin Day began publishing the *New York Sun,* with "It Shines for All" emblazoned on the front page. Within a few years, more of its profits came from advertising than paid circulation. Its success bred competition—the *New York Herald,* begun by James Gordon Bennett in 1837. Both catered to the banal, the sensational, the common. But they also started to carry economic information and editorials as well as gossip (DeFleur and Dennis, 1985, p. 45).

The 1840s brought a tremendous improvement in the amassing and mobilization of news. Because of Samuel F. B. Morse's invention of the telegraph, information could be wired ahead hundreds, even thousands, of miles to newspapers. In the 1840s, the first wire press was formed. Associated Press was the carrier to many small papers that could not afford to have their own roving reporters. Photojournalism later also helped to expand the scope of journalism.

The popular press continued to expand. Joseph Pulitzer built a circulation of 300,000 for the Sunday edition of his *New York World* in the 1890s. His strengths were the combining of reporting with sensational photography. In addition, he introduced color comic strips. His street urchin cartoon character, dubbed the "Yellow Kid," was so popular that its creator was hired away by another famous newspaper magnate, William Randolph Hearst. In 1895, Hearst promoted yellow journalism when he bought the failing *New York Journal* and proceeded to intensify the battle for the public's reading interests (Tebbel 1952, pp. 120–121).

Yellow journalism was known for its concentration on prurient appeals to human nature such as crime, sex, torture, and extortion. The peak (or ebb, depending on one's journalistic viewpoint) of this particular style of writing came in 1898 when the United States got into a short-lived war with Spain over Cuba. The battleship U.S. *Maine* was in the harbor off the port of Cuba when there was an explosion in its hull. Hearst immediately assumed sabotage and offered a large reward for information leading to the culprits, whom he assumed were foreign. There is also evidence indicating that Hearst initiated international military action. He is said to have sent illustrator Frederick Remington to Cuba to monitor the fight that was breaking out. Remington was reported to have sent this cable: "W. R. Hearst, Journal, New York. Everything is quiet. There is no trouble here. There will be no war. Wish to return. Remington." Hearst immediately replied: "Remington, Havana. Please remain. You furnish the pictures and I'll furnish the war. Hearst." (Bessie 1938, pp. 59–60).

The accuracy of these particular statements notwithstanding, it would appear that this era of mass journalism was digging its own grave; the leaders of mass conscience were demanding reform. Clergymen and political leaders were having an obvious influence. Near the end of the nineteenth century, Adolph Ochs took over the failing *New York Times*, determined to right the past wrongs of yellow journalism by printing objective news. Articles on speeches, treatises, and government documents abounded in the *Times*. At last, newspapering had become a respectable profession, no longer a toy at the hands of the whimsical magnates.

Having learned hard lessons from an excessive and rather abusive journalistic past, the American Society of Newspaper Editors in 1923 adopted the Canons of Journalism, stressing the importance of social responsibility and fairness (Emery 1950, p. 245). Nevertheless, yellow journalism was not dead; it came back as *jazz journalism*, a style of writing copied from the London tabloid format, which used much bold print for headline emphasis (Bessie 1938). The *New York Daily News* has long used this format, and it is followed by such tabloids as the *National Enquirer* today.

By the 1960s, newspapers were fighting for survival, as mergers and bankruptcies became common occurrences. Today's newspapers are primarily group-owned and local monopolies. In the late 1960s and early 1970s, a radical so-called underground press flourished in major U.S. cities. Some of the most prominent publications were the *Los Angeles Free Press*, the *Berkeley Barb*, and the *Village Voice*. A newspaper-magazine, the *Rolling Stone*, survives today, but is now considered legitimate press. It is the only one extant of the original radical press. One of the few new developments in the press was the birth of *USA Today* in 1983. It is the first satellite-relayed newspaper and might become the basis for a truly national press (Whetmore, 1985, p. 37).

Magazines

Although the first magazines appeared very early—the *American Magazine* by Andrew Bradford and Benjamin Franklin's *General Magazine and Historical Chronicle* appeared in 1741—it was not until the last half of the nineteenth century that magazines began to stabilize. Most magazines were monthlies targeted for local audiences, much like newspapers and they came and went. Magazines like *McClure's* explored serious public issues, and the authors went out for blood. These *muckrakers*, as they were soon called, exposed crime, corruption, and mismanagement in both business and politics. Muckraking continues today, though it is not confined to magazines.

During the depression era, picture magazines such as the *Post, Look,* and *Life* captured the nation's fancy. These magazines also published short stories by famous novelists like Hemingway and Fitzgerald. Concurrently, news magazines entered the scene, with *Time* leading the way and showing a profit within a year after its birth. By World War II, mass appeal magazines were booming, among them *Collier's, Cosmopolitan,* and *McCall's.* Price wars broke out, but nothing could save the picture magazines from the competition of the television boom: when their advertising revenues declined, they went out of business.

With the growth of television, magazines began to diversify to attract segmented audiences: special interest appeal became the order of the day. For example, *Mad* magazine started as a comic book in 1952. Taking an irreverent look at society, it quickly gained a teenage audience. A year later, Hugh Hefner founded *Playboy* magazine, which responded to loosening social-sexual mores. In 1954, Time Incorporated brought out *Sports Illustrated.* The boom was on for magazines aimed at segmented, or demassified, audiences. A women's rights publication, *Ms.,* became an overnight success in 1972; today, almost every special interest has at least one magazine aimed at it.

Film

The "movies" started out as side show attractions in nineteenth-century carnivals through the use of a zoetrope. This device, called a "wheel of life," was a cylinder mounted on a vertical spindle that produced a natural movement such as a man walking or a horse jumping (DeFleur and Dennis 1985, p. 157). The viewer peered through the slits of the spindle as it spun in order to see the motion.

Initially in the movie business, actors were paid by the footage and not by the content. In the back of warehouses in the 1890s, people watched moving figurines flicker along a bed sheet. By 1896, Thomas Edison was showing these pictures to a more sophisticated public in New York City. And by the early twentieth century, films up to a half-hour in length were being made. The first successes were *A Trip to the Moon* (1902), a whimsical adaptation of an H.G. Wells's science fiction novel; a documentary, *Life of an American Fireman* (1903); and *The Great Train Robbery,* the first Western.

By World War I, 40 million people were going to the movies. Because of the war, Europe fell behind in the industrialization and capitalization of the movie era, and Hollywood became the byword for the new art of cinema. The price of admission had been a nickel at the early nickelodeons, and thus it was the cheapest form of diversion and all-around entertainment. After the war, the United States looked forward to a long period of industrial expansion, one that included movies. New subject matter was introduced into the movies, such as love scenes. America searched for idols and found them in such leading actors and actresses as Rudolph Valentino, Mary Pickford, and Dorothy and Lillian Gish.

The next development was sound. In the 1927–1928 season, Warner Brothers produced the *Jazz Singer,* which offered dialogue and songs to test the audience on its effectiveness and to see if American audiences were ready for the change. The *Jazz Singer* was a hit. Overnight, many stars with other than dramatic voices to match their silver screen images found themselves jobless. Now people could hear as well as see the sounds of love and violence. In 1930, the Motion Picture Producers and Distributors Association adopted the first cinematic censoring code.

During the depression, movies suffered a setback as impoverished audiences stayed home to listen to the radio. And after World War II, television took on and won over the cinematic audience. The movies fought back with gimmicks—3-D movies, "smell-o-vision," Sensurround, and Dolby stereophonic sound—to try to win back audiences.

The mass-audience or family movies that were the most common product through to the 1950s were replaced by films targeted at specific audiences, particularly youth. With the widespread use of cable and home video in the eighties, movie producers have developed important secondary markets for their films. High budget movies like *E.T. The Extra-terrestrial* and the *Star Wars* series co-exist with low budget films ranging from art to comedy to pornography. Together with re-releases of old movies, they fill the growing demand for entertainment.

To warn potential viewers of the contents of movies, the Motion Picture Association of America (MPAA) established a new rating system in 1968. "G" films are meant for all ages; "PG" suggest parental guidance and are primarily for mature audiences; "PG-13" indicates parents are strongly cautioned to give special attention and guidance for children under thirteen; for "R" rated films, those under seventeen must be accompanied by parent or adult; and an "X" rating bars admission to children under seventeen. In reality, a movie is seldom made for a "G" audience unless it is a cartoon show for children, "PG" and "PG-13" is reserved for the teenaged crowd, "R" usually indicates high levels of graphic violence, and an "X" rating usually denotes explicit sexual content.

Broadcasting

Broadcasting was not born with radio, nor was radio born with wireless. The three terms are not really synonymous. *Broadcasting* is defined as the coming of age of wireless radio into the mass media. The common element was the so-called ether waves believed to have carried radio energy through the atmosphere. In the 1860s, Scottish-born physicist James Clerk Maxwell predicted the existence of these radio waves, and in 1886 Heinrich Rudolph

Hertz demonstrated them. By 1895, Guglielmo Marconi, an Italian engineer, was conducting trans-Atlantic wireless radio wave tests. The key discovery in these pursuits was that the "wired telegraph" invention of Samuel Morse forty years before was not necessary to produce and receive electrical energy. Wireless telegraphy was born.

This new industrial revolution into the world of communications created some of the biggest conglomerates that the United States has today, including the formation of the Bell system by Alexander Graham Bell. Soon after Bell showed his telephone in 1876, the Bell Telephone Company changed its name to American Telephone and Telegraph (AT&T). A year later, Thomas Edison formed the Edison Electric Light Company, known today as General Electric. GE was charged with wireless research until after World War I. In 1886, George Westinghouse started what is today known as the Westinghouse Electric and Manufacturing Company. Marconi went to England to patent his invention since Italy would not acknowledge it. He eventually had two Marconi firms: British Marconi and American Marconi.

When World War I broke out, civilian development of the new technologies was halted. After the war, there was much debate as to whether to give the power of radio transmissions to civilians or to have it remain a government monopoly. With the go-ahead for civilian maintenance of this new communications field, Owen D. Young started the Radio Corporation of America (RCA). Now there were two definite groups in the telecommunications industry: the specialized telephone group of AT&T and Western Electric, and the radio group. This duopoly enjoyed unprecedented wealth and power until the advent of television (Smith 1985, pp. 14–15).

Development of Radio

In 1920, a technician from Westinghouse who was also an amateur radio enthusiast, Frank Conrad, became the first acknowledged disc jockey, playing selected records from a Pittsburgh music store. Conrad's boss decided to capitalize on this situation, suggesting to Conrad to keep on with this radio show and he would figure out how to make economical receivers for everyone who wanted to listen. On November 2, 1920, Conrad's venture became the first broadcast station, KDKA Pittsburgh.

What made Conrad's transmission not merely wireless radio but broadcasting is the fact that he had an intended audience. What he had started snowballed. In 1920, the Department of Commerce issued 30 licenses for broadcast use. Within two years, there were 430 more (Smith 1985, p. 19). The means for supporting stations came in various forms. Some people donated money, time, or services. There was discussion of taxing individuals with receivers. In 1922, station WEAF in New York City set aside time for anyone who wanted to and could afford it to come into their studios and use it for programming. This was known as toll broadcasting (Barnouw 1966, pp. 105–106). The first such broadcast came in the form of a ten-minute talk, or commercial, that extolled the virtues of establishing residence at the Queensboro Corporation's Hawthorne Court. Soon sponsored programming flourished, this time with no commercial interruptions.

Although AT&T formed the first network of stations in 1923 when it ran a line between New York City and South Dartmouth, Massachusetts, the first permanent setup was started by David Sarnoff, who in 1926 wrote to his company chiefs advising them of the profit to be made in setting up a radio network. On November 15, 1926, the National Broadcasting Company was formed. And in 1927, William S. Paley, a young public relations man from a cigar company, formed what we know today as CBS.

Until this time, 90 percent of the homes in the United States had no radio sets. Reception was irregular, and the airwaves were being misused with inadvertent jamming and feedback from other stations crowding onto them. In 1927, the federal government developed the first legislation to regulate the airwaves, the Radio Act of 1927. Seven years later, it was expanded to encompass all wired and wireless communications in the form of the Communications Act of 1934, which gave birth to the Federal Communications Commission (FCC) (Barnouw 1966, pp. 31–32, 171).

The field of radio siphoned off most of the talent from vaudeville. Big city stars came from the nightclub and traveling stage circuits to appear on radio in half-hour programs of comedy, adventure, crime, and suspense, with a daily dose of soap operas (so named for their sponsorship by soap manufacturers). When "Fibber McGee and Molly" came on, or when "Amos 'n' Andy" entered living rooms with their special brand of comedy, America stopped to listen.

The golden age of radio began in the 1930s and continued through World War II. Radio provided mystery, comedy, live plays, on-the-spot reports, and many other forms of expression. The radio audience was becoming more sophisticated and increasingly aware of current events. The networks responded with regular newscasts, which infuriated many newspaper publishers, who felt this was their exclusive domain. Even in the year of the Wall Street crash, advertisers sought radio in preference to the press. Newspapers believed radio was a news pirate and thus the cause of their eroding financial base. The last straw was when press copy was read over the air. In April 1931, the Associated Press met in New York to declare war on this practice. But after a couple of years of debating on why and how to curb news on radio, the plan fell apart; many newspaper publishers had bought into radio stations themselves (Emery 1950, p. 196).

Radio carried the sounds of impending war during the 1930s. News commentators H. V. Kaltenborn, Gabriel Heatter, and Lowell Thomas monitored the aligning of the growing Axis powers in Europe. CBS foreign correspondent Edward R. Murrow broadcast in person from Europe events of the Nazi expansion in 1937–1938 (Smith 1985, p. 51).

Although radio was a hero during the war years, all was not well. In 1941, the FCC claimed that the networks were too powerful and dictatorial to their affiliates. It found an undue monopoly within NBC in particular, and a direct result was the selling of a segment of that network. Until 1943, NBC had two national networks and a regional West Coast network. It caved in to FCC pressure and sold off one part. This new network became the American Broadcasting Company (ABC) in 1946 (Barnouw 1982, p. 95).

It was also in the 1940s that radio's supreme reign over the air ended. By 1948, it (and movies) had been eclipsed by an emerging extension of them both, television.

Introduction of Television

David Sarnoff, the radio prophet, also saw the "art of distant seeing" on the horizon. Others before him also had envisioned the projection of images over a great distance. In 1884, German scientist Paul Nipkow devised the Nipkow disk, which scanned movement and was later experimented with in the Bell laboratories (Barnouw 1985, pp. 5–6). But it was a boy from a large Idaho Mormon family who gave television its start. In 1922 Philo T. Farnsworth baffled his high school teacher as he gave the world a preview of the first electronic television camera illustrated on a chalkboard (Smith 1985, p. 30). Running neck and neck with another television experimenter from Russia, Philo received his patent in 1930 (Barnouw 1982, p. 78). Vladimir Zworykin was busily working on his version with RCA. It was Zworykin who gave the world its first look at the electronic world of television at the opening of the 1939 World's Fair in New York.

World War II cut short the development of television until 1946, when television started with six stations on the air (Broadcasting Yearbook 1984, H-55). In fact, so many stations were fighting for air space that the FCC put a freeze on all new applications for an indefinite period. They thought the freeze would last no longer than a few months, but it was 1952 before the freeze was thawed. In the meantime, the stations that were on the air concentrated on programming that was making them and the networks rich. Comedy was popular, Milton Berle on the "Texaco Star Theater" and Sid Caesar on "Your Show of Shows." Variety performances that survived the circus and vaudeville were featured on Ed Sullivan's "Toast of the Town," later dubbed "The Ed Sullivan Show." Live dramatic performances brought new stars to the world of theater. The children were not forgotten, with shows like "Kukla, Fran, and Ollie" and "Howdy Doody."

The 1950s were marked by attempts to purge the media of alleged communistic influences. This began on television before Senator Joseph P. McCarthy brought his crusade before the public. Ed Sullivan put on his show a person who purportedly had red connections, and the furor began. An ultra-right-wing political group developed a list of people with alleged communist connections, including orchestra leader Leonard Bernstein, actor Burl Ives, and FCC commissioner Clifford Durr (Barnouw 1982, p. 122). The downfall of the overzealous senator came when Edward R. Murrow invited him as a guest on his news information program, "See It Now," in March 1954. McCarthy delivered a tirade that the most rudimentary intelligence could see through. After hearings on his attack on the Army, he was eventually censured by the Senate (Barnouw 1982, pp. 179, 182).

In the closing years of the 1950s, television was rocked by a quiz show scandal. Quiz contestants, it was revealed, had been prompted to give right or wrong answers depending on the ratings the public gave them in popularity. They were richly rewarded for playing their parts. Stemming from the basic radio formats of the 1940s, shows like the "64,000 Dollar Question" started out innocently. Within a year, rigged imitations were on the air. When the main star of this era of programming came forth and confessed, the public was quickly weaned from prime-time big quiz shows, and congressional investigations consequently shut them down. It was not until the mid-1980s with the syndicated "Wheel of Fortune," that the game show could be said to have recovered.

In the ensuing years of the Kennedy administration, television broadcasting grew immensely in size, scope, and wealth. Incoming FCC chairman Newton Minow chastised the media, calling the television industry a "vast wasteland" whose banal programming filled the airwaves with mediocrity. A year later, in 1962, the United States and Europe saw the first televised satellite transmission when Telstar swung by the continents many thousands of miles above earth. Camera crews on both sides of the Atlantic beamed transmissions aboard the satellite, which it in turn relayed to the other side of the ocean before millions of viewers. (Barnouw, p. 309). The following year, the television public saw its first presidential assassination.

Each year after that during the 1960s, stunning new visuals were presented to TV audiences. By 1967 all three networks were broadcasting in color. Television provided coverage of the civil rights movements in Alabama, the bombing of black churches, and the uprising in black urban ghettoes. The Vietnam War escalated in the mid-1960s, becoming a major war between 1968 and 1970. All this was covered live and in color on the evening news. Television was on the scene as the U.S. embassy fell in 1975. Television also witnessed the public disgrace of a once-popular president, Richard Nixon; the Watergate hearings went on day after day, with television monitoring it all. The war, the assassinations, the resignations: all were monitored by television, which to many had become not only the most powerful medium, but a power itself in shaping public opinion and political events.

References

Barnouw, Erik. 1966. *A History of Broadcasting in the United States.* Vol. 1: To 1933. New York: Oxford University Press.

———. 1982. *Tube of Plenty: The Evolution of American Television.* Rev. ed. New York: Oxford University Press.

Bessie, Simon Michael. 1938. *Jazz Journalism: The Story of the Tabloid Newspapers.* New York: E. P. Dutton.

Broadcasting Yearbook. 1984. Washington, D.C.: Broadcast Publications.

DeFleur, Melvin L., and Everette E. Dennis. 1985. *Understanding Mass Communication.* Boston: Houghton Mifflin.

Emery, Edwin. 1950. *History of American Newspaper Publisher's Association.* Minneapolis: University of Minnesota Press.

The First 50 Years of Broadcasting: The Running Story of the Fifth Estate. Washington, D.C.: Broadcast Publications, Inc., 1981.

Smith, F. Leslie. 1985. *Perspectives on Radio and Television: Telecommunication in the United States.* 2d ed. New York: Harper & Row.

Tebbel, John. 1952. *The Life and Good Times of William Randolph Hearst.* New York: E. P. Dutton.

Whetmore, Edward Jay. 1985. *MediAmerica: Form, Content, and Consequence of Mass Communication.* 3d ed. Belmont, Calif.: Wadsworth.

NEW TECHNOLOGY AND THE FUTURE OF THE MEDIA

Bruce Klopfenstein

Bruce Klopfenstein earned a B.A.C. degree from Bowling Green State University and an M.A. and Ph.D. from the Ohio State University. He now teaches in the Radio-Television-Film Department of Bowling Green State. His main research interests are on the effects of new media technologies. He is currently studying aspects of home video ownership.

The mass media are by definition products of technology. Their history is littered with technological developments, each of which had its impact on the state of the media at any given time. The first mass circulation newspapers were made possible through breakthroughs in printing press technology. Radio broadcasting developed within the engineering schools of a number of American universities. Clearly any discussion of the future of the mass media must take contemporary technologies into account. At the same time, technology only opens up new paths for the media to take; the direction of those paths is not predetermined.

If you were to return to about 1982, the world of mass media seemed on the brink of a revolution. A veritable alphabet soup of new technologies (CATV, DBS, LPTV, SMATV, VDP) seemed poised to disrupt existing media systems. Newspaper publishers fretted about electronic videotex news services, which seemed to threaten their very existence. Broadcasters, cable operators, and movie studios pondered the future of their businesses in the light of new home video technology. But history is teaching that media institutions are not revolutionized overnight by new technologies. Rather, new technologies are part of the evolution of the media. This reading provides an overview of the technologies shaping the direction of the mass media in the future.

Digital Technology

Digital technology, the basis of several new media technologies, is a direct result of computer technology. Computers work with information in its simplest form, digital bits (literally 1s and 0s). The letter A, for example, can be represented to a computer by the eight bits 10000011. Letters, numbers, pictures, and sound may also be represented as digits that computers can use.

Content of media is also information, and it follows that media content (whether text, audio, or moving pictures) can also be represented by digits. Digital technology as it relates to media refers to the ability to record, store, and transmit information—text, video, or audio—in computer-readable (digital) form. Once in digital form, computer technology may also be used to manipulate the information.

Digital technology is beginning to replace established *analog technology*. Analog technology, as its name implies, records, stores, and transmits imperfect copies of the original source of information (text, video, or audio). If copies are made of the copies, quality diminishes (for example, a photocopied document is not as clear as the original). Digital technology allows perfect copies because they are made from digits.

A simple example will clarify the difference. Making an analog recording is like trying to trace a picture on a sheet of paper. Digital recording is like trying to copy a series of digits. Tracing does not allow for the production of an exact copy, but the replication of a series of digits does, especially when a computer is assigned the task.

Digital technology, therefore, has two general implications for media. First, it is the means by which media content is represented for use with computer and related technologies. Second, it provides a virtually perfect means for recording, storing, and transmitting media content. Thus it is easy to understand why digital technology is taking over from analog technology.

New Technology and the Broadcast Media

Twenty years ago, in the mid-1960s, broadcast technology meant radio and television, with cable television beginning to make its mark in rural areas. Although radio and television continue to be the dominant advertiser-supported electronic media, home video (videocassette recorders), cable, and, to a lesser extent, satellite television have also made their mark as broadcast-related technologies. Each technology is having its effect on the traditional broadcast industry. Home video may turn out to have the most important impacts on television, and it is discussed in a separate section.

Before discussing the broadcast technologies, it is important to understand a little about broadcast spectrum space. Larger chunks of spectrum are required to send larger amounts of information. The broadcast spectrum is divided into units called *kilohertz*. AM radio channels are only 10 kilohertz wide. FM radio channels are 200 kilohertz wide, which is one reason why FM sounds better than AM; more audio information (like two stereo channels) can be broadcast on an FM station than on an AM. Television pictures are made up of much more information than audio, so television channels are 6,000 kilohertz (or 6 megahertz) wide. FM and television stations actually have more channel space than they need, and this opens the door for new services.

Radio

The impact of new technology on radio has been less dramatic than that in television. FM quadraphonic, a major technological innovation involving the broadcast of four channels of audio, failed to get far off the ground in the early 1970s. The last dramatic change in radio came about after the FCC authorized FM stereophonic broadcasting in 1961. Still, the impact of FM stereo was not felt for more than ten years. Since the mid-1970s, however, the combination of FM stereo and FM's inherently cleaner sound have led music audiences (especially younger listeners) to migrate from AM to FM radio. Technological developments to improve the sound of radio continue, however.

AM Stereo. AM radio is trying to win audiences back with stereo technology. Five incompatible AM stereo systems were proposed to the Federal Communications Commission (FCC) in the early 1980s. Instead of selecting one as the industry standard, the deregulatory FCC decided instead to let the radio marketplace work to choose a standard. This strategy, unfortunately, proved to be anything but a catalyst for the struggling AM stereo business, although three of the five systems were weeded out. Motorola's C-Quam system was beginning to look like the industry standard by mid-1986, with over 300 radio stations using it. The only remaining competitor was Leonard

Kahn's stereo system, which was being used by 85 stations, many of those being in larger markets. The battle may become less important to listeners as manufacturers introduce receivers capable of tuning in both systems (*Broadcasting* 1986a).

Some AM broadcasters are hoping that AM stereo will give AM a new lease on life. But although AM stereo is a considerable improvement over traditional AM radio, the fidelity or quality of the sound cannot match that of FM because of AM's smaller channels. The FCC and the AM radio industry are working on other technical ways to improve the quality of AM audio (*Broadcasting* 1986b).

More important to the future of AM radio will be the ability of its programmers to deliver attractive programming to audiences—whether news and talk formats, nostalgic music formats, or innovative new formats. AM stations like WJR in Detroit, WBZ in Boston, and WGN in Chicago continue to attract the largest audiences in their markets with quality programming. The added competition for AM listeners may pose even more difficulties for AM broadcasters. Plans exist to expand the top of the AM band from 1,605 kilohertz (khz) to 1,705 khz as early as 1988, adding as many as 500 new radio stations by 1990 (*Broadcasting* 1986c).

FM. The state of FM radio is much more stable than that of AM. As is the case with AM, however, more FM radio stations may be added before 1990. The FCC is allowing the insertion of eighty new FM channels on the existing FM radio band. This could eventually result in more than 1,000 new commercial FM stations. The FCC began its initial processing of applications for the new channels in late 1985 (*Broadcasting* 1986d, p. 32).

Of all the media, FM's future appears likely to continue to be the most stable. FM can look forward to continuous improvements in sound quality beyond the engineer's ongoing effort to perfect FM transmission. Digital technology has affected radio, and especially FM radio, in the last few years (Gross 1986). Digital audio includes both compact discs and digital audio recording. Digital technology in radio represents the continued progression of sound quality. Although this is good news to music lovers, digital audio is not expected to alter the radio broadcasting business to the extent, for example, that new technologies are changing television.

SCA. Just as stereo broadcasting is made possible by dividing (*multiplexing*) an FM channel into two parts (a left and a right channel), subsidiary communications authority (SCA) further divides the channel for additional specialized broadcast services. A special receiver is needed to pick up SCA services. SCA transmissions are used to broadcast background music services like Muzak to businesses. Medical and legal groups use SCA service to deliver seminars to members of their respective professions. Radio reading services for the blind transmit spoken versions of newspapers, books, and magazines via SCA. Some radio stations lease their SCA channels to users such as financial brokers who broadcast stock prices to area offices. Other subsidiary services that may be broadcast on FM include radio paging services, facsimile (still frame pictures), and even slow scan-video pictures (Whitehouse 1986).

Cable FM. Cable television has the ability to deliver not only video services to the home but FM stereo services as well by connecting a separate cable to a home stereo's FM antenna input. Cable FM (CAFM) services may be distant FM radio stations that have come to be called "superstations," like classical WFMT-FM of Chicago and jazz KKGO-FM of Los Angeles; satellite delivered or taped audio services with no commercials; the stereo soundtracks of cable movie services like HBO; national weather service radio; a locally originated cable-only radio station; or even AM stereo radio stations rebroadcast on CAFM. The leading cable audio services are listed in table 1. Partially due to a lack of marketing effort on the part of cable system operators, CAFM has not received much attention to date and has grown slowly. A cable system usually charges subscribers an additional fee for CAFM.

Satellite Radio. Just as CAFM may receive satellite-delivered audio services, radio stations are getting programming via satellite. Although syndicated weekly programs have been distributed to stations on tape or disc for years, satellite technology allows the live transmission of programming. The most dramatic impact of satellite transmission on radio has been the delivery of entire radio formats twenty-four hours a day. Transtar and Satellite Music Network (SMN), the two most successful satellite radio networks, had 600 and 700 affiliates, respectively, as of mid-1986, which represents one in eight

Table 1
Leading Cable Audio Services

System	Cable Systems	Subscribers
Cable Radio Network	14	1,100,000
KKGO Los Angeles Jazz Radio	15	930,000
Lifestyle/Lifestyle AC	147	2,600,000
Moody Broadcasting Network	65	820,000
Satellite Radio Network	251	740,000
Tempo Sound	80	1,100,000
WFMT	153	1,100,000

Source: *Multichannel News,* June 16, 1986, p. 33

commercial radio stations. SMN began operating in late 1981, and Transtar in early 1982. If these services maintain their growth, soon one in four radio stations may be broadcasting satellite-delivered radio formats.

Each company has several different popular music formats. SMN charges $1,000 per month for its formats, and Transtar charges according to market size (*Broadcasting* 1986e). The affiliated local station has an option of carrying programming all day from the network or using the network only for limited periods such as overnight and/or on weekends. Interestingly, the growth of satellite-delivered national radio programming suggests that radio has come full circle, losing its current local, decentralized character, and returning to the days of network radio.

Audio

Not since CBS's 33 rpm LP ("long playing") and RCA's 45 rpm record replaced the old 78s has the audio industry seen anything like the revolution being brought about by digital technology. The compact disc (CD) player is beginning to replace the turntable. By the end of 1986, about 4 million American homes had CD players.

The CD has two key advantages over the LP: 1) superior sound reproduction and 2) durability. Digital recording of music for CDs allows virtually perfect sound reproductions (some early listeners even felt the reproduction of the high end was too perfect). CD technology is simply mass data storage. In the case of CD audio, the data are music represented digitally. The CD player reads the digitally encoded music much the same as a computer disk drive reads data from a floppy disk. The difference is in the amount of information stored on a CD. It takes plenty of storage for digital audio; a floppy disk can store only three seconds of high-quality audio, but a CD can store up to an hour (Gates 1986, p. xi).

Sony introduced a CD player for the car in 1984 and a portable CD player early in 1985. CD "boom boxes" with radio receivers followed soon afterward, as have CDs with disc changers (Zuckerman 1986). Not to be outdone, recording tape advocates point to digital audiotape, which gives CD-quality sound along with the ability to record. There is no need to discard current phonograph collections, however. Because so many people already own LPs, the market for turntables will probably continue. But as the prices of CD players and turntables converge, and CD recordings multiply, perhaps more consumers will convert to the new technology. Interestingly, the success of the audio CD may play a role in the success of the laser videodisc. Pioneer has introduced the CLD-900 player, which is capable of playing both compact discs and videodiscs (Kaplan 1985).

Television

The impact of new technology on the world of video is no less striking than that in audio. The technologies that will lead television into the 1990s are here today. Chief among them are high definition television, multichannel television sound, and new receiver technologies such as miniature and digital television sets.

High Definition Television. You may be surprised to learn that the resolution of American television is the poorest in the world. The U.S. National Television Systems Committee (NTSC) standard uses 525 horizontal scan lines per frame with 30 frames per second. (The Europeans use 625 horizontal lines. More lines mean a higher resolution or sharper picture.) Because 41 NTSC lines are used for control and synchronization, theoretically 484 lines remain for picture transmission. Due to a number of limiting factors, however, the highest-quality home receivers display only 300 lines, with inexpensive or poorly adjusted sets displaying only 175 lines (Saffady 1985).

A new technology being pushed by Japanese interests and CBS in the United States is high definition television (HDTV). HDTV uses 1,125 scan lines per image and widens the picture from a three-by-four to a three-by-five image. The number of video frames per second is also increased from thirty to sixty frames per second. Not only does this dramatically improve the video picture resolution, but HDTV allows the display of text and graphics material currently limited to high resolution monitors like those used with personal computers (Nadan 1985). Stereo sound is also part of the HDTV standards.

HDTV is not compatible with the existing NTSC system. It transmits more picture information than NTSC, so one HDTV channel requires the same spectrum space as five conventional channels. Another factor that has slowed the move into HDTV is the reluctance of European manufacturers (which are developing their own system) to accept the Japanese—CBS system. Consequently, HDTV standards are not expected to be adopted internationally until 1990 (*Broadcasting* 1986d).

CBS has proposed to use satellites to distribute HDTV programming. This could mean distribution of HDTV programming directly to the home. Another possibility is distributing satellite feeds to movie theaters where audiences would watch a large HDTV projection screen. The adoption of HDTV technology by Hollywood would mean that films could take advantage of the ease and lower cost of videotape editing.

Multichannel Television Sound. The FCC authorized television stations to transmit multichannel television sound (MTS) in 1984. MTS allows stations to broadcast programs in stereo as well as other secondary audience program (SAP) subcarrier services similar to radio SCA. Indeed, television stations can now provide many of the same services as radio SCAs and more of them.

Just as an FM channel is wider than an AM channel, the audio portion of a television channel is two and a half times wider than FM radio's—but television audio has used less space than FM stereo stations do, leaving the extra channel space unused. Even after additional space is used to broadcast the two channels needed for stereo, plenty of room is left over for SAP services. One key SAP service may be a second language track. With the growing Hispanic population in various areas of the United States, for example, MTS can be useful for stations to cast programming in English and Spanish simultaneously.

Television stations are quickly making the transition to stereo broadcasting, and television set manufacturers like RCA and Zenith are pushing stereo television sets. One-fifth of all television stations were broadcasting in stereo within two years of FCC authorization, with others in the process of conversion. NBC (a subsidiary of GE/RCA) quickly grabbed the lead in stereo programming (including past episodes of the "Tonight Show"). The introduction of stereo sound to television could have a direct impact on programming. Shows with considerable musical content like "Miami Vice," "Solid Gold," and a host of music video programs should benefit from stereo soundtracks.

Receiver Technology. Not only are dramatic technological developments changing the way video is distributed to the viewer at home, technology is changing the way the viewer receives the video. Large-screen projection televisions have not taken off as manufacturers hoped due in part to problems with picture quality and high price. New thirty six-inch traditional picture tubes mean that large, nonprojection screens will be available. Manufacturers are also developing thin-wall screen televisions that may be hung on the wall like a painting. Miniature sets like the Sony Watchman have given television its first chance to be as portable as radio. Broadcast television stations (not cable TV) stand to gain viewers through this technology.

Computer technology is starting to make a noticeable impact on receivers. Digital television sets give a better-quality picture and let the viewer watch more than one channel at once. Sports fans can watch one game while having another displayed on a corner of the screen. This is perhaps more than a novelty. Digital television promises to be a real challenge to television research firms like Nielsen, which will have to decide how to count these viewers.

Cable. Cable (community antenna television, or CATV) is no longer a new medium. Originally an inexpensive way for rural television viewers to share a large TV antenna, cable exploded when satellite antennae came along. The booming growth days of the late 1970s and early 1980s are over. Only a few major cities remain unwired. New cable channels are introduced only occasionally rather than seemingly every week. For companies that own cable systems, improving service to cable subscribers is replacing the concentration on building the cable system.

While once there were predictions of a "wired society," the reality is that more than 40 percent of those who have cable available to them choose not to subscribe. Probably more people will have videocassette recorders than will be cable subscribers by 1990 (Beville 1984). The combination of inexpensive videocassette rentals and cable subscriber complaints about movie service program repetition suggest that cable movie networks like HBO face serious VCR competition.

On the technological front, two-way or interactive cable once promised to bring a wealth of new text, shopping, and banking services into the home. Interactive technology allows a cable system to send video signals into the home and to receive signals from the home as well. But videotex services generally have been a great disappointment. To date, interactive cable services have been used primarily as a way of billing cable subscribers for individual video program (pay per view, or PPV).

Cable operators are hoping that PPV will be their new revenue source of the future. PPV events include movies not yet available on the cable networks, concerts, and other live and special events. The average cost of a pay-per-view movie is $4; a special event like a major boxing match has cost more than $17 per viewing (*Multichannel News*, 1986).

Cable Competition. Cable might appear to have no competition. While that is essentially the case, two other services do provide subscribers with cable-like offerings. Satellite Master Antenna Television is a private cable system that feeds satellite-delivered (like HBO) and terrestrial programming services to a small area such as an apartment complex. It serves as a thorn in the side of many local cable operators who would prefer a monopoly in the densely populated areas targeted by SMATV.

Of less significance is multichannel multipoint distribution service (MMDS). Referred to by some as wireless cable, the MMDS system broadcasts cable-like programming using high frequency microwave channels to special receivers. Some of these frequencies were reserved for educational institutions. If they are not being used (as is often the case), the MMDS operator can also lease some of them (Wolf 1986).

Subscribers lease microwave antennae and converters from the MMDS operator, usually paying a hefty installation fee. Microwave, however, is not a good way to broadcast programming because coverage is limited to twenty-five miles and is also subject to interference from, among other things, buildings and even dense foliage. In the few cities still waiting for cable, MMDS can temporarily provide service. One-channel multipoint distribution service (MDS) and subscription television service (STV) have already fallen by the wayside.

Cable may one day get some competition from an unlikely foe, telephone companies. Several U.S. telephone companies have filed applications with the FCC to operate cable systems. Telephone companies by law may not control content; they can only build and manage the video distribution system. Channels could be leased to users like cable program services. As high-capacity fiber optic cables are installed, telephone companies will be in an even better position to provide video service to homes and businesses.

In return, cable operators may compete with telephone companies. Manhattan CATV in New York has been especially innovative in the area of providing telecommunications (data transmission) service to New York financial institutions (Chorafas 1984). Some cable systems even experimented with providing access to a long distance telephone service to their subscribers. Currently, though, the cable–telephone clash does not appear to be gaining momentum.

Direct Broadcast Satellite. At one time, direct broadcast satellite (DBS) looked as if it might compete with cable. The DBS concept represents an innovation in national program delivery in the United States. Whereas network broadcast and cable television is delivered to audiences via local affiliates, DBS would deliver programming directly into the home. True DBS systems as approved by the FCC in 1982 would use new high-powered, high-frequency satellites, which would allow small (less than one meter) home antennae.

DBS had a false start in the early and mid-1980s that resulted in several early corporate pullouts. Publisher Rupert Murdoch's planned five-channel Skyband DBS system folded in 1983. After spending $140 million in more than five years of planning, Comsat's Communication Satellite Corporation abandoned its DBS quest in November 1984, literally without ever getting off the ground. United States Communications delivered a low-power satellite service for a year and a half before folding in early 1985.

While others have applied to the FCC to operate DBS systems (*Broadcasting* 1986d, p. 91), DBS appears to have a brighter future outside the United States. Past domestic systems have proposed fewer channels at higher monthly costs than cable television. Whatever market exists for DBS in the United States may be found only in areas not already well served by cable. In countries that have no cable television, DBS may be viable.

TVRO. Stanford University electronics professor Taylor Howard bought surplus military parts in 1976 for the purpose of building a satellite receiver antenna. Taylor found that he was able to tune in HBO's satellite signal with his thirty-foot wide antenna, a discovery that marked the beginning of a new industry.

Television receive-only (TVRO) satellite antennas (commonly referred to as the backyard dish) originally cost as much as $36,000. By the mid-1980s, prices had fallen well below $1,000; by 1986, over 1.5 million households owned dishes (Barbieri 1986). The industry was growing at 60,000 units per month before the cable programming industry threw cold water on it by scrambling the signals picked up by the dish owners. The difference between TVRO and DBS is that backyard dishes pick up signals not originally intended for individual reception. DBS services would package programming specifically intended for individual reception from new, high-powered satellites.

Congress specifically legalized the reception of unscrambled satellite signals in the Cable Communications Policy Act of 1984. Cable operators were alarmed by the unexpectedly rapid growth of the backyard dish industry, which also represented a potential competitive threat to their industry. (Why pay monthly fees for cable when you could buy a dish and receive pay cable movie channels free?) HBO/Cinemax became the first program supplier to scramble its signals on January 15, 1986. Dish sales dropped to less than 15,000 per month as other program suppliers followed suit (Taub 1986).

TVRO owners, however, can still receive more than one hundred unscrambled channels. Scrambled signals are also available through the use of a leased or purchased decoder (the M/A-COM decoder cost $395 when scrambling began). HBO originally charged $12.95 per month for either HBO or Cinemax or $19.95 per month for both. Other basic cable channels (WTBS/CNN, MTV/Nickelodeon) charge by the year (Tedesco 1986). With the large number of TVRO owners and the move to scrambling by the cable programming services, the time may be ripe for new programmers to begin providing new unscrambled services directly to dish owners.

New Technology and Television Audience Research. Commercial broadcasting is based on advertising. Advertisers buy commercial time on stations based on research from companies like Nielsen, Arbitron, and a more recent entrant, AGB. Any changes in this system can have great implications for television. New technology is affecting audience research companies in two ways: it is making new audience measurement techniques possible, and the new receiver technologies present new challenges.

Nielsen and Arbitron estimate the number of people watching television stations through diaries (in which viewers write down what they watch) and electronic meters (which record to which channel the set is tuned but not who is actually watching). The people meter, developed by AGB Research of Great

Britain, is an electronic combination of the two methods. When the set is turned on, viewers are supposed to check in by pressing an appropriate button. Unfortunately, accurate measurements are based on viewers' willingness to punch in. Nielsen tested its own people meter in 1985, and preliminary results suggested that fewer people were watching television than the diary method showed (Mandese 1985). The television industry asked Nielsen to delay its intended switch to the people meter for the 1986–1987 season (*Broadcasting* 1986f).

Arbitron is developing a new audience measurement technology in a joint venture with another market research company. The venture is called ScanAmerica and if it works could be a dream come true for advertisers. The system not only keeps track of who watches what on television but also what products they buy. When viewers from ScanAmerica households return from shopping, they are asked to record their purchases. This task is made relatively easy by a light pen used to read the universal product code, the bar code on packages. For the first time, advertisers may have the chance to see which people who saw commercials on television also bought the advertised product. Although ScanAmerica is being tested, Arbitron does not expect to have the system ready until about 1989 (*Broadcasting* 1986g).

Audience research firms may have to develop new technology to keep up with the audiences they are trying to measure. The plethora of new programming services has made their job difficult enough. Several cable networks are not satisfied with current measurement techniques for their audiences (Dagnoli 1985). Electronic meters measure only at-home viewing, not portable TV viewing. Some way to count multiple channel viewing on digital television must be found. The use of remote controls has increased rapidly, and their availability promotes channel flicking (changing channels during commercials). Research firms must also be concerned with VCR "zapping" (eliminating commercials while recording) and "zipping" (fast forwarding commercials during replay).

Recording and Storage Technology

Home Video

Perhaps the most significant new technology to hit the electronic media scene has been home video technology, especially the VCR. The VCR has the potential to be the most disruptive new technology to our system of commercial broadcasting because users can easily eliminate commercials. Another home video technology that has yet to make an impact in the United States is the videodisc player (VDP), a technology that may still make its mark in the home in the future.

History of Home Video

Videotape technology was originally developed for the broadcast industry in the 1950s. By 1970, Sony had developed the first compact videotape recorder, the U-Matic 3/4-inch VCR, which used an easily inserted, book-sized cassette. Too expensive for consumers, it found a home as a video training device in schools and businesses. Sony refined the technology and introduced its famous $1,300 1/2-inch Sony Betamax in 1975.

A rival Japanese manufacturer, Japan Victor Corporation (JVC), developed its own incompatible 1/2-inch VCR, the VHS (video home system). JVC designed the VHS to work at a slower speed than Beta, made its cassette larger to hold more tape, and made the tape thinner. Although VHS produces a lower-quality picture than Beta, VHS could record for longer periods. RCA obtained a license to market the VHS and introduced its VCR in August 1977 priced $300 less than the Betamax. Within two years, the VHS controlled 57 percent of the U.S. market. VCR sales rose from 400,000 in 1978 to 4 million in 1983 and nearly 12 million in 1985 (see table 2), with VHS accounting for 90 percent of the market. The future of Beta is now in doubt; several electronics manufacturers that used to produce Beta models switched to VHS in 1986, leaving Sony virtually on its own (Trost, 1986).

One videodisc player (VDP) was developed by RCA, which needed a new product to follow the success of color TV in the market (Graham 1986).

Table 2
VCR Versus Color Television Set Sales

	Total VCR Sales		*Color TV Sales*
1975	30,000	1959	90,000
1976	55,000	1960	120,000
1977	160,000	1961	147,000
1978	402,000	1962	438,000
1979	475,000	1963	747,000
1980	805,000	1964	1,404,000
1981	1,361,000	1965	2,694,000
1982	2,035,000	1966	5,012,000
1983	4,091,000	1967	5,563,000
1984	7,616,000	1968	6,215,000
1985	11,853,000	1969	6,191,000
1986[a]	12,500,000	1970	5,320,000

Sources: Electronic Industries Association (VCR sales figures); U.S. Department of Commerce (TV sales figures).
Note: VCR was introduced in 1975. Color TV was introduced in 1954.
[a]Estimated.

Another was developed by MCA (in partnership with Philips) as an outlet for its movie inventory. Their laservision videodisc can hold up to 54,000 separate video images, or up to one hour of moving pictures, on a side. Philips's Magnavox rushed its $695 Magnavision to market in Atlanta in late 1978. Two hundred disc titles were available, mostly old movies. Technical problems cropped up with both the hardware and the discs (as many as 90 percent were defective), and the player price was soon raised to $775.

RCA introduced its $500 Selectavision VDP in March 1981. Blitzed by the more expensive but versatile VCR, RCA announced in 1984 that it was abandoning its VDP at a loss of $580 million. About 550,000 players had been sold. Far fewer laser VDPs had been sold to consumers. Laser advocates announced in late 1984 that they too would retreat from the home market. A third VDP format, Matsushita's VHD, has found considerable success in Japan and may yet find its way into the U.S. market (Cohen 1985).

While about 40 percent of U.S. households had a VCR by the end of 1986, most experts had predicted only five years earlier that the VDP would be more popular than the VCR. What many of the experts did not appreciate was the usefulness of a player that could also record programs from television. The competition between the Beta and VHS formats led to lower prices and added features. The VDP with limited software was no match for the VCR, which, ironically, also had more prerecorded software than both VDP formats. It cannot be said with any certainty, however, that the VDP could not have been successful had manufacturers adopted different strategies, such as producing original software (Klopfenstein 1985).

Early studies showed that the primary use of VCRs was to record programs off the air for later viewing, a practice known as *time shifting* (Levy 1981). Although the large number of inexpensive rental cassettes has increased the use of the VCR for watching prerecorded tapes, time shifting broadcast programming remains the most frequent use of the VCR (Beville 1986; Gittelsohn 1986). One of the major questions facing broadcasters and advertisers is to what extent VCR owners tape programs and eliminate commercials. One recent study found that only 9 percent of VCR owners surveyed said they watched the commercials recorded on their VCRs (Yorke and Kitchen 1985). Another study suggests that people tend to say they zap or zip commercials more than they actually do (Metzger 1986). Much more research is being done in this area, and the results will take on increased significance as more people become VCR owners.

The VCR has also made its presence felt in the U.S. film industry. In 1985, 100 million people went to the theater to see a movie; about 103 million movie cassettes were rented each month (Green 1986). The theater still has some advantages over home viewing: 1) going to the movies is a social occasion, 2) movies appear in theaters before they appear on cassette, and 3) theaters offer the large, wide screen. As video rentals grow, however, it is clear that these advantages are not critical for many movie viewers.

What is the future of the VCR? While it might be reasonable to assume that most owners of color TVs (more than 90 percent of all U.S. households) will eventually buy a VCR, evidence from other countries suggests a different conclusion. In Japan, Australia, and Western Europe, VCR sales slowed when about 35 percent of households had one (Beville 1986). Forecasts for 1990 VCR penetration in the United States vary from 45 percent to 76 percent, with 60 percent the closest to a consensus (Bortz, Wyche, and Trautman 1986, p. 26). As table 2 shows, VCR sales have outpaced color TV sales at similar sales points in their histories (although the color TV figures are taken five years after color TVs were first being sold in 1954). Unlike color TV, however, the VCR is primarily an entirely new, rather than a replacement, purchase.

8mm Videotape

As VHS has dominated the VCR market in recent years despite added Beta features like stereo sound, Sony decided to back a new format introduced by Kodak in 1984. 8mm is a logical next step in miniaturizing VCR technology, with 8mm videocassettes being close to audio cassettes in size. An effort to market prerecorded software on 8mm tape is being made as well. Blank tapes are twice as expensive as Beta or VHS tapes, however. If consumers equate VCR with prerecorded software, then 8mm may be slow to take off.

Perhaps the more significant innovation from 8mm VCR technology is the miniature camcorder, the combination camera and recorder. (VHS hopes to meet the challenge with its own camcorder and miniature cassette, which can be played with an adapter on a regular VHS VCR). Kodak is interested in seeing 8mm become a new standard for home movies, replacing both VCR formats and what was left of the 8mm film market. The new format also features high-quality digital audio recording. Kodak also introduced an 8mm audio cassette deck, which offers up to twelve hours of recording on one videocassette. Sony has a television set with an 8mm VCR built in (Trost 1986), which could be the kind of innovation that eventually would put a VCR in most households.

Other Videodisc Applications

Although the VDP has yet to be welcomed into the home, other applications of videodisc technology are being made. One of the potentially most useful areas for the videodisc is in the library. The Library of Congress, for example, has placed still photographs, television programs, and films on videodisc.

Placing material on videodisc serves two functions: it makes more material accessible to researchers and helps preserve rare and aging materials (Parker 1985).

New Technology and the Print Media

Perhaps because of their more immediate ties to electronic technology, we tend to think of the broadcast media when new technology is mentioned. The print media, however, are also being affected by new technology. *USA Today* is a prime example of a newspaper that has taken advantage of available technology. Three other technologies may or may not shape the print media in the future: teletext, videotex, and optical disks. It should be noted that although they are only alluded to here, many other developments are taking place in other countries, especially in the areas of videotex and teletext.

Teletext

The FCC authorized television stations to broadcast textual information services, or *teletext*, in 1983. Teletext is an electronic text service broadcast over the air with the station's video and audio signals into the home. A television signal consists of 525 lines of information that carry the picture information, including the twenty-one-line black bar that you see when the set's vertical hold is not adjusted properly. This black bar is called the vertical blanking interval (VBI), and it is the portion of the signal in which teletext is broadcast. (Closed captioning for the hearing impaired uses line 21 of the VBI to transmit a running transcript of the program's audio.)

Depending on the system, from 100 to 200 pages of information are broadcast repeatedly in perhaps ten-second intervals. (If a cable television system devotes an entire channel to a teletext or cabletext service, it can transmit up to 5,000 pages of information in the same interval.) The user selects an item via a keypad from a menu of broad topic areas, such as news, business, entertainment, weather, and sports. When the feature is broadcast during the ten-second cycle, the receiver "grabs" it. This means there is a lag between when the user asks for an item and when it appears on the screen. A teletext decoder is needed to convert the information into text, which is then displayed on the television screen. Text may be superimposed on the television program or viewed by itself. There is no subscription charge for prototype American teletext services, although consumers have to purchase decoders. The teletext dream is that the service will eventually be supported by advertising and compete directly with newspaper classified ads.

Just as it had done with AM stereo, the FCC decided not to institute an industry standard for teletext though there are two competing, incompatible teletext systems. The British were interested in teletext before anyone in the United States, and teletext is already widely available in Britain (Noll 1985). Their World System Teletext (which creates crude pictures by using mosaic-like blocks) was endorsed by Taft Broadcasting and Zenith. Taft has been testing its Electra teletext service in Cincinnati and announced in 1986 that it would begin using the service on all Taft stations. Home users must buy decoders for $300, although some new digital television sets will have them built in at little extra cost. The service has also been available to other television stations via satellite on cable superstation WTBS's VBI. Zenith also has a small teletext printer that gives hard copy of what is on the screen.

A more sophisticated teletext system was developed in Canada in the 1970s. The Canadian system creates more detailed pictures by using different geographic shapes rather than only blocks. AT&T and CBS picked up on the Canadian system, which resulted in the North American Broadcast Teletext Specification (NABTS) standard (Alber 1985). NBC experimented with an NABTS service but quit in early 1985. CBS's teletext service, called Extravision, has been available since early 1983. Although CBS was initially spending $2 million to $3 million a year on Extravision, expenditures dropped to a few hundred thousand by 1986. CBS asks local stations to insert material to supplement national material it provides (*Broadcasting* 1986h). Although NABTS decoders were significantly more expensive than WST, a decoder costing less than $300 was expected to be on the market by late 1986 (*Broadcasting* 1986i).

Teletext has had virtually no impact on the U.S. broadcasting industry, much less the publishing industry. Decoders have turned out to be far too costly to interest any but the most curious consumers. If consumers eventually purchase less expensive decoders or TV sets with decoders built in, the question then becomes how many stations in a given market can offer teletext services. Because television stations can broadcast other services on the vertical blanking interval (such as electronic paging or beeper services), it is possible that many stations will forgo consumer teletext for one of the other services. Another possibility is that stations might lease portions of the teletext service to advertisers and others who may wish to post electronic notices.

Videotex

Videotex (referred to as "viewdata" in Europe) is a generic term for computer-based systems that provide textual and, videotex purists insist, graphic information electronically. Unlike broadcast teletext, videotex services are online and are truly interactive. The user of a videotex service sends requests directly to the service's computer. Not only do videotex users have access to all kinds of information (from airline reservations to stock market prices), they can even type electronic messages to other users.

Videotex requires that the user have some kind of terminal, whether made specifically for accessing the videotex service or a microcomputer with a modem. Although interactive cable television systems have the technological capability to offer videotex services, early efforts were not successful. For the near future, videotex will probably try to make its mark via the telephone or a related telecommunications network.

About 13 percent of U.S. households had microcomputers as of early 1986 (Foley 1985), and those with modems had the ability to tap into a number of services. CompuServe with nearly 200,000 subscribers, Reader's Digest's the Source with 63,000, and Dow Jones News/Retrieval with more than 200,000 mostly business users were the leading national videotex service providers (Fletcher 1985). Subscriber counts may be misleading, however, because some subscribers are not regular users. Indeed, videotex services to the home for the most part have failed in the United States (Lowenstein and Aller 1985). Keycom Electronic Publishing in suburban Chicago announced a goal of 700,000 subscribers when it was launched in 1983. When it folded in 1985, one source counted only a few hundred subscribers (Fletcher 1985). Times Mirror's CATV-based Gateway videotex service (a $20 million investment) and Knight-Ridder's telephone-based viewtron (a $50 million to $60 million investment) videotex service were abandoned within weeks of each other in early 1986 (*Broadcasting* 1986j).

Undaunted, new players have entered the struggling U.S. home information market. IBM, Sears, and CBS have teamed up to form Trintex; AT&T, Time, Inc., and Chemical Bank make up Covi-dea; and RCA (GE), Citicorp, and Nynex form the latest trio of would-be home information players (Moran 1985). Banks have an interest in interactive electronic banking systems, which could be offered as part of a videotex service. It costs a bank much less to have simple transactions like deposits and account transfers done electronically by customers than it does to have them done by bank employees. Some believe that banks will push videotex into the home by assuming some of its costs and therefore offering videotex at lower prices than today.

Optical Disk

Optical disks (spelled with a *k*) are not identical to the laser videodisc developed for home use. Whereas the videodisc player uses a laser to read an analog recording on the disc, the optical disk uses a laser to read digital bits (1s or 0s) from the disc. The optical disk comes in two forms: the 4.75-inch (120 millimeter) CD-ROM (compact disc read-only memory, a technological descendant of the digital audio compact disk), and the 12-inch (300 millimeter) optical disk.

In the computer and publishing industries, CD-ROM became the talk of the mid-1980s. CD-ROM is really a computer peripheral—that is, a storage device to be used with a microcomputer like the IBM PC. The audio CD technology was adapted for use with computers. A CD-ROM disk can hold 550 megabytes of information (one byte equals one character and one megabyte is one million bytes). In practical terms, this means that one CD-ROM disk can hold:

The text content of 150,000 printed pages (enough to fill 250 large books);

Sharp images of 15,000 pages of business documents (enough to fill two tall filing cabinets);

The contents of 1,200 standard 5.25-inch floppy disks; and

A crisp color picture and ten seconds of narration for each of 3,000 segments of an educational or reference program (almost eight hours of content).

Adding to the attractiveness of the storage capacity is random access capability, the ability to locate any piece of stored information (text or pictures) within a second (Laub 1986). GM plans to put an audio CD-based video map and navigation system in all its Corvettes by 1989 (MacNeice 1986).

While the presence of CD-ROM is being felt by the publishing industry, its full impact will be felt in the late 1980s and into the 1990s. The first CD-ROM systems were already available, including the Electronic Encyclopedia, a twenty-volume set on one CD-ROM for $200 (Chen 1986). Because of high costs, however, the CD-ROM will probably be seen in local libraries before it makes its way into the home.

CD-ROM is also expected to compete with some videotex or commercial online database services. In the past, large amounts of electronically stored databases such as magazine indexes had to be stored in a central location and accessed via telephone lines. Now those same data can be placed on a CD-ROM disk and mailed to the library or business office, eliminating telecommunication costs.

As impressive as the CD-ROM's storage attributes are, an older form of digital optical technology, the twelve-inch optical disk, is still more impressive. A single disk can store 5,600 megabytes of information, more than ten times the capability of one CD-ROM. While any need for this much storage in the home is hard to imagine, twelve-inch digital optical disks may prove quite useful for large businesses and government agencies that store huge amounts of information.

The disadvantage of the optical disk is that users cannot record on them. Two optical recording systems, however, are being developed: 1) write-once optical storage, or direct read after write (DRAW), and 2) erasable optical disk, or optical memory disc recorder (OMDR). As the names imply, DRAW technology allows the user to make one permanent recording. OMDR technology allows the user to record repeatedly as if using a VCR or floppy disk drive. If an OMDR technology is developed at a reasonable cost, the ultimate implication for the home user could be a way to store any information—video and text—in one device.

The Technological Future

Speculating about the future of new media technologies is an interesting task. William R. Holm was president of the Society of Motion Picture and Television Engineers (SMPTE) at a time when speculation was rampant that "video cartridges" were on the verge of revolutionizing television. Videodiscs, videotape, and devices that played film cartridges on the TV set were all reportedly nearly ready to be unleashed on the consumer. Holm stepped back from the situation and took a long look. He made some simple observations in an address to a 1971 SMPTE conference in Montreal. They seem appropriate to close this discussion of new media technologies.

Holm defined technology as "science applied to the problems of Society" (Holm 1971, p. 7). Drawing from this definition, Holm concluded, in part, that technology is not useful merely because it exists: it must satisfy needs so that people will buy, which in turn may give birth to future technologies. It is reasonable to suggest that many new technologies will fail: the lessons from history have shown this. Only if new media can provide users with a service that fills a need at a reasonable price will they be successful.

References

Alber, Antone F. 1985. *Videotex/Teletext*. New York: McGraw-Hill.

Barbieri, Richard. 1986. "DBS by Any Other Name." *Channels 1986 Field Guide* 54.

Beville, Hugh M. 1984. "VCR Penetration: Will It Surpass Cable by 1990?" *Television/Radio Age*, July 9, pp. 27–31, 108–110.

Beville, Mel. 1986. "VCR Usage Patterns to Emerge." *Electronic Media*, February 17, p. 26.

Bortz, Paul I., Mark C. Wyche, and James M. Trautman. 1986. *Great Expectations: A Television Manager's Guide to the Future*. Washington, D.C.: National Association of Broadcasters.

Broadcasting. 1986a. "Kahn Won't Quit Despite Rebuff," July 29, pp. 86–88.

———. 1986b. "FCC Prescribes Major Treatment for AM Ills," April 7, pp. 35–38.

———. 1986c. "U.S. Satisfied with AM Conference Results," May: pp. 82–83.

———. 1986d. "Where Things Stand," July 7, pp. 32–33, 90–95.

———. 1986e. "Radio Programming Tunes in the Satellite Sound," May 26, pp. 69–71.

———. 1986f. "People Meter Controversy Aired at NAB," April 21, pp. 54, 56.

———. 1986g. "Ratings Realignment," January 27, p. 33.

———. 1986h. "CBS Makes Changes, Cuts, at Extravision Teletext Service," May 19, p. 75.

———. 1986i. "WBTV's High Hopes for Teletext," March 31, pp. 75, 77.

———. 1986j. "Knight-Ridder Pulls Plug on Viewtron," March 24, pp. 45–46.

Chen, Peter Pin-shan. 1986. "The Compact Disk ROM: How It Works," *IEEE Spectrum* (April): 44–49.

Chorafas, Dimitris N. 1984. *Telephony: Today and Tomorrow*. Englewood Cliffs, N.J.: Prentice-Hall.

Cohen, C.L. 1985. "What Was a Bust in the U.S. Turns into a Boom in Japan." *Electronics*, December 9, pp. 49–50.

Dagnoli, Judann. 1985. "Nielsen Reviews Diaries after Cable Complaints." *Advertising Age*, October 7, p. 54.

Electronic Industries Association. 1986. *Consumer Electronics Annual Review*. Washington, D.C.: The Association.

Fletcher, Carol. 1985. "Videotex: Return Engagement." *IEEE Spectrum* 22: 34–38.

Foley, Mary Jo. 1985. "Revolution Becomes Evolution in the Consumer Market." *Electronic Business*, December 10, pp. 97–98.

Gates, William H. 1986. Foreword to *CD/ROM: The New Papyrus*. Edited by Steve Lambert and Suzanne Ropiequet. Redman, Wash.: Microsoft Press.

Gittelsohn, John. 1986. "VCRs in 6 of 10 Homes by Year-End." *USA Today*, April 11, p. A1.

Graham, Margaret. 1986. *RCA and the Videodisc: The Business of Research*. New York: Cambridge University Press.

Green, Tom. 1986. "Fans Tune in VCRs, Tune out Theaters." *USA Today*, May 15, p. A1.

Gross, Judith. 1986. "Digital Audio: Ready for Radio?" *Broadcast Management/Engineering* (July): 23–41.

Holm, Wilton R. 1971. "Socio-Economic Aspects of Videoplayer Systems—A Perspective." In *Video Cartridge, Cassette and Disc Player Systems*. New York: Society of Motion Picture and Television Engineers.

Kaplan, Gadi. 1985. "All the Comforts of Home." *IEEE Spectrum* (May): 75–78.

Klopfenstein, Bruce C. 1985. "Forecasting the Market for Home Video Players: A Retrospective Analysis. Ph.D. dissertation, Ohio State University.

Lambert, Steve, and Suzanne Ropiequet. 1986. *CD ROM: The New Papyrus*. Redman, Wash.: Microsoft Press.

Laub, Leonard. 1986. "What is CD ROM?" In *CD/ROM: The New Papyrus*, pp. 47–71. Edited by Steve Lambert and Suzanne Ropiequet. Redman, Wash.: Microsoft Press.

Levy, Mark. 1981. "Home Video Recorders and Time Shifting." *Journalism Quarterly* 58:401–405.

Lowenstein, Ralph L., and Helen E. Aller, 1985. "The Inevitable March of Videotex." *Technology Review* 88 (October): 22–29.

MacNeice, Jill. 1986. "Finding Any Street, USA." *USA Today*, June 2, p. 1E.

Mandese, Joe. 1985. "Advertisers Review Nielsen Plan." *Adweek*, October 21, pp. 1, 8.

Metzger, Gale. 1986. "Contam's VCR Research." *Journal of Advertising Research* 26 (April–May): RC8–RC12.

Moran, Brian. 1985. "Perkins to Head $150 Million Videotex Venture." *Advertising Age*, February 24, p. 28.

Multichannel News. 1986. "Pay-per-View Product Comparisons," August 11, p. 37.

Nadan, Joseph S. 1985. "A Glimpse into Future Television." *Byte* (January): 135–150.

Noll, A. Michael. 1985. "Videotex: Anatomy of a Failure." *Information & Management* 9: 99:109.

Parker, Elisabeth Betz. 1985. "The Library of Congress Non-Print Optical Disk Pilot Program." *Information Technology and Libraries* (December): 289–299.

Patten, David A. 1986. *Newspapers and New Media*. White Plains, N.Y.: Knowledge Industry Publications.

Saffady, William. 1985. *Video-Based Information Systems*. Chicago: American Library Association.

Taub, Eric. 1986. "Scrambling Start-up Slowing Dish Sales." *Electronic Media*, March 17, pp. C3, C12.

Tedesco, Richard. 1986. "Most Will Scramble by 1987." *Electronic Media*, March 17, p. C3.

Trost, Mark. 1986. "VCR Sales Explosion Shakes Up Industry." *Advertising Age*, January 9, p. 14.

Whitehouse, George E. 1986. *Understanding the New Technologies of the Mass Media*. Englewood Cliffs, N.J.: Prentice-Hall.

Wolf, Jeffrey L. 1986. "Multichannel MDS: The Start of Something Small." *Channels 1986 Field Guide*: 34.

Yorke, David A., and Philip J. Kitchen. 1985. "Channel Flickers and Video Speeders." *Journal of Advertising Research* 25 (April–May): 21–25.

Zuckerman, Art. 1986. "Compact Discs on the Go." *High Technology* (September): 52–53.

SATELLITES FOR COMMUNICATION

Jon T. Powell

Jon T. Powell, professor of communication studies and instructional technology, and chairman of the Department of Communication Studies, Northern Illinois University, DeKalb, is author of *International Broadcasting by Satellite: Issues of Regulation, Barriers to Communication* (1985).

When satellites are used for communication, the issues related to mass media's role and influence in society take on international dimensions because satellite systems by their nature interconnect the globe. Arthur C. Clarke was the first to describe a communication satellite. In 1945, in an article entitled "Extra-Terrestrial Relays," he wrote that a satellite could link any part of the world; only three could provide world service. He also pointed out that although the initial investment would be high, cost of operation would be relatively low.[1] The signal that reaches up into space and down again creates an electronic connection that in a fraction of a second spans oceans and deserts, mountains and political boundaries.

The average viewer may regard television as a local or national service, but satellite communications have introduced in a short period of time new and little understood international dimensions. Satellite communications have evolved quickly to become a global service. A worldwide network has been created to offer instant transmission of data, facsimile, telephone, telegraph, as well as television. Specialized satellite services for navigation, weather reporting, and teleconferencing are among those available now, with more under development. This variety of uses constitutes the environment within which television can play an influential national and international role.

Communication satellites are examined here from several perspectives: 1) the physical dimensions, 2) the operational dimensions, 3) the social perspective, 4) sociopolitical perspectives, and 5) future trends.

The Physical Dimensions

Webster's Dictionary defines *satellite* as a "man-made object or vehicle intended to orbit the earth, the moon, or another celestial body." The communication satellites in current use are known as *active satellites*. (*Passive satellites* merely reflect signals back to earth.) An active communication satellite receives a signal from earth, amplifies it, and retransmits it on a different frequency back to earth. The reason for the retransmission on a different frequency is to avoid the interference (jamming) that arises from receiving and transmitting on the same frequency.

Satellite communication can take place in three ways. First is *point-to-point communication,* intended to be received by one party only. This type of communication can be and has been received by unauthorized parties, as in the case of the satellite transmissions of Home Box Office or the Movie Channel to cable systems across the country. In order to preserve their point-to-point security, these cable services have scrambled their signal, requiring viewers to use a decoder for acceptable reception.

The second satellite distribution pattern is *point-to-multipoint,* which is used to serve earth stations at different sites simultaneously. International satellite systems are operated with this purpose in mind. For example, the Olympic games have been televised simultaneously in Europe, Asia, and America. In such instances, the signal is received by an earth station for re-transmission to local television stations, which then broadcast the program, all within fractions of a second.

The third distribution pattern involves a *direct broadcast satellite* (DBS), which broadcasts a signal of sufficient strength to be received in the individual home by using a receiving antenna, or dish, approximately three feet across. Although DBS services have been technically possible for a long time, economic and political concerns have slowed implementation.

An active satellite must generate its own power. This is accomplished by using solar panels, which convert sunlight into electricity. The electricity is stored in batteries, which permit operation even when the satellite might not be in sunlight. The communication satellite has its own station-keeping capabilities, including orbit correction or change using on-board jets, receiving and transmitting, and remote monitoring of its operation (telemetry) from earth.

Above all, the communication satellite must be able to fulfill its primary function to act as an electronic link. This function is made possible by a transponder, the operational heart of a communication satellite—a TWT (traveling wave tube) with its ancillary support devices—that can amplify a received signal many thousands of times, providing sufficient power for adequate reception by earth-bound dish antennas. Without the TWT, a miniaturized pencil-sized device, the communication satellite would not have been possible, at least not until launch vehicles could carry very heavy loads.

In order to be electronically visible to an earth station, the communication satellite is placed in a synchronous (also called geostationary or geosynchronous equatorial orbit. Positioned some 22,300 miles in space and moving at a speed of approximately 6,900 miles per hour to match the rotation of the earth, it appears unmoving in space. As a result, an earth station's dish antenna can remain fixed on the satellite, and only three satellites are required to cover the globe.

The physical process of using the communication satellite for a television transmission can thus be described as a series of steps. The picture signal originates on site or in a television studio. It is then relayed to an earth station, which sends the signal up to the satellite. At this point, the earth station acts as an uplink. Upon receiving the signal, the satellite amplifies it and then retransmits down to another earth station, this one acting as a downlink. The downlink passes the signal along to another television station for broadcasting. The electronic signal is moving at the speed of light—over 186,000 miles per second—and must traverse at least 44,600 miles (up to the satellite and down to earth); it takes approximately a quarter of a second on its one-way journey from one television source to another across the world.

As a result of this ability to use space for electronic communication, messages sent by satellite are no longer restricted by oceans, mountains, deserts, or distance. Further, the cost of sending messages anywhere remains essentially the same. This represents a major change from earlier days of written, printed, telegraphic, telephonic, and even radio communications when distance played an important role.

As larger and more efficient satellites were placed in orbit, more voice circuits became available at lower cost. The first satellite, called INTELSAT I, launched in 1965 with a design life of eighteen months, could handle only 240 simultaneous telephone calls. INTELSAT VI, will have a capacity of 30,000 telephone circuits and a design life of ten years.

The Operational Dimensions

Several organizations play a significant role in regulating and operating communication satellite systems. Because the signal, or television program, may originate in one country and end up in another, the process of relaying that information through space and satellite involves both national and international operations, which determines in large part the conditions under which communication can take place.

International Telecommunication Union

The International Telecommunication Union (ITU), an independent agency of the United Nations, was formed by the reorganization of the International Telegraph Union (founded in 1865) in response to the new challenges of radio communications. With some 155 member nations, the ITU is charged with fostering cooperation among nations, studying the techniques of electronic communication, making regulations governing the use of frequencies, and publishing information about telecommunications. All frequencies used for broadcasting and all forms of telecommunication are registered with ITU in the Master International Frequency Register, which contains approximately a half-million frequency assignments.

The international agreements and regulations governing the use of the radio spectrum are generally adhered to in order to avoid the electronic chaos that would result from the interference created by uncontrolled broadcasting on the same frequencies. ITU plays an important role in acting as a watchdog and intermediary, providing technical advice and seeking agreement among nations where conflict occurs.

COMSAT

The U.S. Communications Satellite Corporation (COMSAT) was created by the Communications Satellite Act of 1962 as a commercial enterprise, with government participation, to be operated for profit. The act, which was recognized as laying the groundwork for an international commercial organization, required COMSAT to maintain maximum competition in providing equipment and services for the satellite system and to "maintain and strengthen competition in the provision of services to the public."

INTELSAT

The International Telecommunications Satellite Consortium (INTELSAT) was established on an interim basis in 1964. As a consortium (that is, an international joint venture), the interim agreement included provision for re-negotiation in approximately five years. A new agreement came into force on February 12, 1973. The term *Consortium* was changed to *Organization,* with the acronym remaining the same.

The 1973 agreement (Agreement Relating to the International Telecommunications Satellite Organization "INTELSAT") gave INTELSAT a new legal personality, enabling it to sign contracts, acquire and sell property, and own the satellites used for international communications. The purpose of INTELSAT, as stated in the preamble of the 1973 agreement, was to achieve a "single global commercial telecommunications satellite system." Like the U.S. Satellite Act, it declared itself desirous of expanding services to "all areas of the world" and to "contribute to world peace and understanding." It would also be organized in a way "to permit all peoples to have access" to the system.

INTELSAT has been organized to recognize and protect its members in the context of their rights as representatives of sovereign nations, nongovernmental entities, and investors. As a commercial operation, INTELSAT returns its profits beyond reinvestment to its stockholders. This mixture of nations and companies in a commercial organization has worked reasonably well, although the objective of developing one global system (as a monopoly) has been and continues to be challenged.

INTERSPUTNIK

Because INTELSAT operates under a free marketplace philosophy, the Soviets, for ideological reasons, chose not to participate and organized instead their own international body, INTERSPUTNIK. Member nations, in addition to the Soviet Union, are the nations of Eastern Europe, Afghanistan, Laos, Mongolia, Vietnam, Cuba, and Algeria. The agreement (Agreement on the Establishment of the "INTERSPUTNIK" International System and Organization of Space Communications) makes no mention of commercial goals, instead emphasizing the political sovereignty of the participating nations. Its board, the governing body, approves plans for the development and operation of satellite systems and determines technical requirements for the earth stations, among other duties.

Other Organizations

There are a number of other international and regional organizations charged with developing communication satellite service. One is the European Telecommunications Satellite Organization (EUTELSAT), founded provisionally in 1977 and made permanent in 1982, with its headquarters in Paris. EUTELSAT, whose members include the nations of Western Europe, operate and maintain a communication satellite service for that region. Included in the plans of the organization are the launching of approximately five communication satellites through 1993. Direct broadcast satellites were not included in the planning.

The establishment of EUTELSAT meant a confrontation with a principle laid down by the original INTELSAT agreement that precluded harmful competition with that system. But enlightened self-interest motivated the Europeans to consider that part of the agreement invalid because it was perceived as stifling the growth of telecommunications services in that region, a situation not anticipated at the signing of the original INTELSAT agreement.

Summary

COMSAT, INTELSAT, INTERSPUTNIK, and EUTELSAT are examples of contrasting, competing, and sometimes conflicting efforts to develop satellite communications. Whether the reasons stem from competing ideologies, economic concerns, or simply matters arising out of the evolution of space telecommunications, national interests are clearly at stake. The limitations of orbital slots and frequencies that can be made available to communication satellites, made all the more obvious by increased demand worldwide, can be managed effectively only by careful international cooperation based on enlightened national self-interest.

Social Perspectives

Although the full social impact of communication satellites' bringing global events into the home are still not well understood, some effects can be noted. The United States has never had a foreign war fought on its own soil, but the war in Korea, and particularly in Vietnam, gave ample opportunity to witness the horrors of war first-hand day after day and led to public questioning of the validity of involvement, the wisdom of those responsible, and the outward public expressions that contributed to its end. Had the reporting been delayed and shown in movie theaters as during World War II, one might speculate as to whether the public outcry would have been as strong.

In the international arena, communication satellites have created new situations. The average citizen is perhaps better informed on world politics. No longer can nations engage in private diplomacy immune to the scrutiny of the electronic media. Individual citizens' reactions must be taken into account by those making statements or negotiating across national boundaries. Ideological, social, and economic differences can be brought into sharp focus and must often be explained and justified. The problems of other nations can now be linked quickly and clearly to our own. Much of the privacy formerly protecting international negotiations has been stripped away. The result is that governments are increasingly sensitive to world opinion.

Sociopolitical Perspectives

International agreements, official UN documents, statements by political leaders, and even the verbatim records of international political debates make many references to national sovereignty, the conceptual premise that makes it possible for countries to interact in the international arena while serving their national interests. Without universal recognition of this principle of national sovereignty, there would be no fundamental protection, no legal foundation to justify international negotiations.

One fundamental issue where the technology of satellite communications collides with the international free flow of information occurs in the context of national sovereignty. Divergent national policies for the management of information come face to face as satellite technology makes worldwide instantaneous communications possible at the lowest cost in history. This technology has raised issues about who should control what information for what reasons, or indeed, if such control can ever be justified. At one end of the controversy is the United States, which finds any control of the flow of information unacceptable; at the other end, Soviet ideology requires careful management of information as basic to the responsible operation of party and government and to the maintenance of a stable society. Between these approaches lie the developing nations, whose concerns may extend beyond ideology to the protection of fragile cultures. The developing nations have perceived the opportunities created by satellite as both blessing and curse. Although satellites have occasionally been used for educational purposes, the almost overwhelming problems of economic growth, illiteracy, the preservation of cultural heritage, and political stability can make the prospect of television programming coming directly or indirectly from satellites alarming. The concerns for maintaining a national identity and of ensuring a stable society are made all the more intense by the attractive and pervasive programs from the developed nations, creating demands for consumer goods that cannot be met by governments struggling for survival. Raising the consciousness of an economically deprived population to alternative life-styles can encourage widespread dissatisfaction without offering any solutions.

Future Trends

Regardless of how satellite systems or communication technologies are described, it is clear that not only are they here to stay, but they are expanding. This growth exerts pressure on existing institutions, national and international. The pressures created by the availability of distant and relatively inexpensive communication will increase as more satellites are placed in orbit, more nations become involved in space telecommunications, and more services evolve.

As more instantaneous international communication takes place, greater awareness of events will occur as individuals learn more about the current affairs of other nations than ever before. Consider the contemporary awareness of hunger, nuclear disarmament, balance of trade, U.S.-Soviet arms negotiations, and terrorism. Because knowledge of distant events has become so easily accessible, the individual has become a world citizen whose opinion is becoming increasingly important in the conduct of national and international affairs.

Instantaneous global communication also leads to the possibility of political and cultural confrontation. Conflicts arising from differing customs, personal behavior, attitudes, and even dress become obvious and pressing when transmitted across national borders. Television programming, made even more available by direct broadcast satellites, will continue to raise ideological and cultural issues.

As an international forum, the United Nations and its agencies can be used to explore the issues and search for acceptable solutions. The ITU has a long history of successful cross-national negotiations in the areas of spectrum management and recently in orbital agreements, but its province has been the physical aspects of telecommunications. International communications systems are generally susceptible to cooperation when dealing with the management of the frequency spectrum, but we have yet to find agreement on the arrangements for the program content to broadcast by satellite.

Since satellites have made global communication instantaneous, they have also made it a source of confrontation. For example, direct broadcast satellites without the filtering effect of earth stations can create a confrontational situation in a political or social sense. When this happens, the answer may lie in accommodation, the giving up of absolutes on both sides. Perhaps such accommodation will occur on a regional basis first and then spread globally.

Communication satellites have broadened our outlook and created feelings of neighborliness and responsibility extending beyond national boundaries. This technology has made us more aware of our place in the international arena.

Note

1. Arthur C. Clarke, "Extra-Terrestrial Relays," *Wireless World* (October 1945): 305–308.

HOW COMMUNICATION WORKS

Wilbur Schramm

Wilbur Schramm was formerly Janet M. Peck Professor of International Communication, adjunct professor of education, and director of the Institute for Communication Research at Stanford University. He has been a consultant to several government agencies and foundations, which have recognized his preeminence in communications research. He is the author of fourteen books on communications, including *Television in the Lives of Our Children, Mass Media and National Development, Responsibility in Mass Communication,* and *Classroom Out-of-Doors.*

Reprinted from *The Process and Effects of Mass Communication* (Urbana: University of Illinois Press, 1955), pp. 3–10, 13–17. Used by permission of publisher.

The Process

It will be easier to see how mass communication works if we first look at the communication process in general.

Communication comes from the Latin *communis,* "common." When we communicate we are trying to establish a "commonness" with someone. That is, we are trying to share information, an idea, or an attitude. At this moment I am trying to communicate to you the idea that the essence of communication is getting the receiver and the sender "tuned" together for a particular message. At this same moment, someone somewhere is excitedly phoning the fire department that the house is on fire. Somewhere else a young man in a parked automobile is trying to convey the understanding that he is mooneyed because he loves the young lady. Somewhere else a newspaper is trying to persuade its readers to believe as it does about the Republican party. All these are forms of communication, and the process in each case is essentially the same.

Communication always requires at least three elements—the source, the message, and the destination. A *source* may be an individual (speaking, writing, drawing, gesturing) or a communication organization (like a newspaper, publishing house, television station or motion picture studio). The *message* may be in the form of ink on paper, sound waves in the air, impulses in an electric current, a wave of the hand, a flag in the air, or any other signal capable of being interpreted meaningfully. The *destination* may be an *individual* listening, watching, or reading; or a member of a *group,* such as a discussion group, a lecture audience, a football crowd, or a mob; or an individual member of the particular group we call the *mass audience*, such as the reader of a newspaper or a viewer of television.

Now what happens when the source tries to build up this "commonness" with his intended receiver? First, the source encodes his message. That is, he takes the information or feeling he wants to share and puts it into a form that can be transmitted. The "pictures in our heads" cannot be transmitted until they are coded. When they are coded into spoken words, they can be transmitted easily and effectively, but they cannot travel very far unless radio carries them. If they are coded into written words, they go more slowly than spoken words, but they go further and last longer. Indeed, some messages long outlive their senders—the *Iliad,* for instance; the Gettysburg address; Chartres cathedral. Once coded and sent, a message is quite free of its sender, and what it does is beyond the power of the sender to change. Every writer feels a sense of helplessness when he finally commits his story or his poem to print; you doubtless feel the same way when you mail an important letter. Will it reach the right person? Will he understand it as you intend him to? Will he respond as you want him to? For in order to complete the act of communication, the message must be decoded. And there is good reason, as we shall see, for the sender to wonder whether his receiver will really be in tune with him, whether the message will be interpreted without distortion, whether the "picture in the head" of the receiver will bear any resemblance to that in the head of the sender.

We are talking about something very like a radio or telephone circuit. In fact, it is perfectly possible to draw a picture of the human communication system that way:

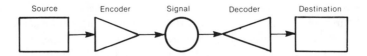

Substitute *microphone* for *encoder* and *earphone* for decoder and you are talking about electronic communication. Consider that the "source" and "encoder" are one person, "decoder" and "destination" are another, and the signal is language, and you are talking about human communication.

Now it is perfectly possible by looking at those diagrams to predict how such a system will work. For one thing, such a system can be no stronger than its weakest link. In engineering terms, there may be filtering or distortion at any stage. In human terms, if the source does not have adequate or clear information; if the message is not encoded fully, accurately, effectively in transmittable signs; if these are not transmitted fast enough and accurately enough, despite interference and competition, to the desired receiver; if the message is not decoded in a pattern that corresponds to the encoding; and finally, if the destination is unable to handle the decoded message so as to produce the desired response—then, obviously, the system is working at less than top efficiency. When we realize that *all* these steps must be accomplished with relatively high efficiency if any communication is to be successful, the everyday act of explaining something to a stranger, or writing a letter, seems a minor miracle.

A system like this will have a maximum capacity for handling information and this will depend on the separate capacities of each unit on the chain—for example, the capacity of the channel (how fast can one talk?) or the capacity of the encoder (can your student understand something explained quickly?). If the coding is good (for example, no unnecessary words) the capacity of the channel can be approached, but it can never be exceeded. You can readily see that one of the great skills of communication will lie in knowing how near capacity to operate a channel.

This is partly determined for us by the nature of the language. English, like every other language, has its sequences of words and sounds governed by certain probabilities. If it were organized so that no set of probabilities governed the likelihood that certain words would follow certain other words (for example, that a noun would follow an adjective, or that "States" or "Nations" would follow "United"), then we would have nonsense. As a matter of fact, we can calculate the relative amount of freedom open to us in writing any language. For English, the freedom is about 50 percent. (Incidentally, this is about the required amount of freedom to enable us to construct interesting crossword puzzles. Shannon has estimated that if we had about 70 percent freedom, we could construct three-dimensional crossword puzzles. If we had only 20 percent, crossword puzzle making would not be worthwhile.)

So much for language *redundancy,* as communication theorists call it, meaning the percentage of the message which is not open to free choice. But there is also the communicator's redundancy, and this is an important aspect of constructing a message. For if we think our audience may have a hard time understanding the message, we can deliberately introduce more redundancy; we can repeat (just as the radio operator on a ship may send "SOS" over and over again to make sure it is heard and decoded), or we can give examples and analogies. In other words, we always have to choose between transmitting more information in a given time, or transmitting less and repeating more in the hope of being better understood. And as you know, it is often a delicate choice, because too slow a rate will bore an audience, whereas too fast a rate may confuse them.

Perhaps the most important thing about such a system is one we have been talking about all too glibly—the fact that receiver and sender must be in tune. This is clear enough in the case of a radio transmitter and receiver, but somewhat more complicated when it means that a human receiver must be able to understand a human sender.

Let us redraw our diagram in very simple form, like this:

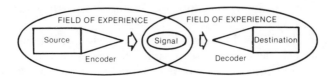

Think of those circles as the accumulated experience of the two individuals trying to communicate. The source can encode, and the destination can decode, only in terms of the experience each has had. If we have never learned any Russian, we can neither code nor decode in that language. If an African tribesman has never seen or heard of an airplane, he can only decode the sight of a plane in terms of whatever experience he has had. The plane may seem to him to be a bird and the aviator a god borne on wings. If the circles do not meet—if there has been no common experience—then communication is impossible. If the circles have only a small area in common—that is, if the experiences of source and destination have been strikingly unlike—then it is going to be very difficult to get an intended meaning across from one to the other. This is the difficulty we face when a non-science-trained person tries to read Einstein or when we try to communicate with another culture much different from ours.

The source, then, tries to encode in such a way as to make it easy for the destination to tune in the message—to relate it to parts of his experience which are much like those of the source. What does he have to work with?

Messages are made up of signs. A sign is a signal that stands for something in experience. The word *dog* is a sign that stands for our generalized experience with dogs. The word would be meaningless to a person who came from a dogless island and had never read of or heard of a dog. But most of us have learned that word by association, just as we learn most signs. Someone called our attention to an animal and said "dog." When we learned the word, it produced in us much the same response as the object it stood for. That is, when we heard "dog," we could recall the appearance of dogs, their sound, their feel, perhaps their smell. But there is an important difference between the sign and the object: the sign always represents the object at a reduced level of cues. By this we mean simply that the sign will not call forth all the responses that the object itself will call forth. This sign "dog," for example, will probably not call forth in us the same wariness or attention a strange dog might attract if it wandered into our presence. This is the price we pay for portability in language. We have a sign system that we can use in place of the less portable originals (for example, Margaret Mitchell could recreate the burning of Atlanta in a novel, and a photograph could transport worldwide the appearance of a bursting atomic bomb), but our sign system is merely a kind of shorthand. The coder has to be able to write the short-hand, the decoder to read it. And no two persons have learned exactly the same system. For example, a person who has known only Arctic huskies will not have learned exactly the same meaning for the shorthand sign "dog" as will a person who comes from a city where he has known only pekes and poms.

We have come now to a point where we need to tinker a little more with our diagram of the communication process. It is obvious that each person in the communication process is both an encoder and a decoder. He receives and transmits. He must be able to write readable shorthand, and to read other people's shorthand. Therefore, it is possible to describe either sender or receiver in a human system thus:

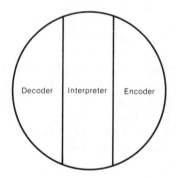

What happens when a signal comes to you? Remember that it comes in the form of a sign. If you have learned the sign, you have learned certain responses with it. We can call these *mediatory responses,* because they me-diate what happens to the message in your nervous system. These responses are the meaning the sign has for you. They are learned from experience, as we said, but they are affected by the state of your organism at the moment. For example, if you are hungry, a picture of a steak may not arouse exactly the same response in you as when you are overfed.

But subject to these effects, the mediatory responses will then determine what you do about the sign, for you have learned other sets of reactions connected to the mediatory responses. A sign that means a certain thing to you will start certain other processes in your nerves and muscles. A sign that means "fire," for example, will certainly trigger off some activity in you. A sign that means you are in danger may start the process in your nerves and muscles that makes you say "help!" In other words, the meaning that results from your decoding of a sign will start you encoding. Exactly what you encode will depend on your choice of the responses available in the situation and connected with the meaning.

Whether this encoding actually results in some overt communication or action depends partly on the barriers in the way. You may think it better to keep silent. And if an action does occur, the nature of the action will also depend on the avenues for action available to you and the barriers in your way. The code of your group may not sanction the action you want to take. The meaning of a sign may make you want to hit the person who has said it, but he may be too big, or you may be in the wrong social situation. You may merely ignore him, or "look murder at him," or say something nasty about him to someone else.

But whatever the exact result, this is the process in which you are constantly engaged. You are constantly decoding signs from your environment, interpreting these signs, and encoding something as a result. In fact, it is misleading to think of the communication process as starting somewhere and ending somewhere. It is really endless. We are little switchboard centers handling and rerouting the great endless current of communication. We can accurately think of communication as passing through us—changed, to be sure, by our interpretations, our habits, our abilities and capabilities, but the input still being reflected in the output.

We need now to add another element to our description of the communication process. Consider what happens in a conversation between two people. One is constantly communicating back to the other, thus:

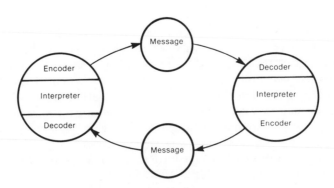

The return process is called *feedback* and plays a very important part in communication because it tells us how our messages are being interpreted. Does the hearer say, "Yes, yes, that's right," as we try to persuade him? Does he nod his head in agreement? Does a puzzled frown appear on his forehead? Does he look away as though he were losing interest? All these are feedback. So is a letter to the editor of a newspaper protesting an editorial. So is an answer to a letter. So is the applause of a lecture audience. An experienced communicator is attentive to feedback and constantly modifies his messages in light of what he observes in or hears from his audience.

At least one other example of feedback also is familiar to all of us. We get feedback from our own messages. That is, we hear our own voices and can correct mispronunciations. We see the words we have written on paper and can correct misspellings or change the style. When we do that, here is what is happening:

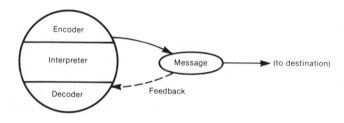

It is clear that in any kind of communication, we rarely send out messages in a single channel, and this is the final element we must add to our account of the communication process. When you speak to me, the sound waves from your voice are the primary message. But there are others: the expression on your face, your gestures, the relation of a given message to past messages. Even the primary message conveys information on several levels. It gives me words to decode. It emphasizes certain words above others. It presents the words in a pattern of intonation and timing which contribute to the total meaning. The quality of your voice (deep, high, shrill, rasping, rich, thin, loud, soft) itself carries information about you and what you are saying.

This multiple channel situation exists even in printed mass communication, where the channels are perhaps most restricted. Meaning is conveyed not only by the words in a news item but also by the size of the headline, the position on the page and the page in the paper, the association with pictures, the use of boldface and other typographical devices. All these tell us something about the item. Thus we can visualize the typical channel of communication not as a simple telegraph circuit, in which current does or does not flow, but rather as a sort of coaxial cable in which many signals flow in parallel from the source toward the destination.

These parallel relationships are complex, but you can see their general pattern. A communicator can emphasize a point by adding as many parallel messages as he feels are deserved. If he is communicating by speaking, he can stress a word, pause just before it, say it with a rising inflection, gesture while he says it, look earnestly at his audience. Or he can keep all the signals parallel—except one. He can speak solemnly but wink. . . . He can stress a word in a way that makes it mean something else—for example, "That's a *fine job* you did!" And by so doing he conveys secondary meanings of sarcasm or humor or doubt.

The same thing can be done with printed prose, with broadcast, with television or films. The secondary channels of the sight-sound media are especially rich. I am reminded of a skillful but deadly job done entirely with secondary channels on a certain political candidate. A sidewalk interview program was filmed to run in local theaters. Ostensibly it was a completely impartial program. An equal number of followers of each candidate were interviewed—first, one who favored candidate A, then one who favored candidate B, and so on. They were asked exactly the same questions and said about the same things although on opposite sides of the political fence, of course. But there was one interesting difference. Whereas the supporters of candidate A were ordinary folks, not outstandingly attractive or impressive, the followers of candidate B who were chosen to be interviewed invariably had something slightly wrong with them. They looked wild-eyed, or they stuttered, or they wore unpressed suits. The extra meaning was communicated. Need I say which candidate won?

But this is the process by which communication works, whether it is mass communication, or communication in a group, or communication between individuals. . . .

How Communication Has an Effect

The chief reason we study this process is to learn something about how it achieves effects. We want to know what a given kind of communication does to people. Given a certain message content, we should like to be able to predict what effect that content will have on its receivers.

Every time we insert an advertisement in a newspaper, put up a sign, explain something to a class, scold a child, write a letter, or put our political candidate on radio or television, we are making a prediction about the effect communication will have. I am predicting now that what I am writing will help you understand the common everyday miracle of communication. Perhaps I am wrong. Certainly many political parties have been proved wrong in their predictions about the effects of their candidates' radio speeches. Some ads sell goods; others don't. Some class teaching "goes over"; some does not.

For it is apparent to you, from what you have read so far, that there is no such thing as a simple and easily predictable relationship between message content and effect.

Nevertheless, it is possible to describe simply what might be called the conditions of success in communication—by which we mean the conditions that must be fulfilled if the message is to arouse its intended response. Let us set them down here briefly, and then talk about them:

1. The message must be so designed and delivered as to gain the attention of the intended destination.

2. The message must employ signs that refer to experience common to source and destination so as to get the meaning across.

3. The message must arouse personality needs in the destination and suggest some ways to meet those needs.

4. The message must suggest a way to meet those needs which is appropriate to the group situation in which the destination finds himself at the time when he is moved to make the desired response.

You can see, by looking at these requirements, why the expert communicator usually begins by finding out as much as he can about his intended destination and why "know your audience" is the first rule of practical mass communication. For it is important to know the right timing for a message, the kind of language one must use to be understood, the attitudes and values one must appeal to in order to be effective, and the group standards in which the desired action will have to take place. This is relatively easy in face-to-face communication, more difficult in mass communication. In either case, it is necessary.

Let us talk about these four requirements.

1. *The message must be so designed and delivered as to gain the attention of the intended destination.* This is not so easy as it sounds. For one thing, the message must be made available. There will be no communication if we do not talk loud enough to be heard, or if our letter is not delivered, or if we smile at the right person when she is not looking. And even if the message is available, it may not be selected. Each of us has available far more communication than we can possibly accept or decode. We therefore scan our environment in much the same way as we scan newspaper headlines or read a table of contents. We choose messages according to our impression of their general characteristics—whether they fit our needs and interests. We choose usually on the basis of an impression we get from one cue in the message, which may be a headline, a name in a radio news story, a picture, a patch of color, or a sound. If that cue does not appeal to us, we may never open our senses to the message. In different situations, of course, we choose differently among these cues. For example, if you are speaking to me at a time when I

am relaxed and unbusy or when I am waiting for the kind of message you have (for instance, that my friends have come to take me fishing), then you are more likely to get good attention than if you address me when noise blots out what you say, or when all my attention is given to some competing message, or when I am too sleepy to pay attention, or when I am thinking about something else and have simply tuned out. (How many times have you finished speaking and realized that your intended receiver had simply not heard a word you said?) The designing of a message for attention, then, involves timing, and placing, and equipping it with cues which will appeal to the receiver's interests.

2. *The message must employ signs which refer to experience common to both source and destination in order to get the meaning across.* We have already talked about this problem of getting the receiver in tune with the sender. Let us add now that as our experience with environment grows, we tend to classify and catalog experience in terms of how it relates to other experience and to our needs and interests. As we grow older, that catalog system grows harder and firmer. It tends to reject messages that do not fit its structure or distort them so that they do fit. It will reject Einstein, perhaps, because it feels it cannot understand him. If an airplane is a completely new experience but a bird is not, it may, as we have said, interpret the plane as a large, noisy bird. If it is Republican, it will tend to reject Democratic radio speeches or to recall only the parts that can be made into pro-Republican arguments; this is one of the things we have found out about voting behavior. Therefore, in designing a message, we have to be sure not only that we speak the "same language" as the receiver, and that we do not "write over his head" but also that we do not conflict too directly with the way he sees and catalogs the world. There are some circumstances, true, in which it works well to conflict directly, but for the most part, these are the circumstances in which our understandings and attitudes are not yet firm or fixed, and they are relatively few and far between. In communicating, as in flying an airplane, the rule is that when a stiff wind is blowing, one does not land cross-wind unless he has to.

3. *The message must arouse personality needs in the destination and suggest some way to meet those needs.* We take action because of need and toward goals. In certain simple situations, the action response is quite automatic. When our nerves signal "pain-heat-finger," we jerk our fingers back from the hot pan. When our optic nerve signals "red traffic light," we stop the car. In more complicated situations, we usually have more freedom of choice, and we choose the action that, in the given situation, will come closest to meeting our needs or goals. The first requisite of an effective message, therefore (as every advertising man knows), is that it relate itself to one of our personality needs—the needs for security, status, belongingness, understanding, freedom from constraint, love, freedom from anxiety, and so forth.

It must arouse a drive. It must make the individual feel a need or a tension he can satisfy by action. Then the message can try to control the resulting action by suggesting what action to take. Thus an advertisement usually tells you to buy, what, and where. Propaganda to enemy troops usually suggests a specific action, such as surrender, subversion, or malingering. The suggested action, of course, is not always the one taken. If an easier, cheaper, or otherwise more acceptable action leading to the same goal is seen, that will probably be selected instead. For instance, it may be that the receiver is not the kind of person to take vigorous action, even though that seems called for. The person's values may inhibit him from doing what is suggested. Or his group role and membership may control what action he takes, and it is this control we must talk about now.

4. *The message must suggest a way to meet those needs that is appropriate to the group situation in which the destination finds himself at the time when he is moved to make the desired response.* We live in groups. We get our first education in the primary group of our family. We learn most of our standards and values from groups. We learn roles in groups because those roles give us the most orderly and satisfying routine of life. We make most of our communication responses in groups. And if communication is going to bring about change in our behavior, the first place we look for approval of this new behavior is to the group. We are scarcely aware of the great importance our group involvements have for us, or of the loyalties we develop toward our several groups and institutions, until our place in the group or the group itself is threatened. But yet if our groups do not sanction the response we are inclined to make to communication, then we are very unlikely to make it. On the other hand, if our group strongly approves of a certain kind of action, that is the one we are likely to select out of several otherwise even choices.

You can see how this works in practical situations. The Jewish culture does not approve the eating of pork; the Indian culture does not approve the slaughter of cows and the eating of beef. Therefore, it is highly unlikely that even the most eloquent advertisement will persuade an orthodox Jewish family to go contrary to their group sanctions and buy pork or an orthodox Hindu family to buy beef. Or take the very simple communication situation of a young man and a young woman in a parked automobile. The young man communicates the idea that he wants a kiss. There is not much likelihood of his not gaining attention for that communication or of its not being understood. But how the young woman responds will depend on a number of factors, partly individual, partly group. Does she want to be kissed at that moment? Does she want to be kissed by that young man? Is the situation at the moment—a moon, soft music from the radio, a convertible?—conducive to the response the young man wants? But then, how about the group customs under which the girl lives? If this is a first date, is it "done" to kiss a boy on a first date? Is petting condoned in the case of a girl her age? What has she learned from her parents and her friends about these things? Of course, she will not knowingly have a little debate with herself such as we have suggested here, but all these elements and more will enter into the decision as to whether she tilts up her chin or says, "No, Jerry. Let's go home."

There are two things we can say with confidence about predicting communication effects. One is that a message is much more likely to succeed if it fits the patterns of understandings, attitudes, values, and goals that a receiver has or at least if it starts with this pattern and tries to reshape it slightly. Communication researchers call this latter process *canalizing,* meaning that the sender provides a channel to direct the already existing motives in the receiver. Advertisers and propagandists say it more bluntly; they say that a communicator must "start where the audience is." You can see why this is. Our personalities—our patterns of habits, attitudes, drives, values, and so forth—grow very slowly but firmly. I have elsewhere compared the process to the slow, sure, ponderous growth of a stalagmite on a cave floor. The stalagmite builds up from the calcareous residue of the water dripping on it from the cave roof. Each drop leaves only a tiny residue, and it is very seldom that we can detect the residue of any single drop or that any single drop will make a fundamental change in the shape or appearance of the stalagmite. Yet together all these drops do build the stalagmite, and over the years it changes considerably in size and somewhat in shape. This is the way our environment drips into us, drop by drop, each drop leaving a little residue, each tending to follow the existing pattern. This personality pattern we are talking about is, of course, an active thing—not passive, like the stalagmite—but still the similarity is there. When we introduce one drop of communication into a person where millions of drops have already fallen and left their residue, we can hardly expect to reshape the personality fundamentally by that one drop. If we are communicating to a child, it is easier because the situation is not so firmly fixed. If we are communicating in an area where ideas and values are not yet determined—if our drop of communication falls where not many have fallen before—then we may be able to see a change as a result of our communication.

But in general we must admit that the best thing we can do is to build on what already exists. If we take advantage of the existing pattern of understanding, drives, and attitudes to gain acceptance for our message, then we may hope to divert the pattern slightly in the direction we want to move it. Let us go back to elections again for an example. It is very hard to change the minds of convinced Republicans or Democrats through communication or even to get them to listen to the arguments of the opposing party. On the other hand, it is possible to start with a Republican or Democratic viewpoint and slightly modify the existing party viewpoints in one way or other. If this process goes on for long enough, it may even be possible to get confirmed party [members] to reverse their voting pattern. . . . But . . . in every campaign, the real objectives of the campaigning [are] the new voters and the undecided voters.

The second thing we can say with confidence about communication effects is that they are resultants of a number of forces, of which the communicator can really control only one. The sender, that is, can shape his message and can decide when and where to introduce it. But the message is only one of at least four important elements that determine what response occurs. The other three are the situation in which the communication is received and in which the response, if any, must occur; the personality state of the receiver; and his group relationships and standards. This is why it is so dangerous to try to predict exactly what will be the effect of any message except the simplest one in the simplest situation.

MASS MEDIA ETHICS

Deni Elliott

Deni Elliott is assistant professor in the Department of Communication at Utah State University. She has written on media ethics for trade, academic, and student audiences. She has taught seminars in ethics for the Poyntee Institute of Media Studies, the Association for Education in Journalism and Mass Communication (AEJMC), the American Society of Newspaper Editors (ASNE), and individual news organizations. Elliott is book review editor for the *Journal of Mass Media Ethics*.

Media ethics is the study of 1) how media practitioners act when making value-related decisions and 2) how they *ought* to act in making these decisions. The first is called *descriptive ethics*, the second *normative ethics*.

All decisions that media practitioners make are value related to some extent. Although the decisions are often called by other names, like *news judgments*, jargon does not change reality. Journalists decide what is "important"—what issues and events to report. They decide what is "relevant"—what information to include in a story. They decide "angle"—what sort of descriptive language, camera angle, or shot to use. These are all value decisions.

Some of the values that influence decisions relate to what journalists perceive as their professional duty. Other principles connect to the person's self-view. Ethical problems arise when values, duties, or principles conflict.

Different media practitioners have different functions in society and therefore different responsibilities. For example, journalists—reporters and editors who seek to inform mass audiences about significant issues and events—have a responsibility to help others understand important issues without attempting to persuade these others to choose one side over another in the debate. Public relations practitioners, on the other hand, work for clients with particular points of view. Their primary responsibility is to persuade an audience to accept certain beliefs about their client. Advertisers have a primary responsibility to sell their client's product. Media practitioners who work in the field of entertainment have a primary responsibility to use print, visual, and electronic media to provide recreation for an audience.

Although each of these media fields has different sorts of ethical questions determined by their different primary responsibilities, they share some basic assumptions. One is that practitioners in each field in fact have some responsibilities. The fact that media practitioners in any field have the power to affect a mass audience in a significant way implies that the practitioners have a responsibility to use that power judiciously.

Law and Ethics Are Not the Same

To some extent, law provides a tether on powerful media. Law articulates minimum standards for how media practitioners must act. Legally, journalists cannot print damaging lies about people; advertisers cannot lie about their client's product.

Morality forms the basis for law, but law expresses only a small part of personal, professional, and societal ethical systems. Although law may be the statement of some moral considerations in society, it is not the law that ultimately makes an action right or wrong. Murder is wrong, for example, and law tells people that they will be held accountable if they commit murder. But there is a law against murder because the action is wrong. It is not the case that murder is wrong because there is a law against it. Refraining from killing other people is one of our individual responsibilities to others, to community, whether or not there is a law on the books.

Media practitioners and organizations set their own standards and rules of conduct that take in a concept of morality far greater than law. To some extent, even deciding to obey the law is a moral decision. Some journalists have decided that certain information is so important that they steal documents, read classified material, or subvert the grand jury process. They cite their duty to inform the citizenry as an ethical reason for disregarding the law.

Media Ethics Is an Offshoot of Moral Philosophy

This responsibility to others, to community, finds its start some 2,000 years ago in the roots of Western philosophy. Philosophers at least since the time of Plato have been searching for answers to the questions, "What is right? What is it that makes some action right and others wrong? Media ethics takes these questions, basic to every rational being, and applies them to a particular professional role. The questions become, How do we know when journalists [or public relation practitioners, advertisers, entertainers] are acting as they should? By what criteria do we judge their professional actions? The variety of ways that people have attempted to deal with these questions can be found in classical ethical theory.

One way that people have tried to answer these questions is called *relativism*. This theory says that each person (or culture) decides on his or her own subjective basis what is right and what is wrong. I decide what is right for me, and you decide what is right for you. It does not make sense, under this theory, for you and me to attempt to talk about what is right for everyone or what is wrong for everyone. Under relativism, the decision is personal.

Many people in our culture believe that relativism is their moral code. U.S. citizens claim to value personal freedom of expression and a plurality of acceptable behaviors. On the surface, the United States may look like the embodiment of relativism, but our easy permissibility depends on some strict, universally accepted beliefs. The U.S. code might be stated this way: "You are free to do whatever you want to do as long as you do not intrude on other people and you are equally tolerant of other people's right to choose to act differently from you. And be careful not to act too far outside the mainstream. Deciding to be a member of the Ku Klux Klan is tolerable; burning a cross on your neighbor's front lawn is not." But even acceptance of this relativistic philosophy rests on some overriding principles. If media practitioners acted under a relativistic theory, then it would be acceptable for writers at the *Podunk Journal* to deceive their readers. If other news organizations told readers the truth, that would be fine, but the news organizations would have no basis for saying that the *Podunk Journal* should not tell lies.

Journalists do judge their peers at other news organizations. Awards such as the coveted Pulitzer Prize highlight the best in journalism each year. Uniform criteria are applied that would be impossible under a relativistic theory.

Journalists criticize their peers as well. When it was discovered in 1981 that Janet Cooke, a *Washington Post* reporter, had fabricated an eight-year-old heroin addict to illustrate the seriousness of Washington, D.C.'s, drug problem, the outcry was heard in newsrooms and journalism classrooms throughout the land. Cooke's actions were clearly wrong. Editors and educators talked about how public trust in the profession had been damaged by Cooke's actions; some used the case to illustrate the editor's need to know exactly who reporters are using as confidential sources. No one responded to the Cooke case by saying, "Cooke can do that if she likes; it's up to her."

Nor will relativism work when applied to other media practices. Society will not tolerate purely relativistic notions about pornography or violence in entertainment. Although communities are allowed to set their standards—to be more conservative than federal law permits—some universal limits apply. Nor can one advertiser blatantly lie to sell a client's product. Some types of persuasive manipulation are wrong for all.

It may be possible to make a case in favor of *cultural relativism* when discussing media practices by pointing out that different countries have different standards. Nudity is common on European television, for example. But whether relativism would hold up when considered on an international scale, it clearly is not an adequate theory for dealing with media ethics questions within the United States.

A second way that people have attempted to answer these basic ethical questions is called *egoism*. This theory says that what is right is the action that is in the agent's self-interest. I ought to act only in ways that help myself. But egoism is as limited as relativism in trying to provide answers to questions of ethics. This theory is questionable even when applied to individuals. Certainly many human actions are motivated out of the person's desire to serve his or her own self-interest, but many other actions are motivated out of a person's desire to benefit others, to keep promises, to act in ways that seem fair, even if the person's self-interest is not directly met through the action.

Media organizations must have some degree of self-interest to stay in business. Privately owned organizations must remain profitable to provide services. But even if the top executives have profits as their primary consideration, the media practitioners who make the initial decisions must have other considerations in mind. More than one news organization has ignored an advertiser's threats and run an important story that hurt the organization's advertising revenue. More than one public relations practitioner has refused to tell a dangerous lie on behalf of a company. In these cases, public interest has overruled self-interest.

Although relativism and egoism provide less than adequate answers for how to approach media ethics problems, classical theory and some current twists on classical theory have provided more usable solutions.

Utilitarianism is a theory that is of some use to media practitioners. The guiding rule in utilitarianism is to do what will benefit the most people. Utilitarianism is concerned with the consequences of action, with an action's effect. For example, the financial interest of a factory may be served if no one in the community knows that it is shutting down in two months. Utilitarianism, however, would dictate that the effect on the employees and their families outweighs the company's financial benefits.

It certainly was in President Nixon's benefit for the Watergate affair to be covered up. There was greater benefit in people knowing the extent of corruption in the federal government.

Another useful theory is *duty-based ethics*. This theory looks less at the consequences of action and more at the rules that govern action. For example, if one has a duty not to lie, then one should never lie under any circumstances. Although most people have difficulty accepting the theory in this ultrasimplistic form, duty-based ethics provides a criterion for media practitioners in dealing with ethical dilemmas. Most journalists act out of their primary duty to inform the public even when they know the consequences may not be favorable. For example, people in a small, conservative community may not want to recognize that a drug or suicide problem exists in their town. Despite potential public outcry, journalists will expose such problems. Citizens may not want to know that construction of a dam, which will bring needed revenue to a city, will also severely damage the environment. The journalist's duty to bring all relevant facts to the community's attention overrides the potentially angry reaction.

Many current moral philosophers base their attempts to provide answers to ethical dilemmas by combining utilitarianism's appeal to consequences and duty-based ethics' appeal to rules in an approach called *mixed formalism*. Although the decision-making systems of philosophers differ, there are some commonalities in utilitarianism, duty-based ethics, and mixed formalism that can help media practitioners caught in moral dilemmas:

1. List and consider all who will be affected by the decision.
2. Consider the consequences to those people. Be sure to consider the amount and kind of harm, along with the amount and kind of benefit for each person or group. For example, a news organization may choose to conceal details about a kidnapping in progress because the death that may result from releasing the facts outweighs the fact that a lot of people might be interested in knowing about the situation.
3. Consider the duty dictated by the profession, and try to state the principle behind that duty.

These considerations will not provide simple answers. One of the hallmarks of ethical dilemmas is that they are complex, multifaceted issues that require careful, rational decision making. Thinking through these considerations does guarantee that media practitioners have a full moral understanding of the situation and that they arrive at a solution that can be explained and justified.

Let us look at some of the problems that have been identified as ethical dilemmas for media practitioners. The catalog of problems here is far from inclusive, but they do encompass basic areas of ethical concern and illustrate how the principles of consequences, duty, and loyalty come into conflict for media practitioners.

Common Areas of Ethical Concern for Journalists

Conflict of Interest

Conflict of interest is an area of ethical concern in which journalists believe they have made the most progress. Journalists have a conflict of interest when they are involved in some other concern that either makes it impossible for them to do their news reporting effectively or when that concern might be perceived by the audience as interfering in their ability to do their job. For example, a travel writer who accepts a free trip to an exotic location might feel obligated to write a positive story about the place and about the trip sponsor. A city hall reporter romantically involved with the mayor's legislative aide might have a divided sense of loyalty and be unable to provide complete, balanced information. A news reporter actively campaigning for a senator's reelection might be perceived by readers as biased in favor of that particular senator. A publisher who serves on the board of directors for the local power company might cause readers to wonder if the newspaper can aggressively cover that company.

Most news organizations no longer allow their employees to accept gifts of any significant value, including meals and trips, in an attempt to keep members of the organization from having, or being perceived to have, a conflict of interest. Most news organizations do not allow news reporters and editors to be actively involved in any controversial issue they may have to cover. A journalist who does not ask for a transfer out of the newsroom when he or she is romantically inclined toward a source is likely to be fired.

Some conflicts of interest are not blatant, however, and thus not easy to solve through company policy. A journalist who truly has no conflict of interest would be a journalist with no interest, no religious affiliation, no political opinions, no beliefs concerning controversial issues of the day. Such an apathetic person would undoubtedly not be a creative and active identifier and interpreter of issues and events.

Deception

Deception is another area that has received considerable attention from journalists. How journalists go about collecting information is sometimes less than above-board. Journalists would have a hard time saying that they never deceive to get a story. But as there are degrees of conflict of interest, there are various levels of deception.

Most news organizations avoid masquerading, the most blatant form of deception. It is highly unusual for a reporter to go undercover as a teacher, a pregnant woman seeking an abortion, or a nursing home attendant to get a story. Most editors say they allow such techniques for an important story that cannot be gotten any other way, but they disagree on what makes a story important enough to employ these techniques, and sometimes it is hard to tell if all other means have been exhausted before turning to provocative masquerading.

Even if news organizations avoid masquerading, most reporters use deception on some level as part of their daily work. Sometimes reporters play dumb during an interview. Or they trick interviewees into telling more than they wish by a reporter who pretends to know things he or she does not. Even this low level of deception causes mistrust in reporters, and their techniques need consideration before use.

Journalistic Role

Another ethical problem in news gathering can be summed up as the journalistic role. Should the journalist be aggressive to the extent of intruding on personal grief to get a story? Are TV reporters who chase sources down the street being aggressive reporters, or are they hounding an individual?

Just as journalists can be too aggressive, they are sometimes criticized for being too dispassionate. Should a photojournalist document a suicide in progress, or should he or she put down the camera and try to prevent the tragedy? Should a reporter write a crime story that names the victim without worrying that the victim may feel he or she has been assaulted once again? What about feigning sympathy or agreement with an issue to get a source to open up? A source will be more candid if he or she thinks the journalist is sympathetic.

Confidentiality

Confidentiality is sometimes a problem for journalists. Sometimes a story source takes major risks to get information out. Other times the source is using a shield of anonymity as a way of safely taking potshots at an opponent or is using this shield as a way of testing reader reaction without taking responsibility for the idea. The reader is at the reporter's mercy when a story is provided by sources who prefer not be named. The reporter is saying, in effect, that readers will have to trust him or her. Just one journalistic mistake in misplaced trust damages the credibility of all stories presented in this fashion.

News Presentation

Although most of the current ethical concerns for journalists seem tied in to their role as news gatherers, there are ethical concerns for presentation of news as well. Language choice is an area of ethical concern. Whether a group is referred to in a story as guerrillas, terrorists, revolutionaries, or freedom fighters will have an impact on how the audience perceives the group in question. The term *fetal material* has a different connotation from *dead baby*. Both terms have been used in stories about illegal abortions.

Common Areas of Ethical Concern for Public Relations Practitioners

In many ways, public relations practitioners seem to have it easier than journalists. Journalists serve that nebulous ideal of truth; public relations practitioners know clearly where their loyalties lie. Yet that does not mean that anything goes for the public relations practitioner. The clarity of loyalty brings about some ethical problems unique to the field.

One of the most difficult ethical conflicts for public relations practitioners is the relationship with news media. The PR person wants good press for the client or company, but it is not clear how far the practitioner can ethically go in getting good coverage.

Journalists know they should not accept gifts that suggest even the appearance of conflict of interest. Does that mean that it is unethical for a company to attempt to seduce the press? Public relations personnel for cities, countries, and corporations know that the quickest way to the people is through the press. If travel writers are brought in at no expense to the news organization and discover through a carefully planned itinerary what a great spot Podunk is, they will write glowing stories about their find.

Public relations practitioners also find less blatant ways to gain free publicity for their clients. The Pillsbury Bake-Off and the children's fashion show sponsored by the local department store do far more than allow regular folks the chance to show off their talents. These sponsored events create a good deal of free publicity for their clients. Do they constitute a misuse and manipulation of news media?

Public relations practitioners also have to deal with the problem of false or misleading statements. How far should a PR person go in protecting a company? When is it acceptable to deceive or lie to the news media? What information should the public relations person disclose no matter what the company wants?

Common Areas of Ethical Concern for Advertisers

Advertising is based on the belief that products should compete in the free marketplace. Theoretically the best detergent will triumph. Advertising can only get the product into the home; once a product fails to perform, no advertising can restore the consumer's confidence. Theoretically, the consumer is a rational individual, able to decide among products and see past cute jingles and clever rhetoric to judge the product being sold. However, this theory is far from reality. The marketplace is made up far more often of parity products (products that have no essential difference among them). Parity raises an ethical problem for advertisers: how to make the client's product seem as good as possible without lying about its performance. Aim toothpaste cannot be called a "better cavity fighter than all the rest," but it can be called "the best money can buy."

Advertisers try to stretch their clients' product claims as far as linguistically possible. The operating convention is to say whatever you can for as long as you can. The Federal Trade Commission decides the claim is deceptive, it will so inform the advertiser. The intention of the advertiser is to deceive. It wants to make the public think something without actually saying it. Toothpaste has little to do with falling in love, but when the singer implores, "Want love? Get Close-Up," advertisers hope the listener will put the question and answer together as though Close-Up is a reasonable answer to the question. Advertisers, like public relations practitioners, have their clients' interests at heart. Does that loyalty justify intentional deception of the audience?

Perhaps the tendency for advertisers to mislead would be less of a problem if the audience were always composed of rational, educated adults. But they are not, and specialized audiences create another ethical problem. It is difficult for educated adults to decipher "the best that money can buy" to understand that it means "no better than any of the rest." Children can hardly be expected to do this sort of logical processing. Nor can children be expected to understand that toys shown in simulated environments will not seem the same in their own homes. Adults can enjoy watching the $20,000 sports car drive off into the sunset in a prime-time commercial and only feel a hint of "wouldn't it be nice?" Children are encouraged to desire expensive toys advertised around Saturday morning cartoons, even though the toy is too expensive for most parents to afford. Yet advertisers often aim their pitch directly at children knowing that children can influence parents to spend money that they otherwise would not.

Product presentation in advertisements must capture the audience instantly on a billboard or print advertisement; there must be instant appeal in television commercials to keep the audience watching for thirty or sixty seconds. Instantly the audience must get the story line—normal, happy family; businessman; housewife. Formula identification like this leads to stereotyping, an ethical concern in advertising and the entertainment field.

The Frito Bandito, a Mexican caricature, disappeared through pressure by Hispanic groups, but questions are still raised about advertising's depiction of other groups, women in particular. The ideal female, young with perfect hair and body, is used to sell everything from guns to butter. On the other hand, the harried and haggard housewife puts in an appearance for pain relievers and some cleaning products. Feminists contend that neither gives a fair representation of women.

Yet while advertisers struggle not to be caught in traditional stereotypes, they may have created a new one, equally false and damaging to women. The idealized Super Mom, the young woman who manages a career and children and still has time to serve as her husband's sex queen in a thirty-second commercial, would not keep her hair in place for five minutes in the real world. Women who have realized through their own hard experience that Super Mom is only another stereotype are offended by the fantasy image.

Ethical Problems Common to the Entertainment Field

Few people need to be introduced to the basic ethical problems that exist for entertainment media. Concerns about violence and other morally offensive material are grist for news media mills. News organizations that refuse to cover other news organizations because they fear being perceived as self-serving cover the debate over what ought to be shown on prime-time TV with glee.

Television is not the only medium that entertains. Well over half of the daily news hole of most newspapers is filled with entertainment material: syndicated advice columns and humor columns, comic strips, and feature stories. Mass media entertainment, in print or broadcast, does more than help people fill time between dinner and bed, entertainment pieces educate and socialize.

We learn about moral heroes through feature profiles—people who risk their lives to help strangers. We learn how to deal with child molestation, drug use, and other crises through watching prime-time situation comedies. Yet when violence is shown, some of the learning may be not what the writers and producers intended. The basic concern about showing violent acts is that the dramatized event may lead people to commit the same acts. Does a TV movie that depicts gang rape encourage similar acts? Psychological experts disagree. Screenwriters and producers must consider the effect that such scenes could have on some members of the audience.

Morally offensive material is another area of ethical concern. Is it acceptable to show drug use, including the use of alcohol, that encourages viewers to do the same? Do depictions of extramarital sex simply reflect real life, or do they contribute to the decline of moral standards?

Media practitioners who work in the entertainment field must consider the educative and socializing affects of their entertaining messages.

Ethics: A Problem for Industry and for Individual Practitioners

Individual practitioners are not completely on their own in dealing with the ethical problems. Laws set some minimum standards for industry, and the industries themselves have attempted to limit their own practice through the formulation of industry codes. All four media fields have some statements of professional conduct or codes of ethics. But these codes do not provide the answers to ethical problems.

The codes are not necessarily accepted by all practitioners. None of the fields requires that their practitioners be licensed or governed by peers, as do doctors and lawyers. Acceptance of a particular code may be prerequisite for a practitioner who wishes to join particular industry groups, but group membership is not necessary for someone to hold a job in the media industries.

Even if the industries were able to coerce practitioners to follow codes, most are not enforceable. For example, according to the Public Relations Society's Code of Professional Standards, members of the Public Relations Society of America "shall adhere to truth and accuracy" and "shall not engage in any practice which tends to corrupt the integrity of channels of communication or the processes of government." According to their code of ethics, members of the Society of Professional Journalists, Sigma Delta Chi, are told, "There is no excuse for inaccuracies or lack of thoroughness." Dictates such as these cannot be enforced without clarifying exactly what the public relations practitioner or the journalist must do to meet these standards, an impossible goal. These are not specific standards for performance; they are descriptions of the ideal professional goals that practitioners should strive to meet.

Although it is clear that, according to these codes, neither public relations practitioners nor journalists should intentionally deceive audiences, truth and accuracy do not necessarily follow. Gaining truthful or accurate information often depends as much on the integrity of sources as the journalist's or public relations officer's motivation. Deadlines and other pressures often make a completely accurate or thorough story impossible. Lack of information may corrupt the channels of communication from a journalist's point of view; silence may be the wisest response a public relations officer can give in some situations.

Codes and statements of professional standards can help practitioners keep in mind the principles on which their profession rests, but the individual practitioner must interpret these goals through practice.

Ethical considerations assume freedom on the part of the practitioner— freedom to make choices among alternative behaviors. Ethical considerations assume responsibility as well—the responsibility the individual practitioner feels toward the profession and toward the public.

Suggested Readings

Ethical Theory, Applied and Professional Ethics

Baier, K. *The Moral Point of View: A Rational Basis of Ethics.* New York: Random House, 1967.

Bayles, M. *Professional Ethics.* Belmont, Calif.: Wadsworth Publishing Co., 1981.

Bok, S. *Lying: Moral Choice in Public and Private Life.* New York: Vintage Books, 1979.

———. *Secrets: On the Ethics of Concealment and Revelation.* New York: Pantheon Books, 1982.

Bowie, N. *Making Ethical Decisions.* New York: McGraw-Hill, 1985.

Feinberg, J. *Rights, Justice and the Bounds of Liberty.* Princeton: Princeton University Press, 1980.

Goldman, A. *The Moral Foundations of Professional Ethics.* Totowa, N.J.: Rowman & Littlefield, 1980.

Goodpaster, K. E., and K. M. Sayre. *Ethics and the Problems of the 21st Century.* Notre Dame: University of Notre Dame Press, 1979.

Nozick, R. *Anarchy, State and Utopia.* New York: Basic Books, 1974.

Olshewsky, T. *Foundations of Moral Decisions: A Dialogue.* Belmont, Calif.: Wadsworth, Inc. 1985.

Rawls, J. *A Theory of Justice.* Cambridge: Harvard University Press, 1971.

Regan, T., and D. Van Deveer. *And Justice for All: New Introductory Essays in Ethics and Public Policy.* Totowa, N.J.: Rowman & Littlefield, 1982.

Taylor, P. *Principles of Ethics: An Introduction.* Encino, Calif.: Dickenson Publishing Co., 1975.

Media Ethics

Callahan, D., W. Green, B. Jennings, and M. Linsky. *Congress and the Media: The Ethical Connection.* New York: Hastings Center, 1985.

Christians, C., K. B. Rotzell, and M. Fackler. *Media Ethics: Cases and Moral Reasoning.* New York: Longman, 1983.

Elliott, D. *Responsible Journalism.* Beverly Hills, Calif.: Sage, 1986.

Goldstein, T. *The News at Any Cost: How Journalists Compromise Their Ethics to Shape the News.* New York: Simon and Schuster, 1985.

Goodwin, H. E. *Groping for Ethics in Journalism.* Ames: Iowa State University Press, 1983.

Haseleen, K. *Morality and the Mass Media.* Nashville: Broadman Press, 1968.

Hulteng, J. L. *The Messenger's Motives: Ethical Problems of the News Media.* 2d ed. Englewood Cliffs, N.J.: Prentice-Hall, 1985.

Journal of Mass Media Ethics.

Lambeth, E. *Committed Journalism: An Ethic for the Profession.* Bloomington: Indiana University Press, 1986.

Merrill, J. C., and S. J. Odell. *Philosophy and Journalism.* New York: Longman, 1983.

Merrill, J. C., and R. Barney. *Ethics and the Press: Readings in Mass Media Morality.* New York: Hastings House, 1975.

Phelan, J. M. *Disenchantment: Meaning and Morality in the Media.* New York: Hastings House, 1980.

Rivers, W. L., W. Schramm, and C. G. Christians. *Responsibility in Mass Communication.* 3d ed. New York: Harper & Row, 1980.

Rubin, B. *Questioning Media Ethics.* New York: Praeger, 1976.

Thayer, L. *Ethics, Morality and the Media.* New York: Hastings House, 1980.

2
The Press

Introduction

The modern newspaper was the first medium of communication with a genuinely mass character. Although some societies have used writing for more than 2,000 years, the development of printing had to await the complex technological achievement of the printing press and the production of uniform paper. Four hundred years more elapsed before social conditions were ready for the daily newspaper. During the American Revolution, there were no daily papers, only irregular pamphlets for the elite. It was not until the 1830s that the population concentration in cities and the spread of mass literacy provided a market for a mass press.

Once imaginative newspaper pioneers discovered that with the aid of advertising revenues they could produce a cheap product like the penny press, they found a ready market in the large metropolitan centers. Like the later electronic media, the founders of the press initially enjoyed bonanza conditions while their audience rapidly grew. Their progress was greatly aided by improved city transportation and the invention of the telegraph. The latter permitted rapid news gathering, and collective services utilizing the wire were organized as early as 1848.

By the 1880s, the period of easy entry for the would-be newspaper tycoon was over, and the industry entered into a period of intense competition. This period witnessed the spread of yellow journalism, the unprincipled use of sensationalism and gimmickry, as major chains, including Pulitzer and Hearst, battled for supremacy and the small papers for survival. Socially and politically influential reformers responded with threats to regulate the news industry. These warnings were heeded, and the papers adopted self-imposed reforms and set up standards for journalism.

Newspaper circulation outpaced population growth as mass transport improved, literacy became more widespread, and the nation became more urban. But in terms of the number of papers sold per household, newspaper circulation reached its peak in 1919. Thereafter, although the total number of papers sold has generally continued to rise slowly, the decrease in competing papers and competition from other media have produced a slow decline in circulation per household.

The first reading, by William Solomon, provides an overview of the newspaper business. It is, first of all, a business and one experiencing an increase in corporate concentration. These factors influence the ways in which newspapers are organized and run. Solomon describes the organization of the newsroom and the decisions that are made to fill the paper's news hole through to production.

James E. Fields next examines in greater detail one of the topics raised by Solomon, the effects of chain ownership. Ownership means different things to various interested parties, and the evidence of the harm or benefit of chain ownership is mixed—and as F. Dennis Hale adds in the next reading, no one wants to pay the price for definitive research to find out. *Editor & Publisher* magazine provides overall statistics on the chains.[1] Gannett leads in most categories; it has 85 dailies (rivaled only by Thompson with 84) and 57 Sunday papers and leads in daily circulation with 4.8 million. Six other chains have a combined daily circulation of over 2 million. They are, in order, Newhouse (26 papers), Knight-Ridder (30), Chicago Tribune (8), Dow Jones (22), Times Mirror (7), and News America (5 papers).

In recent years, the total number of dailies in the United States has declined, though the number of cities being served has continued to rise. Within the cities there is less competition. About 97 percent of all cities served by daily papers have no truly competitive choice; only a few large cities offer two or more independent dailies. Consolidation cannot be blamed entirely on a concerted buildup of newspaper empires. It is also the result of local economies of scale—the sharing of printing facilities, as well as the imperatives of advertising and the competition from radio and television. This concentration has not led to the development of national newspapers with massive circulation, which are common in Europe, although *USA Today,* the *New York Times,* and the more specialized *Wall Street Journal* are expanding in this direction. The lack of a national press is probably due less to transportation and technical difficulties than to the decentralized nature of American politics. Competition is no longer among rival newspapers but between the press and other media.

The two readings that follow are concerned with the content of newspapers. Leonard Leader describes the format of *USA Today* section by section. The short, snappy stories, color, and heavy use of photographs have made it a successful daily. Leo Bogart's survey of dailies shows that several of these features are being adopted by newspapers around the country. The total news content and size of the papers increased between 1977 and 1983. Some trends run against what readers (in opinion surveys) say they want. Thus the move toward more features rather than hard news, more local and less international news, and less regular special interest columns cannot be supported by reader demands.

The other products of the press—books and magazines—often have less of a mass character. Few books sell more than 5,000 copies, although actual readership may be considerably higher for those circulated by libraries. In the United States, the book industry issues about 38,000 new titles per year. Book reading is by and large a matter of personal choice, although book clubs and publicity attempt to create mass markets. The 700 million textbooks sold per year account for about $1 billion to the publishers, a third of their total income. Although textbook readership is seldom voluntary, they certainly provide part of the students' media environment. Paperback trade books may approximate mass circulation by widespread availability on supermarket racks. The book publishing industry, despite mergers and conglomerate take-overs, remains highly competitive, with over one hundred major publishers and hundreds of smaller ones. Entry into the business is easy because the capital required is low (since printing is normally contracted out), but investment entails risk; small publishers come and go rapidly.

Magazine publishing is similarly competitive, and the overall market declined from 1976 to 1983 according to the Audit Bureau of Circulation.[2] *Reader's Digest*, however, has remained strong, with 17.9 million domestic circulation in 1983. Ironically, the second highest mass circulation magazine, *TV Guide* (17.1 million), is devoted to a rival medium. General audience news magazines (aimed primarily at an educated or well-informed reader) fall far below the circulation of the top two: *Time*, 4.6 million; *Newsweek*, 3.0 million; and *U.S. News and World Report*, 2.1 million. *People* magazine has a circulation of 2.8 million. *National Geographic* (10.6 million) is the only major surviving graphic magazine to grace doctors' waiting rooms.

The other top magazines, and the fastest growers, are specialized and can deliver a concentrated group of consumers. They are therefore a good advertising buy for the nonmass producer, and they are often very profitable. *Modern Maturity* has the highest circulation, 9.3 million. The most successful category is women's and home-oriented magazines. The leaders are *Better Homes and Gardens* (8.0 million), *Family Circle* (7.1 million), *Woman's Day* (7.0 million), *McCalls* (6.4 million), *Good Housekeeping* (5.4 million), *Ladies Home Journal* (5.2 million), *Redbook* (4.0 million), and *Cosmopolitan* (3.0 million).

Men are served by *Playboy* (4.2 million), *Penthouse* (3.5 million), and *Hustler* (1.1 million), together with sports and outdoor magazines like *Sports Illustrated* (2.4 million), *Field and Stream* (2.0 million), *Outdoor Life* (1.5 million), and *Sport* (0.9 million). There are magazines for numerous hobbies (*Popular Mechanics, Photoplay*) and participant sports (*Yachting* and *Golf Digest*, which grew from 4,000 circulation in 1970 to 834,000 in 1976 and 1.18 million in 1983). Quality magazines of opinion and the arts (*New

Yorker, Atlantic, Harper's) and the new city magazines (led by *New York*) add to the diversity of American magazines. If current trends persist, the future outlook is for continued specialization of new magazines and fierce competition for the advertising dollar.

Carl Sessions Stepp investigates the growing group of magazines that celebrate personal success. As earlier writing on newspapers showed, those magazines appeal to the audience that advertisers want the most, the affluent young to middle-aged.

Notes

1. *Editor & Publisher*, April 28, 1984, pp. 76–80.
2. *Information Please Almanac Atlas and Yearbook 1985*, p. 508.

THE NEWSPAPER BUSINESS

William S. Solomon

William S. Solomon teaches in the Department of Journalism at the University of Illinois. He has worked at various editing jobs for three daily newspapers, and he has a Ph.D. in sociology from the University of California, Berkeley. His research interests include press criticism, media theory, and technological change.

> The function of the press in society is to inform,
> but its role is to make money.—A. J. Liebling (1975, p. 6)

Liebling's words point up a basic conflict within the U.S. daily newspaper. Like any other business, it is profit oriented, but unlike virtually any other business, a newspaper also is responsible for providing people with the information they need in order to participate in society. (In radio and television, the primary content is entertainment. National news magazines inform, but not about local matters and not daily.) These two purposes, profits and public service, seldom fit neatly together. The result is a steady tension that affects most of the decisions and tasks that go into putting out the paper.

Economics

The daily newspaper is, like most other U.S. mass media, advertising based; most of its revenues come from its advertisers, not its readers. This point is crucial. To pursue maximum profits, a newspaper publisher would seek to publish as many ads as possible while charging as much as possible for advertising space. To do this, the publisher must convince advertisers that it is beneficial to them to advertise in this newspaper because it attracts the kind of readers that the advertisers want to reach.

Newspaper publishers do not take this task lightly. In 1837, James Gordon Bennett, publisher of the *New York Herald,* wrote that the penny press could be a free press "simply because it is subservient to none of its readers—known to none of its readers—and entirely ignorant who are its readers and who are not" (quoted in Schudson 1978, p. 21). But today newspaper publishers are eager to learn who their readers are and to this end large circulation papers use consultants and marketing surveys. Then they try to figure out how to attract people who do not read their newspapers but would be attractive to advertisers.

Who are these readers? Plainly, they are not poverty stricken or the elderly. They are, instead, "affluent consumers 18 to 49 years of age, the heavy buying years, with above median-family income" (Bagdikian 1983, p. 111). How can the paper reach these people? Again, press critic Ben Bagdikian says it succinctly: "The standard cure for 'bad demographics' in newspapers, magazines, radio and television is simple: Change the content. Fill the publication or the program with material that will attract the kind of people the advertisers want" (1983, p. 112).

This simple formula has dramatic effects on newspaper content. On one level, newspapers acknowledge their public service role by printing some news they think the public ought to know about. But increasingly newspapers are far more concerned with profits and print what they think the public wants to know about. This latter approach is well expressed by a marketing consultant who advises newspapers:

> If Procter and Gamble was not doing marketing research on their products . . . Crest toothpaste, for example, would not be the success story that it is.
>
> [Question] (But there's something basically different, isn't there, between newspapers and toothpaste or soap?)
>
> Well, they're—not to keep going to our Procter and Gamble example, but—they're toothpaste. The tubes are different; ingredients may vary

slightly. . . . But . . . newspapers are a commodity . . . and if they're going to build circulation, they've got to give people what they want. (CBS News 1978)

A similar point is made by William Dean Singleton, a Texan who owns twenty-two daily newspapers: "Our philosophy is to edit our papers for readers. To find out what the readers want and edit it that way" (*Editor & Publisher* 1986, p. 12).

To be sure, journalists have long felt obliged to provide human interest stories (Hughes 1940) as well as more serious news. But the current focus on giving the readers what they want has gained importance; the entire newspaper has been revised accordingly to include special sections devoted to food, fashion, life-styles, and the like. Splashy graphics, bigger photographs, and colored inks are part of this trend. The problem is that all this does not mean simply that a newspaper's serious news pages have become surrounded by growing amounts of fluff. Serious news is itself being cut back:

> In the two-year period of 1977–79, a majority of all papers . . . made what their managements described as "substantial" changes in editorial content, graphics, and layout.
>
> Papers of all sizes increased their use of photographs, changed typefaces, and changed the number and width of columns. About two out of five changed the ratio of news to features, and of these nearly three times as many increased features as increased news. (Bogart 1981, p. 150)

So in an increasingly complex world, newspapers are providing less news. Further, the selection of news is done with a mind to attract readers considered desirable:

> Newspapers control the readership by not reporting significantly on neighborhoods of low-income and elderly populations and by promoting their circulation in affluent neighborhoods with the desired characteristics. (Bagdikian 1983, p. 201)

This view is held not only by a press critic. A stock brokerage firm's newspaper analyst recently told a meeting of newspaper publishers that "to survive the next recession . . . publishers will have to drop or drive away subscribers who represent 'demographic targets within markets that are not productive for the advertiser'" (Dorfman 1986, p. 13).

It scarcely would be breaking new ground to say that newspaper economics is perhaps the most powerful influence on newspaper content. What is new is the intensity with which ever-increasing profits are being pursued. In part, this stems from the increasing sophistication with which all advertising-based media are seeking to identify audiences and deliver them to advertisers. Newspaper analyst John Morton (1984, p. 17) says, "In the competition for advertising, everybody is chasing essentially the same dollars." The other main reason is the growing tendency for newspapers to be bought by large corporations.

Ownership Trends

Corporate mergers have flourished during the Reagan administration. So has the media conglomerate, a corporate entity that specializes in acquiring mass media companies. By its nature, the media conglomerate runs counter to the requisites for an independent, watchdog press. The problems involve finance and ethics. The corporate attitude toward the profits–public service conflict is summed up by a production official at a chain-owned newspaper: "A newspaper's business is making money; it's not to serve the public, although we do have to keep that as one of our priorities. But by and large, we're here to turn a profit for the company, and our owners, the stockholders" (Solomon 1985, p. 17).

Inheritance tax laws encourage newspaper heirs to sell the family business. Media conglomerates are eager buyers, in part because corporate tax laws encourage them to invest their profits in more acquisitions. By the end of 1985, newspaper chains—or groups, as they prefer to be called—controlled 77 percent of the 62.8 million newspapers sold daily in the United States (Lorfano 1986).

A newspaper bought by a chain becomes one of that firm's properties. From then on, the newspaper's policies and priorities reflect the parent firm's needs more than the needs of the community in which the newspaper is situated. The primary corporate need is not simply profits but ever-increasing profits:

> The impact of trading newspaper securities on the stock market has meant that news companies must constantly expand in size and rate of profits in order to maintain their position on stock exchanges.
> This has meant the end of a company reaching a steady state of profits in real dollars, and a new ethic of squeezing the maximum from every newspaper unit in the corporation in order to buy ever more properties, not always in the news business, and to declare ever growing dividends. (Bagdikian 1979, p. 24)

A second key problem with chain ownership concerns ethics. Anyone who owns a newspaper needs to be careful about political activities and financial investments if he or she would avoid potential conflicts of interest.

But as a corporation, the media conglomerate has needs that an individual or a family does not have:

> As media conglomerates join the ranks of giant corporations, they require capital to expand and need well-connected executives to run interference with government agencies. Thus, through interlocking directorates, media corporations are tied to the nation's largest banks, corporations, law firms, think tanks and foundations, universities, philanthropies and business policy planning groups. (Dreier 1982, p. 114)

In a study of some 300 directors of the twenty-five largest U.S. newspaper chains, Dreier and Weinberg (1979, p. 51) found "thousands of interlocks with institutions the papers cover—or fail to cover—every day."

Along with the growth of newspaper chains, another trend is a decrease in the number of U.S. daily newspapers. There were 2,433 in 1910 (Lee 1937, p. 723); by the end of 1985 there were 1,676 (Lorfano 1986). One could argue that broadcast media and cable TV have meant more competition for advertising revenues. Yet the newspaper business is highly profitable, or else the U.S. corporate sector would not be buying newspaper businesses.

If newspapers are profitable, why aren't there more of them? First, it is far more profitable—and less risky—to buy a newspaper than to start one. Another reason is the economics of mass advertising. If there are several newspapers in the same town, advertisers have to buy several ads in order to reach all readers in that community. More crucial, in a competitive situation, the newspaper with the biggest circulation can charge the highest advertising rates yet still attract the most advertisers because the advertiser's cost per reader drops as the number of readers increases. The result is that the biggest newspaper in town gets richer while the others fade. In short, the newspaper business is highly profitable but only for the survivors. Newspaper chains hasten this process by closing newspapers in competitive situations (tax write-offs) and buying ones in monopoly situations.

Today, less than 2 percent of all U.S. dailies face competition from another daily covering the same circulation area. As A. J. Liebling said (1975, p. 30), "A city with one newspaper . . . is like a man with one eye, and often the eye is glass."

Structure and Operations

Most newspapers are organized along similar lines: business, editorial, and production. The business side takes care of advertising, circulation, and similar areas; editorial is concerned with nonadvertising content—what we usually call journalism; production runs the presses. The larger the newspaper, the more likely it is that these operations will be subdivided. Business may have separate departments for display ads, classified ads, promotion and market research, and so on. Editorial often has separate operations for the editorial page(s), feature news, sports, and business news, in addition to the newsroom.

Unlike some European newspapers, U.S. newspapers are not run democratically. The publisher picks the top executives, who in turn supervise the hiring process in their respective departments. It is the rare publisher who hires editors with political views he or she dislikes. Further, nearly all U.S. newspaper publishers are white and politically conservative. It follows that in news selection and placement, their newspapers will reflect their general political outlook.

This structure allows the newspaper publisher to claim that he or she does not meddle with the news operations of the paper; in fact, the publisher controls them. If the newspaper is chain owned, the chain of command is extended upward by one step:

> The new owning corporations of our media generally insist that they do not interfere in the editorial product. All they do is appoint the publisher, the editor, the business manager and determine the budget.
>
> If I wanted control of public information that is all I would want. I would not want to decide on every story every day or say "yes" or "no" to every manuscript that came over the transom.
>
> I would rather appoint leaders who understand clearly who hired them and who can fire them, who pays their salaries and decides on their stock options. I would then leave it to them. (Bagdikian 1982, p. 4)

Display advertising, not news, determines the size of a given day's editions. Each paper sets a ratio of news to ads, based on the profit level it seeks. If more display ads are sold for a given day, that day's editions will have more pages. This is why Monday and Saturday editions tend to be thin, while the papers are fat on Wednesdays and Thursdays—days when merchants think people are likely to shop. If there is much news on a day when the newspaper is to be thin, the news is crammed into the available space. The stories will be fewer and briefer, the photos fewer and smaller.

Dealing with such limitations is the province of the newsroom. At a daily news meeting, key staff members make such decisions. Whoever is in charge of the newsroom—often the managing editor, although the title varies—usually decides what stories will go on the front page. The tendency is to aim for a mix of local news and nonlocal news, of feature news and serious news.

Often the managing editor has worked as a reporter and as an editor and has shown a desire to move into management. At many smaller dailies, the managing editor is not yet forty years old. This is because newspaper publishers seek eager, "with it" people who can make the paper more attractive to "desirable" readers.

Other people at the daily news meeting include the department heads from business news, sports, and feature news. The city editor and the wire editor also attend as a rule. Each of these persons brings a list of stories, including some that he or she thinks might go on the front page. Often each person pitches stories to the managing editor. Once the front page is set, each of the meeting's participants has some leeway as to how to fill his or her pages.

Sports reporting is no longer just a matter of who won which game. Drugs, player contract negotiations, strikes, team franchises moving, and similar news items are part of sports. Increasingly such stories appear on the front page.

It has been said that business leaders pay little attention to their local newspaper's business pages, which contain mostly rewrites of their own press releases. Further, only a small percentage of the U.S. population owns stocks or runs businesses. Still, advertisers want to reach such people, and most newspapers emphasize their business news pages. Not surprisingly, there is almost no investigative reporting here. On the rare occasion when a newspaper does report corporate sins, such a story is placed in the news pages. The business pages are reserved for boosterism and for business as usual—trends, transactions, tips, and so forth.

Still, a sound knowledge of business and financial matters is most helpful for reporters and editors in this area; business people often complain that newspaper people lack such understanding. But a critical view of the private sector— much less of corporate capitalism—would likely disqualify a journalist from such work.

As gender roles have changed during the past ten to twenty years, the women's pages have become feature news pages. Such pages now include topics once left to magazines: life-style, health, home furnishings and repairs, science news, and others. The idea is to attract new readers and advertisers. Consequently feature news reporters have more status than formerly. But as with their business page colleagues, their usual role is boosterism. Consumer advocacy does not please advertisers. What is wanted is uncritical reporting on new ways to spend money and enjoy life—from intriguing vacations to high-tech kitchen gadgets.

The tendency toward splashier layouts, bigger photographs, and a more casual writing style is perhaps most evident in the feature pages. It is here that newspapers feel most free to break from convention. Ironically this drive for innovation, because it usually includes writing, often results in a relaxation of the traditional standard of objectivity. Feature news need not be bland. As media critic David Armstrong (1986) notes, "Cultural criticism, rock and book reviews . . . often constitute most of the colorful, opinionated writing in a newspaper."

The newsroom remains the heart of the newspaper. Typically a city editor is in charge of the local news-gathering operation and assigns stories, often suggesting what the news in them is, and then reviews what the reporter submits. The city editor can make revisions in the story's substance, tone, and length, can require the reporter to rework the story, or can even reject it. Almost always the city editor has worked as a reporter. Usually the city editor also assigns photographers. With the current emphasis on graphics, photo-journalists have a better chance to display their work than was formerly the case.

The wire editor is responsible for news not written by the paper's staff. This editor glances through news stories as they are transmitted to the newspaper's computer via telephone, microwave, or satellite. The more wire services a newspaper subscribes to, the more stories there are for the wire editor to read, albeit hastily. Each wire service sends a daily budget listing what it considers to be the top stories. The wire editor usually brings copies of the budgets to the daily news meeting.

After the front page stories are picked, the city editor and the wire editor make final decisions as to which other stories will go in the paper. At large dailies, a metro editor or layout editor may make such decisions. Usually this person also lays out the pages (positions stories and photos around the ads). This work is done on page dummies from the advertising department, which outline the position and size of the ads on each page. *Layout* means deciding what size headline and how much space a story will receive. Then the stories are sent to the copy desk for final editing and for the writing of headlines and photo captions. At small newspapers, copy editors may also lay out the pages.

A typical copy desk will have a chief copy editor, or slot person, and three to six copy editors on the rim. The slot assigns stories, checks them, and sends them to the composing room, the first stop in preparing plates for the printing presses. At large dailies, sports, features, and business have their own layout editors and copy desk. The copy desk does substance editing and technical copy editing. It judges "the significance and quality of the reporting," and it makes "technical corrections in spelling, grammar and sentence structure" (Bagdikian 1984).

Writing good headlines and photo captions means saying much in few words. With their emphasis on graphics, many newspapers value bright, lively headlines as much as, or more than, good editing. Too often the result is a catchy headline on a poorly edited story, a practice that amounts to shoddy journalism.

Perhaps the most basic function of any general circulation newspaper is to provide solid, thorough coverage of local news. In order to participate in their community, people must know what goes on. This is the reporter's job—and very few reporters on the biggest dailies got there without first having proved themselves at smaller papers.

Newspaper reporters work on *beats* or on general assignment. The reasoning behind beats (city hall, the courts, and other specific areas) is that certain parts of the social structure are crucial enough to require a reporter's undivided attention. The problem with this approach to news coverage is that it tends to become "a self-fulfilling prophecy. Under deadlines and competitive pressures, reporters file stories from these beats rather than venture off the beaten track" (Dreier 1983, pp. 23, 26). In short, government officials and corporate executives have far more access to journalists than do the poor and the powerless. As a result, "the structure and ideology of newswork . . . results in a steady stream of 'news' that reflects the hierarchy of power and authority in the larger society" (Dreier 1978, p. 73). Some reporters and editors recognize this problem. But almost no publishers do, and they decide who runs the newsroom. This is why some daily journalists end up working for magazines or as freelancers.

Production and Technology

As with many other workplaces, the newspaper has experienced much technological change in recent years. For the newsroom, the computer has meant that video display terminals (VDT) have displaced the typewriter. Elsewhere in the building, computer-driven typesetting has eliminated production jobs.

Although writing is generally considered to be faster and easier on a VDT, editing is slower and harder (Solomon 1985). The advent of VDTs has not brought a large increase in editing staff. But it has meant that, in addition to their journalistic work, editors have been given responsibility for performing production tasks on the VDTs, such as setting column widths and determining typefaces. The result is less time spent on editing, less job satisfaction, and higher turnover rates (Solomon 1985).

The new newspaper technologies were introduced for other reasons: to shift control of the production process to the newsroom, while eliminating production jobs and cutting production time. (From 1975 to 1984, the total number of workers at U.S. newspapers rose from 377,000 to 441,000. At the same time, the number of production workers, included in these totals, decreased from 168,000 to 166,000 [U.S. Census Bureau 1986, p. 413].) Unlike people, machines do not take vacations, go on strike, become ill or pregnant, or require pension plans. Greater profits and greater control over the labor force are exactly what the U.S. corporate sector values most. So newspapers will continue to use new technologies toward these ends.

Conclusion

From the penny press of the 1830s, the U.S. daily newspaper has evolved into a carefully calculated package of information designed to appeal to specific segments of the population. Ironically, this is reminiscent of the earliest days of the U.S. Republic when only property owners could vote. The current marketing strategy of the U.S. newspaper industry amounts to nothing less than the "deliberate exclusion of a third to a half of the American population" (Bagdikian 1983, p. 202). This strategy is contributing to a two-tier information system in U.S. society. The wealthy, upper tier is information rich. The lower tier—the poor, the elderly, racial minority groups—is increasingly deprived of the information all people need in order to participate in the decisions that affect their lives. In short, democracy is being sacrificed at the altar of ever-increasing profits. Given the steady increase in ownership of newspapers by the U.S. corporate sector, this situation will only worsen.

References

Armstrong, David. 1986. Personal communication, June.

Bagdikian, Ben H., 1979. "More Mergers Mean Less News." *Journalism Studies Review* (July): 21–24, 60.

———. 1982. "New Push for News-Staff 'Voice' Urged." *Guild Reporter*, April 23, pp. 1, 4, 5.

———. 1983. *The Media Monopoly.* Boston: Beacon Press.

———. 1984. Personal Communication.

Bogart, Leo. 1981. *Press and Public: Who Reads What, When, Where and Why in American Newspapers.* Hillsdale, N.J.: Lawrence Erlbaum Associates.

CBS News. 1978. "The Business of Newspapers." Documentary.

Dorfman, Ron. 1986. "Learning Cashbox Journalism." *Quill* 74 (July–August): 12, 13.

Dreier, Peter. 1978. "Newsroom Democracy and Media Monopoly: The Dilemmas of Workplace Reform among Professional Journalists." *Insurgent Sociologist* 8 (Fall): 70–86.

———. 1982. "Capitalists vs. the Media: An Analysis of an Ideological Mobilization among Business Leaders." *Media, Culture and Society* 4 (April): 111–132.

———. 1983. "The Corporate Complaint against the Media." Quill 71 (November): 16–29.

Dreier, Peter, and Steve Weinberg. 1979. "Interlocking Directorates." *Columbia Journalism Review* (November–December): 51–68.

Editor & Publisher. 1986. "A Texan Returns Home," July 5, pp. 11, 12.

Hughes, Helen MacGill. 1940. *News and the Human Interest Story.* Chicago: University of Chicago Press.

Lee, Alfred McLung. 1937. *The Daily Newspaper in America: The Evolution of a Social Instrument*. New York: Macmillan.

Liebling, A. J. 1975. *The Press*. 2d rev. ed. New York: Random House.

Lorfano, Joseph J. 1986. Interview, July 23.

Morton, John. 1984. "Revenge of the Shopper." *Washington Journalism Review* 6 (March): 17.

Schudson, Michael. 1978. *Discovering the News*. New York: Basic Books.

Solomon, William S. 1985. "Technological Change in the Workplace: The Impact of Video Display Terminals on Newspaper Copy Desk Work." Ph.D. dissertation, University of California, Berkeley.

U.S. Bureau of the Census. 1986. *Statistical Abstract of the United States: 1986*. Washington, D.C.: Government Printing Office.

NEWSPAPER OWNERSHIP

James E. Fields

James E. Fields is professor and chairman of the Department of Journalism at the University of Wisconsin in Eau Claire. He received his Ph.D. from the University of Missouri with an emphasis in publishing (finance, law, and technology). He worked as a methods analyst, doing industrial engineering cost and efficiency studies, and for eight years as a newspaper editor, and has been the publisher of several small periodicals.

In the early years of American newspapers, ownership of a newspaper meant owning and operating some wood and metal equipment for setting type and making multiple copies of an inked impression of that type on paper. Two hundred years later, that form of operation has changed thoroughly except in a few rural communities. In the early years, ownership also represented an opportunity to inform and influence the community while possibly earning a modest living from such activity. Those opportunities remain, although earnings are generally far from modest. Newspaper ownership is now a complex responsibility involving many people with varied viewpoints concerning the role of ownership as well as their own roles or relationship to the newspaper.

There are almost 1,700 daily newspapers in the United States with a total daily circulation of 62,723,438; most of those newspapers have a street sale price of twenty-five cents. Newspaper employment increased during 1985 to 453,000 people, of whom 41 percent are women. Newspaper advertising revenue also increased in 1985 by more than 8 percent, to a total of more than $25 billion. When grouped by circulation size, the largest group is medium-sized circulation (10,000 to 50,000 copies). Only about 250 newspapers have circulations of more than 50,000, and only four of those have audited circulation exceeding 1 million copies per day. There are also 7,711 weekly newspapers with an average circulation of 6,497 and a total exceeding 50 million. (Other newspapers are published for special groups, such as people of the same race or religion, but those are excluded from this discussion, as are Sunday newspapers.)

Such figures suggest a healthy, diversified industry offering news and opinion at a price within the budget of most American households. Nevertheless, articles appear regularly in journalism reviews and other publications voicing concern that the healthy industry has a growing illness that could harm American society. This illness can be seen in two trends: 1) concentration of ownership, and 2) limited competition.

Both trends indicate that oligopoly, a feature of even more industries in the United States, is becoming a characteristic of newspaper ownership. Critics may deplore the trend to oligopoly in other industries, such as transportation or electronics manufacturing, but they often seem to accept its inevitability in postindustrial society, possibly because economies of scale associated with some forms of oligopoly may have produced lower prices for consumers.

Critics of newspaper oligopoly are considerably less accepting. The concentration of newspaper ownership has for years remained high on the list of topics that are viewed with alarm. The primary reason for this alarm appears to be a libertarian notion that concentration of ownership will result in a loss of content quality. The worst-case scenario combines a restriction in the flow of information and a decreased number of voices expressing opinion. The result is a citizenry unable to function effectively as members of a self-governing society.

A secondary reason for alarm is the notion that concentration of ownership in the newspaper industry may not produce desirable economic benefits, such as lowered prices for customers or better wages for newspaper workers. The postulate is that newspaper owners may be less ethical and public spirited, or just more penurious, than their counterparts in other industries. Put another way, a newspaper owner who enjoys a market-area monopoly may not behave responsibly toward employees or the public in the manner expected of business firms in an enlightened age.

Scholars have taken an increased interest in both content quality and monopolistic pricing behavior. They have probed the notion that concentration of newspaper ownership will restrict the flow of news, information, ideas, and opinion to members of the public needing this flow to function in their role as self-governing citizens. The research, however, has provided mixed results. One reason, perhaps, is that concentration and its results take different forms, and research may focus on only one. The effect of group ownership (of multiple newspaper properties in different cities) has been studied; so has the single-newspaper city or noncompetitive market. Another research variable is the form of newspaper content—news and opinion. Both have been studied.

Three researchers (Donahue, Olien, and Tichenor 1985, p. 497) found "substantially lower reporting of local conflict in those newspapers with multiple ownership and headquarters outside the state, compared to those with ownership within Minnesota." Three other researchers (Browning, Grierson, and Howard 1984, p. 38), however, concluded that "the effect of chain ownership, be it Gannett or Scripps-Howard, was negligible in news coverage" of a controversial issue in one Tennessee community.

Regarding opinion, one study (Thrift 1977) of twenty-four daily newspapers showed that the editorials published after an independent newspaper was purchased by a chain were less argumentative and controversial. Another study (Hagner 1985, p. 281), in contrast, reported that twenty-five years of research "has not supported the argument that non-competitive marketing areas are disadvantaged"; the free exchange of ideas was not inhibited. Research on editorial page content revealed that opinion writers at both independent and chain newspapers have similar freedom to write as they please, expressing their own views; however, chain owners are more conservative than independent owners in their endorsements of candidates (St. Dizier 1986).

There is virtually no research support for the hypothesis that newspaper owners, particularly the groups or chains, see their properties as vehicles to political influence and will dictate content accordingly. To whatever extent ownership influences content, some other motivation—if there is any—seems more likely.

Some scholars have detected that financial, not ideological, considerations are the more plausible explanation for qualitative differences between independent newspapers and those owned by the chains. Soloski (1979) argued that economics and business management techniques are at the heart of group influence and gave three examples:

1. The group-owned wire service provides copy, which, because of its ready availability, may supplant local news and features.

2. Group-established profit goals influence the local publisher to seek economies; newsroom salaries, including overtime pay for coverage of breaking stories, are vulnerable.

3. Management by objectives can introduce techniques to increase productivity at the expense of quality.

Another scholar (Flatt 1980) found that management by objectives at a different chain newspaper may be used more positively to encourage high-quality journalism.

A recent and thorough research project (Litman and Bridges 1986) explored an economic commitment theory that embraced at least three major variables: size of the newspaper's full-time staff, number of news services purchased by the newspaper, and allocation of space in the newspaper for news content. Those three were tested against four categories of organizational variables: ownership characteristics, intermedia competition, market conditions, and publication structural components such as morning versus evening publication. The objective was to predict newspaper quality or performance. But the impressive methodology and considerable data accumulation resulted in "no definitive and unambiguous conclusions" (Litman and Bridges 1986, 23). Clearly many outside variables, such as population growth in a community, could serve better than oligopoly as the reason for variations in newspaper quality or performance.

A new research construct offers interesting new approaches to the study of newspaper ownership. One of these is the umbrella model (Rosse 1975). It goes beyond the traditional competition of equals to posit competition between layers: metropolitan dailies with regional news coverage, metros emphasizing local coverage, suburban dailies, and a fourth layer of weekly newspapers, including shoppers. As competition within layers virtually disappears, competition and its effects should increase between layers. Study of that competition can examine quality of news and opinion content, but more fertile research ground may be found in the business areas, specifically advertising and circulation, with interesting results. One study of layers found that "weekly publishers felt more competition from small dailies for circulation than vice versa. The reverse was true for advertising. Small daily publishers said they would gain a larger increase in ad sales without weekly competition than weekly publishers said they would gain without daily competition" (Lacy 1984, p. 642). Newspaper owners in every layer should expect continued competition for the foreseeable future with results similar to that found in other industries: survivors will probably be bigger. Also, because most newspapers compete in a limited geographical territory, the winners will gain a monopoly within the conjunction of their layer and market.

Unless it is restrained by some higher power such as government regulation, the newspaper monopolist may exhibit predatory pricing behavior. Because government regulators tread softly where newspapers are concerned, citing concern for the First Amendment, newspapers are freer than some other industries. One study of advertising prices (Blankenburg 1983) indicated that they were higher for newspapers owned by a successful major chain than for independent newspapers. Another study, this one of newspaper chain policy concerning circulation (Blankenburg 1982) describes what seems to be a paradox: chain ownership leads to fewer subscribers but to higher revenues.

Existing tax laws are probably the major factor in the continuing trend toward chain ownership. In addition to inheritance taxes, which encourage families to sell, the tax law differentiation between earnings from dividends and those from capital gains has encouraged newspaper companies to buy other newspapers (Dertouzos and Thorpe 1982). This means that the trend toward chain ownership could continue until chains control 100 percent of the circulation. Then the only escape from taxes would be mergers, large chains acquiring smaller chains, until only a handful of media giants remain. The ultimate chain or monopoly would be a single owner of all the nation's newspapers, though that does not seem likely.

The purchase prices offered by chains for available newspapers in recent years might also encourage a family to forsake its historical stake in a community and become instantly rich. Gannett Co. Inc. paid $200 million for the Des Moines Register and $300 million for the Louisville Courier-Journal. (Matusow 1986, 24)

If neither government nor newspaper owners will abate present trends, we can expect continued concentration of newspaper ownership: only one metropolitan newspaper owner in all but a few U.S. cities, continued acquisitions and mergers, and consolidation of most large dailies into ever fewer newspaper chains, some of which also own broadcast stations and other media properties.

Is there an alternative scenario? The most plausible is an increase in community newspapers with low production costs due to emerging technology. Such newspapers might circulate initially as free shoppers; others might have a modest selling price. But few could be expected to provide much detailed information on events outside the community of publication.

Newspaper ownership in the United States has produced a product that in many ways is better than ever and remarkably superior to its counterparts in many other parts of the world; simultaneously, that ownership operates a complex and efficient enterprise generating attractive profits. The flaw is stagnant circulation levels, sometimes by conscious choice, an unfulfilled stewardship of service to the nation that has nurtured the tradition of a free press.

References

American Newspaper Publishers Association. 1986. *Facts about Newspapers: A Statistical Summary of the Newspaper Business*. Washington, D.C.: AWPA.

Blankenburg, W. B. 1982. "Newspaper Ownership and Control of Circulation to Increase Profits." *Journalism Quarterly* 59, no. 3: 390–398.

———. 1983. "A Newspaper Chain's Pricing Behavior." *Journalism Quarterly* 60, no. 2:275–280.

Browning, N., D. G. Grierson, and H. H. Howard. 1984. "Effects of Conglomerate Takeover on a Newspaper's Coverage of the Knoxville World's Fair: A Case Study." *Newspaper Research Journal* 6, no. 1: 30–38.

Dertouzos, J. N., and K. E. Thorpe. 1982. *Newspaper Groups: Economies of Scale, Tax Laws, and Merger Incentives.* Santa Monica: Rand Corporation.

Donohue, G. A., C. N. Olien, and P. J. Tichenor. 1985. "Reporting Conflict by Pluralism, Newspaper Type and Ownership." *Journalism Quarterly* 62, no. 3:488–499, 507.

Flatt, D. M. 1980. "Managerial Incentives: Effects at a Chain Owned Daily." *Newspaper Research Journal* 2, no. 1:48–55.

Hagner, P. R. 1985. "Newspaper Competition: Isolating Related Market Characteristics." *Journalism Quarterly* 60, no. 2:281–287.

Lacy, S. 1984. "Competition among Metropolitan Daily, Small Daily and Weekly Newspapers." *Journalism Quarterly* 61, no. 3:640–644.

Litman, B. R., and J. Bridges. 1986. "An Economic Analysis of Daily Newspaper Performance." *Newspaper Research Journal* 7, no. 3:9–23.

Matusow, B. 1986. "Allen H. Neuharth Today: What Does Gannett's Guiding Genius Do for an Encore?" *Washington Journalism Review* (August): 18–24.

Rosse, J. N. 1975. "Economic limits of press responsibility." Discussion Paper, Stanford University Studies in Industry Economics, No. 56.

Soloski, J. 1979. "Economics and Management: The Real Influence of Newspaper Groups." *Newspaper Research Journal* 1, no. 1:19–28.

St. Dizier, B. 1986. "Editorial Page Editors and Endorsements: Chain-owned vs. Independent Newspapers." Paper presented at the annual convention of the Association for Education in Journalism and Mass Communication, Norman, Oklahoma.

Thayer, F. 1956. *Legal Control of the Press.* 3d ed. Brooklyn: Foundation Press.

Thrift, R. R., Jr. 1977. "How Chain Ownership Affects Editorial Vigor of Newspapers." *Journalism Quarterly* 54, no. 2:327–331.

AN IN-DEPTH LOOK AT CHAIN OWNERSHIP

F. Dennis Hale

Dennis Hale is associate professor of journalism at Bowling Green State University in Ohio.

Reprinted from *Editor and Publisher*, vol. 117:17 (April 28, 1984). Used by permission.

What, then, is the truth about the widely feared Thomson chain? Does it really suck all the profit it can from its new acquisitions without regard for journalistic quality or employee morale? Or does Thomson simply impose long-needed management reforms that cause resentment among lazy employees?

Reporter Jerry Chaney asked those three questions after visiting Kokomo, Indiana, in 1982 to examine the impact of the Thomson chain on that city. Chaney's in-depth story produced as many questions as answers. Mixed findings dominate the research, reportage, and debate concerning the quality of chain and independent newspapers.

Reporters and editors are themselves divided on the controversy. One year after Thomson bought the *Kokomo Tribune*, the editor was removed. The Thomson publisher said the old editor was insensitive to the needs of the local people. The departing editor said that powerful people in Kokomo hoped to use the new newspaper ownership to reassert their influence over the news.

Journalists from Texas to Alaska both defend and criticize chain ownership. Ben Sargent, editorial cartoonist for the Austin, Texas, newspaper, said chain ownership improved his paper: "A case can be made that chain ownership can render a paper more independent of the local pressures which reduce most small and medium-sized dailies, and many large ones, to anemic, blithering boosterism."

Investigative reporter Bob Porterfield contended that the *Anchorage Daily News* ceased being a "boat-rocker and bush-shaker" after it was purchased by a California chain: "They say they want to build advertising before rocking the boat. I think that kind of philosophy slips over into a lot of these chain acquisitions." (The new ownership vehemently denied Porterfield's allegation.)

Meanwhile, the growth of chains continues unabated. By 1982, 155 chains controlled two-thirds of the over 1,700 dailies in the United States, representing 72 percent of weekday circulation and 75 percent of Sunday circulation. By 1983, 26 "double digit" chains controlled 10 or more dailies each.

The trend continues, even during the recessionary 1980s. Some 104 dailies were sold during the last three years. Six of every seven were sold to chains.

The chain–independent debate is moot and passé, some would argue. Chains own most American dailies and soon will absorb the 533 independents. Chain ownership is the norm. It's a foregone fact.

That argument misses a major distinction. Most chains are small, averaging seven newspapers. In recent years, small chains have been purchased by large chains. That trend and the growth of large chains should be the concern of debaters, researchers, journalists, and policy makers.

To date it has been easy for policy makers to ignore the question. They lacked hard evidence proving that a real problem existed. That now is changing as more research is being conducted that compares chains and independents.

One of the first studies was conducted over ten years ago by Gerald Grotta, who now lives in Forth Worth. His 154-newspaper study compared papers that had changed from independent to chain between 1950 and 1968 with papers that remained independent or chain.

Grotta compared various quantifiable characteristics, many related to news quality, including subscription price, editorial employees, news hole size, editorial page news hole, and proportion of local news. He found no significant differences and concluded that chains benefit chains more than they do newspaper readers: "If there are indeed significant economic efficiencies from larger scale operations in the industry, this study indicates that those benefits are not being passed on to the consumer."

Grotta's analysis of space devoted to non-advertising items and local news is as close as anyone has come to measuring the quality of news in chain and independent papers.

Influence on Editorials

However, three researchers have studied the influence of newspaper ownership on editorials. The most limited of the three studies found no differences. Political scientists from the University of Windsor compared editorials about the 1972 federal election in Canada in three independent papers and four papers from one chain. Regionalism—not ownership–shaped the themes of the 811 Canadian editorials.

Two, more comprehensive, studies found major differences. Three journalism professors at the University of Minnesota analyzed presidential endorsements by most American dailies for four elections, 1960 through 1972. They found that chain papers were more likely to favor the favorite candidate and that papers within a chain were overwhelmingly homogeneous in presidential endorsements. The researchers concluded: "Clearly these data run counter to the insistence of chain spokesmen that their endorsement policies are independent from chain direction."

But what about editorial coverage of local problems, the raison d'être of newspaper editorial pages? A University of Oregon graduate student, Ralph R. Thrift, Jr., analyzed editorials in 24 West Coast papers for the years 1960 to 1975. Sixteen papers had changed from independent to chain during the period; eight remained independent throughout. Thrift found no differences in editorials in the two groups of independent papers during 1960.

However, in 1975, 7.6 percent of editorials in the chain papers fell in the category of argumentative, controversial, and local. This contrasted with 17.6 percent of editorials in the independent papers. Thrift concluded: "But clearly, this study demonstrates that chains have had an impact on the editorial quality of the dailies they have purchased on the West Coast. And certainly, the impact is not helpful to readers who seek guidance on local matters when they turn to the editorial pages of their daily newspapers."

Pricing, Marketing Strategies

William Blankenburg shifted attention to the marketing and pricing strategies of chains. Specifically, the journalism professor at the University of Wisconsin compared the strategies of the chain, Gannett, with other chain and independent papers. Blankenburg's findings will make you sell your house and buy Gannett stock.

In his first study, Blankenburg compared changes in circulation during the 1970s for 35 Gannett and 35 other newspapers. This was the decade when newspapers faced cost increases, distribution problems, and newsprint shortages. Gannett papers managed continued growth in revenue and advertising and subscription rates despite reductions in total circulation and household penetration that exceeded non-Gannett papers. Gannett, with the pooled know-how from over 70 dailies, succeeded at cutting services while increasing prices and revenue.

In his second study, Blankenburg zeroed in on the key revenue source of dailies: local retail advertising. He compared local ad rates for 54 matched pairs of Gannett and non-Gannett papers. Blankenburg used 12 different measures of advertising rates, all derived from current rate cards of the 108 newspapers. Measures compensated for differences in circulation and page sizes. "On the average, it costs a small advertiser, paying the nominal open rate, an average of 84¢ an inch, or 11.2 percent, more to appear in a Gannett daily than in another daily," Blankenburg reported. For one measure, Gannett advertisers paid 18.2 percent more than advertisers in other papers.

The findings of William Blankenburg and others led to my own study of 200 randomly selected, dominant daily newspapers. The "dominant" means that the study was restricted to counties with only one daily in which out-of-county papers reached fewer than 11 percent of local households.

Newspapers were divided into two groups: independents and small chain papers, and large chain papers. Large chains were those with four or more papers. There were 87 independent and small chain papers and 113 large chain papers from 41 states.

The study used 1980 county census data and 1981 magazine and newspaper circulation figures. Cities in the study included Mobile, Ala.; Fresno, Calif.; Des Moines, Iowa; Minneapolis, Minn.; Omaha, Neb.; Raleigh, N.C.; Cleveland, Ohio; Tulsa, Okla.; Memphis, Tenn.; Austin, Texas; Tacoma, Wash.; and Milwaukee, Wisc.

In some respects the two kinds of newspapers and their home counties were identical. Included were the proportions of minorities (Blacks and Spanish speaking), mean value of homes, and percentage of households reached by newspapers.

In other respects, the two groups were quite different. Chain papers were more likely to subscribe to United Press International and less likely to take the Associated Press. Chains were more likely to subscribe to the Sunday supplement, *Parade*, and less likely to take *Family Weekly*.

Magazines circulated more heavily in the counties of large chains. *Fortune* reached 22 percent more households, and the *New Yorker* 24 percent, *Better Homes & Gardens*, *Cosmopolitan*, *People*, *Playboy*, *Reader's Digest* and *Time* had higher circulation. Only *TV Guide* and *Farm Journal* had lower circulation levels in the chain counties.

Most importantly, chain papers charged 14 percent more for a monthly subscription, an average of $6.12 to $5.38. This exceeded what was justified by the one more issue that large chain papers published a month.

Large chain papers existed in more affluent counties. Household incomes averaged $1,300 more a month than in the independent paper counties, and apartment rents averaged $15 more a month. Large chain counties also had a higher percentage of high school graduates and urban residents.

Chain papers subscribed to more news services than the independents, 2.2 to 2.5. The chain's own news service accounted for the difference. Chain counties also had less competition from out-of-county papers, both on weekdays and on Sunday.

Thus a small body of research demonstrates that, indeed, chain papers are different from independents, that chains possess powerful magnets for drawing money out of communities, and that chain editorials tend to be innocuous. None of the research indicates that chains use their superior economic power to provide a better quality of news coverage.

Studies Are Expensive

An empirical study comparing the quality of news in chains and independent papers would be expensive. Where is the financial support for such a study? Private foundations of chains and media conglomerates? Obviously not. University journalism programs? Also unlikely. They have to worry about chain support for buildings, VDTs, scholarships, and the employment of their graduates. The federal government? Not if elected members of Congress have anything to do with it. Just one chain, Gannett, publishes in 34 states. Sixty-eight U.S. senators are concerned about Gannett coverage and election endorsements. State and national press associations? No chance. They are dominated by chain affiliates who have the time to be active in such organizations.

Robert M. Shaw, retired manager of the Minnesota Newspaper Association, recently lamented the resistance of press association members to discussions about newspaper ownership: "Nobody wanted to talk about group ownership because whoever in the room hadn't already been bought out or was currently negotiating was waiting—hoping—to be asked."

Gannett in particular makes a difficult target for officials who wish to limit the size of chains. For Gannett is a progressive corporate leader in the promotion of women and minorities and the protection of the First Amendment. To attack Gannett is to attack a civil liberties crusader.

Chains with reputations for editorial excellence such as Gannett and Cox and Knight-Ridder do not threaten an independent press. The real threat comes from the continued absorption of independents by chains, the subsequent absorption of small chains by larger ones, and the absorption of newspaper chains by corporate conglomerates. Unfortunately, empirical research cannot measure the impact of such economic concentration on the quality of news and commentary.

USA TODAY—USA TOMORROW?

Leonard Leader

Leonard Leader is a lecturer on media history at the University of Southern California's School of Journalism. He received his doctorate at UCLA in U.S. history, specializing in urban history. His career includes years as a journalist and editor.

Reprinted from *The Journalist,* a USC School of Journalism publication, vol. 1:4 (September, 1983). Used by permission.

USA Today was born September 15, 1982, announcing that it was "this country's first nationwide, satellite-delivered, general interest daily newspaper." The founding publishing company, Gannett, called it a giant step in the history of the land.

Will that date take a place alongside the first daily newspaper, the 1783 *Pennsylvania Evening Post;* or with the September 3, 1833, first successful penny paper, the *New York Sun;* or the raucous tabloid child of 1919, *The Illustrated Daily News* of New York? All three found new audiences and changed the face of American journalism.

USA Today is the new brassy, colorful kid on the block. First reactions to the newcomer in the world of the journalists was dismay at the brevity of the printed stories; at *USA Today* they favor "a quick read." Two typical jokes surfaced: Did you hear that a *USA Today* reporter rushed into the city room with a 18-inch story and the editor said, "Good, we'll make it a three part series"? Or the news that *USA Today* won a Pulitzer Prize for "the best investigative paragraph"? The air was full of charges of "junk journalism," "MacPaper," "fast food journalism," "TV journalism"—the verdict was in quickly. *USA Today* was perhaps a logical continuation of printed repetition of the TV tube's news, a very profitable idea, and on the whole a bowl of very thin gruel.

There is much truth to the brevity charge. At *USA Today* they wear the accusation as a medal and point with pride to the fact that only the cover stories in its basic sections—News, Money, Sports, Life—require a continuation. Polls of readers show that most readers do not care for the jumps. *USA Today's* editorial director, John Siegenthaler, says he does not see the national daily doing long or in-depth pieces. The more extended editorial articles are about 400 words in length, about 300 to 350 words less than the average op-ed contribution.

At *USA Today* they have a precise image of the reader they are seeking. Siegenthaler paraphrases Ruth Clark (marketing research analyst with Yankelovich, Skelly and White) who described the reader as "transient, mobile, busy, doesn't have time to read the paper the way you might." Bluntly, the new daily asserts there is an army of people in a hurry—business travelers, in bus and airport terminals, and hotel guests who are potential readers. (We are told that on a given day 1.7 million of us are in hotels and 850,000 are in bus and air terminals.) That constituency is offered two pages with news of fifty states and sports scores down to the local high school teams. The moving crowd is offered a paper away from home; increasing hotels are giving guests free copies of the paper.

While affirming that it is a full newspaper, it still calls itself "a second newspaper" pointing out that local and in-depth news is the mission of the hometown newspaper. The target is the person who will buy two papers. It is not the aim of *USA Today* to cut into the circulation of any other daily.

When *USA Today* was launched, the *New York Times* called it the second national newspaper for a general news audience, noting that the *Times* already sold same-day newspapers in all fifty states. The new paper was not seen as a challenge by Leonard R. Harris, *Times* corporate relations director, who said, "We think of ourselves as a newspaper that will reach the top one percent of the population in terms of education and management or professional position and salary." Allen H. Neuharth, Gannett Company's chairman and president and creative genius of the new daily, adds that *USA Today* is "not designed for journalists."

There is a careful design and plan behind the birth of *USA Today*. Television's style, color, splash, and brevity haunt the new daily. One commentator said the television news scene has been frozen on to the printed page. One daring idea implies that *USA Today* will win TV viewers back to the newspaper. This five-day-a-week daily is on the sidewalks of the nation in colorful simulated 21-inch television sets. (A report tells of a thief who took one home to harbor his portable TV.) The newspaper gives summary sentences on the news in the style of anchor persons; often the front page index item refers one to not much more coverage inside.

At *USA Today* there is open admission that the long periods of planning were influenced by both television news and weekly news magazines. Are we seeing a reversal in media development in which the newer television form influences the older newspaper form?

The decisions on the creation and character of *USA Today* represent much study, research, and polling. Gannett Company owns and uses the survey firm of Louis Harris & Associates and claims to have spent a minimum of $1 million in the prepublication stages. Neuharth's Gannett base is the largest U.S. newspaper chain with eighty-six dailies including *USA Today*, and thirty-five nondailies, plus ownership of seven TV stations, thirteen radio stations, and the largest outdoor advertising firm in the United States and Canada. In 1982 the operating revenues were better than $1.5 billion. The

Gannett Company is number 229 on *Fortune* magazine's list of the top businesses in the country.

The charge of a skimpy TV-like news presentation forces one to examine *USA Today*'s substance in its four sections: News, Money, Sports, and Life. Brevity is the basic style. On occasion some articles run a little longer. A "long read" of many months found substantive pieces on the editorial pages. The cover stories, one per section, do jump inside. There are daily interviews of a half a page in length on the op-ed page, with such well-known figures as General Ariel Sharon of Israel and Mike Wallace of CBS.

I start with the news section A of the edition of Friday, May 27, 1983, a day chosen at random. It was the issue before the Memorial Day holiday. Pluses and minuses become apparent. The story of the death of the first American adviser in El Salvador is two lines far down in the page 1 index. It is backed by almost 20 inches of type, headline, and a one-column picture on page 2. The international economic summit in colonial Williamsburg has a two-column, 2¼-inch index listing alongside a small picture of President Reagan. Inside there are 123 columnar inches on page 7, from which one must subtract 33 inches of pictures and informative captions. Both stories can be described as fair coverage.

Rarely does foreign news get a big play in *USA Today*. The editors rest with their belief that the readers have little interest in news from outside this country.

With the El Salvador death and the Williamsburg economic parley given minimal space on page one, what is played in the prominent place? The big, better than half-page banner headline is "Good ol' summertime!" It is the cover story important enough to jump inside with the holiday news of "Ocean to ocean, time for lotion." A small picture of a sun lotion salesman is cut into the 29 columnar inches. Dominating the front page is a living color picture of the top half of a bathing beauty.

"Family stress hurts I.Q." is the other above-fold page one story. Three lesser article items on the page inform us that "More states ban one-way car windows," "Layoffs are down, output up," and "FCC clears way for FM expansion." The page's bottom corners contain a one-column shot of small flags to be placed on Memorial Day on Arlington National Cemetery graves and the ever-present two column, "USA snapshot." This one is a multicolored graphic on the length of average hospital day stays in ten top states. (On another day the "snapshot" caught the popularity of Mother's Day cards compared to Father's Day and other occasions.)

In short, this pre–Memorial Day page one is wrapped around holidaying. Was there chagrin in the editorial office that mustard and frankfurters were impossible to deliver with each copy? Another day the central page one cover story involved the problems of mowing the lawn.

Continuing our search for substance inside the paper, we learn that Mark

Twain can rest in peace, for *USA Today* has done something about the weather story and directs you inside to a whole page of weather on a national scale in a splashing, waving, color-streaked page-wide map of the USA. The whole page tells nothing but the weather. Not even television has been able to match *USA Today*'s handling of this prime subject. Weather in sixteen local areas from Seattle to Miami; inlets for Alaska and Hawaii; freak weather phenomena get special exciting graphics. Weather in cities around the world marches in a small box, and there is a state-by-state yesterday, today, and before-weekends report. There is more weather than a body can stand!

The graphics of the weather page are part of the general worship for graphics at *USA Today*. The pages are spiced with graphics and charts. Our model issue has more than fifty counting innumerable sports listings. Graphics overwhelm pictures on the pages. Has the ancient Chinese adage on pictures and words to be revised for the primacy of graphics? Cynics charge that a good graphic at *USA Today* will push a story or a picture off page one. Surely the sameness of location for graphics on page one makes for a more rigid layout and crimps the ability to come up with varying page ones.

Money, section B, is the second substantive part of the paper. Making money and managing your finances are reader interests to be served. (Neuharth, stressing that *USA Today*'s aim is to make money, quipped that the accent in Gannett is "net.") It is obvious that Money is not a section for the professional money makers—brokers, financiers, bankers, full-time money makers, and large investors. But there is much in it for the semiprofessional and the amateur who finds the *Wall Street Journal* too detailed. It is a fulsome section. Useful graphics and charts abound. There is no doubt that Money attracts many readers, especially in the 1982–1983 bull market.

Sports, section C, has been hailed by America's sports fans. No one seems to have a critical word for the extensive coverage with its many graphics and charts. (One on college running teams lists USC NCAA titles as twenty-six since 1921, "more than five times as many titles as the next closest schools.") Scores for many sporting events in the fifty states, including possibly your own hometown basketball team, are listed. In general, sports are big. Every *USA Today* front page plays up a Sports item in the top right corner. (The other two snipes refer to Money and Life section features.)

What about the substance of Life, section D? The section has under its tent all the world that News, Money, and Sports do not encompass. It is loaded with short features on movie celebrities, plays, books, TV series, interviews ("Sadat's widow has made her peace" is a 24-inch feature including a one-column picture), rock festivals, "a quick read on what people are talking about," movie reviews, a crossword puzzle, medical fees, suicides, and lots more. (Why are there no comic strips?) The section reflects the popularity of gossip columns, magazines such as *People*, the popularity of psychology, diets, space movies and the latest fads. There is a complete chain and cable TV program with preview items. Life has substance.

On the general content level *USA Today* must be given better than passing grades, operating on Booker T. Washington's thesis of "picking up the bucket from where it is." The multiplicity of items, a veritable smorgasbord, can inundate the reader with so many facts that major issues are lost. One longs for a long article of analysis and a chance to think a matter through, not the machine gun staccato of many small items. Can the forest be seen when the ground is covered with thousands of mere saplings?

Where does *USA Today* stand on the big issues? As with other newspapers, many of the editorial targets are safe ones such as checking off a dollar on your income tax for the Olympic team, against exorbitant funeral industry costs, for citizen neighborhood watches against crime, and against bossism in politics. Alongside marshmallow topics one can find tougher stances: an editorial backing "a decent burial" for the MX missile, a charge that President Reagan had "wrapped himself in the presidential flag . . . waving a blank check for defense." The concept of an editorial page on one theme each day presenting varied and opposing viewpoints is a very good one. Especially unique is a national inquiring photographer asking and receiving viewpoints of men and women across the land. (Pictures were taken at a national event such as a fair and filed to be called in by phone on an issue at a later date— clever, eh?)

The editorial goal is consensus, not confrontation. There is insistence that consensus does not mean lack of independent view and weakness.

The *USA Today* outlook rests on serving its readers, informing them and our nation's leaders, shaking up the journalists, and making it financially by attracting the advertisers. Al Neuharth, chairman and president of Gannett, signed his name to such a credo in the first edition.

Let us consider Neuharth, a model for Horatio Alger, for a moment. He is the son of a South Dakota farmer who died during the depression when Al was two. Raised by a hard-working mother the future publisher sold newspapers at an early age, was a printer's devil at a dollar a week, dropped out of college, served in World War II, and came home to difficulties and final success as he climbed up the newspaper ladder to his present high post. When he spoke at the *USA Today* inaugural day September 15, 1982, in Washington, D.C., he told the attending president of the United States and the countless guests that his country needs "another good 25-cent newspaper" in the tradition of Woodrow Wilson's vice-president Thomas Marshall's call for "a good five-cent cigar." The publisher sees his baby as "The Nation's Newspaper," and he sees it as "Yankee Doodle Dandy" full of pride that always capitalizes USA in the up-beat headlines. (In the downbeat stories it seems that we become plain Us.)

At *USA Today* they believe they are in step with a "return to patriotism in America" and that this will add to the appeal of a national daily. Though the front page lacks the daily Old Glory in color the *Chicago Tribune* used to carry, the spirit is there in the many colors and the endless statistics and polls telling us about our land. Life in our fifty states with its whimsies, cutsies, and foibles is portrayed without end. It is as if the Statistical Abstract and the U.S. Census Reports were worn dog-eared by the editors. Those two sources and the latest studies and polls about American ways are constantly flooding the pages.

The patriotism theme was present in the prelaunch publicity, which had Uncle Sam in a suit and high hat of red, white, and blue reading the new paper. The endless statistics should fill one with pride about the country and increase the cries of "gee whiz," and "I didn't know that," themes that have built and guided the *Reader's Digest*.

Neuharth and the *USA Today*'s philosophy is imbued with patriotism. One sees it in the noncontroversial nature of the headlines and the stories, the generally nonconfrontational editorials, the downplaying of the world scene, the belief expressed in Neuharth's inaugural address that "*USA Today* hopes to serve as a forum for a better understanding and unity to help make the U.S.A. truly one nation."

The diversity of the nation and a strong feeling about it is reflected in the composition of the 250 persons on the staff of *USA Today*. It is not an accident that 43 percent of the staff are women, that 23 percent are minorities. The editorial page staff of ten has four women and two blacks and spans ages twenty-five to sixty-two. This attention to this problem reflects the generally open and egalitarian approach of the Gannett chain, which has a long record of support, practical and financial, of minority integration in the media.

Neuharth speaks of understanding between government and people, free press and readers, all with "the rich diversity and unique unity that makes this truly one nation, indivisible under God." A typical page one streamer stresses: "Grass-roots spirit building in USA." They love those headlines at *USA Today*. One hopes that the unity doesn't become a wallpaper covering holes in the wall.

It is worrisome that there is no embarrassment at *USA Today* when asked what happens to the investigative mission of the press. The powers that be are clear. That is not the mission of this new national daily. Can they even dream of a Pulitzer Prize? What zealous reporter eager for Woodward-Bernstein acclaim can mount a steed here to challenge evils? This nag is too short, too thin, not pointed in the correct direction, and lacks the required wind.

Would they have left the Pentagon Papers closed, the Watergate trail cold, the horrors of Vietnam uncovered? We hope that in the interest of brevity and national unity, *USA Today* does not take itself off the investigative firing lines.

The country will watch *USA Today,* but the past watches too. The probing cartoons of a Thomas Nast join with the cries of muckrakers Lincoln Steffens, Ida Tarbell, and Upton Sinclair. Is there room for the courage of a Heywood Broun who as writer and union builder helped improve journalism, or the voice of an Edward R. Murrow who helped topple a dangerous demagogue? Will *USA Today* be a forum for them as well as for national unity?

USA Today has not reached its full market. The paper has marched across the country in a carefully planned parade not yet covering all fifty states. All signs point to success—maybe a great success—and all experience shows quickly rising circulation figures and greater appeal to advertisers. *USA Today* is getting into rural and thinly spread population areas, and that will be good considering the quality of many small-town newspapers, which sometimes are unable to produce a rich and informative paper. Surely the qualities *USA Today* bring are absent in many a Main Street paper.

When *USA Today* lifts up the quality of news and culture in small-town America, it continues in the tradition of Horace Greeley who shipped a special weekly *Tribune* across the land, and William Rockhill Nelson who made special efforts to get his *Kansas City Star* to farms in his state. It will be a newsy day when the new national daily becomes the habit in Succotash City.

Is *USA Today* good for the people, for the country, for the development of the American media? Are we to agree with the anxiety of one critic, asked if *USA Today* would succeed, who answered, "I am afraid so"? For if the success comes and the circulation figures pass two million and *USA Today* crows it is Number One, what will we have gained? It seems clear that the circulation of most newspapers will not be affected very much. It will be a leap forward and take its place as a landmark in the history of journalism. At *USA Today* they speak of others coming along and developing new national newspapers.

Has the influence of this daily begun to be felt in the media? One senses more use of color, more use of graphics and charts, and a more rapid increase in color photographs. All these are clear to the naked eye, but what about the Trojan horse possibilities of shorter and shorter stories? This might influence some of those editors who run very long articles over many pages. And, what about the erosion of foreign news?

How far should a newspaper go in not covering events because readers are not interested? Should newspapers be followers or leaders? In so many things *USA Today* is a logic of media history. Is it a prophecy of *USA Tomorrow?*

HOW U.S. NEWSPAPER CONTENT IS CHANGING

Leo Bogart

Leo Bogart is executive vice-president and general manager of the Newspaper Advertising Bureau, Inc. The 1983 survey discussed in this reading was directed by Charles Lehman with the assistance of John Kelley.

Reprinted from the *Journal of Communication*, vol. 35:2 (Spring, 1985). © 1985 by the Annenberg School of Communications. Used by permission.

The American press has changed rapidly under the pressures of urban depopulation and transformation, the explosion of broadcast news, and technological improvements in newspaper production methods. The extent and character of the changes have been tracked in a series of four surveys of daily newspaper managements conducted since 1967 by the Newspaper Advertising Bureau. In several significant respects, the editorial changes run counter to the opinions expressed by newspaper readers in surveys conducted during the same period (see Bogart 1981).

In the fourth of these studies, conducted in the spring of 1983, mail questionnaires were returned by 1,310 U.S. daily newspapers, which represent 77 percent of the total number and about 90 percent of the full circulation. The returns have been weighted statistically for papers of different size to make the results projectable to the entire American daily press. The questionnaire asked newspapers about recent editorial and format changes and also about the standing features and columns that they carry on a regular basis (at least once a week or more often) to deal with specialized interests.

The responses show major changes between 1979 and 1983 in editorial content and in graphics or layout.

Two out of three papers report that in those four years, they made "substantial changes" of some specific kind in editorial content, and 71 percent report "substantial changes" in graphics or layout. As table 1 shows, the changes have come most often in larger papers, but even among the smallest papers (under 10,000 circulation) a majority has made such changes.

The most common changes in graphics relate to formatting. On July 1, 1984, American newspapers moved to a standard six-column, 13-inch-wide page designed to facilitate the placement of advertising. (Tabloid papers adopted a compatible format.) The trend toward six columns and narrower

Table 1
Percentage of Newspapers Making "Substantial Changes," 1979–1983

	In Editorial Content	In Graphics or Layout
All papers	64%	71%
Circulation		
100,000 plus	82	83
50,000–100,000	73	77
25,000–50,000	75	76
10,000–25,000	61	74
Under 10,000	55	63

Table 2
Newspapers Showing Increases and Decreases in Average Number of Weekday News and Editorial Pages, 1981–1983

	Average Number of Pages	More Than in 1981 (%)	Less Than in 1981 (%)
All papers	18	52	34
Circulation			
100,000 plus	30	59	28
50,000–100,000	26	44	39
25,000–50,000	21	41	43
10,000–25,000	17	49	39
Under 10,000	14	59	27

page widths was already apparent in our 1979 survey, and the changes have accelerated since then, with 43 percent of the papers in 1983 reporting modifications in column widths, 25 percent in the number of columns, and 38 percent in page size. It is noteworthy that in those four years, 36 percent of papers redesigned the masthead, 35 percent used more photography, 30 percent changed typefaces, and 23 percent went to a modular layout.[1] The proportions are even higher among the larger papers. All this, coming on top of similar dramatic reports of change between 1977 and 1979, indicates that the American press has a very different look than it did just a half-dozen years ago.

A typical weekday paper has an average of eighteen news and editorial pages. A majority of publishers have maintained the size of the editorial package, even in the face of a shift of advertising out of the run of the press and into preprinted inserts.[2] Naturally, the greater the circulation of the paper, the greater the number of news pages. The very largest and the very smallest papers most often increased their total editorial content between 1979 and 1983 (see table 2). In the middle-size range, similar proportions increased and decreased their editorial content.

The number of physically separate sections carried on the average week-day ranges from two for the smallest circulation papers to five for the bigger ones, with an average of three.

For a typical paper, photos and illustrations make up between 10 and 20 percent of the newshole. For 13 percent of the papers, pictures represent less than 10 percent of the editorial content. For 24 percent of the papers, they represent 20 percent or more.

Even before the launching of *USA Today* in 1982, color in editorial matter had been increasingly visible in the American press. Only 17 percent of all papers report that they do not use editorial color at all, and 28 percent are using full color (rather than one or two spot colors plus black) in their weekday editions.

One important development of recent years has been the introduction of geographically zoned editions that include editorial matter as well as advertising. The introduction of zoned editions was in large part a response by metropolitan papers to growing suburban competition and by dailies generally to the rise of free-distributed weekly "shoppers" in the 1970s. Eighteen percent of all daily newspapers, with 43 percent of the circulation, now offer some kind of zoned editorial coverage. Between 1979 and 1983, fourteen percent of all newspapers added editorial zones. (The proportion was 43 percent among the larger papers.)

Another striking change has been sectionalization. In the previous four years, 25 percent of papers added "life-style" sections, and this proportion goes up to 38 percent among papers of over 100,000 circulation.

There have been substantial increases of news coverage in two areas: sports and business. Less than one percent of the papers reported any substantial decrease in coverage for either subject, while two out of five built up each of these important areas. The figures are even higher among the bigger papers that account for a substantial part of circulation. Although readership studies show that sports and business news attract many women readers, both have traditionally been thought of as subjects of special interest to men. There has been no commensurate increase of editorial emphasis in the areas generally considered of primary interest to women.

Op-ed pages are another phenomenon that has been increasingly evident as editors in single-ownership towns seek to avoid charges of media monopoly by presenting an assortment of viewpoints besides their own editorial opinions. In 1979, about one-third of the papers were running op-ed pages at least once a week; about one in five ran them every day. By 1983, over half of all papers, with three-fourths of the circulation, offered op-ed pages, and almost all of those offered them every weekday. Two out of three Sunday papers were also carrying an op-ed page. These pages have become a preferred site for institutional advertising. Only 30 percent of newspapers now report that they would not position corporate ads on the op-ed page if requested. Twenty-seven percent say their decision would depend on the individual ad, and 43 percent take them all as a matter of course.

The trends that emerge from our four surveys of newspaper content are in direct contradiction to the findings of our research among readers about their interest in news. Readers like some kinds of subjects more than others, but they expect the paper to give them both facts and fun and to encompass both the trivial and the earthshaking. Our national surveys of the public's interest in specific items (1972) or reported readership of those items (1982) consistently show that every subject has a constituency among readers, although no reader is uniformly responsive to every subject.

The same surveys show that readers come to the newspaper mainly for the news rather than for the entertainment content. Faced with a forced choice, 49 percent (in 1982) would opt for a paper that is mainly news and 20 percent for one that is mostly features.

On balance, readers are more interested in news of what is going on in the larger world and in the nation than they are in what is going on in their own local areas, though they want to know about both. These conclusions are derived not just by asking people directly in general terms what they are interested in but also by measuring their responses to hundreds of thousands of individual articles and news items. International news items score 29 percent higher than the typical local story; national news scores 11 percent higher (see Bogart 1981, pp. 202–246; Bogart 1984–1985).

However, among the one-third of all newspapers that made substantial changes in the ratio of hard news to features in the period 1979–1983, the ratio runs two to one for more features and less news. This is especially true among smaller papers of under 25,000 circulation.

Almost half of the papers report substantial changes in the ratio of national and international news to local and state news, just within those four years. Nearly five times as many increased local coverage at the expense of international coverage as did the reverse. This is true of papers of every size. Many editors may have been going this route in the belief that people want "chicken dinner news" from their newspapers at a time when television is bringing them battle scenes live from the Middle East and Central America. Some may have become discouraged at the thought of competing with the TV networks in the arena of authoritative reporting on national and world affairs.

As the ratio of hard news to features has decreased, how have these changes been reflected in the "physically separate or otherwise identifiable" or labeled sections of the newspapers?

Table 3
Percentage of Newspapers Carrying Identifiable Sections, 1979–1983

	Every Day	At Least Once a Week	
	All Papers	All Papers	100,000 Plus
Sports	70%	74%	96%
Main news	70	71	95
Entertainment	28	54	68
Food	3	53	85
Lifestyle/women	39	52	72
TV/radio	30	49	38
Second news	41	45	77
Business/finance	25	43	72
Fashion	4	13	38
Home	2	13	20
Food/home	3	9	9
Farm	1	7	3
Travel	1	5	9
Science	1	4	13

Seventy percent of all papers run a daily news section and a daily sports section, but only 25 percent have a labeled business section (table 3). Among papers of 100,000 circulation and over, which represent 55 percent of total circulation, practically every one has a main news and a sports section every day, and over half run a business section. Over the course of a week, these proportions are even higher. (Two out of three food sections now run on Wednesdays.)

Sectionalization makes the newspaper more accessible to readers by making its content more predictable, by packaging content in a convenient and manageable form. Among the expectations with which readers come to their papers is that they will find a certain element in a certain place, whether that element is a comic strip or a political columnist. It is that predictability that develops readers' emotional ties to the features, that brings readers back to the paper day after day, that makes the paper's content seem familiar and comfortable amidst the endless turmoil and daily turnover in the subject matter of the (predominantly unpleasant) hard news.

In our four surveys of content, we have taken an inventory of the standing features or columns that appear either on a daily or less frequent basis. With a few changes made based on our experience, we have tracked about 70 different subjects since 1967 and in Sunday newspapers since 1979.

Regular standing coverage has diminished on almost every single subject of special interest. The trends are documents in table 4. All the numbers are

Table 4
Percentage of Newspapers Carrying Features at Least Once a Week, 1967–1983

| | Percentage of Newspapers | | | | Percentage of Total Circulation | |
| | | | | | Weekday | Sunday/Weekend 1983 |
	1967	1974	1979	1983		
Business, financial	77	78	66	67	87	90
Farm and ranch	53	43	40	34	22	14
Real estate	—	—	—	16	21	57
Security, commodity tables	67	66	56	48	74	74
Automotive	18	18	18	13	25	24
Boating	25	16	—	—	—	—
Outdoors, camping, hunting	64	60	47	44	59	68
Sports	95	99	—	—	—	—
Sports (spectator)	—	—	92	88	91	93
Sports (participant)	—	—	86	78	79	76
Beauty	45	36	36	23	36	25
Fashion, women	57	47	41	26	46	30
Fashion, men	18	20	26	16	31	16
Fashion, teenage	25	28	27	16	29	10
Sewing patterns	62	57	50	44	57	51
Etiquette	31	22	13	12	21	22
"People"	—	—	—	50	70	77
Personal advice	76	82	74	71	81	80
Society, social news	93	95	85	80	69	79
Religion	—	—	58	48	30	40
Home building, repair	47	37	29	22	25	46
Home furnishings, decorating	39	35	28	18	26	37
Household hints	—	—	—	43	44	47
Radio	32	22	—	—	—	—
Radio log	43	29	22	16	38	48
Television	73	80	—	—	—	—
TV reviews	—	—	61	51	73	76
TV log	91	91	85	87	92	96
Gardening	53	47	43	37	39	55
Pets	18	21	14	14	15	34
Photography	17	13	9	6	9	26
Stamps, coins	—	—	8	6	8	43
Computers (personal)	—	—	—	7	16	10
Environment, ecology	—	—	16	9	11	9
Health and medical	68	71	66	63	74	61
Science, technology	34	24	14	9	21	20
Weather	94	98	—	—	—	—
Weather map	—	—	63	65	87	93
Books	49	38	33	25	28	81
Motion pictures	61	60	—	—	—	—
Movie reviews	—	—	46	46	72	69
Movie timetable	—	—	50	48	67	68
Theater	56	56	54	41	64	73
Travel and resort	23	22	19	11	11	81
Music, records, tapes	—	—	37	31	44	61

Table 4 continued

	Percentage of Newspapers				Percentage of Total Circulation	
					Weekday	Sunday/Weekend
	1967	1974	1979	1983		1983
Child care	36	22	17	11	16	11
College	30	33	16	10	8	9
School news	73	66	61	52	36	25
Youth, teenage	61	45	24	24	22	29
Best food buys	—	—	50	50	68	11
Diet, nutrition	—	—	—	44	60	29
Recipes	81	78	78	74	85	40
Restaurants	—	—	—	28	48	38
Wine	—	—	15	14	36	23
Advice on personal finance	—	—	42	38	62	54
Career advice	—	—	15	11	23	26
Consumers (action line)	—	—	28	21	37	35
Retirement, social security	—	—	33	23	28	29
Astrology, horoscope	—	75	78	84	92	92
Bridge	60	62	57	55	78	75
Games and puzzles	—	81	75	78	84	89

much higher if circulation is taken into account, as it is in the two right columns, which show the weekday and Sunday figures for 1983.

Newspapers representing substantial chunks of the total circulation continue to provide, week in and week out, columns and features that speak to an enormous assortment of segmented concerns on a scale beyond the capacity of other mass media. For example, less than half of all newspapers offer a movie timetable or movie reviews on a regular basis, but those papers represent seven out of ten copies sold. Less than one-third of the papers regularly review records and tapes, and only one in four regularly reviews books. Only 11 percent have a weekday travel feature. (Travel, movies, books, records, and performing arts are of special interest to young people, whom newspapers have been seeking to attract.)

What was once called "society news," the minutiae of community life, used to carry its own special heading. While 93 percent of all papers covered it on a regular basis in 1967, that proportion is now down to 80 percent. Only half carry regularly scheduled reviews of television programs at least once a week.

Seven percent of the papers have started a feature for personal computer buffs, but only 9 percent now carry a science or technology column or feature on a regular basis.

There are fewer papers with action lines and career columns. Although the population is aging, fewer papers are now offering a regular feature dealing with retirement and social security matters.

While it is of interest to note the absolute proportions of newspapers providing regular standing coverage of these diverse special interests, more important is the almost universal tendency to cut down on such specialized features in every subject.

The trend holds for papers of every size in every part of the country. (There is one notable exception: newspapers have been increasing their coverage on a regular basis in one field—astrology.)

On many of these subjects, features tend to come predominantly from syndicated sources, as table 5 shows. Thus, the reduction in regular coverage may represent an attempt by editors to increase the amount of staff-written content. It may also be that, as part of the "sectional revolution," papers have been covering subjects of special interest on an individual assignment basis and varying the content from one week to the next, rather than trying to hold to identifiable, labeled features on a week in, week out basis.

Whatever its causes, this trend runs in the face of an increasing segmentation of people's interests in a complex, mobile society. This is what has fueled the growth of specialty magazines, of selective programming on cable

Table 5
Source of Newspapers' Most Widely Carried Standing Features, 1982

	Syndicated (%)	Locally Produced (%)	Both (%)
Astrology	98	2	—
Bridge	96	2	2
Personal advice	92	6	2
Games and puzzles	90	6	4
Health and medical	82	6	12
Weather map	77	16	7
TV log	76	22	2
TV reviews	67	18	5
"People"	49	35	16
Best food buys	29	48	23
Business, finance	24	41	35
Recipes	21	46	33
Op-ed	11	35	54
Sports (spectator)	3	49	48
Sports (participant)	2	61	37
Social news	2	91	7
School news	—	97	3

and radio. Newspapers' mass character derives from the fact that they deal not only with common interests but with innumerable idiosyncrasies. Readership surveys may show that relatively few people share any one particular interest, but they are not likely to show how intensely they feel about it.

Overall, the mix of newspaper subject matter has not changed very much. A sampling of articles in our 1971, 1977, and 1982 surveys did not show dramatic shifts in the proportions dealing with such subjects as crime, public health, taxes, or Hollywood. But even though newspapers may be running as much space in general on fashion or travel as they ever did, they are less likely to be running it in a format that readers can expect, look forward to, and find easily. For stereo buffs or stamp collectors, there is quite a difference between occasionally coming across an article dealing with their peculiar predilections and knowing that there will always be a goody waiting in a regular place.

The substantial changes in both the appearance and content of the American press we have documented are stimulated by new technology, a growing sensitivity to reader interests, and the acute competitive marketing pressures that newspapers face as a business. But three trends can be identified that run counter to the conclusions of research on reader interests: (1) increasing the ratio of features to hard news content, (2) reducing the relative balance of national and world news to local news, and (3) reducing the number of regular standing columns and features dealing with specialized interests. These trends were not set in motion by any conscious policy decisions. They arise from a multitude of small day-by-day decisions that editors make as a matter of course. But over time, these little decisions add up to significant changes in newspaper content.

Notes

1. The use of modular layouts will be spurred as newspapers move to adopt computerized page makeup systems to replace pasteup, which has only recently in turn replaced the metal makeup procedures that had been in use for a century.

2. A separate analysis of 164 papers with circulations over 100,000, representing 56 percent of total circulation, shows that total weekday pages (including advertising preprints) increased by 33 percent between 1977 and 1983, while news and editorial pages increased by 34 percent. Total Sunday pages grew 50 percent and Sunday editorial pages by 40 percent. Although many papers reduced page width during these years, this only slightly offsets the very substantial expansion in the bulk of both news and advertising.

References

Bogart, Leo. 1981. *Press and Public: Who Reads What, When, Where, and Why in American Newspapers.* Hillsdale, N.J.: Lawrence Erlbaum.
———. 1984–1985. "The Public's Use and Perception of Newspapers." *Public Opinion Quarterly* 48 (Winter): 709–719.

LOOKING OUT FOR #1: MAGAZINES THAT CELEBRATE SUCCESS

Carl Sessions Stepp

Carl Sessions Stepp teaches journalism at the University of Maryland. He has been a reporter and editor at the *St. Petersburg Times,* the *Charlotte Observer,* and *USA Today.*

Reprinted from the *Washington Journalism Review,* November, 1985. Used by permission.

Nothing succeeds like success, and many magazines this year have found that out: They're cashing in on the current American infatuation with the good, the rich, the successful life and how to lead it. In an otherwise unspectacular year for magazine advertising and circulation, some publications are reaping big payoffs toasting what *USA Today's* publishing correspondent Karen Heller calls "'Dynasty' themes." They range from simple success (*Self's* "Smartest Self-Improvements To Make Now . . . in looks, guts, daring, selftrust") to exquisite excess (*GQ's* ads for $295 24-karat gold Gucci sunglasses).

Want your career to soar?

Check out "How Leaders Dress for Success" (*Success!* September 1985), "Five Styles of Fashion for the Well-Dressed Man" (*Esquire,* September 1985), or "Successful Career Clothes for Fall" (*Working Woman,* September 1985).

Want to look good?

Try the guide to "The Haircut That's Right for You" (*GQ,* October 1985), the Esquire Collection of fashion and grooming accessories, or *Working Mother's* guide to "Skin That Glows" (August 1985).

Want to feel better?

Turn to "The Necksoother System for Tension Relief" (*American Health,*

September 1985) or "Zen and the Art of Stress Management" (*Working Woman,* September 1985).

Want to rub pinkies, vicariously, with the beau monde?

Gaze upon "Princess TNT—The Dynamite Socialite" (*Vanity Fair,* September 1985) or take a "Gourmet Holiday" to Aragon (*Gourmet,* September 1985).

"The national obsession right now is money. We're in love with things rich," Heller says. "The magazines doing well editorially are devoted to wealth and consumption."

Others see the trend as less toward decadence than toward self-betterment. "It's success," explains Anne Mollegen Smith, editor of *Working Woman.* "It's simmered and come to a boil and now it's blowing the kettle."

Why this has happened is no great mystery. Baby boomers have grown up, traded denim for tweed, and moved upscale and uptown. *USA Today* noted recently that of America's 80 million baby boomers, more than a million qualify as urban professionals making at least $40,000 a year, and fully a third of the baby boomers work in the service community (they're sometimes called "new collar" workers) earning family incomes of $20,000 to $40,000. Together, they form a powerful group of taste makers.

"They've gone through history now, the largest generation in the history of the world, affecting music and politics and cultural norms of all sorts," observes *Success!* editor-in-chief Scott DeGarmo. "Now they're in the workplace, and they're affecting things there."

G. Douglas Johnston, publisher of *Vanity Fair,* says, "Because of the education and sophistication that this group has come to, they turn out to have a pretty good demographic profile—they're all working in good jobs, making good money and living in big cities."

William F. Gorog, president of the Magazine Publishers Association, says, "Meredith Corporation several years ago had a magazine called *Apartment Life.* It was for people just breaking in, and it told how to make a cocktail table from an orange crate—how to do things cheap but still nice. That audience is now 35 years old and taking home a combined income of $60,000 plus, and the magazine has been upgraded and is called *Metropolitan Home.*"

Overall, however, 1985 has proved a disappointing year for magazines. Following a record-breaking 1984, when ad revenues rose 16.5 percent, ad revenues gained only 8 percent in the first half of 1985, and the number of ad pages fell by 1.4 percent. It is estimated that page totals at best will only equal last year's.

Many magazines are nonetheless prospering with the success motif, dishing out lush photos, sumptuous ads and exotic articles on fashion, fitness, health, career development, and stylish living. Through the first half of the year, some have posted impressive numbers: *American Health* (ad revenue up 81 percent, circulation up 28 percent), *Gourmet* (ad revenue up 38 percent, circulation up 78 percent), *Vanity Fair* (ad revenue up 58 percent, circulation up 23 percent, *House & Garden* (ad revenue up 33 percent, circulation up 16 percent).

The hot cover topics now, Gorog says, are "diet, fitness and sex," which can add 20 percent to newsstand sales. What topics to avoid? "The worst is politicians," he says.

In recent times, *Vanity Fair, Success!, Esquire, GQ,* and *House & Garden* all have revamped themselves substantially to lure the trendy, affluent audience. Even *Newsweek* has added sections on family, health, and fashion.

"More and more these days, people really just want a better mind and a better body," says Steven Naftelberg, vice-president and associate media director of New York's SSC&B Inc. ad agency. "I'm OK, you're OK—in both mind and body, in exercise, the mind, work, relationships. We want to look better and feel better, and while those categories used to belong mostly to women, men these days too want to look good and feel good."

And magazines respond to what people want: everything from the contemporary advice of *Working Woman* and the gung-ho pep talks of *Success!* to the cheery self-help tips of *American Health* and the frilly fashions of *GQ*.

On one hand, the idea is simply to help readers get ahead through useful how-to articles and service features. On the other, it is to peep into loftier social strata, in a tone that can border on snobbery or pander to the acquisitiveness and insecurities brought on by moving and shaking. As *Vanity Fair's* "Vanities" column declares, "All is Vanities. Nothing is fair."

Long-time magazine editor Clay Felker, now at *Adweek,* says that, "by definition magazines are marketing responses. They follow the news and the trends. They respond to whatever pockets of audience are thrown up by changing conditions economically or culturally.

"We've got peace and prosperity and a stable country, and people are concerned with their own lives—and that means home, family, jobs, career and personal success. At times like this, people tend to go into more trivial things—literally, trivial pursuits."

Dr. Samir Husni, a magazine authority and journalism professor at the University of Mississippi, says magazines initiate as well as reflect trends by catering to what they perceive as readers' fantasies. "The magazine either will arouse your fantasy world so you say, 'I can't do it but I can live it in my dreams,' or it will make you identify with it and say, 'I can do it,'" Husni says.

GQ, for example, has been remodeled over the past two years from a men's clothing showcase to a broader-based arts, music, dining, and style publication. By using classy writers, deluxe graphics, and featuring "real people," not just models, on its covers, *GQ* has tried to shed its image as a foppish fashion-only magazine of special interest to gay men.

The cover of one ad-rich, 446-page issue boasted of "50 Pages of New Fall Fashions," "Dinner Party Politics," "The Weekend Wardrobe," and "Getting Physical." Articles prescribed "must" clothing for fall and winter, told how to assemble a vintage wine cellar for as little as $1,300, and included pieces on football star Dan Marino, stolen art treasures, T.S. Eliot's tailor, the music of "Miami Vice" and an amazing University of Southern California sorority that wants young women who are "really, really good-looking" and "really, really rich" and that makes initiates, clad in their underwear, kneel in front of live pigs and name the last man they slept with. Beautiful ads marketed handmade Italian crocodile shoes, Raymond Weil Swiss watches, Yves Saint Laurent fragrances, BMWs, and designer clothes.

"Our magazine works on two levels," says *GQ* managing editor Eliot Kaplan. "It's there for those people who can actually buy that stuff. And it works on a fantasy level for people who may aspire to get there some day."

Speaking of her magazine and its peers, *Gourmet* editor-in-chief Jane Montant says, "There must be an awful lot of money around—it's expensive clothes, it's expensive furniture, it's expensive travel."

With more than 2,000 consumer magazines available, generalizing about them can be dangerous. Not every magazine that sells success is rolling in clover, and many publications that head in other directions are doing perfectly well. But the good life is clearly having a good year. Among the ascendant topics:

Fine Living

Joining old standbys such as *Gourmet* and *Food & Wine* are *House & Garden, Vanity Fair, GQ,* and other magazines that exude enthusiasm for high living.

Gourmet ("The Magazine of Good Living") and *Food & Wine* ("The Guide to Good Taste"), along with *Bon Appétit* and others, have long served up tantalizing treats and now may be bigger than ever. "There's a tremendous interest in upscale magazines, and we all know this country is on a real food kick," says *Gourmet's* Montant.

USA Today's Heller calls *House & Garden* "a gorgeous escape book" and points out that "what readers want from magazines is something newspapers can't offer—beauty in their writing and beauty in their look." Certainly *H&G* aspires to beauty, running sumptuous ads for French porcelain, trips to Maui and handpainted china lavatories; elegant house, art, and garden photography; and articles such as "A Young French Family Takes to New

England—Decorator Arnold Copper successfully melds American Greek Revival and Louis XVI styles."

Vanity Fair, reintroduced by Condé Nast two years ago, aims to appeal to the cultural reader. "We're a magazine that scours the contemporary cultural scene and pulls out what's the best," boasts publisher Johnston. Recherché articles and interviews spotlight the media, arts, wines, cruises, restaurants, and travel. Through *Vanity Fair's* often outrageous but charming prose and breathtaking photography, readers venture to the "perfect holiday hideaway" of Mauritius, Martha's Vineyard, or the Hamptons ("The Connecticut shore is stylish, but it doesn't have the wonderful air. The Jersey shore has the air, but it isn't stylish. . . . The Hamptons have always been stylish"). Says Johnston, "This is not a coffee table magazine. It's a bedside table magazine."

Since it was revived in 1983, *Vanity Fair* has struggled, losing perhaps $7 million a year, according to an estimate quoted by the *New York Times*. But Felker, among others, believes it "has found its niche." Ads and circulation both increased this year, and in August the *Times* rewarded *Vanity Fair* with a business section front-page story tagged, "New Success for Magazine."

Fashion and Style, Particularly for Men

After its best year ever in 1984 (ad revenue rose 46 percent), *GQ* saw another 20 percent jump in the first half of this year. Circulation has increased by 50 percent, and total readership has doubled in five years. As the magazine has broadened its scope, fashion has remained central, but style has become the watchword. "Our magazine is about style more than anything else," managing editor Kaplan says. "Fashion is just part of what a man of style is interested in."

New entries in the men's magazine field include *M*, less than two years old, and *MGF* (or Men's Guide to Fashion), launched this spring. Established magazines like *Esquire* and *Playboy* contain more fashion ads and articles than ever. Advertising executive Steven Naftelberg says, "Men have evolved to the point where women might have been ten years ago, where we are more comfortable with wearing fragrances, designer clothes, and so on. We're not afraid of being called sissies."

Women's fashion is doing fine, too. Two of *Working Woman's* top-selling issues have been those devoted to fashion: "not just ordinary clothes, but career clothes," says editor Smith. *Vogue's* annual September fashion issue racked up 550 pages of ads this year (the second best in the magazine's history, behind last year's 604 ad pages).

Newsweek, in a tribute to S.I. Newhouse's Condé Nast fashion empire (which includes *Vogue, GQ, Mademoiselle, Glamour,* and *Self*), called *Vogue* "the ultimate showcase for the chicquest couturiers, the most creative photographers, the hottest models. And, of course, the most ad pages." *Newsweek* also saluted *GQ* for "brilliantly exploiting the growing style consciousness of American males in general."

Fitness and Health

Wanting to look good can lead to wanting to feel good. Dr. Husni of the University of Mississippi says that the third-largest number of new magazines on the market involve fitness. (The largest number are about music, the second largest about computers.)

Conspicuously successful has been *American Health* magazine, founded in 1982. A National Magazine Award for general excellence this year honored its "lively and credible blend of news and service journalism." Editor Joel Gurin thinks *American Health* is successful because "this was a subject whose time had come in a big way."

The magazine, visually attractive and well packaged, has an aggressively upbeat spirit and tries to avoid what medical journalists often call the "disease-of-the-month syndrome." Gurin says *American Health* deals with "nutrition, fitness, selfcare, how to watch what you drink—all the things that tell people how to affect their own health."

It labels its dental column "The Tooth Report," includes articles on folk medicine and such topics as "sport-specific hair" (how "you can have your hair shaped to move with your body in your favorite sport"). One article offers a questionnaire asking, "Does Your Office Have Bad Habits?" (deduct points for a cigarette machine, no nearby gym, elevators that break down, and if "behavior that is irritating to others is tolerated"). Ads tout high-fiber cereals and cross-country skiing simulators.

Other health magazines (and some about running, although their popularity has waned) also do well. Many general-interest publications now are paying attention to fitness, too. *GQ*, for instance, has consolidated its health-fitness-grooming material into a "Body and Soul" column. *Working Mother* plays to its dual interests with departments called "The Healthy Child," "Take Care of Yourself," and "The Guilt Department."

Even *Gourmet* takes notice of the fitness craze. Although Montant says, "We never do a diet and as long as I'm here we're not going to," she adds that the magazine more and more heeds the vegetarian movement; for Thanksgiving it offered two dinners, one with meat, one without.

Career Development

If ever a topic fit the 1980s, this is it. How to advance in a career and how to combine a career and family have become urgent topics for baby boomers on the make.

In October 1984, *Success!* founded by philanthropist W. Clement Stone as a motivational magazine, began to be remade into a more colorful, informational and—of course—"upscale" publication, aimed at an audience mostly of males in their mid-thirties with a marketing or entrepreneurial bent. Through June, ad revenues were up 16 percent and circulation 14 percent. "We are all about helping our readers get ahead," says editor-in-chief Scott DeGarmo. Regular *Success!* features include "One Minute Manager," "New Opportunities," and "Success Scope."

At *Working Woman,* editor Smith says, "We are about success. . . . We put together two strong trends: the women's magazines's closeness to the audience and the informational needs of people in the business world. . . . I don't see this as a self-indulgent, luxury-minded, me-generation thing. These people are strivers. They work hard."

Money forms the core of *Manhattan, inc.*, which earlier this year captured a National Magazine Award for general excellence after publishing for less than a year. *Manhattan, inc.* takes what editor Jane Amsterdam calls "a general-journalism approach to business—and we look at everything as a business." Robust and enterprising, it tells about "power lunches," "power tools," how much people make, what odd things cost (a 30-second personal message on Times Square's Spectacolor board: $50). Says Amsterdam, "It's money—and how it's used or abused or collected or lost."

Celebrities and the Successful

Close behind interest in personal success follows a downright fascination with the success of others. Celebrity and people magazines are booming, paced by their youngish grandparent, the eleven-year-old *People,* whose ad revenues now approach a quarter-billion dollars a year.

Jann Wenner's redesigned *US,* the proposed new *Entertainment Tonight Magazine* and the fact that some 10 million celebrity-oriented publications pass through supermarket checkout stands every week testify to the lure of the people market. *People* assistant managing editor Jim Gaines says Americans use celebrities to "act out our fantasies and in return we will give them fame and glory."

Readers also love stories about the regular-person-who-makes-it (*Suc-*

cess!: "Whiz Kid Becomes Biz Kid . . . At 29, Bill Gates Built an Empire—and He's Just Getting Started") and about young strivers on their way to the penthouse, 272 of whom were identified in the *Esquire* Register as "men and women under 40 who are changing America."

Vanity Fair, with covers on Ronald and Nancy Reagan, Claus von Bülow, and Jerry Hall, and tales like "My Face-Lift" by Viva, takes the *People* formula uptown to what Paul Zuckerman, a senior vice-president at Doyle Dane Bernback Group, Inc., calls "the chichi crowd." One recent issue—which editor in chief Tina Brown dubbed "a cabaret of class acts for a discriminating audience"—zeroed in on Anjelica Huston, Tom Wolfe, Mikhail Baryshnikov, and Dustin Hoffman, among others.

While there's little doubt that smart topics sell big, it can also be said that much of this material represents the quintessence of creampuffery. It's certainly a far cry from the crusading journalism that many of these new magazines' editors recall from the 1960s. As Dr. Husni notes, "Everybody is after the people who are twenty-five to forty. They have the money. . . . Nobody cares about the poor, the lower classes. We leave the tabloids to them."

"It's a subject a lot of people confront with some embarrassment," agrees *Success!* magazine's DeGarmo. "You're not supposed to be too self-interested. But we try to de-mystify that and say it's all right to look at yourself. It doesn't necessarily mean to be greedy."

Joel Gurin of *American Health* concedes that his magazine puts stories in the "best possible light" but says it does so "out of a desire to help people take some kind of action. . . . we never want to be Pollyanna, but we don't want to be gloom and doom, either. . . . Rather than doing a story about how America's ground water is going to hell—a story covered well in the news—we feel we can contribute by telling people, 'You are already worried about this. Now what can you do about it?'"

Working Woman editor Anne Mollegen Smith proclaims herself "guilt-free" about her magazine's fascination with the well heeled. "To me, this for women represents a special opportunity," she says. "I don't see it as materialism. We have so many women supporting themselves and their children. We have so many old women living in poverty. We have a salary gap that won't close. . . . So I feel my readers have a lot of catching up to do, and I'm going to help them in every way possible."

Many of the success-obsessed magazines show a sense of humor that helps keep things in perspective. *Working Woman* looked at "Yuppie love," *Success!* produced an ingenious feature on "what the Mafia can teach you about management," and *Manhattan, inc.* editor Amsterdam, whose magazine offers incisive looks at New York business, likes to find stories that are "devilish or slightly wicked or wonderful at some level."

Since many serious magazines and political journals (the *New Republic,* for instance) also are surging, perhaps today's editors are simply more attuned to their readers, for better or worse.

Says *American Health*'s Gurin, "This isn't just Yuppie merchandising. It's something people really enjoy. . . . You can't really solve every problem in the world with jogging—although it helps with an amazing number of them."

3
Radio

Introduction

Radio was the first electronic medium to serve a mass public. Like the newspapers before it, it had to await the development of technology and people who recognized its potential. Radio has developed from its hobby stage around 1910, to commercial broadcasting, the development of national networks, and the golden age of radio in the 1930s and 1950s. During this latter period, the networks programmed comedy-variety shows, drama, soap operas, and news, very much like network television today without the pictures. When television captured the mass national audience in the 1950s, radio responded by becoming local and specialized. Today's stations program to capture a profitable part of the market based on a target audience characterized by specific demographics (age, sex, ethnicity, and other categories). Different program formats attract differing audiences. The reading by Milan Meeske describes the current formats in some detail: top 40, adult contemporary, album-oriented rock, country, black, and others. Meeske concludes with the strategies employed within the format and the techniques of program directors.

The next two readings give accounts of program consultants, who in effect reduce the local character of radio. While program directors have taken most programming decisions away from disc jockeys, they now seem to be losing control. Karrie Jacob's reading gives an inside look at a consultant at work on a hits station, while Michael Goldberg describes "radio doctors." The last reading in this chapter, by Marc Gunther, describes a trend that could replace local control and the expert adviser, the automated station. As the example shows, it is technically possible to have an automated station that can feed in local spots (ads, news, information) without the need for a fully staffed station.

SPECIALIZATION AND COMPETITION IN RADIO

Milan D. Meeske

Milan D. Meeske is professor of communication and coordinator of radio/TV/film at the University of Central Florida, Orlando. He is coauthor of *Copywriting for the Electronic Media* (1986) and has published extensively in the *Journal of Broadcasting* and *Electronic Media and Journalism Quarterly.* Dr. Meeske has worked in commercial radio and is a freelance copywriter.

Radio is the most pervasive medium of communication in the United States. Over 10,000 stations are on the air, twice the number that existed in the 1960s, and radio reaches 99 percent of all homes. Since 1950, radio programming has undergone a shift in focus as it adapted to the development of new media such as television. Before 1950, radio's main focus was entertaining the family; since then, it has become a personal companion. Almost every automobile has a radio, and seven out of ten adults are reached weekly by car radio. A study by RADAR (Radio's All Dimensional Audience Research) found that over 95 percent of all people over age twelve listen to radio. And the average adult spends three-and-a-half hours per day listening.

The number of radio receivers has increased as well—by 40 percent since 1970. They have also changed to adapt to the more personal function of radio today. Where radio sets were once large and bulky, the emphasis now is on small portable receivers that enable the audience to take radio with them wherever they go.

The basic idea in radio programming is to broadcast programming that will attract a sizeable enough audience to satisfy advertisers. This has become an increasingly complex job. Not only are more stations in operation, but other media are growing in number, and they also compete for the available audience. The government, which once closely regulated radio, now prefers to let marketplace forces decide many programming matters. Stations have considerable latitude in deciding what to program, but their decision is complex because listeners are presented with numerous alternatives.

Radio today is station dominated: stations now produce the bulk of their own programming whether they are affiliated with a network or not. Networks usually supply only news and specialized call-in programs. Station-produced programming consists of music announced by disc jockeys.

Radio Programming Formats

Every radio station adheres to a programming structure called the *format*. Stations strive to maintain a high level of consistency so that listeners know what to expect. Highly structured stations have a rigid format and give disc jockeys little flexibility in what they say on the air or in the music they play. Loose formats allow disc jockeys to express their personalities in terms of what they say and, to some degree, in the music they play. Programming is the most crucial aspect of radio programming. The sound transmitted by a station is the primary product a station communicates to its listeners.

The key factor in selecting a format is *demographics,* an analysis of the composition of the station's potential audience. As stations seek a specialized rather than a general audience, they strive to carve out one small segment of the radio audience. A highly specialized format targeting a highly specialized audience can be highly successful.

Demographics take several factors into account. Age is a particularly important variable since age groups reflect affluence and tastes. The 55–64 age group, for example, has the largest per capita income, but members of it do not buy as many cars, homes, and diapers as those in the 18–34 bracket. Besides age, demographics usually reflect sex, since a format appealing to a given age group may also prefer to attract males rather than females, or vice versa. Ethnic composition, educational level, and other factors may be used to help the program director develop the kind of programming most likely to attract the largest share of the available audience. Once the format has been developed and the audience targeted, the audiences must be constantly monitored to look for changes in tastes, shrinkage of the size of the age group, and the like.

Radio formats come in a number of variations. Some of them overlap, since they include records that are also played in other formats. Table 1 indicates the percentages using various formats.

Music

Top Forty and Contemporary Hit Radio. This is the oldest of the formats yet is constantly being refined. Top forty formats were developed in the late 1950s and became common during the 1960s. The format can be traced back to broadcasters such as Todd Storz in Omaha and Gordon McClendon in Dallas, who discovered that by playing the forty most popular records and emphasizing the personality of the disc jockey, they could win huge audiences. WABC, New York City, was another station that enjoyed tremendous success with the format. It featured a consistent and controlled playlist that rotated the hits about every ninety minutes. The disc jockeys were lively and

Table 1
Format Listening Shares, Fall 1985

Total Audience, Total Week	Shares
Adult contemporary	18.2
Rock and contemporary adult rock	15.5
Album-oriented rock	10.4
Country	9.8
Easy listening	9.8
News/talk	6.4
Urban contemporary	5.3
MOR/nostalgia	4.8
Black/rhythm and blues	4.1
All news	4.0
Spanish	2.8
Soft contemporary	2.4
Golden oldies	2.2
Classical	1.6
Religious	1.5
Variety	0.9

often funny, although they had a limited amount of time to talk (Routt, McGrath, and Weiss 1978).

Top forty was the most important format until the late 1960s. By then, more flexible formats were available on FM stations, which also presented music in stereo. When artists aimed at having single cuts from albums played in an effort to promote the entire album, the emphasis on hit singles declined. Stations responded to the changes with variations of the top forty format. Some increased their playlist to as many as 100 records and many cut back on disc jockey chatter, but by the early 1970s, top forty had found itself again. The personality of the disc jockey was again emphasized, this time as a major ingredient in the station's sound. Today virtually every city has one or more variations of the top forty format.

Today's top forty comes in two basic types: hot hits and contemporary hit radio (CHR). Hot hits shows feature a tight playlist, an up-tempo presentation, and a liberal use of jingles. Nothing but hits are played with an occasional oldie, new record, or up-and-coming hit included. Hot hits stations concentrate on the current and recent hit songs, with little attention to oldies. CHR is not as tightly playlisted as hot hits. Its stations play somewhat more oldies and in some cities appeal to an adult audience during the day while playing more rock music at night. Both hot hits and CHR aim for the 18–24 age group.

Adult Contemporary. This popular format is found in almost every U.S. city. As with other formats, adult contemporary (AC) has its variations. AC radio evolved from the middle-of-the-road (MOR) format, which presented adult music along with news, features, and other information. The problem with the MOR format is that the audience is always changing. One generation thinks of MOR as Peggy Lee, Frank Sinatra, and Tony Bennett; another thinks of MOR as the Beatles and Chicago. Because the audiences keep changing, today's AC stations emphasize the contemporary. Some AC stations do emphasize the adult, but the majority choose music for the youthful, although they avoid that which is too loud or teen oriented.

Adult stations play a lot of oldies from the 1960s and 1970s, while some go back as far as the late 1950s. Many adult stations present a significant amount of news and information, and some devote a sizable percentage of time to sports and talk shows.

AC stations generally emphasize a cheerful, companionable style of presentation that is structured enough to be predictable. Advertisers like the format because it consistently attracts the 25–44 age group. Overall an AC station has broad appeal; it is enjoyable to a wide age spread yet alienates few people.

Album Rock. Album-oriented rock (AOR) is an outgrowth of top forty. When audience enthusiasm for top hits declined in the late 1960s, programmers began to program rock music from albums, often presented by a laid-back disc jockey. Album rock proved to be popular with 18–24-year-old males but not always with other demographic groups.

Two basic types of AOR stations developed. One, free form, was popular in the early years of the format. Free form let the announcers play whatever they liked so each station became highly individualized. But eventually the format became too esoteric for most listeners, and stations moved to a mass appeal AOR approach in which they play only the best cuts from the best albums and occasionally hit singles (Halper 1984).

Today the majority of AOR stations appeal to a mass audience. The nature of an individual AOR station depends on the competition. Some play new music and compete with MTV for the 18–24-year-old audience. Others are a variation of the top forty format, playing hit singles as well as popular album cuts. The drugged-sounding announcers have been replaced with more typical top forty style disc jockeys, often including outrageous and funny morning disc jockeys.

Beautiful Music and Easy Listening. This is strictly an adult format, aimed at listeners over age 25, one confined almost exclusively to FM and one that is sometimes negatively described as elevator music after the background music played in elevators. At one time, beautiful music stations dominated nearly every market, but as the audience has grown older, changes are taking place. A number of these stations have switched to a soft version of AC, and others are experimenting with music mixes that move away from the reliance on lush, orchestral instrumentals to a mix of vocals. One of the problems has always been the availability of suitable recordings. The process of producing the recordings is costly so most of these stations rely on a syndicated programming service to provide the music (*Broadcasting* 1986). Many beautiful music stations attract huge audiences, and the listeners are usually loyal. Still, there are seldom enough listeners to support more than one such station in a market.

Country. Country radio thrives with blue-collar audiences, though it has not been accepted everywhere. Country is popular in the South, the Southwest, and West; it receives mixed reviews in the Midwest and is weakest in the Northeast.

Like other radio formats, country has undergone some alterations because of changing audience tastes. Country stations once used folksy-type announcers who played hillbilly music. Now the announcers are more sophisticated, often top forty in style, and the music has broader appeal, including not only country artists but so-called cross-over performers who appeal to both country and AC listeners. Country music stations have borrowed many ideas from other formats. Some play three or four songs in a row without interruption, some play lots of oldies, and some have little announcer intrusion. As a result, a few cities support several country stations with one using a modern style, one traditional, and so on. Country stations score well with the 25–54 age group and according to a National Association of Broadcasters study they attract the most loyal listeners of all formats.

Nostalgia. Just as there is always an audience for contemporary music, there is also an audience for yesterday's hits. On radio, this can mean a hit from several years back or, in the case of nostalgia, the music that an age group grew up with. Nostalgia stations appeal to an older demographic group, the precise age depending on whether the station appeals to those who grew up in the 1940s or 1950s. Nostalgia has been particularly successful on AM, since the original renditions were not recorded in stereo.

Nostalgia formats come in many varieties. Some have focused on the Big Band era with traditional vocalists like Frank Sinatra and Perry Como. Syndicated versions of some older music are available. Other nostalgia stations include popular vocalists from the 1960s and 1970s, such as Johnny Mathis and Barbra Streisand, if they fit the sound and image of the station. Yet others border on AC, playing such artists as the Carpenters, Neil Diamond, and so on, as long as the selections do not lean too heavily toward rock (Halper 1984).

While nostalgia stations also often provide news and information, and may include a talk show, the emphasis is on music and features that bring back memories to the target age group.

Classical. Classical music has been played on radio since the earliest days of the industry, and although it is common on noncommercial stations, there are only about twenty-five full-time commercial classical stations around the country (Seigerman 1986). The word *classical* has elitist connotations that may alienate the average listener. Still, the stations that program classical music find that the audience is upscale and loyal, though small in number. The format usually appeals to listeners in the 25 and up category. In recent years, however, classical stations have borrowed innovative promotion ideas from popular music stations, such as trip giveaways and summertime concert promotions.

Advertising policies on classical stations differ from other formats. Stations often seek long-term program sponsorship by corporations, a throwback to the days of block programming. Spot announcements are also sold, although stations seek spots compatible with the format.

Religious. Religious radio stations started in the 1920s for the purpose of putting church services on the air (Routt, McGrath, and Weiss 1978). That is still part of the service of religious stations, although commercials, news, and public service programs may also be aired. The programming, however, is mostly religious music. Like others, the religious stations also specialize: the music may be Christian rock, contemporary Christian, southern gospel, traditional, spiritual, middle-of-the-road religious, or a mixture of these types. The nature of the religious music corresponds to the audience sought by the station.

Programming on religious stations may be in block form, with segments of time sold to local and national denominational groups and other religious organizations in the form of recorded worship services and educational religious programs. Disc jockeys on religious stations are expected to carry the image of the station.

Ratings for religious stations seldom are high, but audiences are loyal, over 25 years old, and attractive to some advertisers. The mail response to religious stations is often more revealing than ratings, so some stations do not subscribe to ratings services.

Ethnic Programming

Black. This format has been successful in cities with a large ethnic population. At one time, black-oriented stations (sometimes called soul stations) were confined to the largest cities, but now over 80 percent of the black population is able to hear a black-formatted station.

Black radio stations were once a combination of rhythm and blues, with strong jive-talking personalities. By the 1980s, black formats had become more refined, usually seeking specialized audiences. Some stations labeled themselves disco stations and sought both black and nonblack listeners. Disco, however, was short-lived. Many black stations now refer to themselves as urban, a term thought to have wider audience and sales appeal. Urban stations rely heavily on black music but also choose dance music by nonblack artists. Announcers use a mass appeal style, and whereas black-oriented stations once used only black announcers, urban stations often use both black and white disc jockeys (Halper 1984). Like many other formats, black stations have borrowed much from top forty. The emphasis is on a consistent sound with predictable music, mass appeal announcers, and commercials written to fit the sound.

Hispanic. One of the newest formats is Hispanic radio, which appeals to the fastest-growing ethnic population in the United States. Hispanic stations are found mostly in Florida, the Southwest, and large cities. Since radio is the primary medium that reaches Hispanics, it perhaps helps bridge the gap between Hispanic culture and Anglo-American life (Seigerman 1984). Most Hispanic stations play a quasi-educational role that helps their audiences understand the concepts of living in the United States. News shows on health, legal advice, job openings, and immigration issues are aired. Stations also provide Spanish music from the Caribbean, South and Central America, and Mexico. Hit singles by Anglo artists are included if audience reaction is favorable.

Ratings often are not available for the Hispanic audience, so stations must use trial-and-error methods. Still, Spanish audiences are loyal, listening four to five hours a day. As a result, the one hundred or so Spanish-only radio stations are successful.

News and Talk

Radio has always broadcast news. In the 1920s, reports of sports events and elections were among the items that demonstrated radio's potential to serve the public. News coverage is still important, and now call-in talk shows give listeners an opportunity to express their own views on important topics. News and talk are especially attractive for AM stations since such material does not require stereophonic sound.

News. Radio has a unique ability to cover current events quickly and inexpensively. Most radio stations broadcast news, and some program nothing but news. The cost of running an all-news station is high, but this format can prove successful by attracting affluent audiences, especially the over-50 age category from middle- and upper-income groups. Headline news is most successful. Listeners want news stations to give them constant updates, usually in the form of half-hour (or less) blocks. Extensive coverage and analysis has been less successful, although news stations find that listeners will accept feature material, sports, and weather in each news block.

Listeners want local rather than national news. On-the-scene coverage of events affecting the audience is important, and listeners prefer to get such information from local reporters. Items that require extensive coverage, such as city governments or state legislatures, are difficult for news stations to handle. NBC offered an all-news radio network in the early 1970s, but the lack of local coverage and the emphasis on national and international news doomed the effort.

Because all-news radio is expensive to do well, only large cities with extensive population bases have news stations and then often only one. But once the investment has been made, the news station is usually among the ratings leaders.

Talk. All talk stations exist in the larger markets and often draw impressive ratings. They have been successful since they reach much the same audiences as news stations. Like the news format, talk radio is expensive since competent hosts are hard to find. Intelligent producers are also needed to find stimulating guests and topics.

Talk stations once featured controversial hosts; the emphasis has switched to well-informed hosts who have the ability to listen and ask stimulating questions. A local orientation is preferred in this format too, although network offerings from Mutual, NBC Talk Net, and ABC Talk Radio attract sizable audiences.

The primary content of talk stations is consumer oriented. Topics such as health, work, coping, sex, and money are popular, but important news events also are important topics if they have local appeal.

Program Strategies

Dayparting

Programs, including segments of a radio format, can be timed to coincide with the activities people engage in at various times during the day. Programmers can thus schedule different kinds of program material, or similar program materials in different ways, at various times of the day. The scheduling of programming to match parts of the day *is called dayparting*. The goal of dayparting is to make programming compatible with the activities of the day: getting up and going to work, doing household chores midday, ending the workday and heading home, relaxing in the evening, and passing the small hours of the morning before the cycle begins again.

Dayparting is a major strategy for radio station programming. The challenge is to make each daypart distinct and appropriate to the audience's activities while keeping the station's sound consistent. A rigidly dayparted station should develop a similarity of sound between dayparts. In other words, the station should sound enough alike at all times to be predictable to its listeners while still appealing to the unique audiences available at various times of the day. Too drastic a departure from the desired sound can destroy the consistency of the sound and the effectiveness of the format. For music stations, the essential ingredient in making daypart distinctions is the personality of the disc jockey assigned to each time period (Eastman et al. 1985).

Morning. Morning disc jockeys are friendly and sometimes outrageous. Their shows are service oriented; they present the time, temperature, traffic, and news checks, important items for listeners preparing for work or school between 6 A.M. and 10 A.M.

Morning disc jockeys usually talk more than those of other dayparts, and they may be allowed to violate the format to some extent. Paired morning jocks, perhaps a straight man and a joker, are common. Morning disc jockeys begin the day literally and figuratively, for the prevailing belief holds that if a station can win top ratings in the morning, it can hold them all day. Since morning disc jockeys have a bigger audience than at any other time of the day and anchor the station's team of personalities, they are also the most highly paid.

Midday. The midday disc jockey has a more relaxed style than the morning jock. Friendliness is important, but the music is emphasized during this 10 A.M. to 3 P.M. period. News, weather, and time are not presented as often as in the morning. Instead disc jockeys usually try to appeal to the large female audience at home.

Afternoon. The afternoon disc jockey (3–7 P.M.) is more up-tempo, as is the music, for this daypart. Adults are driving home from work, and teens are out of school, requiring a balance of teen-oriented music with selections appealing to homebound commuters. News, traffic, and weather are important again but not as much as in the morning. The afternoon disc jockey frequently refers to enjoyable evening activities that the audience may be anticipating.

Evening. Many stations program their 7 P.M. to midnight slot quite differently from other dayparts while retaining some consistency. Contemporary formats may play more teen-oriented records at night since teens join the 18–49 listeners. Evening disc jockeys may be up-tempo with an appeal to teens. Telephone lines may be opened to talk to teens on the air.

Night. The all-night hours from midnight to 6 A.M. are a quiet time for the disc jockey to relate to late night listeners: insomniacs, police officers, all-night restaurant and convenience store employees, and the like. Few commercials are scheduled during this period, giving the disc jockey time for uninterrupted music.

Program Wheels

Radio programmers seldom permit disc jockeys to select their own music and other sound elements. The stakes are too high, and the desired results are best obtained through precise scheduling. The station's program director generally determines how much music is to be programmed each hour and in what order. News, public affairs announcements, and commercials are also rigidly scheduled.

Often stations use *program wheels* (also known as *format disks, hot clocks,* or *sound hours*) to slot the presentation of on-air material. Program wheels are posted in the control studio to guide the air people in terms of what is to be broadcast and when each hour. Figure 1 illustrates a typical morning drive time CHR clock. Notice that a top five record is scheduled on the quarter-hour to give the most popular records a prominent position in the program cycle (Keith and Krause 1986).

Many programmers use a set of clocks to reflect the dayparts in the programming; for instance, one clock may be devised for morning drive, another for midday, another for afternoon drive, and so on. In devising the wheel, the programmer must consider competition and market factors. Afternoon drive time may begin at 4:00 P.M. in some cities, and in others it may not begin until 5:00 P.M. The programmer adjusts the clock so that it parallels the activities of the community in which the station is located.

News and talk stations also use program wheels. News stations, like music stations, also want their sound to be predictable each hour. News may be scheduled according to its degree of importance and geographical relevance, such as local, regional, national, and international. News-related items—traffic, weather, sports, and market reports—may be built into the schedule. Talk stations may also use a program wheel, but segments of news and two-way conversation will fill the spaces between commercial spot sets.

Not every station provides announcers with specific programming strategies, but few stations are willing to forgo any programming. Inappropriate

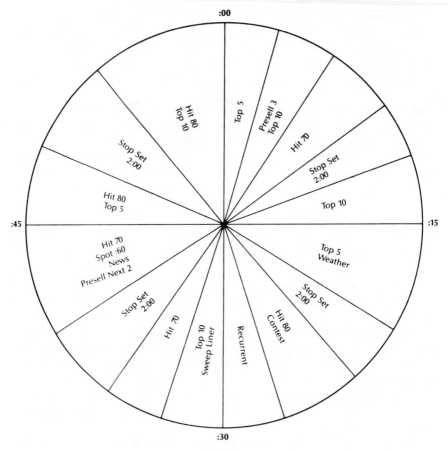

Figure 1. Program Wheel for CHR Station

scheduling and sequencing of sound elements may cause listeners to switch to a competitor.

Program Determinants

A number of factors beyond the choice of format will affect the station's search for listeners. The number of people in the listening area is important because it will determine whether an audience exists for the format. A large metropolitan area may be able to attract a sufficient audience for almost any format. In a small midwestern town, a station may have to program to serve many tastes.

A station in a multistation market will have to consider the programming presented by the competition. Other stations may be doing an effective job of serving the major audience brackets (Busby and Parker 1984). As a result, a station may have to offer an alternative for the minority of listeners with different tastes, or it may have to compete directly with an established station.

A station's resources may limit programming. A competent and dependable staff costs money, but since programming is the product that attracts listeners, cuts in the budget may mean a decreased ability to attract an audience. As a result, programmers must make calculated budget reductions, such as programming more music and less talk.

One of the most important programming determinants is whether a station is AM or FM. FM has the dimension of stereo and lends itself to music better than AM. AM stereo is developing slowly and has not proved to be a significant factor. The consequence is that AM stations often struggle for listeners. They are often used for nonmusic formats, for oldie music not recorded in stereo, or for specialized formats such as religion or ethnic programming.

Research is often conducted to measure the acceptance of music by the target audience. Some songs may appeal to younger listeners, some to older listeners, and some to men more than women. The music selection must be adjusted to meet the tastes of the desired audience.

Finally, audience promotion is significant to program determination. Audience promotion is designed to draw listeners to programming and then keep them. No amount of promotion can keep an audience listening to poor programming.

Radio promotion takes two forms: on air and off air. On-air promotion includes contests, public service projects, and establishment of a station identity disseminated in station announcements, logos, and call letters (WBJW-BJ 105). Off-air promotion includes advertisements in other media (billboards, TV), give-aways (bumper stickers), and personal publicity appearances by station personalities.

Summary

Radio programming is highly specialized. Stations are oriented to the needs and interests of local listeners. The key factor in attracting and holding an audience is demographics. Formats are developed to appeal to a given demographic segment of the audience.

Formats undergo changes as the interests of listeners change. Age also influences formats. A demographic group may literally outgrow the music and approach of a format. When that occurs, a totally new format is needed.

Music is the primary element of formats, but other factors, such as disc jockey personality, news and talk with music, and a variety of promotional activities, are used to stimulate the success of a given format.

Radio broadcasting is highly competitive so few programming matters are left to chance. Programmers look for a void in the market, an audience not being served. In large, multistation markets, a station may already be serving a large audience, and the decision may be to adopt the same programming and split the available audience. In either case, a target audience is selected and a program strategy devised to reach it. Programming, audience research, and promotion go hand in hand in a successful program effort.

The key variable in radio programming is localism. Hundreds of stations around the country may use the same format, but each must make certain that it satisfies local interests and tastes. Therefore the selection of music may vary slightly from station to station; some stations may program local news and public affairs, and some may emphasize high-interest factors such as weather or sports. Still, the stations may sound essentially the same, even in the choice and style of the announcer's chatter.

Radio has become highly specialized, and programming has become a science. But there are also problems. Many AM stations struggle to compete with FM stations for listeners. Programming an AM station is a major challenge, one that requires considerable innovation and creativity.

Still, radio is a dynamic business. Stations are selling for record amounts of money, and advertisers know they can reach listeners by advertising on radio. Not so many years ago, many thought radio was dead. But radio is alive and in most respects well. For the American public, radio is a familiar companion, one that provides information and entertainment. There may not be dramatic changes in the future of radio programming, but more stations will sign on, and programmers will find new and interesting ways to serve the public.

References

Broadcasting. 1986. "Looking at Easy Listening," January 6, p. 182.

Busby, Linda, and Donald Parker. 1984. *The Art and Science of Radio.* Boston: Allyn and Bacon.

Eastman, Susan et al., eds. 1985. *Broadcast/Cable Programming: Strategies and Practices.* 2d ed. Belmont, Calif.: Wadsworth.

Halper, Donna L. 1984. "Choosing a Format." *RadioActive* 10 (February): 6–11.

Josephson, Sanford. 1986. "Easy Listening vs. 'Soft' Contemporary: Shades of Gray." *Television/Radio Age,* March 17, pp. A1–A4.

Keith, Michael C., and Joseph M. Krause. 1986. *The Radio Station.* Boston: Focal Press.

Routt, Edd, James B. McGrath, and Frederic A. Weiss. 1979. *The Radio Format Conundrum.* New York: Hastings House.

Seigerman, Catherine. 1984. "Hispanic Radio," *RadioActive* 10 (November): 8–10.
———. 1986. "The 500-Year Old Format." *RadioActive* 12 (June–July): 12–14.

WATCHING A RADIO CONSULTANT CONSULT

Karrie Jacobs

Karrie Jacobs is a freelance writer based in New York.

Reprinted with permission of *Adweek*, July, 1985.

TOWSON, MD.—"We gotta go after yuppies and we gotta go after baby boomers and we can't lose one teen in the process," declares Rick Sklar. It is Tuesday morning here, and the principal owners of Hot Hits K106, Steve Seymour and Stuart Frankel, along with program director Ralph Wimmer, are seated around a long table in the station's nondescript conference room. They jot occasional notes as radio consultant Rick Sklar coaches them in their quest for bigger numbers in the ratings book.

Sklar, who is based in New York, had come down on the train to Baltimore the previous day with Seymour, counseling him on the advantages and disadvantages of other radio stations in which Seymour and Frankel wish to invest. That evening, Sklar had dinner with Wimmer as they finalized plans to hire a new morning drive-time disc jockey from a Miami station—a move they felt would boost the all-important A.M. rush-hour ratings for K106 (WMKR-FM) but also would necessitate bumping the current morning jock to the less prestigious 10 A.M. slot.

Breaking the news to the soon-to-be-dislocated deejay now was on the agenda for lunch. But first, Sklar—fresh from his five-mile sunrise run—had a pep talk to deliver.

A compact man in his fifties who alternates between fist pounding and a reflective, almost icy deadpan when explaining his methodology to station management, Sklar is one of the handful of radio consultants with national reputations. His own broadcasting career—extending over more than thirty years—parallels the development and ascendance of rock 'n' roll and rock radio.

Much of what a consultant sells to a client is his own success story, and Sklar's is particularly heady. He programmed New York's WABC-AM in the 1960s and 1970s, when that station, fueled by and building on Beatlemania, claimed gigantic 20- to 25-percent shares of the metropolitan area's listening audience. Sklar's winning format combined a short, cyclically repetitive playlist of hit songs; fast-talking, aggressively verbose deejays; and a constant stream of jingles that drilled the station's call letters, slogans and deejays' names ("Cou-sin Bruuu-ceee") until they were etched in the memory of even the most casual listener.

The top forty format lost favor in the mid-1970s as more sophisticated "progressive" and album-oriented-rock FM stations moved to the forefront. Now, however, hit radio is back—this time on the FM band—with all the promotional hoopla and shtick and even shorter playlists. Earlier this year, Sklar left his position as vice-president of ABC radio, and he now is selling his skills to a variety of radio companies. Among his clients are a talk outlet in Oklahoma City, an easy-listening station in Greenwich, Conn., and Hot Hits K106.

"The name of the game," Sklar tells the three men at the table, "is to create a kind of radio over the air that is audience friendly." He explains that what seems like good management and sound programming to the professionals who run the station—those who consider the station's overall format in a twenty-four-hour period—may be the opposite of what attracts the listener who tunes in for twenty minutes at a time. He points out that even a 15 share of the market (nowadays a 5 or 6 share is considered strong in most cities) means that 85 out of every 100 people never listen to the station. "We are trying literally to get five more people out of one hundred because, if that could happen, we'd be the market leader."

Part of what Sklar has done in the month he has been working with K106 has been a winnowing of the record library, tossing out songs that don't have the clout the station is seeking in its rotation. He has instituted a system of surveying local record stores (just as he did twenty years ago at WABC) to determine the top sellers in the area. Those songs can be given maximum exposure on the air. The theory is that the more a record sells, the more popular it is, and the record that sells the most will attract and hold the most listeners. Hit Radio 101. "We've identified 250 songs or so that are popular all over the country," says Sklar. "At this point in time, we're pretty damn sure of most of those records." He emphasizes that they should be added to the cartridge library (the cartridge deck has replaced the turntable at most commercial radio stations) immediately, even if that means buying them rather than waiting for the record labels to supply the discs.

Every trick in Sklar's repertoire is intended to hook listeners. More important, he aims to implant the station's call letters in the minds of the handful of Baltimore-area residents who are selected to keep Arbitron diaries, the arguably dubious but indisputably official basis for ratings that help determine ad rates. Sklar pushes for the institution of a sophisticated program of jingles: "They can do a great many jobs for a station." He advocates putting them on cartridges, in some cases tagged to the beginning of a song with a second jingle or a station ID at the end of the song, to form "multiple-element cartridges." "Look at the station the way a movie director looks at a film, with each cartridge representing a scene," Sklar suggests.

Steve Seymour looks up from a note he's just received from Stu Frankel. "I lost the concept," Seymour confesses. "Go back."

Sklar drops the movie metaphor and tries to clarify the point. The combination of elements on one cartridge scheduled into the day's programming by computer would "force the sound in spite of the deejay." His aim is to "create repeating sound patterns," which he calls "a secret weapon."

"Everything is done," Sklar insists, "not for convenience at this end but for the convenience of those filling out the diary. This damn thing [the Arbitron diary] is an exam book. [The diary keepers] don't like it. It reminds them of school. We have to give them the answers to the exam."

As the morning progresses, Frankel asks Sklar how he feels about the station using syndicated programming from a comedy network. Sklar advises him to "pick and choose," to use the network selectively. They touch on the problem of finding a morning newscaster and debate the merits of using occasional live commercials.

Sklar summarizes what they must do by saying they have to "isolate the hit factor—from hit songs to hit personalities to a hit way of presenting news."

As noon approaches, Seymour, Frankel and Wimmer disperse to attend to last-minute details connected with their first run-through of a new promotion: playing "The Star Spangled Banner" every day at noon until the TWA hostages have been freed by the Shiites. Wimmer has located a copy of the national anthem and had it transferred to a cartridge. Seymour has called the newspapers and television stations and has been told that two different TV news crews will film the airing of the anthem. Somebody has hung a banner with the station's logo—"Hot Hits K106" in orange and magenta graffiti-like letters on a bright yellow background—on the wall in the sound studio and made sure that the deejay, Davey Crockett, is sporting a logo t-shirt.

Sklar assures the staff that even though stations in other cities are doing hostage promos, "as long as we're the first in the market, we're the winner." The station's managers and Sklar take turns enthusing about the promotion, citing its publicity value and its patriotic merit, in that order.

By noon, only one cameraman from one station has arrived. The anthem is aired, and afterward the deejay offers a grave explanation of its significance to the listeners. A station ID is played, followed by the upbeat strains of Katrina and the Waves' "Walking on Sunshine." Seymour, Frankel, and Sklar follow the cameraman out to the parking lot and watch a replay of the video on the television station van's color TV. All are pleased with the visibility of the station's logo in the picture.

By 12:30 they're ready to take the old drive-time deejay to lunch and let him know he doesn't have to get up at 5 in the morning anymore.

Sometime after 2, Sklar, Wimmer, Frankel, and Seymour reconvene in the conference room and are joined by the morning deejay, who seems unfazed by his sudden demotion. They have cushioned the blow with promises of publicity and fanfare for his move to the 10 A.M. slot, including a staged alarm clock smashing and contests for late risers.

Scheduled for this afternoon is a brainstorming session on promotions, particularly ones that will attract adult listeners. The managers need to devise publicity stunts and ongoing giveaways for the fall, but first they have to move on a couple of immediate matters, current events they can capitalize on. Ticket sales have just been announced for the Live Aid extravaganza, a rock festival scheduled to take place simultaneously in Philadelphia and England to benefit African relief organizations. The station has put out feelers in all directions to come up with ten pairs of tickets to give away on the air. Sklar says the giveaway has to be done in a big way, using lots of superlatives. "First the Beatles, then Woodstock and now the biggest concert event of your lifetime" is the pitch he suggests.

Also discussed are ways to wed the airing of the national anthem to a yellow ribbon giveaway. The deejay notes that yellow ribbons would match their logo. Sklar proposes distributing thousands of ribbons stamped discreetly with the K106 emblem.

"Who's the woman who handles this building?" Seymour asks Frankel. "We should call her and see if we can tie a ribbon around it. . . . Find out how thick you can get ribbon."

So goes a typical day in the field for radio consultant Rick Sklar.

It was a day that could have included conferences with deejays, a brainstorming session on jingles ("K106 *music blitz, blitz, blitz*) and a music selection meeting.

A typical day at Sklar's own office might see him sitting back, surrounded by framed black-and-white photos (old ones of Sklar with fresh-faced Beatles and newer ones with Boy George or Juice Newton) and listening to tapes of his stations, making sure his instructions are translated into on-the-air action, taking notes.

There are four times as many radio stations operating in the United States today as there were when Sklar's WABC was at its peak. Simple mathematics implies that rating shares must be smaller than they were in the 1960s. But Sklar thrills station owners and managers with the message that double-digit shares still are possible. "I was talking to a guy yesterday," relates Sklar, "who was happy 'cause he went from a 2.5 to a 2.8. What happens is people get used to these things. They get comfortable with these kinds of shares. You have to try to open their horizons. They could even be bigger if they just believe that they can be and work at it."

THE SEDATING OF ROCK 'N' ROLL RADIO

Michael Goldberg

Michael Goldberg is *Rolling Stone* magazine's West Coast music editor. For over ten years, he has written about all aspects of popular music and the music business. Prior to joining the *Rolling Stone* staff, he wrote for a variety of national and regional publications, including *Esquire, New West, New Times*, the *San Francisco Chronicle, Downbeat*, and England's *New Musical Express*.

Reprinted from *Esquire*, April, 1983. Used by permission.

Lee Abrams does not have fond memories of the summer of 1981. As the most successful radio consultant in America, Abrams, twenty-nine at the time, was earning close to a half-million dollars a year telling album-oriented radio (AOR) stations—the ones that play cuts from albums in addition to singles—which records they should play. Abrams had come to New York to attend the second annual New Music Seminar, which is a conference held by supporters of New Wave rock, the kind of music seldom heard on stations he consults. For the most part, the attendees were not Lee Abrams's kind of crowd, and the minute he stepped onstage at Private's, the club where the radio panel that he was participating in was taking place, he knew he was in for it.

There were boos; there were catcalls. A beer can was hurled at the stage. When Abrams tried to tell them that it wasn't his fault that the public *liked* the mainstream rock typical of his stations, they shouted, "Liar!" When Abrams told them that even *he* was now bored listening to his own stations, they yelled, "Bullshit!" When he told them there was nothing he could do about the fact that New Wave rock wasn't on the air, they snarled, "You're crazy."

Then Bruce Harris, director of East Coast A & R at Epic, stood up and glared at Abrams: "You and mothers like you are responsible for ruining album radio."

Abrams stared back at Harris. Then he looked around the room. He sat there. He said nothing. Because, in truth, there was really nothing for him to say.

Lee Abrams is a radio doctor. He is the guy an AOR station owner or his general manager calls up when his station has been getting bad ratings. To reverse the situation, Abrams may do anything from putting together a TV promotional campaign to replacing staff. But mostly what he does is advise his clients on the particular songs they should put on the air and the frequency that those songs should be played. It is usually enough.

Today Abrams is sitting in a borrowed office at KFOG, a San Francisco station for which he has recently begun consulting. The big desk in front of him is covered with tapes and music magazines and industry tip sheets; thousands of albums are piled on the floor. Grabbing a free moment, he places a call to WKZL, the station he consults for in North Carolina. He opens a scruffy brown leather briefcase and pulls out a piece of paper with notes scribbled all over it. When he's got the station's program director (PD) on the line, he says, "Bump it, I guess," about one record that isn't doing well.

Then Abrams starts tossing out the kind of advice that this station pays him about two thousand dollars a month for. "I think 'Down Under' is a hit. That would be an A. 'Destination Unknown' is probably a hit too. Foghat's doing well for you? Well, add it in P, for two weeks anyway." He's referring to various categories he's created, which indicate how frequently a song should be aired. An A gets played once every five hours; a P gets played every eight hours.

"Did you get that package of themes?" Now he's talking about these old TV themes of "The Beverly Hillbillies," "Mr. Ed," "The Untouchables," and "The Twilight Zone" that he's sent to his stations. Abrams thinks this kind of thing elicits an "Oh, wow!" response from his listeners—makes his meticulously programmed stations sound more spontaneous.

"Mickey Mouse's birthday? How about some kind of tribute? By the way, there's an import version of 'Shock the Monkey' in German. That record's getting burned out. Throw in the import version."

Back in the mid-1960s, "progressive" stations emerged on the FM dial as an alternative to formula top forty radio. They quickly moved into the mainstream. Today, as one promo man puts it, AOR radio is little more than Muzak for teenagers. "What started in San Francisco fifteen or sixteen years ago—free-form radio—certainly doesn't exist anymore," says Joe Smith, former chairman of Elektra/Asylum Records. "And it's the radio consultants and programmers who have changed all that."

What one hears if one tunes in WCOZ in Boston, KLOS in Los Angeles, WQDR in Raleigh, WAPP in New York, or nearly any other AOR station in this country is hits by major stars, past and present. Largely past. The Doors,

Led Zeppelin, Jimi Hendrix, and the Beatles are all played often on the stations, prompting one disc jockey to joke that you have to be dead to get airtime. And much of the "new music" that is played is by established mainstream rockers, the so-called corporate rock bands like Journey, REO Speedwagon, Styx, and Rush, all of whom share the uniform style of tenors singing over a slick, melodic, high-velocity sound sweetened with whooshing synthesizers.

"You used to travel around the country, and when you went to the Midwest you'd get midwestern food, and when you went down South you'd get southern cooking, and now you travel around the country and you get Denny's all over," says Terre Roche, a member of the Roches, a folk-rock group whose three albums have received great reviews from the critics but negligible airplay on AOR radio. "It's the same premise with these radio stations."

Lee Abrams is not the only AOR radio consultant, but he was the first and is still—with something like seventy stations—the biggest. Abrams was the guy who, at seventeen, came up with the basic plan that all the others have imitated, a plan that was based on the brilliant if obvious discovery of what Abrams called "the vulnerable top forty listener."

"This was the type of person," explains Abrams, "that had just started to get into the sound that was happening then. This person didn't listen to the progressive station, 'cause it was just a little over his head. So he listened to top forty but really only liked every third song. He liked it when 'Jumping Jack Flash' came on, but then he'd hear Herb Alpert, then the 1910 Fruitgum Company, tune out, then hear Santana and like that one. So I thought, that's where the gap is. There isn't a format that reaches this person."

Abrams verified his hunch with a variety of unorthodox research techniques, among them the "hitchhiking study," in which he hitchhiked around Fort Lauderdale for a week, surreptitiously "observing people switching stations, why they tune in and out of a station." Satisfied, he went through his record collection and those of his friends to compile a list of about eight hundred songs by "album-oriented artists" that would appeal to the "vulnerable listener." "When I was eighteen or nineteen it was easy putting the list together," says Abrams. "That's the music I was into, anyway. They were the best songs by the best groups. You could instantly hear what sounded right and what didn't. I thought the music should be as commercial as possible without losing the progressive identity." Abrams devised a new radio format from the list and called it Superstars.

The trick of the Superstars system, which is still in use today, is the division of rock artists into a variety of categories based on the artist's popularity. New records deemed suitable for airplay are divided between A, B-1, and P. A records are either hit singles or what Abrams calls "great songs" by album rock artists: the Rolling Stones' "Start Me Up" was an A when first

released, as was Tom Petty's "Refugee." B-1 records are new albums by extremely popular groups: Led Zeppelin, Jefferson Starship, Journey. These albums include three or four cuts okayed for airplay. A and B-1 records are
played five times a day. P records, by semipopular artists, are played three
times a day. Once a record gets old, or, as one program director at an Abrams
station says, "is perceived by the public as not current," it is moved into other
categories (C-1 or B-2) and gets less airplay. Superstars stations currently play
about seven hundred songs repeatedly during a week, but they tend to be by
the same twenty or thirty artists.

Prior to Superstars, disc jockeys at an FM station could play anything
they wanted. But at Abrams's stations, the disc jockeys use a "flow sheet," a
piece of paper with the categories printed down the left side. Moving down
the list, they first play a cut from the A category, then one from the D-2
category, and so on. The point of all this is to give the station a consistent
sound; whether you tune in at 9 A.M. or 4 P.M., you'll hear the same mix of
old and new songs.

Another innovation was shifting the emphasis from the song to the artist.
"In top forty formats, listeners are acquired and retained through the 'Familiarity Principle,'" wrote Abrams in a brochure that explains the format to
potential clients. "With top forty, the familiarity is with the song; with the
'Superstars' format, the familiarity is with the artist." Thus one hears a disc
jockey announcing that he's just played the Rolling Stones; he doesn't mention that the cut was "Jumping Jack Flash."

First used at WQDR in Raleigh in 1972, when Abrams was the PD,
Superstars was a hit; based on its success, Abrams went into the consulting
business. By 1973 he had hooked up with Kent Burkhart, a top forty consultant who was looking for a way to pick up more client stations. The two
formed Burkhart/Abrams, and Superstars took off. As time went on, they
found ways to keep in touch with changing tastes: they phoned record stores
on a weekly basis to see what was selling locally, kept an eye on the weekly
trades, and made note of listener requests. Abrams and Burkhart also passed
out questionnaires, attached feedback cards to rock albums, and held focus
groups—semiencounter groups where twenty kids listen to records and talk
about what they like and dislike.

With the success of Superstars, free-form radio began to die out slowly,
and between 1974 and 1977, dozens of stations were hiring the consultants.
"It was like one a month," says Abrams. Usually, when he went up against a
free-form station, he won the ratings battle. As one former disc jockey says,
"Match a machine against 'whatever happens, man'—the machine wins every
time."

For a long time, Abrams was the only AOR consultant worth talking
about. But then, in 1981, a man named John Sebastian came along to throw
a monkey wrench into the prevailing methodology. Sebastian decided there

was a way to find out *exactly* what the mass audience wants to hear or, maybe more to the point, *doesn't* want to hear. He started using what he termed "call-out" or "passive" research, employing a team of "researchers," usually high school girls, to go through the phone book and make random phone calls in search of, for instance, twenty- to twenty-four-year-old males who listen to rock radio. Once one of these males is on the line, the researcher aims to find out which songs will *not* cause him to tune out by playing a series of thirty or so seven-second excerpts from songs. After each excerpt, the man on the phone is asked a few questions: "Have you heard the song? Did you used to like it? Do you like it now?"

Sebastian treated the "actives," the kids who phone in to request a favorite song or write the station, as an insignificant percentage of the listening demographic. With the record business in a slump, he also began to ignore sales charts. If fewer people were buying records, he figured those charts weren't accurately portraying what all the radio listeners who weren't buying records really wanted to hear. "We can tell if people like a song or not, not whether people would go out and buy it," he says. "And there's a distinct difference. Everybody doesn't just go out and buy a record 'cause they happen to like it."

"Call-out" allowed John Sebastian to tap into what he saw as the "silent majority" of AOR radio listeners—and it certainly worked. In Boston, one year after he became PD at WCOZ, that station's ratings rose from 4.1 to a 12.6, the highest rating any AOR station had ever achieved in a top twenty-five market. (Just a one-point rise in the Arbitron ratings can mean a million-dollar increase in advertising revenues.) Then he did what any PD who has just won the Super Bowl of radio would do: he started up his own consulting firm.

What Sebastian did in creating his format was take Superstars and tighten it up, make it closer to top forty in form, if not content. When he first arrived at WCOZ, he quickly reduced the record library from five thousand albums to five hundred. "Prior to his arrival, there was everything," says former WCOZ music director Kate Ingram. "From Bonnie Raitt to the Sex Pistols. Plenty of black music. As soon as John came in, he took things out right and left." He also even further reduced the disc jockey's freedom. Unlike Abrams, Sebastian provides cards that tell the disc jockey *exactly* what to say on the air. Slogans like "Playing a wider variety of rock 'n' roll, or [station's call letters], with one great rock 'n' roll song after another, or [jock's name], guaranteeing no less than six in a row or we'll pay you ten thousand, six hundred dollars"—these phrases are repeated three or four times an hour on a Sebastian station twenty-four hours a day.

Call-out worked to such an extent that two other radio consultants—Jeff Pollack and Dave Hamilton—began to use it. But "passive" research also has detractors who charge that the method is only effective when used to test old records, such as "Stairway to Heaven," since it's difficult for someone to express an opinion on seven seconds of a song they've never heard before.

Not surprisingly, Abrams is among those critics. "One reason is, sometimes there are records that people like but don't want to hear on the radio. Also, I think it leads you to make real safe conclusions that certainly have their competitive value, but can make a station dull after a while. From what I hear, the Police never tested well. So they [Sebastian's stations] weren't too much behind the Police."

Sebastian counters by claiming that his methods are the most democratic way to program a radio station. "See, as a consulting company, we don't dictate which records are played at all," he says. "While other programmers *subjectively* decide what should be played and what shouldn't be played, we don't. We don't choose to believe we have golden ears."

Of course, Sebastian doesn't really ask people what they like. He asks them to rate the songs *he's* chosen. If you offer somebody a choice between a Jumbo Jack and a Big Mac, you are offering them a choice, but you're still only talking about hamburgers.

Still, the irony of this debate is that though the consultants all claim to use a different combination of research techniques to determine their play lists, they all end up playing the same stuff. A look at the recent top twenty for each of the top four consulted stations (which is printed each week in an AOR radio tip sheet called *The Friday Morning Quarterback Album Report*) shows the lists have fifteen out of twenty bands in common.

Radio consultants have no shortage of detractors, but their economic success is inarguable. "The appeal of AOR radio used to be very, very small," says John Sebastian. "We have widened that appeal. And now album-oriented rock is one of the most successful formats in the country. It is making money and it is going to survive."

Shelley Grafman, executive vice-president at KSHE in St. Louis, says that his station, which began programming free-form rock in 1967, was taking in between five and seven thousand dollars a month in the early days. "In those days, if you had receipts for eighty or ninety thousand dollars a year, you were doing pretty well. There was nothing but losses in terms of economics." Today, a leading AOR station in a top twenty market may bill as much as three million a year. "When we had the ratings success at WCOZ," says John Sebastian, "they went from charging about seventy dollars a commercial minute to, at times, charging as much as three hundred dollars a minute."

Because of their success, consultants are very powerful men. The four most influential—Abrams, Sebastian, Pollack, and Hamilton—directly control the sound of more than 120 rock stations. That's about a third of the stations that count—and that doesn't include the influence the consultants have had over others who listen to the consulted stations and imitate their play lists.

The consequence of a system in which, as a former research director at a

Sebastian station puts it, "if your new record comes out and all the consultants go on it, you already have over a hundred stations in every market playing that record and it slams through the charts," is a certain oligopoly of taste. "That the record gets played doesn't mean anyone's buying it," says the director, "it doesn't mean anyone really likes it. It just means that a few guys decide to make their stations play that record."

The power of the consultants is such that record companies will sometimes even edit songs at their request. Sebastian, for example, thought the eight-minute live version of Bob Seger's "Let It Rock" was too long, and Capitol Records gladly agreed to press up a shorter version.

But perhaps the most serious consequence of this power has been its influence on the type of rock music many bands now make and the kinds of bands record companies are willing to sign. "When you know something is not in vogue at the radio station, you don't sign the act," says Joe Smith. Many worthwhile acts that do get signed don't get played on AOR. Black musicians, for instance, are seldom programmed by the consultants. And one of the more important kinds of music currently out of vogue with the consultants is black music. To take just the week of November 19, 1982, one might think that black musicians had stopped making records: the FMQ "song index," which lists the hundred most-played songs of the week (not including oldies) on AOR radio, includes no songs at all by black artists. And no black artists appeared in the individual top twenty charts that Abrams, Pollack, Sebastian, and Hamilton each provide, either.

The situation is not unique to black music, however; New Wave, punk, folk—virtually all other forms of pop music have been almost completely excluded from airtime. Given this state of affairs, it is difficult to see how new bands ever get played. Rumors that the consultants take bribes in exchange for advising their stations to play a record are denied as often as they spring up. But all of the consultants say that they (or their associates) simply listen to the new rock records and advise their stations to play the stuff that fits their sound. Abrams says that in addition to "gut feeling" he uses sales charts, focus groups, and other soft research techniques. In any case, the type of new music that does make it on the air almost always sounds a lot like the records they're already playing, or that are already being played on other stations in the market.

At the beginning of the 1980s, Lee Abrams started showing up at radio conferences admitting that even he, the man most responsible for the one-sided uniformity in AOR radio, was bored by the format. He said he couldn't listen to his stations anymore.

In a sense, Superstars had become too successful. "I think maybe its success made it look too easy," says Abrams. "Superstars sort of became the standard and everyone sort of felt, 'Well, that's the way to win in AOR.' But that's not necessarily true. It's just one way."

But if Abrams is slightly uncomfortable with the monster he's created, he says he can't really feel guilty about it. "Just came up with the thing, after all; sorry if it worked," and then says, "It's not my fault. It's just like, 'Come on, can't anybody come up with something different?'"

And then somebody did.

In April 1979 a fellow named Rick Carroll became PD at KROQ, a tacky little low-rent radio station in L.A. that played mostly punk and New Wave rock in an extremely loose, free-form format. Like other PDs and consultants, Carroll took the music programming out of the hands of the disc jockeys. But unlike the others, he kept the focus exclusively on New Wave rock 'n' roll. He limited the number of songs and set up an almost top forty–like rotation. KROQ became known as the station where you could hear the Ramones and Devo, Talking Heads and the Plasmatics, the Sex Pistols and the B-52's, X and Bananarama—in other words, all the stuff that the other AOR stations were ignoring.

Three years after Carroll took the job, KROQ was the number-one rock station in L.A., and last July [1982] Carroll went into the consulting business. Though he's only got four client stations at the moment, he says twenty others are considering his top forty–styled, "modern music" format.

To date, the only other consultant who has put a New Wave format into practice is Lee Abrams. Even before KROQ was a hit, Abrams had begun to develop what he calls the Superstars II format and last October [1982] the new format debuted on KFOG in San Francisco. Now Sebastian says he has plans to announce *his* "revolutionary new format" in June. If it's anything like Abrams's program it probably won't be too bad, but even progressive music, when it's packaged like this, has its limits. Abrams calls the format Timeless Rock, and that hints at the strategy. For what Abrams is up to is shifting the target from the vulnerable top forty listener to what he calls "the weekend hippie," an older listener whose taste in rock was set in the late 1960s and early 1970s, who thinks fondly of Joni Mitchell and the Rolling Stones but can't stomach AC/DC or Styx. So Abrams programs about thirty "modern music" records from the softer side of the New Wave (like Peter Gabriel) along with a selection of compatible mainstream artists (like Tom Petty) and lots of oldies.

Abrams claims he would eventually like to switch many, if not all, of his old-line Superstars stations over to the Timeless Rock format. He also expresses some regret over the death of free-form. "I sort of thought the old progressive radio was good," he admits. "The intention was not really to go in and destroy them." The Superstars II format would be closer to that old system, but much of its future hinges on the success of KFOG. "You can't just go into a station that's really successful with Superstars I and say, 'We're going to change.' We got the word from the presidents of these companies: 'Hey, we're very successful; don't go screwing around with it.'"

PUTTING RADIO ON AUTOMATIC PILOT

Marc Gunther

Marc Gunther, a reporter with the *Hartford Courant,* often writes about the media.

Reprinted from the *Washington Journalism Review,* July/August, 1983. Used by permission.

Say good-bye to your local deejay. Forget the "happy birthday" announcements in the morning, and don't bother calling up to request a favorite record. Radio—the most personal and local of the media—is going national. Listen to the silky smooth voice of Bob Leonard, a thirty-four-year-old disc jockey on the rise:

To KTXY-FM in Jefferson City, Mississippi: "FM-107, Jefferson City, serving Columbia, the Lake of the Ozarks, and all of central Mississippi with your favorite music in stereo, 24 hours a day. It's 9 o'clock."

To KAAM-AM in Dallas: "You're with Bob Leonard this morning and I've got great oldies and more for you right here on Radio 1310."

To KROW-AM in Reno, Nevada: "The morning team of me, Bob Leonard, C. M. McMullen—I call her Connie—and Tom Lilly—I call him Tom—are all ready to go when you get up."

Bob Leonard is not in Jefferson City. He is not in Dallas. He is not in Reno either, and he has probably never even met Connie McMullen or Tom Lilly. Leonard is in Mokena, Illinois, population 4,578, a town with little more than a few cornfields and a spanking new radio studio, where some say a revolution is occurring in radio.

Bob Leonard chatters to the nation over the Satellite Music Network, the first and most successful of a small group of new radio networks determined to dominate American radio. The networks offer local stations round-the-clock programming based on exhaustive research in musical tastes and some of the best on-the-air talent in the country. They even help create slogans and sell ads. Buying the whole package can be cheaper than running a local station without it.

"There's no question that in ten years, 50 percent of all the radio stations in the United States will be on a twenty-four-hour satellite," says Kent Burkhart, a part-owner of Satellite Music Network. "It's one of those revolutions that happens. It's here. It's now."

While some worry that the new networks will pack the airwaves with dull or predictable sounds, they are proving irresistible to local station owners who can essentially flip a switch, sell some ads, and wait for the profits to roll in.

In less than a year, Satellite Music Network has attracted more than 125 affiliates and a crowded field of competitors. Ted Turner's Cable News Network launched a twenty-four-hour all-news radio network in April [1982] by simply using the audio portion of CNN2, a cable television network featuring half-hour cycles of hard-hitting, fast-breaking news. Radio's CNN2 already has a dozen affiliates.

ABC, meanwhile, offers TalkRadio, an eighteen-hour-a-day cascade of words from the West Coast. It is also preparing, with much hoopla, for this month's debut of ABC Superadio, a round-the-clock music network with a star-studded lineup of disc jockeys lured away from the country's top markets.

"I think we will dominate radio," says E. Karl, senior vice-president of Sunbelt Communications, which runs yet another satellite network called Transtar. "I would venture to say you won't even recognize the industry."

Many listeners will not even know it when their local station goes satellite. Perhaps the most ingenious feature of the new national networks is that they can be engineered to sound local. Leonard, for example, tapes dozens of "local" spots every month (such as the ones quoted above) that are shipped to affiliates of Satellite Music Network. The taped spots are then inserted automatically into the national programs, triggered by cues that come over the satellite. So Leonard can be heard introducing a local newscaster in Reno, promoting that night's Astros game in Houston, and describing the weather in Portland ("cloudy skies and temps in the sixties this afternoon").

"We can localize weather, we can localize time checks, we can localize a whole bunch of things," says Michael Hauptman, vice-president in charge of ABC Radio Enterprises. "All of this is done in ways that are completely undetectable. Your listeners will not know it's coming from anywhere but your station." Local station owners concur, saying they frequently get calls for network disc jockeys. Some hang photographs of the deejays in their lobbies.

So, if listeners cannot tell the difference, who cares where the programs are coming from? Television has relied heavily on network programming for years, and newspapers fill pages with canned features or wire service copy. Even some radio stations, especially those with so-called beautiful music formats, use hours of taped music.

The difference, critics say, is that the new radio networks allow local stations to become turnkey operations with no attachment to their communities. "The problem is the absence of any requirement that the broadcaster provide service to the local community, based on the needs and problems of the local community," says Andrew Jay Schwartzman, executive director of the Media Access Project in Washington. "The removal of any need for local input is horrifying."

The temptation for local station owners to go national has become harder to resist since the Federal Communications Commission voted to deregulate radio. In January 1981, the commission lifted requirements that stations devote a minimum percentage of airtime to news and public affairs programming.

Now, Schwartzman warns that stations using satellite programming will be ill equipped to serve the public, either with routine announcements or during emergencies. "Supposing the hospital calls up and says, 'We need type-O blood.' If you don't have a studio anymore, you're not going to invite people in to do local PSAs [public service announcements]," he says.

Local disc jockeys are not happy, either, about the satellite networks, for an obvious reason—their jobs are being eliminated. Some warn that the networks will homogenize radio, sweeping aside regional diversity, offbeat announcers, and innovative programming.

"They're taking the fun out of radio," laments Bruce Morrow, who owns four suburban radio stations in New York and New Jersey. As Cousin Brucie, Morrow was the dominant personality on the nation's most listened-to radio station, WABC in New York, during the 1960s.

Morrow still practices an intensely personal approach to radio, taking regular shifts at his own stations and making frequent public appearances. "I'm out in the community constantly, signing autographs at McDonald's," he says.

Some local disc jockeys and programmers doubt the satellite jockeys will be able to compete with those on the scene. "In a comparative situation, there's no question that a station programmed locally can win," claims Daniel W. Hayden, program director at WHCN-FM, Hartford, a successful rock station. "We can take the morning show out to someone's kitchen and broadcast live. We try to get out two or three times a week."

"Contemporary radio cries out for localism," Morrow says. "The [network] concept has been around for many years, and it's failed. I really believe it will fail. The listener will lose touch with his world."

Network executives respond that they encourage local stations to blend their own programs with network broadcasts. Ed Fritts, owner and general manager of automated station WPAD-AM in Paducah, Kentucky, signed up for Satellite Music Network's country format last year but still retained programs tailored for Paducah. He broadcasts six local newscasts daily, sports from the University of Kentucky, and even a midday swap-and-barter show.

Fritts says the satellite network offers a high-quality sound at a low cost. "You cannot employ the quality of voices they use in a small town like this," he says. "We sound better than we could sound any other way."

The satellite networks, made possible by new technology, are in fact a throwback to radio's early days. Network radio ruled the airwaves during the 1930s and 1940s—Fritts's WPAD had been a CBS affiliate for thirty-seven years—before giving way to television as the medium of entertainment. Some network programs hung on—remember Arthur Godfrey's morning show on CBS?—but the networks became primarily news and sports services that distributed their programs over costly and ineffective land-lines.

Since the launch of RCA's Satcom I in 1975, first cable television and now radio programs have been distributed by the satellites that orbit 23,000 miles above the earth. For radio, the sound quality is excellent, and the cost of equipment needed to receive the signals has tumbled faster than anyone expected.

Owning a radio station, meanwhile, has become a risky business. As the number of stations has grown from 4,000 to nearly 8,000 in the past fifteen years, FCC studies have reported that as many as four in ten are losing money.

"The competition among radio stations for a piece of their market has increased, as FM has emerged," ABC's Michael Hauptman says. "You're sharing roughly the same audience with twice as many radio stations. Competition is fierce."

Satellite Music Network charges $1,000 a month for its programs, boasting that it costs affiliates only $1.37 an hour and promising annual savings of up to $67,000 in small markets and $300,000 in major ones. Generally, local stations also give up one or two minutes of commercial time each hour to be sold to national advertisers by the networks.

While the financial arrangements vary, signing on with a network enables most owners to cut their payroll dramatically and rid themselves of other headaches. "Satellite doesn't smoke, drink, spill Cokes, come to work reeking, pregnant, lie, steal, gossip, leave on lights, pout, get jealous, leave early or come in late," says Lou Meyerhoffer of WTTC in Lewisburg, Pennsylvania.

The same economics of scale that can bring top talent to places like Paducah and Jefferson City also apply to promotion and marketing. ABC Superadio will compose jingles, provide billboards, and run contests, complete with prizes, for local affiliates. Transtar bills itself as "America's First Full Service Radio Network," promising everything from videotape training sessions for advertising salesmen to daily wire service-type bulletins covering industry trends, new recordings, even the monologues used the night before by Johnny Carson.

Network programming is designed by industry gurus such as ABC's Superadio's Rick Sklar, who made his reputation at WABC, and Burkhart, whose radio consulting firm has about 150 clients and has been adding about 30 a year. The consultants, sometimes called "radio doctors," keep abreast of America's musical tastes by holding panel discussions, sending out questionnaires, and conducting shopping center surveys (sample question: "What tune did you hum when you woke up this morning?"). Burkhart's firm reportedly conducts half a million interviews a year.

"We spend one hell of a lot of money on it. We think it's vital that we know what the public wants to hear," he says. "We find out what colors are hot, what magazines are read, what movies people have seen. . . . It makes the listener feel we're on top of things."

Nothing goes on the air that has not been thoroughly tested first. When Satellite Music Network's deejays chat about Ann Landers and *People* magazine, you can bet it is because more listeners are reading them than "Dear Abby" and *Time*. The policy of sticking with the tried and true extends to music as well.

"Familiarity is something that adds audience," Burkhart says. "We find it in our best interests to program all familiar [music]. We play what people want to hear."

Satellite Music Network has two formats, soft rock (Barry Manilow, Barbra Streisand) and contemporary country (Dolly Parton, Willie Nelson). Transtar offers adult contemporary (Simon and Garfunkel, Barbra Streisand). And ABC will air an adult contemporary format playing what Sklar calls "music that is the national consciousness." A typical artist? Barbra Streisand.

It's precisely this kind of thing that worries some radio buffs, though. Burkhart insists that his research merely reflects public opinion, without shaping it. "If people want their hemlines to come up," he says, "they're going to come up."

It seems clear, however, that a new musical group—or an entirely new style of music—will have a hard time breaking into a network-dominated industry. Now, local and regional stations can experiment with a new band or format.

Take the case of WOMN in Hamden, Connecticut, a small daytime station that made national news in 1979 by pioneering a format of nonsexist music for young women under the banner of "Woman Sound." The station also aired daily discussions of such issues as women in the business world, changing life-styles, and the equal rights amendment.

But it didn't sell. So, after a brief flirtation with a rock format, WOMN changed its name to WSCR and hooked onto Satellite Music Network's "Country Coast to Coast." As feminist folk singer Holly Near gave way to Elvis and Kenny Rogers, ratings shot up, and John Saville, WSCR's program manager, was delighted. "Right out of the box, we got a three share during the week and a nine share on weekends," he said. "You could probably have given away the radio station before."

When WOMN flopped, station officials had no choice but to try something different and seek higher ratings. Yet something is lost here, just as something has been lost since WABC, a one-time broadcasting giant, dropped out of the competition with FM music stations and turned to talk.

As for WABC's deejays, all familiar voices for years to New Yorkers, Ron Lundy and Dan Ingram have signed with ABC Superadio. Cousin Brucie, though settled happily in the suburbs, still mourns for his old station.

"They didn't take a radio station off the air. They stopped a life-style," he declares, sounding every bit like his old self.

He is just getting warmed up: "People want a guy who knows what's going on in town—where the potholes are, where the accidents are, what hospital needs blood. Radio is the medium . . . that takes showers with you, that has sex with you. I believe in radio with a feeling. You turn on the radio, you find a friend."

4
Recording

Introduction

Recording is a large component of today's mass media. Records provide most of the programming for radio and are the basis for TV's biggest recent boom, the music video. The recording industry is large. As Don J. Hibbard's reading notes, since 1972 the total sales of records and prerecorded tapes were greater than the combined revenues of theaters, movies, and all professional sports. To a certain degree, the record is a personalized medium. As with magazines, the user can enjoy records at leisure, and the recording is relatively permanent. But although the record purchaser may think that his or her choice is purely personal, the record business clearly operates on a mass scale and attempts to influence what we buy. Top records sell in the millions (to go platinum, a record must sell 1 million copies), and the most successful, Michael Jackson's *Thriller,* sold an estimated 25 million.

The record business, although large, has been a stagnant part of the economy in recent years. Total sales for the industry peaked at $4.13 billion in 1978. Since then, sales have dropped, stabilizing at around $3.6 billion. The industry had grown dramatically since the 1960s—why, then, did it stop? There appear to be several explanations. One is the increase in home taping. In 1978, 65 million blank tapes were sold; in 1983, the figure was 215 million, and most are used to record music. In the 1980s, video games also used up young people's money that might otherwise have been spent on records. Finally, the quality of music may have declined, and the choices of new recordings dropped from 4,170 new LPs in 1978 to only 2,300 in 1983. It should be noted, however, that about 80 percent of new releases fail to make a profit.[1]

Over the years, the main product sold by recording companies has changed. By the 1970s, long-playing records overtook the sales of singles and became the major market. Eight-track tapes grew to over a third of market sales by 1978 but are now obsolete. They have been replaced by cassette album tapes, which now sell more than vinyl discs. The compact disc (CD) is growing rapidly. Although there are currently only 3 million CD players in the United States, compared to 98 million turntables, the CD owner is a heavy record buyer.[2] The high-quality sound encourages the audiophile to replace entire record libraries, and rerelease discs sell well though they cost about twice as much as conventional records or tapes.

The record-buying audience is primarily young, and the recording industry produces heavily for them. The fifteen- to twenty-four-year-old group buys about 40 percent of all records, and women spend more on records than men. Much of the market is therefore aimed at young women. They are the audience for Madonna and the new female performers (although males may like their videos) and, more important, for the continuing stream of male idols—dream lovers for the young women. Males appear to use music less for emotional attachment than release; heavy metal exists largely for young male audiences.

Both sexes may find music an important part of their life, particularly in association with both good and bad memories. The teens and early twenties are dramatically changing periods of life, and it is not surprising that music becomes associated with important life events. Nostalgia radio aims at triggering the memories of thirty- to forty-year-olds with music, and each generation (perhaps about a four-year span of popular music) can identify with its music. Love is a constant theme, although not all is teenage love anymore. Older pop artists like Bob Seger, Bruce Springsteen, Pete Townshend, and even the Rolling Stones now often have middle-aged themes to their songs.

The division of music sales by type of music reflects the tastes of the audience. According to the Recording Industry Association of America, the largest shares in 1983 went to rock (35 percent) and pop/easy listening (14 percent) music. Black/dance (11 percent) and gospel (5 percent) accounted for another market sector. Country (13 percent), classical (5 percent), children's (3 percent), jazz (2 percent), shows/soundtracks (3 percent), and other (9 percent) made up the remainder of the market.

Rock is clearly king of the music market. The first reading, by Don J. Hibbard, looks at the impact of rock on popular music. In the 1960s, music became part of the youth culture. The decline of art rock in the early 1970s was therefore not just a change in musical taste or just the effect of commercial domination. The author describes the corporate structure (and mergers) of the business but still sees some cultural spirit left in music. The recent Live Aid and other charitable events indicate that music may not have completely lost its soul.

Although rock was an American invention, foreign artists, particularly the British, have played an important part in its development. Table 1 shows the popularity of different nationalities of artists by their U.S. *Billboard* success. It shows that the British have been a fairly constant component of the U.S. market. Although they have had peaks in success, they have never gone away.

Table 1
Sources of Top Fifty Annual U.S. Pop Singles, by Nationality, Sex, and Race, 1955–1985 (Scores and number of records)

	British[a]	Other Foreign[b]	American White Male	American Black Male	American White Female	American Black Female	Total
1955		104 (3)	689 (25)	66 (6)	275 (10)	62 (2)	1,130 (44)
1956		22 (2)	755 (30)	124 (5)	191 (7)		1,253 (48)
1957		73 (2)	825 (33)	222 (9)	99 (4)		1,196 (46)
1958	35 (1)	126 (4)	758 (28)	216 (9)	61 (4)		1,085 (43)
1959		43 (1)	829 (33)	87 (4)	60 (4)	70 (3)	1,232 (49)
1960		29 (3)	929 (34)	105 (3)	168 (6)		1,232 (46)
1961		13 (1)	840 (34)	230 (7)	97 (5)	47 (1)	1,262 (49)
1962	82 (3)		645 (26)	235 (7)	159 (8)	137 (5)	1,176 (46)
1963	46 (1)	21 (1)	694 (27)	93 (3)	223 (10)	77 (3)	1,190 (47)
1964	292 (12)	70 (2)	544 (20)	111 (5)	106 (5)	96 (4)	913 (36)
1965	383 (17)	36 (2)	436 (15)	139 (5)	130 (5)	102 (5)	856 (31)
1966	257 (11)	47 (1)	676 (28)	58 (2)	85 (3)	69 (3)	971 (38)
1967	259 (12)		705 (24)	54 (3)	90 (3)	85 (4)	1,016 (38)
1968	157 (9)	14 (1)	863 (30)	113 (3)	69 (2)	38 (3)	1,104 (40)
1969	176 (6)		660 (27)	226 (9)	5 (1)	12 (1)	1,099 (44)
1970	187 (7)	112 (4)	493 (21)	296 (11)		118 (4)	976 (39)
1971	278 (9)	73 (5)	422 (14)	111 (6)	198 (7)	39 (1)	925 (36)
1972	148 (8)	65 (3)	503 (19)	403 (14)	44 (2)	49 (1)	1,062 (39)
1973	172 (8)	81 (3)	409 (15)	261 (10)	163 (5)	84 (2)	998 (37)
1974	137 (6)	173 (9)	546 (19)	231 (9)	89 (2)	19 (1)	965 (35)
1975	252 (9)	73 (3)	500 (20)	149 (6)	45 (3)	68 (2)	950 (38)
1976	288 (10)	42 (2)	458 (19)	244 (8)	13 (1)	99 (4)	945 (38)
1977	254 (9)	36 (1)	388 (17)	160 (9)	214 (8)	88 (2)	985 (40)
1978	398 (13)	216 (10)	295 (14)	51 (2)	51 (2)	71 (3)	661 (27)
1979	239 (8)	20 (1)	312 (14)	118 (5)	108 (4)	236 (9)	1,016 (41)
1980	313 (9)	105 (3)	316 (14)	146 (8)	64 (2)	121 (6)	857 (38)
1981	244 (11)	174 (6)	367 (17)	157 (6)	155 (5)	32 (1)	857 (33)
1982	249 (8)	172 (7)	589 (21)	89 (4)	86 (6)		854 (35)
1983	197 (7)	188 (7)	524 (20)	75 (4)	106 (5)	5 (1)	890 (36)
1984	325 (11)	33 (3)	357 (15)	306 (10)	103 (4)	146 (6)	917 (36)
1985	513 (18)	69 (3)	282 (12)	99 (4)	125 (4)	101 (6)	693 (29)

Source: Compiled from: Peter E. Berry, *And the Hits Just Keep on Coming* (Syracuse: Syracuse University Press, 1977); Joel Whitburn, *Joel Whitburn's Pop Annual, 1955–82* (Menomonee Falls, Wisc.: Record Research, 1983); and *Billboard* annual charts, 1983–1985.

Note: Each record was given a weighted score, ranging from 50 points for the year's top recording to 1 point for the fiftieth entry. Number of records is shown in parentheses.

[a]Includes British-American groups.
[b]Includes foreign-American groups.

British musicians entered the American charts as a serious force with the arrival of the Beatles in 1964 in what has become known as the "British invasion." Playing American black-derived music, the Beatles had already generated mass hysteria in Britain in the early 1960s. Their hallmark was simple love songs, sung with an innovative harmony. Indeed, the Beatles became musical revolutionaries only after they were famous, borrowing from Caribbean and blues music and employing Indian sounds and classical arrangements.

Having replaced American stars in Britain, the Beatles proceeded to generate the same following in the United States. Other British bands followed, and despite some fluctuations, British musicians have maintained their presence at around a 20 percent share of the top fifty scores. (See table 1). The black-originated disco movement of the 1970s did not exclude the British for long; the Bee Gees, the Rolling Stones, and Rod Stewart joined it.

From 1970 on, other foreign artists have perhaps gained from the earlier acceptance and popularity of British artists. As table 1 shows, the best years for other foreigners were 1974, 1978, and 1981 through 1983. The peak years for combined foreign impact (British and other foreigners together) on the singles charts were 1964, 1965, 1978, and 1985. The last two years had higher foreign music scores than the first invasion peak of 1965. The most recent peak was not 1983–1984, as the press saw it, but 1985.

What was the impact of this foreign invasion? As the format of rock changed after the initial British invasion, women were relegated to a back seat.[3] Few knew how to play the new electronic instruments, and women certainly risked more severe social disapproval for mouthing the obscenities of the male groups. Another problem women encountered was that the most frantic new fans, according to Lloyd Grossman in *Social History of Rock,* were interested in fantasy boyfriends, which of course women rock stars could not provide. Grossman argues that because of this fact, the low potential of rock careers for women is likely to continue. Although this may have been partially true initially, the long-range effects are more complex.

The impact of the foreign invasion on different groups of American artists can also be seen in table 1. It shows that in the early period of the invasion, both white male and female American musicians lost more ground than did blacks. In 1971, white and black males lost most; in the mid-1970s, there were evenly distributed losses for American artists. For 1978 and 1980–1982, the foreign gains accompanied losses by white males and black females, but in 1984–1985, it was white males and females who lost ground. The influx of foreigners, therefore, does not appear to discriminate systematically against one category of American artists. Since the foreigners are predominantly white males, the losses of the most successful domestic category (white males) are to be expected.

R. Serge Denisoff and John Bridges look at the musicians who make the recordings in their reading. The top "superstars," of course, make millions of dollars and travel the globe in style. Many, it seems, succumb to an "easy money" syndrome of excesses. Most musicians, however, do not fit such a pattern. The authors describe three types of musician—the starting band member, learning to play and looking for an audience; working performers, ranging from barroom acts at the bottom up to "show acts"; and, the most successful, recording acts. Their sample draws on biographies of the latter—artists who have recording contracts. The large majority are white males in their early thirties who are high school graduates. Almost half play rock, followed in numbers by country, soul and R&B, and jazz performers. Even with a recording contract, however, few are really "big time," much less wealthy, artists.

Country music is the subject of Don Tomlinson's reading. The new rock 'n' roll of the 1950s took most of the market from traditional country music. In response, Chet Atkins and others developed a modern commercial form of country, the Nashville sound. The country nature and even the word *country* was downplayed to appeal to urban audiences. This music grew rapidly in the 1970s, but the boom collapsed in 1984. To some degree, it had been a fad. Tomlinson describes what has happened since, particularly the emergence of the new traditionalists. He profiles several of the new country artists and groups who are gaining acclaim by rejecting Nashville and returning to the roots of country music.

Notes

1. Leisure Time, *Industry Surveys*, November 29, 1984.
2. *Rolling Stone*, August 28, 1986.
3. Lloyd Grossman, *Social History of Rock* (New York: David McKay, 1976).

THE ROCK REVOLUTION

Don J. Hibbard with Carol Kaleialoha

Don Hibbard is the director of the Hawaii State Historic Preservation Program within the state's Department of Land and Natural Resources. He received a Ph.D. in American studies, with an emphasis on American art history, from the University of Hawaii. He has taught courses on rock music, American art and culture, and American history at the University of Hawaii and Boise State University. Besides *The Role of Rock*, he has published several books and a number of articles on American art and architecture.

Carol Kaleialoha Sing holds a B.A. from the University of California at Los Angeles and an M.A. from the University of Hawaii. She has taught sociology and political science and worked on numerous research projects.

Reprinted from *The Role of Rock*, Prentice-Hall, 1983, pages 133–138, 146–149. Used by permission.

Over the past three decades rock has undergone a number of transformations. It has moved from an abscessed adolescent obsession streaked with rebelliousness, through a consciousness-raising stage that articulated alienated utopian ideals, to reach the present day's multiplicity of styles that self-consciously perpetuate the rock tradition. By continuing to perform previous functions, the stylized rock retains a vital position within society, addressing not only adolescent but adult concerns. It carries a zip, a zing, but little zeal. The earlier sense of collective joy and freedom, of shared common experience, has all but disappeared from the rock scene. A glossy shadow of its former self, rock moves on down the line, a background sound in a world that keeps turning around us, a declaration of alienation and/or joy that goes no further than the periphery of its own musical dimension.

However, rock's impact runs deeper than today's music. The music of the late 1960s made an indelible mark on society, and its imprint still remains. To perceive the extent of rock's cultural influence, forms other than today's music need to be examined. However, prior to undertaking such an investigation, we need to move back to the period from 1969 to 1971 and reconsider the dissolution of the rock revolution. Such a step will further illuminate the rock stance of the 1960s against the dominant culture, and provide a better position from which to evaluate the effect of that music.

Snap, Fizzle, and Poof

The rock forms and energy supporting the counterculture gradually faded during the opening years of the 1970s. Their disappearance was a profound and noticeable change, and people were quick to comment upon it. In an attempt to explain the evaporation of the rock revolution three major arguments came to the fore:

1. Rock had become too pretentious and had lost sight of its original purpose.
2. Rock, as a commercial product, could not sustain any viable attack upon the economically oriented dominant culture.
3. The audience did not follow the precepts elucidated in the songs.

None of these viewpoints perceived what was happening and instead reflected the immediate reaction to the moment rather than any accurate appraisal of the situation.

The first argument myopically viewed rock as primarily a musical form rather than a social phenomena. Arnold Shaw, the author of *The Rock Revolution* in a *High Fidelity* article from April 1969,[1] accurately discerned the rock audience's retreat "into the woods and hills of mountain music" and their acceptance of soul and vintage rhythm-and-blues. He ascribed this shift in taste to a rejection of rock's increasing artiness, which led to a loss of "the raw vitality, eroticism and simplicity of its birth phase." Shaw viewed rock essentially as part of a popular music tradition rather than an integral part of a social movement. Instead of considering the change in musical preferences in terms of the social scene, he claimed that popular listeners could tolerate only a minimal range of deviation and artistic license. However, such an explanation confuses symptoms with causes. The rejection of artiness accompanied the change in taste but did not cause it. During the height of the counterculture's energy burst, the music's artiness and increased complexity were lauded as positive values, and such well-received albums as the Beatles's *Sergeant Pepper,* the Jefferson Airplane's *Surrealistic Pillow,* and Jimi Hendrix's *Are You Experienced?* deviated from previous popular music in a much more dramatic manner than any of the more pretentious rock material of 1969 and 1970. Also, such aspiring "artists" as Frank Zappa, Pink Floyd, and the Jefferson Starship continued to have large followings in the 1970s, as did many new stars such as David Bowie, Roxy Music, and numerous art rock and New Wave bands, indicating that at least a portion of the rock audience continued to support the pretentiousness posited by Shaw as a motivation for the movement toward the more mellow country-rock sound. As such, an increased artiness may not be viewed plausibly as the trigger for the 1969 turn to different musical forms. Instead . . . deeper cultural factors were at work.

Rock as a Commercial Product

Another more popular explanation for the demise of the rock revolution focused on the music's economic context, its status as a commercial product. In a June 1969 *Ramparts* article, "Rock for Sale," Michael Lydon summarized this position.[2] He recognized rock's "undeniably liberating effect" but also realized rock was "a product created, distributed, and controlled for the profit of American (and international) business." Such a relationship ultimately doomed rock "to a bitter impotence" as the music remained subservient to those whom it attacked, turning a profit for corporate America.

Without a doubt rock is a commercial product, a popular art form with a wide appeal, thanks to mass distribution and advertising. Furthermore, rock has been largely responsible for the enormous growth of the music industry over the past quarter-century. Since 1955 record sales have increased phenomenally, moving from a total of $277 million to over $0.5 billion by 1959. By 1968 sales has advanced to over $1 billion, and ten years later that figure had tripled. By 1972 the sale of records and tapes brought in more money than did movies, professional sports, and the theater *combined*. Rock concerts grossed close to five times as much money as Broadway plays. By this time at least fifty music superstars were earning between $2 million and $6 million a year, which represented a salary range three to seven times higher than America's highest paid corporate "capitalist pig." Rock does make money, and makes it in large quantities.[3] The expansion of the music industry has been stupendous, and as the age bracket of rock's audience continues to broaden, the industry appears to have growth potential, as long as the economy remains sound.

As big business the music industry has developed along lines similar to those of other corporate establishments. During the 1950s the major companies, RCA, Columbia, Decca, Capitol, MGM, Mercury, and later ABC-Paramount, controlled less of the rock 'n' roll market than the independent companies, which included Atlantic, Dot, Chess, Speciality, Sun, Herald-Ember, Cadence, Liberty, and Imperial. Most of these companies, both the majors and independents, were fairly new to the field, with only RCA, Columbia, and Decca operating prior to World War II. The majors primarily differed from the independents in their capital investment. They not only produced records but owned manufacturing plants and directly controlled distribution outlets. RCA and Columbia, the two dominant companies in the industry, held their positions mainly due to their affiliations with their parent communications organizations: the Radio Corporation of America and the Columbia Broadcasting System.

The majors approached the peculiar, new rock 'n' roll fad with caution, signing only a moderate number of performers: Elvis (RCA), Bill Haley and Buddy Holly (Decca), Gene Vincent (Capitol), Conway Twitty (MGM), and the Big Bopper (Mercury). In comparison, many of the independents already operated within the rhythm-and-blues market, and thus easily flowed into the new rock 'n' roll scene. From 1955 to 1959 they produced over one hundred top ten hits as compared to forty-six by the major companies.[4] Even through the early 1960s, the independents dominated the charts with Roulette, Cameo, Parkway, and Chancellor boasting such stars as Bobby Rydell, Fabian, Frankie Avalon, Jimmy Rodgers, and Chubby Checker.

However, the reign of the independents was short-lived. Commencing with the purchase of Dot by ABC-Paramount for $2 million in 1957, the independents slowly but surely sold out to major companies, with Warner Brothers-Reprise's purchase of Atlantic in 1967, Electra in 1970, and Asylum in 1973 among the more significant later deals. By the late 1960s the majors were in fairly tight command of the music scene. Capitol featured the Beatles; RCA, the Jefferson Airplane; Decca, the Who; ABC, Steppenwolf; MGM, the Animals; Warner Brothers, the Grateful Dead, Jimi Hendrix, Jethro Tull, Joni Mitchell, James Taylor, Led Zeppelin, and Crosby, Stills, Nash and Young; and Columbia, Bob Dylan, Simon and Garfunkel, the Byrds, Janis Joplin, and Santana. A majority of the independents operated under the majors and relied upon them for distribution, although a few companies such as Motown and A&M remained completely autonomous.

The 1970s brought further consolidation of the industry as the smaller majors had to merge in order to attain a more financially efficient scale. MCA, which resulted from the combination of Decca, Kapp, and Uni records in the late 1960s, added ABC to its organization in the late 1970s, and in the early years of that decade Mercury, MGM, and Polydor records were united under Polygram. This corporation has since added Casablanca, Capricorn, and RSO to its ranks. Thus, as the 1980s began, the "Big Six" (Warner Communications, Columbia Broadcasting System, Polygram, RCA, Capitol-EMI, and MCA) held a firm position in the music industry, with 1977 figures indicating that Warner controlled 23 percent of all record and tape sales, Columbia 19 percent, and Polygram 14 percent.

The immediate association with outrageous wealth and an increasingly consolidated corporate system surely has affected rock but in all likelihood did not contribute to the declining spirit of revolution. By 1968 annual record sales already had surpassed a billion dollars, making the sense of wealth, of churning capitalism, very much a part of rock's revolutionary stream. This presence, however, neither stemmed the flow nor contaminated the water.

Indeed, it might have contributed to the stream's floodlike appearance. The record companies filled a demand, and although much of the rock of the late 1960s explicitly stood as the antithesis of the corporate way of life, these companies exerted little or no censorship over rock material. When they did intervene, their concerns usually revolved around the use of obscenity, as in the clash between RCA and the Jefferson Airplane, which the band eventually won.

Thus the revolutionary content of the music was not diluted by the music industry. Indeed, the existence of the record companies as figures of authority, as representatives of the corporate world, heightened the rebellious tension in the songs in certain instances. For example, the Jefferson Airplane's fight to use explicit language became one in a series of metaphors that enhanced the spirit of change, the feeling of us versus them, and the role of musicians as exemplars of the new ways. Their victory transcended their individual battle, representing a step forward for the counterculture itself. As such "Eskimo Blue Day" (1969) and "Volunteers" (1969) carried a triumphant message that outstripped their lyrical and musical contents.

Further evidence of the minimal impact of any corporate influence on the rock revolution may be obtained by a comparison of Abbey Road (1969) and The Beatles (1968), which the Beatles produced under their own Apple label, with their earlier Capitol works, Sgt. Pepper and Magical Mystery Tour. Certainly the freedom of their own label did not precipitate a more radical dialogue in their music. The same can be said for albums produced by other musicians who operated their own independent labels such as the Beach Boys, Frank Zappa, the Rolling Stones, the Jefferson Starship, and the Grateful Dead.

Thus the highly commercial character of the music industry did not directly mitigate any of rock's revolutionary fervor. Nor did it do so in an indirect, coopting manner as Steve Chapple and Reebee Garofalo postulated in *Rock 'n' Roll Is Here to Pay*. These investigators of rock's commercial core more or less revamped the theories of the German philosopher Theodor W. Adorno and applied them to rock. Adorno premised all his perceptions of music upon the fact that with the advent of improved mechanical reproduction and more sophisticated means of distribution, a "commodity fetishism" had increased in all areas of modern music, both classical and popular. Music, once freed of its more traditional context of ritual and use, had come to function primarily as a commodity with a value of exchange. Adorno found popular music, including jazz, to be corruptions of earlier forms, a standardized product with a "pseudo-individual" veneer, the sole end of which was its consumption by the masses. This music produced a "commodity listening," which ideally dispensed, as far as possible, with the need for any attentive efforts on the part of the audience; it was "easy listening" music. As a commodity in a capitalist system, popular music implicitly reflected and legitimized the establishment, replicating working conditions within the context of a leisure time. To Adorno, the product orientation of the music destroyed any revolutionary potential which it formerly might have harbored.[5]

Many of Adorno's observations apply to mainstream popular music, and indeed they are quite applicable to much of the rock scene of the 1970s. However, Adorno so intently examined the commercial form of music that he overlooked the range of audience reactions to it and thus, for example, failed to differentiate between the extremely diverse reactions aroused by jazz in comparison to easy listening music. Similarly, the proponents of "rock as a commercial product which coopted the revolution" failed to acknowledge adequately the tremendous impact rock had on the late 1960s. Rock was the voice of the counterculture; without it no sense of revolution would have existed. Furthermore, people did not passively listen to this music; they "dug on it" and embraced its reality. Espousing alienated values, rock did more than provide merely an illusion of freedom; it conveyed an alternative vision to the prescribed ways of life. By articulately reflecting and reinforcing the social flux of the period, this music transcended its role as a commodity; it was a human force pushing for a better tomorrow. . . .

Within the recent past three major events have revealed the hold that the musical spirit of the 1960s still exerts on contemporary American society. The lingering longing to reaffirm the faith of the young burgeoned forth with the funeral obsequies following the assassination of John Lennon, the Central Park reunion concert of Simon and Garfunkel, and the Rolling Stones' 1981 American tour. All three events represented a coming together of masses of people to publicly express, if not reaffirm, their sense of identification with the values of the 1960s, to feel once again that common hope and to remind themselves that the spirit still abides within them. Embraced not only by the aging members of the psychedelic youth culture, but surprisingly, also by many still in their youth, these events were not acts of nostalgia, but rather displayed a veneration for a shared sensibility.

The first, and by far the heaviest, of these events started on Monday night, December 8, 1980, with the shocking murder of John Lennon. His death shattered any dream of a Beatle reunion and represented the loss of a major icon within the reposing counterculture.

Countless people—over 100,000 in New York's Central Park, another 30,000 in Liverpool, several thousand in Boston, Chicago, Melbourne, and other urban areas around the globe, and still smaller groups in numerous towns and hamlets—fittingly observed a silent vigil in his memory at 2 P.M. Eastern Standard Time, December 14, 1980. For months afterward, Beatles songs somberly issued forth from the radio, a consistent, haunting eulogy for the man and the era. John Lennon was truly everywhere, and his spirit became again deeply imbued within the American psyche.

The death of the man did not signal the death of the era. If anything,

Lennon's assassination fixed within the minds of people the tremendous impact the 1960s and its music had made on them and the world. In part, this consciousness led half a million people to gather in Central Park nine months later to listen to the reunited Simon and Garfunkel. Stirred by a rekindled memory, one of the largest crowds in the history of American music,[6] almost doubling Woodstock's attendance, assembled on September 19, 1981, to hear once again the sounds of silence and reexperience the sensation of unity, of coming together and enjoying the pleasure of the shared moment. The autumn nip in the air could not refute that the summer of love was still alive.

Equally telling was the Rolling Stones' 1981 American tour, which opened to a crowd of ninety thousand at Philadelphia's John F. Kennedy Stadium six days after the Simon and Garfunkel performance. Building on the energy generated in Central Park, Stones fever inundated city after city, laying them to waste. "The World's Greatest Rock 'n' Roll Band" played to packed house after packed house during the three-month tour, with ticket demands far outstripping seating capacities. Every Stones' tour is something special, as a sense of transcendent autonomy, tinged with malevolence, pervades the concert atmosphere. The energy, drive, and aura of the band surpass audience expectations, and through the live performance the Stones' mythic image, so finely honed in the 1960s and maintained in the 1970s, is renewed, perpetuated. The audience, having partaken of a transdimensional ritual, return to their lives replenished. Yes, a Stones tour has always been an incredible, memorable event. However, the 1981 American tour, viewed by over 2 million paying people, assumed an even greater air.

Constant speculation over this being the aging band's last tour helped generate numbers of fans. People reached out to garner a final memory for the future, grasping at the Stones as a major presence, a vestige of an era about to pass. The turnout was tremendous. In Seattle, the Kingdome was filled to capacity twice, a crowd equal in size to nearly a quarter of the city's population; the two San Francisco shows drew the largest paid crowds in Bay Area rock history; and in New York 4 million ticket requests were received by mail in a fifty-six-hour period for the five metropolitan area shows, which would accommodate approximately one hundred thousand. Couple such numbers with the enormous stage set in Philadelphia, the giant video screen in Syracuse, the cherry picker in Los Angeles, tremendous amounts of money (with ticket sales alone grossing over $34 million), the incessant programming of Stones' hits on the radio, and the extensive national media coverage, and the tour took on epic proportions, presenting a stunning statement on the group, their time, and their music.

All three events—the Lennon funeral, the Simon and Garfunkel concert, and the Rolling Stones tour—derive their significance from the overwhelming response they elicited. But more than just numbers, these events also had a spirit. They were not belated acknowledgments of the past, as was the rock 'n' roll revival of the early 1970s, nor were they comebacks of the order of Neil Sedaka or Frankie Valli. Rather than exercises in nostalgia or resurrection, they were large-scale demonstrations that the good vibrations had not as yet disappeared, that the invisible atmosphere which surrounded the late 1960s sensibility was still capable of generating high energy. These three highly charged moments were but events in a continuing tale, fragments to show us once again that "The Time Has Come Today." Without a doubt, the time will come again, and again.

Notes

1. Arnold Shaw, "Rocks in Their Heads," *High Fidelity* (April 1969): 48–51.
2. Michael Lydon, "Rock for Sale," *Ramparts* (June 1969): 19–24.
3. These figures appear in "The Rockers Are Rolling in It," *Forbes*, April 15, 1973, pp. 28–30; "The Gorillas Are Coming," *Forbes*, July 10, 1978, pp. 41–46; and Steve Chapple and Reebee Garofalo, *Rock 'n' Roll Is Here to Pay* (Chicago: Nelson-Hall, 1977), p. 14.
4. Charlie Gillett, *The Sound of the City* (New York: Dell, 1972), p. 76.
5. See Theodor W. Adorno, "On Popular Music," *Studies in Philosophy and Science* 9, No. 1 (1941); Theodor W. Adorno, "A Social Critique of Radio Music," *Kenyon Review* 7, No. 2 (Spring 1945); and Gillian Rose, *The Melancholy Science, An Introduction to the Thought of Theodor W. Adorno* (New York: Columbia University Press, 1978).
6. The only crowd to surpass the Simon and Garfunkel audience converged on Watkins Glen in 1973 to participate in the Grateful Dead and Allman Brothers Band's Summer Jam.

POPULAR MUSIC: WHO ARE THE RECORDING ARTISTS?

R. Serge Denisoff
John Bridges

R. Serge Denisoff is professor of sociology at Bowling Green State University. John Bridges is in the Department of Sociology at the University of Notre Dame. An earlier version of this article was presented at the American Culture and Popular Culture Association joint meetings in Detroit, April 19, 1980. The authors wish to thank Professor Richard Zeller for his help with sections of this article.

Reprinted from the *Journal of Communication*, Winter 1982. ©1982 by The Annenberg School of Communications. Used by permission.

An analysis of the links between the "who-what-where" of performers and their music.

One of the least examined aspects of the music industry is the recording artist. Social scientists have generally ignored the "creator" of sound in favor of content analyses of lyrics or studies of organizational structures such as record companies or studio work (2).

The few studies of artists in the music industry have largely focused on individual relationships with the audience, musician interactions (especially in the field of jazz), or the role of the musician. Schutz treated the social interactions and communication processes between composer, performer, and listener as joint participants in the musical process (14). Becker's study of Chicago jazz musicians (1) reported on the contempt of the jazzman for the "square" audience. Stebbins, Peterson, and Nanry have discussed the components of the "jazz community" (9). Faulkner (4) focused his attention on studio musicians in Hollywood, and Sanders (13) examined the relationships of folk music artists in clubs.

Recording artists in the popular field have received little attention. In an early study, Coffman treated the role conflict of rock artists in a corporate industry structure (3). Lewis (8), in a rather cryptic analysis, and Hunter (7) have dealt with the recruitment of popular musicians. Gonzales's fictionalized account of a band, Jambeaux, is an outstanding account of the socio-psychological process impacting on contemporary musicians. He traced the careers of four musicians from Houston "skull orchards" to fleeting stardom, while highlighting industry demands and interpersonal relations (5).

Still, the characteristics of those who "make the songs" in the popular music field remain largely unexamined. A major factor is the problem of accessibility. One doctoral candidate was not able to contact any performers until his project was advertised in an influential *Los Angeles Times* entertainment column (6). Even in this instance, the sample left much to be desired.

Record companies, a potentially rich resource for scholarly research, are not terribly helpful to academics. In the arena of artist data, this resistance is not malicious or ill-willed; most companies simply have little in the way of archival material. If options are not renewed or the artist changes labels, marketing materials, including biographies and photos, are discarded.

The usefulness of the print media as a source of artist data is badly tainted. Most press accounts, even in specialty publications like *Billboard* or the more widely distributed *Rolling Stone,* tend to feature "name" stars and more sensational artists.

An additional source of data is the so-called "rock encyclopedias" that list various artists (10, 12). Again, however, problems are apparent. Most performers listed have enjoyed a "hit" record, and the biographical material is either too cryptic or nonexistent. Musicians' union (American Federation of Musicians) files might be helpful if properly organized and open to examination.

Given these conditions—unavailability of artists, lack of industry cooperation, and media agenda-setting—obtaining data dealing with artists has been a major problem. In this study we have attempted to partially circumvent some of these obstacles.

Based on artist biographies from printed sources, and personal observation and experience, we developed an "ideal type" using three hierarchical categories of artists.

By ideal type we mean a model depicting what appears to be a general pattern of behavior (although obviously exceptions can always be found). The three categories of recording artists most commonly found in the literature are starting bands, working bands, and recording acts.

Starting bands are informal performing units without overt professional aspirations. These would include high school groups and amateur entertainers of various sorts. These performers usually lack commitment and a high level of musical skill. Their dropout rate is extremely high; however, from this pool of individuals some begin to take the avocation seriously and may graduate to the second level.

Working performers can be subdivided into two categories: barroom acts and show acts. Barroom acts are strictly in the process of "paying their dues," that is, acquiring the necessary musical skills and equipment. Most bar bands never transcend this level of being a "human jukebox." For most barroom acts, performing is a secondary occupation or a form of musical moonlighting. Rarely can these performers support themselves from their music. Many give up in disgust, while others find nonmusical employment more economically rewarding. The attrition rate is high.

Showroom or lounge acts tend to be in limbo in the music industry. Generally they have developed their stage presence and have obtained fairly expensive professional equipment. These musicians capitalize on their musical dexterity and audience rapport, which is developed while playing numerous circuits of hotels, lounges, and middle-class night clubs. While such performers can make a living playing current hits and "all-time" favorites, they are unlikely to catch the attention of record companies, which search for artists with new and unique material. Many show bands are not afforded the opportunity to develop new material, since the club owners who employ them tend to be guided by the adage "people like what they know and know what they like." A show band can try to break out of this cycle by playing one-nighters at colleges, youth centers, and outdoor festivals, or as opening acts at concerts.

Recording acts represent for most performers the Mount Olympus of the business. Recording acts have record contracts and frequently perform on regional or national concert tours in an attempt to boost record sales. They are not necessarily "superstars," who may be defined as artists whose concert appearances and records are considered guaranteed successes. "Shipping gold or platinum" and "selling out a concert" are the chief characteristics of superstars. While superstars garner the vast majority of media attention, it is important to remember that nearly 80 percent of the albums released annually "stiff"—that is, they do not return their initial investment or production cost. Still, for most acts, record contracts are all-important, and we will focus here on those performers who have earned them.

Our data come from published artist biographies obtained from various record companies covering the period between 1970 and 1979.

The record companies examined include both major and independent operations such as Capitol, Columbia, RCA, Warner Brothers, MCA, Atlantic, RSO, Capricorn, Casablanca, A&M, and many others. These labels may be considered representative of both the recording industry in general and the popular music industry in particular. The few "specialty" labels appearing in the analysis were those directed primarily to jazz audiences, such as Blue Note, Galaxy, Milestone, etc. No artist, musical style, or recording company was systematically preselected or excluded in any fashion. The sample was not constructed around random techniques, since an attempt was made to include all biographies received during the time period indicated. However, those biographies that lacked a number of pertinent demographic data were eliminated from consideration.

Recording artists are broadly defined as those performers who have earned and signed recording contracts in the United States and those artists of other nations for whom distribution rights have been obtained by U.S. labels. Members of groups and ensembles were coded individually (regardless of their status as "leader" or "sideman" within the same unit), as were solo artists. Motion picture soundtracks and Broadway musicals, which appeared infrequently in our sample, were absorbed into the more dominant categories for coding. The actual numbers of artists from each musical style in the sample is proportional to those numbers found in the industry. "Rock" musicians therefore outnumber jazz musicians, who are more plentiful than noted "classical" players, and so on.

Finally, a distinction was made between individual demographic data and those "industry variables" related to the artist's position in the industry and his/her musical career.

> *Race.* We attempted to define both race and/or nationality. Initial coding included white, black, Mexican/Spanish, or other native-born Americans. Artists of British or European origin were also noted and a residual category was included. Collapsing of categories was necessary for statistical analysis.
>
> *Sex.* Male artists accounted for nearly 90 percent of the 667 artists.
>
> *Age.* The age of each artist in the sample was calculated through December 31, 1979. The ages of only 35 percent of artists could be ascertained (mean = 32.6 years). For analysis, age was grouped into tens of years.
>
> *Education.* Level of education was calculated in U.S. standards for all artists. The biographies of those artists who were not from the U.S. normally did not discuss education. Honorary degrees were not included in the analysis.
>
> As shown in table 1, over 90 percent of the recording artists for whom educational information was available had at least graduated high school. The numbers of artists become progressively smaller at each stage of higher education. The few individuals who had graduate degrees may have been involved in musical styles demanding more fluent "musical literacy" (such as jazz, big bands, or orchestral ensembles); or they may have held, or aspired to, positions as arrangers, composers, or studio musicians, for whom the ability to sightread proficiently is most often a prerequisite to steady employment.
>
> A final demographic variable was *geographic region,* which refers to the artist's community of origin. In those instances where an artist's family

Table 1
Distribution of Recording Artists by Level of Education

	Number	*Percent*
Less than high school	23	7.0
High school graduate	139	42.2
Some college	87	26.4
College graduate	75	22.8
M.A. or Ph.D.	5	1.6
Total	329	100.0

may have moved during his or her childhood, consideration was given to those areas wherein the artist spent formative years, and acquired education and musical skills and influences.

The following industry variables were considered:

Market of migration. An effort was made to determine those cases in which the artist had migrated from his/her community of origin to a major musical market, presumably in order to achieve success in the industry. Although less than half of the sample was determined to have made such a move, a strong pattern emerges when migration is correlated with musical style, as will be discussed below.

Level of previous act (beginning, working, or recording). In cases where the artist's record contract was obtained without working through the hierarchy, the level held before the contract was awarded was coded.

Stature. The stature of the artist (at the time of coding) was determined by his or her number of successful ("hit") recordings—those that had placed on national charts. A minor artist was considered one who had had either one hit, or was still trying for the first; a marginal artist had two or three successes; and a major artist had four or more hits.

Musical style. The musical style variable was among the more difficult to code, due to the lack of a stylistic typology within either the industry or academic research. The stylistic designations initially conformed to those published in a *New York Times* article (11). Collapsing of data took place in the final stages of analysis.

The "generic" breakdown of musical styles is shown in table 2. As the table indicates, rock musicians comprised the largest portion of the sample. Since the biographies were not preselected in any fashion, there is no reason to believe the actual number of recording artists performing

Table 2
Distribution of Recording Artists by Musical Style

	Number	*Percent*
Rock (top 40, heavy metal, hard, soft, album-oriented, progressive, art, experimental, punk, Southern)	268	46.9
Soul/rhythm and blues/disco (delta blues, gospel, funk, salsa, reggae)	89	15.6
Easy listening (soft pop, standards, middle-of-the-road)	35	6.1
Country and western (folk, country, outlaw, Tex-Mex, bluegrass, country-rock)	99	17.3
Jazz (bop, funky jazz, jazz fusion, jazz)	76	13.3
Classical	3	0.5
Other (comedy artists, pure electronic artists)	2	0.3
Total	572	100.0

in this style differs from this proportion. The next three most prevalent musical styles—jazz, country and western, and soul/rhythm and blues/disco—combined total only 46.2 percent of the sample. The remaining three styles accounted for less than 10 percent of the sample.

Our data support the notion that artists "pay their dues" before attaining success.

Table 3, which compares artists by stature and by level of previous act, shows that there is a basis for the generally accepted notion that major artists have "been around" longer than the marginal or minor artists, have had previous recording experience, etc. Because of unequal cells, the numbers in table 3 are more informative than the percentages. Of the major artists in the sample, more have had previous experience as recording artists than have moved directly to major status without recording experience. Minor artists tended to be signed as beginners.

Table 4 presents a cross-tabulation of artists' race/origin and musical style. The table indicates that, as expected, race/origin is related to musical style. White artists tend to be found in rock and country and western music; more black artists are found in soul/rhythm and blues/disco and in jazz than in the other styles combined. The predominance of rock in the "other" racial category, which includes all those who are not native-born white or black Americans, stems from the large number of British rock artists in the sample.

An examination of musical style and geographic region of artists' origin (see table 5) shows that artists are influenced by the style of music dominant where they grew up. In the Southeast, country and western music, a predom-

Table 3
Level of Act at Time of Signing Current Contract by Stature of Recording Artist

	Stature					
	Minor Artist (0–1 successful recordings)		Marginal Artist (2–3 successful recordings)		Major Artist (4 or more successful recordings)	
Level of Previous Act	n	%	n	%	n	%
Beginning	75	45.1	33	22.6	77	27.0
Working	40	24.1	38	26.0	90	31.6
Recording act	51	30.7	75	51.4	118	41.4
Total	166	99.9[a]	146	100.0	285	100.0

$\chi^2 = 26.09$; df = 4; p < .001 (n = 597)
[a]Rounding error.
n = Number; % = Percent.

Table 4
Comparison of the Musical Style and Race/Origin of Recording Artists

	Race/Origin of Artist					
	White American		Black American		Other	
Musical style	n	%	n	%	n	%
Rock	141	54.2	2	2.9	75	57.7
Soul/rhythm and blues/disco	21	8.1	36	52.9	6	4.6
Easy listening	11	4.2	2	2.9	14	10.8
Country and western	63	24.2	1	1.5	15	11.5
Jazz	22	8.5	26	38.2	19	14.6
Classical	0	0.0	1	1.5	1	0.8
Other	2	0.8	0	0.0	0	0.0
Total	260	100.0	68	99.9[a]	130	100.0

$\chi^2 = 187.98$; df = 12; p < .0001 (n = 458)
[a]Rounding error.
n = Number; % = Percent.

Table 5
Comparison of the Musical Style of U.S. Recording Artists and Their Geographic Region of Origin

| | Geographic Region | | | | | | | |
| | Southeast | | Northeast and East Coast | | Midwest, Central | | West Coast, Southwest, Far West | |
Musical Style	n	%	n	%	n	%	n	%
Rock	14	19.2	74	65.5	40	53.3	27	29.0
Soul/rhythm and blues/disco	22	30.1	6	5.3	7	9.3	17	18.3
Easy listening	5	6.8	8	7.1	4	5.3	0	0.0
Country and western	29	39.7	8	7.1	15	20.0	30	32.3
Jazz	3	4.1	17	15.0	7	9.3	18	19.4
Classical	0	0.0	0	0.0	1	1.3	1	1.1
Other	0	0.0	0	0.0	1	1.3	0	0.0
Total	73	99.9[a]	113	100.0	75	99.9[a]	93	100.1[a]

$\chi^2 = 95.24$; df = 18; p < .0001 (n = 354)

[a]Rounding error.

n = Number; % = Percent.

inantly white style, and soul/rhythm and blues/disco, a predominantly black style, are the two most significant musical styles. In the Northeast, rock and jazz are more dominant. Rock and country and western seem to be big in the more conservative Midwest, while the West Coast offers a more even mix of country and western, rock, jazz, and soul/rhythm and blues/disco.

Table 6 compares musical style with the sex of the recording artist. As noted earlier, only 10 percent of the total sample is female. The data suggest that soul/rhythm and blues/disco and country and western are the strongest fields for females—again, mediated by race. The recent successes of Pat Benatar, Deborah Harry, Christie Hyde of the Pretenders, Sheena Easton, and others lead one to suspect a comparatively great increase in the number of female performers in rock music, although our figures indicate a rather substantial gap yet to be bridged.

Table 7 shows the age range of recording artists in our sample by musical style. Again, due to the unequal cells in the table, the actual numbers are more informative than the percentages.

Most of the rock artists are between the ages of 30–39, followed by 20–29. This same pattern is found for country and western artists. Soul/rhythm and blues/disco styles reverse the pattern slightly, with more artists between

Table 6
Comparison of Musical Style and Sex of Recording Artist

Musical Style	Male		Female	
	Number	Percent	Number	Percent
Rock	266	51.0	10	17.2
Soul/rhythm and blues/disco	71	13.6	18	31.0
Easy listening	25	4.8	10	17.2
Country and western	85	16.3	14	24.1
Jazz	71	13.6	5	8.6
Classical	2	0.4	1	1.7
Other	2	0.4	0	0.0
Total	522	100.1[a]	58	99.8[a]

$\chi^2 = 41.13$; df = 6; p < .0001 (n = 580)
[a]Rounding error.

Table 7
Comparison of Musical Style and Age of Recording Artist

Musical Style	15–19		20–29		30–39		40–49		50+	
	n	%	n	%	n	%	n	%	n	%
Rock	2	66.7	39	51.3	57	56.4	2	10.0	0	0.0
Soul/rhythm and blues/disco	0	0.0	9	11.8	4	4.0	1	5.0	1	10.0
Easy listening	0	0.0	3	3.9	9	8.9	0	0.0	0	0.0
Country and western	1	33.3	7	9.2	23	22.8	5	25.0	2	20.0
Jazz	0	0.0	17	22.4	8	7.9	12	60.0	7	70.0
Classical	0	0.0	1	1.3	0	0.0	0	0.0	0	0.0
Total	3	100.0	76	99.9[a]	101	100.0	20	100.0	10	100.0

$\chi^2 = 63.30$; df = 20; p < .0001 (n = 210)
[a]Rounding error.
n = Number; % = Percent.

20–29 than 30–39. Among jazz musicians, older artists (30–50 and over) predominate. Those jazz musicians between the ages of 20 and 29 consist primarily of "fusion" players, making the effort to link jazz with rock and other styles.

Table 8 shows the relationship between educational level and musical style. Overall, there is a fairly even division between artists with high school education or less, and those with at least some college. Easy listening and jazz

Table 8
Comparison of Musical Style and Education of Recording Artist

Musical Style	High School or Less		Some College or More	
	Number	*Percent*	*Number*	*Percent*
Rock	63	47.7	72	46.5
Soul/rhythm and blues/disco	25	18.9	13	8.4
Easy listening	3	2.3	11	7.1
Country and western	26	19.7	29	18.7
Jazz	15	11.4	29	18.7
Classical	0	0.0	1	0.6
Total	132	100.0	155	100.0

$\chi^2 = 12.81$; df $= 5$; p $< .05$ (n $= 287$)

musicians tend to be better educated than soul/rhythm and blues/disco artists. Among country and western artists and rock artists, equal numbers have high school and college-plus educations.

Our final consideration was the importance of migration to the artist's professional career. In 245 cases, artists made a move to an entertainment center that was indicated as pivotal to their career success. Table 9 lists the market areas artists chose, presumably based in large part on their musical style. (There may of course be other reasons that these moves were made, such as proximity or chance.)

Among rock artists, more moved to the West Coast and the East Coast than to other areas. Soul/rhythm and blues/disco musicians gravitated primarily to the East Coast and West Coast. Easy listening artists tended not to move to the South, while country and western artists moved primarily to the South (presumably because of Nashville) and to the West Coast. Jazz artists were evenly split between moves to the East and West Coasts. Thus the New York and Los Angeles markets, along with Nashville, receive virtually the entire influx of musical migrators.

The present research has sought to define certain demographic and migratory characteristics of recording artists. Much of our data offer empirical confirmation of "taken for granted" assumptions about the recording industry. There is a strong relationship, for instance, between race/origin of artists and musical style; the industry is shown to be male-dominated artistically; the average age of artists does appear to be over 30; and so on. We have also defined an apparent hierarchy of artistic statuses within the business. Migration was found to be of critical importance to the careers of approximately

Table 9
Comparison of Markets to Which Recording Artists Migrated and Musical Style

	Rock		Soul/Rhythm and Blues/ Disco		Easy Listening	
	n	%	n	%	n	%
East Coast (New York, Philadelphia, Boston)	33	30.6	16	45.7	8	44.4
West Coast (Los Angeles, San Francisco, Las Vegas)	50	46.3	10	28.6	6	33.3
Southern (Nashville, Miami)	10	9.3	2	5.7	0	0.0
Midwest (Chicago, Memphis, Detroit)	15	13.9	7	20.0	4	22.2
Total	108	100.0	35	100.0	18	99.9[a]

	Country and Western		Jazz		Classical		Other	
	n	%	n	%	n	%	n	%
East Coast (New York, Philadelphia, Boston)	4	9.3	18	47.4	1	100.0	0	0.0
West Coast (Los Angeles, San Francisco, Las Vegas)	14	32.6	18	47.4	0	0.0	1	50.0
Southern (Nashville, Miami)	24	55.8	1	2.6	0	0.0	1	50.0
Midwest (Chicago, Memphis, Detroit)	1	2.3	1	2.6	0	0.0	0	0.0
Total	43	100.0	38	100.0	1	100.0	2	100.0

$\chi^2 = 87.56$; df = 18; p < .0001 (n = 245)
[a]Rounding error.
n = Number; % = Percent.

37 percent of the artists in our sample. While we acknowledge some methodological difficulties with the sample, it is hoped that our findings will both stimulate and be of use to further research on contemporary recording artists.

References

1. Becker, Howard. "The Professional Dance Musician and His Audience." *American Journal of Sociology* 56, 1951, pp. 136–144.
2. Bridges, John and R. Serge Denisoff. "PMS in Retrospect: A Look at the First Six Volumes." *Popular Music and Society* 7, 1979, pp. 2–7.
3. Coffman, James. "Everybody Knows This Is Nowhere: Role Conflict and the Rock Musician." *Popular Music and Society* 1, 1971, pp. 20–32.

4. Faulkner, Robert. *Hollywood Studio Musicians*. Chicago: Aldine-Atherton, 1971.
5. Gonzales, Lawrence. *Jambeaux*. New York: Harcourt Brace Jovanovich, 1979.
6. Goodykoontz, William. "Becoming a Star: An Interactionist Perspective On the Presentation of Onstage Identity." Unpublished Ph.D. dissertation, University of California, Riverside, 1979.
7. Hunter, Ian. *Reflections of a Rock Star*. London: Flash Books, 1976.
8. Lewis, George. "The Pop Artist and His Product: Mixed-Up Confusion." *Journal of Popular Culture* 4, 1970, pp. 327–338.
9. Nanry, Charles (Ed.). *American Music: From Storyville to Woodstock*. New Brunswick, N.J.: Transaction, 1972.
10. Nite, Norm. *Rock On: The Illustrated Encyclopedia of Rock 'n' Roll*. New York: Thomas Crowell, 1974.
11. Rockwell, John. "From 'Doo-wop' to 'Shlockrock.'" *New York Times*, February 4, 1979.
12. Roxon, Lillian. *Rock Encyclopedia*. New York: Grosset and Dunlap, 1969.
13. Sanders, Clinton. "Psyching Out the Crowd: Folk Performers and Their Audiences." *Urban Life and Culture* 3, 1974, pp. 264–282.
14. Schutz, Alfred. "Making Music Together." In A. Brodersen (Ed.), *Collected Papers*, Volume 2: *Studies in Social Theory*. The Hague: Martin Nijhoff, 1964.

COUNTRY MUSIC: WHAT PRICE PROGRESS?

Don E. Tomlinson

Don E. Tomlinson is an assistant professor of journalism at Texas A&M University. Prior to joining the A&M faculty in 1985, Tomlinson lived in Nashville, Tennessee, where he was a communications and entertainment lawyer and country music video cinematographer at the production and programming arm of the Country Music Television Network. His music video credits include "The Yellow Rose," which has become a country music video standard.

Traditional country music can be defined as a native American musical form that features lyrical and musical simplicity and evolves from the rural southern way of life. Modern country music is a constructed musical form exemplified by the Nashville sound, a marriage of traditional country music and pop music. This bond results in a commercial smoothness that appeals to diverse musical tastes but to country music traditionalists is plastic.

During the late 1970s and early 1980s, the popularity of modern country music reached an all-time high. But in attracting a wider audience, record company executives moved country music as far from its roots as they could without destroying it. Now it has been jolted back to reality by a new generation of traditionalists like Ricky Skaggs who, when he admonishes his fans, "Don't get above your raisin," might as well be admonishing country music itself.

Traditional country music was in its heyday in the decade after World War II. It enjoyed wide popularity among young people until rock and roll. Country music historian Bill Malone writes, "The teenage market had, in fact, accounted for much of the success of country music [during the postwar years]. In the mid-fifties, this market, taking in the ever-increasing youthful segment of the population, turned toward another product of grassroots America" (Malone 1968, p. 241).

Although rock and roll, which arguably began in 1954, came on fast in terms of acceptance by fans, it did not begin to erode the popularity of country music until 1957 when, Malone writes, it became clear that "the music was not faring as well as it had in previous years" (p. 246). Bill Ivey, director of the Country Music Foundation, says country music is lucky to be alive today in any form considering what almost happened to it when rock and roll came along: "If you had looked at country music in 1957, you would have said it was effectively over. Wesley Rose at Acuff-Rose studios tells how in 1957 they used to close down shop and play softball all afternoon because there was just so little to do" (Lundy 1986, p. 6). During the late 1950s, country music was reeling from the effects of rock and roll. Elvis Presley was taking the country by storm, other rock acts were making it big, and a musical steamroller seemed to be running wild.

It also seemed that country's fans had deserted their music. Or maybe the slump occurred because so many families had moved from the farms to the cities in the population shifts after World War II, where they succumbed to the near mass hysteria of rock and roll. Further, practically everyone in the music business wanted to get on the economic bandwagon created by the mass popularity of rock and roll. Whatever the reasons, the popularity of country music was fading fast. The magic formula of simple lyrics and even simpler music that for years had ensured success could no longer be counted on. Country record sales declined, and radio stations with country formats started switching to rock. Country was going to have to adapt by coming up with something new to fight rock and roll and bring country back from the brink. It could meld with rock and cease to exist as a separate musical form, or it could move toward rock but keep enough distance not to be absorbed while attempting to regain its share of the market.

Since rock had supplanted so much of the music of the time, the question became whether there was a void, an unfilled niche. Was there a sizable segment of the market that did not like rock (too harsh), jazz (too unmelodious), pop (too insincere), rockabilly/honky-tonk (too raucous), or country (too twangy) and would gladly accept what was left if someone could figure out just what that was?

In 1960, Chet Atkins, a guitar player and Nashville record company executive, with several other Nashville innovators took what were considered to be the best elements of each style and came out with country music, easy listening style (Hemphill 1970). Country music became the Nashville sound. Or was it the Nashville sound that became country music?

The Nashville sound was successful, and it endured. The market was larger than expected. Country sales went back up, and more radio stations than ever were playing country music. To be sure, a segment of country music has retained that old hard edge, but it has been dwarfed by the mainstream. Over the years, the mainstream has included Eddy Arnold, Anne Murray, Barbara Mandrell, and Gary Morris (who in the summer of 1985 starred in the off-Broadway production of the Italian opera *La Boheme*).

The Nashville sound changed over the years. New people came to sing it and play it. It was middle of the road and was attracting more fans all the while. Through the 1960s and 1970s and into the 1980s, it was the glue that held together the country music industry (Oermann 1983).

Any description of the Nashville sound and the state of country music through the early 1980s would have to include the idea of homogeneity:

1. the hard edges were smoothed;
2. lyrical content was banal; songwriters were writing not from the heart but from a sense of commerce;
3. all instruments sounding anything like a steel guitar were banished from the recording studios, and violins—not fiddles—along with background singers, were added to make the final product country-pop;
4. synthesizers and drum machines were becoming standard studio fare;
5. studio musicians, technically excellent, were playing country but feeling rock, pop, or jazz;
6. artists were singing what their producers told them to sing;
7. producers were producing what they thought the record company executives wanted them to produce;
8. record company executives wanted to move country even closer to the pop sound;
9. disc jockeys and program directors were constructing their playlists based on the output of the major record companies; and

10. there was talk of changing the name *country music* to *American music.* (Indeed the word *country* is conspicuous by its absence in the name of the Nashville Network, country's flagship cable television network, which premiered in 1983.)

The record company that won *Billboard* magazine's new independent country label of the year award in 1982 was AMI. The first two letters stand for "American music." Although the label's roster of artists has included Vern Gosdin, who clearly fits the traditional country mold, company president Mike Radford (1986) says he named the company as he did because "in 1981, when we got started, it seemed to me that country music was becoming American music. The big theme in radio at the time was 'We don't call it country; we call it American. This is music for all the people; not just part of them.'" Radford says he viewed American music as nothing more than a symbol or label: "I didn't think that just because the music got called 'American' that it still wouldn't really be country. The word 'country' has a negative connotation to some people. I just thought it was good marketing strategy for the name to make the same product more acceptable to a larger group of consumers." Apparently, however, many country radio stations had other ideas. "We went through a period of time where the radio stations calling their format 'American,'" Radford says, "wouldn't play Vern Gosdin because they said he was too country for their format. So we said: 'Well, if you aren't playing country music anymore, who is?'"

David Gates reported in *Newsweek,* "At a time when the country music audience had reached an all-time high, the music's actual country content seemed to have hit rock bottom. A few uncompromising traditionalists like Merle Haggard and George Jones refused to abandon the sobbing steel guitars, keening fiddles, biting guitar leads and the taut, passionate singing in unashamedly Southern accents that characterize hard-core country music. Until recently, though, few new singers seemed interested in re-creating this bittersweet sound" (Gates 1984, p. 93).

Country traditionalists had never embraced the Nashville sound. At the time it got started, though, most of them realized it was that or nothing. Even so, they would not concede the death of traditional country music, only that it was hibernating. They longed for the opportunity to revive their kind of country. They got their chance but not before the Nashville sound erupted into a record sales frenzy beginning in 1979. The excitement eased in 1984, to the point, music industry writer Mark Humphrey says, that "Nashville reacted to its changing fortunes with a mixture of good ol' boy fatalism and corporate panic. Porky artist rosters were trimmed to the bone at all the majors" (Humphrey 1986, p. 52).

What accounted for the sudden frenzy and the equally sudden decline? Many people believe the 1979–1984 boom was false in the sense that country music was not as popular as the boom seemed to indicate and that other, larger forces were at work. Ivey says the boom was a fad: "Country benefitted from the exotic quality of the country lifestyle that was being touted at that time. The urban audience was having a massive flirtation with that lifestyle then. We knew that was a fad. I was quoted in 1980 concerning the [boom], and basically I said people were not going to wear Western shirts, cowboy boots and Stetson hats in New York when the next fashion fad came along. We also knew that some people who were buying records because it was stylish wouldn't continue, either" (Lundy 1986, p. 6).

At that time, because record company executives were seeking to capitalize on this seeming urban taste for the Nashville sound, country music had been moved about as far as it could get from its traditions. Jim Foglesong, president of the Nashville division of Capitol Records, sums up the views of many of his fellow executives in commenting on what happened to country beginning in 1979: "During the euphoric boom, we wanted more and more of a good thing. When something gets hot, we have a tendency to jump on the bandwagon, saturate it and kill it" (Lundy 1986, p. 6).

By 1984, America's love affair with modern country music had ended. Because the country product was still being tailored to a big market that had significantly decreased in size, "country's share of record sales dropped from 15 percent ($600 million) to 10 percent ($430 million)" in 1984. "The reason would appear to be that too many . . . country recordings sound[ed] alike. And that's because Nashville music factories [were] so eager to keep cashing in on pop-country [or crossover] recordings that much of what [was] called country . . . [had] only the most attenuated relationship to the core traditions of the music: Bill Monroe, Hank Williams . . . George Jones and Merle Haggard" (Hentoff 1985, p. 40).

When the rock-pop audience decided it did not like country music as well as it thought it did, country music traditionalists seized the opportunity to bring country home. Humphrey welcomes the return to traditional country music: "Nashville perfected the hue and cry of honky-tonk [in the 1950s], then went soft in search of middle-of-the-road money [in the 1960s] when rock drew away the younger audience. The outlaws brought back some kick (and younger listeners) in the mid-seventies, but proved paunchy in the end. Country's young traditionalists have come up with the first fresh Southern sound in a decade" (Humphrey 1986, p. 65).

Traditional country music not only was alive, it was making a strong comeback. Writer Wayne Robins reports that the death of traditional country music was greatly exaggerated: "The good news is that a new group of performers is putting the kick back in country. It's an insurrection not unlike the outlaw movement of the early seventies when Willie Nelson, Waylon Jennings and others turned their backs on Nashville altogether and took their music back home to Texas. Some of these new artists are going back home to the gritty roots of a music that until the fifties was known as hillbilly" (Robins 1986, p. 3).

Hentoff, whose column for the *Progressive* is called "Indigenous Music," hails the arrival of traditionalists such as Skaggs and George Strait, whom he believes may signal the beginning of a turnaround. As evidence, he cites Skaggs's winning the entertainer of the year award from the Country Music Association plus Strait's award as male vocalist of the year, both in 1985 (Hentoff 1985, p. 40).

Humphrey sees the new movement as having begun when "a crew of young buckaroos and buckarettes from the South and Southwest took it upon themselves to revitalize country plain and simple. . . . Young country traditionalists such as . . . Skaggs and John Anderson began to insist that the simplicity of basic country had more guts and drive then the baleful sophistication of the stuff called 'crossover'—the musical equivalent of a Tennessee tickhound with a poodle perm. Skaggs and Anderson were the vanguard of the back-to-basics movement. Since then the ranks have swelled to include Strait, Reba McEntire, the Whites, the Judds and Dwight Yoakam. Individually, each has a distinctive sound that owes much to some aspect of country tradition, be it bluegrass, honky-tonk, rockabilly or western swing" (Humphrey 1986, p. 52).

Country music continues to be diverse in the sense that while traditional country music is rebounding, other segments of country (modern and various hybrids) are here to stay. Foglesong does not see any major trends developing in the next few years to equal the 1979–1984 rise and fall: "I think it's going to be diverse. There are new traditionalists, sounds that are quite contemporary, even fifties and sixties music with contemporaneity" (Lundy 1986, p. 6).

That country music unit sales are down significantly since the end of the boom period in 1984 is no secret. What should be noted, however, is that although country sales are down, they are still considerably higher than before the big upsurge of the late 1970s and early 1980s.

The associate executive director of the Country Music Association, Ed Benson, says the boom period produced a big rise in the number of radio stations with country music formats and that, surprisingly, the number of country radio stations did not drop when the record boom was over: "We have 2,300 full-time stations out of 8,500 in the country. That's more than a quarter, and that's significant. Surveys show that country is second only to [the] adult contemporary format in listener popularity" (Lundy 1986, pp. 1, 6).

The number of stations listing themselves as having country formats is not the only thing that is happening in radio. Thankfully, Radford says, the pendulum is swinging back from the effect of the American music idea: "Since 1984, lots of radio stations have decided they would be better off to be *blatantly* country than to be homogenized country so they can completely distinguish themselves from the pop stations in town" (Radford 1986).

Although rock music clearly is ahead of country music in unit sales and all other financial categories, country leads in overall popularity. A Harris poll on the popularity of music in the United States, conducted January 3–7, 1986, shows that "a substantial 59 percent say they like country music and 27 percent name it as their favorite, putting it in first place in both categories" (Harris Survey 1986, p. 1). The results of the poll also indicate, somewhat surprisingly, that two rather disparate groups find country music particularly enjoyable: the baby boomer generation and those fifty years of age and older.

The Nashville Network, with 25 million subscribers, earned cable's top prime-time Nielsen rating in April 1986 (Nashville Network 1986, p. 1). Clearly it is a force to be reckoned with. New traditional artists have been able to use TNN to their advantage: Vic Faraci, senior vice-president of marketing at Warner Brothers' Nashville division, says TNN "was a tremendous help in establishing [Yoakam's] country identity" (Bessman 1986, p. 1).

Another opportunity that many traditionalists are not passing up is country's other cable network, the Country Music Television Network. A twenty-four-hour per day country music video service founded in 1983, CMTV has 6.5 million subscribers, according to Mike Abney, its vice-president of network operations (Abney 1986). Although the network airs all varieties of country videos, it "pays the heaviest attention to [the] core country audience" (Abney 1986). Ricky Skaggs, George Strait, and the Judds, among other traditional country artists, have received heavy airplay of their music videos on CMTV.

Based on indicators like unit sales, concert bookings and attendance figures, radio airplay, record chart performance, and industry accolades and awards, there is a resurgence of traditional country music. What does it say about American society?

Radford says the elusive factor *is* society:

> I believe the adult population's taste in music is reflective of the mass media in general. I think the history of the music business will bear me out when I say that traditional country music is most popular when traditional ideas in general are popular. Right now, patriotism is big; conservatism is big; nostalgia is big.
>
> In other words, what the population is exposed to in general through the media influences its musical tastes. Right now there is traditional atmosphere generally—not just musically. (Radford 1986).

Rock and pop seem to be flirting with traditionalism as well. Reporter Steve Morse believes rock and pop are abandoning the keyboard synthesizer sound of the first half of the 1980s for a return to the instrument that was

largely responsible for launching rock and roll in the 1950s: the electric guitar. He sees this as a "back-to-basics" movement (Morse 1986, p. 2D).

Buck White has never had to get back to the basics because he never left
them to start with. White, who is in his mid-fifties, has been playing country
music all his life. He is the leader of the Whites, a traditional country music
group that features, in addition to himself, his two daughters (one of them,
Sharon, is married to singer Ricky Skaggs).

White believes traditional country music is gaining in popularity because
listeners do not seem to be ashamed of their enjoyment of it: "The average
country fan wants to hear basic country again. For a while, [traditional]
country music was kind of kept in a closet. If people like[d] it, they might
not [have wanted] their society friends to know they did because it was
looked down on" (Humphrey 1986, p. 52).

Dwight Yoakam, a fast-rising performer and an ardent spokesman for
traditionalism, agrees: "Country was thrown on the garbage heap. It's tragic
that we ignored the ethnic American music of the majority for so long"
(Humphrey 1986, p. 52).

Who are these latter-day traditionalists? Why is traditional country music so important to them? What is it about them that the record-buying, con-
cert-going public seems to like so well? Let us briefly review the growing
careers of some of the leading new artists.

Just as sure as the trend toward traditionalism in country music is a coun-
terrevolution, it was begun by Ricky Skaggs. "The beginning of the eighties
was almost the beginning of the end for country music. Musically, it got *so*
sterile—syruped with strings, background voices, and synthesizers. I *knew*
what country music was, and I wasn't hearing it on the radio," Skaggs says
(Humphrey 1986, p. 52).

Singer Reba McEntire knew what it was too, and she was not hearing it
either: "Ricky Skaggs kind of started it off by saying he's going to do what
he wants, regardless. Everybody liked it, and it gave the rest of us the notion,
'Well, if people are likin' this kind of music [again], and we like it, why aren't
we doing it?'" (Humphrey 1986, p. 52).

One of the most time-honored policies of the Nashville sound is that no
artist of any stature less than a Dolly Parton or a Kenny Rogers even thinks
about asking his record company to allow him to produce his own recording
sessions, that is, to choose the songs to go on his albums and to determine
the style(s) in which to record them.

Skaggs was fully aware of this policy as he was negotiating his first major
recording contract with CBS Records in 1980. But he made it clear that he
would sign only if the contract were modified to allow him to be his own
producer. CBS agreed. His first album on CBS, *Waitin' On the Sun to Shine*
in 1981, brought together his bluegrass "raisin'" and the country-rock sound
that he helped invent as Emmylou Harris's Hot Band guitar player in the late

1970s. The album spent nearly a year at the top of the charts, and produced four hit singles.

The nation met Ricky Skaggs the night he gave his acceptance speech on live network television on receiving the Country Music Associations' 1985 award as Entertainer of the Year. After thanking various persons and God for his good fortune, Skaggs said: "Some radio folks who call themselves country music disc jockeys aren't playing records by the Ricky Skaggs Band because they say we're too country. If we get to the point where country radio stations don't play country music, we're in a lot of trouble" (Hentoff 1985, p. 40).

Of Skaggs, Nat Hentoff says: "When you hear him on radio, there's no way you would mistake him for some fellow from New Jersey who went down to Nashville, put on a cowboy hat, hired a dobro player, and called himself a country singer. Skaggs is real" (Hentoff 1985, p. 40). Ray Charles put it a little differently, but it means the same thing: "Skaggs, man, he's somethin'! He's got that 'way-back-in-them-hills' shit in his voice" (Humphrey 1986, p. 52).

Skaggs himself is supremely confident. When once asked whether traditional country music would exist in the year 2000, he replied: "Yeah, buddy. Unless the Lord comes and raptures us all real soon." When the interviewer allowed as how the Almighty might like a traditional country tune Himself, Skaggs said: "Oh, I *know* He does" (Humphrey 1986, p. 65).

Women are also a part of the new country sounds. When the Judds, a mother and daughter who have had a string of country hits, began singing in 1984, they did not know anything about traditionalism versus the Nashville sound. Their production is spare, to achieve an old-time sound that is definitely traditional country but does not quite fit any of the subcategories. The mother, Naomi, sings the harmonies, and Wynonna, her daughter, sings lead. Legions of country music critics have said Wynonna's voice is the purest country voice since Patsy Cline, whose career in the 1950s was cut short by her death in an airplane crash. David Gates says: "The Judds touch women's hearts: they're middle-American fantasy come to life, a which-one-is-the-mother pair right out of a TV commercial" (Gates 1985, p. 60). Wynonna adds that "Women out there support Mom because she stands for the home, the family. So many mothers are terrified their kids are gonna run off and leave 'em" (Gates 1985, p. 60).

Dwight Yoakam is probably the least well known of the group of country performers usually credited with being at the fore of country traditionalism, but he may be the most fervent traditionalist of all. Having been rejected by the Grand Ole Opry in 1977 and 1980 as "too country," Yoakam, a Kentucky and Ohio native whose grandfather was a coal miner, headed for California where he honed his skills as a true honky-tonker in clubs mainly frequented by second- and third-generation transplanted Okies and other southerners.

In 1984, he produced an independent album, *Guitars, Cadillacs, Etc., Etc.,* on the Oak label. The album met with such critical success that it earned him a major recording contract.

Yoakam's new boss at Warner Bros.' Nashville division, executive vice-president Jim Ed Norman, says of Yoakam: "[He] has such a strong, strong relationship with his past, his history. He deals with it in a purely emotional, esthetic sense, where there is an obligation to remind people that what he's giving is the real truth, the hard edge, rather than some watered-down version that's more accessible to mass-appeal, adult contemporary radio" (Robins 1986, p. 19).

So there it is: traditional country music versus modern/hybrid country music. What price progress? While the Nashville sound brought empty commercial success, the new, back-to-the-roots artists are carving their own share of the market. Their diversity may preserve country music as a populist art form far into the future.

References

Abney, Mike. 1986. Telephone interview. July 25.

Bessman, Jim. 1986. "Labels Cheer Exposure Opportunities at the Nashville Network." *Billboard,* May 10, p. 1.

Gates, David. 1984. "Country Purists Fight Back." *Newsweek,* January 9, p. 93.

———. 1985. "Nashville's New Class." *Newsweek,* August 12, pp. 58–61.

Harris Survey. 1986. *Country Music Most Popular; Rock Second.* Orlando: Tribune Media Services.

Hemphill, Paul. 1970. *The Nashville Sound: Bright Lights and Country Music.* New York: Simon and Schuster.

Hentoff, Nat. 1985. "Country in Trouble." *Progressive* 49 (December): 40.

Humphrey, Mark. 1986. "Young Country Traditionalists." *Spin* (March): 52–54, 65.

Lundy, Ronni. 1986. "Country Music: Alive and Well." *Louisville Courier-Journal,* March 30, sec. 1, pp. 1, 6.

Malone, Bill C. 1968. *Country Music U.S.A.* Austin: University of Texas Press and American Folklore Society.

Morse, Steve. 1986. Electric Guitar Stages Pop Music Comeback." *Bryan-College Station Eagle,* July 31, p. 2D.

Nashville Network. 1986. *TNN Was the Highest Rated Single Cable Network in Primetime in April.* Stamford, Conn.: Group W Satellite Communications.

Oermann, Robert K., with Douglas B. Green. 1983. *The Listener's Guide to Country Music.* New York: Facts on File.

Radford, Mike. 1986. Telephone interview, July 25.

Robins, Wayne. 1986. "Country Changes Its Tune." *Newsday,* April 20, part 2, pp. 3, 19.

5
Television

Introduction

The United States was the first country to introduce television on a mass scale. The technology was available in the 1930s, and broadcasting began at the end of the decade, although television sets were not mass produced until after World War II. With the postwar boom, television became an item first of prestige and then of mass consumption. An estimated 8,000 sets were in use in 1946, 1 million by 1948, 4 million the following year, and over 10 million in 1950. There were about seventy stations in 1948 when the Federal Communications Commission (FCC) suspended new licensing for four years to allow necessary organization and allocation plans for the thirteen VHF frequencies available nationwide. When new licensing resumed, station expansion was rapid and spread to include nearly all of the country in viewing range. By 1955, more than 37 million sets were in use, more than three for every four households; in 1960 there were slightly more sets than households (57 million sets, 53 million households).[1] In 1984, 98 percent of all U.S. households owned television sets.[2]

The market for television sets has apparently nearly reached saturation. New sets are sold primarily as replacements for earlier or defunct models. The demand for a second set in the household is almost certainly less pressing than it was for the first. Domestic sales figures in recent years have shown a large drop in monochrome receiver sales and a steady increase in color set purchases. Total sales, however, have declined. Yet because of the much higher unit price of color, dollar sales have continued to rise.

Color television has grown rapidly. By 1984, 75.8 million homes in the United States had color sets.[3] The color boom occurred in the late 1960s and early 1970s, similar to the video player boom of the 1980s. The proportion of households with these more expensive sets can safely be predicted to rise but primarily through replacements for old monochrome sets. Thus despite the introduction of color, the industry is no longer experiencing the bonanza expansion associated with a totally new product and virgin markets.

The wide distribution of television sets means that the potential audience for transmitting stations is large. Although television developed earliest in the Northeast, by 1956 it served more than 60 percent of potential viewers in all regions. Large cities had the best coverage, but there was good coverage even in farm districts. Differences were very small in the coverage of national markets stratified by income, education, family size, age of housewife, or age of children.[4]

The time spent watching the medium is prodigious, but it probably will not grow much in the future. In 1983 the average viewing day was 7 hours, up from 6.6 hours in 1980 and 5.9 hours in 1970.[5] High-income families spend more time watching TV than poor, with the middle class the heaviest viewers. Households with elderly women view less than those with young or middle-aged women. Viewing increases with the number of years of the head of the household's education through to high school. Households headed by an individual with some college education are the lowest viewers, however. Homes in the East Central region of the United States seem to have their sets on more than those in other regions of the country.[6]

From the outset, television broadcasting in the United States has been overwhelmingly a commercial undertaking, though the airwaves are recognized by law, if not by the industry, as public property. The FCC has a weak regulating authority over the medium's operators, consisting primarily of the power to grant or refuse licenses to transmitting stations. The commission is now strongly committed to deregulation. Past interference by the FCC in commercial operations was strongly resisted by the corporations, and public sympathy usually went to the local men of the "public" corporation rather than the government. The government is often just another customer that must follow the dictates of the networks. A striking example of this is network treatment of politicians, who as legitimate representatives of the public presumably have some right of access to the public airwaves. They do, if they buy broadcasting time. Otherwise they must be interrupted by advertisements just like everyone else.[7]

The triumph of commercial television was by no means inevitable. Governments in Europe, Canada, and Japan have retained more regulatory power, though this often means they must subsidize the medium. Great Britain and Germany, for example, derive revenue by imposing licensing fees on television receivers. Britain runs its own noncommercial network, and Germany limits advertising and prohibits interruption of programs for commercial spots.

Public television in the United States is clearly no political match for commercial interests, and it lags behind its European counterparts. It is continuously short of capital and remains heavily dependent on private contributions. For many years NET (National Educational Television) was further handicapped by the educational label that it carried. It has now been absorbed by PBS, the largest noncommercial network that runs many cultural and general interest programs in addition to daytime school programming. The public stations are expensive and require tax money and contributions. The financial burden of public broadcasting falls most heavily on those who contribute voluntarily. The widely held belief that commercial television broadcasting is free while public broadcasting is a luxury or a liability is encouraged by the major networks. For example, they were opposed to pay TV because they claimed it would constitute the selling of public property and deny the right of the individual owner to tune in free.

H. J. Skornia has argued that commercial broadcasts are, in fact, by no means free to the consumer. There are, he says,

> many channels through which funds are secured from the citizen to pay for broadcast service. They are indirect, and they may or may not be too high. They include what he pays for receiving equipment, installation, upkeep, and electricity or batteries; part of the [cost of] ... television-advertising products goes to pay for television time and talent costs and various other expenses.[8]

Presumably receiver costs would have to be borne under any system. Most of the broadcasters' expenses are met directly by advertising fees, but these, says Skornia, are passed on to the consumer in the form of higher prices. The standard apologia for advertising—that it increases market size, which leads to subsequent economies of scale in production, distribution, and marketing, and hence lower consumer costs—Skornia rejects as a myth. He finds no instances of price reduction after any successful advertising drive. Good advertising means good profits for the manufacturer, advertising agency, television networks, and stations. The stations do not reallocate their surpluses to provide better public service, nor do they cut back on commercial spot sales. They do what any other corporation does to benefit itself: they diversify and expand.

The networks ostensibly program what the public wants, but it is unclear who constitutes the public, although to commercial spokespersons, it is apparently the biggest minority at any given time. Nor is it readily apparent how the desires of the public, however defined, are determined. Many program decisions obviously are made initially by the networks and their sponsors. The audience is consulted, and then extremely haphazardly, only after the program is aired. The networks are far from perfect as a public forum for two-way communication.

In 1984 commercial television organizations broadcast from 841 stations. There were 734 stations in 1980, 677 in 1970, and 515 in 1960.[9] The recent growth in stations is due mainly to the licensing of new UHF transmitters.

The big three networks—NBC, CBS, and ABC—have long dominated commercial television. Between them they shared $8.3 billion of advertising revenues in 1985. Their share of viewers, however, is on the decline due to increased competition from cable and independent programming. In 1980 they had 85 percent of the prime-time audience but in 1985 only 73 percent. They have recently attempted to cut costs (NBC earned a $333 million profit, CBS $202 million, and ABC $133 million in 1985) and have been vulnerable to corporate takeovers. ABC fell to Capital Cities Communications and NBC and its parent company RCA to General Electric.[10]

Even before the mergers, the networks were not autonomous entrepreneurial establishments in any real sense. NBC is a subsidiary of RCA, as are Hertz, Commercial Credit Co., Random House, Sunbury and Dunbar Music, and Defense Electronic Products. CBS's family is reported to include Creative Playthings, Baily Films, and the book publisher Holt, Rinehart & Winston. ABC-TV and its international divisions were part of the greater ABC-Paramount organization, which was linked to Gulf and Western.[11]

The networks actively promote the ideology of free commercial television, programming for mass markets, time priority for advertising, and resistance to regulation. Alan Thomas has pointed out that each television viewer has three distinct roles: as audience, viewers want to be entertained and to indulge themselves; as market, they are open for a sale; but as public, they rationally dictate what they need for their own good. In Canada, Thomas explains, the

> public strongly supports the Canadian type of broadcasting, although as audience many of the same people may watch television programs from United States stations along Canada's borders. The Canadian Public is very Canadian. The Canadian Audience and Market are essentially American—very much like the people of the United States in the same roles.[12]

U.S. television, with minor exceptions, serves only audience and market.

One alternative to commercial television, public TV, has been modestly successful in its programming, especially in its airing of English imports, children's programs, (e.g., Sesame Street), and extensive news coverage. It gleaned its record audience in 1973 for nightly coverage of the Senate Watergate hearings. Financing, however, remains a major problem.

Cable television (CATV) is the newest alternative to current forms of television operation. For a monthly fee, a cable system links homes by coaxial cable to a centralized community antenna, improving picture reception and adding otherwise out-of-reach stations. This system has long been employed in remote and mountainous communities. Since the channel capacity is much greater (twenty or more) than that of over-the-air reception and since program origination can be done cheaply within the system, cable offers the potential for great diversity. Several commentators, however, suggest that cable still has a long way to go if it is to fulfill its promise.[13]

The entire television audience may soon be joined in a national web of cable. In 1960, there were 640 operating cable systems with 650,000 subscribers. Five years later, there were 1,325 systems and 1.3 million subscribers. In 1970, 4.5 million subscribers were hooked up to 2,490 systems. By 1980, 15.5 million subscribed to over 4,000 systems, and the pace has continued (30 million subscribers in 6,200 systems by 1984).[14] Cable, then, is growing rapidly (it now gets over $6 billion in revenues) and along with other new technologies (like home video) may reshape television in the United States.

Cable's most successful services include CNN, the cable news network, and its separate Headline News, both part of the Turner media empire. For children, there is Nickelodeon (a Warner Communications/American Express venture) and the Disney channel, while Playboy and others program for adults.[15] Music television (MTV) has created something of a new art form and along with other music services (such as the Nashville Network) now perhaps competes with radio.[16] There are religious networks, sports networks, and major city superstations offered nationwide (WGN, Chicago; WTBS, Atlanta; WOR, New York). To complete the competition with the networks, pay movie channels are available: Showtime, The Movie Channel (Warner), and HBO (Time-Life).

The first reading, by Robert Abelman, describes the history of television in the United States and the crucial role of the networks in TV production and distribution. From 1948 to 1955, Abelman claims, sponsors controlled programming. The following years saw a growth in creative and network control, and soon the networks owned the rights to programs. The 1970–1971 FCC rules forced syndication changes and cut back network prime-time programming to two and a half hours. The changes, Abelman claims, helped the networks more than program producers. Currently networks like Metromedia are rivaling the big three with syndication of major network rejects and some new programming, and the new deregulation rules that permit ownership of twelve VHF stations may encourage more competition.

What types of programs are successful on television, and who makes them? David Marc in the second reading gives some answers in his article on MTM, a highly successful production company with a string of hits, including, recently, "Hill Street Blues" and "St. Elsewhere." Their programs have the great advantage of appealing to the affluent young adults favored by advertisers. Patricia Geist and Harvey Jassem next investigate how stations choose their programming, particularly how they keep controversial material off the air. Program managers rely primarily on their feelings, aided by network alerts, press warnings, and audience responses. John Wicklein then uncovers some problems that plague public TV. The current mood in Washington threatens to pressure public TV to follow its political dictates. Government funding is uncertain, and some public stations may go commercial. The public system, Wicklein claims, needs rebuilding, and he suggests ways that it might be done.

One type of successful program is the daytime soap opera and its prime-time versions like "Dallas" and "Dynasty." ("Dallas" holds the record for the highest-rated single program, with over 53 percent of the audience on November 21, 1980. Others in the top twenty list include several superbowls, "Roots" episodes, "Gone with the Wind," and the "Ed Sullivan Show.")[17] Much has been written about the soaps. Muriel Cantor and Suzanne Pingree have written a book that sketches the history of soaps, describes in detail how they are made, and examines their audience.[18] Entertainment programs in fact tell us much about American culture.[19]

Notes

1. Information in this paragraph is derived from Melvin L. DeFleur and Sandra Ball-Rokeach, *Theories of Mass Communication* (New York: McKay, 1975), pp. 97–101. For a useful history of the early days of television, see Eric Barnouw, *The Golden Web* (New York: Oxford University Press, 1968).

2. U.S. Bureau of the Census, *Statistical Abstract of the United States, 1985* (Washington, D.C.: Government Printing Office, 1986), p. 542.

3. Ibid.

4. Leo Bogart, "The Growth of Television," in Wilbur E. Schramm, ed., *Mass Communications* (Urbana: University of Illinois Press, 1960), p. 108.

5. *Statistical Abstract*, p. 542.

6. C. S. Aaronson, ed., *International TV Almanac* (New York: Quigley Publications, 1977), p. 10A.

7. The head of state is an exception; U.S. presidents can preempt television time.

8. H. J. Skornia, *Television and Society* (New York: McGraw-Hill, 1965), p. 90.

9. *Statistical Abstract*, p. 542.

10. See Thomas Moore, "Culture Shock Rattles the Networks, *Fortune*, April 14, 1986, pp. 22–27.

11. For a good summary of network operations and their business connections see Hyman H. Goldin, "The Television Overlords," *Atlantic* (July 1969): 87–89, and Alan Pearce, "The TV Networks: A Primer," *Journal of Communication* (Autumn 1976).

12. Alan Thomas, *Canadian Broadcasting*, Occasional Paper no. 7 (University of British Columbia, Department of University Extension, April 1960), cited by Skornia, *Television and Society*, p. 122.

13. See Nicholas Johnson, "The Myth of the Marketplace," *Technology Review* (January 1983); and William Andrews, "Cable's Broken Promises," *Video* (April 1984).

14. *Statistical Abstract,* p. 542.

15. See "Tale of a Bunny and a Mouse," *Time,* September 12, 1983.

16. See "Sing a Song of Seeing," *Time,* December 26, 1983.

17. *Les Brown's Encyclopedia of Television* (New York: Zeotrope, 1982), p. 490.

18. Muriel A. Cantor and Suzanne Pingree, *The Soap Opera* (Beverly Hills: Sage, 1983).

19. See, for example, Mike Budd, Steve Craig, and Clay Steinman, "Fantasy Island: Marketplace of Desire," *Journal of Communication* (Winter 1983): 67–77; Nancy L. Buerkel-Rothfus, Bradley S. Greenberg, Charles K. Atkin, and Kimberly Neuendorf, "Learning about the Family from Television," *Journal of Communication* (Summer 1982): 191–201.

COMMERCIAL TELEVISION: HOW IT WORKS

Robert Abelman

Robert Abelman is an associate professor in the Department of Communication at Cleveland State University. He has published two textbooks and over thirty research articles and has written for numerous popular publications on the relationship between television and society. He is a board member of the National Council for Families and Television, a nonprofit organization devoted to educating media professionals, regulators, and consumers regarding children's associations with television.

Despite the increasing prevalence of cable and home videocassette recorders, valiant efforts by the Public Broadcasting Service, and the threat of a fourth commercial network by corporate moguls Rupert Murdoch, Ted Turner, and others, American television *is* ABC, CBS, and NBC. Together these three networks reach over 80 million households on any given night. According to a recent CBS report, by 1990 the three networks will have an estimated combined revenue of over $15 billion as a result of their capacity to capture a mass audience. Les Brown (1982, p. 26), editor of *Channels* magazine, refers to commercial television as a "beautiful business: three networks in one vast sellers' market. . . . The networks' main challenge has been in dividing up the audience. One year, NBC ran a poor third and still made record profits. Quite a business—sweet and failure-proof." That is why Capital Cities paid $3.5 billion for the acquisition of the ABC network in 1985, and General Electric purchased RCA, NBC's parent company for which it generates 40 percent of the corporate profits, for $6.3 billion in 1986.

Upon close examination, however, the heartbeat of commercial television does not resound from the networks alone. Rather, the networks are one of four interrelated, mutually dependent components of the American television industry. Commercial broadcasting would not be successful without nation-wide distribution, but it would not be feasible without production houses to make programming, advertisers to buy airtime within programming, and the over 700 TV stations through which to deliver this fare to the masses. Over the years, the networks—the carriers and distributors of programming—rose to power, prestige, and accumulated wealth.

How did this happen, and how do the production houses, advertisers, and TV stations benefit from their role in this multibillion dollar industry? As we shall see, the current structure and stature of the television industry is the result of a multiphase evolution in the relationship among these four components, an evolution still in the state of flux.

The Beginning, 1948–1955

During the early days of television, the advertisers were in control of the industry. As a carry-over from radio, companies and corporations, through advertising agencies, owned and sole sponsored programming. They selected a program that best suited the company's image or, more likely, promised to be the most lucrative, and produced it themselves or had it made by independent production houses. These programs bore the company's name when they were broadcast on the air, and, because they were the sole sponsor, the companies were in a position to control program content. Consequently the networks, TV stations, and production houses were dependent on advertisers for programming and revenue.

For making these programs, production houses typically received the cost of making the program plus a 10 percent profit from the advertising agency. Producers did not retain ownership of the programs or program idea they generated for advertisers. However, in the hope of making a greater profit and retaining ownership, producers often sold their wares directly to individual TV stations or to regional or local sponsors. As television became more popular and the number of stations across the country increased, producers were able to negotiate price with a growing supply of interested buyers. All in all, it was a seller's market for producers.

Owners of television stations obtained their revenue by selling their sole commodity, airtime, to advertisers. The stations received 30 percent of the fee they would charge local advertisers when they aired network distributed programming. The 70 percent loss of potential revenue was easily justified by local broadcasters, for they received a better-quality show than would have been produced locally, they were the recipients of the prestige that came with being part of a nationwide network, and they received all this without having to solicit business. They simply signed a contract, received the network feed through telephone wires (now received through microwave and satellite), aired the program to their local viewers, and reaped the benefits. Their biggest decision was with which network to affiliate.

Affiliation was a tougher decision than it is today for, in the beginning of television, numerous television networks surfaced in an effort to capitalize on the promising future of the new medium. Clearly ABC, CBS, and NBC were in the forefront, having gained prominence and experience in the radio industry and early experimentation with television technology. The Dumont Television Network and the Westinghouse corporation, however, attempted to jump on the bandwagon and serve as go-betweens for the stations and the advertisers.

Indeed that was the early function of networks: to serve as national sales agents. They cleared time with the stations, collected fees from the advertiser, and arranged for the program to be distributed to participating stations. In return, the network collected a fee for its services. For several years, this symbiotic relationship among advertiser, producer, broadcaster, and network was mutually satisfactory. Each component stood to make money, and the function of one component was dependent on the others.

Eventually, however, the networks came to realize that they were the most depended upon component as the all-important link between these other parties but did not generate the most money or have the greatest control over programming.

Transition 1: Creative Control, 1955–1958

The networks first attempted to generate creative control over the programs they distributed and in so doing created problems for advertisers. According to David Sontag, former vice-president of 20th Century Fox and self-proclaimed "survivor of the Golden Age of television" (Newcomb and Alley 1983, p. 12), it was relatively easy for the networks to take control: "Program and time costs were relatively inexpensive . . . allowing the networks the option of accepting or turning down programs which advertisers had bought directly and were attempting to place on the network."

The shift in control created some problems for producers. Because the networks started pulling their weight in terms of approving or disapproving material they disseminated, the advertiser would buy the program from a producer subject to network approval. This problem was confounded when the networks began expanding the news and sports programming they produced to include more popular fare, such as daytime soap operas, thus competing with the producers who were seeking approval for their programs. Often the networks found the programs they produced more acceptable for distribution through their stations than programming offered by an outside producer. Many production companies quit, others learned the new rules, which included paying the networks a fee in return for creative counseling and advice to make their programs more acceptable for distribution.

Transition 2: The Quiz Show Scandal, 1959

The networks' next step toward control was to remove advertisers from programming decisions completely and require the producer to deal directly with them. At about the time network executives were trying to figure out how to go about such a dramatic move, a major scandal broke involving one of television's most beloved genre, quiz shows. Several winners of CBS's "The $64,000 Question," one of the most popular programs on television from 1955 to 1958, confessed that the shows were staged and scripted rather than truly intellectual and legitimate contests.

One of the results was the removal of all intellectually based prime-time quiz shows from the airwaves. (Only recently, over twenty-five years later, have these programs resurfaced with some level of success.) The first major consequence of the scandal affected producers. CBS took advantage of the public uproar by reminding their audience and government officials that the quiz shows had been made by independent producers, not the networks, and were brought in by advertisers. The other networks claimed that they too had no control and did not know what was going on in programming. They followed CBS's lead by taking control of the programs they distributed to their affiliated stations.

From that time forward, producers with a program to sell had to go directly to one of the three networks rather than to any of the hundreds of potential advertisers. Furthermore, the networks limited their use of independent producers in an effort to cut down on the cost of program production. Instead they established relations with major film studios, which could produce programs faster and for less money because of their expansive facilities. The networks would then become the owner of the program or go into partnership with the film studio and control the program's future. Before long, the networks owned, at least in part, nearly every show they telecast.

By this time, many programs were recorded on film (videotape came later) rather than performed and aired live, and their future consisted of national and international syndication (reruns). Ownership entitled the networks to sell their programs to individual stations across the globe. It also meant that they could withhold U.S. syndication of a popular program in order to prevent the program from cutting into the ratings of their first-run shows.

The second major consequence of the scandals concerned advertisers. Many advertisers, having lost faith in television and perceiving the scandals as the first sign of television's demise, placed their advertising dollars elsewhere. Advertisers still interested in investing in television had to do so under the control of the networks. Rather than offering a program to the networks, the advertisers now found themselves in the position of being offered a series of shows over which they had no control or ownership. Thus, they paid money to the networks not only for the airtime of the TV stations but also for the programs themselves. With fewer advertisers interested in television, the networks found it more expedient and profitable to do away with sole sponsorship and offer numerous advertisers one-minute pieces of the same programs. Thus, in the course of just a few years, advertisers found themselves going from sole ownership and sponsorship of programs to competing for airtime with other advertisers on network-owned programming.

The third major consequence concerned the TV stations. With advertisers now buying pieces of programs, the companies wanted some guarantee that they were reaching as large an audience as possible during their commercial minutes. Consequently national ratings became more important than ever before, and the networks charged advertisers on a dollars-per-thousand viewers basis. The networks then paid their affiliated stations on the basis of the average number of people the stations were capable of reaching. For a successful show, the advertiser paid an increased amount for gaining access to so many viewers. The broadcasters received no additional monies from the networks for airing a popular program than they did for running a poorly attended program.

Independents, or nonnetwork affiliated TV stations, were also influenced by the scandal. Independent stations survive on the selling of local and national advertising for movies, locally produced programming, and, primarily, off-network programs purchased through syndication. When the networks gained control of syndication rights, they also controlled the existence of these independent stations. When the networks limited syndication distribution, they cut off the life's blood of many of these stations.

Transition 3: FCC Intervention and Deficit Financing, 1971

Eventually the Federal Communications Commission (FCC) and committees of both houses of Congress expressed an interest in the demise of syndication and the subsequent reduction of competition in the marketplace. Of paramount concern was the fact that the networks controlled both the production and distribution of television programming. In 1970–1971, the FCC initiated and enforced a series of unprecedented rulings designed to disrupt the growing network monopoly.

First, the FCC forced the networks out of major involvement in entertainment program ownership through the financial interest and syndication rule. This rule prohibited the networks from producing and owning its own prime-time programming and acquiring any interest or ownership in a program produced by an outside party beyond the right of exhibition. Second, the FCC mandated that the networks would no longer acquire syndication rights, called back-end profits, or engage in the selling of programs to anyone, anywhere in the world. Instead the network retained the right to show a program twice (typically during the regular season and again during the summer), and the production houses received syndication rights. Third, the FCC adopted the prime-time access rule, imposing a limit of two and a half hours that affiliates in the top fifty markets would be allowed to clear for network entertainment each weeknight in an effort to allow network-affiliated stations to choose alternative programming. The intention was to inspire locally produced programming and form a new market for producers without network interference.

Much of the good intention behind these rulings resulted in problems for producers and benefits for the networks. By the 1970s, the cost of producing a network-quality prime-time program had skyrocketed. The networks were finding it expensive to maintain big studios and the staff necessary for producing nearly two dozen programs for weekly distribution. They were already farming out productions to private companies to cut costs when the FCC ruling to get out of production came into play, which then served as a final release of what had become the financial burden of production.

The prime-time access ruling was also beneficial for the networks, for it reduced the amount of available prime-time commercial time below advertiser demand and drove up the rates the networks could charge their advertisers. This ruling was especially advantageous for ABC, which had been running hopelessly behind the other networks in the ratings. Forced to cut its schedule to two and a half hours, ABC happily discarded seven series from its large roster of losers, thereby narrowing the gap between it and its rival networks, and allowing it to become a full-fledged competitor for the first time.

Although it appeared as if the producers would greatly profit from getting back the business of program production and obtaining back-end profits, it was actually one of the worst things to happen to producers since the inception of television. Because the producers now owned syndication rights, the days of cost plus 10 percent were over, and the networks were just paying producers the average cost of producing a program—typically $400,000 for a situation comedy and $900,000 for an action-adventure show in today's market. And the networks were once again in control of accepting or rejecting a producer's program.

Consequently, in order to make a program more attractive to the networks and increase the likelihood of its acceptance, producers often created one episode of a program (*pilot*) that cost twice what they received as payment from the networks. Producers made up the difference of this deficit financing from their own pockets, an acceptable expense for the possibility of having a hit show and making a fortune from syndication. And fortunes were to be had. When "M*A*S*H" went into syndication in 1977, stations paid $250,000 per episode; today episodes are being sold for $900,000, and there are eleven years of episodes. "Magnum P.I." went into syndication in 1986, its producers receiving $1.7 million per episode. NBC's popular program "The Cosby Show," which will be going into syndication in 1989, is expected to accumulate $3 million per half-hour episode in national revenues (Brown 1986b, p. 72).

Here is where the problems come in. Approximately 5 percent of all pilot programs are accepted by the networks. Consequently the producers run the risk of losing $400,000 to $900,000 for every pilot episode that fails. And if the program is accepted by the networks and is successful, the networks continue to pay the standard rate for a program but expect the same quality program they received in the pilot episode. As a result, the producers find themselves having to pay twice what they receive from the networks for every episode they produce. It is not uncommon for a producer to lose $5 million to $15 million a year producing a successful program while the network makes a profit in advertising sales. For example, the producer of the successful TV drama "The Waltons" was paid approximately $275,000 per one-hour episode; the network received $600,000 in advertising revenue for that same one-hour program (Reel 1979). It is not until syndication that the producers make their money.

Herein lies the biggest problem of all: very few shows get to the point where they can be syndicated. In order to be syndicated, there need to be about one hundred episodes so individual stations can *strip* the show (that is, place an episode of the program at the same time every weekday). It usually takes from four to five years before a producer has generated that many episodes. Of ten shows that get on the air as a series, seven will be immediate failures, two will run for just a year, and only one will be a lingering success. That means that producers have no back-end profit on nine out of ten shows made. They literally lose fortune after fortune in the hope that a program lasts four or more years. And the duration of a program's run is dependent on the network's perception of the program's ability to attract a large audience of 20 million people or more.

Only extremely large production houses, typically film studios, can afford to lose millions of dollars in the hope of eventually striking it rich with one success. All totaled, television program syndication in 1985 amounted to a $1.7 billion industry (Guttenplan 1986), led by the following production houses and their 1985 syndication revenues: Coca-Cola, which owns Columbia Pictures and Embassy Communications ($400 million); Paramount Studios ($375 million); Universal Studios ($275 million); 20th Century Fox ($225 million); and Lorimar/Telepictures ($216 million) (Brown 1986a). Clearly syndication is a lucrative business, but it has led to the near elimination of small production houses.

It was originally thought that the prime-time access ruling would enable small production houses to sell programs directly to individual stations and survive. According to the FCC, the aim of the ruling was "to make available for competition among existing and potential program producers, both at the local and national levels, an arena of more adequate competition for the custom and favor of broadcasters and advertisers" (FCC 1970, p. 326). In order to make this type of arrangement feasible and the cost to producers affordable, however, the program must be sold to stations in the largest markets in the country that would pay the largest fee. Unfortunately for producers, the largest stations in these markets (New York, Los Angeles, and Chicago) are owned and operated by the organizations that kept them off the air to begin with—ABC, CBS, and NBC.

Although the prime-time access ruling seemed to have helped TV stations by lessening the networks' hold over prime-time entertainment programming, it too hurt the stations in the long run. Rather than produce local programming, broadcasters took financial advantage of this access period by buying off-network syndicated programming. This type of programming did not reflect the intent behind the ruling but was more attractive to local advertisers and thus generated a greater profit for stations than the production of their own programming or the purchase of original programming from producers. However, in response to this ruling and the reduced number of hours stations carried actual, on-network programming, the networks decided to modify their pay scale to local stations. Rather than simply paying the stations on the basis of the size of audience they were capable of delivering, the networks created the network-station rate (NSR) for each individual station.

The NSR is a figure negotiated by the network and the station based on how much money the network will pay for each equivalent hour that the station carries a network program. Prime time (8–11 P.M.) has the greatest audience and is worth one equivalent hour. Early evening (5–7 P.M.) typically has half the prime-time audience and is worth 50 percent of an equivalent hour. Daytime (9 A.M.–5 P.M.) has the smallest audience and is worth only 35 percent of an equivalent hour. The actual NSR is determined by the size of the market in which the station exists. The NBC station in Cleveland,

Ohio, for example, gets approximately $5,000 per equivalent hour; the NBC affiliate in New York City gets approximately four times that amount.

The network then figures out the total equivalent hours based on the total number of hours of programming the station carries across the various time periods. Twenty-four equivalent hours are automatically subtracted every month to compensate the network for overhead costs of providing their programming service. The total number of equivalent hours are then reduced to 30 percent. (Recall that since the beginning of network-station affiliation, broadcasters received 30 percent of the fee they would charge local advertisers when they aired network distributed programming.) The remaining equivalent hours are then multiplied by the NSR, and that is the amount of money the station would receive for carrying network programming, minus 3.59 percent for artist royalty costs. This was quite a dramatic change from the early days but still worth the trouble for local broadcasters. Aside from being an independent station, network affiliation was the only game in town—until the next transition occurred.

Transition 4: Ad Hoc Networks, Early 1980s

Traditionally programs cancelled by the networks are given up for dead by producers. Unless enough episodes were generated for syndication, the producer absorbed the substantial financial loss, and the program went out of production. Similarly advertisers for cancelled programs simply sought new vehicles for their commercials. TV stations whose local audiences loved a program that the networks subsequently cancelled had no recourse. Recently, *Ad hoc* networks have been forming that give promising but cancelled programs a second chance to make money, offer advertisers and TV stations new episodes of cancelled favorites, and are giving ABC, CBS, and NBC a run for their money.

Ad hoc networks are comprised of organizations that own and operate stations in at least three of the largest U.S. cities and four stations in other major markets (at this time, seven television stations—five VHF, two UHF— is the maximum number a company can own). Most stations are independents, allowing them to be relatively free to take on programming from non-network sources. Independent stations reach only 65 percent of U.S. homes, however, so it is also necessary for an Ad hoc network to get a substantial number of network affiliates to join the club in order to establish a truly nationwide network. With these stations lined up, the Ad hoc network encourages producers to continue production of their well-known but cancelled programs and then proceeds to distribute that programming to the various stations and sell time to national advertising.

202 · *Mass Media and Society*

Metromedia Television, an example of an organization setting this trend, resurrected "Fame," which was cancelled by NBC after two years of generally lukewarm ratings, and "Too Close for Comfort," which had three respectable seasons on ABC when it was released (Zuckerman and Brown 1983). Note that Ad hoc networking is not being referred to as a new trend, for this phenomenon has all the components of the TV industry through its various stages of transition. As with the beginning of television, the Ad hoc network is merely serving as a clearinghouse and distribution agent. Producers own their product, advertisers buy pieces of the program, and stations purchase the program as they would with any other form of syndication.

In addition to the resurrection of off-network programming, Ad hoc networks are generating original programming. Operation Primetime is one example, distributing such distinguished programs as "A Woman Called Golda," with Ingrid Bergman, and "Smiley's People," with Alec Guinness. Films rejected by the networks and cable movie channels are also being distributed by Ad hoc networks.

There is evidence that Ad hoc networks are having an impact on the TV industry, though minuscule in scope. At the NBC affiliate convention in 1982, the network announced that its prime time program availability had fallen to 97 percent of all television homes; in the daytime, NBC was off by as much as 5 percent. According to network president Pierson Mapes (Zuckerman and Brown 1983, p. 46), that translates into millions of dollars in lost revenue each year. This effect afforded greater revenue and creative freedom for producers, however, who had felt restricted by the limited types of programming appropriate for the major networks. Furthermore, the prevalence of Ad hoc networks no doubt made the networks less cavalier about cancelling programs that still showed signs of popularity, thus offering greater security to producers. Similarly, Ad hoc networks offered stations greater variety of programming, although network-affiliated stations were somewhat limited in the amount of nonnetwork programming they could accept without raising the wrath of their mother network.

Transition 5: FCC Deregulation, Mid-1980s

The current FCC chairperson, Mark Fowler, is committed to deregulating broadcasting as much as possible, a stance quite the opposite of that held by the FCC during its era of intervention in the 1970s. The FCC has recently relinquished some of its early forms of restrictive regulation of the networks and created new avenues of entrepreneurialism for those with enough money to play the game.

One such form of deregulation has been to expand the limit of corporate television station ownership from seven to twelve stations. Furthermore UHF stations, because they do not typically attract as many viewers as VHF stations, count as only one-half of a station in the scheme of ownership. Consequently it is possible for a corporation to own as many as twenty-four (UHF) television stations across the country.

While this ruling affords Ad hoc networks a greater opportunity to expand their services and opens uncharted territories for independent producers, it also allows the already powerful networks to further their strong hold on the television industry. Each network can now reach 25 percent of the total television audience through its twelve owned and operated stations alone. As a result, the networks not only collect the national advertiser's fee (as it would for all network program distribution) but receive the income from local advertiser fees sold by the station and do not need to pay the station for carrying network programming.

It is no surprise, then, that television stations are currently being bought and sold for enormous prices and at breakneck speed. Boston's WCVB-TV was recently bought for $450 million, more than doubling in value in only three years. Los Angeles' KTLA-TV sold for $510 million in 1985, more than doubling in value in only two years. In Houston, the eleventh largest media market, KHOU-TV sold for $342 million in 1984. Even in smaller markets, such as Minneapolis, KITN-TV sold for $25 million, over twice its going price just sixteen months earlier. Consequently owning a television station stands to be more lucrative than ever. Because of the escalating prices, however, only large corporations can afford to partake in these endeavors. As was the case with program production for the networks, where the smaller production houses were slowly eliminated from participation, small-time broadcasters are being pushed out of the industry by large conglomerates.

Another form of deregulation focuses on program production. The FCC loosened the financial interest and syndication ruling, permitting the networks once again to engage in prime-time program production and ownership, albeit on a much more limited basis than was previously permitted. Once again the networks are given permission to compete with producers for the valuable commodity of prime time. And once again, the networks have some voice in the well-being of syndication-dependent independent stations.

The Outlook

Although cable and various forms of new technology have not yet dramatically transformed the television industry, it is safe to say that yet another transition is in the making. Proponents of direct broadcast satellite claim that they will render the networks obsolete by providing households with programming direct from production houses via satellite transmissions. Similarly efforts are being made to bypass network programming and off-network program syndication through the creation of regional television, in which either individual television stations or a corporation that owns several stations contribute to the overall cost of program production. In return they receive limited partnership of the program and a network-quality program for a cost similar to local production. Clearly the power of cable is not to be undermined when it reaches its estimated 65 percent national saturation in 1990.

There is every indication that the evolution of the relationship among the four key components of the industry is continuing and prone to dramatic change and the introduction of other key components. The industry is still in a state of flux, but it is certain that television will remain one of the most active and volatile communication industries in the future.

References

Brown, L. 1982. "Are the Networks Dinosaurs?" *Channels of Communication* 2(2):26–29, 57.

———. 1986a. "Running the Numbers." *Channels of Communication* 6(1):72.

———. 1986b. "Running the Numbers." *Channels of Communication* 6(2):72.

Brown, M. 1986. "The Real Action in TV—Station Trading." *Channels of Communication* 5(5):25.

Federal Communication Commission. 1970. "Amendment of Part 73 of the Commission's Rules and Regulations with Respect to Competition and Responsibility in Network Television Broadcasting." Washington, D.C.: Government Printing Office.

Guttenplan, D. D. 1986. "Syndication's New Superteam." *Channels of Communication* 5(5):58–61.

Newcomb, H., and R. S. Alley. 1983. *The Producer's Medium*. New York: Oxford University Press.

Reel, A. F. 1979. *The Networks: How They Stole the Show*. New York: Charles Scribner's Sons.

Wellesley, A. 1980. "Behind TV's 'Angelgate' Mess: How Shady Deals Work—and Why Hollywood Loves Them." *Panorama* 1(9):34–39, 93.

Zuckerman, L., and L. Brown. 1983. "Autumn of the Networks' Reign." *Channels of Communication* 3(3):45–48.

MTM'S PAST AND FUTURE

David Marc

David Marc is an assistant professor of American studies at
Brandeis University. He is the author of *Demographic Vistas:
Television in American Culture* and has written on television
and popular culture for many publications, including the *Village Voice, Video Magazine,* and *American Film.*

Reprinted from *The Atlantic,* November, 1984. Used by permission of the
author.

Cable penetration is slowly bringing about the Balkanization of the
American television audience. That audience, roughly identical to the U.S.
population at large, is gradually declaring its independence from three-network cultural hegemony and reconstituting itself into dozens of smaller but
more cleanly defined "taste culture" viewing groups. Whereas once CBS,
NBC, and ABC were the Sears, the Montgomery Ward, and the K-Mart in a
shopping center without boutiques, now the industry offers viewers opportunities for more personalized services.

For thirty years the Big Three could assume that at any given prime-time
moment, more than 90 percent of those watching television would be tuned
in to one of their programs. These days, however, it is not unusual for the A.
C. Nielsen Company to report the total network share of the viewing audience as less than 75 percent. With HBO, Showtime, and the Movie Channel
offering recent Hollywood features, with ESPN, USA, and SportsChannel
running every athletic event from junior-college lacrosse to all-star heavy-
weight wrestling, with Bravo and Arts & Entertainment importing *le cinéma*
and the opera, with The Nashville Network producing C&W sitcoms (have
you seen "I-40 *Paradise*"?), with CMTV featuring Merle Haggard videos
(that's right, CMTV), and with the Christian Broadcasting Network and the
national Christian Network dueling with "800" numbers for the audience's
very soul, what are the odds for survival of the quaint cop shows, doc shows,
and sitcoms that viewers dependent on antennae have been watching during
these early years of telecasting? The familiar programming genres constitute
the Greek drama of television. Will the fragmentation of the audience force
them into a state of suspended animation in the reruns?

Despite the multichannel cable converters that are becoming unremark-
able furniture in American living rooms, the major television-production
companies are still forced to sell their wares in a preposterously narrow marketplace dominated by three likeminded customers. None of the cable net-

works can easily afford the high cost of independently produced episodic television drama.

The predicament of MTM Enterprises during this transitional period is illuminating. MTM has produced what is arguably the most interesting and innovative collection of weekly series in the thirty-eight-year history of network television. Since the company's inception it has been harassed by network censors for the post-Victorianism of its scripts and characters. It has also been under constant pressure to attract the larger audiences necessary for mass marketing, yet despite these constraints, it has not taken advantage of the new technological opportunities to circumvent the three-network system.

In 1978 the studio attempted its first end run on the networks by putting together a series for public television. Although "Going Home Again"—the continuing story of an affluent Santa Barbara family set amid the cultural and social changes of the years following the assassination of John F. Kennedy—was ambitious in conception, it never progressed beyond the pilot stage. Some members of the Corporation for Public Broadcasting may have looked askance at the notion of committing any of public television's limited resources to a successful commercial studio, no matter how good its reputation. Moreover, the corporation refused to commit itself to a set price for each episode. Geared up for high-overhead commercial production, the studio was unable to proceed on such uncertain ground, and the project died.

Perhaps the most obvious strategy for MTM would be to establish itself as a supplier of programs to cable TV. Indeed, Nielsen studies point to an inordinate number of pay-cable subscribers among the audiences for MTM's current shows. The studio's vice-president in charge of public relations, Larry Bloustein, asserts that "a look at 'Hill Street Blues,' 'St. Elsewhere,' or any of today's MTM shows could be a look at the cable shows of tomorrow."

The pay-cable vendors—those that charge a fee beyond the one for basic service—generally sell themselves as movie exhibitors. Nevertheless, they have displayed some curiosity about series television. In 1982, for example, HBO made an effort to pick up "Taxi," after that sitcom was canceled by ABC. "Taxi" was not an MTM property, but it was created by James L. Brooks, Stan Daniels, David Davis, and Ed. Weinberger—all veterans of the old "Mary Tyler Moore Show" production team. Although NBC, the last-place broadcast network, easily outbid HBO, the first-place cable network, and won the rights to the series, the ice had been broken on cable's interest in series television. More recently "Brothers," the first made-for-pay-cable sitcom, had its premiere on Showtime. The series is written by Weinberger, Daniels, and yet another MTM veteran, David Lloyd.

Thus far MTM has not been as lucky in the wired world as its alumni have. Harlan Kleiman, a well-known cable-industry operative, was hired by the company in 1983 to develop cable projects. His tenure, however, was brief. The economic conditions of the still-growing cable industry prevented him from striking any deals. As it is, a one-hour episode of "Hill Street Blues" costs approximately $875,000 to produce, and NBC pays MTM only $800,000 for its trouble. Whatever profit the production company makes will have to come from syndication of the reruns, which cannot begin until 1987. MTM might be lucky to get $400,000 per episode from a cable service. The figure is likely to increase as cable subscriptions proliferate, but in the meantime the company's refusal to compromise its highly respected production quality to suit the constraints of a cable budget prevents it from cracking the market.

In yet another effort to come up with an alternative means of distribution, MTM has tried to develop theatrical movie projects. So far, only one picture has been produced: "A Little Sex," starring Tim Matheson, Kate Capshaw, and Edward Herrmann, and directed by Bruce Paltrow, the executive producer of "St. Elsewhere." Though the film didn't do much business at the box office in 1982, when it was released, it has since become popular with cable-movie audiences.

According to Bloustein, the dominant sentiment in the studio is that MTM ought to continue to fight for space on the prime-time network schedules. He says that the greater artistic freedom that playing to an upscale audience of cable subscribers, public-television viewers, or moviegoers might offer could not compensate for the loss of the chance to speak to the national consciousness; the latter is still possible only on ABC, CBS, and NBC.

MTM's history is more or less concurrent with a broad shift in American marketing from the building of mass audiences to the cultivating of class target groups. The studio reflects this evolving process not only in the problems involved in distributing its shows but also in the content of the shows themselves. By looking closely at several of MTM's series, one can find a dramatic concordance to the recent history of American consumer culture.

MTM was founded in 1970 by Mary Tyler Moore, Arthur Price, and Grant Tinker. In less than a dozen years it created such situation comedies as "The Mary Tyler Moore Show," "The Bob Newhart Show," "Rhoda," and "WKRP in Cincinnati," and such hour-long drama series as "Lou Grant," "The White Shadow," "Hill Street Blues," and "St. Elsewhere." MTM's shows have not all enjoyed astounding ratings, but the successful ones have been distinguished by their consistent ability to capture the interest of well-educated people—a segment of the audience that tends not to be enthusiastic about television's standard offerings. There isn't another studio in Hollywood with a comparable track record.

Norman Lear became a household name in the 1970s as the behind-the-scenes mastermind of "All in the Family," "The Jeffersons," "Maude," and a half-dozen other revisionist portrayals of an American family that had become stranded in the 1960s—one eternally obsessed with race relations, menopause, inflation, and the defense budget. During those same years, however, MTM was creating a comedy of manners in which the nuclear family was conspicuous by its absence. Allan Burns and James L. Brooks, who created "The Mary Tyler Moore Show," had originally imagined Mary as a divorcée. In 1970, however, CBS was still hitting the Nielsen top ten with wacky widows ("Here's Lucy," "The Doris Day Show") and did not believe that fans were ready to accept a sitcom heroine who had renounced sacred vows. Michael Dann, the network's programming chief at the time, told Burns, Brooks, and Tinker that his own research had proved conclusively that there were three types of people Americans didn't want in their situation comedies: people from New York, people with moustaches, and people who were divorced. In this, the first of MTM's many censorship battles, the studio capitulated to the network. Mary arrived at the WJM newsroom in September of 1970 in the guise of a never-wed single bouncing back from a broken long-term romance. (It was not until 1975 that Norman Lear, always the politician, decisively cracked the divorce barrier, with "One Day at a Time.") But as it turned out, the significance of "The Mary Tyler Moore Show" lay not so much in Mary's reason for being single as in her ability to survive—and even flourish—without the encouragement of a family. Woodstock Nation had become Planet of the Singles; the Age of Soup for One had begun.

Miss Moore's transformation was a watershed in American teleculture. No longer married to Rob Petrie (Dick Van Dyke), Laura Petrie of suburban New Rochelle re-emerged as Mary Richards of gentrified Minneapolis. The Petries had flaunted New Frontier credentials: they were unabashedly young, attractive, and educated; they were friends with a Jew (Morey Amsterdam, no less); and Rob worked in middle management (as the chief writer for a prime-time comedy show) while his wife tended their single-family detached house and progressively brought-up child. "The Dick Van Dyke Show" is a missing link between "The Donna Reed Show" and "Three's Company." "The Mary Tyler Moore Show" is another. Mary Richards took an apartment for herself in the city, was the friend of a Jew, and worked as the associate producer of a six o'clock news show—a job that proved to be far less powerful and glamorous than its title suggested. In the signature montage, there was one exquisite shot of Mary reading the price on a plastic package of supermarket meat and looking up at the gods in exasperation. The long-suffering TV career woman—from Ann Sothern in "Private Secretary" to Sally Rogers in "Dick Van Dyke"—was redeemed in the beautiful but familiar, capable but human, compassionate but logical Mary Richards. Mary transcended not only the model moms of the "Father Knows Best/Leave It to Beaver" era but also the more recent efforts at witches (Samantha), genies (Jeannie), and dingbats (Edith) that had replaced them. Unlike Marlo Thomas in "That Girl," Mary didn't need a steady boyfriend to define her sexual identity. As if to emphasize the point, she had an affair with "That Girls'" eternal fiancé, Ted Bessell, which ended after only a few episodes.

On "The Mary Tyler Moore Show," family was eclipsed by support group. Rhoda (Valerie Harper), who, like Al Jolson in *The Jazz Singer*, had forsaken New York ghetto life for the lure of the American West, was the perfectly imperfect *upstairsnik* for a splendid midwestern shiksa like Mary. Though stylistically at odds, the two shared a point of view on the bread-and-butter issues of the heart. Their emotional solidarity served to underline the trendy, pretentious silliness of their married downstairs neighbor and landlady, Phyllis Lindstrom (Cloris Leachman). In a reversal of sitcom tradition, the single women enjoyed an active, fulfilling relationship and their married friend was the odd one out. Mary's friendship with her coworker Murray (Gavin MacLeod) introduced to television the notion that a relationship between a woman and a man could be nonsexual without being asexual. In a sitcom of the 1950s or 1960s, if a married man was seen merely talking to an attractive single woman, it was grounds for his wife to pack a suitcase and go directly to her mother's house for the duration of the episode. But Murray's wife, Marie, didn't seem to mind his office friendship; in fact, she liked Mary. Lou Grant (Ed Asner) was a father figure, to be sure, but his marital problems (culminating in a midseries divorce), his bottle, and his less-than-superhuman capabilities prevented the specter of Robert Young from rearing its condescending head. Ted Baxter (Ted Knight) was among the show's formidable sitcom innovations, though the opportunities offered by the character in the early episodes were never fully realized. True hate, as one can find it in almost any modern office, remained an emotion beyond the purview of the sitcom, and thus Murray's exchanges with Ted never transcended witty repartee.

The "Mary Tyler Moore Show"—like most of the other sitcoms and dramas that MTM has produced since—took place in a white, middle-class, metropolitan America in which idealistic urges and ironic reflexes created a confusion of lost hopes and found ambitions. Years before the movie *The Big Chill* was released, the survivors of that same fallen post-sixties world were characters in MTM's television shows. Rhoda (still following Jolson's path) returned to New York. She got married; then she got divorced; then she turned her attention to her career. The widowed Phyllis, cocky and incompetent, moved away to San Francisco to start a new life. Bob Newhart, the "button-down" humorist of the pre-Beatles world, reemerged in the 1970s with a Ph.D. in psychology, offering group therapy at popular prices. No member of the group seemed to make any progress—least of all Bob, who would doggedly return to his stylish Chicago Gold Coast apartment only to find Bill Daily (an astronaut on "I Dream of Jeannie," a civilian airline navigator on this show) raiding his frost-free refrigerator in a bourgeois reprise of Ed Norton's assault on Ralph Kramden's icebox in "The Honeymooners." Bob's wife, Suzanne Pleshette, had her career in teaching to worry about and could offer her husband no better solace than the admonition "Physician, heal thyself." Like WJM in Minneapolis, "WRKP in Cincinnati" was staffed by attractive, reasonable, even admirable people, with the Ted-like Herb Tarlek (Frank Bonner) thrown in just to keep things irritating and honest. Despite such excellent personnel—or perhaps because of them—WKRP (again like WJM) was a loser in the (fictional) ratings. One can suppose that WKRP's program director, Andy (Gary Sandy), was meant to be a male Mary. The character, however, lacked an issue, such as was implicit in the feminist thrust of Mary's independence, and never found direction. Despite his good looks and modern heart of gold, Andy got lost in the glare of Loni Anderson's sudden pin-up stardom and the more exotic personalities of the station's disc jockeys, Dr. Johnny Fever (Howard Hesseman) and Venus Flytrap (Tim Reid).

The sitcom, which for many people had epitomized all that was distasteful and moronic in television—and in mass culture in general—achieved a kind of maturity in the early and middle 1970s, though this "golden age" did not last the decade. If Norman Lear was the Emile Zola of the genre, and if "M*A*S*H" gave the lie to the old wisdom that left-wing politics won't play in Peoria, the MTM shows contributed to the genre a new configuration of social relations. Whereas once the family had been the anchor of social being, in MTM America there were few marriages (and some of those ended in divorce) and fewer children. Dating, formerly an activity reserved for teenagers, became a way of social existence for adults. Money was shown to be tougher to come by than it had been for Ozzie Nelson or Ward Cleaver, but a genteel life was still available for those who were willing to work hard for it. What's more, in the 1960s, America had invented and perfected the notion of "life-style," and therefore had become a much better place in which to spend one's money and be happy. In short, what is now called the Yuppie— the young urban professional—was predicted, perhaps partially created, by the studio that had chosen a meowing kitten for its symbol.

Few weekly series are according the honor of being brought to a macrodenouement. Dr. Richard Kimble achieved the satisfaction of seeing the one-armed man confess to the murder of Mrs. Kimble and then die at the hands of Lieutenant Gerard in "The Fugitive." But most shows are too busy praying for renewal to produce this kind of climactic episode. When Miss Moore announced that despite respectable ratings she had decided to terminate production of the series at the end of the 1976–1977 season, MTM gave narrative closure to "The Mary Tyler Moore Show" with a farewell half-hour in which a new owner bought WJM and fired everyone in the newsroom—save Ted. The basic unfairness of the world was reiterated as the grand punch line of the comedy. Irony won out over justice, as it often does in the real world.

Institutions are heartless and cold, and all a modern professional can do is add a line to the old résumé and seek the protection of another corporate body.

In the diaspora from Minneapolis that followed, MTM once again broke with tradition by creating television's first cross-genre spin-off, "Lou Grant," for the 1977–1978 season. This new show pointed the way to MTM's future of socially concerned hour-long dramas set amid the frustrating perplexities of the American inner city. Much to MTM's credit, the studio became a source of issue-oriented episodic television at a time when most of its competitors were wrapped up in negotiations for the rights to comic-book superheroes. To be sure, touches of the humor that MTM had perfected in its sitcoms survived the studio's shift from the comedy of manners to social realism. Lou Grant was as much at home trading one-liners with Billie and Rossi and even Mrs. Pynchon as he was at practicing socially conscious journalism. Nevertheless, the balance of the show clearly was tipped in favor of frank concern about the problems of racism, poverty, ecological survival, equal justice, and so on.

"The White Shadow," the story of a white victim of NBA knee problems (Ken Howard) who became the basketball coach at a predominantly black inner-city Los Angeles high school, had its premiere on CBS the following season. Both "The White Shadow" and "Lou Grant" were in harmony with a set of values shared by most Americans to the left of Scrooge McDuck and to the right of Che Guevara. And both shows won effusive praise from many critics and educators, who saw them as lonely defenders of social morality on TV schedules dominated by warmed-over slapstick ("Laverne & Shirley"), ritual car chases ("The Dukes of Hazzard"), and pop video journalism ("That's Incredible!"). Given the muckraking concerns of "Lou Grant" and the integrationist didacticism of "The White Shadow," the attitude of the shows could be loosely described as "liberal." At the same time, however, both were quite conservative in form. Each week a familiar, flawed hero encountered a contemporary social problem that adversely affected those around him. By the end of the episode, the problem was alleviated at the local level, but there were wistful references to its persistence in the larger scheme of things. "Lou Grant" and "The White Shadow," coming as they did half a dozen years after much of their audience had retired from political activism, can be seen as romantic, escapist fantasies for deskbound Yuppies.

"Hill Street Blues," MTM's next important effort, appeared on NBC in January 1981. Fred Silverman, then the president of NBC television, had asked two members of the MTM team, Steven Bochco and Michael Kozoll, for a traditional police shoot-'em-up set in Fort Apache—the South Bronx precinct notorious for its high crime rate. At first Bochco and Kozoll balked at the suggestion. "We didn't want to do it. We were sick of doing cop shows," Bochco told a writer for *TV Guide*. But Silverman, who had performed the "miracle" of ABC's rise to first place in the 1970s, was sorely in need of some magic for NBC. He promised that the network would give MTM some room to breathe in terms of sex, violence, and even narrative continuity. What has resulted is a powerful synthesis of "Naked City," "Dallas," "The Edge of Night," and "Dragnet," shot partially with a hand-held camera. In its studied vacillation between idealism and cynicism, "Hill Street Blues" has almost singlehandedly relieved the television cop show of its conventional obsession with symmetrical justice and has thrust it into the gap between modern and postmodern art.

Captain Frank Furillo (Daniel J. Travanti) is the picture of educated, well-tailored, middle-management success. Furillo is the point of identification for the relatively wealthy, noticeably well-educated, and predominantly male audience that "Hill Street Blues" has attracted, but the perspective of his wife, Joyce Davenport (Veronica Hamel), is of equal importance. Joyce is a public defender who sees no conflict in her love for both Miranda and Furillo. The two previously divorced, workaholic professionals have come together as the middle-class Everycouple for jogging, computer-crunching, white-wine-sipping America. As in all MTM series, heroic modern Americans are suspicious of utopian panaceas but never back off from their immediate social responsibilities; the latter is apparently a sin committed only by wimps, psychotics, the underprivileged, and the overprivileged. "Hill Street Blues" is racially and sexually integrated beyond the aspirations of "The Mod Squad" and goes out of its way to traverse the peaks and valleys of the American class system. But Pizza Man and the Counselor for the Defense are the show's centers of consciousness.

The working-class cops—Renko, Bobby Hill, Lucy Bates, and Coffey—are idealized visions of blue-collar virtue and vice. Though a bit rougher than middle-class propriety might dictate, they are capable of great impulsive courage. One way that these good yeomen are distinguished from the heroic MTM gentlefolk is that they don't know a thing about how to handle money. The comic subplots of many episodes make this point clear: Bobby Hill hits the lottery and squanders the pile, the cops invest in a narcoleptic nightclub comedian named Vic Hitler, and so on.

At the end of the 1980–1981 season "Hill Street Blues" had such low ratings that it seemed sure to be cancelled. The show won an unprecedented eight Emmy Awards, however. Languishing in third place, NBC renewed the series and heaped congratulations upon itself for this demonstration of its commitment to quality in the face of ratings anemia. But the renewal of "Hill Street" may have been more than a charitable donation to American culture. Though "Hill Street's" total audience was small by prime-time standards, the series showed remarkable strength with certain groups of viewers, including POMs (professionals, owners, and managers), the college-educated, those making $30,000 a year or more, and—perhaps most important to the networks these days—those subscribing to one or more pay-cable channels. Was there really such a thing as a weekly series—a cop show—that people would rather watch than HBO?

In the spring of 1982, a year after Grant Tinker replaced Fred Silverman as president of NBC, MTM's next series for that network—"St. Elsewhere"—went into production, under the supervision of Tinker's son, Mark. Meanwhile, the total audience for "Hill Street" had grown appreciably during that show's second season, prompting speculation that the show's early Yuppie following had flexed its "opinion-maker" muscles and was leading the masses to "Hill Street." NBC went out of its way in its promotional campaign for the 1982–1983 season to associate "St. Elsewhere" with "Hill Street," hoping that the snowballing popularity of the high-IQ cop show could be duplicated in the doc-show genre.

"St. Elsewhere's" upscale audience is comparable to "Hill Street's." According to Nielsen, a "St. Elsewhere" episode draws only about 83 percent of the viewers that a typical prime-time show can be expected to draw. However, that smaller pool of viewers is likely to contain more POMs, college graduates, and pay-TV subscribers than the average prime-time show's audience. The main difference between the audience of "Hill Street Blues" and that of "St. Elsewhere" is gender. While "Hill Street" delivers a high concentration of Yuppie men, "St. Elsewhere" delivers an even higher concentration of Yuppie women. And in comparison with the average prime-time show, a typical "St. Elsewhere" episode is likely to draw 60 percent more college-educated or professional women, according to Nielsen's *National Audience Demographics*.

Tom Fontana and John Masius, two producers on the "St. Elsewhere" staff, point out that St. Eligius, the teaching hospital in Boston where the series is set, is a workplace very much in the MTM tradition: WJM had the lowest-rated news show of any station in Minneapolis; WKRP was a marginal Cincinnati radio station teetering on the brink of bankruptcy; "The White Shadow's" Carver High was an underfunded Los Angeles ghetto school; Lou Grant struggled to keep *The Trib* alive in the age of television; "Hill Street" is the most dangerous and embattled precinct in Innercity, U.S.A. And so it is with St. Eligius. The building, a ponderous but friendly Second Empire confection, sits crumbling and decaying next to an elevated subway. Inside, a staff of hard-working, compassionate, witty, and ironic middle-class Americans (and their allies) show what they can do despite the odds. They are not the omnipotent, eternally understanding superpeople whom lifelong viewers might expect to find on the staff of a TV hospital; they blunder in ways that must make the AMA shudder. At St. Eligius performance does not always match intention, and sometimes intention isn't all that admirable. The doctors—like the viewers—spend a good deal of their time fretting about money and their sex lives. According to Fontana, "The personalities of the characters in the MTM shows are very much like the personalities of the people who run around the [MTM] lot." Masius says, "It's like they—and we—are all doing time together."

The show is extraordinary in nighttime television for its decentralization of persona. The doctors, support staff, and administrators are organized mainly along generational lines. The old guard is dominated by Dr. Westphall (Ed Flanders), Dr. Craig (William Daniels), and Dr. Auschlander (Norman Lloyd). While all three are exemplary practitioners of the art/science to which they have given their lives, Craig's suburban Republican excesses and Auschlander's struggle to survive liver cancer leave Westphall, the chief of medicine, at the antiheroic/heroic center. Though certainly no Yuppie, Craig's impatience with anything less than "quality" surely rings a bell for a subculture willing to pay a dollar for a chocolate-chip cookie. But Craig's demands for excellence occasionally carry mean-spirited and even racist overtones, removing him from the heroic realm. Auschlander, for his part, is a professed agnostic whose reminiscences of childhood egg creams on the Lower East Side of Manhattan suggest the surviving spirit—and values—of the old socialist, immigrant left. Auschlander's traits are admirable or at least human enough to elicit sympathy, but he is offered to the viewer as a dying (if precious) echo of another time. Bruce Paltrow, "St. Elsewhere's" executive producer, describes the workaholic manager Westphall as the "soul of the hospital." Standing squarely in the political center, a widower with a college-age daughter and an autistic son, the *pater familias* of the young doctors, Westphall eclipses Frank Furillo in his ability to sail a sinking ship: he, too, is the manager as modern hero.

In the second echelon of the hospital's administrative hierarchy is a group of characters who are rarely central to the important story lines: Dr. Cavanero (Cynthia Sikes), Dr. Caldwell (Mark Harmon), and city-hospital liaison Joan Halloran (Nancy Stafford). Caldwell, the dashing plastic surgeon, and Halloran, the woman from city hall, carry on an affair of Furillo-Davenport proportions. Cavanero struggles with a contemporary identity crisis: Am I a dedicated doctor with no time to be a swinging single or just an old maid in progress? This group functions like a kind of emotional DMZ for the greater personality conflicts that erupt between the senior doctors and the residents.

The lives of the young residents are where the attitudes of sitcom, soap opera, and social drama intersect with maximum complexity. Dr. Morrison (David Morse) wears flannel shirts and corduroy jeans, the traditional costume of his native Pacific Northwest. The early episodes of the series flattered Morrison's sensitivity, indicating that this all-American boy might become the center of identification. "If network Broadcast Standards had its way, we'd be mostly doing Marcus Welby–Steve Kiley scripts for Westphall and Morrison," John Masius claims. (Indeed, "St. Elsewhere" has had running battles with NBC's censors, over such topics as the use of the word *testicular* and the portrayal of Irish partisans; the network has consistently asked for more-traditional and happier scripts.) But Morrison has turned out to be no Steve Kiley, despite NBC's desires. His wife died in a freak accident soon after the birth of little Pete. More surprising than this is Morrison's less than superb competence as a physician. Morrison's strong suit is bedside manner—no small thing, especially on television—but his diagnostic skills are mediocre and he is frequently indecisive. In one episode he was actually let go from the staff by an evaluation committee composed of Westphall, Craig, and Auschlander, and was saved only when bulimic Dr. Armstrong (Kim Miyori) killed herself after the courts failed to convict Dr. White (Terence Knox), who had raped her.

The other residents are a cross-section of Yuppie possibilities: Ehrlich (Ed Begley, Jr.) is a blond California space case who was brought up by his aunt (Louise Lasser!) and who now serves as surgeon's apprentice to the dictatorial Dr. Craig. Fiscus (Howie Mandel) is a wiseguy of Bill Murray magnitude, the son of Lithuanian immigrants, a Red Sox fanatic, and a crackerjack emergency-room doctor to boot. Chandler (Denzel Washington) is a black doctor with Ivy League speech and manners whose preppy sensibility is caused much anguish by the shuck and jive of Luther (Eric Laneuville), an orderly from the Community. Cathy Martin (Barbara Whinnery), a pathologist straight out of "The Addams Family," brings life to the house of death by making love with her friends right on the autopsy table.

MTM's good track record with the educated and the well-to-do is a liability to advertisers who need sheer numbers. The networks set prices according to the size and makeup of the audiences delivered. A show with an audience that is relatively small but specifically desired by advertisers may cost as much as a show with an audience that is much larger but less easily categorized. "Hill Street" was the first series in television history to get a regular advertising commitment from Mercedes-Benz, but it is not a good buy for General Foods and other bread-and-butter sponsors: the price is too high for the numbers delivered. Likewise, if "Hill Street's" audience were larger and more diverse, the show would not be a good buy for Mercedes. Why should Mercedes make a pitch to millions of viewers who can't afford its product?

Officials at MTM play down the idea that their shows are aimed at any "target" market. "Television must be a mass medium, and TV shows must have mass appeal," Lary Bloustein says. "A show can't survive on network with only cult appeal. Think of it this way: "St. Elsewhere" may have a core of cult supporters among the wealthy or the well educated or whoever it is they're saying. But if that's true, those upscale viewers aren't likely to be as loyal to television watching as, let us say, the audience of "Dynasty." People with money and education like to do other things, like go to the theater and the ballet and even talk to each other. The point is, we need all the "Dynasty" viewers we can get—people who watch a lot of TV and don't miss their favorite shows week after week."

The survival of "Hill Street" and "St. Elsewhere" notwithstanding, it seems to be becoming harder and harder for MTM to beat the marketing demands that are probably inevitable when advertisers, rather than viewers, pay for television shows. MTM had not contributed a single new show to the networks this fall [1984]—a decision based at least partially on the disastrous failure of its terrifically expensive "Bay City Blues" series, which was canceled by NBC after only four episodes last season. A minor-league baseball epic in the "Hill Street/St. Elsewhere" mold, the series had solid MTM credentials: a sensitive, complex, divorced, middle-aged team manager and a bed-wetting, clutch-hitting left fielder. "The Duck Factory," a sitcom set in a Hollywood cartoon studio, was tried by NBC last year [1983] as a midseason replacement, but it, too, was taken off the air.

For all of the network system's faults, the only material cost to a viewer of CBS, NBC, and ABC over the past thirty-eight years has been a few pennies on each month's electric bill. But television is gradually catching up with clean drinking water, noncarcinogenic foods, and a decent place to live: if you want the good stuff, you're probably going to have to pay for it.

CONTROVERSY AND COMMERCIAL TELEVISION GATEKEEPING

Patricia Geist
Harvey Jassem

Patricia Geist is an assistant professor of communication at the University of Hartford. Her research interests include decision making, identification, and control in contemporary organizations.

Harvey Jassem is an associate professor of communication at the University of Hartford. His research interests include media policy and the future of telecommunication.

In recent years, there has been growing concern about objectionable television programming. Faced with increased competition for viewers from cable television and home video, changing audience mores, and bolder program producers, television stations are constantly dealing with difficult programming decisions. Stations in many cities make literally million dollar programming decisions that affect both their audience and their bottom lines. We recently interviewed program managers, representing a wide array of commercial television stations, to gather information about their decisions regarding what people get to see on television. To understand television gatekeeping when programs are deemed problematic or controversial, one must examine the sources of programs, the warnings signaling controversy, and the ways in which stations handle the problems.

Sources of Programs

Television programs come to television stations from several sources. Stations may produce their own or ready-made programs from syndicators or networks. When television stations create and produce their own programs, the stations are in full control of the programs and ensure that nothing inappropriate is incorporated into the show.

Most television stations buy the rights to air programs made by someone else. These syndicated programs include movies, old network shows, and some new programs such as "P.M. Magazine" and game shows such as "The Wheel of Fortune." A third source of programming is the television networks, which pay the stations to carry their programs, with commercials included. In the case of syndicated and network programs, the television station generally receives complete programs suitable for airing all over the nation. Although syndicated programs generally may be edited, network programs usually may not be edited by the station.

For the most part, the program manager does not screen or make gatekeeping decisions about individual programs or episodes or even parts of programs. On occasion, however, he or she does. Indeed, on occasion, programs are screened, and gatekeeping decisions are made by or with the program manager's superiors. Thus the question to be asked is, What causes some programs to be culled out for review, and what criteria are used in evaluating them?

Warnings Signaling Controversy

The general criterion of potential offensiveness is utilized in making programming decisions. Content areas that typically raise concern regarding offensiveness include sex, nudity, violence, language, abortion, feminine hygiene products, racism, and religion.

Information about potentially problematic programs comes to the program managers from a variety of sources. Because most programs do not originate at the individual television station, program managers rely heavily on outside sources to alert them to such programming. These sources include program suppliers such as syndicators and networks, special interest groups, the press, and the audience. Program managers may also be alerted to problematic program content by internal station sources such as the film editor, sales manager, general manager, producers, or corporate officers.

Network

In the case of a network offering, the network often notifies its affiliates of a potentially problematic program and prefeeds the program to affiliates so they can review it prior to its scheduled showing. Indeed there is an extraordinary reliance on the networks to flag their own shows. The networks alert stations by telephone or TWX telex that an upcoming network program contains material the stations might be concerned about. In addition, the network often feeds the program to the affiliates before the airdate to give stations an opportunity to decide whether and how to handle the program. There is a general, though not necessarily unanimous, feeling that, as one program manager put it, the networks "are very good about that, and we do rely on them doing that." Another told us that the network her station was affiliated with generally flags controversial programs:

> They generally say we think you should view this before airing it, we think you should show it to community leaders who are involved in this problem. . . . You should view it first and see how you feel about it, you should bring law enforcement officials in and have them view it, let people know that there's going to be tough talk, there's going to be tough scenes, or whatever. . . . They let us know a month or two in advance.

In most cases, we found that program managers do not have a great deal to worry about with respect to network-supplied programs: "All stations affiliated with a network would say, [the network] is going to run it, it must be all right. Their censors are probably a lot stricter than ours. They have people and that's all they do. So they say if this goes through why are we worried?" Such confidence is sometimes unwarranted, however.

Syndicator

Off-network syndicated programs rarely present a problem because they passed through network review years earlier. However, program managers do rely upon syndicators to flag potentially controversial programs. Syndicated programs (and movies) are also generally accompanied by story synopses. If a synopsis hints that sensitive areas are dealt with, the program manager or the film editors review the episode or movie. Movie ratings serve the same flagging function. Not only are movies with R or PG-13 ratings more carefully screened than their G counterparts, but so too are the trailers or ads for such films.

Program managers also look to the source of the program for clues about possible or likely content. Programs produced or supplied to the station by political, some religious, or special interest groups are often routinely checked by the station before they are accepted for airing. One program manager remarked that "one of the flags could be just the fact that it's paid programming. People are buying airtime from you instead of you paying them a license fee. . . . Most often . . . they are buying that time because they are trying to solicit funds in one way or another, or present a point of view, which is really not what we are looking for."

Press

Should the network or syndicator fail to flag a program, the program manager may be alerted to a potential problem by the press (popular and/or trade). As one respondent said, "All the TV guides and trades talk about upcoming programming months in advance, especially what's controversial so you know what's coming. I can't think of any time I did not know that something controversial was coming up." When alerted by the press, the program manager (or editor) often reviews syndicated or local programs and may ask the network for an early feed for station review. One program manager related the case of a CBS docudrama that dealt with the Atlanta child murders. Serious questions about the program were raised in the *New York Times*, the *Washington Post*, and other broadcast stations before the program aired. This program manager asked and received from CBS an early feed of the program, which he screened. Programs that present a potential problem are generally reviewed by a team consisting of program manager, editor(s), and general manager. Their decision is based on their assessment of local audience tastes. Some program managers noted that different cities and different regions have different tastes, and hence different standards apply.

Audience

Audience responses to programming are recorded and acted upon, providing another signal for concern about a program. One program manager in a fairly large market noted that if he received twenty letters on a particular program or issue, he would carefully examine the program or issue; if he received one hundred letters asking for something, he would probably acquiesce. The program manager of a small market station noted that it was "very unusual to get more than three responses in letter form objecting to a show or saying 'we didn't like that show.'" Seven or eight letters, he continued, say "it's out of the ordinary, there's something wrong; we have to do something. Now, had there been 20 letters we might have said 'O.K., we'll take it off right now.'"

Local Producers

Although most commercial television stations produce little of their own programming, when they do, their producers are in close contact with the program managers. Hence program managers generally know about and sometimes play a role in local productions during the production and pre-production stages. It is rare, then, for a program manager to be unpleasantly surprised by the problematic nature of content in a locally produced program.

Film Editors

Films are typically edited at the stations for matters of taste, length, and commercial insertions. Editors generally are instructed to share any potential problems they find with the program manager. Film editors who watch films and listen to the language make judgments about taste and editing based on the time the program will air and on published corporate and station policies or, more often, unpublished and unstated guidelines. A film editor who experiences difficulty in making the decision turns to the manager.

Program Manager

Once the program manager is alerted to the questionable content of a program, the decision of what to do typically rests with him or her. The program manager rarely makes the decision alone, however. Discussions with others inside and outside the station aid the program manager in making a final decision about such programs. In our study, we found that the discussions and decisions usually focus on several criteria, including concern for sex, profanity, politics, drug abuse, inappropriate program themes or timing, as well as the perceived values of coworkers and superiors. Program managers report heavy reliance on their instincts: One told us that:

> Instinct is the first thing. I think the number of years that you have worked with a place makes a difference. . . . You pretty well know your people [general manager, station manager] . . . you put yourself in their place: "What would they think?" Based on . . . years [of] experience . . . you know whether to say: "O.K., I better talk to them about it."

Over the years, program managers develop specific criteria they rely on to judge a program as potentially problematic. *Questionable material* is a generic phrase used to describe programs whose content goes beyond what is normally anticipated or tolerated by an audience. Poor timing is one of the specific components of questionable material most often cited by program managers in explaining past programming problems. In one example, the program manager noticed that a "Donohue" program on lesbian nuns was scheduled to be aired the day after Easter. In describing his response to the timing of this program, the program manager said:

> I just didn't feel it was appropriate timing to broadcast that kind of an issue on what amounted to and was part of a religious holiday. Schools were out that week. It was, in my mind, not a good day to carry that issue. If it had been two months later I wouldn't have cared at all.

In this instance, the program manager made the decision to flag the program on the basis of timing. He brought the program to the attention of others, including the network affiliate relations representative and the station's general manager. As a result of these discussions, the episode was replaced with a file tape, and the lesbian nun tape was put on the shelf for a later airdate.

Another incident involving timing and "Donohue" did not work out quite as well. Aired on the day after Thanksgiving when, as one program manager put it, "every school child in the world was home," this episode of the program included the broadcast of a live childbirth, "complete with intimate feminine parts." The program manager did not flag the program before it aired because the program's synopsis was vague and did not indicate the extent of the detail depicted. Calling it the "worst experience in my broadcasting life," the program manager explained that the program had "invaded what is normally a housewife and mother's world and when the children turn on the set, is she suddenly going to be embarrassed by an eight-year-old child saying to mommy, 'What's that?'"

Another example of poor timing illustrates a program manager's sensitivity to what might be in the best interest of broadcasters, if not viewers. In this case, a program manager alerted others to join with him in expressing the opinion that the movie "Spring Break" should not be aired. Although the problematic content in the film related to the excessive use of alcohol by teenagers, this manager suggested to the network's affiliate relations person that airing the film at that time would be inappropriate because broadcasters were fighting to maintain beer and wine advertising on television. The network decided to delete the film from its schedule. Such success in achieving changes in network programming plans are the exception rather than the rule, however. This same program manager noted that "networks are very stubborn about changing something. Once they make their minds up to do something, you have to move heaven and earth to get them to change."

Regarding matters of taste, program managers agree that they must be sensitive to the community their station serves. Thus, no single set of standards applies nationwide. Managers tell of making different decisions in different communities, what might be acceptable in one community might be considered poor taste in another. What constitutes important issues differs from community to community. One of the program manager's jobs is to know the community and program the station accordingly.

Controversy and Programming Decisions

Program manager concern for broadcasting content appears to be standard, though thresholds for what is or is not permissible vary. One program manager stated, "We are a guest in people's home, and so programming must not upset people or put people in a position of having to censor programming for the children." The manager qualified this statement by describing the distinction between judgments of controversy—objective, concrete, and usually political—and judgments of taste—subjective, not as strictly mandated, and usually involving individuals inside the station. The general criterion cited by program managers for making decisions regarding whether a program or part of a program is in good enough taste to be broadcast is its propensity to upset or offend the audience. Program managers want to preview programs that could potentially offend audience members. (Interestingly, none of the commercial broadcast station program managers noted the stress this philosophy puts on the First Amendment, which is designed to protect offensive speech.)

The problems presented by potentially offensive programs are handled in a multitude of ways, each with costs and benefits. Once a program is deemed problematic, the station may choose to run it as is and take a chance, it may decide not to air it at all, or it may run the program in an out-of-the-ordinary fashion (for example, with warnings or disclaimers preceding it, with the problematic material edited out, or with a discussion program following the program that deals with the controversial issues raised). In some cases, stations may decide to air the program later in the day when children are not likely to be in the audience or at a later date if local contexts or holidays make the program unsuitable for airing as originally scheduled.

Determining the best solution requires an assessment of the problem and a determination of the ability of the station to implement its desired solution. For example, if editing is deemed to be the ideal solution, the station may do that work if the program is one it owns or has purchased the rights to show from a syndicator (given the syndicator's or producer's permission to edit the program). (Editing, of course, may cause artistic or continuity problems.) In such cases, the film editors may edit the program or movie without involving the program manager or may discuss the work with the program manager prior to the final editing. In the case of a network-supplied program, however, station editing is not an option. The station may request that the network edit a program differently; it may even notify the network that unless certain changes are made, the station will not run the program, but ultimately the network or the program's producers make these editing decisions.

The networks are under the same pressure as the stations to attract a large audience without upsetting viewers; hence, they are interested in the comments of affiliates. But because they feed the identical program to each of their two hundred or so affiliates and because issues and standards differ in the markets served by their affiliates, the networks do not have programs reedited every time one or a few affiliates want it. The station's program manager is chiefly responsible for maintaining good relations with the network. Any serious station differences with the network are explained to the network by the program manager. Although the station has the right to refuse any network offering, neither the station nor the network views such refusals lightly. It is important for the network to have its programs and advertisements showcased nationally. If a station refuses to air a program, that decision creates problems for the network whose advertisers bought that market along with the others the network provided. The network's displeasure is of importance to the affiliate because the network affiliation contract is a major revenue asset. Networks might not renew their affiliation contract with an ornery station; similarly, they might increase the amount of financial compensation they give to a cooperative station. Several of the program managers we interviewed indicated that these elements were considered when dealing with their networks.

The overall station picture for dealing with programs that present controversy suggests that once the potential problem is noted, decision making involves more than the routine number of people at the station. Managers and editors evaluate the problem and attempt to reach consensus regarding a solution.

In general, then, the program manager is centrally located in the network of communicative interaction in terms of program decision making. Although the communicative network is not solidly or formally established, the findings paint a picture of the program manager as the individual who initiates the decision-making process as the result of acquired information. The information that stimulates decision making comes from a variety of sources—either as a result of the program manager's search or as a result of information supplied by other sources.

Program managers show great similarity in their use of information. They rely on ratings for the programs they consider purchasing for the station. They also rely on what is most often called gut feelings, knowledge of the community, and interactions with similar people inside and outside the station. Programming decisions are often not completely rational but are often presented to superiors and clients as such based on data (such as ratings) that managers acknowledge privately are hardly good predictors. Information in such cases may be more important as a way to justify a decision than it is to the making of the decision.

The decision-making process that occurs in those rare controversial programming situations is indeed different from that of the routine situation. It involves group management discussion, evaluation, and decision and is triggered when the station's goal (to make money) is threatened. If a program manager is considering purchasing an expensive program or thinks the content of a program is so questionable that it might cause viewers to turn away from the station (hence giving her or him less to sell the advertiser), group management decision making takes place. Controversy warrants exceptional decision making in these stations because of its relationship to the bottom line. One program manager discussed the purchase of "Scared Straight," a controversial program filled with shocking language. The decision to purchase that program (though not necessarily to air it) was his alone. He consulted no one at the station. His explanation was that the program rights did not cost much; hence there was not much of a risk in purchasing them, even if the station chose not to air the program. Ironically the airing of that program, more than its purchase, might trigger the group decision-making process. Conversely, a similar group decision-making process is instituted for the purchase of very expensive programming, even if that programming is not likely to offend anyone.

Program decision making is a collaborative effort, particularly when the decision significantly involves the station's bottom line. The collaborators include program suppliers, advertisers, audience, and several representatives and levels of station management and staff. The less routine the program situation, the more these constituencies are considered and involved. In more routine programming situations, there is little need for extensive collaboration, since the presumed interests of these constituencies are served automatically.

In general, we found that television decision makers deliberated the most about programming that they felt would offend their audience. Although there are many different sources of concern and counsel for the television program manager, the audience members must be aware that they can be an important one. Audience input, it should be remembered, is most effective when it demonstrates the potential to affect the broadcasters' bottom line.

THE ASSAULT ON PUBLIC TELEVISION

John Wicklein

John Wicklein is director of the Kiplinger midcareer program for print and broadcast journalists at Ohio State University. From 1980 to 1984, he served as news and public affairs program officer for the Corporation for Public Broadcasting in Washington. He spent eight years as a reporter and editor with the *New York Times* and then managed the television news operations at WNET/Ch. 13, WCBS, and WABC in New York. He was Washington bureau chief of the Public Broadcast Laboratory of National Educational Television. He has produced or been executive producer of over one hundred news documentaries. He is author of *Electronic Nightmare: The New Communications and Freedom.*

Reprinted from the *Columbia Journalism Review,* January 1986 ©. Used by permission.

> Are you really contemplating abandonment of *"The Lawmakers"?* I know not what course others may take . . . but I shall find it difficult to stay the course of my heretofore strong support of the Corporation for Public Broadcasting if the Corporation . . . effectively denies to the public this excellent view of what their Congress is doing.
> —Representative Andy Jacobs, Jr., in a letter to Edward J. Pfister, then president of the Corporation for Public Broadcasting, December 1, 1982

Why was the congressman exercised? Because he and 534 other lawmakers who control federal appropriations for public broadcasting know what they like. They like a program that presents favorable profiles of their leaders, shows members making ringing speeches on the floor of the House and Senate, and presents soft features about their stewardship in carrying out the public's will. WETA, the public television station in Washington, gave them that program in 1982. The series was called "The Lawmakers," and Congress thought it was wonderful. The public, which did not, tuned out. Public stations around the country dropped the program or buried it in their schedules. The Corporation for Public Broadcasting, which had provided money for its airing nationally on Public Broadcasting Service, told WETA it could not justify continued funding.

The response on the Hill was swift and clear. Thirty-five members of Congress, including Tip O'Neill and George Bush, who as vice-president sits as president of the Senate, made phone calls and wrote letters to CPB, many with direct or implied threats to cut the corporation's appropriation if it did not restore the program's support. The pressure worked; "The Lawmakers" was kept on the air.

"The Lawmakers" affair was a classic instance of the application of political influence—*bipartisan* political influence—by powerful congressmen to see to it that they have ultimate control of content in the system. As a public television administrator commented, "It's the Golden Rule: them that's got the money makes the rule." In attempting to control content, the senators and representatives have violated the basic principle for federal funding established in the 1967 act that created the corporation. Responding to a recommendation of the Carnegie Commission on Educational Television, Congress set up CPB as an independent, private entity and directed it to "carry out its purposes . . . in ways that will most effectively assure the most freedom on noncommercial educational television and radio broadcast systems and local stations from interference with or control of program content." Another provision, however, effectively undercut this intention. Rejecting a Carnegie Commission proposal that the system be financed by a 2 percent excise tax on television sets, Congress decided instead to provide money through annual appropriations.

Congress is by no means the only group that seems bent on undermining the independence of public broadcasting. A succession of administrations has also attempted to do so. Ronald Reagan has never concealed his antipathy toward the whole notion of an independent broadcasting system. His original plan was to kill it. *Broadcasting* magazine's head on a January 26, 1981, story summed up the incoming president's position nicely: "Reagan Transition's Verdict on CPB: Termination with Extreme Prejudice." Nixon was equally hostile. Believing that public broadcasting was in the hands of liberals, he first tried to kill federal funding for it; when that effort failed, he threatened to veto any appropriation bill if the system insisted on producing national public affairs programming.

Nixon was particularly outraged by the appointment in 1971 of two men he regarded as liberals—Sander Vanocur and Robert MacNeil (now co-host of "The MacNeil/Lehrer NewsHour")—to anchor a political program under the auspices of the National Public Affairs Center for Television in Washington. He ordered his staff to see to it that "all funds for public broadcasting be cut immediately," according to Nixon administration papers released in 1979 in response to a Freedom of Information Act request. Clay Whitehead, who as head of Nixon's Office of Telecommunications Policy had been leading the attack, told him that this would not fly, politically. But there was another route: under the 1967 act, the president appoints all CPB board members. An internal White House memo showed how this could be put to political use: "The President's basic objective [is]: to get the left-wing commentators who are cutting us up off public television at once, indeed yesterday if possible. We need eight loyalists to control the present CPB board and fire the current staff who make the grants."

By 1972, Nixon had brought that off. The new board voted to discontinue funding "the networking of news, news analysis, and political commentary," and rescinded a staff commitment for multiyear funding of the National Public Affairs Center for Television. Nixon had won a major victory: strong public affairs programming was not to surface again until well after he was driven from office by Watergate.

After Nixon, the Ford administration was quiescent toward public broadcasting, while Jimmy Carter, who supported its goals, proposed raising its appropriation. In presenting this proposal to Congress, he stated that public broadcasting must be protected against political interference. When push came to shove, however, the Carter administration tried to block a program it did not like. The program was "Death of a Princess." Coproduced by WGBH in Boston and scheduled to air in May 1980, it told of the beheading in 1977 of a princess in Saudi Arabia for having openly had an affair with a commoner. The Saudis protested vehemently to its being aired; Warren M. Christopher, acting secretary of state, forwarded the protest to Larry Grossman, then head of PBS. In a covering letter, Christopher asked Grossman to show "programming judgment" and, by implication, suggested that the program be canceled. The Mobil Corporation, a major underwriter of PBS, also brought pressure to bear. After wavering, Grossman decided that the program would be aired.

Like the Nixon administration, but far more successfully, the Reagan administration has resorted to various stratagems designed to kill, gut, or otherwise drastically alter the nature of public broadcasting. The manner in which public broadcasting has been buffeted by Reagan over the past five years provides a clear demonstration that, if public broadcasting is to maintain the independence envisioned for it by its founders, new methods of financing and administering the system are required.

The first budget drawn up by David Stockman had *zero* funds in it for public broadcasting; his fallback position called for phasing out all federal funding in five years. The Reagan argument was that, if people want public broadcast programming, they should pay for it, in the same way they pay for Home Box Office, for example. (This would mean, of course, that people who cannot pay would not see and hear news, public affairs, and cultural programming that may give them a perspective other than the pap normally offered by marketplace programming.) In his first year in office, Reagan the landslide winner was able to get Congress, in an unprecedented action, to rescind $35 million of the $172 million already appropriated for public broadcasting for 1983. That forced CPB to cut community service grants to the stations by 20 percent. As a result, two smaller stations went under, and several large ones nearly did. On the Hill, the talk was that the administration hoped more would fail so that their licenses could be taken over by commercial stations.

Failing in 1981 and 1982 to persuade Congress to knock out *all* federal funding, Reagan took another tack: convert public broadcasting into a commercial system whose programming would be based on marketplace values. Reagan officials inspired a bill to permit an eighteen-month pilot program in which ten public television and ten public radio stations would broadcast commercials.

William McCarter, president of WTTW in Chicago, and Jay Iselin, president of WNET in New York, were converted to the idea. McCarter said he wanted WTTW to be a commercial station that continued to broadcast public television fare; Iselin said he thought ads were "inevitable." The presidents of both PBS and CPB, however, were adamantly opposed to advertising. The executive committee of the National Association of Public Television Stations argued that public broadcasting should continue to be an educational medium that is supported by the people who use it, and also by the federal government. "Any attempt to inject commercial advertising into the mix," the committee declared, "would change the flavor, purpose, and intent of public broadcasting as it exists today."

A Temporary Commission on Alternative Funding, created by Congress at the administration's urging, reported after a two-year study that limited advertising was unlikely to produce enough revenue to replace federal funding. Dissatisfied with the report, Reagan continued to push the system to support itself commercially. He twice vetoed CPB appropriations in 1984. Then, taking a leaf from Nixon's book, he appointed several of his supporters to the CPB board in the expectation they they would bring its programming in line with his thinking. (That Reagan should borrow this tactic from Nixon was not surprising. After all, Pat Buchanan, one of the chief architects of the Nixon plan to subvert public broadcasting, is now Reagan's director of communications.)

Before Reagan came in, the board majority appointed by Carter had voted in 1979 to take themselves out of program-by-program decision making. To do this, they set up an independent Program Fund with about $25 million a year to commission national programming in news, public affairs, and cultural areas. The fund's charter stated that it was to be "protected from outside influences"—specifically including board members—"in selecting programs." Thus, CPB, designed as a "heat shield" (the phrase used in the original Carnegie Commission report) against outside pressures on programming, had installed a second layer of insulation.

In its first couple of years, the Program Fund operated without feeling the presence of the board. It commissioned a ten-part documentary series, called "Crisis to Crisis," in which independent producers investigated controversial issues. Eight out of the ten documentaries won national or international awards. It established "Frontline," an award-winning weekly series of news documentaries supervised by David Fanning at WGBH in Boston, now in its fourth season. It provided initial funding for the "Inside Story" series, which has won four Emmys for its critiques of journalism. And, through an "open-solicitation" process in which the Program Fund's officers ask for proposals from independent producers and producers at member stations, the fund has selected and financed fifteen to eighteen hour-long documentaries each year, to be shown as PBS specials. (By contrast, the networks have steadily decreased the number of documentaries they produce.)

A Charter Ignored—and an Activist Board

With a Reagan majority now in control of the board, the concept that members should not meddle with program decisions has been eroded. One Reagan appointee, R. Kenneth Towery, a former deputy director of the United States Information Agency, said at a board meeting that the Program Fund should not give another cent to "Frontline." Another, Richard Brookhiser, a senior editor at *National Review,* objected to PBS's airing of "Concealed Enemies," a docudrama on the Alger Hiss case, because the show left "an agnosticism" about whether Hiss had, in fact, been guilty of spying for the Russians.

Sonia Landau, board chairman and head of Women for Reagan/Bush in the 1984 campaign, has also made her views clear on what sort of programs the fund should support. Last January, ignoring the board's own written policy, she sat in on an open-solicitation review panel. She said she thought the fund should be used for more historical public affairs programming, such as a series explaining the Constitution. Several panelists and staff members felt that both her presence and her comments violated the principle of insulation set forth in the fund's charter.

In a recent telephone interview, Landau said, "I see nothing wrong with expressing my views at a panel meeting. If we [the board] are going to use taxpayers' dollars, we should have an opinion on programs and know what they are putting on. [But] the Program Fund director makes up his own mind."

A regional public television administrator pointed out, however, that since the board hires and fires the director he is likely to pay *some* attention when Landau intervenes as she did at the review panel meeting. "Sonia has to come to terms with the fact that, in such a case, she's a two-thousand-pound canary," this administrator said.

In any event, Ron Hull, the current Program Fund director, told a meeting of San Francisco Bay Area independent producers that he agreed with Landau "one hundred percent." He said he favored "the education model" for CPB and thought it should do more programming in history, including the Constitution. The independents took this to mean that, from now on, the Program Fund would shy away from controversial public affairs documentaries. Because PBS is one of the few remaining outlets for this kind of documentary, independent producers fear that they will no longer be able to place their work on national television.

System officials who deal on a regular basis with the Program Fund say that this change in funding priorities is less the result of direct edicts from the board than it is a result of trying to read the board's mind.

This mind-set became crystal clear at a May 15, 1985, board meeting at which Landau and other pro-Reagan board members voted to cancel a marketing trip to the Soviet Union that the CPB International Affairs Department had organized as one of a series by station executives who hoped to sell and exchange programs in other countries. Reading the transcript of that meeting is like reading a tract by right-wing ideologues. The marketing project had been cleared by the State Department. But Reagan appointees Brookhiser, Towery, and Howard Gutin let it be known that they looked on this as trading with the enemy. "If we are going to be opening the doors to wonderful Soviet ideas on their history or something, that is just disastrous," said Brookhiser. Landau commented: "I am concerned that an institution that operates on federal money is dealing with the Soviet government."

CPB president Edward J. Pfister was put in the bizarre position of having to explain to Landau and the Reagan majority on his board that CPB "is a public broadcasting entity; it is not a government agency." The next day, in the wake of the six-to-four vote to cancel the trip, Pfister resigned. He said that political motives had influenced the vote and that it represented an "encroachment on the independence of the corporation." Landau, informed by the *Washington Post* that critics had charged her with moving CPB to the right, retorted: "From where? To the right of George McGovern? Yeah, you're right." She denied, however, that the vote had anything to do with politics.

Interviewed more recently, Landau asserted that the board was *not* taking orders from the Reagan administration and that the CPB had *never* been subjected to pressure from Congress on programming. "In fact," she said, "it's been quite extraordinary. They may buck a few letters to us from their constituents but that's the extent of it." She added, however, that the board is part of "the body politic." The kind of thinking exhibited by the board does not reassure producers who want to do investigative stories on public television—many of whom left commercial broadcast news operations because they had not been permitted to dig into controversial subjects.

A willingness to defer to the board's pro-Reagan majority is not the only reason viewers are less likely to see strong news and public affairs programming on their local stations. Another is that local boards are often composed of fat cats appointed for their fund-raising skills or their ability to contribute funds themselves or, on the other hand, of politicians foisted on them by state officials. These board members don't like the heat good reporting can generate. Moreover, as often as not, they show little understanding of the mission of public broadcasting. In more than one instance, the anchor of a local public affairs program has been replaced because a board member did not like his politics; and many station managers tell of instances in which a board member has insisted on reviewing a program before it aired, then asked the manager to pull it from the schedule.

To address this problem, a group of station managers last year [1985] organized the Wingspread Conference on Editorial Integrity. "It's an ethical issue," says Virginia Fox, president of the Southern Educational Communications Association and the leader of the conference. "We've got to insulate editorial integrity regardless of the source. We've got to reduce undue influence, whether it's a 'Friends' [of the station] group, or a politician, or AT&T. We came to see the boards as the cure."

The group's statement of principles, which members of the conference are working to get boards across the country to adopt, begins: "We are trustees of a public service." As such, board members pledge to create a climate in which station management can "responsibly exercise the editorial freedom necessary to achieve public broadcasting's mission effectively."

Enter, Bearing Money, the Big Corporations

As presently financed and administered, public broadcasting is vulnerable not only to political pressure but also to pressure from large corporations. Corporate underwriters now select many of PBS's prime-time programs. "Great Performances" segments are picked by programmers at Exxon; "Masterpiece Theatre" miniseries are picked by programmers at the Mobil Corporation. Corporations rarely fund enterprising news programs or investigative documentaries because the ideas expressed might run counter to their commercial interests. The exceptions are safe public affairs programs such as "The MacNeil/Lehrer NewsHour." AT&T chose to sponsor "the nation's first hour-long news program" because this would help to position it, in the public's mind, for its planned emergence as electronic information provider to the nation. All AT&T had to do was dangle $10 million in front of station managers' eyes at the 1982 public television Program Fair, and they immediately saw the need, not felt before, to extend "MacNeil/Lehrer" to an hour.

In the scramble for corporate dollars, PBS and the public stations have tossed their former conflict-of-interest standards concerning underwriting out the window. Now we have "enhanced underwriting," with credits that are often blatant plugs. And we find ads such as one in *TV Guide* promoting "Air Force One," a documentary that the ad said was "sponsored by" (not "underwritten by") the Boeing Company, which manufactures Air Force One.

Many programmers and producers in the system say that the tendency today is to shape content to suit the purposes of potential corporate underwriters. In the words of one independent producer, "It's getting so that you have to pitch programs to corporate underwriters in the same terms you pitch shows to commercial sponsors."

"High Tech Times," a series about consumer electronics that was originally supported by an insurance company, was later pitched to an industry group promoting products directly related to the series's content. Its host, former FCC commissioner Nicholas Johnson, objected to the change. "There is an inherent conflict of interest," he said recently, "in having a program on consumer electronics underwritten by something called the Consumer Electronics Group of the Electronics Industry Association." Johnson, who has since parted company with the producers (WHA-TV in Madison, Wisconsin), says that the same criticism can be applied to any program in which the underwriter has a clear economic interest in the way the subject matter is presented—"say, for example, a brokerage firm underwriting a show about the stock market." Louis Rukeyser's "Wall Street Week," one of the most popular programs in the PBS schedule, is underwritten by Prudential-Bache Securities.

None of this commercialism, of course, is conducive to program independence. Despite that fact, no one in the top leadership is trying to change the system fundamentally. "I don't see a great need to tinker," says Bruce Christensen, president of PBS. He would, however, like to see a program endowment of up to $1 billion created from private sources, as a counterbalance to federal funding. Peter Fannon, president of the National Association of Public Television Stations, says he thinks the present sum of many parts works quite well. But, he adds, it must develop many sources of funding to keep control away from one entity. Landau of CPB says, "I don't feel it has to be changed at all."

These attitudes differ sharply from those of public television journalists, who often have to be creatively subversive to get around the system and do good work. For them, this is no way to run a railroad.

How the System's Integrity *Could* Be Saved

At best, the funding system established by Congress encourages timidity in programming; at worst, it invites political and commercial interference. If we want a public broadcasting service whose news and documentary programs provide a real alternative to what the networks have to offer, there must be a radical overhauling of the way public broadcasting is financed and administered.

What form would a reorganization have to take to guarantee the system's independence? One thing is certain: it cannot be "the BBC solution" often proposed by people not familiar with public broadcasting in the United States. The BBC has some good arrangements that *could* be used here—production and scheduling of news and public affairs programs are done through the same organization, and the BBC has a guaranteed and insulated source of programming funds, through license fees on television and radio sets. But it is a *national* system, without independent local affiliates. The intent in this country was to establish independent local stations, and this must be kept in mind in any reorganization.

First and foremost, Congress and the administration must agree to take funding out of the politics of direct appropriations. To do this, the Corporation for Public Broadcasting must be abolished. In its place, Congress could establish an Independent Public Broadcasting Authority, supported by a 2 percent tax on the profits of commercial broadcasting companies. These broadcasters have been given the use of the public airways—free—to produce those profits, estimated at $21.3 billion for 1983. Such a tax, bringing in more than $400 million a year, would end the need for direct appropriations, greatly reduce the need for corporate underwriting, and provide the funds necessary for a first-rate national program service.

With public broadcasting costs now running nearly $1 billion a year, local station operations would still have to be financed from state funds and subscriber contributions. Today, support for the system breaks down to: federal funds, 16 percent; state funds, 29 percent; business underwriting, 16 percent; private contributions, 23 percent; and the rest from a variety of sources. The federal appropriation for 1986 is $159.5 million.

Funding from a 2 percent tax on commercial broadcasters would bring to about $5 per person the amount provided for public broadcasting from all sources each year in the United States. By way of comparison, Canada provides $25; the United Kingdom, $18; and New Zealand, $38 per person.

In return for this tax, commercial broadcasters could be released from their present legal obligation to serve the public interest in their programming, allowing them to concentrate entirely on programs that maximize profit. Henry Geller, director of the Washington Center for Public Policy Research, suggests that, since the commercial broadcasters would benefit financially from this arrangement, they should be willing to give up a small share of their earnings to support a nonprofit system devoted to public interest programming. This would be especially appropriate if the public stations agreed, as an added inducement, to abandon the idea of selling commercials on their own.

An Independent Public Broadcasting Authority could use its funds in two ways: 50 percent could be given as a straight pass-through to the stations for their own program productions and acquisitions. And 50 percent could be allocated to national programs produced and acquired by the authority's program staff.

Rather than develop a single take-it-or-leave-it network in the commercial mold, the staff could program a multichannel service via the authority's satellite interconnection. This would have a core service of news, public affairs, and cultural programs that could be promoted and advertised nationally, plus several other services for the stations and for public cable channel operations. One of these could be devoted to the work of independent producers—in the last decade, independents have provided most of the exciting fare in news and public affairs documentaries.

A multichannel service could also be provided for public radio programming. One channel, centering on "All Things Considered" and "Morning Edition," could provide the first national all-news radio service.

To take the authority out of the politics of presidential appointments, it could be run by a director selected by a search committee of nongovernment leaders in journalism, the arts, education, business, labor, and so on. Policy could be set, not by a board of political chit-holders, but by the director as chairperson of a panel that would include one representative of PBS, one from NPR, one elected by independent producer groups, and one elected by the station's existing community advisory boards.

Naysayers to complete reorganization are right in saying that political and system opposition to this is formidable—but wrong in saying it cannot be overcome. It can't happen, obviously, under the Reagan administration, which is actively hostile. And public broadcasting has no champions now in Congress; they would have to be encouraged to come forward or be elected. But an administration—possibly even the next one—that is more dedicated to the public interest in communications *could* provide the climate, and the drive, required to overhaul the system. Progressive forces inside public broadcasting and media reform groups should be forming a national coalition now to draft a plan to be put into action as soon as the time is ripe.

6
Film

Introduction

Although film does not have access to an instant mass audience as does television, it is clearly a mass medium. All major films are distributed nationwide. Paid attendance has passed its peak, but over a number of years, successful films can reach a large segment of the public. Few Americans have not seen old movies like *Gone with the Wind* and assorted Disney films, and seeing *Star Wars, E.T.,* or even *Rambo* has become a common experience for a large part of the population. Major films also have a worldwide audience and are made with soundtracks in several languages. In addition to their direct impact in movie theaters, films constitute a large component of television content and video sales and rentals. Films are increasingly commissioned specifically for television or made with a view toward TV and video sales after a period in the cinema circuits. A glance at *TV Guide* shows that films from the 1940s on are an important program source. If television (especially cable) is permitted to relax its sex and violence standards for late night programming, most of the films made today will eventually be televised.

The motion picture was developed from the technology of still photography, and penny arcades drew thousands to their Kinetoscopes around 1900. Risqué shorts soon gave way to longer movies with simple plots and much slapstick. By the 1920s, elaborate, though silent, films and sumptuous picture palaces were common, and the Hollywood mystique and big star system were well established. Sound was added in the late 1920s. From then until about 1950, film was a true mass medium, with attendance little affected even by the Great Depression. In 1930 and again in 1946 and 1948, average weekly attendance was an estimated 90 million persons. With the advent of television, attendance fell drastically—to 60 million in 1950, 40 million in 1958, 21 million in 1965, to 15 million in 1972. By 1983, weekly attendance had increased again, to over 23 million per week. In that year, Americans paid over $3.7 billion in admissions. There are over 18,000 theater screens in use, many in small multiscreen cinemas rather than the huge, increasingly obsolete palaces of the 1930s. Almost the entire audience (86 percent) is under forty years old, and one-quarter of the total audience is aged sixteen to twenty. Over half of all teenagers (age twelve to seventeen) are reported to attend a movie at least once a month.[1] The medium has therefore moved from a mass business aimed at a generalized audience to a specialized one increasingly aimed at teenagers.

The boom years at Hollywood and the major film studios were the late 1940s. When television hit the film business, Hollywood responded with the wide-screen epics of the 1950s and 1960s and the relaxation of the Production Code, which permitted the filming of formerly taboo topics. But the industry had lost its general audience, and the younger, more sophisticated moviegoers discovered foreign and experimental films. Movies from Italy, France, and England, and the films of such directors as Andy Warhol and Paul Morrissey made inroads into Hollywood's remaining audience. Since 1965, the new independents have often outproduced the major studios in Hollywood, and international ventures have blurred the distinction between American and foreign products.

The first reading, by Steve Buss, describes the basic operation of the movie business. The studio system of the earlier golden age of film has now broken up. Buss describes three routes to making a movie: through the majors, the minimajors, or the independents. He examines the problems of production, distribution to cinemas, and exhibition. It can be a very expensive process, and usually one with a fairly high economic risk.

The second topic of this chapter is movie criticism. Mark J. Shaefermeyer discusses the many approaches of critics, who may employ different types of semiotic, structuralist, or contextual methods. Good criticism of all types can help us to understand and get more meaning out of movies. Dennis Holder then provides a picture of an outrageous reviewer of drive-in "trash" movies, Joe Bob Briggs. As Holder indicates, once this critic was invented, he took on a life of his own. Clearly he loves movies that most critics despise.

David Altheide encourages us to investigate the underlying, often political, message of movies. By political, he means generally the images of what is right and wrong. Movies employ everyday ideas—our feelings, knowledge, experiences, and so on—to make us feel involved with the movie and indirectly to buy its message (usually also familiar to us). He sketches the ways in which movies often portray the family and friends, how males and females are supposed to be (gender), age, horror, courage, and conflict. Often the theme of the latter is the struggle of the individual versus some sinister enemy (often the Soviet Union). This glorification of individualism is a common theme in American culture. It is not, however, a complete reflection of society: the country was not built entirely by loners—any society needs cooperation. This, however, is usually downplayed in our culture. For example, football is very much a team game. It requires very elaborate coordination of effort (much more than baseball). But its salary structure, star system, and the way it is described by journalists and commentators lead us to actually *see* it as a clash of *individuals*.

Note

1. *The International Motion Picture Almanac* (New York: Quigley Publishing Co., 1985), pp. 28A, 30A, 32A.

THE MOVIE BUSINESS

Steven Buss

Steve Buss received his B.A. and M.F.A. in cinema production (with an emphasis in film business) from the University of Southern California. He has worked in Los Angeles for various production companies and in San Antonio, Texas, where he has produced and directed a large number of educational films, videotapes, and slide-tape presentations, some of which have won national awards. He is currently a freelance director/cameraman and an assistant professor in the Communication Studies Department at California State University, Sacramento.

With the birth of movies in the early 1900s, one company would shoot the film, develop and edit the negative, make a print, and then rent a place to exhibit it to paying customers. With the money from these customers, the company would make another movie. Anything left would be profit.

As movies became more popular and profitable, companies became more specialized. Now one company would produce the movie, another would distribute it, and still another would exhibit it. This specialization meant that each company became expert in its area of concern; it also meant that each was at the other's mercy. Exhibitors might complain that the movies were not good enough to draw customers. Distributors might complain that not enough movies, good or bad, were being made to rent to the exhibitors, who wanted to change their programs at least twice each week. Production companies would complain that the distributors and exhibitors would not work hard enough or spend enough money to promote the movie. The production companies also felt that when a movie was a success, the distributor and the exhibitor kept too much of the profit for something they did not even produce. All three branches of the movie business still have the same complaints today.

To cut through these problems and maximize profits, some companies decided that the one-man-band company idea was not so bad after all. One large company could handle all three areas of the business, and that is just what Warner Brothers, Fox, Paramount, and others decided to do. This was the birth of the studio system, which was powerful in the 1930s and 1940s.

Under the studio system, actors were owned by studios. Unless he or she was loaned out to another studio, the actor worked in, say, MGM movies, which were made on MGM's lot, shot with MGM-owned equipment by an MGM production crew, and under the helm of an MGM director. The completed movie, through an MGM distributor, was seen at an MGM theater. In business, this is known as vertical ownership.

Not only did a studio have total control over movies from script to screen, but all profit went back to the studio. This vertical ownership gave the studios the chance to make lesser, or B, pictures, which would fill out a double bill in their theaters. B pictures also served as a training ground for new talent the studio had under contract and were bringing along slowly. By this system, an unsuccessful film usually was not as detrimental to the business health of the company. A flop could be carried by another movie that was a hit. And if the flop was a real "stinker," as they say in the movie business, the studio could pull it quickly before too much damage was done to the stars or the company. Because the studio owned the theater, it could easily cut its losses by pulling unpopular films and maximizing its profits by playing a hit for as long as it made money.

Vertical ownership is a sweet deal for those on the inside and because the studios owned not just a few but a large number of theaters, the studios also had what is called horizontal ownership. For small independent producers, distributors, or exhibitors, it looked like an illegal monopoly. The result was that in the late 1940s and early 1950s, the Supreme Court ruled against the eight major studios in what have come to be known as the Paramount decrees. The Court ruled that the studios could own only two areas of the motion picture business and would have to let one go. The studios chose to keep production and distribution and divested themselves of the exhibition business. Let us look at each of these segments of the business as they are run today.

Production

A movie can begin as a novel, a play, or just an idea, but usually it begins as a screenplay. After the screenplay has been written, the next step is to try and get the money together to shoot the film. There are four main options: the producer can supply the money, go to a major studio, go to a minimajor, or go to an independent producer.

The differences among majors, minimajors, and independents are not always clear, but as a rule of thumb, it can be said that a major studio (such as Universal, 20th Century Fox, or Disney) has three things: 1) money (or access to it), 2) a distribution division (domestic and foreign), and 3) sound (shooting) stages. A minimajor (Orion, Lorimar, and Malpaso, for example) usually has 1) access to some money (but not as much as a major has), and 2) a multipicture deal with a distribution company. (In the past, minimajors did not own sound stages; some now do.) Finally, an independent producer typically has to go looking for money (from banks, distribution companies, or private investors) to produce movies. Independents must sell each picture on an individual basis to a distributor and must rent sound stages if they are needed.

Majors

Let us say that you have written a screenplay and you decide to start at the top; you send it to Universal. They promptly send it back. Not only won't they read it, but they will not even open the package you sent it in. They take only solicited material. Thus you must go through an established literary agent. The agent would have to read the material, like it enough to sign you to a contract, and submit the screenplay to the studio for you.

Once your agent takes it to Universal, it goes to the story department where a reader writes a synopsis of your story and makes a recommendation on it. If the recommendation is positive, it goes to the head of the story department, who (if he or she agrees with the reader) will submit it to a vice-president. Vice-presidents, however, rarely deal with ideas that come up through the Story Department because most of their efforts go into scripts submitted to them by known producers who have bypassed the story department altogether. In other words, the odds of your script getting past an agent, past a reader, past the head of the story department, and to a vice-president are astronomically bad.

But let us say that luck and a very good screenplay are on your side. The vice-president reads it, and likes it enough to pass it on to the head of production for the studio. If the head of production thinks that this would be a good film for the studio to make, it goes to the president of Universal. The buck stops here. If the president says yes, a contract is drawn up, and the budget is prepared.

The budget is important. If it is too high, the studio will tell the producer or the writer to rewrite the script so that the film will be less expensive. Or the studio might pass on the project if they feel that it will cost more than it is worth.

Most studios have budget departments that work with other departments on the studio's lot to determine the proposed movie's *negative cost,* or the amount of money needed for preproduction (development and planning), production, and postproduction (finishing costs such as music and editing). These costs are typically very high: A Sci-Fi movie, for example, can easily cost over $10 million.

Basically, a production budget can be broken down into two areas: above the line costs and below the line costs. Above the line costs (story rights and screenplay purchase and expenses) are very flexible, while below the line costs (all filming costs for personnel and sets plus processing) are not.

Also the budget includes 1) insurance, 2) a contingency, and 3) often a completion bond. Insurance is an expensive item. A feature movie must have at least eleven different types of insurance encompassing such items as cast insurance, negative film and videotape, and faulty stock, camera, and processing.

A contingency fee, which is 10 percent of the budget, is added before the completion bond. This fee helps fill in for something that has been either forgotten or cannot be foreseen, and it gives the producer and director a little breathing room.

Finally, although the completion guarantee bond is listed apart from insurance in the budget, it still is a type of insurance. The bond is a guarantee to whomever is putting the money up for the movie that not only will a movie be made but will be completed on time, within budget, of professional quality, and close to the story in the screenplay. The company that puts the bond up has the power to take over the production (fire the director) at any time if it feels that any of these conditions is not met.

Minimajors

If a major studio turns down your idea, you could try a minimajor. Most minimajors do not have a story department, but even when they do, they will not often look at a screenplay unless it comes through an agent. At a minimajor, the project has to go through only two or three people. Because minimajors already have distribution deals, they do not have difficulty getting the money from the distributor or a bank to make the movie.

So why not go to a minimajor in the first place? Because your chances are just about as bad getting a movie off the ground with them as it is with a major. Although a project does not have to go through as many levels of bureaucracy as it does at a major, the minimajor cannot produce as many movies as a major because their deal with a distributor is for only a limited number of pictures. (The exception is minimajors that distribute their movies.) Because filmmaking is such a gamble the minimajors try to keep the odds down by working with producers and writers with a track record. Minimajors thus have more in common with the majors than not.

Independents

If all the majors and minimajors turn your project down, an independent production company or producer can take it on and try to raise the money to get it made. Independents cannot turn for money to distributors (which might buy the movie for distribution, but only after it has been completed) or banks (like any other loan, a bank wants some form of collateral). Instead they turn to forming limited partnerships and try to find investors or investment groups. Here the problem is that because only a small number of completed independent feature films ever find a distributor, the chance that an investor will get the investment back and make a profit is low. Nevertheless investors can be found, and for the same reason that people go to Las Vegas: the glamour, the excitement, and the chance to reap a sizable return.

No matter which of these three routes—major, minimajor, or independent—it takes to get a movie made, once the movie is in production, the producer is responsible for the overall control of the budget. In many cases, the producer's profit percentage is tied in with the budget, so if the movie goes over the budget, the producer loses *points* (a percentage of the profits).

Distribution

Distributors, like production companies, can be large, medium, or small and with a lot of cash and credit or little. Producers always want their movies to go to a large distributor, which, they hope, will spend sizable amounts on advertising and get each movie into the right theaters at the right time. In reality, an independent producer will take whatever he or she can get. And even a producer who has a major or minimajor behind him or her still needs to be powerful enough to get the best terms and make demands on the distributor.

Because distributors need a product to rent to exhibitors, they will look at any completed or almost completed movie. If they like it, they can pick it up. However, unless a major distributor has either made the movie through its own production company or in agreement with a minimajor, the movie will usually be passed on (rejected), and the producer will have to take the movie to a smaller distribution company.

Many independent movies, and a few major ones, are never shown in theaters because they cannot find a distributor. Distributors, like production companies, have to take large risks once they decide to handle a movie. With the costs of advertising, prints, and a large staff, the average movie today costs about $5 million to distribute. So even if millions of the distributor's dollars were spent to make the movie, if the distributor thinks the film will fail commercially, it will release the movie only on a limited basis—or not at all.

Let us say that the movie is very good with excellent commercial potential. First the distributor works out contract terms with the producer. The distributor usually agrees to give the producer a large cash advance, which is often paid back to the distributor out of the producer's profits, promises to spend a specific amount of money for advertising and prints, and typically agrees to a profit split in which the producer gets 70 percent.

The exhibitor will take its share of the money before the distributor sees any cash flow. Once the money does come to the distributor, all expenses must be deducted before the books show any profit to be split with the producer. Remember that it costs millions to distribute a movie so the movie has to be a smash to pay for production, pay for distribution, and still make a profit. The rule of thumb is that in order for an average budget movie to break even, it must gross three times its negative costs. In the case of a $10 million movie (an above-average budget), the movie would have to gross over $30 million just to break even.

For domestic distribution, the United States is broken down into thirty-two territories. Major distributors have offices in every territory, but smaller distributors have to subcontract some of the selling to a subdistributor, which also takes a percentage of the box office receipts.

Foreign distribution can bring in anywhere from 40 percent to 50 percent of the total movie rental income. As in the domestic market, the major distributors have offices in most of the foreign sales territories. Smaller U.S. distributors must work with foreign distributors and give them a percentage of the box office receipts.

The distributor has, besides the quality of the movie, two major concerns that can make or break a movie: how to market it and when to market it. Marketing can include designing, producing, and buying television and radio spots, newspaper ads, posters, and billboards. The distributor knows that how the film is marketed is one of the most important decisions that will be made. If a movie is good, word of mouth will play a major role in bringing more people into the theaters, but the distributor must get the first audience through marketing.

Distributors spend time and money on research to find out how to market each movie. The most common type of research is the sneak preview, where the movie is shown once in selected theaters. The audience is asked to fill out survey cards after they have seen the movie, and the distributor will work out a marketing plan based on their comments. It will use this research, along with other factors, to help decide when to release the movie. The Christmas holidays and summer months are thought to be the most lucrative time to release most types of high-quality movies, but each major distributor knows what and when other major distributors plan to market, knowledge that will be considered in ad decisions and play dates.

Exhibition

A movie can make money with network television sales, cable sales, home video sales, and nontheatrical sales. The producer can also make money by selling certain rights such as book spinoffs, merchandising, and soundtrack albums, but the one area where a movie must be successful for any of these other markets to open up considerably is in theatrical exhibition.

Exhibitors rent movies from the distributors. If there is more than one exhibition chain in a city (there usually is, along with a few independents), the theaters must bid for the first run of the movie. The distributor provides information to the exhibitors about the movie and its projected release date in a *bid letter.* The letter asks the exhibitor to meet or beat a nonrefundable cash guarantee, play the film for a specified number of weeks, and pay a certain percentage of the income from the movie back to the distributor after the exhibitor has subtracted taxes and overhead from the ticket sales. The percentage of the split starts at anywhere from 90/10 (90 percent for the distributor and 10 percent for the exhibitor) to 50/50, with 70/30 being the most common. This figure changes each or every other week, with the exhibitor getting a larger percentage of the ticket sales as the movie plays longer. The distributor can also ask the exhibitor to help pay advertising costs. After the bid letter has been sent out, the exhibitor has seven days to reply.

Sometimes the distributor will preview the movie for the exhibitors, but generally when the bid letter goes out, there is nothing, or little, to show because the movie is still in production or, at best, postproduction. When the exhibitor is asked to bid on a movie without seeing it, the process is called *blind bidding* (and is banned in some states as illegal).

Conclusion

The production companies, the distributors, and the exhibitors need each other. They need to work together as much as possible to help each other through the lean times and share in the profits when the business is on an upswing. The movie business is expensive and a gamble. It can also be glamorous and fun. Between production, distribution, and exhibition, the movie business is also large. It employs thousands of people and puts a large amount of money into the national economy. And through foreign distribution, it puts American culture on the movie screens in every corner of the globe.

FILM CRITICISM

Mark J. Schaefermeyer

Mark J. Schaefermeyer is an assistant professor in the Department of Communication Studies at Virginia Polytechnic Institute and State University, Blacksburg, Virginia. In addition to criticism, his major research interests center on the relationship between rhetoric and aesthetics in film.

The place occupied by movie critics in the popular media is perhaps stronger today than it ever has been. The success of Gene Siskel and Roger Ebert in moving from PBS to syndication with their self-described movie review program is evidence that the medium is not without those who are paid to pass judgment on it. Paperback books that describe and rate all the films available on television abound; local news programs often have a critic of their own or regularly utilize a video version of the syndicated columnist. Major news magazines and large city dailies regularly review films; even the smallest of newspapers offers a column discussing the film industry's latest releases. In some cases, movies are reviewed a second time when they are released in videocassette format.

And yet these instances of criticism are only part of the effort that goes into analyzing film. This reading puts into perspective the act of film criticism while providing an overview of the critical approaches currently being used. The bulk of this essay will focus on academic criticism versus the more popular media forms. The general public is aware of and utilizes criticism that is more aptly termed *movie reviewing*. Movie reviews are meant to recommend or not recommend particular films to the potential viewing public. In one sense, the popular media critic is a consumer watchdog keeping a wary eye on the film industry's attempts to obtain the viewers' dollars.

Distinguishing the popular media form of criticism from academic or scholarly criticism is not to suggest that the former is unscholarly or a poor cousin to the latter. Movie reviews are meant for a specific audience, and they perform a specific function: to assist consumers in choosing what films to see. For the most part, movie reviewers rely on such categories as plot, characterization, or strength of the actors' performances to arrive at their assessment of the film (this is probably a holdover from the early beginnings of such criticism when reviewers of this new medium generally were drama critics taking on additional duties). In most cases today, reviewers' closest comments regarding purely filmic qualities are related to a director's use of particular techniques.

In contrast, academic critical pursuits are directed toward publications intended for fellow academicians and/or filmmakers. Their purpose is to foster a better understanding of film as a medium and as an art form. Hence scholarly criticism of film invariably touches the medium's history, functions, practitioners, techniques, or aesthetics. In most cases, such criticism attempts to answer questions about the film's history and other issues in order to further our knowledge about art, ourselves, and the world.

Sidney Pollack (1986), director of the critically acclaimed and successful films *Out of Africa* and *Tootsie,* has stated that each film is a revelation of the director's perceptions about how the world operates. Each film is thus a communication of the director's overall vision of the world. Those who seek to understand a film implicitly seek understanding of what the director has communicated. In many cases, what is communicated is not always obvious to the viewer or the critic. Close analysis is necessary to reveal, interpret, or merely aid the viewer's understanding.

There are a variety of methods and critical models imposed on films, all of which propose to answer specific questions about those works of art. Indeed, the question of what the filmmaker "meant" is not an appropriate query (many critical theorists have long ago abandoned the quest for artist's intent). Rather, the meaning of a film is just that: what the film (or work of art) communicates. The film's meaning, then, depends on how it is perceived, by whom, and with what particular perspective(s).

This situation appears to indicate that film meanings vary and therefore criticism as a method for arriving at that meaning must be fruitless pursuit. Quite the contrary is true. Works of art will often hold different meanings for people because of their varied experiences and backgrounds. Hence, each viewer approaches a film with different sets of expectations and prejudices, as well as a distinct worldview and knowledge base. The variety of critical perspectives allows each individual to explore the perspective most meaningful to that person. More important, for those of us studying the mass media, an additional gain from the variety of critical perspectives used to analyze film is the differences that are highlighted and what those differences tell us about ourselves, others, and the human condition in general.

The remainder of this reading will be composed of two major sections: an overall perspective of criticism and its functions and, a review of the various types of film criticism, with examples for each type of criticism. Although no particular perspective should be viewed as more useful or proper than any other, no doubt each reader will find one or two of those discussed to be more functional than the others. The key is that no perspective should be dismissed out of hand; each has its own merits as well as faults. Like the cinematic works of art they attempt to analyze, some critical methods work for us, and others do not. To aid us in our understanding of film as a mass medium and as an art form, it is necessary to be acquainted with the basic theory and the tools utilized by critics of film.

Criticism

The number of definitions for criticism is perhaps as numerous as the number of theorists who have written about criticism. The earliest works on literary criticism, by Aristotle, Horace, Longinus, and others, were generally discussions about the elements that comprise literature of good taste and quality. Aristotle's *Poetics*, for example, treats such subjects as origins of poetry, nature of tragedy, catharsis, plot, characterization, and epic poetry. Such works can be viewed as examples of theoretical criticism—the study of the poetic aesthetic—answering questions such as, What constitutes poetic merit? Examples of practical criticism, on the other hand, seek to understand particular works of art and answer questions such as, What does this say? Is it good?

Although there are numerous critical works prior to the eighteenth century, there are few, if any, concise definitions of criticism until 1783 when the Reverend Hugh Blair, in volume 1 of *Lectures on Rhetoric and Belles Lettres*, declares true criticism to be "the application of taste and good sense to the several fine arts" (1965, p. 36). Specifically, Blair maintains that the object of criticism is "to distinguish what is beautiful and what is faulty in every performance; from particular instances to ascend to general principles; and so to form rules or conclusions concerning the several kinds of beauty in works of Genius" (*Lectures* 1965, p. 36).

Blair admonishes his students (and readers) that practical criticism is necessary for the establishment of aesthetic rules and conventions prior to any foray into the theoretical brand of criticism, which seeks to establish the aesthetic of the art form under examination. Blair has thus provided support for the contention that a variety of critical models and methods, along with their use in critical analyses of films, are prerequisite to understanding fully the nature of film as mass media art form.

More recently, John Dewey (1958) addressed the subject of criticism. For him, "criticism is judgment" (1958, p. 298), and judgment, based on established criteria, has certain functions to perform: discrimination and unification (p. 310). Judgments must delineate the constituent parts (discrimination) and discover how those parts form a whole (unification); the execution of these functions is known as analysis and synthesis, respectively (p. 310).

In his discussion of analytic judgment, Dewey notes the critic must have knowledge of an art form's traditions. One who does not is limited, and "his criticisms will be one-sided to the point of distortion" (p. 311). More important, however, for the viewer-critic, Dewey asserts that judgment grows out of the object as it enters into the critic's experience by interaction with the critic's perceptual field, knowledge, and past experience (p. 309). Again, the very nature of criticism accounts for the variability of critical responses from however many critics are engaged in film analysis. Each critic's experience of the object will be unlike those of other critics. And yet just as much, if not more, is learned from their differences of perception and experience as from the similarities. Above all, criticism is not fault-finding but judgment based on discrimination among values (Dewey 1930, p. 12).

Criticism also has a unifying function. After distinguishing the parts of an art form, the critic should find a unifying thread or pattern that runs through the details. The goal of unification is to distinguish particulars and parts with respect to their weight and function within the whole. Thus, the critic finds a particular structure or strand and illuminates it so clearly that there is then a new guide for the reader's perception of the work of art. Dewey is quick to point out that there are many unifying ideas of themes to a work in proportion to its richness. As such, this is additional validation for the variety of critical methods manifested in contemporary film criticism.

A more recent definition of criticism blends together those of Blair and Dewey in declaring that criticism is a "systematic process of illuminating and evaluating products of human activity" (Andrews 1983, p. 4). The process of illumination and evaluation must necessarily perform the discrimination of individual parts called for by Blair and Dewey. In evaluation, the critic breaks down the art work to determine whether individual elements are appropriate (in Blair's terminology, there is judgment as to that element's beauty).

The process of evaluation is comprised of judgment based on values. These values should be based on the objective qualities of the work of art— that is, qualities that are as far removed from simplified judgments of good and bad as the critic can manage. In most cases, the act of evaluation relies on established norms, traditions, and conventions associated with the history of the art form; in other cases, the values are based on violations of those norms, traditions, and/or conventions.

The practicing critic must base the evaluation on particular criteria. Some examples of film criticism will use criteria based on filmmaking techniques and conventions; other types will derive the analytic criteria from specific disciplinary methodologies (rhetoric, psychology, semiotics, literary theory, and others). It is important that the criteria used are relevant to the work of art. For example, analyzing a black and white film based on color balances or vividness is absurd. Yet how many times have we overheard similar versions of this fallacy when an acquaintance (or critic) dismisses a film because "it was not what I thought it would be." We must examine the film based on the methods and techniques inherent in the work itself. Our analysis is not whether a work of art shows what we would have chosen as the artist; rather, it should be based on what choices the artist made and whether they achieve success in that context.

Equally important is that justification for making the evaluation must also be made apparent. When the critic knows the reason behind making an evaluation of a work of art, there is less tendency to practice the type of criticism mentioned by Frye (1957) and Dewey—criticism that itself is a form of literary art (more appropriately, a noncriticism). Reader and critic must understand the purpose for and gains accrued from evaluating the work of art.

Finally, it seems fitting to review comments on criticism from a film critic. John Simon says that a good critic is a teacher, an artist, and a thinker. All of these roles are related to criticism's justification for existence: "Without criticism, there would be no dialogue. . . . Without criticism, the artist receives no serious answer" (Simon 1967, p. 2). Simon argues that the artist needs some response, positive or negative, to his or her work in order to gauge his or her progress in the craft or art form. Without criticism, the artist might assume that his or her work is all good or all bad. Silence is the most devastating response to an artist.

Critical Methods in Film Criticism

Each of the critical approaches to film discussed here falls within one of three categories:

Semiotic: realist, formalist, rhetorical, mise-en-scène.

Structuralist: mythic, political, feminist, psychoanalytic, sociological, phenomenological

Contextual: auteur, genre, historical.

Grouped within the *semiotic* category are methods that tend to focus on the meaning of the filmic signs (shots and shot transitions), the relationship of these signs to other filmic signs, or the effect of the signs on the film viewer. Methods that fall under the *structuralist* category seek to define and understand the structures into which individual films and/or from where they are derived. Those under the *contextual* heading focus on aspects of film in the context of other aspects of film.

Semiotic Studies

The most logical place to start in the review of critical approaches with a semiotic impetus is with both the *realist* and *formalist traditions* within film theory. The *realist* tradition focuses on the use of film to re-present reality based on the power of photography's ability to render the real world objectively (Bazin 1967). Bazin argues that long takes, depth of focus, location shooting, sunlight, and the use of nonprofessional actors all contribute to a film's realist aesthetic. In his analysis of Visconti's *La Terra Trema* (1971), Bazin discusses how the film is "real" by virtue of the manner in which the narrative is presented: without the trappings of montage (where reality is fragmented through such techniques as close-up shots and excessive editing). "If a fisherman rolls a cigarette, he [Visconti] spares us nothing: we see the whole operation; it will not be reduced to its dramatic or symbolic meaning, as is usual with montage" (Bazin 1971, p. 43). In a review of De Sica's *Bicycle Thief*, Bazin praises the realist use of location shooting (nothing has been filmed in the studio) and actors without any previous experience in theater or film (Bazin 1971, p. 52).

Analyses using the *formalist* approach have a different focus. Because of his influence on the early history of filmmaking, the Russian filmmaker and theorist Sergei Eisenstein is most often linked (above other theorists) to film's *formalist* tradition. Eisenstein's theory of dialectical montage is influenced by the Japanese hieroglyph, as a pictorial representation of language symbols, and by Hegel's dialectic. First, Eisenstein believes that the Japanese language was built on the principle of montage. For example, the picture symbol for a *dog* plus the symbol for *mouth* means "to bark" (1949, p. 30). The combination of "two hieroglyphs of the simplest series is to be regarded not as their sum, but as their product, i.e., as a value of another dimension, another degree; each, separately, corresponds to an *object*, to a fact, but their combination corresponds to a *concept*. From separate hieroglyphs has been fused— the ideogram" (Eisenstein 1949, pp. 29–30).

Eisenstein theorizes that film relied on the same process: a shot combined in the editing process with another shot created a new concept. Paralleling this approach is the influence of Hegel's dialectic. *Thesis* and *antithesis* combine to form a *synthesis*—a new concept that is no longer reducible to those ideas that in combination make up the editing (as well as any other art form). Montage is the collision of independent shots (shots that are opposite to one another) (Eisenstein 1949, p. 49). Meaning in film, then, evolves from the juxtaposition of film shots that manifest conflict. The differences might be in lighting, shot composition, shot length, conflict of volumes, lines, movement of objects, or something else. Excluding Eisenstein's philosophical and political (or Marxist) orientation, the basis of his theory is film construction: shot plus shot plus shot . . . Hence, any critic interested in how the shots of a film are combined to "mean" would essentially be conducting formalist criticism.

Ted Perry's essay (1970) on Michaelangelo Antonioni's film *L'Eclisse* argues that the meaning of the film depends on certain cues given within the film. In distinguishing between what he calls *fact context* and *value context,* the author argues that the film's meaning is born of the formative forces within the film (p. 79). Perry's analysis relies heavily on the notion of combination. The value context (the attitudes, impressions, and values by which the film frames the fact context) influences the viewer's reading of the fact context (the elements that represent the actions, objects, and events of the physical world depicted in the motion picture images). This analysis reflects the formalist tradition in its focus on meaning that is built upon the combination of shots.

A third type of analysis within the semiotic orientation is *rhetorical* in focus. This type of criticism examines the film as a rhetorical artifact that exhibits intentional meaning and structure. It is an approach based on traditional notions of rhetoric as a means to persuasion. Often relying on critical models from other disciplines, the rhetorical criticism of film deals with the communicative potential of film.

In "Image and Ambiguity: A Rhetorical Approach to *The Exorcist,*" Martin Medhurst (1978) examines the key images in six of the film's episodes in order to define the film's central stance: a rhetoric of choice. The author argues that certain recurring images combine in clusters to foster the contention that people have choices to make: "Humans must choose between the forces of good and the legions of evil. . . . They must consciously will the good and then by a step of faith act on that choice. This is exactly what Damien Karras does in the climax of the film. He consciously chooses to assert that Regan will not die and then proceeds to act on the basis of that assertion" (Medhurst 1978, pp. 90–91).

Medhurst (1982) has also analyzed Alain Resnais' *Hiroshima, Mon Amour* as a film about the problem of knowing reality. In essence, Medhurst's analysis is traditionally rhetorical in his focus on the filmmaker's "cinematic statement": "Resnais has built into the film the very paradox which forms its thesis. . . . Resnais has been able to take his thesis and transform it into a cinematic resource. . . . To know reality, Resnais seems to be saying, is no easy task" (Medhurst 1982, p. 370). Clearly in evidence is the rhetorical quest concerning what the filmmaker means. Both of the Medhurst essays ostensibly rely on examining and interpreting the filmmaker's message.

The final type of semiotic-oriented criticism relys on *mise-en-scène*—the environment of the film, which is created by its lighting, sets, costumes, movement, and any other features that comprise the scene as photographed by the camera. Film analysis that focuses on these elements and on the expressive function of the individual shots is the basis of mise-en-scène criticism (Stromgren and Norden 1984, p. 265). Mise-en-scène criticism lies in the boundary zone between formalism and realism; it is "largely concerned with stylistic or expressive qualities of the single shot . . . in contrast to Bazin's perception of the long take as a transparent realism . . . and in sharp distinction to Eisenstein's herding of all expressive categories under the single umbrella of montage" (Nichols 1976, p. 311).

One notable example of mise-en-scène criticism is Place and Peterson's "Some Visual Motifs of *Film Noir*" (1974). Here, the authors define visual style by utilizing the technical terminology of Hollywood. Their analysis reveals a style reliant on low-key lighting, night-for-night photography (versus day-for-night where the scene, shot in the bright sunlight of day, is manipulated to create an illusion of night), depth of field (the entire shot is in focus), and antitraditional camera setups and angles: "The 'dark mirror' of *film noir* creates a visually unstable environment in which no character has a firm moral base from which he can confidently operate. All attempts to find safety or security are undercut by the antitraditional cinematography and *mise-en-scène*" (Place and Peterson, p. 338).

All of these types of criticism have semiotic underpinnings: each attempts to understand and/or interpret the meaning of cinematic signs, the relationship of cinematic signs to each other, and their meaning to the viewer. There are not always clear-cut boundaries between the varying elements. However, the distinctive features of the type are clear: The primary focus is on cinematic features and the use of film theory. This is contrary to the structuralist studies, which utilize literary-cultural features. They are, in effect, extracinematic (outside of cinema).

Structuralist Studies

There are several types of structuralist methodology. Each method attempts to impose its own orientation or structure on the film; each argues that the film exhibits particular features of the society within which it is produced.

The *mythic* approach asserts the presence of one or more specific myths that, by virtue of their preeminence, are found (or likely to be found) in a society's aesthetic artifacts. Dale Williams's essay (1984) on the religious nature of Stanley Kubrick's *2001: A Space Odyssey* is an example of criticism that uncovers the meaning of the film by defining its mythic overtones. Using the theories of Kenneth Burke (1969), Williams argues that *2001* revolves around the concepts of order and redemption, sacrifice and rebirth, self-denial, and communion with God (Williams 1984, p. 321). Similarly, Martha

Solomon (1983) argues that British-made *Chariots of Fire* was successful in the United States because it reflects two contradictory facets of the American dream—what Fisher (1973) calls the materialistic myth and the moralistic myth. The film's success, in part, is due to its reaffirmation of both competing myths for an audience likely to follow, individually, one or the other. *Chariots,* according to Solomon, functions both mythically and metaphorically in its depiction of a series of successful, archetypal quests by the film's mythic hero characters (p. 275).

The *political* approach to criticism is likely to focus on films and their relationship to the areas of history, ideology, economics, and social criticism. Jeffrey Richards's essay (1970) on Frank Capra illustrates how the films of a single director can contain political undertones. In this case, Capra's films reflect ideals of the populist party: self-help and individualism versus political machines and big government. Richards finds the presence of Capra's emphasis of populism in the motifs of anti-intellectualism, wealth, pursuit of happiness, and the quintessential good neighbor. Capra's films in the postwar era cast aside these themes because the world had progressed, and the forces of organization had won out.

The *feminist* perspective in criticism has gained sufficient status as a category, though it could be argued that its impetus is political in nature. Most of the feminist critics analyze films' treatment of women as they support or negate the role of women in contemporary society. For example, Diane Giddis (1973) explores a woman's dilemma (the fear that love represents loss of autonomy) in her analysis of *Klute*. Giddis finds that the film reflects woman's need to love and make a deep emotional commitment—a commitment unnecessary, to the same degree, for men. Constance Penley (1973) analyzes Ingmar Bergman's *Cries and Whispers* in the perspective of Bergman's other films. Penley's analysis runs counter to the majority of the film's reviews; she sees *Cries* as another example of Bergman's excessive portrayal of woman as victim, temptress, evil incarnate, and earth mother.

Psychoanalytic and *sociological* criticisms are likely to use models of analysis from accepted theorists or contemporary social concerns. Rushing and Frentz (1980), for example, derive their analysis of *The Deer Hunter* from the psychological theories of Carl Jung. In a sociological critique, the critic uses sociological concepts, such as class, status, interaction, organization and culture, to analyze a film. They may also use the perspective and language of social movements.

Finally, the *phenomenological* approach to criticism is concerned with the manner in which viewers perceive the film and/or its images (always, however, in relation to the whole) (see Andrew 1978). An example of this type is Janice Schuetz's analysis (1975) of *The Exorcist*. Schuetz utilizes the symbols of yin and yang from the *I Ching* as a paradigm for explaining the viewer's perceptions of the film. She argues that the film "presents reality in an organismic way, showing goodness and evil, doubt and faith, despair and hope, secular and sacred . . . as realistic representations of an integrated reality" (pp. 100–101). In addition, the images are sufficiently ambiguous to permit viewers to attribute meaning based on their own frame of reference (p. 101).

Contextual Studies

The three types included here—auteur, genre, and historical—have in common the study of film(s) within a specific context: directorial style (in its broadest sense), narrative type, and impact on or development of the film industry and/or the film as art form. Examples of each type are readily available in single texts, film periodicals, and collections of essays.

The most controversial of the three types is *auteur* criticism. Auteur theory assumes a certain amount of directorial autonomy in film production regardless of the fact that film is a product of producers, screenwriters, cinematographers, actors, musicians, film editors, and others. The film's creation and the stylistic choices made are assumed to be those of a single person— the director. Auteur criticism, then, focuses on film directors and the style manifested in two or more of their films. Directors such as Alfred Hitchcock, Charles Chaplin, John Ford, Howard Hawks, and Orson Welles have indirectly generated numerous auteur studies. No doubt, and not far off, there will be studies of George Lucas and Steven Spielberg.

Andrew Sarris (1968) uses auteur theory to rank various directors. Relying on three criteria—technical competence, stylistic identity, and communicability of worldview—he estimates their worth as directors. John Simon's analysis of Ingmar Bergman (1972) is an auteur study that looks at four films that Simon thinks represent Bergman's best work up to the early 1970s. Ian Cameron's two-part essay on Hitchcock (1972a) is another example of auteur criticism. It analyzes a specific feature of the director's overall style, his ability to create suspense in his films:

> Having arrived at such a disturbing view [everything is a potential threat], Hitchcock paradoxically relishes it and loves more than anything to torture his audiences by making them find the most innocuous thing alarming so that he can surprise and terrify them when the real threat is revealed. (Cameron 1972b, p. 34).

By examining a single film, *The Man Who Knew Too Much*, Cameron validates his auteur assumptions about Hitchcock's style. Another typical example of auteur criticism is Michael Budd's essay (1976) on visual imagery in John Ford's Westerns.

Genre criticism focuses on the narrative structures common to film: Westerns, war films, musicals, gangster films, and so on. This type of criticism also categorizes films according to specific characteristics. Thus, to be able to classify an object, to know where it fits, is a means toward understanding it better. We are then able to analyze a certain film based on how well it fits a particular genre and "how the director of that work used the elements of the genre—its *conventions*—to make a statement unique to that film" (Stromgren and Norden 1984). (For additional comments on genre criticism see Kaminsky 1974; see also, the extensive bibliography of genre studies in Cook 1981, pp. 691–692.)

Finally, *historical* studies inevitably analyze the entire scope of the film's development. Cook (1981), Ellis (1985), Giannetti and Eyman (1986), and Mast (1986) are fine representatives of historical criticism. In addition, studies of particular studios (Buscombe 1975; Gomery 1976) analyze the film industry from economic, political, or corporate perspectives or the impact of new technology. A relatively new annual series edited by Bruce A. Austin, "Current Research in Film: Audiences, Economics, and Law," publishes original essays on corporate structure, film financing, legal issues, marketing and promotion strategies, and others in an attempt to provide a place for those critics whose interests and work lie outside of the scope addressed by existing film journals.

Conclusion

There is a danger in establishing category systems. Inevitably examples of criticism exhibit features appropriate for more than one type of critical method. Judgment as to the correct placement of each of the examples here is left up to the reader. However, no apology is made for the classification contained within; what these essays accomplish is typical of the category they exemplify. Nor are they to be considered examples of superior criticism. In some cases, they create as many questions as they answer.

There will continue to be a need to analyze the best, worst, and average output of the film industry. Although the ultimate arbiter for judging a film's success may be its box office receipts, those with expertise should continue to analyze film with the express purpose of better understanding it as a mass media art form. Critics of both kinds, public and scholarly, can always hope that filmmakers, and ultimately audiences, will benefit from their efforts.

From the opposite viewpoint, those who practice film criticism have no monopoly on perfection. Critics must continue to read other critical analyses of film in order to improve their own craft. Like the student in a public speaking course, critics benefit from witnessing the successes and blunders of other critics. New methods are tried and either validated or rejected. In a rapidly progressing world, there is comfort in the thought that our critical stance and methods also continue to progress.

References

Andrew, Dudley. 1978. "The Neglected Tradition of Phenomenology in Film Theory." *Wide Angle* 2:44–49.

Andrews, James R. 1983. *The Practice of Rhetorical Criticism*. New York: Macmillan.

Bazin, André. 1967. *What Is Cinema?* Vol. 1. Translated and edited by Hugh Gray. Berkeley: University of California Press.

———. 1971. *What Is Cinema?* Vol. 2. Translated and edited by Hugh Gray. Berkeley: University of California Press.

Blair, Hugh. 1965. *Lectures on Rhetoric and Belles Lettres*. Vol. 1. Edited by Harold F. Harding. Carbondale: Southern Illinois University Press.

Budd, Michael. 1976. "A Home in the Wilderness: Visual Imagery in John Ford's Westerns." *Cinema Journal* 16:62–75.

Burke, Kenneth. 1969. *A Rhetoric of Motives*. Berkeley: University of California Press.

Buscombe, Edward. 1975. "Notes on Columbia Pictures Corporation, 1926–1941." *Screen* 16. Reprinted in Nichols 1985:92–108.

Cameron, Ian. 1972a. "Hitchcock and the Mechanics of Suspense." *Movie Reader*. New York: Frederick A. Praeger.

———. 1972b. "Hitchcock 2: Suspense and Meaning." *Movie Reader*. New York: Praeger.

Cook, David A. 1981. *A History of Narrative Film*. New York: W. W. Norton.

Dewey, John. 1930. *Construction and Criticism*. New York: Columbia University Press.

———. 1958. *Art as Experience*. New York: G. P. Putnam's Sons.

Eisenstein, Sergei. 1947. *The Film Sense*. New York: Harcourt Brace Jovanovich.

———. 1949. *Film Form: Essays in Film Theory*. Translated and edited by Jay Leyda. New York: Harcourt, Brace and World.

Ellis, Jack C. 1985. *A History of Film*. 2d ed. Englewood Cliffs, N.J.: Prentice-Hall.

Fisher, Walter. 1973. "Reaffirmation and Subversion of the American Dream." *Quarterly Journal of Speech* 59:160–167.

Frye, Northrop. 1957. *Anatomy of Criticism*. Princeton, N.J.: Princeton University Press.

Giannetti, Louis, and Scott Eyman. 1986. *Flashback: A Brief History of Film*. Englewood Cliffs, N.J.: Prentice-Hall.

Giddis, Diane. 1973. "The Divided Woman: Bree Daniels in *Klute*." *Women and Film*, nos. 3–4. Reprinted in Nichols 1976:194–201.

Gomery, Douglas. 1976. "Writing the History of the American Film Industry: Warner Brothers and Sound." *Screen* 17. Reprinted in Nichols 1985:109–119.

Hess, John. 1975. "*Godfather II*: A Deal Coppola Couldn't Refuse." *Jump-Cut*, no. 7. Reprinted in Nichols 1976:86–90.

Kaminsky, Stuart M. 1974. *American Film Genres: Approaches to a Critical Theory.* New York: Dell.

Mast, Gerald. 1986. *A Short History of the Movies.* 4th ed. New York: Macmillan.

Medhurst, Martin. 1978. "Image and Ambiguity: A Rhetorical Approach to *The Exorcist.*" *Southern Speech Communication Journal* 48:54–72.

———. 1982. "*Hiroshima, Mon Amour:* From Iconography to Rhetoric." *Quarterly Journal of Speech* 68:345–370.

Nichols, Bill, ed. 1976. *Movies and Methods: An Anthology.* Berkeley: University of California Press.

———. 1985. *Movies and Methods.* Vol. 2. Berkeley: University of California Press.

Penley, Constance. 1973. "*Cries and Whispers.*" *Women and Film,* nos. 3/4. Reprinted in Nichols 1976:204–208.

Perry, Ted. 1970. "A Contextual Study of M. Antonioni's *L'Eclisse.*" *Speech Monographs.*

Place, J. A., and C. S. Peterson. 1974. "Some Visual Motifs of Film Noir." *Film Comment* 10. Reprinted in Nichols 1976:325–338.

Pollack, Sidney. 1986. Interview on CBS, "West 57th St.," July 2.

Richards, Jeffrey. 1970. "Frank Capra and the Cinema of Populism." *Cinema,* no. 5. Reprinted in Nichols 1976:65–77.

Rushing, Janice Hocker, and Thomas S. Frentz. 1980. "*The Deer Hunter: Rhetoric of the Warrior.*" *Quarterly Journal of Speech* 66:392–406.

Sarris, Andrew. 1968. *The American Cinema.* New York: Dutton.

Schuetz, Janice. 1975. "*The Exorcist:* Images of Good and Evil." *Western Journal of Speech Communication* 39:92–101.

Simon, John. 1972. *Ingmar Bergman Directs.* New York: Harcourt Brace Jovanovich.

———. 1967. *Private Screenings.* New York: Macmillan.

Solomon, Martha. 1983. "Villainless Quest: Myth, Metaphor, and Dream in *Chariots of Fire.*" *Communication Quarterly* 31:274–281.

Stromgren, Richard L., and Martin F. Norden. 1984. *Movies: A Language in Light.* Englewood Cliffs, N.J.: Prentice-Hall.

Williams, Dale E. 1984. "*2001: A Space Odyssey:* A Warning before Its Time." *Critical Studies in Mass Communication* 1:311–322.

JOE BOB BRIGGS: DRIVE-IN MOVIE CRITIC

Dennis Holder

Dennis Holder is a Dallas writer.

Reprinted from the *Washington Journalism Review,* Vol. 6:2 (March, 1984).

Remember *Mad Monkey Kung Fu* and *Bloodsucking Freaks?* Remember *Screwballs, Hell's Angels Forever* or *I Dismember Mama?* Probably not. Not unless you live in Dallas and read Joe Bob Briggs's weekly drive-in movie reviews.

Joe Bob Briggs is said to be the world's first drive-in movie critic. And with a regular column in "Weekend," the *Dallas Times Herald's* Friday entertainment tabloid, a distribution contract with the Los Angeles Times Syndicate, and a book contract with Dell, he is on the verge of introducing the rest of America to his weird world of exploitation films and good ole boy misadventures.

In Dallas, where people laugh at the unsophisticated, macho, bigoted Texas stereotype while frequently living up to it, Joe Bob's column is one of the best-read regular features in either of the two, fiercely competitive daily newspapers. Since he was introduced, January 15, 1982, Joe Bob has become a cult figure to readers who appreciate parody and a friend in the wilderness to those who don't. He has been written about in the *Wall Street Journal,* the *Philadelphia Inquirer, USA Today, Playboy, US,* and the *Manchester* (England) *Guardian.*

In a slow week, Joe Bob draws about thirty letters from as far away as New York, Denver, and Washington State. When he campaigns—Joe Bob is nothing if not crusading—the mail floods in. An attack [in 1983] on the "french-fry head mayor of Irving" (A Dallas suburb), for tearing down the drive-in screens at Texas Stadium, garnered nearly 900 letters. A 1982 call for readers to nominate the best exploitation films in history brought 1,000 ballots in the first two weeks and a two-month total approaching 2,500.

Joe Bob Briggs, is, as *Times Herald* managing editor Kerry Slagle puts it, "a redneck for the masses." He loves America, beer, popcorn-without butter, and his 1972 Toronado with curb feelers and a No-Pest Strip dangling from the rear-view mirror. He hates indoor theaters, communist-speaking countries, a woman he refers to as "Ugly On A Stick," and anything to do with suspect regions like New York or Washington.

"Joe Bob is every Texan and southern cliché you ever heard all packed into one personality," says John Bloom, the *Times Herald*'s regular film critic. Because of the similarity in initials, Bloom is often accused of writing the Joe Bob column. "The tastes of Joe Bob Briggs are exactly the tastes of the audience exploitation movies are designed for," Bloom says.

Those tastes include an appreciation for the key elements of the great B movie: severed heads, unearthly beasts, car crashes, kung fu, and naked females. No matter how many beers he drinks or how insistently May Ellen Masters tries to glue him to the seatcovers, Joe Bob exercises his reporter's instincts to note the important facts:

> That's what I like about this flick. Honesty. All on-camera chainsaw deaths are absolutely necessary to the plot. Heads roll twice. Arms roll. Legs roll. (In the last scene, something rolls that the *Times Herald* high sheriffs won't let me put in the paper, but I'll just put it this way: I can still feel it. If you know what I mean, and I think you do.) Nine living breasts, two dead breasts. No motor vehicle chases. Good kung fu. Eight corpses. One beast with a chainsaw. Four gallons blood. Not much talking. Drive-in Academy Award nominations for Paul Smith, as the ugly gardener who likes to diddle around with a chainsaw, Dick Randall and John Shadow, who wrote this sucker and didn't put a lot of talking in it, and J. Piquer Simon, the director who keeps things moving.

Although Joe Bob is billed as a drive-in movie critic, film commentary frequently is merely incidental to his columns. In a full tabloid page each week, he often rambles on about his own misadventures, his friends, and life as he sees it. His earthy command of the language is often expressed with such words as "nookie" and "garbonzas." All women are bimbos, dumber than a box of rocks. The French are frogs. Turkish sailors are slopeheads. And anyone who works in an office, visits a health spa, or drinks anything from a stemmed glass is a wimp, jerkola or communist. With "the boys," Joe Bob is slightly more tolerant:

> Hey, I know all about "the boys" because I was in the Army one time for two weeks. And all I got to say is, so what you turkeys, this is America and as long as they don't tell me how to play "Dance Fever" on the mouth harp, I don't tell them how to butter their toast.

Among his pals is Rhett Beavers, who recently escaped from the Garland jail and took off for Arkansas to harvest polio weed. There's Chubb Fricke, a 300-pound bowling enthusiast who hasn't spoken to Joe Bob since they argued about whether the diving pig at Aquarena Springs was still alive or not; Ugh Barclay, who is handy to have around because "it's easy to meet people when you have a person named 'Ugh' with you"; and Junior Bodine, the first man ever turned down for service in Nuevo Laredo's red-light district. And there's Stookie McMahay, who got a hair transplant by mailing in a coupon to *Fling* magazine and is making regular payments "in the high two digits" to Wanda Bodine, who said she wouldn't marry him for less than $10,000.

Wanda, of course, operates a beauty parlor and Rockabilly Glamourcize studio in a trailer house on the Grapevine Highway. Formerly called Le Bodine, the business was renamed Institut De Beaute Bodine—"Look Like a Hundred Francs"—after Wanda followed Joe Bob to France for the Cannes Film Festival last year.

Other women in Joe Bob's circle include Cherry Dilday, who is "tougher than a 50-cent steak," and May Ellen Masters, who was Joe Bob's favorite date for the drive-in until she ran off in his car without even unhooking the speaker.

These characters and others weave in and out of Joe Bob's life in a soap opera—part fact, part fiction and unerringly funny.

Any movie that starts off with a woman being diddled by a giant katydid can't be all bad.

"Cicada."

That was Horace Busby disagreeing with me. Horace works at TI so he thinks that entitles him to use words like "cicada." I can't say "cicada," so I ignored Horace. Horace drives a Mercedes: I guess that makes him think he has the right to say anything.

As I was saying, it was a giant katydid. It came lurching out of the trees and ripped this woman's clothes off and had insect sex with her.

This reminds me of this guy I used to know named Burl who kept tarantulas in a glass box on top of his microwave. Burl used to say that tarantulas had sex through those little hairs that stand up on their kneecaps. I told him that tarantulas don't have kneecaps. He said that they have little hairs where their kneecaps should be. Burl wasn't a very intelligent individual when it came to insect sex.

So when I went to see this movie called *The Beast Within*, I took Horace Busby with me because Horace works at TI, and I figured that's a place where they would know about ladies who have katydid babies. Actually, we went in Horace's Mercedes because my car is up on blocks and Gus Simpson took out the motor last week and lost part of it. Plus the fact that Horace refuses to ride in my car anyway.

The first thing Horace asked me was what I meant by diddled.

I know that Horace has a Ph.D. from the University of Arkansas at Jasper so I ignored the question. So Horace piped up like a jerk.

"What happened is that the protagonist was raped by a cicada which appears to be one of the larger species."

I said, "What?"

There is no way to discuss adequately the phenomenon of Joe Bob Briggs without speculating about his real identity. It is widely assumed that Joe Bob is really film critic John Bloom, an award-winning former investigative reporter who periodically ducks into Institut De Beaute Bodine to change his alter ego. But Bloom will tell you this cannot be so.

"I'm not even from Texas. I'm from Arkansas," argues Bloom, who speaks slowly and quietly in a faintly chicken-fried baritone. "I drive a Toyota. Besides, I don't have any sense of humor. I couldn't be Joe Bob."

It is, in fact, as difficult to imagine John Bloom creating Joe Bob Briggs as it is to imagine Clark Kent turning into Superman. Bloom is a tall, thin, fragile-looking young man with pale complexion and a meandering stack of wavy, dark hair. No one is sure just what Joe Bob looks like, but he ought to be chunkier. He must have a tan.

Bloom tends to dress like Dan Rather, and he has been known to have lunch in a new-wave oyster bar. Joe Bob would spot him as a wimp for certain, probably for a communist.

Bloom's film reviews are sensitive and restrained. He decries gratuitous violence and unnecessary nudity. He delights in reporting in depth on the ins and outs of big-business Hollywood.

But, despite the contradictions, despite Bloom's initial denials, John Bloom and Joe Bob Briggs are indeed one and the same.

"At least half of the mail Joe Bob gets is from people who take the column seriously," Bloom says. "They don't necessarily believe all of the stories he tells in the paper, but they think he's just lying, telling tall tales. They still believe in the character. I think if we came out and told them who Joe Bob really is, they would be disappointed. It would be like telling a kid there is no Santa Claus."

To protect his privacy and the illusion, Joe Bob has repeatedly refused requests to appear in public or on radio and television talk shows. When he turned down "The David Letterman Show," producers asked for John Bloom instead. Bloom said that he could not speak for Joe Bob Briggs. Other programs have offered to interview a shadow or to hide Joe Bob behind a curtain, but the answer has always been no.

"I get request after request for TV interviews and radio interviews," Bloom says. "Several want to adapt the column for TV. That it is a purely literary creation, nobody can understand. They think everything has to have an electronic expression.

"This thing is so fragile that the last thing you'd want is to remove the mystery and magic through the cold reality of a camera. If you ever gave Joe Bob a specific face, or even a voice, some of the power would be lost. Some people see him as fat. Some think of him as lanky, stringy. Some hear the southern twang in his voice. Some don't. To use a ridiculous example, the reason Helen of Troy is thought of as the world's most beautiful woman is that no one ever described her."

Editors at the *Dallas Times Herald* could not have predicted such popularity for Joe Bob Briggs when the column was introduced. The feature was actually created largely by accident, a mischievous device to report a tired topic.

"The whole thing started as a Sunday feature assignment," recalls special sections editor Ron Smith. "Everyone had been writing stories about the death of the drive-in movie. We thought that was bullshit. Drive-ins still are alive and well, at least in the Southwest. We wanted to find out why that was true and what kind of people actually go to the drive-in. It would have been just another Sunday story if Bloom hadn't come up with the idea of writing it from the perspective of a drive-in regular."

Bloom says the idea percolated almost from the time he joined the *Times Herald*. He saw it as a way of serving readers interested in the films typically shown at drive-ins without taking the movies too seriously.

In a previous stint with the *Times Herald* as a reporter, Bloom won two Headliner awards and a Robert F. Kennedy award for social reporting for articles on the Ku Klux Klan, an investigation into the death of a Mexican-American at the hands of police, and a series on police abuse of minority groups in the Southwest. But he had never worked as a movie critic and wasn't quite sure how to approach the assignment.

"When I started as film critic, I felt it was my responsibility to review everything that opened in this market. I was turning out columns with four or five straight reviews and then a couple of films like *Dead and Buried*. After a few weeks, it struck me as silly to review these as art. I wanted to find a way to treat them as they were meant to be treated, as product. Ron [Smith] and I got together on that idea and Joe Bob was the result."

By the time of his first appearance, Joe Bob had evolved from a Sunday story to a possible occasional feature for an unused page of "Weekend." Bloom introduced him with a longish biographical sketch. Joe Bob, he explained, was about nineteen years old, had at least three ex-wives (he may have forgotten a couple), was unemployed, and claimed to have seen 6,800 drive-in movies, counting triple features.

In a comparatively straight, six-paragraph review at the bottom of the page, Joe Bob Briggs was born.

> *The Grim Reaper* is this movie about a guy who will use a meat cleaver when he has to, but usually he just uses his mouth. (I know what you're thinking: you're thinking vampire. So was I. But you're wrong.) I won't tell you the whole deal, but the Grim Reaper is not a monster; he's a believable human being who likes to kill people and then chew on them for a while.

Smith and Bloom began the drive-in movie review quietly, without even mentioning the column to their senior editors. For several weeks it ran unnoticed. "We were convinced that because of the place it was played, nobody in management was reading it," says Bloom. "We were right. By the time they found out about it, we had received so much response they couldn't afford to stop it."

Slagle, who at that time was assistant managing editor for features and was on leave when the first Joe Bob columns appeared, confirms Bloom's account. "There were some raised eyebrows around here when management found out this was in the paper. It was so off-the-wall and so different that no one seemed comfortable with it. Nobody loved it at first, but everybody loved it after they found out how popular it was."

No figures are available on the number of telephone calls and letters the early Joe Bob Briggs columns elicited, but Slagle says it was obvious by about the third week that it ought to be a regular, weekly feature. With help from Smith and Slagle, Bloom began to flesh out the character.

"Joe Bob's personality, his love life—it all grew out of the movies he reviewed," says Bloom. "The movies came first and the persona just evolved. We tried to imagine what a person who liked these movies would be like and to create a consistent character. I began giving him friends and girlfriends and so on.

"Readers let me know what they liked and what they thought did not ring true. Once I introduced a character named Vida Stegall. She was a nice person, a kind of girl next door. She was very unpopular. Readers didn't want any nice women. They only wanted sluts and bimbos. Vida Stegall is still around, but Joe Bob doesn't talk about her very often."

While Joe Bob was an immediate success in the Dallas area, early attempts to syndicate his column were rebuffed. When they received tear sheets, most major syndicates said they didn't like the idea or had too many movie reviews already. One or two did like the concept but claimed they had no idea how to market it to other papers. It didn't fit their package.

In the fall of 1982, when the *Times Herald* enlisted the director of the USA Film Festival to help present Joe Bob Briggs's "First Annual World Drive-In Movie Festival and Custom Car Rally," syndicate skepticism began to dissolve. The festival itself was a failure—although B-movie king Roger Corman flew in to accept the Joe Bob Briggs Lifetime Achievement Award engraved on a '57 Chevy hubcap—but it prompted the *Wall Street Journal* to write about Joe Bob on November 10, 1982.

Under the page-one headline, "Aficionado of Trash at the *Times Herald* Is a Big Hit in Dallas" *WSJ* writer G. Christian Hill declared, "*Joe Bob Goes to the Drive-In* is reactionary, in bad taste and just about the most popular feature in either of this city's two big, fiercely competitive newspapers."

"As soon as the *Wall Street Journal* article came out, we were getting calls from all over," says Bloom. "A couple of syndicates called and said they would like to take another look at the column. Several newspapers—the *San Francisco Chronicle*, the *Kansas City Star*, the *Denver Post*, and a few others—called to inquire about running Joe Bob. We had publishers offering contracts to produce a Joe Bob Briggs book. The whole thing just completely took off."

In the year and a half since the *Wall Street Journal* made Joe Bob Briggs a star, Bloom has hired an agent, signed with a syndicate, and shopped for the biggest book advance he could get. The book, an autobiography of Joe Bob Briggs, is due from Dell. . . . Its title: *A Guide to Western Civilization.* The Los Angeles Times Syndicate, which will offer *Joe Bob Goes to the Drive-In* nationally beginning March 12, currently is talking with Bloom about a second book, a collection of Joe Bob columns.

According to Bloom, Joe Bob Briggs's columns are among the easiest writing he has ever done for pay. Each column requires about three hours of his time, he says—two hours to see the movie and one to write 1,200 to 1,500 words. Syndication, he adds, will neither increase the workload—except perhaps for answering mail—nor change the flavor of the column. "I may make it a little less local in the references to Dallas personalities, but I will keep the geography. I think the local color is one of the big strengths of the column."

Asked whether he might eventually grow tired of Joe Bob Briggs and want to give it up, Bloom answers, "I don't know. It isn't the sort of thing that can go on forever. I imagine reader interest will die out after awhile. But I guess I'll be writing Joe Bob for at least the next four years. That's the length of my contract with the syndicate."

Wanda Bodine hired this new shampoo girl that everybody calls Chloris. Everybody except me. I call her Ugly On A Stick.

Chloris weighs about 27 pounds and stands six-foot-eight. (That's not counting when she has on her platform clog shoes.) She has these little beady eyes like a Pekinese dog that was hit by a bakery truck and still remembers it. Sometimes, she'll start whining and carrying on and bothering all the other employees at Le Bodine until Vida Stegall agrees to give her a manicure. It don't help.

One time I went in the trailer house right after Ugly On A Stick started working there, and the first thing happened is Vida pulled me aside and said, "Joe Bob, I just want you to know that there's a new girl in the back."

I said, "What?"

Vida said, "She's a very nice person and she's ugly."

I went back to take a look, and Chloris had her head bent over the sink and was mixing up some kind of super industrial-strength hair-spray remover, and at the same time she was yelling over at Audrey Tullis that she needed some new seat covers for her Vega, or a new Vega, whichever one she could get out of this guy named Curtis. From what I could tell from the back end, Curtis was a student at Texas School for the Blind. Before I could get away, she turned around and folded her lips together like a piece of cellophane that's been all wadded up for five minutes and then you sit around and watch it pop out full size again—that's what Ugly On a Stick's lips looked like, only they'd been wadded up more than five minutes.

"Hi," she said. "I'm Chloris."

"Rhett Beavers," I said. (What the hey, the man's in jail, he don't give a diddly.)

Chloris said, "I hope you don't mind that I'm ugly."

"It doesn't bother us that Joe Bob Briggs probably will offend some people," says Angela Rinaldi, managing editor of development for the Los Angeles Times Syndicate. "Controversy attracts readers. Besides, this is an extremely good-humored and well-controlled kind of offensiveness. I don't think Joe Bob is on the level of offensiveness of James Watt, for example."

In fact, *Times Herald* editors concede, some readers have been offended—make that outraged—by Joe Bob Briggs's preoccupation with nudity, sex, and violence. Perhaps 20 percent of the letters the column generates are from readers who hate it. Occasionally, a letter ends with the words, "Please cancel my subscription to the *Dallas Times Herald.*"

One Baptist minister in Tyler, Texas, a city 95 miles east of Dallas, has publicly declared Joe Bob a "sick mind" and has urged his congregation to pray for the writer's immortal soul. He also has forbidden his three sons to read Joe Bob.

Even drive-in theater owners don't like the column, Bloom says. "They don't think Joe Bob is typical of the average drive-in movie patron. They think he creates a bad image for the drive-ins. They've been trying to bill themselves as family entertainment since 1946. It has never worked, but they don't like to be represented as the garbage pit for exploitation movies."

On the other side, *Times Herald* editors contend the column attracts more readers than it loses, and it gets the newspaper talked about. "We get letters from people in New York and Washington State who want to subscribe to the paper just on Fridays so they can keep up with Joe Bob," says Smith. "We have people who come in and buy back issues of Friday papers they miss when they are out of town. I don't have any hard numbers, but I think that in terms of readership, it nets out to a definite plus."

According to Slagle, the *Times Herald* has carefully considered and formally proscribed the column's boundaries of taste. Early in Joe Bob's writing career, Slagle says, then-executive editor Ken Johnson asked for guidelines describing "just how far this thing is going to go." Slagle and Smith drew up a set of rules specifying, among other things, which risqué words would be permitted and which ones should be taboo. As Joe Bob's editor, part of Smith's job is to enforce those rules.

"Joe Bob has a little more latitude than most other writers," Smith says. "But I can't let him go too far. John just keeps chipping away, trying to get a little more latitude, to break new ground. 'Twat' is the word he tried to get in the most. He's tried to get it in three times that I know of. I'm the high sheriff that takes it out."

Responds Bloom, "I know the limits so well that I know when I write something what's going to trigger the taste police. I ask, 'Are you going to let me say that? If they say no, I go back and have Joe Bob say, 'They won't let me say it.' The column is very honest in that respect. Readers like it."

Readers do like it. But there is room to ask whether it is a legitimate function of a daily newspaper to push the limits of good taste. There even is room to ask whether this is journalism.

In a signed column, *Dallas Morning News* editorial writer William Murchison recently attacked Joe Bob for condoning violence as depicted in exploitation movies. "I don't think anyone takes Joe Bob Briggs seriously," says Murchison, "so he's probably pretty harmless. But the movies he reviews do celebrate violence, and I don't think that's a good thing in our society.

"Feminists find his column extremely offensive," Murchison adds. "Those films treat women as objects, and his columns take it one step further. He makes jokes about a lot of things that aren't very funny. I think there is a legitimate argument to be made that a lot of what he writes is in pretty bad taste."

Joe Bob responded to Murchison's critical column by asking his readers: "Is Bill Murchison a royal wimp or has Hell frozen over?"

"I'm sure Joe Bob offends the journalistic purists," says Slagle. "There are a lot of journalists, including quite a few on the staff of this newspaper, who don't think we ought to be doing it. They say, 'Is this really the kind of thing that a serious newspaper ought to be doing?'

"I haven't thought about it much from a journalistic or philosophical viewpoint. I just know it's crazy, it's fun, it's popular. I look at it as one part journalism, one part pure fun, and one part parody. And to the extent that some of our readers have any interest in these exploitation movies, it is a little bit of a service item."

Despite the fact that Joe Bob Briggs is his creation, Bloom laments that his red-neck spoof has proved more popular than some of his serious work.

"It's funny," he muses. "*Texas Monthly* associate editor Jim Atkinson and I spent two years researching and writing a book on the Candace Montgomery murder case. It is a serious piece of journalism, and we thought it would be fairly commercial because the case was so sensational. But we had to beg agents to handle it and publishers to look at it. When we finally got a publisher to take it, we got almost no advance. [Called *Evidence of Love,* the Bloom-Atkinson book was published in 1984.]

"But then Joe Bob comes along, and I have publishers begging me for a book. I think it says something about the publishing industry and about readers' tastes when you can't give away a book of serious reporting but everybody wants the low-brow humor."

OK. Now somebody out in East Texas sent me a letter last week about "gratuitous nudity" and I believe that individual knows who he or she is so we won't single him out here in the newspaper because I'm feeling like a heck of a nice guy today. Here's my opinion of gratuitous nudity:

I only approve of gratuitous nudity when it's necessary to the story.

Or when it's a real boring movie and you need some nekkid women to liven things up.

Also, I keep getting these letters from bimbos who say, "Hey, Joe Bob, you seem to have this *thing* about garbonzas and female flesh, so why don't you ever talk about *male* nudity, because we like to look at (a male nickname not allowed by the *Times Herald* high sheriffs unless it has a capital letter on it)."

Answer to that one: I am not a United Way agency. This column is not for a bunch of nympho bar bunnies working in a (*sic*) insurance office somewhere, trying to get their jollies out of the paper because they cain't get a drink poured down their dress at Confetti. This is a movie review column. There's still a few of us who take our job seriously and don't go around asking people to write kinky bull-stuff so they can hide it under the Sealy Posturepedic and get it out after the Letterman show. There's still a few of us who have some ethics.

MOVIES AND THE POLITICS OF EVERYDAY LIFE

David L. Altheide

David L. Altheide is a professor in the School of Justice Studies, Arizona State University, where he also serves as field research director at the Center for Urban Studies. He has reported on various aspects of rational and official information in TV news, bureaucracy, and everyday life. Among his major works are *Creating Reality: How TV News Distorts Events; Media Logic* (with Robert P. Snow); *Bureaucratic Propaganda* (with John M. Johnson); and *Media Power*.

The politics of communication involve the selection, organization, emphasis, presentation, and consequences of messages. We want to understand how aspects of everyday life are incorporated into movies because these familiar images, scenarios, and practices can reinforce the movie content and our general understandings about appropriate and inappropriate behavior.

Popular depictions in movies of personal, institutional, and social affairs involve some features of feelings, knowledge, skills, and experience with which the audience is already familiar. From this perspective *the politics of everyday life would include those behaviors, problems, topics, strategies, styles, and emotions apparent in the selection, organization, emphasis, and presentation of movie scenarios.*

This reading focuses on the way some of these mundane, yet critical, features of daily life are artistically presented in movies. Following a brief discussion of movie logic and everyday life, we will then illustrate how movies contribute to the politics of communication in terms of family and friends, age, gender, technology and culture, horror, mass media use, and courage and conflict.

Communication Formats

Specific media routinely perform their communicative tasks through the use of *formats*, or rules of thumb, for selecting, organizing, emphasizing, and presenting messages (Altheide and Snow 1979; Snow 1983; Altheide 1985). The nature of a specific format will depend to some extent on the technology used, the basic character of the medium (linear, aural, visual), and the purpose of the medium (for example, to entertain in order to earn money). Each of these points is rife with political features. But there is an added dimension to be considered: communication with any audience entails drawing on the audience's communicative experience, knowledge, and assumptions about language, situations, scenarios, roles, and emotions. This does not mean that films simply reflect society as it is but that many features of everyday life are used to enlist the audience involvement in the construction of scenarios and meanings (Snow 1983, p. 208; Combs 1984). In this sense, our understanding and appreciation of a movie is grounded in our familiarity with culture, including everyday life routines and our cultural stocks of knowledge (Schutz 1967).

Perhaps one of the most basic points about everyday life in movies is that people are featured in specific situations with which the audience is familiar. The audience's knowledge provides a context for providing a definition and sense for locating a novel and bizarre scenario next to a familiar one. In this sense, movies may have abstract messages, themes, and morals, but the message is carried through rather specific interaction and implied feelings in context. As articulated by Robert Snow (1983, p. 209), "Given the intensity of emotional involvement afforded by movies, the genre and content of films develop a powerful potential for influence." At the core, then, is a critical question: What makes movies recognizable and intelligible to an audience, especially a heterogeneous one? Consider a few examples.

Everyday Life Experience in Movies

Family and Friends

Several recent movies have explored the interpersonal conflicts and problems of family and friendship; *Terms of Endearment, Ordinary People,* and *The Big Chill* are examples. Emotions, personal relationships, history, bureaucratic organizations, and social institutions provide the context of experience, which is presumably shared by the characters and the audience members. Moreover, the action—like in much of everyday life—consists of individuals making claims, and offering accounts, to intimates about past, present, and future concerns.

The family—or friends as substitute family in *The Big Chill*—is depicted in these movies as the source and solution of emotional traumas, including misspent affections, individual meaning and fulfillment, and competition. The family members in a variety of roles provide the context for emotions and action rather than individuals in pursuit of romantic love. The significant social actors in these movies include children, who are involved in significant conurturing relationships with adults and are not just spectators or props for their parents. In this sense, some recent movies proclaim that the silver screen version of family and friendship is less exclusive but also more vulnerable to expectations of self and others.

Gender

The movies *Yentl* and *Tootsie* offer a look at the complexity of how women must present themselves in society. *Yentl* stresses religious exclusionary practices and their impact on the development of strategies for self-presentation of a woman who wants to do what only men are permitted to do. In *Tootsie,* a talented male actor disguised as a woman gets a job playing a "woman character cast by a man," and we are given somewhat the same message but with an ironic twist: a man can learn about men by engaging in a role performance expected of women. Moreover, it is suggested that other women find such characterological traits in men to be quite appealing. The audience member's awareness and empathy is drawn on in these depictions of loving, caring and insensitivity (Zimmerman and Pollner 1970).

Age

Few popular movies explicitly deal with age, although character portrayals of youth, middle-aged adults, and the elderly are apparent in movies. Children tend to be presented as innocents in science fiction movies, such as *ET* and *Close Encounters,* and horror movies about demonic possession, as in

The Omen. In both instances, a political statement is being made about the incomplete socialization of children, which makes them more accepting of novel experiences, including lacking the proper ego defenses to avoid becoming the devil's agent.

Adolescence tends to be depicted in certain activities and styles. Adolescent sexual behavior is a common topic in a variety of movies, such as *Fast Times at Ridgemont High*. We are privy to the enactment of innocence, as in discussions about oral sex, and the politics of peer pressure for an offending member to pay for an abortion. In *War Games,* an adolescent who is skilled with a computer accidentally cracks the Defense Department's code and unwittingly plays the game of thermonuclear war. Here it is the youth who winds up apologizing to the authorities rather than the adult buffoons who intended and developed the game scenario in the first place. The depiction of such hackers as irresponsible people with strange ways of having fun easily fits within our version of the politics of everyday life.

Old people are seldom major characters in movies. Although the elderly wise role is clearly portrayed by Yoda in *Return of the Jedi.* That wisdom looks old is a common assumption of everyday life.

Technology and Culture

The politics of everyday life is also depicted in movies as an answer to the questions: What does technology look like, what has modern culture done to us, and what will we become? Without speaking to the validity of movie versions of answers, we can nevertheless identify some recent answers found, respectively, in the films *ET, Iceman, Never Cry Wolf, and Road Warrior.*

In the first two movies, but especially *Iceman,* the notion of "man is bad, nature is good" is offered. More is involved here than an antiscience statement: rather, the interest is in the social interaction, language, appearance, and manner through which the problem and issue are illustrated.

In some examples, certain characters act contrary or out of role in a way that filmmakers believe the audience will understand. In the *Iceman,* a scientist articulates a higher value and lets the Iceman escape rather than sacrifice this creature from the past to the whims of scientific experiments. With *ET,* it is a child, not an adult, who has the initial curiosity, humanity, and love to enable this extraterrestrial stranger to thrive and learn rather than quickly destroy him. This, too, is a political statement.

Never Cry Wolf invokes a seemingly barren and hostile environment to bring forth life, learning, and love of nature. A naturalist learns the ways of wolves by looking at them on their own terms and in the process undergoes experiences that invalidate prevailing stereotypes about dangerous and aggressive wolves. The movie illustrates the clash of wills between the naturalist, who seems to represent the wolves, and the northern natives, who can earn money by shooting the wolves for bounty and hides. The natives understand that many beliefs about the danger of wolves are incorrect, but they do not care; they would rather earn money. The naturalist believes that it is wrong to kill wolves, especially if they are not the menace to other animals and civilization that some people claim they are. For this individual, preserving and understanding part of nature is important in its own right.

Futures may appear to be tenuous and uncertain, but in movies, we can know them as surely as we know the past. In *Road Warrior II*, the lessons take place in a barren environment, essentially devoid of customary architecture. In this way, even the most basic physical surroundings become visual statements about the circumstances and conditions of the future. The characters in *Road Warrior* are the survivors of a nuclear war who battle for the most precious of all goods, gasoline. Those who have it must protect it.

The politics of everyday life in the future resemble those in the present in one important way: the good guys and the bad guys are clearly distinguishable by their dress, manner, and styles. The costuming in this futuristic scenario depicts the bad guys as a composite of bikers and punks. They wear football helmets, catchers' masks, and, above all, use off-road racing vehicles. Their weapons are crossbows, muzzle loader handguns, and spears, and vehicles look like dune buggies chopped out of Oldsmobiles and Buicks from other decades. In short, the look of future hoodlums and desperadoes is portrayed as not unlike current outcasts and deviants.

Horror

Horror at the movies looks like our imaginations and primordial fears. Movies about the demonic world of possession and evil give horror a specific look. What we have to fear from this standpoint is the world of the unknown. The politics of helplessness and despair are apparent in horror movies. Another source of horror is the psychotic random murderer, who uses the most grizzly of crude instruments, such as a chain saw or an axe. We feel defenseless against such irrational assault.

The personalization of horror in everyday life has been shown in recent movies about the Vietnam War. *Apocalypse Now* shows the horror caused by a brilliant officer gone crazy. Brutality and inhumanity can be represented in hand-to-hand combat, horrified faces and screams, and dark colors. But there is more to it. Another side of horror in Vietnam and other military films is the bureaucratic mind-set and accounting procedures that relied on body counts to measure military progress and condoned the spraying of deadly herbicides to achieve an objective. This feature of the craziness of war is more complicated and thus not easily told in close-up visuals.

Mass Media

With a few exceptions, the major media play a small role in most movies. Characters are seldom seen watching TV or reading. But there are a few exceptions: *Being There, Moscow on the Hudson,* and *Splash.*

In *Being There,* the extreme media effects on one's knowledge of the world, style, and taken-for-granted assumptions are depicted in Peter Sellers's version of Chauncey Gardener, a recluse whose major contact with life was his TV set. His TV clichés are mistaken as wisdom when he ventures out into the world.

The way visitors to our culture rely on media imagery for everyday life problems is illustrated, with different slants, in *Splash* (a mermaid) and *Moscow on the Hudson* (a musician from the Soviet Union). As the characters study and imitate TV phrases, facial expressions, and body posture, they are guided through a variety of situations. In this sense, the major question of how reality is communicated and constructed is partially answered by these movies to include the mass media.

Courage and Conflict

Movie formats are organized to join basic values of the audience with story lines. The aim is to enlist the expectations and beliefs of moviegoers to fill in a lot of assumptions and lend credibility to the plot. Individual courage is one cultural value that can be illustrated in a variety of story lines that show an individual in conflict with an adversary. Who that adversary is, how they look, and what they do is relevant for the politics of everyday life. In recent years, the courageous individuals have been featured in conflict against foreigners who are cast as agents of an enemy government. Performances by Sylvester Stallone as Rocky and then as Rambo, and Tom Cruise's character, Maverick, in *Top Gun,* are good illustrations of the use of the lone warrior to champion the values and causes shared by the audience.

Stallone's fame emerged from his portrayals of Rocky Balboa, a tough boxer who demonstrated individual courage in overcoming great odds to become champion. In *Rocky IV,* he defends America's honor against the Soviet Union's champion, Ivan Drago. Perhaps the most important point is the way the two champions are presented. Rocky is humane and kind, has a sense of humor, and trains "naturally" by pulling wagons and lifting logs on a farm in the Soviet countryside. Drago, by contrast, is like an automaton; he seldom smiles and is trained with science and drugs in laboratories. He is managed and controlled by others; Rocky is his own man. In the end, the Soviet fans cheer Rocky, who invites them to cooperate in winning world peace.

Since moviegoers know Stallone as Rocky, it is not surprising that Stallone became Rocky in the public mind. When other versions of the lone warrior were released featuring Stallone as a psychotic Vietnam veteran, John Rambo, it is not too far-fetched to say that in viewers' minds, they were seeing Rocky Rambo. Like Rocky, Rambo does what he thinks is best, including shooting up towns, getting revenge, and doing all of the things that can be shown visually to demonstrate courage in conflicts with the law, rednecks, and international adversaries.

The individual initiative of Rambo is also apparent in *Top Gun,* a film about navy fighter pilots. This musical video centers around the exploits of an appealing pilot whose call sign is Maverick. We get the impression that a rough-cut individual who deviates from a lot of rules can still be successful with beautiful women and against the enemy. There is a clear sense of belonging to a team and working together as fellow pilots support each other and in turn depend on aircraft carrier crews.

Like an earlier movie in the 1950s, *Rebel without Cause,* starring James Dean, *Top Gun* appeals to younger people because of the action, drama, and rebellion. There have been numerous reports about skyrocketing enlistments in the navy since the movie, and a two-day (July 26–27, 1986) Blue Angel air show at Miramar Naval Base, the setting for the movie, drew more than 650,000 spectators. In these and other movies, courage is demonstrated with toughness and a moral stand against traditional adversaries. In this sense, the movies reinforce conventional propaganda about our fears and the manner of courage to help us survive.

Conclusion

Dictators and others who would seek to control freedom like to attack the mass media, particularly visual media. Although their aim is to control public information, in more specific terms, they are seeking to provide a uniform set of everyday life images and understandings. The essence of political control is to reduce ambiguity by increased uniformity of messages. This is why it is important to understand the connection between the politics of everyday life and movies.

For a movie to be intelligible to an audience and to make an entertaining and/or interesting point, it must provide familiar features of everyday life. The drama, excitement, horror, and general emotion associated with a pay-for-thrill source of popular culture like movies will also use and develop themes and images as a feature of the broader experience. The way that family and friends, gender, age, technology and culture, horror, the mass media, and courage are portrayed and visualized as part of routine activities invites an inquiry into the politics of everyday life as a feature of political communication.

Future research into this topic could include comparisons of topics in movies compared to TV, both cross-sectionally and over time. The aim should be to identify the way everyday life is used as both a topic and a resource in movies and other major media. This research challenge is made somewhat easier because of the availability of numerous old movies and TV programs. The method used will be a rather unique form of ethnographic content analysis in which structured coding categories develop after an initial inquiry and never totally dominate the analysis; room must always be made available for detailed description on a case-by-case basis.

One brief example of the power of comparative ethnographic content analysis is Monya Katzson's (1983) study of adult and children roles on "Leave It to Beaver" and "Silver Spoons." In noting that the former show had adults and children much more firmly implanted in their roles while the latter program lets roles travel more, Katzson wrote (1983, pp. 36–37):

> Adults are people who remain in control. Kids are people who have no con-trol. Kids are incompetent, dependent on adults for approval. Adults only hope that their children won't shame them by doing too many incompetent things. Roles are at rest in the Cleaver family. They do not move about . . . children are lesser beings. They stumble puzzled through life, their eventual salvation inevitable only as they age. . . .
>
> In the Stratton household ["Silver Spoons"] roles travel. Adults and chil-dren pop in and out of situations as competence in doing and talking travels from one situation to [another]. Adult/adult and child/child roles still exist, but two new forms have emerged, the child/adult and the adult/child. . . . This traveling of roles and thus diffusion of competence blurs the distinction between the generations.

In brief, everyday life and political communication are not dissimilar; they are components of any communication effort to make meaningful state-ments to a heterogeneous audience. Identifying the nature and use of this mode of political communication will clarify the interaction among the movie producers, movie images, and the viewing audience.

References

Altheide, David L. 1985. *Media Power.* Beverly Hills, Calif.: Sage.

Altheide, David L., and Robert P. Snow. 1979. *Media Logic.* Beverly Hills, Calif.: Sage.

Combs, James. 1984. "Movies as Political Communication: A Theory of Popular

Representation." Paper presented at the Annual Meeting of the International Communication Association, San Francisco, May 24–28, 1984.

Katzson, Monya. 1983. "Reflections on the Inward Eye." Seminar paper, Arizona State University.

Schutz, Alfred. 1967. *The Phenomenology of the Social World.* Evanston, Ill.: Northwestern University Press.

Snow, Robert P. 1983. *Creating Media Culture.* Beverly Hills, Calif.: Sage.

Zimmerman, Don H., and Melvin Pollner. 1970. "The Everyday World as a Phenomenon." In Jack D. Douglas, ed., *Understanding Everyday Life,* pp. 80–104. Chicago: Aldine.

7
Advertising and Public Relations

Introduction

> Many people have expressed uneasiness about the advertising enterprise in our time. To put the matter abruptly, the advertising industry is a crude attempt to extend the principles of automation to every aspect of society. Ideally, advertising aims at the goal of a programmed harmony among all human impulses and aspirations and endeavors. Using handicraft methods, it stretches out toward the ultimate electronic goal of a collective consciousness.[1]

The far-reaching overall effect and the aims of advertising suggested by McLuhan in this quotation may be valid topics for exploration. Certainly advertising's importance to the mass media is not subject to any doubt, for the advertising industry is vital to their support. Newspapers and magazines could not be marketed at existing prices, nor could commercial radio and television be broadcast without massive advertising revenues. We have already seen how changes in medium preference affected magazines and how the switch to cable television may change network revenues. In return for current levels of financial sponsorship, considerable time and space are devoted to advertising. Television advertisements may run as high as eighteen minutes per hour, and news magazines devote about 30 percent of their space to their sponsors. Large-circulation newspapers such as the *New York Times* use about 40 percent of their space for advertising, and smaller local papers may be as much as 60 percent advertising, excluding classified ads. This is about three or four times more space than they usually devote to international, national, and local news combined.

The advertising industry is a sizable part of the U.S. economy. In 1966, the total expenditure on advertising amounted to $16.6 billion, or 2.6 percent of the national income. Newspapers and magazines received the greatest share—almost 42 percent—radio's share was 6 percent, and television obtained 17 percent.[2] In 1984, total advertising volume was over $88 billion.

The share taken by newspapers and magazines had declined to 32.5 percent, while radio and television had gained a larger share, 6.6. and 22.6 percent, respectively.[3]

The advertising agency is one of the most curious enterprises in the economy and perhaps one of the most competitive. Since its main product is ideas, it requires little more than a typewriter, a desk, and access to photographic and drawing equipment. An ad agent creative enough to hold down a few good contracts is in business. Agencies can go from virtually nothing to multimillion dollar operations in a few years. But even the largest agencies can never be fully secure since their clients can easily switch agencies and may do so every few years as a matter of policy. Some corporations will then give a new, spectacularly successful agency their business.

The tried and tested giants at the top are big enough to survive the loss of a few clients, even major ones. Large agencies like J. Walter Thompson, Young and Rubicam, and McCann-Erickson have domestic billings in the hundreds of millions of dollars, and they have extensive operations overseas. Together with many leading advertisers, they are becoming increasingly international concerns. Such agencies clearly have sufficient economic strength to be a powerful influence on the media industries (and society in general) if they choose to exercise their potential.

The type of advertisement placed in each of the media varies considerably because of the different types of audience they reach. Newspaper advertising consists primarily of local plugs for retail stores. Magazines and television enjoy the bigger product-oriented contracts, including public relations pitches on behalf of major corporations such as chemical companies, which do not sell directly to the consumer, and power companies, which are sole suppliers.

Commonplace activities—eating, drinking, housekeeping—are heavily urged in the new electronic age through its most advanced medium. Of course, everyone needs to do them, and the market is truly a mass one for these products, so advertising is justified. On the other hand, people can be expected to fulfill their basic needs without the urgings of advertising, although perhaps a few would be less well scrubbed and overfed. Competition is strong among the producers of these goods, and they compete with each other through advertising rather than price. Some corporations, such as those that manufacture detergents, carry this to the extreme of promoting their own rival products against each other. The standard rationale for advertising—that it disseminates useful product information and thereby stimulates the market—is not accurate in the case of such products.

George Kirstein asked about the overall effect of advertising on society by imagining what would happen if a total moratorium were imposed on advertising.[4] (Since attempts have been made to ban all advertising on children's TV programs, perhaps his ideas will not remain entirely speculative.) He thinks that papers and magazines would immediately become much more expensive, and broadcasting would have to convert rapidly to a subscription pattern. Product information would be considerably improved. Sales of *Consumer Reports* would skyrocket, books would become more valued, and landscape and airwaves would be more aesthetic and better suited to an advanced civilization. The economy would not collapse, as the advertisers' rationale would lead us to predict. Kirstein's dream, however, is not likely to come true, for a total ban on advertising would require not only the self-conscious action of a well-organized majority of consumers but also their ability to outflank the powerful media interests that would be destroyed in the process. Advertising control is a matter of high finance and power, not a matter of public interest. The ads are here to stay.

The first reading, by Robert Illidge, argues that advertising is valuable. Illidge claims that it provides useful information, raises our standard of living, and supports most of the media. Ad production is designed to get our attention, hold our interest, raise our desires, and provoke action. He describes in detail how advertising agencies are organized and the duties each department performs. As he shows, theirs is not a simple task.

Robert Snow next questions why we respond to ads the way we do. He examines three explanations: Freudian, which stresses the subconscious workings of the mind and can be influenced by subliminal suggestion;[5] behaviorism, which claims that consumers are conditioned by constant repetition; and a traditional approach to emotions that argues they must be released. He prefers a different approach that focuses on what people say about their own behavior and that of others. We are emotionally involved with ads, but we use them selectively to help develop our identities. Advertising therefore uses aspects of everyday life, draws on our emotional experience, and sells us the "sizzle." Despite the sophistication of ad techniques,[6] however, control remains with the audience.

In the following reading, Rick Berkoff is more critical in his evaluation of ad content and techniques.[7] Ads sell us *end benefits,* and many promise more than they can deliver. Berkoff offers a "short guide to some tricks of the trade" that advertisers use to mislead us. They include parity claims; borrowed interest; playing on guilts and fears; arousing emotions; and using "holy" words, cartoon characters, celebrities, and adorable women, babies, and animals. The result is that we often lose sight of the product in the barrage of distortion. But apparently it works.

The remaining readings in the chapter deal with public relations. The goals of PR are similar to advertising; in fact, advertising is usually part of a PR campaign. It includes much else, however, including gaining free publicity and representing the client to the public, peers, government, and other organizations. Public relations has a long history intertwined with advertising.[8]

Davis Young describes what he believes to be the ethical responsibilities of public relations. Although PR is essentially a business, it should move toward professionalization. It should stress accountability, full disclosure, legality, and honesty. To be successful in the long run, PR must above all else enhance trust. Finally, Patrick Jackson adds that PR must be concerned with the overall well-being of human society, and he suggests ways in which PR might help.

Notes

1. Marshall McLuhan, *Understanding Media* (New York: McGraw-Hill, 1964), p. 227.

2. International Advertising Association, *Advertising Investments around the World, Eighth IAA Biennial Report* (New York: IAA, 1967).

3. *Advertising Age,* May 6, 1985, p. 47.

4. "The Day the Ads Stopped," *Nation,* June 1, 1964, pp. 555–557.

5. This idea has been developed by Wilson Bryan Key, who believes that advertising uses hidden sex and death imagery to influence us. See his *Media Sexploitation* (New York: Signet, 1976). His ideas have received heated denials, for example, Jerry Goodis, "Help! There's Sex in My Soup," *Quest* (February–March 1979).

6. An excellent description of how an ad is made is John J. Arlen's *Thirty Seconds* (New York: Penguin, 1981). Lynn Hirschberg's description of the top TV ad directors is also interesting: see her "When You Absolutely, Positively Want the Best," *Esquire* (August 1983): 53–56.

7. Others have warned that we need to be armed against advertising deception. See Samm Sinclair Baker, *The Permissible Lie* (Boston: Beacon, 1968); Paul Stevens, *I Can Sell You Anything* (New York: Ballantine, 1972); and D. A. Kehl, "Learning to Read between the Lies," *English Journal* (October 1983): 32–38.

8. For a lively, brief account, see P. J. Corkery, "For Immediate Release," *Harper's* (March 1982).

THE ADVERTISING BUSINESS: PURPOSE, PRODUCTION, EFFECTS, AND CAREERS

Robert J. Illidge

Robert J. Illidge has been an assistant professor in the Journalism Department at the Wichita State University since 1983 and department chairperson since 1986. He has been a copywriter and creative director for agencies in Kansas City and Wichita, Kansas, as well as account executive at Bruce B. Brewer Advertising Agency in Kansas City, advertising manager for Smith & Loveless, a division of the Union Tank Car Corporation, in Lenexa, Kansas, and account executive and vice president for Associated Advertising Agency in Wichita. He continues as advertising/marketing consultant to certain firms in the Wichita area.

Purpose

To some, advertising is the practice of advertising itself; to others it is the ads themselves; and to still others it is the profession. There is yet another definition: "any paid form of nonpersonal presentation and promotion of ideas, goods, or services by an identified sponsor."[1] To the end of that definition we can add: "who hopes that the target market will act in the way the identified sponsor wants it to act." In sum, advertising is about getting more customers and keeping the ones you already have. It will not succeed in its basic task if it is not honest and believable and unless it speaks the language of its prospects to them with memorable impact and with enough frequency to get the job done.

Advertising must be paid for. If it is not, it does not satisfy all requirements of our definition. (Public relations, for example, strives to make many presentations in the mass media without paying for the space or time used.) It must also be nonpersonal. Thus the saying, "the best kind of advertising is word-of-mouth advertising," does not meet this criterion. Word-of-mouth advertising is more accurately termed salesmanship. And it must have an identifiable sponsor. If the sponsor is not clearly identified, the effort is, at best, a waste of the advertiser's money. At worst, an unidentified sponsor might be, in reality, a wielder of propaganda.

Although the purpose of advertising is clearly understood, there are no guarantees that it will work as planned. Do you buy every product about which you have read an ad or have seen a television commercial? Of course not. Do you switch political affiliation simply because a radio spot urges you to do so? Definitely, no.

"Making Good Ads"

Paid communications by a nonpersonal, identified sponsor can include all media: newspapers, consumer magazines, farm publications, business publications, television, radio, outdoor, transit, direct mail, specialities, and point of purchase. In all of these, the advertiser wants ads that are effective.

"Making good ads" requires imagination, a command of the language, a sense of color, design, and proportion, an understanding of business, an awareness of the competition, an affinity for the prospects' wants and needs, and sometimes even a comprehension of music and how people respond to its many variations. To be truly effective, advertising must be the end result of a carefully thought-out advertising plan whose specific objectives have been agreed upon by those involved. But this plan should not stifle creativity. On the contrary, it should enhance it. It *must* enhance it because good advertising must break through the "boredom barrier." The "boredom barrier" is the protective shield used by the consumer to protect against the constant exposure to advertising messages—more than 1,000 such messages every day!

Many advertising professionals use a simple formula when producing ads, known by the letters AIDA (attention, interest, desire, and action). Those four areas must be covered effectively if the ad is to accomplish its task.

Advertisers must first gain *attention,* which can be accomplished in a variety of ways. In print advertisements, the size of the ad and use of color are attention getters. It is hard not to pay attention to a two-page spread (two facing pages) in a publication, for instance. The dramatic use of full color pictures in an advertisement does much toward pulling the reader into the rest of the ad. Position of the advertisement in the publication also plays an extremely important part in gaining attention. Ads positioned on the inside-front, inside-back, or back cover of a magazine will attract more readers than those positioned elsewhere. The same is true of a television spot placed strategically at the conclusion of a highly dramatic show rather than at an early station break.

After the attention is gained, *interest* in the idea, goods, or service being advertised must be built. One way to build and maintain interest is to present the message with the prospect in mind. In other words, the advertisement should feature benefits to the consumer, not features of the product. To say, for example, that a razor is extremely sharp is to list a feature. To report that because the razor is extremely sharp (feature), it provides a comfortable, smooth shave (benefit) is to present the message with the prospect in mind. One of the hardest-working words used in advertising production continues to be *you*. The advertiser who directs the communication to "you" reaps the profitable benefits.

Once attention has been flagged and interest built, the job of the advertisement is to move the prospects into the area of desire: wanting the product or service being advertised. This is not easy because prospects harbor two basic conflicting feelings: 1) skepticism and 2) a desire to believe. Although the prospect is leery of the sponsor's story, he or she wants to believe it. Advertising professionals have learned that one way to overcome one feeling and build on the other is to back all claims with believable, substantiated proof—perhaps testimonials from recognizable experts, celebrities, or "just plain folks"; guarantees or warranties; or product demonstrations.

The final step in the AIDA formula is *action*. All well-produced advertisements ask the prospect for some sort of action. The asking can be as straightforward as "write in immediately and get your catalog," or it can be implied, as in becoming aware of a particular brand or product or remembering the idea put forth by a certain political candidate. Whatever the idea, the goods, or the service, the interested prospect knows what to do.

The production of good advertising is not as simple as following some formula, however, because there are too many variables that also play a role in producing good ads: These include the budget size, the medium to be used, the time of day (or week or month) the advertisement is to appear, and the national and international business and political climates in which the advertisement will run.

And there are variables within the variables. A big production budget does not automatically mean that a successful ad or spot for magazines or television will be produced. Nor does a small budget automatically mean that only small returns on the advertising investment can be expected. One of the most successful ads of all times was produced for very little money. It was a small black and white ad with no illustration, only copy. The advertiser got right to the heart of the matter by getting the attention of the prime prospect and overcoming any skepticism with a rock-solid guarantee. The headline of this famous ad (which also used the body to build interest and spell out the action asked for) was: "Corns. Gone in 5 days or your money back!" A bigger budget would not have improved that ad, which ran unchanged for years.

The Effects of Advertising

One of the effects of advertising is knowledge. Without advertising, people would not know about new products on the market, new uses for old products, new prices being offered for goods and services of all kinds, the business hours of a restaurant, job openings, courses being offered at the university, or how to help in the fight against drunk driving. This gain of information is one of the effects of advertising.

Proponents of advertising point to another tremendous effect of advertising: it helps to raise our standard of living. They use this rationale:

1. Advertising helps create more sales.
2. More sales stimulates the need for more goods and services.
3. Production of more goods and services opens up more new jobs.
4. More jobs means more spendable income to fuel the economy further.

Thus, the standard of living is raised.

Newspapers and magazines, TV, and radio generate the bulk of their revenues from advertisers. *Look* magazine, for example, ceased publication in 1971 because it could not supply advertisers with the same audience as television at a competitive price, and without advertising, it was not possible to continue publication.

How would television survive without the tremendous revenues generated by the commercials? Would there be constant fund-raising drives similar to those on many of the public television stations today? Would the programming change dramatically? The same questions can be asked of commercial radio, which has no other source of income.

Is advertising's effect on this country something to ponder? It certainly is—especially when one considers that the top ten advertisers alone spent nearly $6.5 billion in just one twelve-month period to tell you about their goods and services.[2] The top ten advertisers, ranked by dollars spent in 1984 (courtesy of *Advertising Age*) were:

Rank	Company	Advertising Expenditures
1	Procter & Gamble Co.	$872,000,000
2	General Motors Corp.	763,800,000
3	Sears, Roebuck & Co.	746,937,000
4	Beatrice Cos.	680,000,000
5	R. J. Reynolds Industries	678,176,000
6	Philip Morris Inc.	570,435,000
7	American Telephone & Telegraph (AT&T)	563,200,000
8	Ford Motor Co.	559,400,000
9	K mart Corp.	554,400,000
10	McDonald's Corp.	480,000,000

Just ten advertisers, in one year. And this figure includes only measured media. It does not begin to count the dollars spent in other areas by these same ten advertisers, or the money they invested in the basic production of the advertisements and commercials in the first place. And don't forget the hundreds of thousands of other advertisers in this country, with their own stories to tell, and their own advertising budgets.

On the other hand, some say that the media would survive without advertising, although under a different format. Moreover, these people argue that doing away with advertising would have a positive effect. Many vocal groups decry the questionable effects advertising has on society, particularly on young children. Is the constant bombardment of advertising messages directed toward the young producing detrimental side effects? Where does society have a real responsibility? Should it criticize, even ban, advertising of cigarettes yet allow the manufacture of cigarettes to continue? Should advertising for motion pictures of questionable moral tone, full of excessive violence and explicit sexual scenes, be stopped—while the movie continues to be shown? These and many other equally important questions need to be addressed.

In our society, we have the framework with which to build upon our strengths and overcome our weaknesses. So long as we keep ourselves informed—we can work and progress. And it is good to remember that advertising, with all its faults and shortcomings, is responsible at least in part for helping to bring the finest in literature and music to untold numbers who would never have the opportunity to be exposed to it otherwise. Information, education, and entertainment of unquestioned high quality and value have been presented with the necessary financial aid coming basically from advertising. In many ways, advertising has helped us grow and understand.

Careers

According to the American Association of Advertising Agencies, nearly one-third of those employed in the advertising business work in advertising agencies. Agencies vary greatly in size—from the one- and two-person shops handling a few local advertising accounts to huge agencies employing thousands of highly skilled professionals in dozens of offices throughout the world. The usual way to classify an advertising agency is not, however, by the number of people it employs but by the amount of money it spends for its clients in a twelve-month period. This money is generally referred to as the agency's *billings*. The size of advertising agencies ranges from under $100,000 in billings to billions of dollars.

Depending on its size, the advertising agency's exact organization will vary. A solid, successful agency in the $15 million billing category will probably have six major departments reporting to the agency head, president, or chairman of the board: account service, art, copy, media, production, and administration.

Account Service

Common job titles in the account service department are account supervisor, account executive, and assistant account executive. The account executive (AE) is the liaison between the agency and the client, or *account,* as the client is often called. The AE's responsibility also includes the preparation and presentation to agency management and to the client of marketing–advertising–public relations plans encompassing proposed objectives, strategies, creative thrust, media, and production timetables and budget.

Upon approval of a plan, it is the responsibility of the account executive to implement all phases of the plan. This means working closely with the creative team of copywriters and art directors; the media department, which is in charge of ordering space and time for the placement of ads and commercials; the production department, whose task is to produce the ad and deliver it on time; and the administration, to ensure that billing the client for space, time, and other agreed-upon items is handled properly.

The account executive must have many skills, not the least of which is the ability to deal effectively with talented, sensitive professionals who display a variety of emotions when working under the constant pressure of deadlines.

Art

Common job titles in the art department are: executive art director, art director, illustrator, designer, and paste-up artist.

The art director (AD) is responsible for the visualization of the advertising message, either in all forms of the print media or in television. Thus the AD must have the ability to direct typographers, printers, photographers, and cinematographers from outside the agency as well as those from within. He or she must pull together the various elements in a print ad—for example, the headline, illustration, body copy, and company signature—into an overall shape that will attract readers. An AD does not have to be a master artist but must be able to visualize the final product and turn that concept into reality.

Copy

Leo Burnett, founder of one of the most successful advertising agencies in the United States, placed high value on copywriters and their ability to take a blank sheet of paper and fill that page with persuasive, selling advertising copy. Writing advertising copy is no mean feat. Almost anyone can write an ad, but to create the believable, convincing rationale that will persuade a stranger to buy a product or service based on words alone is very difficult.

Common titles in the copy department are creative director, copy chief, and copywriter. The copywriter's responsibilities begin with the words, as the art director's responsibilities begin with the pictures. But simply writing the words does not begin to cover it all. A good copywriter must also be able to visualize the entire advertisement or commercial just as the art director does. Thus, an appreciation of graphic design, of form, of color, is essential. Even more basic, the copywriter must have at least an awareness of why people act as they do, what benefits they are looking for, and the reason they prefer one product over another. In short, a good copywriter will have a thorough understanding of consumer behavior, psychology, philosophy, and sociology, in addition to having mastered both verbal and visual skills.

Media

Let us say that you are the marketing officer for a full-service bank in Wichita, Kansas, a metropolitan center of approximately 280,000 persons located in the south-central part of the state. Your bank is the fifth largest in the city, with the two largest banks being well out in front in terms of deposits, while your bank and two others are scrambling for the third, fourth, and fifth spots. The total number of banks listed in the local telephone book is thirty-six, with a similar number of savings and loan institutions and credit unions. Your bank's management gives you, and your advertising agency, the objective of increasing deposits by 3 percent during the next twelve months. Your advertising media budget is about $200,000. How are you going to invest your advertising budget in order to gain the greatest return on your dollar? The media department at your agency can help you decide where to advertise.

There are four television stations in Wichita, and this does not include all the cable signals available. There is one large, daily metropolitan newspaper, plus numerous weeklies targeted toward various publics in the area and papers published by the local high schools, college, and universities, along with a shopping news or two. There is an outdoor advertising company with billboards on all major arteries, thoroughfares, and streets. A transit company has advertising signs on taxicabs and the metropolitan bus line. There are seventeen commercial radio stations. There are two general interest magazines plus two dozen or so special interest periodicals directed to certain ethnic, social, business, and educational groups. Each medium has its unique advantages and disadvantages. Each entity within the medium has its strong and weak points. Which one or ones do you choose? And why? How much of the budget will each command? And why? When will the ads and commercials run? And why? These and a myriad of other questions must be answered. The media department basically does the answering.

Common titles in the media department are media director, media planner, time buyer, and space buyer. All positions require persons who are willing to negotiate for better deals for the client, who can boil away much of the extraneous material about a medium and get to the heart of the matter, who have the ability to look at recommendations fairly, objectively, and critically. The media department also ensures that all advertising appears as ordered.

Production

Common titles in the production department are production director, production administrator and assistant, and creative coordinator. Staff members in the production department work with members of all other departments to ensure that materials are prepared to proper specifications in every regard, on time, and within budget.

This department is responsible for working with outside suppliers, getting job estimates, and making sure the work load is equally distributed and that the work is moving smoothly through the agency's departments with no bottle-necks. It requires a wide variety of skills in graphics, printing, budgeting, and accounting, plus the dedication and tact required to complete a job using the diverse skills and talents of many different professionals.

Administration

Common titles in an advertising agency's administration department are treasurer, comptroller, accountant, and computer operator. As with any other for-profit organization, an advertising agency is in business to make money. The administration department of the agency has prime responsibility in that area. It must ensure that internal and external operations of the agency are kept within budget, that all personnel requirements are met, that billing and invoicing are accurate, on time, and paid, and that the day-to-day affairs of running a complex organization are handled in a highly professional manner.

Other Opportunities

Many times a larger retailer or a manufacturer has an advertising manager on staff to work with the advertising agency or to handle the advertising function in place of the agency. The advertising manager's job requires many of the same skills as the agency's account executive. It is a vitally important position, and many times the advertising manager is also on the executive committee of the company.

There is a saying in the graphic arts industry, "If you don't know printing, know your printer." The same can be said of media: "If you don't know media, know your media representative." Good media representatives can make the difference between an average media schedule and an outstanding one. Good media reps do not merely take orders from the media buyers at an advertising agency; they add their own creativity to aid in reaching the desired audience. They are an invaluable source of up-to-date information of all kinds: research, costs, format changes, audience profiles, and more. Many successful advertising leaders began in this area of representing newspapers, radio and TV stations, farm publications, magazines or other media.

Notes

1. American Marketing Association, *Marketing Definitions* (Chicago: The Association, 1963), p. 9.
2. *Advertising Age,* September 26, 1985, pp. 1, 3.

EMOTIONS IN ADVERTISING

Robert P. Snow

Robert P. Snow is an associate professor in the Department of Sociology at Arizona State University. He has authored and coauthored articles and several books (*Media Logic* and *Creating Media Culture*) on the interaction between mass media and American culture. His current research interest is the relationship between media and social rhythm.

Looking at advertising ranks as one of the most common everyday life activities in our culture. A person must escape to the wilderness to avoid a bombardment of advertising on every imaginable product. In one sense, advertising is the pervasive scenery of American consumerism, a scenery that we love to hate and attack. But drawing from Shakespeare, perhaps we protest too much. At least secretly we not only like and enjoy a great many ads, we deliberately seek out these messages and use them as important information for personal gain.

One of the reasons that advertising can produce spirited discussion and heated response is that it strikes at the heart of questions on human nature. Are humans always capable of exercising free will and making rational decisions, or are there times and situations in which we can be manipulated by appeals beyond our conscious rational process? No one likes to admit to the possibility of being molded, shaped, and otherwise caused to succumb to impractical and irrational suggestion, yet we all think thoughts, commit acts, and buy products that in the light of another day seem to defy rationality.

The popular understanding of advertising's persuasive power seems to rest on a combination of Freudian psychology, B. F. Skinner's radical behaviorism, and a traditional approach to the nature of emotions. From Freudian psychology it is assumed that everyone possesses a subconscious realm in their psyche, a realm containing impulses, drives, and desires that are ever present as potential behavioral motivators. Tapping or releasing these motivational agents is believed to be the key to certain kinds of persuasion, such as appeals through mass media or from charismatic personalities. A popular acceptance of this general notion ranges in degree from a tempered recognition of preconscious states that must be mediated by strong ego mechanisms to the unconditional belief in subliminal suggestion. At one end of the continuum are those who grant the potential power of a subconscious but feel it usually can be counterbalanced with vigilance, resourcefulness, and rationality. At the other extreme of the continuum is the view that particular cues can bypass the conscious rational process and directly trigger subconscious impulses and activity. This belief in subliminal suggestion can result in a fear of advertising.

In contrast, Skinner's behaviorism suspends all judgment on the existence and content of a subconscious. Instead behavior is thought to be stimulated from the motivating power of observable rewards. For Skinner, sex need not be a subconscious impulse; it can be clearly recognized and consciously pursued. Indeed, why all the mystery over such an obvious and common drive? From a behaviorist perspective, advertising conditions the consumer to respond to product stimuli with the promise of personal reward. In place of subliminal cues, the behaviorist would recommend repetition of a message that demonstrates the association between a particular product and some commonly recognized reward.

The pop psychology approach to advertising seems at ease with a marriage of these aspects of the Freudian and Skinnerian models. One deals with subconscious motivation and the other with conscious motivation. Both would agree that ads are potentially powerful persuaders, and both place the locus of power outside or beyond the full control of the individual. In short, free will is a limited resource, if not totally absent, in Freud and Skinner's thought. On the other hand, with either of these theoretical approaches, no one need accept personal responsibility for behavior that may be attributed to conditioning or appeals to the subconscious. Fault lies with the agents who construct the conditioning process or deliver the subconscious cues.

The traditional theory of emotion is closely allied with the determinism of Freud and Skinner. Emotions are commonly thought of as feelings that exist in a reservoir and can be evoked under the right circumstances. It is taken for granted that we are born with our emotions and can do little, if anything, to change them. Furthermore, emotions are thought to be essential to our well-being. These emotions, such as fear, love, and hate, may be expressed in many sophisticated variations, but essentially they are not subject to rationality or easily controlled. Testimony to this notion is the common-sense dictum that it is unwise to keep emotions checked or controlled for too long, or disastrous results will follow. Once triggered or evoked, emotions supposedly must be released. This assumption certainly underlies the power attributed to advertising.

Ironically all three views rest on theories that have been seriously challenged. In Freudian psychology, the existence of a subconscious continues to be taken purely as an assumption, without empirical proof. With respect to Skinner's approach, the connection between stimulus and reward ignores the interaction and negotiation process through which something becomes established as a reward. In fact, it is difficult to identify exactly what is rewarding in a particular behavioral exchange. As for the traditional theory of emotion, there has always been considerable confusion as to exactly what an emotion is and how it is produced: are they evoked in a manner similar to subconscious impulses or stimulated feelings, or are they social constructions, feelings made appropriate for particular situations? Regardless, advertising is commonly thought to be the cause or culprit, and consumers are the effect or victim. To this notion, I propose an alternative that shifts responsibility—and freedom—back to the consumer.

An Alternative Approach

An alternative to understanding the apparent power of advertising is based on ideas from symbolic interaction theory in sociology and attribution theory in psychology. These models share a strict adherence to data that can be observed: what people say about their behavior and the behavior of others. No assumptions are made about the existence and power of a subconscious or a reservoir of emotions. In dealing with advertising, it is assumed that a person's attention to and involvement with an advertisement is done consciously and selectively. Consequently the aim is to understand the interaction process between advertisement and potential consumer. It begins with the consumer and asks why people watch advertisements.

In discussing many media-related topics with children, adolescents, and adults, I have encountered only a few individuals who cannot cite details about specific ads they like and dislike. Indeed many individuals have familiarity with a rather extensive repertoire of ads in both their recent and distant past. People can even mark periods in their life according to the style and content of specific ads. A few examples to jog the memory include antacid products and various brands of soap, cigarettes, beer, toothpaste, and automobiles. Although a typical consumer may not be able to recall the ads that appeared on a favorite TV show an hour ago, these same people have ads they love and love to hate.

To analyze an individual's emotional involvement with ads, note the words and inflection used in explaining what is liked or disliked in a particular advertisement. Quite often these responses are animated and effusive, agitated and ebullient, or they are expressed with the outward calm of internal seething. Typically "good" ads are described as fun, exciting, dramatic, bizarre, goofy, or even sensitive and romantic. Rarely do people use pragmatic terms, such as *accurate, sensible, humane,* and *practical.* An insulting ad is referred to with the ire of "How dare they!" or "What do they take me for, an idiot?" This is not the dispassionate argument or response of someone who has made a rational decision based on careful analysis of evidence. It is the remark of a person whose self-esteem has been wounded. And this is the key: *advertisements are identity statements.*

Advertising and Personal Identity

Social psychologists generally agree that people are self-oriented. In other words, life is a process of attempting to create, establish, maintain, and enhance various conceptions of self (identities), such as female, young adult, cosmopolitan, athlete, student, Baptist, nature lover. This is not as selfish as it sounds; we often find it advantageous to reciprocate and act with altruism toward others. The most important point is that social activity of any kind involves an identity establishment and maintenance process. People are identity conscious and are always ready to recognize responses from others that will validate their own identities. It is this readiness that makes advertising powerful.

A major factor in the willingness of consumers to pay attention to advertising is the relatively high potential for ambiguity and emotional instability in modern urban life. Compared to the more stable and slow-changing character of rural and small town life, the urban condition is characterized by many fleeting relations, specialization that tends to limit how much one knows about another person, physical change that reduces familiarity and disrupts routine, and a hurried sense of pace that turns time into a precious commodity. These and other features of urban life mitigate against achieving success and security in the multiple identities that characterize the typical city dweller. In short, who and what we are can be fairly problematic a good deal of the time. Although there may be safety in the anonymity that urban life affords, it can also be quite lonely in the crowd. In an effort to obtain at least a vicarious sense of stability and security, many people turn to mass media. Soap operas, for example, provide ready-made families that are routinely available, and radio talk shows provide instant contact with a community of others. To excite the imagination, magazines offer exotic and glamorous images.

Within the plethora of mass-mediated social settings, advertisements are integrated almost without interruption. Ads are part of the flow of media culture offering the same form and content as "General Hospital," "Miami Vice," or "Cheers." The art deco of "Miami Vice" is repeated in a wine cooler advertisement, and Whitney Houston does her stage act for a soft drink product. The only major difference between an ad for a low-calorie beer and the sitcom "Cheers" is that brand names are missing in "Cheers." Television viewers can obtain the same vicariously social gratifications from advertisements as they get from the main stories, games, and contests, and in many instances the ads are at least as exciting, interesting, and humorous—perhaps more so. When people talk about their favorite ads, it is clear that their orientation is to the social scene in the advertisement more than the product.

People will claim that ads are watched or heard simply because they are there—with nothing specifically in mind. Obviously, a person does not tune in "The Cosby Show" to watch an ad for pudding. On the other hand, when an advertisement is watched, what does it mean to the viewer? It is possible that a viewer would not be selectively attentive to a particular ad which would then have meaning only as an interruption in the program. The viewer could also orient to an ad as the continuing flow of the form of the medium, cognizant only of the rhythm and tempo of the advertisement. This in itself could be part of the emotional appeal of advertising. In reading magazines, a person may flip through the pages and enjoy the brilliant flow of colorful images without interpreting the content of those images. Therefore when a person claims to watch an ad simply because it is there, he or she could be emotionally involved in the form of the advertisement rather than the content.

On the more rational side, we occasionally seek information from ads that facilitate the enactment of practical identities. Grocery ads, classified ads, and other sale ads enable us to act as shoppers and bargain hunters. These ads can also aid in fostering feelings of enjoyment and excitement in anticipation of finding a treasure or saving a few dollars. However, many ads, especially those on television and in magazines, emphasize an emotional context that is relevant for experiencing, feeling, a particular identity or general sense of self. Consider the following model.

An Identity-Emotive Model

An advertisement designed for television or other wide-distribution media contains at least four social psychological dimensions.[1] First, an ad must project an identity and suggest the importance of that identity for the consumer.

Second, a situational context for the enactment and experience of that identity is portrayed. An important dimension of this portrayal is the mood or feeling that may be experienced by an individual who is engaged in this situation. Third, a product is associated with the identity, the situation, and the mood. Finally, if necessary, a motive or justification is offered to explain why the product is important for achieving and maintaining that identity and experience.

Although this model may be applied to an analysis of any commercial advertisement, concern here will be with national campaign ads carried over the major media. As a category this would consist of the typical thirty-second spot on prime-time television, full-page or fold-out spreads in magazines, canned radio spots, and national ads in local newspapers. The primary features of any advertisement in this group will promote what it feels like to use the product. For example, recent prime-time television ads included a fast food chain that focused on the experience of small town rural life; a nonstick cooking product created a fast-paced visual collage that followed a music video format; an American automobile ad used computer graphics to promote the image of exciting elegance; and a package express company showed the demolition of a large building with a statement, "Don't let your business collapse around you." None of these advertisements referred to the rational or utilitarian properties of the product. They all sold emotion—the so-called sizzle.

The importance of selling moods or even primary emotions is not that advertisers deliberately try to deceive the consumer or avoid talking frankly about the product. Rather, advertising emphasizes an aspect of everyday life that consumers readily recognize. The general context for consumer behavior is that affluent American culture is currently oriented toward experiencing a leisure life-style involving creative consumption. The sizzle is an important element of this quest. It may be argued that this quest is too superficial and lacks substance, but the sizzle is still what many people want. Even those who frequent health food stores and exercise emporiums are at least partially involved in obtaining the proper sense of emotional involvement. Consequently ads for health spas emphasize the pleasant side of "no pain, no gain." Therefore care must be taken to avoid defining the apparent superficiality of the sizzle as something that is nonessential in the social-psychological process of maintaining a sense of self and self-esteem.

Although orienting to the overall emotional tenor of an advertisement may be significant, it does not capture the more fundamental importance of emotion as a justification or motive for behavior. Most people will admit that the most important criterion for establishing the authenticity and legitimacy of anything is how it feels. Indeed, our vernacular expressions commonly use the word *feel* as a substitute for *think*. Typically questions on opinions and attitudes are worded "How do you feel about _____ ?"

rather than "What do you think about _____ ?" If this seems like a hair-splitting matter, people usually will comment that when forced to make a difficult decision, they will review the rational evidence and then go with a feeling—"It feels right." This is not to say that feelings are beyond rationality or that feelings manifest magically at the right moment. The point is that people verbally claim that feelings are the bottom line. Whether emotion should be viewed as a causal factor is irrelevant at this point. The fact is that people refer to emotion as a reason for their behavior. Consequently the identity establishment process is as much an emotional process as it is a rational process. And if the sizzle helps develop the appropriate emotional experience, then people will not only pay attention to the sizzle in ads, they will demand it. The fast food industry discovered this some years ago. McDonald's does not just sell fast food; it sells the McDonald's experience.

In conceptualizing emotion as a stated motive or justification for behavior, attention must be directed to how emotion is constructed in an advertisement. As an illustration, consider a recent thirty-second prime-time television ad for a soft drink. The scene opens with a large, strange-looking truck rapidly disappearing down a dark and wet street in the industrial section of a city. With the camera at street level, we see steam rising from a sewer and red neon lights blinking in the distance. A metal box the size of a milk crate falls off the truck, and an antenna rises from the box. Immediately four preadolescent boys ride up on their hi-tech motocross bicycles. The boys appear to be prowling aimlessly; their visual images are almost ethereal. The music suggests science-fiction. The boys are wearing heavy jackets, jeans, baseball caps, and headphones. One of the boys says, "It must be a generator." Just then, a door on the box slides open to reveal a television screen with a silver-haired, alien male who announces that he is a "Max Headroom." One of the boys peers into the screen and repeats the alien's statement as a question: "A Max Headroom?" The boy is drinking the soft drink. The alien interrupts his narrative to state "Ah a _____ologist!" (referring to the soft drink). He continues, "Where there's a wave there's a _____ . Ya'know, more people prefer _____ to _____ ." At that point the boys decide to take the box home (another close-up of the boy drinking the soft drink). They slap the box on the back of one of the bikes, and the camera follows them down the street. As they disappear, we hear the alien's voice trailing off saying, "Now's your chance _____ drinkers. Catch the wave. Become a _____ologist." The ad ends with a graphic of a computer-generated wave and the soft drink can superimposed over the late-night street. In all there are twenty-four separate scenes or edits in this thirty-second period.

From a rational standpoint, the advertisement shows typical middle-class boys in middle-class clothing, and we hear a statement about more people preferring this soft drink to another. Beyond that nearly everything else was a fantasy–adventure scene that could easily be conjured up by an average

294 • Mass Media and Society

imaginative boy. With twenty-four separate scenes in thirty seconds, the pace of the ad was adequately rapid by music video standards. The background was richly detailed, but the night lighting obscured most of it in order to emphasize the cool feel of mystery. As a story, it was clear and simple; more important, it was humorously bizarre, and the soft drink was definitely part of the total experience. It is difficult to imagine any boy failing to consider this ad as pure fun.

A potential criticism of the soft drink advertisement is that since the product itself is designed for pleasure, the ad should convey emotional involvement. However, it might be difficult to find a product advertised on prime-time television that does not have an emotional theme. In the context of entertainment television, advertisements should sell emotional involvement and justification. For example, a prime-time advertisement for a home builder emphasized "the home for the new American life-style." In a thirty-second spot with nine edited scene changes, each scene separately depicted the leisure activities of the back yard barbecue, playing touch football on the front lawn, lounging in the bathtub, and doing aerobics next to the pool. For each of these scenes, the words *functional, fun, intimate,* and *open* were used. The scene for *functional* showed the father-husband holding a roasted crown rib roast. In a thirty-second ad for a national brand of gasoline, there was only one scene, a sunset viewed from a lonely mountain road. The narration over the scene was simple and emphatic: "This gasoline guarantees that automobile fuel injectors won't clog." During the narration, a tow truck drives up the road towing a disabled car. At the end of the ad, we see another car whizzing down the road into the sunset. The narration in the ad is a straightforward rational statement; the scene depicts what it might feel like to be disabled at night on a lonely mountain road compared to the carefree feeling of a well-tuned automobile. And if the viewer does not care about gasoline, there is always the pretty sunset to gaze at for thirty seconds.

A sample of any number of prime-time television ads will demonstrate that the construction of emotional experience or a setting for emotional experience is a major feature of almost all advertisements. Although data are needed on the meanings that viewers ascribe to the advertisements they encounter, anyone can easily compare their own experience with the model presented here. What remains is to clarify how advertisements promote the emotional characteristics of an advertisement. For this, attention is directed to the grammar of media and advertising language.

The Grammar Factor

All communication occurs through language, and all languages follow grammatical rules that govern the usage of language elements. Syntax governs the order or organization of words, such as the relationship of subject to object and the relationship of dependent to independent clauses. Inflection covers the placement of accent or emphasis, and vocabulary consists of the words (symbols) used to establish meaningful content.

The emotional dimension of grammar is primarily located in inflection. These are the rules that provide a sense of movement in the language. Specifically, the movement or flow of communication is achieved through techniques that establish rhythm and tempo, or beat and pace. Using music as an illustration, rhythm can be a steady 4/4 beat, a gliding 3/4 waltz beat, a bouncy 2/4 common in country swing music, or it can be a more complex 6/8 time. Listen to speech patterns; after a few moments, the rhythm or cadence of an individual's speech becomes apparent. In fact, failure to discern the rhythm of a person's speech will usually result in a high degree of misunderstanding. For example, a person from the United States who speaks English may have great difficulty understanding a Scot in Glasgow. Regional dialects are also a good example; variations in pronunciation are in part a matter of inflection. Whereas rhythm is the cadence of movement, tempo is the pace or speed at which the movement proceeds. Just as music is slow, moderate, or upbeat, speech and written prose vary in apparent pace.

The grammatical features of language are not restricted to a formal language but may be applied to any other form of communication, such as mass media. Television, radio, newspapers, film, and other mass media have developed grammatical strategies in presenting subject matter to audiences. Inflection strategies in television programs vary from the steady rhythm and slow pace of soap operas to the varied rhythms and rapid pace of network news programs. Compare the visual rhythm and tempo of a current music video to the oral rhythm and tempo of 1950s rock 'n roll. In addition, the overall rhythm and tempo of one medium may influence another medium, such as the influence of television on the press, as exemplified by *USA Today,* or intramedium influence, as vividly illustrated by the impact of music video on dramatic programs, such as "Miami Vice."

As a form of communication, advertising also develops grammatical strategies, clearly demonstrated in the differences between billboards and radio ads or magazines and newspapers. By and large, the grammatical characteristics of an advertisement are consistent with the grammatical characteristics of the medium in which the ad appears. Ads for television follow the general characteristics of television grammar; newspaper ads are consistent with newspaper grammar. In addition, some ads are tailored specifically for particular subject genre, such as soap ads for soap operas, and the inflection of an ad may be designed for specific seasons of the year, such as the beer company Christmas card/carol ads prior to the Christmas holidays. On the other hand, it is common for advertisers to exaggerate slightly the inflection characteristics of the medium in which the ad appears. Television ads often have a slightly brighter rhythm and faster tempo than the program itself in order to keep the attention of the viewer. The same holds true for radio. Some magazines, such as *Better Homes and Gardens* and *Good Housekeeping* are memorable primarily for their colorful ads.

Returning to the question of what makes a good advertisement, the answer, in part, is found in the grammar of advertising communication. For television, viewers are oriented toward entertainment, and entertainment is intended to be an emotional experience. Consequently the grammar of television entertainment consists of inflection techniques that facilitate emotional involvement in program content. Prime-time television advertisements must flow with or slightly exaggerate the rhythm and tempo of television entertainment. In short, good television ads are good television.

Who Has the Power?

Despite the temptation to focus exclusively on advertising and media characteristics, it must not be forgotten that the viewer-consumer is still the key factor in this analysis. The ultimate meaning of an advertisement is established by the audience. The primary element in making an advertisement relevant to a consumer is the announcement of an identity or definition of self in the ad that an audience member will find appropriate to himself or herself. In a mass audience, many people could relate to having clean teeth; fewer would be interested in a beer drinker identity; even fewer would be concerned with buying bird seed. However, in a highly specialized audience watching a nature program on cable TV, nearly everyone might be interested in bird seed.

An identity must have a social and emotional context to make the identity socially viable. As such, a person could be attentive to an ad with the appropriate identity and then find the situational and emotional context presented in the ad inappropriate. For example, an ad showing beer being consumed at a church social would be inappropriate for many beer drinkers. Similarly, a soft drink can would be inappropriate at a formal dinner. Consequently the announced identity in an advertisement must be presented within an appropriate social and emotional context. Finally, the product must seem reasonably appropriate for establishing and maintaining the identity within the described social and emotional context. The consumer can reject the advertisement at any of these points.

This analysis must also be concerned with examining the identity and the social and emotional context of the consumer at the moment the advertisement is seen or heard. Obviously there are situations in which an individual will not be attentive to a deodorant advertisement. Therefore advertisers attempt to catch consumers when they are most likely to be attentive to the products. The fact that bizarre used-car ads are not run during local news programs is not due simply to the cost of ads during that time segment. And denture creams are not advertised during sporting events, while pizza, beer, and automotive products are.

Given the social-psychological dimensions of the relationship between consumer and advertisements, it should not be surprising that some ads result in extreme positive feelings, while others are hated. Ads defined as sexist will draw the ire of anyone supporting the cause of equal rights for women. An advertised product line that is consistently lily white will be denounced by blacks and supporters of the black community. Any advertisement derogatory to an important identity among audience members will result in a negative response from those members. Furthermore, any advertisement that places an identity in an inappropriate or negative situational context will also draw fire from the audience. But positive and negative responses from the consumer audience will only occur as long as advertising is an important source of identity information and potential emotional support.

The soft drink slogan "Be a Pepper" may sound a bit flip, but it summarizes the argument about emotions in advertising. A pepper is an identity, and to be a pepper conveys emotional involvement and experience. In this sense, emotions are not manipulated by hidden persuaders; they are deliberately sought and purposefully established whenever possible. That advertising through mass media aids in facilitating emotional experience may speak to a lamented condition of modern urban life. On the other hand, many people have come to terms with this condition. At the very worst, advertising presents images about ourselves and our life-style that reveal our darker and more shameful side. To the extent that these images go unchallenged, advertising becomes a means for their persistence. On the other hand, advertising is a colorful, humorous, outrageous, fantastic, and glamorous world of vicarious pleasure. As such, it can provide emotional justification for a variety of behaviors. And at a mundane level, ads may simply facilitate the rhythmic flow of the day or evening. We have the power to assign whatever meanings we wish to advertisements. We can be selectively attentive or inattentive; self-assured or paranoid; positive or negative; excited or bored. In any case, the power is ours.

Note

1. Robert Snow, *Creating Media Culture* (Beverly Hills: Sage, 1983), pp. 243–247.

CAN YOU SEPARATE THE SIZZLE FROM THE STEAK?

Rick Berkoff

Reprinted from the *Journal of Popular Culture*, Fall 1981. Used by permission.

People in the advertising business like to say: "Don't sell the steak; sell the sizzle!" In other words, an advertisement should concentrate on selling not the particular product or service, in and of itself, but what is called its "end benefit."

What's an end benefit? Well, when you drink a Coke, it supposedly refreshes you. That feeling of being refreshed is the end benefit. Likewise, you don't buy a lawn mower for the sake of simply having a lawn mower (at least most people don't); you buy it because you want your grass cut. A trim lawn—and perhaps peer approval—are the end benefits here. And what about the dream merchants? Revlon isn't selling a face cream—it's selling beauty, youth, and hope.

There's nothing wrong with emphasizing end benefits—within reason. But much of the advertising we see has a way of taking indecent liberties with these end benefits, carrying them to their absolute extremes. The result: lots of promises that can't be delivered. Sizzle that oversells.

Problems inevitably result when we allow ourselves to become dazzled by the sizzle and romanced to a point where, as consumers, we forget ourselves, losing touch with reality just when we need our good judgment the most—when we're being motivated to buy.

In the two decades since Vance Packard wrote his now classic study of the role of motivational research in modern advertising, *The Hidden Persuaders,* much has been said and written on the subject of "M.R." But even today most of us take advertising too much for granted. We have little notion of how it's actually constructed, and we care much less. But our lack of apparent interest makes us no less susceptible to advertising's charms—and costly charms at that.

Hence this short guide to some tricks of the trade.

There's Nothing Better Than a Good Parity Statement

When you've got nothing really unique to plug, sometimes the best you can do is make a parity statement. Especially if you're selling something you can't make any special claim for. (In advertising, that special claim is often called the "Unique Selling Proposition," or USP.)

One example among many is the tagline used for years by Personna Double II, a twin-blade razor made by a subsidiary of Philip Morris. Personna Double II liked to say: "There's no finer razor made. Period." This is a seemingly strong and certainly a dramatic sounding statement, but what is it really saying? Only that Personna Double II is as good as its competition. Personna Double II never for a moment claimed superiority, only that their product was as good as the rest, and no worse. All the blades could claim was parity. They were equal to their competition, and nothing more.

Unfortunately even the cleverest parity statement lacks the appeal of the USP. It might do to ask whether you really need any product about which its advertisers can think of nothing special to say.

What Liz Told Jackie about Borrowed Interest

"Borrowed interest" is interest that exists in one thing, or person, and is borrowed for use somewhere else, and for a different purpose. When advertisers use borrowed interest, they take a product or service that is inherently dull and without interest, and they give it some excitement by borrowing for their use something which in itself has interest.

A recent TV commercial for duPont spends nearly all its time showing us a bride on her wedding day, in a world of white—white gown, white invitation, white carpeting even—all made lily white and possible by virtue of the use of titanium dioxide. Consider the ingenuity of linking all the positive feelings we hold for a bride on her wedding day, or linking up that romance—that sizzle—to titanium dioxide. That's borrowed interest. And it does the trick very nicely. It gets us to watch the beautiful bride, even while the ugly bridesmaid—some chemical compound—catches the bouquet.

Typical of the most common ads and commercials using borrowed interest are those that take us to sea to sell us Nescafe coffee and to the moon to sell us Tang breakfast drink. And what about the spot that carries us to the eighteenth green and asks the memorable question: "Orange juice after a golf tournament, Arnold Palmer?" "Sure," says Arnie, "it isn't just for breakfast anymore." Question: Is Arnold Palmer some kind of expert on the subject of orange juice? Of course not. But what a stroke! And he sure can command attention. From an advertiser's point of view, that's a smart start for any TV spot.

Playing On—and Purging—Our Guilt and Fear

We all have our guilts and fears, and motivational studies have exposed many of these to advertisers eager to capitalize on them. The mother of young children is particularly vulnerable. A Pampers TV commercial, for instance, asks the question: "Doesn't your baby deserve Pampers dryness?" This question implies both that Pampers offers more dryness than its competition and that mothers who don't buy Pampers are failing to give their babies what they deserve. Another Pampers spot has a woman claim, "I'd wash a million cloth diapers myself if it meant they'd keep him as dry as Pampers." What an ingenious way around the guilt mothers feel for not using the more tradi-tional—and time-consuming—cloth diapers!

Then there's the spot for the Playtex nurser, telling us that it "gives mother one less thing to worry about." Now, what is that one less thing to worry about? Nursing itself? Or which substitute nursing device to use? The calculated vagueness works to this product's clear advantage.

And, finally, there's the commercial for toilet bowl cleaner that whispers the insidious words "People *will* look!" Spare us.

Kentucky Fried Chicken commercials now tell us how "it's nice to feel so good about a meal." This plays on the good psychological feelings you pre-sumably will have if you buy their chicken. These words "position" KFC as something quite different from, say, McDonald's hamburgers. The difference is that, while McDonald says, "You deserve a break today" (in other words, "Get out of the kitchen and out of the house for a change"), the chicken people want you to think of home, and home cooking, when you think of their product. Much as people love the convenience of eating at these fast food places, they suffer guilt because they're not cooking it at home. So in order to combat this guilt, KFC tells us, "It's nice to feel so good about a meal." They sing it to us and we believe it, because we want to believe it.

We're also accosted by commercials that play on our fears—even our fear of making mistakes. H&R Block commercials now feature people saying, "I shoulda come here last year." They feel what can only be described as retro-active guilt. This campaign takes us enigmatically to task with the gnarled self-criticism: "It's already too late, so hurry!"

And what about the ever-growing number of smoke alarm spots, usually showing smoke and flames and families in crisis? One of these opens with a presenter—he appears to be a dangerous intruder with thoughts of arson on his mind, a flaming torch in hand—asking the unanswerable question: "Are you really safe there in your bed?" (Strings dramatically up.) Probably the only rule to come out of this is: Never rush out to buy anything while you're still in a cold sweat from the advertising you've been watching. Sleep on it. If you can.

The Cardinal Sin of Omission

It's every bit as important to know what is not being said as what is, because it raises a pertinent question we should habitually ask ourselves: "Is this ad-vertisement telling us the whole story?"

Example: TV commercials for American Express Travellers' Checks focus on hysterical people—who haven't been wise enough to use American Express checks and have used other companies' checks, instead—suffering the loss of their money and belongings. These spots, with Karl Malden as their spokesperson, have in the past, said: "What to do? Get American Express Travellers' Checks. If they're lost, you can get a full refund at over 600 places."

By committing the sin of omission, American Express created the impression—through implication—that its competition will not offer full refunds on lost or stolen checks. This is absolutely contrary to the truth, and a successful court suit brought by Thomas Cook Company has forced American Express to amend its commercials, which in their new versions now include that other travelers' check companies also do, in fact, make refunds.

Eager to climb on the conservation bandwagon, Commonwealth Edison, the northern Illinois electric utility, ran an advertisement some time ago showing a female water chemist testing the water used to cool one of Com Ed's nuclear power facilities. The newspaper ad had this chemist say: "The water our power plants use is just as clean coming out as going in. It's my job to make sure of it." These words allay our concern about possible problems that could result from Com Ed's using millions of gallons of Lake Michigan drinking water to cool their engines. Most people feel good when they read that ad. But what they aren't told is that the water coming out of these nukes may be clean all right, but it's also substantially warmer than it was before being diverted to the utility's use, and this warmer water can have the effect of changing entire ecosystems.

Sins of omission are like the black holes of space. They draw you in and swallow you whole. So watch where you walk. And what you hear.

Doin' the Sidestep, or Leaky Balloons That Don't Hold Up

You'll never have problems recognizing this dandy, since your typical reaction is a double take. You hear the pitch and nod in agreement; then you slap your forehead and curse the curve ball.

Example: "What's in Bayer is what doctors recommend most." Now what is that supposed to mean? Does Bayer contain an ingredient, the mystical workings of which we mere laymen cannot comprehend? Or is the truth, more likely, that Bayer contains precisely what every aspirin product, by definition, must contain: acetylsalicylic acid?

The point here is that often the only difference between a brand name drug and its generic equivalent is the price. Trademark-advertised brand names often sell for 50 percent more than the generic pharmaceuticals their names are designed to obfuscate. It is estimated that over a year's time, the average consumer can save up to $125 or more by buying generic drugs instead of the more heavily advertised brand names.

To show how cannily the Bayer words dance the sidestep, let's look at them from another angle. Let's pretend that we have created a product that is 99 percent water and 1 percent sugar. We call it Goodie Juice, and we sell it with words like, "You can't live without what's in Goodie Juice" or "What's in Goodie Juice can save your life."

It comes to this: If what's in Bayer is what doctors recommend most, then what's in Bayer is what I want. Not Bayer itself, necessarily, but what's in Bayer. And that's generic aspirin.

Rule: Carry your critical sickle always at your side, to cut away the camouflage. It's a jungle out there.

Who's That A-Tuggin on Those Ol' Heartstrings O' Mine?

Into this giant category fall all those advertisements so hard to hate because they are triggered to touch us way deep down. They play on our emotions, and unless we are cold or un-American, it's hard not to respond. Ma Bell's "Reach Out" campaign is a perfect example. We're told to "reach out and touch someone." And we're shown all sorts of people, reaching out and touching those they love. Go ahead. Just pick up the phone. Nothing to it. But consider reality here. A monopoly utility is spending our money—it has recently upped the cost of phone calls in many areas—in order to increase service and make more money. Really, now, do most of us have to be reminded of the phone?

The Jellyfish in Sheep's Clothing

The jellyfish is about as transparent as the aforementioned leaky balloon. Consider Orson Wells, for Paul Masson Wines, uncorking this beauty: "We will sell no wine before its time!" The drama, the vibrato, the strength of these words of commitment! But what is the Paul Masson Wine Company committing itself to? Do they promise us thirty-year-old wine? No. Ten-year-old wine? No. Not a word of it. All they say is that they will sell no wine "before its time." Now maybe that time is a year, maybe it's six months. Who knows? What we do know is that these words play upon our desire to gain prestige when we quaff wine. And they work. What could be more prestigious than to get your hands on a good vintage wine? Say a rich, robust [1987]...

The Advertising of Joy

Like the classic hearttuggers, the advertising of joy is usually mounted on behalf of those major companies that can afford to enhance their images with magical positioning words like "Coke Adds Life." Words like these, linked with pictures of happy people drinking coke, work through the power of suggestion. Forget the fact that Coke cleans the rust off your fender panels. "Just give me a smile with everything on it, and I'll pass it on."

Advertising like this may require that we mentally take a step away from it in order to appraise it more objectively. But usually it's so well put together that we fall into it, taken by its charms. Perhaps we are underestimating Coke's value as a secret weapon in fixing our new relationship with China.

Holy Words

These are words designed to sound not only believable but semisacred, words to be taken as gospel. Words like "Geritol every day." They have the fine fit of a rule of habit and behavior. Another example, again from American Express, is for the American Express card: "Don't leave home without it." Your American Express card is like your socks or briefcase or car keys or kissing your wife. At least that's how the folks at American Express want you to think.

Selling You "Where You Live"

Finding out "where you live" is the specialty of the motivational researchers. What's your sex? Age group? Income profile? Are you female, 18–34? Virginia Slims sells to you by saying "You've come a long way, baby!" But most truly liberated females want to scream, "Save us from the stereotyping!" After all, being cast as some pseudo-siren of [the 1980s] in a slinky gown is no less degrading than being cast as some pseudo-suffragette sneaking a smoke in 1919.

Are you America's typical macho male? You're gonna love it in Marlboro Country, a territory of the mind so well established in full-color magazine ads that the mere sight of one evokes the desired response patterns. Health hazard? What's that?

Many, if not most, of the ads we see play on our desire to conform. The popular "Dewar's Profile" of the average Dewar's whiskey drinkers shows us precisely the sort of person who drinks Dewar's. Want to be like the skydiver or the rising young stockbroker? Drink his brand of alcohol. Do people really take to this approach? They do! They do! And companies can trot out sales figures to prove it.

Charley the Tuna and Other Red Herrings

Charley the Tuna, as well as Tony the Tiger, the Jolly Green Giant, Snap, Crackle & Pop, the Pillsbury Doughboy, Ernie Keebler, and all the rest of the netherworld of cartoon characters created by advertising agencies are simple symbols designed for the purpose of creating certain mental associations in our minds. Again, these little charmers are image builders. The Giant, for example, isn't going to tell you that his niblets are on sale this week. What he wants you to know is that the vegies growing in his valley are the very best. The Giant is making what is called a "generic" sale. He's selling you the concept of overall quality.

Unfortunately, product quality is often outstripped by sheer "cartoonability." Take, for example, the advertising of kids' cereals, many of which use cartoon personalities like Tony the Tiger, Frankenberry, and Count Chocula to hawk their sugar-laden wares to kids who, without the advantage of a discriminating judgment, know only that they like the taste of sugar and who watch these same heroes adorning their cereal boxes come alive on Saturday mornings in TV commercials piped into their rooms.

The trick is to look beyond our own initial, subliminal, sympathetic reactions in order to find the real product story. Let's go back to our friend Charley the Tuna. Charley's job is telling us what tastes good. He plays to our worries over having to make do with second best. The fact is that while tuna may vary somewhat from one grade to another, the difference is mostly in color, consistency, and medium (oil or water). Canned tuna—is pretty much—canned tuna. Our "taste" is largely learned. Charley is helping to teach us to like the most expensive cuts—his boss's cuts.

When it comes to these seemingly innocuous little creatures, beware. The tasteful little tuna may be trying to hook you.

Great Big Irrelevant Attention Getters
(Not Red Herrings—Just a Lot of Carp)

No area of advertising can claim to be innocent of this technique but somehow automobile dealers—particularly on the local level—seem to act as though irrelevancies are their special province. Noteworthy are those dealers who regularly take sledge hammers to new cars and vans. Although this wanton destruction is surely pitiable, it is more entertaining than all those dealers who play violins, sing for their supper, or put their little ones to work to show you what terrific family men they are. What does this tell you about their product? Goose egg zero.

Digging Out Those Buried Warnings and Admissions

Back to those beautiful two-page spreads for Marlboro cigarettes, with the mustachioed macho-men and the horses and the wide-open spaces. It's time to reach into those saddlebags, partner, and grab your spyglass. Now scout the countryside. You'll find what you're looking for—eventually. There under the sagebrush and the boulders, in the lower corner of Marlboro Country, like a small headstone, rests the surgeon general's warning that "Cigarette Smoking is Dangerous to Your Health." Of course this caveat is treated by the advertiser as completely incidental to the thrust of the ad as a whole, and that's how it comes off.

It's up to you to notice warnings and pay attention to their true importance. When a company is required by law to print a warning, they're not going to give it any more prominence than they absolutely have to.

That also goes for what are called "qualifier words," which often appear in premium offers. You'll see the word "FREE," followed in substantially smaller type by the words which "qualify"—that is, limit—that offer. "FREE . . . with 2 coupons," for example, or "FREE . . . with purchase of regular size." Financial advertisements often include an abundance of qualifying words, like "Substantial Interest Penalty for Early Withdrawal," which flash on and off the screen in . . . a flash.

Admissions are ingeniously finessed by ad agencies, and the tired albatross hung around the company's neck can be made to come off like a soaring eagle, so pay attention. Especially when Ford Motor Company, under pressure of litigation growing out of its Pinto's lethally located gas tanks, ends up talking about the new Pintos in terms of their bold new design, with no direct mention of the original problem whatsoever.

Likewise, Listerine brushes by its admission that it doesn't stop colds, an admission forced upon it by court order. Listerine promises less to us now than it did [a few years] ago, but do most of us pick that up?

Untying Those Gordian Knots

The words that win the Gordian Knot Award are so carefully turned that they turn in upon themselves, like a pretzel. They take you from A to B and back again to A. You know you've been traveling, but you suspect that you haven't gotten anywhere for your trouble. Take this award winner: "The world needs more of what Allis Chalmers makes." The AC people don't want to bore you by telling you specifically what it is they make. They just want you to know that, whatever it is, it's important in our lives. But how can people who won't even tell you what it is they're in business to make expect you to take this leap of faith on their behalf? Words that take you nowhere ought to leave you cold.

Music Hath Charms
(So Hath Marvelous Art Direction, Computer Animation, Clever Ideas and Snappy Editing)

Ad agencies often subcontract work to "jingle houses." These are production studios that make music, developing soundtracks for use in radio and TV commercials. These jingles are often built around important campaign words, or taglines, which are at the semantic roots of the campaign. For example, listen again to McDonald's popular "You deserve a break today." As you speak them aloud, you can hear these words set to their familiar music. (Starting out much the same, incidentally, as Walt Disney's "When You Wish upon a Star.")

It's hard not to love the well-coiffed results of expensive production, with its commissioned music, top directors, producers, editors, and the finest commercial talents—composers, arrangers, musicians, designers, writers and animators—all working together on one project built to run probably thirty seconds—although on countless occasions. With all the talent a big budget buys, you can clothe the barest idea in the finest raiment.

We end up looking at these beautiful print ads, listening to these clever radio spots, and watching these overproduced TV commercials, and we can't help loving the actors, the sets, the story turns, and production values, the very sureness and tightness of it all.

The question, of course, is whether we're loving the lady for her clothes or for her heart. Which takes us back to the sizzle on our steak. And our ability to separate the two.

Women, Babies, Animals—

Even the least jaded among us must admit that advertising, if only by virtue of its charge to get and hold our attention, coopts absolutely everything we hold most dear. Chief among these ideals are women, babies, and animals. We see them in advertising everywhere. One good question to ask is whether their presence is contributing to our understanding of product benefits. Another question is whether their absence would damage our understanding, or only give us less to look at.

—And Stars

The stars are out every blessed night. And every day, too. On every channel [celebrities try to sell us products]. . . . But what do the stars tell us? How have they legitimized the products being advertised? Does the fact that [astronaut] Neil Armstrong walked on the moon make him more believable as a spokesperson for Chrysler cars? The Chrysler commercial offers us the link, talking about Chrysler's respect for "machines solving problems." And Armstrong goes no further than to say that "Chrysler cars are exciting, innovative approaches to the needs we all have today." Now, when you look at these words on paper, it appears that they may belong several categories back, back among the jellyfish in sheep's clothing. After all, to say that your products "are exciting, innovative approaches to the needs we all have today," is to use the safest, most nebulous words in the dictionary. Most—if not all—companies advertising hard goods could feel fairly comfortable using those same words themselves. Words as general as that come pretty cheap.

Is the Name the Game?

Advertising people know the value of a well-chosen name for their product, and agencies go to incredible lengths to find that perfect name, using group interviews, questionnaires, and other research tools in order to find the right words to attach to what is sometimes only an idea on the way to being born as a product on your grocery shelf. When an agency first takes on a new product assignment, that product may already have a position, a name, even a package. But, more likely, and especially if the agency has the opportunity to work in close creative association with its client company, that agency will have basic responsibilities for developing ideas, sometimes even from inception; taking them into test markets; finding the right names, packages, sizes, colors—everything. A good agency is continually testing and making changes, like a tailor custom fitting your new suit.

Sometimes you can take a name and give it meaning; sometimes you can take a word or set of words that already have meaning and lay them on a product. It depends on what you're trying to accomplish.

Take "Hamburger Helper." From the point of view of the merchandiser, this is a solid gold name. It describes what is generally called a "food stretcher," and it describes it with just the right nuance. The two things this name tells you are really everything you need to know about the product; it works with your hamburger (not your steak); and it does something good to it. Yet any name, by itself, cannot answer all our questions. Using "Hamburger Helper" as an example, you might ask whether it really is helping your hamburger or just your budget. You may end up deciding that, using food quality as an indicator rather than sheer stretchability, you can help your burgers more in other ways.

Often new product names do the real work of positioning. New products such as Heinz's "Chili Fixin's" and Swift's "Soup Starter" have the names they do so that consumers will recognize that they are intended not as end products but as "ingredient" products. Most research indicates that homemakers reject the concept of instant dinners, even though they welcome convenience features. To circumvent this problem, merchandisers have wisely left a few things for consumers to do themselves. We are instructed to add an egg to the cake mix and ground beef to the Chili Fixin's. Presto! We've got dishes we can pretend we've prepared from scratch. And so these new products are positioned not as instant dinners, not as means in themselves, but as "starters" or "add-ons." The trick is to leave us with a sense of usefulness. Left only to add water, we rebel.

Insofar as naming goes, the promise held out by Hamburger Helper seems innocent when compared with hot little numbers like "Night of Olay." There are people sitting around, day and night, conjuring up names that capture our imagination and . . . fantasies. In sheerest ecstasy we buy the dream soap. And what've we got? Soap. The dreams you can't buy.

Advertising undeniably packs a wallop. You can pretend to be immune to its influence, but unless you watch no television, listen to no radio, and read no newspapers or magazines, you are, more or less—and like all the rest of us—under its spell. No one is completely immune. That is why we need to develop our defenses through self-education as to how advertising works. It begins with our paying more attention, not less, to advertising.

WE ARE IN THE BUSINESS OF ENHANCING TRUST

Davis Young

Davis Young is president of Young-Liggett Public Relations, Cleveland, Ohio.

Reprinted with permission from the January 1986 issue of the *Public Relations Journal*. Copyright 1986.

After the rise and fall of the Roman Empire, but before the rise and what may be the fall of Apple Computer, God created the first public relations person.

Many people—perhaps with justification—might argue that God did not create that person in His own image.

But if God on the one hand asks us to strive for high standards, He is equally quick to forgive our transgressions. God understands what employers and clients do not, which is that public relations people are not perfect.

Let me step up onto the public confessional and confess that I have been guilty of public relations sins in the last twenty-two years. I will probably be guilty again in the future. However, if not sinning were a qualification to talk about ethics, the subject would never be discussed. So like other sinners before me, please allow me the privilege of addressing this sensitive and important subject in my own awkward and imperfect way.

Do we, in fact, have an ethical responsibility? Yes. All businesses and professions do. And all people do. So we are not unusual in that respect. What gives us a point of departure from other types of activity is that our ethical responsibility is based on the fact that significant numbers of people make important decisions because of what public relations practitioners do and say. People buy and sell stock, take jobs, purchase products, and cast votes as a result of public relations programs. Therefore, we not only have an ethical responsibility, but we have that responsibility to a very special degree.

If we are to meet the responsibility more perfectly (or at least less imperfectly), then we need to devote some attention to several issues. We must:

• Publicly recognize the nature of our business. Stop equating public relations with some divine calling. Only public relations people look in the mirror and see Albert Schweitzer. Public relations is a business. It is not a profession. It can, however, be a business practiced with professional standards. Confront what we are, then decide how we can practice our business within honorable professional tolerances.

• Put into effect a long-range program that will get us to a true professional status. Ultimately, this will require some uniform educational requirements, continuing-education or professional-development standards, and a program of strict certification.

• Recognize that being held accountable for results is an intellectually honest direction in which to go. In the best of all worlds, we would find a way to measure all public relations work. At the very least, we need to agree employee-to-employer, or counselor-to-client, on expectations in advance and some means of reconciling what is done against those expectations.

• Place the same emphasis on full, accurate, and understandable disclosure as we do on timely disclosure. Too often ours is a business of selective disclosure on a timely basis. When companies and clients understand that enlightened programs for disclosure are in their self-interest, they will respond more positively than they do today. This does not mean release of legitimately proprietary information related to technology, marketing strategies, sensitive personnel matters, or other such areas. It means being open and accessible for reasonable areas of inquiry.

• Place less emphasis on the bells, trains, and whistles of our craft and more on the substance of what it is we are trying to communicate. Ultimately, what we have to say is far more important than the way we say it. In cases where this is not true, we should avoid saying anything.

• Pay as much attention to the spirit of the law as to the letter of the law. Technical compliance with the letter of the law is frequently far outside the intended spirit.

• Go out of our way to avoid even the appearance of potential impropriety. The opportunities for the appearance of impropriety—even when no impropriety exists—are rampant in our business. In this case, the perception does, in fact, become the reality.

• Refrain from the tendency in our business to search for quick fixes, easy answers, magic solutions. There are no quick fixes, easy answers, or magic solutions to tough problems, and it is dishonest to advance substitutes like these in lieu of substantive ideas.

• Strive for the day when having our name on a news release or other piece of communication carries the same weight as the certification of a Big Eight auditing firm in an annual report. That, of course, implies that our words would be as clean as their numbers.

• Finally, the issue of ethics in public relations (or any field) raises the question of doing all that we can, as individuals, to advance in terms of professional development. None of us ever stops learning. The opportunity to pursue knowledge and new techniques is one of the great attractions of the public relations field. Thus I throw into the ethical mix the issue of cheating ourselves when we fail to take advantage of such opportunities. Surely cheating oneself is an ethical issue of great magnitude.

Public relations relates to *enhancing perceptions of trust.* That's our business—getting people to have trust in products, services, other people, companies, institutions, governments, and so on. Take a moment to think about that. Nobody really makes important decisions in this life without having some measure of trust. If ours is a business that influences decision making, then enhancing trust gets to the real core of public relations.

We are in the business of enhancing trust. The only real objective of a communications program is to enhance trust. That is such a simple, fundamental concept that it is tempting to dismiss it out of hand. Please don't. Think about it. The only real objective of a communications program is to enhance trust—trust in a product, trust in a service, trust in its quality and its service. That is the first commandment of communications in the 1980s. The winners will earn that trust. The losers will be perceived to be unworthy of trust. The difference between winning and losing may well be the effectiveness of communications programs.

If ours is the business of enhancing trust, then our effectiveness is in direct relation to whether people trust us. Let's be honest with each other. That has been a problem. We should address that problem more effectively and with greater courage than we have in the past.

TOMORROW'S PUBLIC RELATIONS

Patrick Jackson

Patrick Jackson is senior counsel at Jackson, Jackson & Wagner, Exeter, New Hampshire; editor of *PR Reporter;* and a former president of the Public Relations Society of America (PRSA). This article is adapted from one that previously appeared in the *IPRA Review* (November 1984) and in *Perspectives,* a publication of the Ball State University Department of Journalism, Muncie, Indiana.

Today's encompassing issue is whether humanity will eradicate itself—through nuclear weapons, chemical warfare, or perhaps genetic misengineering. Of the disciplines available for dealing with this ultimate problem, the one that is directly relevant here is the science and art we know as public relations.

Denis Gabor put it forthrightly in 1964: "Until now, the problems of mankind have been ones of nature. From now on they will be ones of *human nature.*" Solutions are no longer in technology but in taking account of actual human behavior. Indeed the wonders of computer-age technology more often create social problems than solve them.

Speaking in 1976 at the World Congress in Boston, Sanat Lahiri of India, the president of the International Public Relations Association (IPRA), made the linkage. "We must be more than public relations technicians," Lahiri said, "We must be *public relations humanists.* For the goal of public relations is to reach and touch the hearts and minds of men and women."

For years, Edward L. Bernays has been defining practitioners as "societal technicians with the skills to bring about accommodation in the court of public opinion."

Edward Robinson wrote in the foreword to his 1966 book, *Communications and Public Relations,* "Whenever a public relations situation is analyzed, it inevitably boils down to some sort of attitude and behavior change or maintenance problem. That is, the practitioner is either trying to change or maintain someone's or some group's behavior and attitudes. That is why I have defined the public relations practitioner as an *applied social and behavioral scientist.*"

Are We Slow Learners?

These commentators see public relations dealing effectively with even the most difficult world problems. Their messages reached us years ago. Were professionals listening? On one hand, there's little concrete evidence that we were, or even are. Too many practitioners still act and talk as if communications were an end in itself, with magical powers to change attitudes and motivate behavior. Scholars punctured these assumptions decades ago.

On the other hand, practitioners do know the power—and the social responsibility—of our profession. The difficulty has been in applying these lofty principles to daily practice in hospitals, schools, corporations, government, and associations.

Few professionals will ever have world peace as a client. But, just as public opinion consists of an agglomeration of individual opinions, so widespread human behavior depends on the attitude expressed in every workplace, marketplace, and social grouping. We *can* influence the policies and actions of *our* organizations in the direction of public relations philosophy. I am convinced public relations is a philosophy more than anything else. It is a belief that human dignity is invaluable, that people are capable of governing themselves, and that they are entitled to a voice in decisions that affect their lives.

The Near-Term Future

The need is for each of us to provide clients-employers with programs and skills that recognize these realities. We are playing catch up, but I believe we can pull it off. Here is what I predict professionals will be doing very soon:

Raising our sights. A maxim of practice postulates that to change others' attitudes, we must first examine our own. So we had better ask what our attitudes about public relations are. Topical issues like whether we should call it public relations or public affairs, whether it is a profession or a vocation, are insignificant beside the query: Do I truly believe this field has an underlying body of knowledge based in the behavioral sciences and the humanities? More to the point, do I know the science of public relations? Am I able to apply it to my work?

Learning without end. This body of knowledge is growing so fast that continuing education is becoming a necessity. (If you dislike continuing professional development, leave the field. You'll be a drag on your colleagues.) In addition to basics like diffusion process, two-step flow, group psychology, communications modeling, methods of persuasion, and applied semantics, here are some subjects to be studied. You might call them "new product development" for the profession:

Organization Development: How to be an effective agent of change.

Policy Sciences: How to make consensus decisions.

Diplomacy: How to say no without stiffening resistance.

Arbitration: How to effect compromises and accommodation.

Learning theory: How to educate instead of just "talking at" people.

Visual literacy and graphic psychology: How to reach and motivate people beyond words.

Systems dynamics: How the sociopolitical economy really works.

Strategic planning and futures forecasting: Anticipating problems and opportunities instead of being surprised.

(I hear some of you saying we should know all of this already, but remember we are playing catch up.)

Embracing research. All sound public relations begins with research and ends with evaluation. The most potent word in our practice is *evidence*. Research provides it. We should master informal research techniques as well as use the blind statistical sample. Would you want your doctor prescribing medication without making a careful diagnosis? Your lawyer going into court without touching law books? Those activities are often uncomplicated in comparison to what we do when venturing into the court of public opinion.

The Longer-Term Future

By adopting a can-do attitude and powerful skills of the "New Public Relations," these are among the things professionals will be doing before too long:

Becoming "managers of change" rather than "defenders of the faith." No more reactively apologizing but actively gaining approval of plans that anticipate issues and events.

Going by the book. Presenting recommendations to our management colleagues within frameworks that explicitly demonstrate the body of knowledge and our ability to apply it. "I think" will give way to "Here are the options and what we can predict for each from research and proven theoretical concepts."

Avoiding the victory syndrome. Building public relationships has no room for winners and losers. Yet our model has been victor and vanquished. Now our goal is success, not victory . . . because losers rise again. We will seek consensus or at least compromise.

Learning to trust the people. Less telling them what is best for them, more listening to what they really expect of our organizations. Going into the court of public opinion carries with it the risk of failing to win consent. We will waste less time and money in protracted, enormously expensive battles like those over nuclear power, efficient automobiles, or releasing pollution into the environment—where all of society is the loser because a few recalcitrant executives did not understand the court of public opinion. Participation is basic to the public relations philosophy.

A two-track reward system whereby you can practice your profession or even a specialty within it and still get the income and honors now reserved for those willing to become full-time managers. And, like accountants in the 1950s, our ranks will swell from one or a few per organization to large staffs. Organizations exist by public consent, and we have just begun to realize the many ways that winning consent can influence the bottom line—whatever it is for your outfit. So we will put more manpower into the challenge—mainly new practitioners with excellent preprofessional education.

Policy not publicity. Most important of all, practitioners will learn the true role and power of the mass media. That is, they will recognize that publicity lacks the power to deal with most public relations problems. Then we will stop expecting the media to do our job for us and get out there and build relationships, not one-way communications. To do that, we will think more about organizational policy, rather than publicity.

The Uncertainty

In a world changing as swiftly as ours, public relations is a survival skill for organizations and the ideas they represent. The future of public relations is thus assured. The prognosis for present-day practitioners and our obsolete methods is less certain.

But destiny is a matter of choice, not chance. Whether we attain our potential role in society—or perhaps even whether we survive—depends on our will to create the future—quickly—along lines similar to those outlined above.

One more point: I hope you agree or disagree enough with what I've written to take issue. Debating our future makes it far more likely that we will demand ownership and take action.

8
The News

Introduction

The age of mass media has coincided historically with a vast increase in the use and importance of propaganda. This is by no means accidental. The mass media inevitably speak for a select number of people who control the key means of persuasion in society. In modern societies, people are expected to have opinions on a wide range of topics and, according to Jacques Ellul, have a strong need for propaganda:

> The public will accept news if it is arranged in a comprehensive system, and if it does not speak only to the intelligence but to the "heart." This means, precisely, that the public wants propaganda, and if the State does not wish to leave it to a party, which will provide explanations for everything (i.e., the truth), it must itself make propaganda. Thus, the democratic state, even if it does not want to, becomes a propagandist state because of the need to dispense information.[1]

The news in the press and electronic media serves this purpose.

Because there are often discrepancies between the government's interpretation of events and that offered by the mass media, neither of which is necessarily compatible with public opinion, the United States is internally vulnerable to credibility gaps. This is normal in a democracy; but as Ellul has pointed out, competition in the Cold War—clearly a contest heavily dependent on propaganda—may demand a united voice, which is the antithesis of democracy.

Terence Qualter has outlined the main techniques of propaganda.[2] His definition of the term, like Ellul's, goes beyond that of most laymen, who tend to see propaganda as persuasive lies told by some person or organization they do not like. To Qualter, propaganda is any message that "works on the minds of other men, seeking to influence their attitudes and thereby their actions." Thus propaganda may be political, commercial (advertising), religious; good, evil, or neutral. Those who know the techniques readily switch from one type of persuasion to another, thus justifying the utility of this broad definition. For example, skilled advertisers may handle not only consumer goods but also religious revivals, political campaigns, and national image making directed at foreign countries.

Robert Cirino has investigated propaganda in the American media.[3] Contrary to the claims of conservatives in government, he concludes that the media are inherently conservative and represent the views of the establishment. Cirino, who has amassed considerable evidence supporting this position, points out that the media label leftist viewpoints as propaganda but do not label their own bias. We are seldom consciously aware of the status quo viewpoint of our own press or of the way in which sports entertainment—the Super Bowl for example—is turned into a nationalist celebration.[4]

Similarly, some research indicates that the press is often not an adversary press but plays into the hands of the government and yields to presidential pressures.[5] Other commentators note that the press is selective in its news coverage and biased toward the interests of the upper middle and upper class. A low proportion of the public own stocks, for example, but there is much coverage of the stock market. The meaning of market gains or losses, too, is never made clear. Most people probably assume a rising market is good. It is for the seller, but is it for the buyer or prospective buyer? The news seldom covers labor unions, which have millions of members, and when it does, the coverage is usually unsympathetic.[6] Business, however, gets largely favorable coverage, while decisions that may have serious long-term repercussions—like the deindustrialization of the United States—are ignored.[7]

Others claim the news has a liberal bias. Edward Jay Epstein does not fault the system as a whole, but he does find built-in biases in network news.[8] The news production process originates in New York City, and it stresses only big city news. The networks must create news, and their need for visual material places the emphasis on violent and sensational events. Epstein suggests organizational changes that would remedy some of these built-in biases. Numerous polls, however, indicate that TV anchors have high credibility—above that of politicians—and network news is the public's first choice for information. Newspapers, it seems, are considered elitist and less trustworthy by the public.[9]

Similar opinions have been expressed about journalists' bias in the printed press. Thomas Griffith has defended reporters from charges of bias, and his position is probably representative of the thinking of many journalists. He argues that facts do not "speak for themselves" but must be interpreted to have meaning. Reporters' personal views clearly influence their interpretations, but, Griffith claims, this does not prevent them from being professionals. He thinks that intelligent readers should respect the journalist who demonstrates a well-reasoned point of view.[10] The claim of objectivity, it should be noted, is often used as a smoke screen to cover hidden bias.[11]

Columnist Robert D. Novak's conclusions are directly opposite to the conservative bias claims of Cirino.[12] He argues that the Washington press corps is becoming more and more like the liberal leadership of the Democratic party in its basic beliefs and scores "advocacy" journalism for espousing liberal causes.[13] Similarly, Louis Banks claims that the values of the media do not reflect those of their audiences.[14] And a survey of top media newspeople has claimed to verify their liberal biases, a claim that is viewed as irrelevant by many who see the media as essentially businesses.[15] As Michael J. Robinson has said, there is a long history of blaming the press; certainly it is nothing new.[16]

The first reading, by Lawrence Jankowski, provides an overview of electronic news. He defines news and what is newsworthy and describes the process by which news is produced. Television news is much more expensive than radio, and in large markets a station retains a large news staff. He describes the duties of producers, directors, assignment editors, reporters, and support staff. The news, he demonstrates, is a highly complex process and demands a high degree of coordination.

The next reading looks at the network's competitors. Tina Rosenberg describes the changes in local news and the part played by news consultants. Although there is still much that could be improved, the show biz excesses of the 1970s appear to be over.

The press is sensitive on the issue of its credibility. A recent survey commissioned by the American Society of Newspaper Editors, for example, showed that the public trusted television more than the press, much to the chagrin of the latter.[17] Andrew Radolf here reports on a Times Mirror Co. poll conducted by the Gallup Organization. Its conclusion was that the credibility of the press is not a major problem, but the public does believe that the media are influenced by special interests.

The last reading, by Sondra Rubenstein, examines the legal structure in which the journalist must operate. She examines the court decisions that limit the newsperson's right to travel, enter government buildings, gain access to government records and meetings, court proceedings, and the journalists' right to protect sources. Whether reporters are free enough depends on one's political and perhaps ethical beliefs. To many they are "free enough," but for others wanting a growth in civil liberties, the journalist needs more freedom.

Notes

1. Jacques Ellul, *Propaganda,* trans. Konrad Kellen and Jean Lerner (New York: Knopf, 1966), p. 250.

2. Terence H. Qualter, *Propaganda and Psychological Warfare* (New York: Random House, 1962).

3. Robert Cirino, *Don't Blame the People* (New York: Random House, 1971).

4. See Michael R. Real, "Super Bowl: Mythic Spectacle," *Journal of Communication* (Winter 1975). Michael Novak, however, has argued that sports are not treated by the press as serious ritual—as they should be. See his "The Game's the Thing," *Columbia Journalism Review* 15 (May–June 1976). Dan Hallin, "The Myth of the Adversary Press," *Quill* (November 1983): 31–35.

5. Richard Senter, Jr., Larry T. Reynolds, and David Gruenenfelder, "The Presidency and the Print Media: Who Controls the News?" *Sociological Quarterly* 27 (1986): 91–105.

6. Michael Hoyt, "Downtime for Labor," *Columbia Journalism Review* (March–April 1984): 36–40.

7. David Moberg, "Smokestacks and Smoke Screens," *Quill* (April 1984): 24–30.

8. Edward Jay Epstein, "The Selection of Reality," *New Yorker,* March 3, 1973, pp. 41–77. Foreign news, when covered by the media at all, is biased by nationalism and sensationalism. See John A. Lent, "Foreign News in American Media," *Journal of Communication* (Winter 1977).

9. See Philip Meyer, "Elitism and Newspaper Believability," *Journalism Quarterly* (Spring 1973): 31–36.

10. See Thomas Griffith, *How True: A Skeptic's Guide to Believing the News* (Boston: Atlantic Monthly Press, 1974).

11. For a provocative scholarly treatment, see Gaye Tuchman, "Objectivity as Strategic Ritual: An Examination of Newsmen's Notions of Objectivity," *American Journal of Sociology* (January 1972): 660–676. See also Edward Jay Epstein, "Journalism and Truth," *Commentary* (April 1974): 36–40.

12. Robert Novak, "The New Journalism," in *The Mass Media and Modern Democracy,* ed. Harry M. Clor (New York: Rand McNally, 1974).

13. The term *new journalism* refers to both advocacy journalism and the news-based fiction of writers like Tom Wolfe, Norman Mailer, and Truman Capote. For a valuable summary and analysis of writing on this topic, see James E. Murphy, "The New Journalism: A Critical Perspective," *Journalism Monographs,* no. 34 (May 1974). For opposing views, see the series on objectivity—Theodore L. Glasser, "Objectivity Precludes Responsibility," William E. Rowley and William V. Grimes, "Three Dimensional Objectivity," and Sharon M. Murphy and James E. Murphy, "A New Look at the New Journalism"—in *The Quill* (February, March, and April 1984, respectively).

14. Louis Banks "The Rise of the Newsocracy," *Atlantic* (January 1981): 54–59.

15. S. Robert Lichter and Stanley Rothman, "Media and Business Elites," *Public Opinion* (October–November 1981). See also Peter Dreier, "The Corporate Complaint against the Media," *Quill* (November 1983): 17–29.

16. See Michael Robinson, "Fifty Years in the Doghouse: Blaming the Press Is Nothing New," *Washington Journalism Review* (March 1986): 44–45.

17. See Andrew Radolf, "A Credibility Shocker," *Editor and Publisher,* April 6, 1985, pp. 9–10, and "Newspaper Survey: TV Most Trusted," *Broadcasting,* April 15, 1985.

TELEVISION NEWS: HOW IT WORKS

Lawrence J. Jankowski

Lawrence Jankowski is an associate professor of broadcast journalism at Bowling Green State University and executive director of the Northern Ohio Scholastic Press Association. Besides his writing, Jankowski has produced numerous audiovisual materials for educational use in geology.

Television news is something most Americans take for granted. In most studies conducted on how audiences get most of their news and information, television repeatedly heads the list, followed by radio, newspapers, and magazines, in that order.

Critics of television and radio have often stated that these media can only provide the broad outline of stories. They can hardly rival the in-depth reporting of magazines or newspapers. They also report only a fraction of newsworthy events. But television has never tried to compete with newspapers or magazines. It serves a different need and usually a different audience.

Collecting and reporting the news on television is a complex and sophisticated process that has evolved a great deal. In its early days, television did not report as much news as it does today. Then, newscasters did little more than read current newspaper articles to the audience. It was not long until stations realized the potential of television coverage. It was an instant medium. Unlike the newspaper, it could interrupt a program to report an important breaking news event. Like radio, it could announce a story to the world and show what was happening. Television has been there to show the events surrounding the Kennedy assassination, the explosion of the space shuttle *Challenger*, the extravaganza in honor of the one hundredth birthday of the Statue of Liberty, Watergate, the attempted assassination of President Ronald Reagan, the hostage situation in Iran, and numerous terrorist actions. Television has connected the world together in what Marshall McLuhan called the global village. We may not like what we see on television, but like a giant magnifying glass, it highlights important events going on in the world.

News: A Definition

Exactly what is news? News could be defined as whatever people are interested in hearing about. Sometimes this news is little more than gossip or a staged public relations event such as the grand opening of a new shopping center. To be defined as news, an event should contain one or more of the following elements: 1) timeliness; 2) proximity; 3) significance; 4) conflict; 5) prominent people, places, or events; and 6) human interest. Let us take a closer look at each of these elements of a news event.

Timeliness is an important ingredient in broadcast news. Radio can go on the air with a story just minutes after something has happened. Because radio does not have to depend on pictures, it is the simplest of the broadcast media. A reporter can make a call to the station and be live in just a few moments. The attempted assassination of a public official makes timely news.

News is what happens close to us, *proximity*. If a small town decides to raise property taxes, this decision will affect many people. Most people are also interested in how the local high school did in the football championships.

A third element of news is *significance*. A fire in an abandoned tire factory may be important to residents in the town because heavy smoke may damage their property.

A fourth element of news is *conflict*. There are many conflicts with which most people can identify—a handicapped person fighting the city transportation system because local buses lack adequate lift facilities or some struggle of people against nature: the residents of Hawaii who watch lava move over their valuable farmland, the coastal landowner who watches the season's first hurricane destroy his property; or the Xenia, Ohio, homeowner who lost everything when a tornado sweeps through the subdivision. Probably one of the main reasons that so many stories like this are featured on television news is because it offers such dramatic footage of the event. In television news, pictures can often tell more than a thousand words.

A fifth element of news is what happens to *famous people, places, or things*. If you catch a flu virus, hardly anyone even seems to notice, let alone care. If the president has a runny nose, his affliction will probably be mentioned in the evening news. The more famous a person is, the more people want to know.

Finally, there is the *human interest element*. If people are genuinely interested in something, it can be considered news. A local widow decides to do something about the rising crime in her neighborhood. She makes the rounds of her streets and organizes the residents to set up a block watch program. After a year, the crime statistics start to fall, and home values begin to rise.

TV News Departments

The news departments vary widely across television stations. Small stations in remote areas may use only one or two people to report the news; television stations in the major markets, like New York, Houston, and Cleveland, may employ up to a hundred people to report, write, edit, and produce the daily newscasts. Large city television news operations are very complex, requiring videographers, photographers, graphic artists, engineers to maintain and design the television equipment, set decorators, set designers, lighting technicians, make-up artists, electronic news producers, editors, and video librarians.

Although there is no one set format for television stations in the United States, there are a few general practices that most stations perform. Most stations, for example, subscribe to a wire service. A news department pays a standard fee based on the size of its audience for the use of this important service. The wire services continually update news stories and provide headlines and hourly news summaries.

A tremendous amount of work, skill, and technology is necessary to produce the news. The production of a half-hour network newscast requires the work of hundreds of people from across the world. For news stories received from networks, the assistance of correspondents stationed around the world and major American bureaus is necessary.

A news department's most visible person is the *anchor,* also called the *on-air personality.* Although some newscasters are no more than announcers who read prepared news scripts, many on-air anchors are also excellent reporters and writers. The newscaster will usually edit wire copy, write and rewrite stories, and help to decide which stories are to be aired.

The *assignment editor* is a key person in the news operation. This person's job is to choose which events to cover from all the things happening in the news area of the station. The assignment editor will give stories to reporters and photographers and line up interviews throughout the day. The information may come from a variety of sources—telephone calls, wire copy, police or fire calls, or network feeds. The assignment editor must know how long it will take a news crew to get from one place to another across town or across the country. This editor is one of the primary gatekeepers in the station. A story idea or upcoming event may be shelved because the editor may not want it aired. However, the assignment editor makes it a point to be fair and balanced. If an antiabortion rally is covered this week, he or she must include a proabortion viewpoint soon after. The editor will keep a "futures file" containing information on upcoming events. When the newsday begins, the editor already has a number of possible stories.

A key element to any news operation is the *reporter.* Although a great deal of news comes over the wire or through the network, the reporter gathers it at the local level. Much of the time the reporter gathers and reports the news from the field in the form of *voicers* (stories recorded for later broadcast or voiced reports on videotape). The reporter will also do on-camera reports delivered live from the field or recorded on videotape for broadcast later in the day.

A station may make use of a beat reporter who covers a certain person or place each day. Beat reporters may cover news from the courthouse, city government, education, medical, consumer reports, science, or entertainment. Other stations, especially those in smaller markets, use general assignment reporters, who cover just about anything. In the morning, the general assignment reporter may be out covering a local strike and in the afternoon covering the arrival of an important celebrity to that city.

A news crew is usually made up of a reporter and a *cameraman*. The cameraman must not only know how to photograph a subject or event but must also know something about news judgment, creative editing, and composition skills.

Large stations may hire *writers* who work on anything from headlines to news documentaries and from wire copy to original feature material. Reporters are not to be confused with writers. A writer does not usually go into the field to cover a breaking story; this is the job of the field reporter.

At the local level, the station's *news director* has the responsibility of filling up the half-hour slots with news events. The director works with the assignment editor who sends out crews to cover stories of interest to the viewing audience. He or she may send out a crew to cover a press conference that has been scheduled for weeks. Of if a story breaks immediately, the director may reassign crews or get in extra help to cover the story.

Crews vary in number depending on the size of the market and the size of the station. Small news operations may have only one person, who both writes and photographs a story. Larger stations usually send out two or three persons. At the network level, there is usually a reporter, a cameraman, a sound man, and a field producer, who will accompany the news crew and the reporters to oversee production of in-field coverage.

The development of electronic news gathering equipment (ENG) has increased the effectiveness and efficiency of newscasting. In addition to studio cameras, there are smaller, more portable television cameras, called *minicams*, that record sound and picture on magnetic tape. These cameras are lightweight, and the tape requires no processing time. The pictures and sound can also be transmitted back to the studio live by means of telephone lines or sent by means of microwaves to the station for rebroadcast. Such revolutionary electronic news gathering permits stories to get on the air much faster than in the past. Electronic news-gathering vans are also useful. An electronic technician lines up a microwave antenna with a fixed relay point, such as the top of a large building, and transmits the signal directly back to the station.

Back at the station, additional labor, skill, and technology are required during editing and telecasting. When the reporter returns to the station, he or she will look at the videotape shot in the field. Usually there are three ingredients to each television story: the interview, the stand-up or narration, and the cutaway.

The *interview* usually focuses on a particular story or event, or it can consist of a spokesperson or expert speaking about a particular area of interest. If a city council member decides to run for mayor, the reporter may interview the candidate on camera. If an earthquake occurs in a nearby state, the reporter may call on the local college geologist or seismologist to explain what has happened.

The second ingredient of most news packages is the *stand-up* or *narration*. The reporter may just include his or her voice in the report. The story will present the basic information: the who, why, what, when, and where. Depending on the type of story, the reporter may want to be included in the report—perhaps by standing in front of an office building while giving the story to add impact. The reporter may decide to include himself or herself in the close of the story, either to present a certain image to the community or because the audience has learned to trust various reporters, and their presence may help to increase this trust.

The third ingredient of most television news packages is the *cutaway*. The videographer will shoot a great deal of tape during any one story. The cutaways, edited pieces of this tape, are selected to show what happened and at the same time reduce the number of "talking heads" on the television screen.

The final edited story is ready for broadcast once the executive producer decides on the lineup of the newscast. The producer has the flexibility of moving stories around within the program to meet any last-minute changes in the format. The television newscast is a dynamic event. The program lineup could change at any time. Moments before a news program begins, a big breaking story might take place. Details might be very sketchy, so the news director keeps a close eye on the wire machines and the network feeds. Often the entire program has to be revised because of this late-breaking event.

A news program may also change from a particular lineup because of technical difficulties, such as a faulty videotape playback machine. Sometimes a story is not even completely edited or finished when the newscast begins. Reporters and editors work frantically to get the package completed by the end of the news program. Thus newscasters must retain their composure even under a great deal of stress. They may be handed a bulletin to read that they have never seen before. Sometimes the news is as devastating for the newscaster as it is for the viewer.

The producer assembles a *road map*, a final order of the news within the program. Often it is completed only moments before the program is to go on the air. The television director is now called into action. He or she must pull all of the pieces of the show together and assemble the live newscast. The director calls all the shots from a control booth in the TV station or from a remote van if out on location for an important breaking story.

Time is critical; the program must be counted down to the second. Many local newscasts have a more relaxed atmosphere, and a great deal of padding is incorporated into the program. The co-anchors may chat on the set or make some comments to the weather announcer or sports personality. At the network level, however, there is little padding.

During most newscasts, the director must also time the breaks for commercials. Generally there are about seven minutes of commercials distributed at intervals in the typical half-hour format. During the newscast, there must be constant communications between the control room and the studio technicians, videotape room, electronic graphics, the announcer's booth, and audio control. This is achieved by special wired telephone circuits with clamp-on headsets and mouthpieces. The control room may be situated to look into the studio, or directors may work from a blind control room or from a remote van, where they depend solely on TV monitors.

Another important piece of equipment in a newsroom is the *character generator,* a small word processor that stores words or graphics on magnetic tape. At the cue, these words or graphics can be placed on the screen. The character generator has almost eliminated the art department in television stations. In the past, if a chart or graph was needed, the reporter had to make a request to the art director. The studio artist then made up the design, executed it, and had a slide made up. This process took time, so materials had to be ordered well in advance. Now all a technician has to do is type into the computer, and it will quickly produce a graphic. The increased use of graphics helps to organize information and makes it easier for viewers to understand a complicated issue or story.

Another important breakthrough in the news department is the use of satellites. In the past, television signals had to be sent from one place to another by means of telephone lines. Today a signal can be sent to a satellite, and this signal can then be bounced to some distant spot on the earth's surface. At the receiving end is a large, dish-shaped antenna, which picks up the signal and puts this over the air immediately, or it may be videotaped for replay later. With the increasing use of satellites, it will be possible to develop new television networks and so-called superstations. Ted Turner's WTBS in Atlanta is one such station. This independent station sends its programs via satellite to cable stations all over the United States. The cable system in turn offers this additional channel, also used by Cable Network News, which offers a twenty-four-hour news service to subscribers.

Local television stations are also beginning to use satellites more. A station may buy into a feature or news service in Washington, D.C. Rather than send a reporter and photographer to Washington to get a local angle on a national event, it may hire a news service. The service will send a reporter to cover the event, edit the story, and send it via satellite to the local station. Most TV stations now have some type of receiving dish or downlink that allows them to pick up the story and rebroadcast it. Because of the advances of satellite technology, local stations have many new sources for producing their newscasts. This is especially important for sports, where so many different athletic events are being played at about the same time. Satellites allow a station to offer highlights of a particular team though it might be playing a game far away. Satellites are also being used more for foreign news. After the Mexico City earthquake in 1985, videotape of the destruction was sent out by satellite because it was so difficult to get in or around the city.

Television news departments are also beginning to make use of helicopters. Stations are willing to invest considerable sums to get camera crews and reporters to a news event before the competition. Helicopters also allow a cameraman to record a story and beam it back to the station by microwave antennas. In this way, news can be sent long distances. In disasters such as fires, floods, and earthquakes, a helicopter can get to locations even if roads are blocked. After the devastation associated with the 1980 Mount Saint Helen's volcanic eruption, the helicopter and small plane was the only way that the world was able to see exactly what had happened. Since time is such an important factor in television news, the helicopter has been proving itself an important investment. It is also a visible symbol, which helps a station's image.

Other behind-the-scenes workers who help put the show on the air include studio floor directors, who work with the director; the technical director, who ensures that the right video and audio source are put on the screen; the audio and video engineers, who make the correct adjustments so that the home viewer receives the best possible picture; the studio camera operators, who work in the studio; and the set designer and carpenter, who provide an environment from which to deliver the news.

The anchors on newscasts are only the tip of the news iceberg. News involves a team of many skilled and creative people working together. The end result is almost two hours of news each day at the local station.

LOCAL TV NEWS TAKES THE SMILE OFF ITS FACE

Tina Rosenberg

Tina Rosenberg is a Washington writer.

Reprinted from the *Washington Journalism Review,* Vol. 6:7 (November, 1984). Used by permission.

It seemed in the 1970s as though a cult of idiocy had taken over local television news. There was the time at WLS in Chicago that local anchorman Joel Daly, sportscaster Mike Nolan and weatherman John Coleman recited on the air the nursery rhyme "Ding Dong Dell." And the year, 1970, when WFIL in Philadelphia ran through as many as thirty news stories in each half-hour of local news. And the evening in January 1974 that KGO in San Francisco on its 11 o'clock news spent four minutes and twenty-five seconds on sex stories, including segments on a *Cosmopolitan* centerfold, the mother of a *Playgirl* centerfold, nude sun bathing, a Tennessee masher, and a North Carolina massage parlor. On another night, KGO broadcast seven crime stories in a row—killings, rapes, and robberies—all in one half-hour of local news.

The blame for these local news orgies fell not on the stations themselves but on their news consultants. The television consultants, who were hired by station managers to improve ratings, surveyed viewers over the phone or in person, showed them tapes of anchors and segments from news shows, and asked them what they liked. Then the consultants recommended new sets, music, pacing, features, and, most important, new on-air talent, based on what viewers had said they wanted. In his 1977 book, *The Newscasters,* Ron Powers, who is now CBS News TV critic, called these consultants "the principal architects of cybernetic news."

Local TV news is almost a decade older now, and it is obvious that reports of its death as a serious purveyor of news were greatly exaggerated. Individual stations still overdo the crime stories and many local news shows overemphasize personalities and soft features, but the excesses of the 1970s have, for the most part, subsided. Most local news shows today do a slick, respectable job of reporting the news. Dare we admit it? Local television news is getting pretty good.

The transformation, however, did not take place because consultants disappeared. They are still with us, and their business is better than ever. In truth, they were never as responsible for the excesses of local news as the critics claimed. Consultants did not invent the demolition derbies, comedy routines, and breakneck speed of local news; they merely encouraged them.

The consultants mirrored the changes in local television news and, more basically, the gradual education of newscasters and their viewers. When TV news was in its infancy, neither newscasters nor viewers had clear standards—stations tried widely varying formats, and viewers seemed receptive to almost all of them. But as both groups came to understand the restrictions and potential of local TV news, a more sophisticated news show emerged.

In the 1960s, local television stations broadcast news primarily to ingratiate themselves with the Federal Communications Commission, which required programming "in the public interest, convenience, or necessity." News, however, was not a moneymaker, so station executives did not give it much money or much thought. "In the early days, stations just translated a newspaper style of reporting to TV," says John Bowen, vice-president of the consulting firm McHugh & Hoffman. "An anchor read wire copy or wrote out long stories and read four or five in a half-hour. Field reports were at a minimum. But during the civil rights movement and Vietnam war, people realized TV could portray what was going on in the world and in their city in dramatic ways. I remember sitting in Detroit in 1967 glued to my TV set, watching riots."

As a result, the ratings of local news rose and with them advertising revenues. "After all those years of losing money, stations started to realize that if you do this right, you can make more money on news than on 'I Dream of Jeannie' reruns," says one former researcher for Frank N. Magid Associates, the largest TV consulting firm. Today, a local station can make 35 to 50 percent of its revenues from news. On its 11 P.M. news show, a rise of one rating point for a station in a major city can be worth a million dollars a year.

The light of profitability in local news started dawning, at least at NBC and CBS. ABC (which started as an offshoot of NBC) had not reached full television citizenship in the 1960s. "ABC had no commitment to news," says Richard Salant, former president of CBS News. "They were three years later than CBS and NBC in going from fifteen minutes to half an hour for their evening news and they lacked seven-day-a-week news." While NBC and CBS spent more than $60 million apiece to cover the news in the eventful year of 1968, ABC spent only $32 million. That network's ambivalence toward news pervaded its five owned and operated (O&O) local television stations: WABC in New York, KABC in Los Angeles, WXYZ in Detroit, KGO in San Francisco, and WBKB (now WLS) in Chicago.

At WBKB in 1966 things looked bleak. WBKB news was rated fourth in Chicago, trailing not only the CBS and NBC-owned stations but also WGN, the *Chicago Tribune*–owned independent. Richard O'Leary, WBKB's general manager, then saw an opportunity. "There was a conflict then between the 'adult' values of the Eisenhower era and the tremendous emphasis on the self of the 1960s," he says. "Both the CBS and NBC stations were establishment voices. There was no alternative viewpoint. I thought if I could put together the right kind of organization, we could humanize and popularize the news in the best sense of the term."

O'Leary convinced his bosses at ABC that there was little to lose and much profit to be gained by trying something new. He started searching for on-air talent across the country and hired new anchors from Cleveland and from the CBS Chicago station, WBBM. He placed commercial breaks *within* segments on the news, weather, or sports rather than between them and coached the anchors to chatter happily at each transition. "They used a lot of rough humor," he says, something reporter Morey Roth of *Variety* soon dubbed "happy talk." O'Leary also started new features and began promoting in ad campaigns upcoming stories, especially crime stories, that "were so salacious and titillating that they went about 50 yards beyond the story," says Elmer Lower, then president of ABC News. "I was ashamed of them."

But it worked. By 1973, WLS (it changed its call letters in 1968) was number one in Chicago, and O'Leary was number one with ABC, which pulled him to New York to work the same magic at ABC's other owned and operated stations. Gradually, each station went from third in its market to first. The changes cost ABC a lot of money, but, O'Leary says, the shows became profitable so quickly that "the money was coming in almost before the bills were due."

During this period, ABC hired the two biggest consulting firms—McHugh & Hoffman and Magid—which were making their reputations during that time. The consultants "were believers in understanding the audience," says O'Leary, a philosophy that exactly coincided with his own.

McHugh & Hoffman, based in Fairfax, Virginia, started out in 1962 and advised its first clients, the six Storer Broadcasting stations in Toledo, Atlanta, Detroit, Cleveland, Philadelphia, and Milwaukee, to use more film and field reports. Four of the six moved to first place in their markets. Today, McHugh & Hoffman has thirty-four clients.

Frank N. Magid opened his one-man firm in Marion, Iowa, in 1957 to do market research. Gradually, he and his researchers started making recommendations to television stations; in 1970, they officially began a consulting division. Magid today employs 315 people and has clients in more than 100 of the country's 211 markets and in 22 of the 25 largest markets. Last year, Magid moved from ABC to NBC, where he works for its five O&O stations and the "Today" show. Magid boasts that between 70 and 80 percent of his clients eventually have become number one in their market.

The consultants' recommendations reflected what viewers wanted—or thought they wanted—from local TV news in the 1970s. Consider, for example, Magid's work for WXYZ, the ABC-owned station in Detroit. Before

1972, WXYZ's local news programs at 5 and 11 P.M. were the TV news version of a lemon. They consistently came up third in the ratings. The sets looked like stark holdovers from a standard 1960s office, the production was clumsy, and viewers were indifferent to most of the on-air talent.

By the fall of 1972, Magid and his colleagues had interviewed Detroit viewers and suggested changes to the station. Based on Magid's recommendations, Vice-President and General Manager Jim Osborn hired Jac LeGoff, John Kelly, Marilyn Turner, and Jerry Hodak from WJBK in Detroit and Diana Lewis from KABC in Los Angeles. He promoted the new talent in a campaign that used the brazen slogan "We Got Who You Wanted." Anchor Bill Bonds and his new coanchor Kelly were placed in a new set that put them up front surrounded by warm brown, and they were shot from new camera angles "designed to let the viewer perceive the warmth," according to Osborn.

New human interest stories and regular features appeared. One, which ran to the music of "The Entertainer," was a 90-second newsreel of five different stories from around Detroit. "We wanted to counter the perception that the other stations had more film," says Osborn. Another feature, called "Jim Harrington Is," showed reporter Harrington trying his hand at different jobs, including that of riverboat gambler, telephone lineman, and limousine driver. In 1975, WXYZ news became number one in Detroit. It has not slipped in the nine years since then.

Magid also consulted—briefly—for WTVJ in Miami. But his suggestions were so unpopular that WTVJ Vice-President and News Director Ralph Renick persuaded the station to drop Magid after he gave his recommendations in 1971—recommendations that found their way into the duPont–Columbia University Survey of Broadcast Journalism in 1975. Among the forty-two changes Magid suggested were: "More stories should be covered; a number of stories should be shortened"; "Broward County news should not be reported in great detail"; "Minority group stories should be used only when really news; should be presented by a member of the minority group"; "A slogan emphasizing friendliness and warmth of WTVJ news should be employed"; "Serialized mini-documentaries should not be used"; "Initiate Action Reporter feature"; "Initiate consumer protection feature—once/week one minute," and "Develop team atmosphere through conversational interchange. . . . Develop atmosphere which will produce genuine spontaneity."

Such recommendations produced some of the worst distortions of local news in the 1970s as other stations copied—and exaggerated—them. The trademarks of this 1970s style local news were:

Happy Talk. Happy talk was prompted by research showing that the people on the air are the number-one reason viewers pick a station. O'Leary and the consultants encouraged anchors to be likable—i.e., spontaneous and warm; some stations embraced that idea too ardently.

"General managers would go to WLS, watch the broadcast and say, 'Ahh, I know what they're doing, they're making jokes.'" says McHugh & Hoffman's Vice-President Bowen. "But the issue wasn't jokes, it was making the anchors warm human beings."

Blood, guts, and sex. When CBS's "60 Minutes" monitored the news shows in San Francisco for an assessment of that city's news during the 1973–1974 season, it found 55 percent of the stories on the 11 o'clock news at ABC-owned KGO, known as "Kickers, Guts, and Orgasms," were about fires, crime, sex, accidents, exorcisms, or tearjerking events.

"I invented that stuff and it was a success," says Pat Polillo, news director of KGO from 1970 to 1973. "We became number one without a single promotion—just by catching viewers who left their set on after 'Marcus Welby' (the Tuesday lead-in to the late news that rated first in its time slot)." Even a Magid staffer says, "We used to wince when we watched those newscasts."

As with happy talk, the "if it bleeds, it leads" newscast spread because stations mindful of KGO's success overreacted to the consultants' recommendations to use action-filled film stories.

More stories, shorter stories. In the spring of 1970, Polillo, then news director of WFIL in Philadelphia, started running twenty-five or thirty stories in the half-hour 11 o'clock news. "We had to get a film story on within 18 seconds to keep people from tuning out," says Mel Kampmann, who became news director when Polillo went to KGO. "We ran a lot of fires as the lead story." By May 1971, WFIL, last in the market for twenty-one years, was number one. Magid, who consulted for WFIL, "actually came back eighteen months later and told us to slow down," says Kampmann.

Although today Magid says, "I cannot recall in any case recommending a strict time limit on stories," at least three news directors report that Magid consultants said exactly that. "The recommended length of a film story was a minute and a half at the outside, regardless of the story's importance," the news director of WCVB in Boston wrote to the duPont–Columbia University 1975 Survey.

Franchised news. Consultants such as Magid made it easy for smaller stations to copy the successful innovations of larger stations. "News directors get together and compare notes," says a man who used to be one. "Magid gives the same set recommendations in Cleveland as in D.C. He recommends the same features in each city. I guarantee you, you could go into any city in America and pick out the Magid station."

Magid consultants disagree. "The answer is whatever works," says Richard Sabreen today. Sabreen was Magid's director of consultation in the late 1970s. "Sometimes a young anchor is successful, sometimes a person twice his age." But when one Magid station runs a popular new feature, Magid often recommends it in other markets or actually tests tapes on viewers. Although his competitors often copy his signature features, they are easy to spot: the "On Your Side" reporter who checks out viewers' complaints about shoddy business practices, the George Plimpton—style reporter who tries running a ferryboat or trading pork bellies, the "Anonymous Witness" segments, in which a reporter reconstructs a crime and asks viewers with tips to phone them in, and the specialists such as psychologists, pediatricians, greengrocers, or money managers.

Although many news directors complain about it, franchised news was probably the consultants' most significant contribution to local news' evolution. "Small stations tended to be isolated outposts," says Bob White, a former news director at WXYZ who is now vice-president and general manager of KMGH in Denver. Consultants prompted stations where lone anchors read wire copy, to develop (and spend money for) field reports and graphics—in short, to use TV's technology with sophistication. "Magid has singlehandedly, and not by design, upgraded news in this country," says a talent agent. "He began to make a format and structure for people to function in that will succeed in every little jerkwater town if you put orangutans in the role."

Reducing the influence of the news director. The consultants competed with news directors for dominance over the program. Consultants presented a station manager with a scientifically researched book of recommendations cloaked in statistics that could cost as much as $100,000 today. "A general manager only knows his station is running third," says Elmer Lower. "He's not from news—he doesn't know if what the consultant says is good or bad. Particularly if his news is third, the news director has no muscle at all. He has to follow the consultant or the general manager will move him out."

It's not news. News for profit also challenged the accepted definition of news: "What happened that people need to know?"

"Unlike earlier concepts of 'What is news' which defined the product as what people should know, Action News is defined as 'what people want to know,'" a 1972 Magid memo to KFMB-TV in San Diego read. This standard began gaining acceptance as soon as station managers realized local news could be profitable. "The general managers got together at National Association of Broadcasters conventions," says Lower. "They said, 'O'Leary's making headway in Chicago, maybe I ought to try it.' It's copycat. Consultants just provided them with the formula."

Local TV was no more susceptible to what the audience supposedly wanted than the other news media. CBS management was very interested in Dan Rather's "Q" rating—the measure of likability—before it made him anchor of the "CBS Evening News." Newspapers also use consultants to tell them what their readers want. Magid claims between forty and fifty newspaper clients.

For the most part, however, the network newscasts have not succumbed to the same temptations as local news. One reason is they were not always expected to bring in that much money. "When I was at CBS the news was not asked to be a profit center," says Salant. In addition, newspaper and network reporters are guided by long-established traditions of journalism. "Some people at ABC in the 1960s, when we were third, thought if there was a *Daily News* tabloid way to promote the news at the network basis, we would succeed," says Lower. "But you couldn't get people like Howard K. Smith or Harry Reasoner to do that. A lot of these guys grew up with Edward R. Murrow as their idol. You aren't considered a very serious journalist if you go schlock."

If local television news in the 1970s seemed like the teenager who ran around the neighborhood wrecking trash cans, today it has settled into comfortable Yuppiehood.

Detroit's WXYZ broadcasts five hours of news and magazine shows every weekday. Its reports vary from one-line voice-overs to a 35-minute examination of the recommendations of a blue-ribbon panel on Detroit's financial crisis. A large part of the newscast goes to "Anonymous Witness," psychology and medical tips, consumer stories, and a weekly lesson on how to make a local chef's favorite recipe. It runs "Close-Up" almost every week on such topics as the job market, toxic waste dumps, and a nuclear power plant in Midland, Michigan, 150 miles away. "They were heavily into flash and trash in the late 1970s," says *Detroit Free Press* Television Critic Mike Duffy, "but now they do a very slick, complete job of the news. They focus on a personalized story—how the news affects you."

WXYZ is like many local news stations today. Gone are the forty stories per half-hour, demolition derbies, and weathermen showing up on the set with rubber ducks on rainy days. "They speak American, but they don't spend a lot of time tickling each other," says Ernie Schultz, executive vice-president of the Radio and Television News Directors Association.

The two-hour early evening shows now running in most big cities (three hours in Los Angeles) allow time for popular features without artificially dolling up or truncating the hard news. New videotape and satellite technologies allow stations to go "live" from a picket line or toxic waste cleanup site.

And local news viewers have become more demanding. "They're busier," says Pete Hoffman of McHugh & Hoffman, "and as education levels increase and more families have double working spouses, they have a greater interest in what's going on around them."

"Viewers ask, 'Why did you tell me that?'" says Neil Wasserstein, research director of McHugh & Hoffman. "They don't want their time wasted. They want a constructive newscast that tells them why a story is beneficial."

Most important, news executives have set standards for themselves. "We have a better understanding of the role local news plays in peoples' lives," says Bob White. The fact, he says, "that so many people depend on local newscasts for their news scares the hell out of me." General managers and station managers are more likely to be former news directors themselves, White says, and therefore more protective of news and less likely to follow formularized recommendations.

Certainly, some flaws in local news remain: First among these is the continuing fascination with on-air talent. Although popular anchors have always been important, today they are an obsession. Because of increased competition from cable and satellite stations and because copying another newscast's style or new feature is so easy, Magid says, "more attention is focused on people" to distinguish one newscast from another.

The emphasis on talent has blurred the distinction between journalism and entertainment. For example, five out of ten Miss America finalists this year said they planned to become television anchorwomen—but only one mentioned anything about reporting. And consider the example of NBC-owned WRC in Washington, a Magid client since 1981. In the most hard-news-oriented city in the country, Channel 4 promotes its "Team 4 News" reporters in commercials showing them playing football, feasting on crabs, and decorating birthday cakes together.

And with so much emphasis on service features, some viewers may not notice how little real news they are getting. The trend now is to "emphasize news you can use as opposed to the state capital," says Schultz of the Radio and Television News Directors Association. "Twenty years ago, city hall, police, and school board were the primary beats. Now it's health, consumer, and business news. Police news has to compete with things that weren't considered news before."

"You could tune into a half-hour of a two-hour show and think you've got the front-page news," says Ralph Renick, "when you've really seen the Lively Arts section." A randomly selected half-hour of Washington's WRC News from 5:30 to 6 o'clock one September day shows that some local news programs are still not broadcasting grown-up news. WRC that day aired a story on sports, two health features, a story on the upcoming Jacksons' concert, a "whatever happened to" story, and an interview with the star of "Sky King," a Saturday show for kids in the 1950s.

After announcing the next day's program would cover a man who does public relations for movie stars and advice on money management, anchor Lea Thompson closed with this wishful message for viewers: "Stay tuned for another full hour of news."

WHAT CREDIBILITY PROBLEM?

Andrew Radolf

Reprinted from *Editor and Publisher*, January, 1986. Used by permission.

There is "no credibility problem for the media," but there is a problem of the media's perceived independence from the "establishment" and special interests, according to a Gallup Organization survey commissioned by Times Mirror Co.

"At a minimum, the independence issue is something of a surprise," Gallup said. "Contemporary press critics usually argue that the media have become arrogant, even imperial. The public sees the press as anything but.

"The independence issue emerges as central when the public tells us why it feels the press performs badly: more often than not, the public sees press failures as a consequence of external influences."

The survey found, however, strong public support—"to the point of enthusiasm"—for the media's role as the "watchdog" of government. Majorities said that the media, through its watchdog role, protect the democratic process, keep political leaders from "doing what should not be done," and keep the nation militarily prepared.

Called "The People and the Press," Times Mirror commissioned the survey over a year ago [1985] to resolve some of the "puzzling inconsistencies" of earlier research and to "expressly uncover the public's most basic attitudes towards the media."

The survey said that "if credibility is defined as believability, then credibility is in fact one of the media's strongest suits."

The survey also found that "print news organizations are not seen as any more or less believable than electronic news organizations." It found that print news organizations, however, get both the highest and lowest believability ratings from the respondents.

The survey also found that President Reagan "was seen as less believable than all of the major anchors and major news organizations that appear in the survey."

The president was also "less favorably regarded than all of the major [news] organizations which comprise the press establishment."

The survey found that 71% of the public rate President Reagan as either mostly favorable or highly favorable. For both national and local television, the favorable rating was 89%, radio news's favorable rating was 90%, while local daily newspapers enjoyed a favorable rating of 86%. "Nationally influential daily newspapers" received an 81% favorable rating.

In believability, 68% of the respondents said President Reagan was either believable or highly believable. The *Wall Street Journal,* CBS News, and ABC News received believability ratings of 87%, while 86% called NBC News either believable or highly believable.

Local daily newspapers were rated believable by 84% of the respondents, as was Cable News Network and radio news. The Associated Press was viewed as believable by 82%.

Nationally influential newspapers were seen as believable or highly believable by 78% of the respondents, but *USA Today* was called believable by 73%.

Walter Cronkite, though he left his news anchor post in 1981, is still the believability champ with a 92% score. Peter Jennings and David Brinkley scored 90% in believability, followed by Dan Rather and John Chancellor at 89%, Ted Koppel and Tom Brokaw at 88%, Mike Wallace at 83%, Diane Sawyer at 80%, Sam Donaldson at 79% and Barbara Walters at 78%.

George Will scored 74% in believability, but Jack Anderson came in lower than President Reagan with a 62% believability score. Phil Donahue scored 60%, while Ann Landers came in lowest in the survey with a 49% believability score.

Cronkite is also the best-known news personality, with only 6% of the respondents unable to recognize a photograph of him. Rupert Murdoch, on the other hand, was not recognized by 84% of the respondents who were shown his photograph.

As for accuracy of the news media, Gallup found "there is no evidence that the nation has grown more suspicious about the facts."

The survey noted that in the 1930s, polls done for *Fortune* by Roper found about one person in three expressed reservations about the accuracy of the media. In its survey, Gallup found the numbers basically unchanged. Fifty-five percent of the respondents said the news media "get the facts straight," while 34% said the media are "often inaccurate."

The survey also found that a majority, 52%, feels the media "stand up for America," while 30% said the media are "too critical."

However, 53% of the respondents said news organizations are "often influenced by powerful people and organizations," compared to 37% who view the media as "pretty independent."

"More telling, perhaps, is the fact that large portions of the public feel that news organizations are often influenced by a wide spectrum of political and social groups in the way they report the news," the survey stated. "Heavy majorities see the press as often influenced by the federal government (78%); business corporations (70%), advertisers (65%), and labor unions (62%).

"Clear majorities also believe news organizations are often influenced by Republicans (60%) and by Democrats (58%). Half see the military as often influencing the way the press presents the news."

Forty-eight percent of the respondents said liberals influence the way news is reported, but 45% "thinks that conservatives exert influence on news work."

Those seen as least influential were blacks, Catholics, and Jews. These were the only three groups "not seen by a majority" as able to influence news reporting on a regular basis.

The survey found "mixed evidence" that the news media have a liberal bias. Forty-one percent said the press is liberal, but only 22% said the news reporting is "liberally biased."

Nine percent believe the news reporting shows a conservative bias.

Yet a total of 45% believe news reporting is politically biased, compared to 36% who feel it is not. Fifty-three percent said news organizations favor one side in their reporting, versus 34% who said the media are fair to all sides.

But 78% of the respondents said the news media are fair to President Reagan in their coverage of his administration. Only 12% said news organizations are unfair to him.

News organizations were seen by 79% as caring about the quality of their work, while 72% said they are "highly professional."

Fifty-four percent viewed news organizations as moral, compared to 13% viewing them as immoral, but only 35% of respondents believed the media care about people they report on. Forty-eight percent said they don't care.

The belief that news organizations have no regard for people's privacy continues to be "one of the most widely held criticisms of all," the survey said, with 73% of respondents saying news organizations are likely to invade privacy. Only 21% felt the news media respect people's privacy.

The criticism that the media also dwell too much on bad news also persists. Sixty percent said news organizations pay too much attention to bad news, while 36% said there is "not too much" attention paid to bad news.

The "need for attracting a big audience" was the leading factor cited for the media's failure to do a good job of reporting (23%), followed by pressure from special interests (21%), not keeping opinions out of stories (17%), and government keeping the story from the press (11%).

The public "all but dismisses the notion" that budgetary restrictions keep the press from doing a good job, with only 3% citing it as a factor for poor performance. "Nor does the public consider the incompetence of newspeople a major factor in press failures," the survey said, noting only 6% cited lack of skills or background as a reason for bad reporting.

Advertiser pressure was also dismissed, with only 8% saying it was a factor in poor press performance.

HOW FREE ARE REPORTERS?

Sondra M. Rubenstein

Sondra Miller Rubenstein has a Ph.D. in political science from Columbia University. She is an assistant professor of communication theory at Hofstra University and is the author of *The Communist Movement in Palestine and Israel, 1919–1984* (1985). She has taught courses in censorship and international communication.

Although American journalists are freer than journalists elsewhere in the world, many lament the reality that they do not enjoy an absolute freedom to gather information, to protect their sources, or to publish whatever they wish regardless of whether it damages someone's reputation or invades someone's privacy. For many, dismay over a series of Supreme Court decisions—particularly in the areas of news gathering and source protection—stems from their belief in a common law origin of these rights, their interpretation of the First Amendment guarantee, and their refusal to accept any restraints, claiming an absolute freedom for the press.

The underlying principle of modern libel and invasion of privacy laws, which places limitations on the press, was a reaction to the common law practice that permitted the duel to rectify an insult and to protect and restore one's honor. Positive law (that which was promulgated) evolved to guard against the resultant breach of peace caused by the perceived need to duel. It is thus relatively easy to explain and justify the origin of, and the need for, legal constraints in the areas of libel and invasion of privacy and to dismiss reporter abhorrence of these press constraints. Indeed, most journalists accept the legal precedent in these areas because Supreme Court decisions, beginning with *New York Times v. Sullivan* (1964), showed an understanding and a sympathy for the day-to-day pressures on the press, its need to cover prominent people and events, and the inevitability of occasional error in the rush to deadline.

Because legal decisions in the areas of news gathering and source protection have been consistently less sympathetic to the press, if not (in the view of many) actually hostile, there is greater controversy and lack of acceptance of the legalistic thinking behind court opinions that have separated the issue of access to information from the act of publishing. Speaking on this subject in 1975, following his controversial opinion in *Pell v. Procunier* (1974), Associate Justice Potter Stewart said: "So far as the Constitution goes, the autonomous press may publish what it knows, and may seek to learn what it can." Yet, Stewart noted,

> this autonomy cuts both ways. The press is free to do battle against secrecy and deception in government. But the press cannot expect from the Constitution any guarantee that it will succeed. There is no constitutional right to have access to particular government information, or to require openness from the bureaucracy. . . .
>
> The Constitution . . . establishes the contest, not its resolution. Congress may provide a resolution, at least in some instances, through carefully drawn legislation. For the rest, we must rely, as so often in our system we must, on the tug and pull of the political forces in American society. (Stewart 1975)

For their part, reporters have generally claimed that the right to publish is meaningless without access to information and source protection. This reading therefore focuses on these two areas and examines several cases in which the decision was viewed as an attack against the public forum role of a free press in the United States.

Under common law, legally compelled disclosure of confidential exchanges was not applicable to certain relationships: husband-wife, attorney-client, doctor-patient, and clergyman-penitent. As written or positive law developed, the lawmakers and courts were reluctant to include the reporter and his or her source among those who received this qualified legal protection, and, in fact, since the press was generally seen as an adversary in most countries, its role was proscribed.

In the United States, the press has traditionally played the role of society's watchdog and has assumed a privilege of access to government-originated information, as well as source protection, as an integral part of the First Amendment's guarantee of the right to publish. The Supreme Court has consistently taken the position that reporters have no greater rights (either based in common law or in the Constitution) than those afforded the general population. In fact, since the 1970s, nearly all Supreme Court cases involving news gathering have gone against the press, leading many to conclude that the increasingly conservative Supreme Court (often dubbed "Nixon's revenge"), unlike the previous court led by Earl Warren, was antipress. Now, with the retirement of Chief Justice Warren Burger and the appointment of Associate Justice William Rehnquist to his position, it is likely that this trend will continue for some time.

To answer the question, "How free are reporters?" one is first obliged to ask: "To do what?" How free are reporters to travel where and when they wish, to enter areas and buildings under government control, including jails to interview prisoners, to have access to any government records, agency, and court proceedings, or to protect their sources during testimony? A quick answer would be that they are as free as, and no freer than, any other citizen of the United States. Claims to any greater privilege, based on the journalist's self-appointed role of public representative entitled to a front-and-center seat, have met with support only in the dissenting opinions of such First Amendment absolutists as the late Supreme Court Associate Justices William O. Douglas and Hugo L. Black. In short, a reporter is not absolutely free to gather information and to protect sources.

Right to Travel

In 1956, *Baltimore Afro-American* reporter William Worthy traveled to the People's Republic of China despite a ban by Secretary of State John Foster Dulles. On his return, Worthy's passport was revoked, and the State Department refused to issue another. Worthy attempted to regain his passport by taking the matter to court, but he lost in both the trial court and in the court of appeals, which held:

> The right here involved is not a right to think or speak; it is a right to be physically present in a certain place. . . .
> Freedom of press bears restrictions. . . . Merely because a newsman has a right to travel does not mean he can go anywhere he wishes. He cannot attend conferences of the Supreme Court, or meetings of the President's Cabinet or executive sessions of the Committees of Congress. He cannot come into my house without permission or enter a ball park without a ticket of admission from the management. (*Worthy v. Herter*, 270 F.2d 905, D.C. Cir., 1959)

When the Supreme Court refused to hear the case (361 U.S. 918, 80 S. Ct. 255), it left in place the court of appeals holding that it cited as precedent in 1965, in *Zemel v. Rusk*. Zemel had argued that the State Department's ban against travel to Cuba interfered with his right as a citizen to inform himself. The Supreme Court acknowledged the resultant obstruction to a free flow of information but supported the government's denial: "The right to speak and publish does not carry with it the unrestrained right to gather information" (85 S. Ct. 1271–1281, 1965).

Right to Enter Government Buildings and Areas

On August 21, 1971, three San Quentin staff members and two inmates were killed during an escape attempt. Prison officials blamed their previous liberal press policy, which permitted access to and interviews of inmates who had attracted press attention because they had flouted prison regulations. The authorities believed these inmates had gained in notoriety and influence, encouraging noncooperation among other prisoners. As a result, two days later, on August 23, § 415.071 of the California prison regulations was adopted. It was this provision that was challenged by journalists Eve Pell, Betty Segal, and Paul Jacobs, whose requests to interview certain prisoners had been denied.

Pell v. Procunier, as the landmark case became known, reached the Supreme Court in 1974. Writing for the majority, Justice Stewart recalled the San Quentin events and attributed them to the celebrity status acquired by inmates interviewed by the press. He justified the press restriction:

> The sole limitations on news-gathering in California prisons is the prohibition . . . of interviews with individual inmates specifically designated by representatives of the press.
>
> The Constitution does not . . . require government to accord the press special access to information not shared by members of the public generally. It is one thing to say that a journalist is free to seek out sources of information not available to members of the general public. . . .
>
> It is quite another thing to suggest that the Constitution imposes upon government the affirmative duty to make available to journalists sources of information not available to members of the public generally.

Such a proposition, he wrote, "finds no support in the words of the Constitution or in any decision of this Court" (94 S. Ct. 2800–2810, 1974).

With *Pell v. Procunier* as precedent, the Supreme Court, in *Houchins v. KQED* (1978), issued a more restrictive opinion on the issue of general reporter access to jails and other areas under government control. The judgment of the Court was announced by Chief Justice Warren Burger, who acknowledged the historic role and importance of the media and the "powerful and constructive force" they can be in "contributing to remedial action in the conduct of public business." Yet, he concluded,

> The media are not a substitute for or an adjunct of government, and . . . they are "ill-equipped" to deal with problems of prison administration. . . .
>
> The public importance of conditions in penal facilities and the media's role of providing information afford no basis for reading into the Constitution a right of the public or the media to enter these institutions, with camera equipment, and take moving and still pictures of inmates for broadcast purposes. *This Court has never intimated a First Amendment guarantee of a right of access to all sources of information within government control* (emphasis added). (98 S. Ct. 2588, 1978)

Right of Access to Records and Meetings of Government Agencies

When, in 1966, President Lyndon B. Johnson signed the Federal Public Records Law, soon called the Freedom of Information (FOI) Act, proclaiming that "a democracy works best when the people have all the information that the security of the Nation permits," journalists cheered and then bombarded government agencies with requests for information (Nelson and Teeter 1986, p. 464). In addition, reporters hailed the Sunshine Act, which initially mandated open meetings for the regular sessions of some fifty government agencies.

Attorney General Ramsey Clark said of the FOI Act that it imposed on the executive branch "an affirmative obligation to adopt new standards and practices for publication and availability of information. It leaves no doubt that disclosure is a transcendent goal, yielding only to such compelling considerations as those provided for in the exemptions of the act" (Nelson and Teeter 1986, p. 465).

There were soon nine categories of exemptions under the FOI Act and ten under the Sunshine Act. During the Nixon and Carter administrations, the exemptions were tightened and revised. By 1978, despite changes in eligibility requirements to receive information, government agencies were complaining about the costs in dollars and personnel to fill the deluge of requests by journalists, law firms, commercial competitors, and foreign agents. The Treasury Department cited a cost of $6 million, and the CIA gave the figure of $2 million, with 257,420 man-hours required to fill requests not covered by any exemption written into the law (Nelson and Teeter 1986, 467). Finally, in 1983, with strong support from the Reagan administration, the Ninety-seventh Congress passed a number of measures authorizing the further withholding of information by agencies dealing with trade, consumer product safety, income tax, energy, and health.

Writing about what she calls the "tight-lipped presidency" of Ronald Reagan, Donna A. Demac (1984) discussed the prepublication review provision of the president's national security directive, his directive on lie detector tests for all federal employees and contractors, the Paperwork Reduction Act, the effect of budget cutbacks on statistical operations, including the elimination of the Statistical Policy Office in the Office of Management and Budget, and reductions in agency staffs. She concludes her litany of complaints with a warning:

> The politics of secrecy began long ago. It is an intricate mosaic of tangibles and intangibles carried out directly through laws, lies, and misinformation

and indirectly through insider habits that shield those in office from public scrutiny.

. . . The information restrictions of the Reagan government are of historic value: they will outlast his administration or reappear in amended form in the future, unless appropriate measures are taken to prevent this from happening. (Pp. 141–142)

Right of Access to Court Proceedings

In 1979, in *Gannett v. DePasquale,* the Supreme Court ruled that neither the public nor the press has a right to attend pretrial criminal hearings. Speaking for the Court, Associate Justice Potter Stewart wrote:

> The whole purpose of such [pretrial] hearings is to screen out unreliable or illegally obtained evidence and insure that this evidence does not become known to the jury. Publicity concerning the proceedings at a pretrial hearing, however, could influence public opinion against a defendant and inform potential jurors of inculpatory information wholly inadmissible at the actual trial.
>
> . . . Closure of pretrial proceedings is often one of the most effective methods that a trial judge can employ to attempt to insure that the fairness of a trial will not be jeopardized by the dissemination of such information throughout the community before the trial itself has even begun. . . .
>
> The Sixth Amendment, applicable to the States through the Fourteenth, surrounds a criminal trial with guarantees such as the rights to notice, confrontation, and compulsory process that have as their overriding purpose the protection of the accused from prosecutorial and judicial abuses. Among the guarantees that the Amendment provides to a person charged with the commission of a criminal offense, and *to him alone,* is the "right to a speedy and public trial, by an impartial jury." *The Constitution nowhere mentioned any right of access to a criminal trial on the part of the public; its guarantee, like the others enumerated, is personal to the accused* (emphasis added). (99 S. Ct. 2898, 2905–2096, 1979)

As many trial court judges subsequently misinterpreted this decision (and the conditions listed to justify closure) to mean that reporters could generally be kept out of the courtroom, the Supreme Court felt the need to clarify its decision by differentiating between the necessarily closed hearing to determine the admissibility of evidence in a subsequent criminal trial and the public's historic right to attend criminal trials. Thus, in *Richmond Newspapers v. Virginia* (1980), Chief Justice Warren Burger, delivering the opinion of the Court, narrowly defined the issue as "whether the right of the public and press to attend criminal trials is guaranteed under the United States Constitution." Prior to our own Bill of Rights, criminal trials in the United States and in England, he wrote, had always been "presumptively open," and public access to trials has long been seen as a necessary and important element to ensure fairness in the trial process.

To the state of Virginia's arguments that neither the Constitution nor its amendments contain any guarantees of a public right to attend trials, Burger responded:

> Notwithstanding the appropriate caution against reading into the Constitution rights not explicitly defined, the Court has acknowledged that certain unarticulated rights are implicit in enumerated guarantees. For example, the rights of association and of privacy, the right to be presumed innocent and the right to be judged by a standard of proof beyond a reasonable doubt in a criminal trial . . . appear nowhere in the Constitution or Bill of Rights. *Yet these important but unarticulated rights have nonetheless been found to share constitutional protection in common with explicit guarantees* (emphasis added). (100 S. Ct. 2814, 1980)

Although *Richmond* clarified the issue of press access to criminal trials, the right of the press to cover various pretrial matters remains uncertain, as the three conditions justifying closure of pretrial hearings listed in the *Gannett* decision have sometimes been ignored. These conditions are the presence of convincing evidence that there will be irreparable damage to the defendant's fair trial rights, there are no other means to deal with the publicity, and there is clear indication that closure will be effective (that is, that no leaks will occur).

Because many trial judges find it easier to ban the press from their pretrial proceedings rather than to deal with the *Gannett* conditions and because pretrial matters play such a major role in the criminal justice system, many reporters have taken to carrying some version of what is called the "Gannett card." This clearly identifies the individual as a reporter for a specific newspaper and politely raises objection to a proposed closing while respectfully asking to be heard through counsel, who is prepared to present arguments against the closing.

Right to Protect Sources during Testimony

When Paul Branzburg (*Louisville Courier-Journal*), Paul Pappas (a television reporter in New Bedford, Massachusetts), and Earl Caldwell (*New York Times*) refused to testify before grand juries during 1970 and 1971, they asserted a privilege that they and most other journalists believe is guaranteed as part of the free press clause of the First Amendment. Supreme Court Justice Byron R. White delivered the opinion in what is called the *Branzburg* decision, dealing with all three cases and rejecting the reporters' arguments on the grounds that there is no constitutional or common law basis for granting special privileges of any sort to journalists:

> Newsmen are not exempt from the normal duty of appearing before a grand jury and answering questions relevant to a criminal investigation.
> . . . Grand juries address themselves to the issues of whether crimes have been committed and who committed them. Only where news sources themselves are implicated in crime or possess information relevant to the grand jury's task need they or the reporter be concerned about grand jury subpoenas. . . .
> We are admonished that refusal to provide a First Amendment reporter's privilege will undermine the freedom of the press to collect and disseminate news. But this is not the lesson history teaches. . . . The common law recognized no such privilege. . . . From the beginning of our country the press has operated without constitutional protection for press informants, and the press has flourished.

The decision noted that while a number of states have passed shield laws, providing statutory privilege, most have not, and there is no federal statute granting source protection to journalists.

In 1978, a shield case arose in New Jersey in connection with the famed "Dr. X" case, the murder trial of Dr. Mario Jascalevich. Myron Farber, a *New York Times* reporter, was subpoenaed to bring documents to court for their inspection in private. The trial judge turned down Farber's demand for a hearing before he would agree to turn over the materials. Farber was charged with contempt of court and sentenced to jail (where he remained for forty days), and he and the *Times* were fined $101,000 plus $5,000 per day until the materials were brought to the judge's chamber. The judge ruled that in order to determine applicability of New Jersey's shield law, he would first have to examine the documents. On appeal to the New Jersey Supreme Court, Farber and the *Times* lost. The Court cited *Branzburg* and flatly rejected the notion that the First Amendment provided any privilege to Farber to remain silent. The *Times* and Farber, the Court ruled, should have submitted the documents for private examination by the judge as a preliminary step to determining shield law applicability (*In re Farber*, 78 N.J. 259, 394 A.2d 330, 1978).

At the end of an eight-month trial, Dr. Jascalevich was acquitted. The judge ordered Farber's release from jail and suspended the penalties imposed against him and the *Times*. Debate over the effectiveness of the New Jersey shield law continued in the state legislature, where a bill was presented to prevent a recurrence of the Farber incident. The substantially strengthened new shield law of 1981 provides for a pretrial hearing at which a criminal defendant must prove that the subpoenaed journalist's materials are relevant and unavailable elsewhere.

We can conclude that, at best, certain states grant reporters a qualified privilege to protect their sources. There remains an absence of a federal statute granting similar protection. The *Branzburg* decision, denying any special testimonial privileges to reporters subpoenaed before a federal grand jury, continues to be the relevant precedent.

In an address delivered at Rutgers University in 1979, William J. Brennan, Jr., associate justice of the U.S. Supreme Court, set out to clarify the thinking of the Court on issues of news gathering and source protection. He argued on the basis of two "models": the traditional speech model and the structural model. In the former, "the press requires and is according the absolute protection of the First Amendment." This model sees the press as an important public spokesman and as a collection of individuals who speak out on various issues. In the structural model, the concern is with the relationship of the press to functions of communication as required by a democratic society in which many interests compete. In this model "the press' interests may conflict with other societal interests [for example, a fair trial] and adjustment of the conflict on occasion favors the competing claim." It falls to the Court to weigh the social interests involved and to decide which is more important. Thus, according to Brennan, the *Branzburg* case can best be understood in the light of the structural model:

> The reporters in *Branzburg* . . . argued that if they were compelled to reveal confidential sources or notes before a Grand Jury, their ability to gather the news would be impaired. The case did not involve any substantive restrictions on press publications. The contention of the press was simply that reporters must be excused from duties imposed on all other citizens because the fulfillment of those duties would impair *the press' ability to support the structure of communications protected by the First Amendment.* In its decision, the Court acknowledged that First Amendment interests were involved in the process of news gathering, but concluded that these interests were outweighed by society's interest in the enforcement of the criminal law (emphasis added). (Devol 1982, pp. 139–147)

How free are reporters? The answer depends on whether you are a libertarian supporter of the Douglas-Black school of absolute freedom of the press, wherein the First Amendment is interpreted to mean exactly what it says: "Congress shall make *no* law . . . abridging . . . freedom of speech, or of the press." In that case, you will want to add, "nor, should the Supreme Court 'legislate,' through its power of judicial review, constraints on our press, when none were intended by the Founding Fathers, who chose their words with such care." You will speak of the "chilling effect" the Supreme

Court and the Reagan administration have had on the free flow of information, and you will see the press as a natural ally of the people. You can still have a healthy skepticism toward everything you read, but whenever government acts, you will go to the press knowing that some reporter will ferret out the facts, as occurred in the Watergate affair (1972–1974). So, how free are reporters if you are a libertarian thinker? Not free enough.

On the other hand, perhaps you are a social responsibility advocate. In that case, Brennan's structural model will suit you fine. You will, of course, point to such things as national security and executive privilege and conclude that the press has become too powerful, too influential. You will speak of balancing, weighing, and compromising to ensure an orderly society. You can also argue that all rights contained in the first ten amendments, regardless of whether listed as the first or the sixth, are equal and must be considered equally. In the end, to the question "How free are reporters?" you will answer, "As free as any other citizens, and that's free enough."

References

Demac, Donna A. 1984. *Keeping America Un-Informed: Government Secrecy in the 1980's*. New York: Pilgrim Press.

Devol, Kenneth S., ed. 1982. *Mass Media and the Supreme Court*. 3d ed. New York: Hastings House.

Franklin, Marc A. 1982. *Mass Media Law—Cases and Materials*. 2d ed. New York: Foundation Press.

Nelson, Harold L., and Dwight L. Teeter, Jr., 1986. *Law of Mass Communications—Freedom and Control of Print and Broadcast Media*. 5th ed. New York: Foundation Press.

Stewart, Potter. 1975. "Or of the Press." *Hastings Law Journal* 26:631.

9
Politics and the Law

Introduction

The instruments of mass communication in the modern world have an enormous potential for shaping politics. This is particularly obvious in totalitarian countries, where the media are under direct political control. Misuses in our own society are less obvious but real enough, and in recent years public concern has grown over such issues as political bias and control, the effect of the media on campaigns, and the long-range implications for the political system.

Perhaps the most important political effect of the media is an unseen one: their ability to set the agenda of public debate. This ability, claims McCombs and Shaw, is shared by politicians, news reporters, and editors working together.[1] They, along with the reporters and editors of the wire services, decide what is newsworthy.

The news and public issues exposed by these organizations to a large degree constitute what we know of politics. Sidney Kraus has summarized what contemporary research findings show about political socialization, the ways in which the media shape political opinions and actions.[2] Because young voters today, unlike their parents, have grown up with television, says Kraus, they are much more likely to have learned political concepts from that medium. Not only has television brought them direct political information, it has also shaped their view of the country and the rest of the world—a view that is both more sophisticated and less optimistic than that of their elders. Kraus concludes that since much research still ignores the possibility that the media are important in forming political beliefs, more research and reevaluation is called for.

Harold Mendelsohn and Irving Crespi have examined the media-politics problem.[3] They trace the growing use of the media by Franklin D. Roosevelt and his successors and the changes this has wrought. Personality, images, and celebrity have replaced political experience, real issues, and integrity in politics. Because access to the media means political strength, the executive has a distinct advantage over the legislative branch of government. The president is a single personality who can project a human image, while Congress is a body of a few hundred disputatious people, many of them unknown to the general public. Personality politics is based on media exposure—hence, the escalation of election expenses, the increasing employment of marketing techniques, and the emergence of what Mendelsohn and Crespi call the "pseudo campaign."

The mechanisms of one such campaign have been described from an insider's level in a now-classic book by Joe McGinniss.[4] The guiding forces in Richard Nixon's 1968 presidential campaign came from show business, marketing, and public relations. The Nixon team was not dealing with deep political ideas; rather, it was applying professional advertising skills to the campaign. This style of campaign was not limited to former President Nixon nor the Republican party nor the infamous Committee to Re-elect the President in 1972, which played image politics but added dirty tricks and criminal acts to their methods. George McGovern tried the "new politics" of participation in 1972 for philosophical and financial reasons (he lacked wealthy corporate backers), but he also used image methods, as did Jimmy Carter and Ronald Reagan in the next three campaigns. Today all serious candidates for major office use similar techniques of persuasion. Emphasis falls on images and personality—show business celebrities become prime political material—while party platforms and ideologies fade into insignificance.[5]

A related problem arises once a successful candidate is in office. The reporter must often rely on the politician for news (the president, of course, can "make news" whenever he pleases). This puts considerable potential for manipulation in politicians' hands. To a degree all influential persons, elected or not, have this power. If a news reporter offends them, they will stop cooperating. An outspoken, crusading journalist is likely to become an unemployed one. At presidential news conferences, for example, the nation's top officeholder is quizzed by men and women who must stay in some favor if they wish to pursue their work in Washington or even be called on again for a question.

David Halberstam has looked at the overall relationship between the press and the recent presidents; he concludes that they got the news treatment they deserved.[6] White House reporters, he claims, are willing to be manipulated by an executive who gives them access to government spokesmen. But if they are treated with suspicion, they react with hostility or even with malice. Much depends on the personality of the president and his underlying feelings about the press. John F. Kennedy, despite his occasional anger at the press, maintained good relations with the press. Lyndon Johnson lost their trust. Nixon brought a long-time fear and distrust of the press into the White House and was treated accordingly. Many members of the press and much of the public believe that the Watergate coverage by the *Washington Post,* perhaps the most significant piece of journalism in U.S. history, was instrumental in driving the president out of office.[7] The Nixon resignation marked the all-time low in presidential press relations. Although more friendly relations were resumed during the Ford, Carter, and Reagan administrations, the press will probably never again be as naive and accommodating to the chief executive as it was in the Eisenhower–Kennedy era.

While politicians rely on the press, the media in turn must operate within the context of a complex political and legal environment. The mass media are regulated in part by internal pressures and in part by public opinion. Professional codes of ethics constitute the former. In addition to audience size and sales to the public and to sponsors, public influence includes complaints of citizens' pressure groups and of organized reviewers (critics in other media, press councils). Citizens' groups, such as Action for Children's Television (ACT) and the Office of Communication of the United Church of Christ, appear to be most successful when they mobilize a public and then put pressure on regulatory and legal agencies rather than directly on the medium.

There is also formal regulation, the legal structure under which the media operate, and the government regulatory agencies devised by public law. The mass media are regulated by many different government agencies. The basic guidelines come from the executive branch of government and congressional legislation. On a day-to-day basis, both the Justice Department and the Federal Trade Commission are involved with enforcing the general laws, but the most important regulatory agency is the Federal Communications Commission (FCC), whose specific task it is to regulate the electronic media. The FCC has the authority to license stations, suggest broadcasting regulations to Congress and the president, and prosecute stations and networks for alleged violations of existing laws. But the television industry has gained the upper hand in many of the disputes that are crucial to its operation. Partly because of its public image as the donor of "free" services and its powerful control of the communications media themselves, it has been able to portray the FCC as an intruding organization that works against the public interest. In addition, the FCC itself is now committed to deregulation.

The weakness of the FCC relative to the private television industry could be attributed to confusion between the regulator and the regulated, by the interlocking of elite personnel. A retired commissioner, for example, is admirably suited for lucrative posts in the private industries that he has regulated during his FCC tenure, and, as with other government officers, such changes in employment are not unprecedented. However, although a few commissioners may have relaxed controls to keep open future employment channels, conflict of interest is difficult to prove and certainly does not apply to officials like former commissioner Nicholas Johnson, whose continuous attack on the networks scarcely endeared him to the industry's leaders and more compliant commissioners. The commission's weakness is probably not due to the doubtful integrity of commissioners but to the more basic structural defects of its organization.

The FCC has an enormously wide range of responsibilities, many of which are only vaguely defined, in the nation's sophisticated and expanding communications channels. These range from space satellites to telegraph and telephone use to the protection of individual privacy in new wire-connected computer systems, and from all public and private broadcasting to the licensing of pocket paging devices. The commission is responsible for applying the fairness doctrine—the rules relating to advertising, political campaigning, and personal attack—to each of these stations. The commission has to fulfill these multiple tasks with a staff of fewer than 1,500 employees and a small budget. This hardly indicates the dominance of big government in mass communications.

Despite the government's attempt to regulate the electronic media and its incursion into educational public broadcasting, the U.S. system is overwhelmingly a commercial enterprise. The profit motive and economic imperatives place the emphasis on mass entertainment rather than the maximum spread of public information or artistic creativity. Thus, for example, film producers readily accept military censorship in return for cut-rate hire of battleships, tanks, bombers, and thousands of armed services extras.

Because broadcasting is a business operation, it must first serve its stockholders and only then the public (as, presumably, newspapers, film, and mass-circulation magazines do). Major broadcasters are linked to the economy by their dependence on corporate advertising and by other less obvious interests. This is especially clear if the medium's parent company is tied to the military-industrial complex by holding companies seeking defense contracts or engaged in overseas activities. In such cases, despite seemingly autonomous news staffing, the conflict of interest in reporting military and foreign news is readily apparent.

There has been much attention recently to the limits of the central principle of law under which the media operate, the First Amendment. Sig Mickelson thinks that the fairness doctrine has modified the principle of free speech (for the broadcasters) by generating pressure for public access to television time and for counteradvertising.[8] Due to its public service guidelines, then, the application of the First Amendment to broadcasting remains ambiguous. Ben Bagdikian is more critical of the media's performance.[9] He finds that print journalists often used the First Amendment self-righteously, but the government and courts also have displayed heavy-handed arrogance. Donald McDonald[10] argues that the media themselves may be the worst violators of the First Amendment and that the courts may increasingly stress the "public's right to know."[11]

Benno Schmidt has analyzed the *Nebraska* decision of the U.S. Supreme Court.[12] While it was overall a victory for press freedom, it may also limit press access to criminal trial information. The conflict between the First (free speech) and Sixth (fair trial) amendments has not been resolved by the *Nebraska* case and will continue to be a problem,[13] along with the media's constant struggle with libel laws.[14]

The first reading in this chapter studies the central problem between the government and the press: how can reporters get at the truth when officials try to hide or disguise it? Anthony Marro first gives some examples of government "misinformation," from half-truths to outright lies, that journalists have come to expect. Politicians apparently find it necessary to manipulate the press and public to their own advantage. The Reagan administration has even claimed that the literal truth is not important. Many politicians and people in the press argue that lying is sometimes necessary, particularly in cases of national security. The danger is in determining what constitutes security. Others fault the press for not doing their job well enough. Marro concludes with the issue of secrecy: how much should a democracy allow?

The next two readings continue the analysis of politics and the media. Charles McDowell examines the influence of television on political campaigns. He has covered all national political conventions since 1952, when Eisenhower won the first crucial televised confrontation to win the Republican nomination and the presidency. Since that time, the image of the candidate has been important. Today's politics bypass political parties and, aided by political action committees, appeal directly to voters. This has serious repercussions for politics. Greg Schneiders examines the press coverage of Congress. Unlike the flash of the election campaign, the activities in the House and Senate are not glamorous. Although the results are the crucial part of democratic government, the press does a poor job of coverage, and the public remains uninformed.

The last reading gives an overview of the media and the law. Jay B. Wright first traces the history of freedom of expression, from its English origins to the First Amendment and its interpretation by the courts. He then weighs these rights against the rights of individuals. At issue are laws concerned with defamation, invasions of privacy, and fair trials. Wright then outlines the laws concerning government secrecy and obscenity. He concludes with two special problem areas: the legal structure for advertising and public relations and the regulation of electronic media.

Notes

1. "Structuring the 'Unseen Environment,'" *Journal of Communication* 26 (Spring 1976).

2. Sidney Kraus, "Mass Communication and Political Socialization," *Quarterly Journal of Speech* 59 (December 1973).

3. Harold Mendelsohn and Irving Crespi, *Polls, Television and the New Politics* (New York: Harper & Row, 1970).

4. Joe McGinniss, *The Selling of the President* (New York: Trident Press, 1969). See also Jeff Greenfield, "Campaign Reporting: Advice from a Double Agent," *Columbia Journalism Review* (July–August 1975).

5. For a recent account, see Charles McDowell, "Trust Me," *Washingtonian* (May 1986): 134–150.

6. David Halberstam, "Press and Prejudice," *Esquire* (April 1974).

7. See, for example, James McCartney, "The Washington Post and Watergate: How Two Davids Slew Goliath," *Columbia Journalism Review* (July–August 1973): 8–22. Edward Jay Epstein argues strongly that the press has exaggerated its own role in uncovering Watergate; the FBI and judiciary were much more important. See his "Did the Press Uncover Watergate," *Commentary* (July 1974): 21–24.

8. Sig Mickelson, "The First Amendment and Broadcast Journalism," in *The First Amendment and the News Media*, Final Report, Annual Chief Justice Earl Warren Conference on Advocacy in the United States, June 1973. For a useful historical account of the changing use and meaning of the amendment, see Charles Rembar, "The First Amendment on Trial," *Atlantic* (April 1973). Fred Friendly, "Television and the First Amendment," *Saturday Review*, January 8, 1972, pp. 45–54, argues that broadcasters often feign attack on their rights to hide their own inadequacies. See also his *The Good Guys, the Bad Guys and the First Amendment* (New York: Vintage, 1977). For a general treatment, see Howard Simons and Joseph A. Califano, Jr., eds., *The Media and the Law* (New York: Praeger, 1976).

9. Ben Bagdikian, "First Amendment Revisionism," *Columbia Journalism Review* 13 (May–June 1974).

10. Donald McDonald, "The Media's Conflict of Interests," *Center Magazine* (November–December 1976). See also responses to this article by Tracy Westen, Steve Shiffrin, Richard Kipling, Joseph J. Schwab, Ronald K. L. Collins, Arnold Paul, and Clifton Fadiman in the March–April 1977 issue of the magazine; and Edwin Knoll, Douglas Cater, Nicholas Johnson, and others in the January–February 1977 issue.

11. See Richard A. Schwarzlose, "Journalism and the Law," *Columbia Journalism Review* 16 (July–August 1977).

12. Benno Schmidt, "Nebraska Press Association: An Expansion of Freedom and Contraction of Theory," *Stanford Law Review* 29 (February 1977).

13. See Lyle Denniston, "The Struggle between the First and Sixth Amendments," *California Lawyer* (November 1982).

14. See Steve Weinberg, "Libel: The Press Fights Back," *Columbia Journalism Review* (November–December 1983): 65–67; Karen Rothmyer, "Westmoreland v. CBS," *Columbia Journalism Review* (May–June 1985): 25–30; Lyle Denniston, "The Law Giveth, the Law Taketh Away," *Quill* (November 1984): 46–49; and Michael Massing, "The Libel Chill: How Cold Is It Out There?" *Columbia Journalism Review* (May–June 1985): 31–43.

WHEN THE GOVERNMENT TELLS LIES

Anthony J. Marro

Anthony J. Marro has served as a reporter in *Newsweek*'s Washington bureau (1974–1976) and in the Washington bureau of the *New York Times* (1976–1979). He then served as chief of *Newsday*'s Washington bureau, and in 1981 became managing editor. Marro holds a master's degree from the Columbia University School of Journalism. This reading was the winner of the Joseph L. Brechner Freedom of Information contest at the University of Florida College of Journalism and Communications.

Reprinted from the *Columbia Journalism Review*, March/April, 1985, ©. Used by permission.

NOVEMBER 25, 1957—Dwight Eisenhower, sixty-seven years old and recently recovered from both a heart attack and abdominal surgery, is in his office. He tries to pick up a document, and can't. He tries to read it, and fails. The words, he later says, "seemed literally to run off the top of the page." He tries to get up, and nearly falls down. He tries to tell his secretary what is wrong, but she can't make any sense of what he is saying. His physician realizes almost immediately that Eisenhower has suffered some sort of a stroke.

The president has developed "a chill," the press office tells reporters. It is not until twenty-four hours later that the nation is told that its president is seriously ill.

DECEMBER 7, 1971—Henry Kissinger is briefing the press on the government's position on the India-Pakistan war. "First of all, let's get a number of things straight," he begins. "There have been some comments that the administration is anti-Indian. This is totally inaccurate." A briefing paper has been handed out at the start of the session. The first sentence reads: "The policy of this administration towards South Asia must be understood. It is neither anti-Indian nor pro-Pakistan."

A month later, Jack Anderson publishes the transcript of a meeting attended by Kissinger on December 3, just four days before the briefing for the press. "I am getting hell every half-hour from the president that we are not being tough enough on India," Kissinger is quoted as saying. "He wants to tilt in favor of Pakistan."

APRIL 22, 1980—Jody Powell, President Carter's chief spokesman, is talking with Jack Nelson, Washington bureau chief for the *Los Angeles Times*. No military operation is being planned to rescue the hostages in Iran, Powell tells him. A blockade might be feasible, somewhere down the road, but a rescue mission just wouldn't make any sense.

354 • Mass Media and Society

The newspapers with Nelson's story, which says that the Carter White House considers a rescue operation impractical, are still scattered around in living rooms all over Los Angeles when the members of Delta Team board airplanes for the raid on Tehran.

OCTOBER 24, 1983—Larry Speakes, the White House spokesman, is asked by reporters whether U.S. troops have landed on Grenada. He checks with a member of President Reagan's national security staff, and relays the response. "Preposterous," he says, and goes on to deny that any invasion is planned.

The landing takes place the next day.

For starters, Stephen Hess probably is right. The Brookings Institution scholar, who has studied both Washington reporters and government press operations, says that most government spokespersons don't like to lie. For one thing, telling the truth is official U.S. government policy. For another, they prefer telling the truth. To lie, he says, is to "fail to play fair with reporters and the public, to diminish their self-esteem, and to complicate their work."

But complications and crises are of the essence of government, and trying to put the best face on a sensitive situation also is part of the job. Political posturing, face-saving, honest error, bad judgment, and legitimate national security concerns also play a role, and so, to different degrees in different administrations, do arrogance, deceit, disregard for the public, high-handedness, and attempts to cover up stupidity and criminal conduct. The result is that reporters have come to accept some level of deception as part of the routine and to expect, as Hess delicately phrases it, "less than full candor" on the part of their government.

In fact, Washington reporters over the years have had to deal with a steady barrage of deceptions, half-truths, and outright lies—deceptions about national security operations that were so sensitive that they probably wouldn't have published the information even if they had been able to obtain it, and deceits so petty that they wondered why anyone would bother to lie in the first place.

There was the time in 1960 when Lincoln White tried to explain away the crash of the U-2 airplane in the Soviet Union. It had been on a weather mission and had just strayed off course, the State Department's chief spokesman said. "Now, our assumption is that the [pilot] blacked out. There was absolutely no—N-O, no—deliberate attempt to violate Soviet air space. There never has been." Within days it became clear that the pilot, Francis Gary Powers, was alive, that the Soviets had him, and that he was talking. The principal attachment to the airplane was not a thermometer but a camera, and its mission was not weather reconnaissance but spying.

There was the time in 1966 that Lyndon Johnson claimed that one of his great-great-grandfathers had died at the Alamo (not true), and the time in 1971 that the White House claimed that Tricia Nixon's wedding cake had been based on an old family recipe (it apparently had been created by a White House chef).

There was the time in 1975 when FBI director Clarence Kelley said that while there had been some warrantless break-ins by FBI agents in the past, they had been confined by and large to foreign espionage and counterintelligence matters, and had been ended by J. Edgar Hoover in 1966. In truth, there had been thousands, all of them illegal, most of them against American citizens, many of them against people never charged with any crime, and some as recently as 1972. Kelley's aides were left to explain that the head of the nation's most sophisticated police agency had been misinformed.

There was the time in 1954 when Henry Cabot Lodge, ambassador to the UN, described fighting in Guatemala as "a revolt of Guatemalans against Guatemalans," despite the fact the uprising was being orchestrated, in large part, by Frank Wisner, the deputy director for plans for the CIA. There was the time in 1981 when the Reagan administration released a white paper on Central America that attributed authorship of key documents to several guerrilla leaders who clearly had not written them. There was the time, during the Bay of Pigs invasion, when the government lied in saying that the bombings were being conducted by defectors from Castro's own air force and then, when reporters discovered the lie, groused because the reporters did not create lies of their own to help protect the government's lie.

There was the time in a televised debate last October [1984] when President Reagan insisted that more people were receiving food stamps than ever before (actually the number had dropped by about 400,000 since he had become president) and when Walter Mondale claimed that Reagan had sought to "terminate" a housing program for the elderly (in fact, the Reagan administration had made major cuts in the program but hadn't tried to abolish it).

There was the time that John Mitchell, the former attorney general, was indicted for lying about Watergate, the time that Richard Helms, the former head of the CIA, was indicted for lying about Chile, and the time that Rita Lavelle, a former official with the Environmental Protection Agency, was indicted for lying about the EPA's handling of toxic waste.

There was the time that Ron Nessen, President Ford's press secretary, began a response to a question by saying, "To tell you the truth . . ." only to be overwhelmed by sarcastic applause.

The Manifold Forms of Deception

I.F. Stone has said that "Every government is run by liars, and nothing they say should be believed."

James Deakin, who covered the White House for many years for the *St. Louis Post-Dispatch*, pretty much agreed with Stone but worded it differently. "Every government is run by people who seek to wield and retain power," he wrote in *Straight Stuff,* his brilliantly witty book on Washington journalism. "To do this, they must convince the public of certain things: That their policies are correct. That their facts and explanations should be accepted. That they are in control of events and situations. That sounds nicer [than Stone]. And it comes out at the same place."

To achieve these things, it's necessary not only for governments to deceive, but also to hype, slant, tilt, and gloss over, trying at the same time to present a situation in its most favorable light, while hiding, or hedging on, or deflecting reporters away from any information that might conflict with its version. Indeed, Stephen Hess has written, "It is hard to find a discussion of modern government's relations with the press that does not include the words 'manage,' 'manipulate,' and 'control.'"

It probably is a fool's errand to try to measure degrees of deception from one administration to the next or to try to show whether Democrats are more or less deceptive than Republicans. Clearly, much misinformation was produced by the Reagan administration during its first four years, on such matters as the invasion of Grenada, revolution in Central America, its concern for the handicapped, and its commitment to civil rights. But there is no way of assessing how it compares with, or whether it's even in the same league with, the massive amounts of misinformation put out by the Johnson administration during the Vietnam War for example, or by the Nixon administration during the Watergate years.

For one thing, it often takes years for deceptions to surface. It took congressional hearings, criminal prosecutions, and serious reporting by people like Nicholas Horrock and John Crewdson, both then working for the *New York Times,* to expose the degree to which the FBI had been staging illegal break-ins against American citizens. And even in 1985, fifteen years after the fact, we were still learning in the libel trial of General Westmoreland against CBS about the degree to which key officials in the Johnson administration knew that, despite their public statements to the contrary, there wasn't any light at the end of the tunnel. For another thing, there is the question of degree, and the issue of whether and at what point, numerous small deceptions begin to equal major ones.

There was a time, early in the Reagan administration, when the president's aides argued that it didn't matter whether some of his stories were literally true—his numerous misstatements of fact, his confusion about detail, and his repeated anecdotes about supposed welfare cheats that no one was ever able to confirm, for example—because they contained a larger truth.

"We've been dealing with four years of an administration that freely states—and stated early—that literal truth was not a concern," says Bill Kovach, the Washington news editor of the *New York Times.* "This is the first time I've heard that literal truth is not important to the presidency."

There also is the matter of attitude. "This administration is much more arrogant with the press," says one career government official who has served through several administrations. "The attitude is, 'Screw you, we don't need you. The Reagan administration is going to be successful despite the editorials in the *Washington Post* and the *New York Times,* and the cartoons in the *Los Angeles Times.*'"

And Morton Halperin, the director of the left-leaning Center for National Security Studies, says that many key officials in the Reagan administration have a philosophy of government that doesn't include public discussion and debate. "These guys came here straight out of 1946," he says. "They came out of World War II, when the government lied all the time, and it was all right to lie. The whole Normandy invasion, and the covert operations that surrounded it, are an important part of that mind-set. . . . They still think fundamentally that foreign policy should be left to the executive branch and that people shouldn't even try to find out what they're up to."

Deceptions by government officials take many forms, and it's not always easy to show what they amount to. They can include simple face-saving, such as Geraldine Ferraro claiming she felt "vindicated" by a House report critical of her failure to disclose her husband's financial interests, and routine political posturing, such as the White House announcing full support for people like Anne Burford and James Watt, when both had clearly become major liabilities and were on their way out of the government. And there is the endless, predictable attempt by administrations to portray themselves in the best light as Reagan did in a speech to the National Council of Negro Women in July 1983. "We have authorized for filing three school desegregation cases, more than were authorized by the previous administration during its first thirty months in office" he said.

At first blush, this looks like a simple statement of fact. But when James Nathan Miller took a look at the numbers, he concluded in an article in the *Atlantic* on Reagan's civil rights record that "this seemingly straightforward twenty-four-word sentence contains three carefully crafted semantic deceptions."

To begin with, Reagan's administration hadn't actually filed more cases than Carter's. His Justice Department had filed only one, while Carter's had filed two. Second, while Reagan seemed to be saying that he had filed more cases, he hadn't really said that. What he had said was that his administration had *authorized* that the suits be filed. And third, while he implied that he was talking about his record and Carter's on the same terms, in truth he was using an apples and oranges comparison of legal suits his people had authorized (but not yet acted on) with suits that Carter actually had taken to court.

The fact that it took Miller about twelve hours' worth of digging just to deal with that one sentence gives some notion of the problem at hand.

The Reagan Twist—and John Mitchell's Maxim

The problem, in the view of many, is very real, not necessarily because face-saving and political posturing are outrageous in themselves but because a pattern of routine and systematic deception has very real costs, both in terms of loss of confidence by people in their government and in terms of citizens not learning until it is too late just what it is that their government is up to. And while it is not clear that the Reagan administration is any more duplicitous than others, it unquestionably has gone well beyond other recent administrations in its attempts to bottle up information to prevent public access to government officials and records, to threaten and intimidate the bureaucracy in order to dry up sources of information, and to prevent the press and the public from learning how their government is functioning.

This goes well beyond just shielding the president from questions (Reagan has had fewer official news conferences than any president in modern times) and doing silly things like revving up the helicopters while he's getting ready to leave for Camp David so that reporters won't be able to make themselves heard over the din. The administration's proposals for limiting the Freedom of Information Act, censoring the public statements of government officials even after they leave office, and using polygraphs to search out people who talk to the press all have the effect of restricting access to information, and of making it harder for reporters to report on the way Reagan is running the government.

Jack Landau, who heads the Reporters Committee for Freedom of the Press, goes so far as to say that such actions by the Reagan administration constitute the greatest restrictions on public access to government information since World War II. There is no question but that the Reagan administration is seeking restrictions and kinds of censorship in peacetime that Eisenhower, Kennedy, Johnson, and even Richard Nixon didn't ask for in times of war.

There is a temptation to shrug that politicians have always lied and that the Republic nonetheless has survived. But David Wise, in *The Politics of Lying*, argues that to dwell on historical examples of lying is to miss the point entirely because it was only in the 1960s that government deception came to be *perceived* by large numbers of citizens. Many actually were shocked to learn at the time of the U-2 incident that their government would tell such a lie. And once large numbers of people come to distrust their government, he says, a new political environment is created in which the president can no longer assume that most people believe what he says.

According to Wise, a former bureau chief for the *New York Herald Tribune*, this is a dangerous situation in a society in which the government is supposed to operate with the consent of the governed. Indeed, writing in 1972, he termed the erosion of confidence between people and government—an erosion that was documented by University of Michigan studies—"perhaps the single most significant political development in America in the past decade."

Wise laid much of the blame for this erosion on official deception, and he in turn laid the blame for much of the deception on the growth of the nation's intelligence-gathering agencies since World War II. Once the government began running covert operations, it had to have cover stories to hide them, and that required government-sanctioned lies. The chief criterion thus was not truth but just the opposite—developing lies that would be plausible enough to be accepted as truth. "Thus the standard is not truth," Wise wrote, "but fashioning lies that will be believed."

Sissela Bok, in *Lying: Moral Choice in Public and Private Life*, argues that it is dangerous to let public officials get away with even minor lies or lies that they feel are for the public good. "Some come to believe that any lie can be told so long as they can convince themselves that people will be better off in the long run," she writes. "From there, it is a short step to the conclusion that, even if people will not be better off from a particular lie they will benefit by all maneuvers to keep the right people in office. Once public servants lose their bearings in this way, all the shabby deceits of Watergate—the fake telegrams, the erased tapes, the elaborate cover-ups, the bribing of witnesses to make them lie, the televised pleas for trust—become possible."

And Jody Powell, President Carter's press secretary and a man who admits to at least one lie that he still believes was in the national interest, argues that while there are long-range problems for a democracy if people don't trust their government, there can be more immediate consequences, too. "An administration that has a reputation for being not credible, for evoking 'national security' to cover political embarrassments and things that don't involve any real national security matters at all, that sort of administration is going to have a harder time protecting national security secrets when there's a need," he said in a recent interview. In short, if reporters come to distrust an administration's officials, they won't believe them even when the matter is serious and the officials are telling the truth.

All three—a former journalist, an academic, and a former press secretary—would argue that it is important that the press not shrug off lies as just part of the routine but must, instead, set out aggressively to expose them and to hold officials accountable for them. The reason is not just to expose deceptions for the sake of exposure (although Bok, more than the others, would argue that this is an important goal in itself) but to make it possible for people to know how their government is working.

To this end, the best piece of advice for reporters was offered by John Mitchell, the former attorney general and no particular friend of the press. His words: "Watch what we do instead of what we say." In truth, he wasn't talking to reporters at the time (he was talking with a group of people concerned about the direction of civil rights law enforcement under Nixon), and he never did much to help reporters learn what his department was doing. But sorting out the difference between what a person, or a government, is saying and doing is at the heart of reporting and central to the role of the press in a democracy. Among other things, this means getting access to information about the process, about alternatives that were debated and discarded, about how a decision came to be made, and about all the predicted results of the decision, not just those that the government sees fit to release.

This also means being able to report on the decision-making process while it is still underway and while it is possible to show what the alternatives are. On this point, Deakin says, the press is very much like Lyndon Johnson, who when he was Senate majority leader used to complain to the White House that Congress wanted to be "in on the takeoffs as well as the crash landings."

Letting the public in on the takeoffs means telling it what an administration really is up to—whether it really had a commitment to enforcement of civil rights laws, whether it really is providing a "safety net" for the helpless, and how far it really is prepared to go in trying to prop up allies in Central America, for example—and what the likely consequence of its actions will be. And the single biggest complaint of many reporters now working in Washington is not just that the government has deceived them in major ways but that it has taken unprecedented moves to try to prevent them from getting behind the deceptions.

Does Government Have a "Right to Lie"?

It is not known who first argued that the government has a right to lie to its citizens, but the person who touched off the greatest furor by saying it was Arthur Sylvester, a Defense Department spokesman during the Kennedy administration. On December 6, 1962, during a dinner meeting of the New York chapter of Sigma Delta Chi, Sylvester was asked by Jack Fox of UPI what he thought about half-truths and deceptions by government spokesmen.

This was in the aftermath of the Cuban missile crisis of October 1962, and many reporters were still fuming about some of the misinformation that had been released during the crisis. For one thing, Kennedy had cut short a political trip to Chicago and had rushed back to Washington to deal with the evidence that the Soviets had placed offensive missiles in Cuba. Instead of telling the nation that a major confrontation with the Soviets was brewing, however, Kennedy's aides explained the sudden return to the capital by saying that the president had come down with a cold.

Later in that same week, with tensions rising and questions flying thick and fast, Sylvester had authorized a press release from the Pentagon that read: "A Pentagon spokesman denied tonight that any alert has been ordered or that any emergency military measures have been set in motion against Communist-ruled Cuba. Further, the spokesman said, the Pentagon has no information indicating the presence of offensive weapons in Cuba."

The first sentence may have been technically correct. The second was false, a government-planted lie at a time when Kennedy had made the decision to confront Khrushchev but before all the strategy for the confrontation had been worked out.

In authorizing the release, Sylvester later said, he had come down on the side of the "Lying Baptists" and against the "Truthful Baptists." His reference was to a dispute between two groups of Baptists that had erupted at Long Run, Kentucky, back in 1804. The issue was whether a man with three children who had been captured by marauding Indians was justified in lying to the Indians in order to conceal the fact that a fourth child was hiding nearby. The "Lying Baptists" argued that the father had the right to lie and thus save the child. The "Truthful Baptists" disagreed, saying that, no matter what the consequences, the truth should be told.

This is a philosophical and ethical debate that far predates Arthur Sylvester, the Cuban missile crisis, or even the 1804 dispute among the Baptists of Long Run, Kentucky. Discussing a similar hypothetical situation, albeit one without Indians or the possibility of nuclear holocaust, Immanuel Kant argued that truthfulness cannot be avoided by any person, no matter how serious "may be the disadvantage accruing to himself or another." Samuel Johnson's view was more in line with that of the "Lying Baptists" and Sylvester. "The general rule is, that truth should never be violated; there must, however, be some exception," he said. "If, for instance, a murderer should ask you which way a man has gone."

Others have argued that the key question is whether the person seeking the information—a murderer in Sam Johnson's London or a Miami resident who suddenly has Soviet missiles aimed at him, for example—has any right to it. At what point did the American people have a right to know that their president was wrestling with a major crisis, not just a cold, and that Soviet missiles had been placed in Cuba?

Sylvester's argument was that the stakes were so high that deception, both of the Soviets and of the American people, was necessary, at least until the president had decided on his next move.

Jack Fox, in his story for UPI, gave what Sylvester later said was a fair summary of his statement at the Sigma Delta Chi dinner. "He [Sylvester] said that the government must not put out false information, but later added, 'I think the inherent right of the government to lie to save itself when faced with nuclear disaster is basic,'" Fox wrote.

Others made more of the "right to lie" part of the statement and less of the caveats, to the point where Sylvester, in an article written for the *Washington Star* in 1967, complained that they had "distorted my remarks beyond recognition, howling that they were proof that the government was not to be believed, under any circumstances."

"He got a raw deal on that," Hess said recently. "It's always been taken out of context, as though he said the government has a right to lie, period. He said a lot more than that."

In his article in the *Star*, Sylvester said that as assistant secretary of defense for public affairs, he had always taken the position that the prime requisite for a government information program was that it be truthful. And he went on to argue that it was totally wrong for any press aide to lie for personal or political reasons.

Many press secretaries would agree. There is considerable evidence to back up Hess's contention that most of them don't like to lie, not just because it makes them feel bad—Lincoln White, who lied about the U-2 flight in 1960, later told Patrick Sloyan, then working for UPI, that it was "my darkest moment"—but because credibility is important to their job. To be effective, a press aide not only has to be able to generate favorable stories but has to be able to stop bad ones. And a press aide who isn't trusted will have a whole lot more trouble trying to head off a bad story than one who is trusted. "All you need is one lie, and five years of credibility goes right down the drain," says Homer Boynton, who acted as chief spokesman for the FBI from 1973 until 1980. "So when you're giving it out, you goddamn better be right."

Sylvester's statement touched off an angry debate at the time. But the fact is that many reporters and editors agree with it, at least in principle. Philip Geyelin, for example, complained in a recent article in the *Washington Post* that the Reagan administration seemed to be squandering its credibility with a pattern of deception in its statements about Central America. But he began the piece by saying, "We will get nowhere without first stipulating that, while circumstances alter almost any case you can think of, the president has an inherent right—perhaps even an obligation in particular situations—to deceive." And he went on to argue that, when it comes to troop movements and placement of weapons, a certain ambiguity of purpose is, as John Foster Dulles used to say "a necessary art."

Bill Kovach, who runs the *New York Times*'s Washington bureau, says that, "as a rational human being, I'd have to say yes, if lives really are at stake. But [the occasions] should be so few and far between that we talk about them for years. And it's better for [press aides] to try to avoid answering the question than to give out real misinformation, because the next time they won't be believed."

Even Jack Landau, the head of the Reporters Committee for Freedom of the Press and one of the most vocal advocates of the public's right to know, says that in some legitimate national security cases, "I would guess . . . [lying] would be all right." And Jack Nelson, who was lied to by Jody Powell during the Iran hostage crisis, also thinks there are times when a government can justify some forms of deception. "I didn't like being lied to. I didn't like being used. But I didn't have a great deal of problem with [Powell's] doing it," he says. "If it was a real matter of life and death, and he thought it was, I can't argue with what he did."

What Powell did was to tell Nelson flat-out that there was no chance that a rescue mission would be launched in the near future—a lie that Powell still argues was proper, given the circumstances. At the time he told the lie, the preparations for the raid were well underway, and in less than forty-eight hours the U.S. planes would be entering Iranian air space. Not only was he fearful that a story suggesting a raid was possible would alert the Iranians, but he felt that a flat statement to the contrary would "reinforce the web of deception" that had been constructed to protect the mission.

In *The Other Side of the Story,* his book on his years as President Carter's press secretary, Powell argues that there are two reasons why the government can, and sometimes should, lie. The first is that the "government has a legitimate right to secrecy in certain matters because the welfare of the nation requires it." The second is that the press, for the most part, has a right to print what it knows. Freedom of the press is so important to democracy, he says, that when there is a conflict with legitimate national security needs, it is probably better for the government simply to lie to the press than to try to limit it, censor it, or restrict it through prior restraint.

But Powell admits to at least one other lie that had nothing to do with national security or life-and-death matters. It was a question that, as Powell put it, "involved the personal life of a colleague and that of his family." Powell says he decided to lie because to respond with the truth would have resulted in "great pain and embarrassment for a number of perfectly innocent people." And, besides, he didn't think that the matter was of any legitimate public interest to begin with. Powell thus goes a step beyond Sylvester and argues that it is sometimes permissible for a government to lie to protect the privacy of public figures, as well as to protect the security of the nation.

Powell, now a Washington columnist, says he has come to understand more clearly than he used to why it is that "journalists get so damn skeptical about what people [in government] tell them." He says he has no doubts at all that he acted properly in the Iran situation but has mixed feelings about the second lie. "That's harder to defend without getting into the details, which I won't do," he says, adding that he would probably lie again in that situation, too.

"The minimal line you can draw there is that you can absolutely say that lying to cover up your own embarrassments is not permissible," says Powell. "Once you get past that, you get into areas where, unfortunately, things tend to be mixed. Then you have to weigh in the sort of long-term impact, not just in terms of the credibility of a particular administration, but the credibility of the government over the long haul. If you contribute to the idea that people can't believe anything their government tells them, that's awful. It's also dangerous."

In his book, Powell cites other cases in which he thinks a government sometimes might have a right to lie, including protection of intelligence sources and methods, protection of an innocent person whose name had cropped up during a Justice Department investigation, and a pending decision by the Treasury Department that could have major financial consequences to individuals and to the nation.

And it is here that he runs into conflict with many others, including Hess, who argue that there is a big difference between lying to protect legitimate national security matters and lying to protect anything less. "It's very easy to slop over into other areas . . . and I'm less sympathetic when it does," says Hess. "Just because something might concern the 'public good,' that isn't enough" to justify government lying. "It has to be to save lives, as in the Iranian hostage thing, or similar wartime activities."

But while many people in government and in the media agree that, in some circumstances, the government has a right to lie, they also agree that the people have a right to know what their government is really up to. And they argue that a chief reason that the government gets away with as much deception as it does is that the press, for all of its bluster and all its professed skepticism, is far too willing to take the government at its word.

Sylvester, for example, placed much of the blame for misinformation about government activities on the laziness and ineptitude of reporters, saying that they relied too much on handouts and failed to ask the right questions "Every sophisticated [reporter] knows the federal government puts its best, not its worst, foot forward," he said. "That being so, it is [the reporter's] function to penetrate this protective coloration behind which all men attempt to mask their errors. If there is a credibility gap, it measures the failure of newsmen to do their job."

This is a charge that not only was valid when it was made, and remains so today, but also had been a particular matter of controversy just a decade before, when Joe McCarthy was at the height of his influence and there was much debate within the media over the lengths to which reporters should go to try to unmask deception and lies.

Joe McCarthy: Testing the Limits of "Objective Reporting"

To understand the controversy that surrounded McCarthy and the press, it is necessary to understand not just that many of the charges by the Wisconsin senator were considered by many reporters to be reckless but also that the press in the early 1950s was very different from what it is today. There was much less analysis and interpretative reporting in news sections (analysis and most forms of comment being reserved for the editorial pages), and almost none was provided by the wire services. The "objective reporting" standards of the day held that if a U.S. senator was going to make charges of treason, espionage, and communists in high places, that in itself was news, and it wasn't necessarily the job of a reporter to determine the validity of the charges or to hold the senator accountable for them.

"We let Joe get away with murder, reporting it as he said it, not doing the kind of critical analysis we'd do today," William Theis, a former reporter for International News Service, told Edwin Bayley, whose book *Joe McCarthy and the Press* analyzes the coverage and finds much of it lacking. George Reedy, who covered McCarthy for United Press and later became a press secretary to Lyndon Johnson, told Bayley that his frustration at trying to cope with McCarthy's charges was a major consideration in his decision to quit newspaper work. "We had to take what McCarthy said at face value," he told Bayley. "Joe couldn't find a communist in Red Square—he didn't know Karl Marx from Groucho—but he was a United States senator. . . . It was a shattering experience, and I couldn't stand it."

As McCarthy's influence grew, the debate over how to cover him and his charges grew also. Much of the debate was over the nature of "objective" reporting, but the debate itself tended to be partisan in the extreme. Editors and publishers who approved of McCarthy tended to argue that they wanted his statements reported as they were made, without heavy doses of analysis or perspective. And they, in turn, put pressure on the wire services, which provided the bulk of the daily coverage, to report the charges in a straightforward way.

Others, including many who disapproved of McCarthy's politics as well as his tactics, argued that reporters who simply wrote down what he said, along with the subsequent rebuttals and denials, were playing into his hands, because they were not addressing the large number of inconsistencies and proved inaccuracies that marked his attacks on supposed communists.

Some papers developed strategies specifically for McCarthy. The *Milwaukee Journal*, for example, began adding bracketed inserts to stories about McCarthy's charges, using the brackets to add explanatory information. Here is an excerpt from a May 8, 1950, article about McCarthy and Owen Lattimore, whom the senator had accused of helping to shape foreign policy to the benefit of communist governments:

> McCarthy said that Lattimore has "long been referred to as the architect of the State Department's Asiatic policy."
> [State Department officials and three former secretaries of state have denied that Lattimore played any part in forming policy.]
> The Young Republicans guffawed as McCarthy joked about "individuals with peculiar mental aberrations as far as sex is concerned."
> [The individual referred to by Mr. McCarthy here is no longer in government service.]

According to Bayley, this got to the point where, in September 1952, the *Journal* had bracketed thirteen inches' worth of such inserts into a fifty-two-inch story. "McCarthy's tactics produced lasting changes in the media," Bayley observes in his book. "Newspaper people realized that it was not enough simply to tell what had happened and what was said, but that they had to tell what it meant and whether or not it was true. By 1954, interpretative reporting and news analysis had become standard practice; these functions were no longer left to the editorial writers."

And these devices were to become more important in the following decades, not just because of the massive amounts of misinformation released by the government during Vietnam and Watergate, but because, as Wise argues effectively in *The Politics of Lying*, cover stories and deception became a significant part of government operations.

Four Kinds of Lies—and the Problems They Pose for the Press

Not all deceptions are equal, of course. There is a big difference between a Joe McCarthy making harsh, and often groundless, charges of treason and the sort of political posturing that causes a president to defend an aide who has done something dumb. After several years of studying the press-government relationship from both sides, Hess has concluded that some reporters tolerate, even welcome, minor deceptions, because exposing deceptions helps them to display their skills. While studying the State Department press operations during Reagan's first term, he says, he found many examples of deception, most of them minor, and didn't detect much outrage on the part of the reporters there. "It is only the Big Lie, the deliberate and consistent pattern of misstatement on a matter of importance, that turns Washington reporters into inflamed civil libertarians," Hess writes in *The Government/ Press Connection*.

Hess cites four broad categories of government deceptions. On a scale of decreasing acceptability to the press, he says, are so-called honest lies, inadvertent lies, half-truths (which include many forms of political posturing and selective release of data), and flat-out lies. An honest lie, for Hess, is a legitimate national security matter, such as Powell lying about the raid on Teheran. Even if they don't approve of such a lie, most reporters can understand the need for it, he says.

Reporters also tend to forgive inadvertent lies, because they know from their own work that mistakes happen when things are done in a hurry. Bill Beecher, a former Defense Department information officer and now a reporter for the *Boston Globe,* has said that "half the initial internal reporting within government in a crisis is wrong."

It is with half-truths, a specialty at the State Department, that some reporters begin to get resentful. The chief technique here is for a press officer to define the question as narrowly as possible and then answer it that way. Here are two examples Hess cites in *The Government/Press Connection.* Both, he said in an interview, are real examples, with the facts altered just slightly "to protect the guilty."

> Q—Has the assistant secretary of state been invited to China?
> A—No. (Meaning: He will go to China as an adviser to the vice president. It is the vice president who has been invited. Therefore, I am not lying. Rationale: I have to say this because protocol requires that the Chinese must first publicly extend the invitation.)
> Q—Will the ambassador-at-large go to Egypt?
> A—No decision has been made. (Meaning: A "decision" is made when the Secretary of State signs the cable. The cable will be signed tomorrow. Therefore, I am not lying. Rationale: I do not have the authority to give a premature confirmation.)

In the Reagan administration, examples of all four types of deception can be found in the invasion of Grenada. Larry Speakes himself may not have known that he was telling a lie when he said that it was "preposterous" to think U.S. forces had invaded and that no invasion would take place. But Rear Admiral John Poindexter, who told Speakes it was preposterous, knew that the landing would take place the next day and kept Speakes and other press aides in the dark about it. Speakes did not respond to a request for an interview, but Hess and Powell and a number of the journalists interviewed for this article argued that, even if he had known and then told the lie, it might have been justifiable.

The initial claim by the government that there were no civilian casualties appears to have been inadvertent. The Pentagon says that it didn't know about the bombing of a mental hospital by a Navy plane (at least seventeen persons were killed) until several days after it occurred, and no one has yet proved otherwise.

The claim by the administration that leaders of other Caribbean countries urged it to take action appears to be in the nature of a half-truth. The administration said that the urging from other leaders came after the assassination of Maurice Bishop, the Marxist prime minister of Grenada, on October 19. But Stuart Taylor, Jr., in a lengthy piece in the *New York Times* on some of the misinformation put out by the U.S. government during and immediately after the invasion, quotes the prime minister of Barbados as saying that U.S. officials had been talking about possible action at least as early as October 15, four days before the killing.

And while it's hard to determine whether the government was telling an outright lie when it said it had prevented reporters from accompanying the troops because of concern for the safety of the journalists, subsequent comments by Secretary of State George Shultz seem to give some sense of the real reason for the ban. "These days, in the advocacy journalism that's been adopted, it seems as though the reporters are always against us and so they're always trying to screw things up," he said. "And when you're trying to conduct a military operation, you don't need that."

It is difficult to know whether some of the most important misinformation was deliberate or inadvertent because the degree of the deception depends on whether there was any intent to deceive. Reagan, in a television speech to the nation, said there were an estimated 400 to 600 Cubans on the island and that they were "a military force" rather than construction workers. The next day, Admiral Wesley L. McDonald said that captured documents showed that there were at least 1,100 Cubans on Grenada and that they were all "well-trained professional soldiers."

Eventually, the State Department said that the Cuban government's own figure probably was right—that there had been 784 Cubans on the island. Still later, U.S. military authorities on Grenada said that, after interrogating them, they had concluded that most of the Cubans really had been construction workers and that only about 100 had been combatants. "Thus, over three days the Pentagon estimate of the number of Cuban fighters who had met the invading force seems to have plunged from more than 1,000 to fewer than 200, including the estimated 30 to 70 Cubans who were killed," Taylor wrote.

What difference does it make whether there were 784 Cubans on Grenada or 1,100 and whether they were "well-trained professional soldiers," as Admiral McDonald insisted, or construction workers, as the Cuban government claimed? One answer, of course, is that one version suggests an attempt to take over a country and perhaps export revolution (which the Reagan administration said was the case), while the other version suggests that Cuba might only have been providing economic aid to a government that it considered an ally.

The inflation of the number of Cubans, and the initial characterization of them as a military force, was part of the data that were used by the Reagan administration to argue that a Cuban takeover was at hand, that American students were in danger, and that, as many newspapers repeated in their headlines, "We got there just in time."

Grenada also highlighted a major problem in trying to counter deception and misinformation. The president was able to give his version on national television, to a huge audience, and was backed up by carefully selected and edited television film clips. The challenges to the official version came over a period of days and weeks, and they were fragmented and uncoordinated. One paper would challenge one statement, a second paper would challenge a second one, and a television report would challenge a third. A large number of Americans heard the president say, "We got there just in time." But it was only in a disjointed and scattershot way, over a period of weeks following the invasion, that the press raised the two immediate and obvious questions, neither of them yet fully answered.

Did we?

In time for what?

This issue arose again during the presidential campaign, when George Bush claimed in his television debate with Geraldine Ferraro that Mondale had said that the American Marines who had died in the bombing of the embassy in Beirut had died in "shame." Mondale denied this and pressed Bush for a retraction. And in the process Peter Teeley, Bush's press secretary, brought the whole problem into focus.

"You can say anything you want in a debate, and eighty million people hear it," he told reporters. "If reporters then document that a candidate spoke untruthfully, so what? Maybe two hundred people read it, or two thousand or twenty thousand."

Which makes the point that, particularly in the television age, reporters need to be aggressive in documenting and pointing out deceptions, half-truths, and outright lies, unless governments and officials are going to be allowed to lie with impunity.

How Some Journalists Cope with Official Misinformation

There are some kinds of misinformation that quickly become apparent on their own. For example, there was Tricia Nixon's wedding cake. According to the White House, it had been based on a recipe for old-fashioned pound cake, a favorite of Tricia's, that had been in Mrs. Nixon's recipe box for years. But when the White House released a recipe for the wedding cake, scaled back down to family size, there was a problem. Housewives and amateur cooks all over the country, including food writers for several newspapers and magazines, rushed to test it. The result in many cases was a porridge-like glob that overflowed the baking pans and messed up the ovens.

When asked for an explanation, the White House first said there must have been a miscalculation in the attempt to scale down the recipe. There was hemming and hawing when it was suggested that the White House should simply produce the original recipe, from Mrs. Nixon's recipe box. There was bobbing and weaving when it was noted that most recipes for pound cake call for whole eggs (this one called only for the whites), while the White House chef was quoted as saying that his pastry chef had gotten the recipe, "where I don't know." This in itself was of no great import, except that the whole episode suggested that a White House that would put out misinformation about the origins of a cake recipe probably couldn't be expected to tell the truth about the war in Cambodia. Which it didn't.

It's not possible to test all government statements as easily as a cake recipe, of course. Some deceptions are so major and so long-running and so tightly held that it takes the combination of Congress, the courts, and the media, working over a period of years, to unravel them. But Patrick Sloyan, a Washington reporter for two decades and now *Newsday*'s London bureau chief, argues that basic reporting, common sense, and "simple math on a pocket calculator can often deflate the biggest government lies."

One of the easiest and most obvious ways to challenge official statements is simply to go to the opposition. When Reagan claimed that his administration had made "great progress" in its efforts to protect the environment, Francis X. Clines, of the *New York Times,* made clear that officials of some of the nation's leading environmental groups didn't know whether to laugh or cry at the statement. For specifics, he went to Representative James L. Florio of New Jersey, who noted that of 22,000 hazardous waste sites identified by the EPA, only six had been cleaned up by the Reagan administration in four years, and that even as the president was trumpeting his record on the environment, he was opposing proposals in Congress to combat acid rain.

Many such claims are more a matter of opinion than fact, of course, and going to the other side is a first lesson of journalism. But some of the most basic kinds of reporting can be used to provide a second, often different, view of events and issues. And in covering an administration that works as hard as Reagan's does to control and shape the information being released, basic reporting is particularly important.

Go to the Scene

During the invasion of Grenada, Reagan and the Pentagon camera crews combined to show American television viewers warehouses on the island that seemingly were stacked to the rafters with automatic weapons. The president said there were enough of them to "supply thousands of terrorists." But when reporters themselves got to the sites, they found some of the warehouses half-empty, some of them stacked with cases of sardines, and many of the weapons antiquated, possibly more suited for defense by an island militia than for the export of terrorism and revolution.

Go to the People Affected

The Reagan administration insisted that its changes in the Social Security disability law were intended only to get rid of people who had no right to the government aid in the first place. The people being removed, it said, were able-bodied people who had managed to slip through loopholes and get themselves into the program because of lax monitoring and ambiguous standards. But it turned out that a third of a million persons, including many with serious physical handicaps and mental disorders, had been cut off from the payments in a massive purge of the rolls, often on the basis of reviews of their health records by doctors who had never examined them in person.

Here is how Bob Wyrick and Patrick Owens of *Newsday* began a series that grew out of a months-long study of persons whose benefits had been taken away:

> Lyle Ely was blind in one eye and had tunnel vision in the other. He could not, as he complained in one of the many forms he filled out in the last years of his life, see well enough to read, drive a car, or watch television. His partial blindness, along with the convulsive seizures that also plagued him, was caused by a tumor that grew to the size of a large orange in the front part of his brain. But claims examiners and reviewing physicians who had never seen him found him well enough to work, cancelled his Social Security disability pension, and reaffirmed the cancellation when Ely applied for reconsideration.

Go to the Documents

In February 1981, the State Department issued a white paper on El Salvador, which it said "presents definitive evidence of the clandestine military support given by the Soviet Union, Cuba, and their Communist allies to the Marxist-Leninist guerrillas now fighting to overthrow the established government of El Salvador." It said that the evidence was drawn from captured guerrilla documents and war material, and had been "corroborated by intelligence reports."

The white paper was accepted by much of the nation's press, was used by State Department officials to drum up support in Europe for Reagan's Central America policy, and was used on the Hill by White House lobbyists to persuade Congress that more funds were needed to help counter the outside aid being given to Salvadoran guerrillas. But when Jonathan Kwitney of the *Wall Street Journal* began a study of the documents a few months later and went back to the people who had drafted the white paper, he found the evidence something less than it had been made out to be.

"Several of the most important documents, it's obvious, were attributed to guerilla leaders who didn't write them. And it's unknown who did," he wrote in the *Journal*. "Statistics of armament shipments into El Salvador, supposedly drawn directly from the documents, were extrapolated . . . and in questionable ways, it seems. Much information in the white paper can't be found in the documents at all. This information now is attributed by the State Department to other, still-secret sources."

Kwitney's article did not totally discredit the conclusion of the white paper, which was that some weapons and supplies were being sent to the rebels by communist governments overseas. But it made clear that the evidence cited by the State Department, which had been accepted at face value by much of the press, wasn't as clear or as precise or as unambiguous as the government had claimed.

So, too, with Grenada. Admiral McDonald said on October 28 that captured documents showed that "341 more officers and 4,000 more reservists" had been scheduled to arrive from Cuba as part of a plan for "the Cubans to come in and take over the island." But Stuart Taylor of the *New York Times* reported that the captured documents, when finally released, showed an agreement by the Soviet Union and North Korea to provide Grenada with $37 million worth of equipment; the only reference to more Cuban soldiers was a promise by the Cubans to provide twenty-seven military advisers to train Grenadian troops.

A senior Pentagon official was quoted by Taylor as saying that McDonald had been mistaken about the 4,341 additional troops—they were to have been Grenadians, not Cubans. And he went on to report that "there is no evidence . . . that the Cubans had planned to take over Grenada either in the documents released Friday or in any other materials made public by the administration."

Check the Numbers

When James Nathan Miller set out to examine Reagan's civil rights record, he went to the data that Reagan himself had used to illustrate what he termed "our unbending commitment" to civil rights. What Miller found were not outright lies—he did not once use the word "lie" in his *Atlantic* article—but a selective use of information that told only a part of the story. For example, Reagan had touted the fact that his Justice Department had reviewed 25,000 proposed changes in the Voting Rights Act and had vetoed 165 of them because it felt they would be discriminatory. When Miller looked at the actual record, however, he found that the veto of 165 proposed changes was not an unusually strong enforcement of the law but a dramatic reduction in the rate of objections. From 1965 until Reagan took office, the department had vetoed 2.4 out of every 100 proposed changes it had examined. But the figures that Reagan cited amounted to a veto rate of .7 per 100—a decrease of 71 percent.

Again, in a speech to the American Bar Association, Reagan said that in his first thirty months in office the Justice Department had filed more than a hundred cases charging criminal violations of citizens' civil rights. This, he said, was not just a respectable number but was "substantially more than any prior administration during a comparable period."

In terms of *criminal* cases, the Reagan administration actually was ahead of where the Carter administration was after the first thirty months. Reagan's Justice Department had filed 114 criminal cases, while Carter's had filed 101. But the civil law has been a potent weapon for civil rights in recent decades, and when the number of *civil* cases was added, the Reagan administration fell well behind the record of the Carter administration at thirty months—a total of 225 civil and criminal suits filed by Carter and only 156 filed by Reagan.

"Almost every one of the major points I made in the article was being made for the first time," Miller says. "The people in the daily press, even those covering civil rights, had simply printed the statements without any serious attempt to check their validity."

The Need for a More Aggressive Press

It is not necessary to challenge every statistic to make a point, and readers of most major newspapers have been told repeatedly that the Reagan administration has a philosophy about enforcement of civil rights laws that is very different from that of most recent administrations. But Miller nonetheless has a point when he says that for reporters to accept such numbers on their face is to allow themselves and their readers to be manipulated and deceived.

The challenge is likely to become greater as Reagan, immensely popular . . . , moves ahead with his stated goals for limiting the flow of information to the public. Already, his administration has supported bills that would exempt the Secret Service, the CIA, and most FBI activities from the Freedom of Information Act and has imposed a rule at the Defense Department that any person with access to classified information must submit to lie detector tests whenever asked to. It has reversed the Carter administration policy and now allows the FBI and CIA to infiltrate the media if the attorney general finds it in the interest of the national security to do so and has set regulations that allow the FBI to infiltrate and monitor domestic groups, including the press, while conducting investigations of organized crime or terrorism. It has slashed the budget of the indexing staff of the National Archives, meaning that access to historical records, including the Nixon tapes, will be delayed for years. It has created mechanisms for monitoring contacts between White House staffers and reporters and has issued guidelines telling officials handling FOIA requests to be stingy in giving fee reductions to journalists, scholars, and authors. It has rewritten the classification system to insure that more, rather than less, information will be classified. And it has made proposals— already implemented in some agencies—that would require all officials who have had access to classified information to come back to the government for the rest of their lives and submit for prior censorship any speeches, letters to the editor, news articles, or works of fiction.

Nick Horrock, of *Newsweek,* who has worked in Washington for most of the past two decades, says that some of the changes are atmospheric and not entirely caused by Reagan. "There has been a shift back to an atmosphere much more like it was in the early 1960s," Horrock says. "During the Vietnam War and Watergate, a lot of dissidents were in the government, and they were quick to speak out, to tell reporters that things weren't working the way they should. Now, there aren't so many dissidents. It's not popular to take risks. Being a whistle-blower is no longer popular."

In a recent article, William Greider, the former assistant managing editor for national news at the *Washington Post* and now national editor of *Rolling Stone* magazine, argued that the press, too, seems to be in retreat. "It seems to be pulling in its lances, taking fewer risks, avoiding the hard and nasty confrontations it would have zealously pursued five or ten years ago . . . ," he wrote. "The trend I see is deep and subtle—a shift toward 'hard news,' which means narrow splinters of unexamined fact, a turning away from more provocative explorations of subjects that have not been legitimized by official sources."

If he's right, and many in the media agree that he is, it is happening at a particularly bad time. The history of the press-government relationship since World War II shows that administrations have claimed a right to lie in some circumstances and have been unable to resist the temptation to deceive in a great many others. And this particular administration, headed by a tremendously popular president, has made clear that it wants to make information about government operations harder to get and, in terms of threats to their careers, more dangerous for civil servants to provide.

That means that the press needs to be even more aggressive, not less, if it is to follow the John Mitchell rule for covering government: Don't watch what we say. Watch what we do.

TRUST ME

Charles McDowell

Charles McDowell earned his MS in journalism from Columbia University and has been a reporter and columnist for the *Richmond Times-Dispatch* since 1948, and their Washington correspondent and columnist since 1965. Author of three books and numerous magazine articles, he has also been a regular panelist since 1977 on PBS's "Washington Week in Review" and has participated in many other PBS programs. He won the 1984 award from the Millar Center of Public Affairs at the University of Virginia for "an enduring contribution to the understanding of the American presidency."

From *Beyond Reagan: The Politics of Upheaval,* by the reporters of "Washington Week in Review," Warner Books, 1986. Reprinted from the *Washingtonian* magazine, May, 1986. Used by permission.

In the summer of 1952, television dawned on American politics. The occasion was the Republican National Convention at Chicago, and, yes, there was one of those camera towers blocking the front of the hall, and the floodlights cutting through the traditional layers of cigar smoke seemed suddenly to be exposing a mystic rite. But the true dawning was the glow of 18 million little screens on which politicians walked and talked and looked citizens in the eye in their living rooms all over the United States.

Television had made a pass at the conventions in 1948, but only about 400,000 squinty sets were in use then. The coverage was a limited curiosity, not a national experience.

By 1952 television was ready to become a force. There would have been television interest in the convention as a folk festival, but the Republicans were offering more, a classic confrontation: the popular hero from World War II, General Dwight D. Eisenhower, taking on Senator Robert A. Taft of Ohio, who was not called Mr. Republican for nothing.

An austere and respected conservative, Taft had the support of the party bosses and nominal control of the convention machinery. He figured to hold off Eisenhower by using his insider's power in the ruthless custom of these things.

The first stage of Taft's nomination for president would take place in the convention's credentials committee, where his supporters expected to use their narrow majority to reject the Eisenhower side's challenge of fifteen Taft delegates from Louisiana. There was a case to be made that the delegates had been chosen unfairly in Louisiana, but Taft needed them.

I was in Chicago for my first national convention. When I showed up for the credentials committee hearings in the Gold Room of the Congress Hotel, no seats were available for junior reporters from the provinces. An official explained that television had to be accommodated in the press space. Alas, it was the beginning of that, too.

A kindly security guard let me slip into the serving kitchen adjoining the Gold Room, and from there I covered the credentials contest for a couple of days. The huge tiled kitchen, with its racks of glasses, stainless-steel sinks, and signs saying "Keep It Clean," became the caucus room for the members of the committee.

While witnesses testified and the committee argued before the television cameras in the Gold Room, the leaders of the Taft and Eisenhower factions came to the kitchen to talk tactics. I was taken for a hotel functionary of some sort and overheard a lot from both sides. By the morning of the second day, the Taft managers were talking about conceding the Louisiana delegates to Eisenhower.

What was happening was that people back home, following the debate on television, were telephoning and telegraphing their delegates to say that Taft's case was coming through as weak. Republicans of consequence were saying that a steamroller approach would look bad on television and hurt Taft more than yielding the delegates.

I particularly remember a Minnesota member of the committee, technically a backer of the dark horse, Harold Stassen, bringing Taft partisans from the Gold Room to the kitchen to persuade them of their public-relations problem. He rested an elbow on a dishwashing machine as he talked. He was earnest and deep-chested and had a big, hollow voice, and there was no trouble in hearing him tell the Taft people that they could ruin their candidate if they insisted on arrogantly running over Eisenhower in this little controversy. The Minnesota delegate was Warren Burger.

Taft's manager on the committee, Congressman Clarence Brown of Ohio, recommended to the candidate that he concede Louisiana as a public-relations gesture. He was talking to Taft headquarters by telephone from the kitchen. The candidate was instinctively against conceding Louisiana but told Brown to do what he thought best.

The concession would be on television in the Gold Room. Up to now in the debate, the Taft spokesmen had tended to be the crusty elders of the party. The Eisenhower spokesmen were somehow younger, trimmer, clearer of eye.

To make their motion to seat Eisenhower's Louisiana delegation, to claim acquaintance with fairness, the Taft side passed over the elders and chose a young, clean-cut, well-spoken committee member from Virginia: Eugene Worrell. Two days into the era of television politics, and everyone was beginning to catch on.

Worrell's talk of fairness in Louisiana only encouraged the Eisenhower supporters to press the same case in the Texas delegation and others. The Taft side became adamant and held the line in the committee. The Eisenhower managers announced they would appeal the decision and went before the cameras to explain their case again and to lecture on sportsmanship. The document of appeal was called the "fair play amendment," and in retrospect that name will do for me as the first great artifact of the television era in politics.

So the crucial battle was fought amid the turbulence and drama on the floor of a national political convention, all on television. It became a morality play. Here was a national hero standing above politics and demanding simple justice from the cynical bosses of what had always been a closed process. By the rules of the Republican party and the customs of American politics, the merits of the proposition were at least doubtful, but there was no doubt about the public perception of the struggle. The telephone calls and telegrams poured into Chicago; public opinion was pro-Eisenhower.

The convention ended with the "I Like Ike" signs dancing in the almost blinding light. And there was the general on the platform with his arms thrown up in a V for victory and his smile beaming out to all those little screens. We could write like poets on the press stand or broadcast it faithfully on the radio, we could explain and analyze the event in the context of the great issues of the day, but now politics was acquiring a new reality and its medium was television.

Politics would never be the same again in a country where people in their living rooms could watch their politicians at work. Thirty years later, the *Economist* of London was still trying to help us get used to it: "Today's are the first politicians since the Athenian statesman Pericles, in the fifth century BC, to be seen by all their electors."

The people see the picture—moving, instantaneous, compelling. It is a personal experience, and the reaction is intuitive and emotional as well as logical. In this circumstance, the personal qualities of politicians matter very much. Television becomes a medium of personal trust—or mistrust or yawns.

In the time of Ronald Reagan, we have seen personal trust for a president at the core of an administration's viability. Over the long haul in politics, I would say, television's inherent function as a medium of personal trust is far more significant than all the passing sensations that often dominate discussions of the subject.

One way to trace the relentless rise of television in American politics is through the presidents who used television most successfully.

John Kennedy, going for the Democratic nomination in 1960, hardly could have been a candidate without television. Besides being personable, he was running in a political landscape that had undergone tremendous change since television came on the scene in 1952. The nominating process was evolving into a whole new game.

In the selection of national-convention delegates, primaries were replacing the old state conventions and back-room appointments. Presidential candidates were not soliciting party leaders' support as much as before; they were campaigning more among the people. Television liked it: local color, crowds, hands to shake, competition out where you could see it.

There were only sixteen primaries in 1960, but we sensed watching television that somehow they had eclipsed the old system. Kennedy, campaigning in Wisconsin or West Virginia, was being seen and heard in all the states. An individual primary on television was a national event, and a sequence of strong showings in several primaries could become a national bandwagon.

When the Democrats gathered for their convention in Los Angeles, Kennedy had already done what had to be done. His first-ballot nomination was dramatic but a formality. In the first decade of TV politics, a young, Catholic, back-bench senator, and not one who had shown extraordinary promise in Congress, had knocked over Hubert Humphrey and Democratic elders in the primaries, then controlled the convention easily against Lyndon B. Johnson, the fabled inside operator and acknowledged leader of his party in Washington.

John Kennedy's successful campaign against Richard Nixon is remembered mainly for their four debates on television. More than 100 million adults watched. The issues, which both candidates discussed skillfully, are not much remembered.

At the time, people who heard the debates on radio were fairly evenly divided as to who had won. But on television, Vice-President Nixon had problems. One was Kennedy. Not only was the upstart young senator more engaging, more relaxed, and cooler than Nixon, but he came through as more mature and thoughtful than the Kennedy many people expected. He turned out not to be a boy, somebody said. Other Nixon problems were pallor, five-o'clock shadow, and perspiration on his face.

Twenty-five years after Kennedy beat Nixon in an extremely close election, media experts still have difficulty assessing the relative effects of performance and substance on the public perception of a politician. Of course substance matters.

The crucial ability in the new era is to be heard and felt as an authentic person in a living room, one on one. The person, the performance, and the message merge. Television pulls the viewer past literal information into intuitive responses. It invites, almost demands, judgments on personal trust.

Tony Schwartz, the political consultant and disciple of Marshall McLuhan, says in his book *Media: The Second God:* "Radio, and then television, drew our attention away from issues and caused us to focus on the more personal qualities of the candidate, his ability to speak, and his style of presentation."

Voters watching candidates, Schwartz says, "Look for what they consider to be good character: qualities such as conviction, compassion, steadiness, the willingness to work hard. That is why we have so large a party-crossover vote. This emphasis on people and feeling is the product of an instant-communication environment."

The good vibes received from a Kennedy or a Reagan do not convert droves of committed Republicans or Democrats. But 20 percent or more of the electorate have little or no commitment to party, and these are the people who decide most elections.

Long before television came along, many of these people were wary of politics in general. They voted for "the best man." Television gave them access to the personal evidence they wanted. And it increased their numbers, according to Edward J. Rollins, Jr., director of the 1984 Reagan campaign. While some of his brothers talked about a realignment of the parties, Rollins insisted that the major political phenomenon of his time was a "dealignment" attributable to television.

Isn't print journalism supposed to be in there somewhere, calling the voters' attention to the issues and away from personality? Yes, and the print press can seem gray and boring as it stakes out the important issues and summons television to the serious agenda.

But day by day in routine coverage, the print press is drawn into the same lore of personality and performance that all those millions watching television are interested in. A combative exchange, a line misspoken, a sweaty brow—they become news if only because so many people are watching.

The press watches television and vice-versa. A provocative sound bite from a campaign is validated for the television producers when the press writes about it, and it gets another round for reaction on the evening news, which makes it fodder for the weekend talk shows, which brings it back into the Monday morning papers as something the syndicated heavyweights may want to write a column about, and on it goes.

Television on occasion conveys a truly important issue to the consciousness of the country, and with awesome effect. That has happened when television has been able to show the essence of the issue and not just politicians and commentators talking about it.

The Vietnam war is the classic example. When television gave the war reality night after night for American families at home, public opinion began to sour. At the same time, reporters in both print and television were becoming more aggressive in contrasting the government's claims and reassurances with other versions of reality. President Lyndon Johnson, one of the most accomplished politicians of the old school, decided in failure and frustration not to run for a second term in 1968.

In covering the civil-rights movement, television explored the historical background, the constitutional arguments, and the muffled themes of moderation in the South, but television's transforming power was simply in its pictures of events. The images defined the crisis in the starkest terms: There were the peaceful black protesters, the preachers of nonviolence, the marchers singing hymns, the children walking solemn and brave to school, and then there were the white hecklers and haters, the swaggering sheriffs, the Klan and the neo-Nazis, the violence. The impact was cumulative. The Reverend Martin Luther King's eloquent call to conscience went out from the Lincoln Memorial to tens of millions of television sets, where it was received amid the echoing images of the police dogs of Birmingham.

In its own time, Watergate was an event closed to cameras. It was uncovered by newspaper reporters and explored relentlessly in print as the third-rate burglary expanded into a constitutional scandal.

The television coverage had a second-hand quality; it could not seem to engage the issue on its own terms. But when television put Senator Sam Ervin and the Nixon staff conspirators on the screen for weeks at a time in 1973 and put the House impeachment inquiry on the screen in 1974, public opinion was mobilized to support the removal of the president from office.

Disillusionment with Watergate set the stage for Jimmy Carter, a presidential candidate who personified moralism and skepticism about politics. And he was as fascinating a television phenomenon as any we had seen before 1976.

Here was an obscure former governor of Georgia, distinctly from the boondocks, not a commanding presence personally, not a leader of any established movement, an outsider to the traditional political fraternity—and he came from nowhere to defeat a clutch of veteran liberal Democratic candidates for the nomination. Then he defeated the incumbent Republican president, Gerald Ford.

Carter understood how television had revolutionized the nominating system. He was willing to concentrate a couple of years' effort on the earliest tests, Iowa and New Hampshire, betting that a good showing would be a sensational payoff because expectations for his candidacy were so low. He was right, and he became a national figure within several weeks.

Carter believed that the delegate-selection process was subject to a sequential effect, state by state. He believed in momentum. With a front-runner's access to television and the conferred charisma of a miracle worker in Iowa and New Hampshire, he offered a vision that was essentially antipolitical.

Carter knew people had long been skeptical of the whole pack of politicians and their big talk, big government, red tape, inside deals, and slickery. Well, he personified opposition to all that. The very look and manner of the man set him apart. He was slight, almost shy. He had a high voice and a drawl. He was a farmer and small-business man, trained as an engineer. For him problems had logical solutions. A plain, practical man without a politician's bombast and wheeler-dealer ways might impose some common sense and efficiency on Washington. He would stand up for morality, too, and was not too sophisticated to keep saying so. He was a religious man, a Sunday-school teacher in a fundamentalist church, and he called attention to his religion often. But he was not a hypocrite; he lived his commitment.

The crucial issue that blended into the image of Jimmy Carter was civil rights. It authenticated him as a southerner who could be president. In his long-shot bid for the nomination, his record in Georgia on behalf of civil rights brought him the support of southern black leaders, some of them associates of Martin Luther King. With black leaders seen around him from the beginning of the campaign—and going as his missionaries to the North and West—Carter overcame the suspicions that many liberals had of a white southerner and a relative conservative in the Democratic field. In the primaries, Carter ran strongly in predominantly black precincts, North and South, against famous liberals of his party.

Carter's defeat for a second term had a major television component, and it consisted of far more than Ronald Reagan, the Great Communicator. President Carter's fortunes had faltered at home and abroad.

The worst was the Iran hostage crisis, which obsessed television and the country for more than a year. In a regular ritual of humiliation, television counted off the days that the American hostages had been held by terrorists in a pitifully backward country while the United States engaged in futile diplomacy, empty threats, and, finally, failed military rescue.

Meanwhile, the terrorists demonstrated a keen sense of American television. By allowing crews from the West to televise images of the hostages and to interview their captors, Iran gained leverage over a superpower. As in the case of the TWA hostage crisis in Lebanon five years later, the American public's very personal concern for the safety of their fellow citizens soon began to dominate the policy options of the American government.

In the incident in Lebanon, the hostages on television—sometimes under threat of death as they spoke to us—tended to become our national authorities on the nature of the terrorists, their point of view, their demands, and the best American approach to the problem. Indeed, television became a medium of diplomacy. A representative of the terrorists was drawn out on possible settlement terms by network anchors and morning-show hosts. Officials in the State Department confessed that in some of the crucial moments of the crisis they had been watching television, trying to keep up. If that seems unsettling, that is because it is.

Carter's hostage crisis was not resolved quickly, as Reagan's was. For Carter, the preoccupying misery stretched out month after month and into a second year. What that did to Carter was to make him the living image of the country's humiliation, pain, and loss of confidence. And we had to watch that image on television. Understandably, there was not much inclination to reelect it.

Ronald Reagan came to office running against the hapless Carter but also against Washington and politicians generally, thus ironically doing what

Carter had done. He was a Republican and a conservative, but he presented himself more as a citizen-reformer who would save us from politics. In saving us, he would reduce the cost, the size, and the meddlesome power of the federal government at home, strengthen it militarily in the world, and restore patriotism, religious values, adventurous free enterprise, and confidence. All this came to be called a conservative revolution.

But for many voters assessing Reagan in 1980, the big test was not whether he should have a mandate for his revolution. The test was whether he seemed safe enough to justify voting the incumbent out. He passed easily, although he was older and more ideological than many who voted for him would have wished. Reagan looked undeniably vigorous; the visible evidence minimized the age issue. As for the extremely conservative views he expressed, his temperate, amiable personality took the edge off. It was true, as the old Hollywood story had it, that Ronald Reagan just naturally fitted the role of best friend.

He had the qualities of a best friend on television, all right, and this level, likable man soon had the personal trust of much of the population. That Reagan had been an actor most of his life has been cited—beyond all previously known limits of redundancy—as the explanation for his success in communicating on television.

In my minority opinion, acting background is an all-too-convenient, point-missing rationale for Reagan's effectiveness on camera and microphone. Oh, experience might help him read lines and not squint into the lights and not trip over cables. But what makes Ronald Reagan effective on television is that he is authentic. He knows who he is; he is himself. He is comfortable with that, and he knows not to act.

This confident, consistent sense of self makes the compelling presence on television. A political scientist at the University of California at Berkeley picks up the argument that Reagan "knows who he is"—and carries it right back to Hollywood. Professor Michael Rogin says, "Ronald Reagan found out who he was by whom he played on film. Responding to typecasting that either attracted him or repelled him, making active efforts to obtain certain roles and to escape from others, Reagan merged his on-screen and off-screen identities."

Reagan seems especially effective because the television performance level of so many other politicians of the day is so low. They tend to strike attitudes. They project or hold themselves in. They work at television and remember what the media consultant told them about posture and gesture and pace. They try to be natural while getting the effect they want. They act.

If Reagan himself is consistent and fairly uncomplicated, his presidency has been full of paradoxes. He is remote but somehow very much in charge. He has left an almost unprecedented proportion of his job to staff, yet he has to be ranked with the assertive, strong presidents.

He is an ideologue who frustrates the Republican pragmatists in the Senate, and he is a pragmatist who disillusions the Republican right wing. He takes unyielding public positions on principle, and then allows them to be compromised—without apology, sometimes without conceding that they were compromised.

He holds relatively few news conferences, preferring set pieces to the risk of error in give-and-take, but he seems the most accessible president in the world as he walks from his helicopter on the White House grounds giving good-natured, noncommittal answers to the bumptious, shouted questions from Sam Donaldson of ABC—a ritual both Donaldson and the White House find useful for their own purposes.

Reagan is the natural man, just being himself, yet his staff spends more time than any in memory moving him around to appealing and symbolic settings, keeping him visible, contriving events to play to his credit and obscure his failings, and always promoting and briefing him for television appearances as if he were a forgetful old actor.

The paradoxes all are accommodated in the positive perception of Ronald Reagan. It is not that the people are fooled; many seem to be quite aware of both sides of each paradox. In crowds of Reagan supporters, reporters constantly encounter fans who will talk about his flaws. Public-opinion polls keep showing large blocs of voters who disagree with Reagan on this or that issue, or a whole swath of issues, but give him high ratings as president anyway.

Mary McGrory, the liberal columnist, has written in some despair: "Reagan has a lock on the affections of the American people. They are almost blindly fond of him. He is not exactly a father figure—he is rather too jaunty and nonchalant for that. He is more a jolly, reassuring uncle who comes to call amid much laughter and many stories. Never mind his views—wrong, but strong, they are generally considered, and they add to the fondness."

Christopher Matthews, who is on the staff of the Speaker of the House, says Reagan is "the nation's host." Matthews says Reagan has redefined the presidency: "He is not *in* government, but some place, previously uncharted, *between* us and government."

If we take this seriously, and we should, it carries us well beyond personality in explaining Reagan's success. His approach to the function of being president seems to be to reassure people that he has not given himself over to Washington. He shares the public prejudice about government and politics, and he keeps his distance. He would rather talk to the people.

Henry Fairlie, a journalist with a British background, made this observation in the time of Reagan: "The American presidency is being transformed into a radically popular institution—more and more dependent on, and at the same time able to exploit, a direct and uninterrupted relationship with the people. . . . For some years now almost every important development in the American political system has been encouraging the direct relationship between the president and the people. These include the weakness of the parties and disarray of the party system; the dissipation of power in the House and Senate; the reliance on direct mail and media consultants in election campaigns; and, of course, the new prominence of the media, dominated by television."

That assessment is not far out of line with the views of many American academics, politicians, and political reporters, although I would insist that television is not just one of the developments but the driving force behind all the others.

Politicians and consultants lavish creative energy and money on television commercials to make points already market-tested by pollsters. In buying their own airtime—the record shows Republicans can afford it more often than Democrats—candidates get at the viewers without intervening questioners or editors. For the television news shows, they contrive short, provocative statements that will intrigue producers and resist editing. Former governor Jerry Brown of California is said to have been able to talk in twenty-second sound bites, stringing them together, each with a beginning, middle, and end.

For debates, an important strategy is to come up with one-liners catchy enough that they will become enduring images in a campaign—such as Walter Mondale's line to Gary Hart: "Where's the beef?" Spontaneity is rehearsed until it's right.

The political fraternity studies the personal quirks and presumed political biases of correspondents, morning show hosts, news anchors. Conservatives take for granted a liberal bias in the networks; it is part of their ideology and has some public following. Liberals gripe less about philosophical bias; they complain about assorted slights and failures of judgment in the coverage of themselves.

The professionalism of network journalists is often admirable, but they are coping with burdensome logistics, ridiculous little time slots, and the need to shoot for the gist of a story on a visual medium whose impact is monstrous. So television news executives rarely get through a day without having to consider criticism of inconsistencies, sensationalism, superficiality, and perhaps plain irresponsibility in the snapshots they take of politics. When the networks really monkey with the minds of the electorate, as in broadcasting "exit polls" and "projections" while people are still voting, everyone from righteous print journalists to congressional committees comes down on them.

So television is subject to pressure and control from both outside and inside. Assignment editors, reporters, cameramen, producers, network management, and the Federal Communications Commission are forever making decisions that influence what is shown of politics. Politicians are forever devising strategies, ploys, and gimmicks to gain advantage on the tube.

Much of the apprehension about television politics arises from all this manipulation, and there is a notion that the effect is vast. This is exaggerated. For one thing, the television audience often knows when it is being used. It has lived with television and has some sense of illusion; what the audience will accept on a game show or a melodrama it will not necessarily treat the same way in true-life public affairs.

True, politics is trivialized when it is played for television. But that is only a part of the larger reality: Politics has been transformed by the very existence of television. Yes, the medium is the message. The medium itself has changed the way people connect to politicians and the way the political system works. As Reuven Frank, the former president of NBC News, has said, "The truly serious criticisms of television can be reduced ultimately to the proposition that it shouldn't have been invented in the first place."

It *was* invented, and in 1952 at the national conventions it became part of the presidential nominating process. There has not been a contest that went past the first ballot at a convention since 1952.

The nominees since then have been designated before the conventions in a burgeoning series of televised primaries and caucuses. These contests in the states are open, competitive affairs for ordinary voters, not closed convocations of wrangling, deal-making factions and bosses. The old, closed process could not survive under television's eye.

Of course, television's eye did not really pick up the meaning of the old conventions. All that wheeling and dealing was a national political party negotiating among its constituencies, balancing its interests, compromising its differences. Such conventions were uniquely American, and political scientists gave them a lot of the credit for the stability of two-party government, for avoiding extreme swings to the right and left.

What is the purpose of the conventions now? Surely more than being a kind of electoral college to certify the results of the primaries and caucuses. Surely more than voting "aye" on the nominee's draft of a platform and choice for vice-president.

Besides those pro forma functions, recent conventions have settled for being reconciliation rallies to kick off the presidential campaign. But how long will the networks be willing to give away a week of prime time for that sort of enterprise? At the 1984 Democratic convention, even the rally was a charade because everyone in the hall knew Walter Mondale could not beat Ronald Reagan.

Aha! That became the unstated point of the convention, and prime time was devoted to showcasing likely Democratic candidates in 1988. Governor Mario Cuomo of New York was the hit both as a television performer and as a prescriber for the party's future. Is the evolving role of the convention to present the candidates and themes not of the campaign at hand but of the next one after that?

The primaries are the nominating system now. In 1952 there were twelve primaries, and they bound only a small fraction of the national-convention delegates. By 1980 there were thirty primaries, and they elected more than 75 percent of the delegates. A slight reduction in the number of primaries in 1984 only increased the number of state caucuses, which usually were merely another format for popular voting to pledge the delegates to a candidate. The field was winnowed quickly in the first few contests, for they were crucial to a winning image and campaign contributions.

Over the years it evolved that the first caucus, in Iowa, in the winter before the late-summer national convention, would establish the contenders in rough order. Then the first primary, amid the frosty scenery and commercialism of New Hampshire, would narrow the race to two serious possibilities, or maybe one—such was the national impact of the television battle.

The primary schedule ran on, from February into June.

The candidates, not the constituencies of the party, controlled the delegates elected in their names by the voters in the primaries and caucuses. The presidential nominee in such circumstances was less a product of a party process than an independent operator with his own political base and organization, his own obligations and agenda.

When I think I overstate, I reread Professor David B. Truman, formerly of Columbia University, who said the primary system "tends to destroy accountability. It does so because it disintegrates and ultimately eliminates the political party as an organization which the voter once could hold accountable for the performance of a government. The single-issue groups, political-action committees, faceless image makers, and professional media manipulators that occupy the resulting vacuum cannot be held accountable for the results that they produce. They are basically irresponsible and ultimately subversive of the common good."

Most observers would agree anyway that political parties have undergone a drastic decline in the age of television. The party program can be a burden to a candidate appealing to voters essentially as an individual. Politicians are less dependent on the party as an organization that develops leaders and promotes them through the ranks. Now the sharp ones can promote themselves.

In the matter of campaign finance, where television advertising is a wildly escalating cost, the parties' role is far less important than it once was. Television candidates increasingly rely on contributions directly to themselves from individuals and from that booming new source, political-action committees.

PACs represent special interests—insurance companies, defense contractors, all kinds of corporations, labor unions, trade associations, a mind-boggling assortment of ideological groups—and often a PAC's concern is so narrow that it comes down to a single issue. The distinctive thing about most PACs is the sheer specificity of what they want in return for their contributions; they don't trouble the officeholder for accountability on any issues but theirs.

Ten years ago there were 600 PACs. In 1984 there were 4,000 of them raising and distributing campaign money. Presidential elections, which are federally financed, are somewhat insulated from this influence, but Congress is up to its knees in PAC money.

Senate and House candidates, especially incumbents on key legislative committees, frequently get more financial help from PACs than from their own parties. For the last election, PACs raised $288 million. The total receipts of the Republican party were $300 million; of the Democratic party, $97 million.

The PACs delivered a much higher proportion of their receipts directly to individual candidates than the parties did. That was because each party spent so much to sustain itself as an organization and to promote itself and its entire team of candidates as representing a coherent political philosophy. Meanwhile, as the PACs grew, a candidate could pay less attention to parties and coherent political philosophy and rely more on his own conglomerate of assorted special interests.

If strong parties really matter in the American system, if accountability is a good thing, if compromise is the essence of viable politics, then some of the trends since the dawn of television are troublesome at best.

Maybe the political system will adapt without severe damage; it has adapted to new conditions before, though not to a universal, instantaneous communications technology that keeps throwing off secondary effects that nobody expected. Those secondary effects are organic changes in the system—the erosion of old institutions, including the conventions and the political parties themselves, the rise of the distorted sequence of primaries, the quantum leap in the cost of campaigning, and the emergence of the mighty swarm of disparate new special-interest lobbies to finance the new politics.

Meanwhile, the primary effect of television—to focus the attention of huge audiences on the visible personal qualities of politicians—will presumably endure. And there will be those compelling presences on the little screen reassuring us that they are not politicians at all but something more independent and righteous.

I, for one, lament the passing of politicians who are frankly politicians. For it is still the politicians who balance competing interests, negotiate coalitions, see a wisp of glory in the notion of consensus, and make our kind of government work.

We are a diverse people. We are a collection of factions, minorities, and ideologies. More than television is needed to hold us together.

What does hold us together, as from the beginning, is the practice of politics under a Constitution drawn up by politicians.

WHY TV COVERAGE OF LEGISLATION FALLS SHORT

Greg Schneiders

Greg Schneiders, who worked in the Carter White House and on Senator John Glenn's presidential campaign, is now senior vice-president of Hamilton & Staff, a political consulting and research firm.

Reprinted from the *Washington Journalism Review*, Vol. 7:6 (June, 1985). Used by permission.

If the picture of Congress presented by the network news seems to be fading, don't adjust your set. The problem is not there. It's in the executive suites of network headquarters in New York. And the picture *is* fading.

In fact, the number of stories involving Congress on the network nightly news today is less than half the number aired in the late 1970s. From 1980 to 1984, the three networks produced 3,545 stories about Congress for the nightly broadcasts, compared with 7,824 for the previous five years, according to the Vanderbilt University TV news archives. (Figures for four months of 1984 are estimates.)

The downturn is merely the official separation in a marriage that began with great promise but, in recent years, has obviously been in trouble. When TV started covering Congress in the early 1950s, the two institutions seemed perfectly matched. The Army-McCarthy hearings in 1954 brought real life drama—charges of communists in the military and vivid confrontations between Senator McCarthy and Eisenhower administration officials—into the nation's living rooms. Once the networks realized Hill hearings made good television, they wanted more and they got it—the McClellan hearings on union corruption in the 1950s, among others.

But, before long, it became obvious that television and Congress had problems of incompatibility. Television news requires a steady diet of pictures, color, personalities, and stories that can be told in a minute and a half. Congress dwells on issues that are arcane and often complicated and lumbers through a legislative process that is slow moving and often dull. Occasionally a sensational story, such as the McCarthy or the Watergate hearings, turns up, but usually television has to struggle to package Congress for the nightly news.

Today, coverage has decreased, and almost nobody on Capitol Hill has a good word to say about network coverage of the legislative branch. "It is a terrible distortion" says Republican Senate Whip Alan Simpson (R–Wyoming). Representative David Obey (D–Wisconsin) says, "The job they do is so poor that I studiously avoid appearing on any network television program." "Day in and day out they have their attention all in the wrong place," says Senator Christopher Dodd (D–Connecticut). Even Phil Jones, the veteran congressional correspondent for CBS, says, "We don't do as well as I would like and I think we leave a lot of things untouched, which, as a journalist, as a pure reporter, frustrates the hell out of me."

Part of the problem, as Simpson points out, is that "legislating, if done properly, is the very driest form of human endeavor."

Legislating is not only dry, it is nonvisual. There are a few good pictures. Although the sight of a United States Senator challenging a leader of organized crime produced high drama in the 1950s, the novelty soon wore off. Now the networks show little interest in broadcasting committee hearings despite congressional efforts to make them "good television."

Until the late 1970s, the ban on televising floor debate in the House of Representatives and the Senate was often blamed for TV's inability to tell the congressional story. But in 1979 the House began televising floor proceedings using its own cameras and making the pictures available to the networks. Gone were the archaic artists' renditions of the scene. Now there were talking, moving pictures to illustrate the correspondent's story. But enthusiasm for televising floor proceedings was short-lived. Soon it was clear that the House Chamber was mostly empty. Moreover, after hearing the debate, it was clear why.

Still, members of Congress hunted for good "visuals" for the evening news. They had auto wrecks towed to the East Plaza in front of the Capitol to dramatize legislation against drunk driving. Or they sat down to a lunch of ketchup to protest the Reagan administration's school lunch cutbacks. Not all their efforts succeeded.

"We've had some interesting 'battles of the visuals' around here," says Christopher Matthews, Speaker Tip O'Neill's press secretary. He remembers the day "they had the Republicans out here with fifty shopping carts showing how much you'd save because of the Reagan tax cut and [social justice advocate] Mitch Snyder shows up with fifty shopping carts showing how much food [Reagan's] cutting from social programs." It was so confusing the networks didn't use any of the shots that night. "They couldn't figure out what was going on with all these shopping carts," says Matthews.

Network correspondents and producers are as interested in covering congressional "color" as the Congress is in providing it. Some of their efforts are sensible. Increasingly they are going outside Washington for pictures to illustrate a congressional story, often to good effect. Clips of deteriorating cities illustrate a housing bill story; pictures of Trident submarines and MX missiles replace talking heads in a piece on defense legislation.

But some observers think the search for the vivid and unusual goes too far. "They look for the colorful," says Simpson. "They look for the witticism. They look for the extraneous with the exclamation point that doesn't have anything to do with the issue and it's distorted." Michael Robinson, a professor of political science at George Washington University, says, "They cover the floor in not a hysterical so much as a sensational way. They like the colorful."

The legislative process—committee meetings, subcommittee meetings, markups, joint concurrent resolutions, conference committees, reconciliation—is difficult to tell in segments only one and a half to three minutes long. "Congress is not designed to be covered in pieces that are one minute-30," says Norm Ornstein, resident scholar at the American Enterprise Institute.

Covering Congress has become even harder since the networks have reduced their coverage. "There's been a definite change," says Phil Jones. "It used to be we tracked legislation . . . [now] you take all the events that have happened over a month-long or two-month-long period and put that into a package that eventually amounts to two and one-half minutes."

Network correspondents struggle to explain the complexity of Congress, and the importance of covering it to their bosses in New York. NBC's Bob Kur, who covers the House, says: "I have had conversations with people in decision-making jobs at NBC News who say, 'Well, gee, you know there are a few hundred guys there and they all look alike and they wear their gray suits and they stand before the microphone and I don't want to see it unless I have to.'"

The broadcasting that results has often been described as a "headline service." Kur admits that "'headline mentality' is reinforced when you are constantly reminded, 'Just tell us who won and why.' The interest fades very quickly after that," he says.

The need for "visuals," the shortness of the pieces, and the complexity of Congress may be unavoidable institutional problems, embedded in the conflicting natures of Congress and the networks. Many congressmen find an additional failing in television's reporting on Congress: the cynical attitude of the TV correspondents who cover it.

Even Representative Tony Coelho (D–California), normally a defender of network coverage of the Hill, complains, "There is an impression [at the networks] that the House is only made up of people who take junkets, who collect big salaries, who really aren't that bright and I think that's unfair."

"[Network reporting] is a smirking way of covering this institution . . . just one more raindrop eating away at the rock of public understanding of a very complicated institution," says Obey. Simpson says in a typical network interview, "They run up to you with a mike, stick it under your nose, grab the camera man and the sound man, and say, 'Simpson, you've failed, haven't you . . . your bill is dead.'"

There is some empirical evidence to support this criticism. Professor Robinson and assistant Kevin R. Appel reviewed all the stories about Capitol Hill on NBC, CBS, and ABC during a five-week period in early 1976 and coded them positive, neutral, or negative. Eighty-six percent of the stories were "neutral"—mostly reporting events that had taken place that day. The rest were "negative." In five weeks there had not been a single positive story on Congress.

These findings do not surprise Robinson, who says the networks "have an institutional beat that is negative and, in some ways, adversarial and ascerbic. . . . It's just East Coast high-charged journalism—'let's have a spin'— and, of course, the 'spin' on Congress has always been and will always be the same: 'Oooh Congress!'"

Others are more concerned. Obey says, "I've been told by television reporters . . . that they have gotten instructions from their editors in New York to make sure that there is not a positive spin on the story as far as Congress as an institution is concerned." "It's a business," says Dodd, "and I think too many people still think of the networks as being public service operations. They're not. Business decisions have to be made . . . [and] I think the media plays off the [negative] public reaction to Congress that's been around for generations. It's good business because it's appealing to the consumer."

Network correspondents deny that they are more negative about Congress than print reporters or, for that matter, the American public. "I don't think we're cynical. I think we're realistic," says John Dancy, who covers the Senate for NBC. Steve Gerstel, veteran Hill bureau chief for UPI, says the low esteem in which some TV reporters hold Congress "is probably deserved. It stems from things [the members] do."

Even Phil Jones, however, acknowledges that a reporter's "close"—his comment at the end of a piece—can often be tough. Jones says: "There are times when a close may have a little too much bite to it. . . . There's no question that closes have to have a little style. They're not like a newspaper story that when you're finished you're finished and you stop."

"Face it," says NBC's Kur, "you don't only report facts; I mean that's not news. There's a little bit of interpretation in what we do . . . and therein comes the entertainment portion of television—the fact that the correspondent is trying to catch your interest."

The pattern of television coverage of Congress may be more damaging to the institution than its negative tone. Network reporting often shows Congress *reacting* to the president in ten-second sound bites. Robinson says the networks are "not going out for the story. They're waiting for the bounce from the Congress after the bounce from the president."

"The institution of the presidency is much more television-oriented than the Congress. . . ." says Matthews. "It's a very simple thing to say, 'I wonder what the king is thinking tonight.' That's a hell of an interesting story. It's not interesting to say, 'I wonder what 535 [congressmen] are thinking tonight.'"

One thing many of those 535 are pondering is how to survive and prosper in this new environment. Some of the older members avoid TV. Most younger members developed their television survival skills along the road to Congress. "I know how [to get on the air]," says Dodd. "I think in 20-second clips. . . . Every one of us has that little machine going and we know exactly what these guys are interested in."

Matthews believes that younger members of Congress have learned to play their reactive role well on TV. "They know what the networks need and they also are attuned to what the story is that's being packaged for that night. . . ." he says. "If you're in the package, you're in. If you're not in, you're not going to get on [the air] on your own."

But he wonders about the effect of this new sophistication on the members. "[If you got] here through TV, you love TV because it is what brought you here," says Matthews. "[But] the people who got here because of people never forget it. They keep close to the people. The people who got here because of the tube sometimes forget people. They think about the tube all the time."

For reporters covering the Hill, the difficulty of getting their stories on the air takes a toll. "Their lives are crises," says Senator Simpson. "You can see them hurtling around like the 'hounds of hell'. . . . It must be terrible for them. . . . [They] look very calm and composed and say, 'So-and-so at the Capitol' . . . [when] they've just been jerked over there, memorized this thing . . . and interviewed you in the meantime. It's not clean stuff."

The people "jerking" the Hill correspondents around are their New York producers, who have also been instrumental in deciding to air fewer stories about Congress. Most of them came of age when Washington dominated the nightly news programs. They believe that their new approach is better.

"Years ago we were limited by our own technology. Washington was a big bureau, and it was easy to get pieces out of it and so more of it got on the air," says Bill Lord, executive producer of ABC's "World News Tonight."

"[The reduced congressional coverage] is a direct result of decisions made at CBS two and one-half years ago to 'de-Washingtonize' our coverage. . . ." says Lane Venardos, executive producer of the "CBS Evening News." "The theory is simply one of making the coverage of issues more meaningful by showing people who are affected by these issues and the locations where they are happening instead of showing a group of people around green felt tables uttering sound bites."

Issue stories—as distinct from congressional stories—are better than ever, according to many network producers and correspondents. "Issues are not being ignored. In fact, they're being presented in a much more interesting and meaningful way. . . ." says Lord. "When you're talking about issues that are potentially boring you certainly want to present them in as interesting a way as possible."

John Dancy says that network coverage "is evolving. We're learning how to make issues interesting to people because if you're not interesting, you're dead."

Of course, the nightly news is not the only network coverage of Congress. The morning programs, ABC's "Nightline," CBS's "60 Minutes," and the Sunday morning interview programs provide a "news hole" that often did not exist before. But the nightly news shows are where most Americans get their news, and, for those viewers, the picture of Congress continues to fade.

"Any viewers who think that they're getting all the news they need from the networks are woefully mistaken," says Venardos. Adds NBC's John Dancy, "We will never replace newspapers in the amount of content or interpretation that we're able to give a news event. People will just simply have to read if they want to be informed."

Even the network correspondents worry about the effect their diminishing coverage may be having on the balance of power between the executive and legislative branches. Reduction of Hill coverage, says Dancy, "makes the presidency much more important than Congress and I don't think that was the intention of the framers of the Constitution. . . . By making the decision that we made we aid the White House in its attempt to influence what people think."

Professor Robinson is more sanguine: "The Congress and the Constitution," he says, "are much bigger than our communications system." That may be, but for 70 million viewers of the evening news, Congress, at least, is getting smaller all the time.

MASS MEDIA AND THE LAW

Jay B. Wright

Jay B. Wright is a professor at the S. I. Newhouse School of Public Communications, Syracuse University. He is coauthor of *The First Amendment and the Fourth Estate: The Law of Mass Media* (third edition, 1985) and *The First Amendment and the Fifth Estate: Regulation of Electronic Mass Media* (1986) and editor of *Legal Handbook for New York State Journalists* (1986). He is executive director of the New York Fair Trial Free Press Conference, New York State's bench-bar-press organization. Wright has a Ph.D. in mass communications from Syracuse University and a master's degree in law from Yale Law School.

The rules of society are formalized in its laws. Not even mass media, protected though they are, are immune from legal scrutiny. Just how much legal scrutiny there should be, and what form it should take, has been the subject of discussion for centuries. In the United States, the press is largely protected from government interference, but cases inevitably arise in the courts that test our willingness to let the press operate without restriction. The most important of those cases are decided by the U.S. Supreme Court and shape and reshape media law.

Historical and Philosophical Background for Freedom of Expression

Our roots are clearly in the libertarian tradition. John Milton's famous essay *Areopagitica,* published in 1644, expressed dismay at the English system of censorship, which required advance permission from the government before a license could be obtained for publication. English philosopher John Locke and others believed that truth and falsehood should be allowed to mingle in a free marketplace of ideas, that people were intelligent enough to sort out the truth from the fiction, and that it was better to allow an intellectual free-for-all than to give a government censor the power to regulate what people said or wrote.

When the Bill of Rights was added to the U.S. Constitution, the first of the amendments specified, "Congress shall make no law . . . abridging the freedom . . . of the press."—a strong proscription against government interference. The Fourteenth Amendment subsequently extended the press's protection by prohibiting state infringements.

Some people believe that the First Amendment totally prohibits any governmental interference with the press, but governmental interference in the form of libel law and obscenity law is part of the legal tradition and is generally accepted today as permissible. (Although one has freedom to swing one's fist in the air, that freedom ends when someone else's chin is in its way. Similarly, although one has the freedom to say what one wants, that freedom may be limited when someone else's reputation or privacy is "in the way.")

The courts have found it necessary to interpret the First Amendment in such a way as to balance First Amendment rights against competing interests. Some of those interests are state interests (interests of the government or the citizens collectively, and others are individual interests, like libel and privacy.

More than anything else, the First Amendment has been seen as a protection of the right to publish without censorship. Such a freedom is a freedom from prior restraint on publication. In *Near v. Minnesota* (283 U.S. 697 [1931]), the Supreme Court struck down a state statute that had been used to close down an offensive newspaper. The Court established the principle that prior restraints are almost always unconstitutional. Wartime, obscenity, and incitement to violence provide possible exceptions.

In a variety of cases (see, for example, *Schenck v. United States*, 249 U.S. 47 [1919]), by contrast, the Court has upheld subsequent sanctions in freedom of expression cases. Distributors of obscenity, for instance, have been punished by being put in prison or being fined; media that have libeled people have had to pay damages as the result of civil lawsuits.

Balancing First Amendment Freedoms against the Rights of Individuals

A true libertarian would be willing to let individuals suffer the consequences when their reputations are unfairly damaged by others' false and harmful statements about them, when their privacy is invaded, or when their rights to a fair trial are endangered by prejudicial news accounts. Society has been less willing to sit back and let the individual suffer, but we still bend over backward to protect freedom of expression, so the balancing act is delicate. In the first two instances, involving libel and invasion of privacy, the law makes it possible for individuals who have been harmed to sue to be compensated for the harm done to them. In the latter instance—interference with a criminal defendant's right to a fair trial—a defendant can appeal the conviction based on a claim of unfairness resulting from the news accounts.

Defamation

In its broadest sense, the term *defamation* means the taking from one's reputation. Normally when the media publish something that is truthful but harmful, the law protects the media. But when something false and harmful is published, the media can be in trouble. Slander and libel are two kinds of defamation. Although people frequently try to simplify by saying that slander is oral and libel is written, the distinction is somewhat more complex. Because the media reach large audiences, their messages—regardless of whether they are printed in a newspaper or oral on television or radio—are more likely to result in suits for libel than in suits for slander.

Prior to 1964, the news media were strictly liable for any damage they did to individuals as a result of false and harmful statements. In other words, no matter how careful they tried to be, no matter how much they believed what they published, the media were responsible for any libels they published. If the media are businesses, which they are, one of the costs of doing business was the occasional compensation of the people who were accidentally harmed as a result of the publication.

A famous 1964 decision by the U.S. Supreme Court put an end to strict liability when the person defamed was a public official. *New York Times v. Sullivan* (376 U.S. 254), a case involving a Montgomery County, Alabama, city official who claimed he was defamed in a paid civil rights advertisement in the *New York Times*, resulted in a major change in libel law. Creating a new constitutional defense in libel, the Supreme Court decided the case in favor of the *Times* because the newspaper had not demonstrated "actual malice" by publishing the advertisement. *Actual malice* is a term of art; the Supreme Court has defined the term, both in words and by example, but its definition is not the same as an ordinary dictionary meaning of the term. An ordinary dictionary might define *malice* in terms suggesting ill will; the Supreme Court chose to define it as prior knowledge of falsity or reckless disregard for the truth. In subsequent cases, the Court made clear that reckless disregard meant not merely a failure to check the facts of a story but in fact "entertaining serious doubts" about a story and publishing it anyway or having a high degree of awareness of probable falsity.

Because the Court concluded that the *New York Times* had handled the advertisement in a reasonably appropriate way, the errors notwithstanding, it held that public official L.B. Sullivan lacked sufficient proof of actual malice and could not win his suit.

It thereafter became far more difficult—but not altogether impossible—for public officials to win libel suits. They have to show not just that something libelous was published, that they were identified, and that they suffered harm from the publication, but they have the additional burden of proving actual malice. Although some people thought this might be unfair to public officials (that they could be unfairly hurt and could not be compensated for that hurt), the Supreme Court thought it was justified in the interest of having open and robust public debate about public officials. Public officials, the Court thought, generally can make their views known through the media—

they have access to the media—so harm to them from erroneous statements was perhaps more tolerable than harm to other kinds of people.

Since 1964, the Supreme Court has wrestled frequently with libel cases. It has held that public figures also must prove actual malice. Public figures are either *all-purpose* public figures (those widely known in society) or *vortex* public figures (those who enter a controversy attempting to resolve it).

In 1974, in what is widely thought to be the most significant libel case since *New York Times,* the Supreme Court held that private figures need not necessarily prove actual malice. The case was *Gertz v. Robert Welch, Inc.* (418 U.S. 323), and it involved a prominent Chicago lawyer, Elmer Gertz, who sued the John Birch Society (under its corporate name, Robert Welch, Inc.) as a result of accusations in their magazine *American Opinion* that Gertz was a Marxist and a Communist fronter. Gertz won. The Court found him to be a private figure despite his prominence in Chicago legal circles; he had not, in the Court's view, voluntarily entered the public eye.

In recent years, some libel plaintiffs have sought enormous amounts of money. Lawsuits for $40 million and $120 million make big headlines. Fortunately for the media, high damage awards by juries are usually reduced by appellate courts. It is impossible to say how much is the largest amount of money ever paid to a plaintiff by a defendant in a libel case because cases are frequently settled out of court, with secret settlements. The largest settlement may have been close to $1 million, in Carol Burnett's suit against the *National Enquirer* for erroneously portraying her as loud and drunk in a Washington, D.C., restaurant.

Private figure libel plaintiffs need not necessarily prove actual malice to win compensatory damages (to compensate them for the harm done to them), but they must prove actual malice to receive punitive damages (to punish the defendant). The Supreme Court has permitted the states to define for themselves the standard of proof necessary for private figure plaintiffs. Some states have settled on an actual malice standard; others something more like a simple negligence test.

Invasions of Privacy

Should it be legal for a newspaper to print someone's picture even though he or she does not want it to? Should it be legal for a television camera crew to walk into a restaurant uninvited, cameras rolling, and cause a disturbance while trying to get a news story at the restaurant?

Few things about the media are as disturbing to the public as invasions of privacy. How many times have we heard people complain about "unconstitutional" invasions of privacy? Actually, the word *privacy* is never mentioned in the U.S. Constitution, but we generally assume that it is one of our most basic rights.

A famous law review article published by two young Boston law partners, Samuel Warren and Louis D. Brandeis ("The Right to Privacy," 4 *Harvard Law Review* 193 [1890]) is credited with creating a whole new area of law: privacy law. Today the Warren and Brandeis article is cited when one talks about invasions of privacy by computer, by electronic eavesdropping, and by other means, but Warren and Brandeis had in mind the gossipy nature of the Boston press.

Different states recognize different kinds of invasion of privacy, and there is no guarantee that a case decided one way in one state would be decided the same way in another state, where the law may be entirely different. It is clear, however, that we are dealing with a variety of different kinds of invasion of privacy. Each is a separate wrong or injury—what the law calls a *tort*.

The following are privacy torts:

Putting the plaintiff in a false light in the public eye.

Publication of embarrassing private facts that tend to violate ordinary decencies.

Intrusion on the plaintiff's physical solitude.

Appropriation of some element of the plaintiff's personality for commercial use.

A more recently recognized tort—some say it is just a branch of the *commercial use* tort—is violation of a plaintiff's right of publicity.

Not until 1967 did the U.S. Supreme Court decide a case involving an alleged invasion of privacy by the mass media. *Time, Inc. v. Hill* (385 U.S. 374) was a suit against *Life* magazine by the James Hill family. The Hills had been held hostage in their suburban Philadelphia home in 1952. Subsequently a best-selling novel, *The Desperate Hours,* was published about a fictional family with a similar name. The author had based his story on the real-life experiences of several families, including the Hills. In 1955, when a Broadway play based on the novel was previewing in Philadelphia, *Life* magazine ran an article with photographs of the actors at the home the real Hill family had since sold. Headlined "True Crime Inspires Tense Drama," the story created the impression that the dramatic events depicted had actually happened to the Hills. The Hills, on the contrary, had emphasized that they had not been mistreated by their captors. The Hills sued Time, Inc., under a New York State statute for commercial use—stressing that the article and photographs commercially promoted the play. (The courts generally have considered journalistic uses not to be commercial uses and have reserved the commercial use tort for advertising and marketing uses, but the New York statute recognized only commercial use.)

The Hills had won in the New York courts, but Time, Inc., appealed to the Supreme Court. Their attorney was Richard M. Nixon. This was just three years after the Supreme Court had introduced the actual malice rule in libel. Drawing from it, the Supreme Court treated the case primarily as a false light case because of the erroneous impressions created about the Hills. The Court decided for the magazine because there was no proof of actual malice on its part. It is far from clear that the case would be decided the same way today, given the Court's greater protection, in libel law, of people, who, like the Hills, are involuntarily drawn into the public eye.

The second mass media privacy case to come before the Supreme Court was also a false light case. In *Cantrell v. Forest City Publishing Co.* (419 U.S. 245 [1974]), the Court considered a suit against the *Cleveland Plain Dealer* newspaper by the widow of a man killed in a bridge collapse. The newspaper published an article by a freelance writer in its Sunday magazine supplement. The article said Mrs. Cantrell "will talk neither about what happened nor about how [she and her children] are doing. She wears the same mask of non-expression she wore at the funeral." Actually, Mrs. Cantrell had been absent from her home when the reporter visited. The Court concluded that there was deliberate falsity here and held for Mrs. Cantrell.

In *Cox Broadcasting v. Cohn* (420 U.S. 469 [1975]), the Court held for a defendant television station that had broadcast the name of a gang-rape victim despite a Georgia law making it a misdemeanor to do so. The seventeen-year-old rape victim had died, and her name had been included in a court document available in a courtroom when six youths charged with the crime were indicted. The Court found this kind of accurate reporting from an open public record to be protected. (More commonly, media voluntarily choose to withhold the names of living rape victims, or names of victims are withheld by law enforcement authorities.)

Zacchini v. Scripps-Howard Broadcasting Co. (433 U.S. 562 [1977]) presented a different problem. Zacchini, a carnival performer billing himself as "the human cannonball," sued a television station that had broadcast, over his objections, a videotape of his entire fifteen-second act of being shot by a cannon into a net 200 feet away. The Supreme Court decided the case in favor of Zacchini, thus establishing the right of publicity. The case's application may be limited because it is so unusual that an entertainer's act would be so brief.

The fact that there have been so few privacy cases before the Supreme Court makes it difficult to generalize about the law in this area. Ordinarily, however, publication of embarrassing private facts can be successfully defended by the media on the basis of newsworthiness. Newsworthiness, however, does not justify trespassing or intrusion onto another's property where one is uninvited.

Fair Trial versus Free Press

Few other topics have engendered the amount of heated discussion generated by the fair trial–free press issue. The problem is one of balancing the rights of the media to report on the administration of justice against the right of individuals to have trials that are fair—free from the type of prejudice that sometimes results from heavy media coverage.

The problem is hardly new. As long as there have been crimes committed and people to gossip about them, the public has demonstrated a seemingly insatiable appetite for crime and trial news. The stories often are laden with human drama and suspense. Alleged criminals may have nicknames, weeping mothers, and mysterious motives; all are reflected in the media coverage.

Lawyers and judges—trained to believe that the best way to arrive at the truth in a court of law is to expose the jurors only to the sort of sterilized information that is acceptable ("admissible")—are disturbed, even outraged, by what they term the sensational publicity surrounding some crimes and trials. But one person's sensational publicity is another's thorough news coverage; and although both the media and the law may be aiming to discover the truth, inevitably there will be conflicts.

The Supreme Court has considered this problem a number of times since 1961—first in a series of cases in which convicted defendants sought to have their guilty verdicts overturned on the basis that prejudicial publicity made their trials unfair, and then in a series of cases in which media alleged that restrictions interfered with their First Amendment rights.

Leslie Irvin, the appellant in *Irvin v. Dowd* (366 U.S. 717 [1961]), was an incorrigible youth accused of, and ultimately convicted of, a series of "mad dog" killings in Indiana. The Supreme Court agreed that his first trial had been unfair, and he was retried. The result was another conviction. Wilber Rideau (*Rideau v. Louisiana*, 73 U.S. 723 [1963]), confessed to a Louisiana bank robbery on television before the trial. The Supreme Court held that his trial too had been unfair. At retrial, another conviction resulted.

Flamboyant Texas financier Billie Sol Estes, who had highly placed political friends, was tried in Texas when it was one of only two states that permitted cameras in courtrooms. Estes (*Estes v. Texas*, 381 U.S. 532 [1965]) appealed his conviction, was retried, and convicted again.

The exception was the case of Dr. Sam Sheppard, accused in the brutal murder of his pregnant wife, Marilyn, in a Cleveland suburb on July 4, 1954. Sheppard's trial attracted national attention and resulted in his conviction. Appeals were rejected, and Sheppard spent ten years in jail. A young attorney, F. Lee Bailey, persuaded the Supreme Court to hear Sheppard's appeal. In *Sheppard v. Maxwell* (384 U.S. 333 [1965]), the Court held that Sheppard's trial had been unfairly prejudiced by the news coverage and editorials in the Cleveland media. On retrial, Sheppard—unlike Irvin, Rideau, and Estes—was acquitted.

The Court's decision in *Sheppard,* combined with a conclusion by the commission that investigated the assassination of President John F. Kennedy that Kennedy's assassin could never have received a fair trial because of the publicity, helped to prompt the American Bar Association to appoint a committee to deal with the problem. That committee, which came to be known as the Reardon committee, promulgated guidelines for pretrial and trial news coverage. News media resisted the attempts by the established bar to tell them how to do their own jobs, but subsequent state bench-bar-press organizations, which adopted similar sets of guidelines with media participation, have met with somewhat greater success.

It is easy to pick up the erroneous impression from *Irvin, Rideau, Estes,* and *Sheppard* that every convicted person who claims his or her first trial was unfair will get a new one. That is not so. In *Murphy v. Florida* (421 U.S. 794 [1975]), the Supreme Court upheld Jack Murphy's conviction despite the fact that the media had widely identified him by his nickname, "Murph the Surf," and had reported prior to the trial that he was a notorious jewel thief. The Court was satisfied that the first trial was sufficiently fair. In contrast with Irvin's first trial, at which 430 potential jurors had to be questioned before a jury could be seated, only 78 potential jurors were examined at Murphy's trial before a jury was chosen.

Although the Cleveland newspapers took much of the blame for what went wrong in the Sheppard trial, the Supreme Court put the responsibility squarely on the trial judge's shoulders. Other trial judges took note and in the 1970s tried a variety of means to protect defendants' fair trial rights. The Supreme Court eventually ruled on the constitutionality of these means. In *Nebraska Press Association v. Stuart* (427 U.S. 539 [1976]), the Court held unconstitutional a Nebraska judge's attempt to gag the press by issuing an order against disclosure of prejudicial information. In *Gannett v. DePasquale* (433 U.S. 368 [1979]), the Court found acceptable a trial court judge's closure of a pretrial hearing held to determine whether information should be suppressed. In *Richmond Newspapers v. Virginia* (448 U.S. 555 [1980]), the Court ruled that trials should generally be open. In *Globe Newspaper Co. v. Superior Court* (457 U.S. 596 [1982]), the Court held that automatic trial closures (such as one providing for closure of rape and other sexual assault trials during the testimony of minors who are victims) are inappropriate— that the media and public ought at least to have the opportunity to present arguments in favor of openness. Then the Court ruled, in *Press-Enterprise Co. v. Superior Court* (464 U.S. 501 [1984]), that the examination of potential jurors should presumptively be open to the public and later, in 1986, that pretrial proceedings should generally be open.

Because the First Amendment and Sixth Amendment are equals, the attempt to balance the media's rights against those of defendants is a never-ending process.

Balancing First Amendment Freedoms against the Rights of Society

Government Secrets

Here we have a true dilemma: you cannot successfully run a government in the 1980s without keeping some secrets, but you cannot have a totally free press if it is a crime to publish everything the government stamps secret.

The Pentagon Papers case, *New York Times v. U.S.* (403 U.S. 713 [1971]), provided a dramatic example of a confrontation between the federal government and the news media. The *New York Times* received illegal copies of pages from a forty-seven-volume, 7,000-page top secret government-sponsored study of the history of the U.S. decision-making process on Vietnam policy. Under a cloak of secrecy, the newspaper began editing the materials in a New York City hotel and then, on a Sunday in June 1971, began publishing them. The government sought a court order to stop publication. The case moved with extraordinary speed through the courts and was decided by the Supreme Court only two weeks later. The Court lifted the restraint, saying that the government had failed to prove that the danger posed by the publication would justify the prior restraint on the news media.

Another illustration of government concern for protecting secrets is the 1979 case involving the *Progressive* magazine's attempt to publish information about the hydrogen bomb in *U.S. v. The Progressive* (467 F. Supp. 990 [W.D. Wis. 1979], appeal dismissed 610 F.2d 819 [7th Cir.]). There the government successfully sought in federal court an injunction stopping publication, but the government withdrew its complaint, and the case was dismissed after the *Madison Press Connection* published a letter containing information that the *Progressive* had been enjoined from publishing and the *Chicago Tribune* announced it planned to publish the same letter.

Landmark Communications, Inc. v. Virginia (435 U.S. 829 [1978]), involved an appeal of a conviction by a newspaper found guilty of violating a state statute prohibiting the divulging of proceedings of a commission investigating charges against judges. Writing for a majority of the Supreme Court, Chief Justice Warren Burger said, "We conclude that the publication Virginia seeks to punish under its statute lies near the core of the First Amendment, and the Commonwealth's interests advanced by the imposition of criminal sanctions are insufficient to justify the actual and potential encroachments on freedom of speech and of the press which follow therefrom."

Obscenity

Few other problems in communications law have been as vexing as obscenity. How does one preserve adults' rights to see sexually explicit materials if they choose to, while looking after society's interest in protecting children from such materials? The courts have tended to view some sexually explicit materials—pornographic materials—as legally acceptable and within the realm of First Amendment protection. Other sexually explicit materials, including "hard-core" materials, have been viewed as illegal, or obscene, and therefore excluded from First Amendment protection.

To make such a distinction, the courts need a definition of the word *obscene* that is more precise than an ordinary dictionary definition. Over the years, a three-part test has evolved for determining whether the content of materials is obscene:

> (a) whether the average person, applying contemporary community standards, would find that the work, taken as a whole, appeals to the prurient interest, (b) whether the work depicts or describes, in a patently offensive way, sexual conduct specifically defined by the applicable state law; and (c) whether the work, taken as a whole, lacks serious literary, artistic, political, or scientific value. (*Miller v. California,* 413 U.S. 15 [1973])

All three parts of the test must be met; something that appeals to prurient interest and describes sexual conduct in a patently offensive way may be saved from being obscene by having serious value. The Supreme Court has not described the conduct as offensive; it is the way the conduct is depicted or described that may be patently offensive.

In addition to the content criteria for determining obscenity, the Court has established conduct criteria. Convictions have been upheld for (1) pandering, or commercially exploiting the sexual content of material in the way that it is advertised or distributed (*Ginzburg v. U.S.,* 383 U.S. 463 [1966]); (2) variable obscenity, or distributing materials to a minor (*Ginsberg v. N.Y.,* 390 U.S. 629 [1968]); and (3) invading people's privacy by confronting them with sexually explicit material they do not wish to see (*Miller v. California,* 413 U.S. 15 [1973]). Also, the use of children in the making of pornography (promoting a sexual performance by a child) is reason for upholding of a conviction (*New York v. Ferber,* 458 U.S. 747 [1982]).

Special Problem Areas

Advertising and Public Relations as Commercial Speech

Is expression any less protected by the First Amendment just because its source is a business and it takes the form of an advertisement or public relations release? The area of commercial speech law was once referred to indelicately as no more important than a "pimple on the chin of communications law," but it grew to new importance in the 1970s.

A 1942 case, *Valentine v. Chrestensen* (316 U.S. 52), set the law in this area for decades. Chrestensen owned a surplus submarine, which he exhibited as a tourist attraction in New York City. New York City police stopped him from distributing handbills on the street advertising the submarine, citing a requirement of the city's sanitary code that prohibited such distribution because it could cause a littering problem. The Supreme Court held that advertising, like Chrestensen's, was not protected by the First Amendment; commercial speech was outside the realm of expression the framers of the Constitution sought to protect.

In some important cases from the 1970s, however, some advertising came to receive protection under the Supreme Court's decisions. In *Bigelow v. Virginia* (421 U.S. 809 [1975]), the Court held in favor of a newspaper editor who had published an advertisement for an abortion referral service that told Virginia women about the possibility of legal abortions in New York.

The following year, the Court recognized a First Amendment protection in advertising in *Virginia State Board of Pharmacy v. Virginia Citizens Consumer Council, Inc.* (425 U.S. 748 [1976]), a challenge to a restriction against the price advertising of prescription drugs. In 1980, in *Central Hudson Gas & Electric Corp. v. Public Service Commission of New York* (447 U.S. 557), the Court spelled out criteria to be used in such cases: (1) is the communication neither misleading nor related to unlawful activity? (2) is there a substantial state interest in the restrictions? (3) is the regulatory interest in proportion to that interest? and (4) is the regulation likely to achieve the state's goal?

These cases established a series of precedents in which advertising—sometimes controversial advertising but always truthful advertising—was protected by the First Amendment. Then, in mid-1986, the Supreme Court surprised many observers with its decision in *Posadas de Puerto Rico Associates v. Tourism Company of Puerto Rico*. The case involved a prohibition against certain advertising by Puerto Rican gambling casinos.

Puerto Rico sought to avoid encouraging its own residents from entering the casinos but allowed advertising directed primarily at tourists. The Court applied the four-part test from *Central Hudson* and concluded that the regulation did concern lawful activity and was not misleading, that the government's interest was substantial, that the regulation directly advanced the government's asserted interest, and that the regulation was no more extensive than necessary to serve the government's interest. Therefore the government's prohibition against such advertising was permissible. By upholding the restrictions, the Court clearly suggested that commercial speech—even truthful commercial speech—does not always have the same protection as noncommercial speech. The decision's full impact has yet to be seen, but it raises questions about the future of tobacco advertising, given the arguments that could be made for a governmental interest in discouraging smoking.

Regulation of Electronic Media

The First Amendment protection of a free press has been interpreted generally as protecting the electronic media as well as the print media. First Amendment law that has resulted from Supreme Court decisions in such areas as libel and invasion of privacy applies to electronic as well as to print media; the rules are basically the same. But the electronic media must cope with something the print media can largely ignore: regulation.

The Federal Communications Commission (FCC) regulates the electronic media; there is no comparable federal commission for print media. Because there are only a finite number of over-the-air broadcasting frequencies and channels available, regulation has been a necessity, but that scarcity rationale breaks down in the face of cable and other newer technologies with seemingly limitless possible communications channels.

Some have suggested that the FCC should be merely a traffic cop, making sure that only one station at a time broadcasts over any given frequency or channel but ignoring the content of the broadcasts. The FCC has carved out a much fuller role. In looking out for the public "convenience, interest, and necessity," the FCC has sought to improve the content of broadcast messages.

Congress, through the Communications Act of 1934, established the FCC and gave it the authority to promulgate rules and regulations. In that sense, the FCC is a quasi-legislative body; it is also quasi-judicial. Its commissioners decide cases involving broadcasting, and appeals of those cases can go to a federal appeals court without any trial in a federal district court.

The FCC has tried to maintain fairness in broadcasting through the equal opportunities rule (section 315 of the Communications Act of 1934, frequently called the equal time rule) and through the fairness doctrine. (By contrast, that fairness is not legally mandated in the print media.) The equal time rule applied only to political candidates and mechanically requires broadcast licensees to give candidates for the same office equal time. It does not apply to bona fide newscasts.

The fairness doctrine, by contrast, applies to all kinds of controversial issues but leaves much more to the discretion of the licensee. It was developed by the FCC, and it requires broadcasters to cover controversial issues of public importance and to make sure that important contrasting views are presented. The views may be presented by the licensee or by others. Under the fairness doctrine, an individual who is the subject of a personal attack should be given opportunity to respond. The Supreme Court upheld the constitutionality of the personal attack rule in *Red Lion Broadcasting Co. v. Federal Communications Commission* (395 U.S. 367 [1969]).

The spirit of deregulation in Washington in recent years has combined with the advent of new technologies to yield considerable weight to the movement to do away with, or substantially reduce the scope of, the equal opportunities rule and the fairness doctrine.

Summary

The U.S. Supreme Court continues to shape mass media law by interpreting the First Amendment and deciding the constitutionality of federal and state statutes. Cases involving prior restraints on publication, libel, invasion of privacy, fair trial–free press, obscenity, government secrets, obscenity, commercial speech, and regulation of electronic media are an important part of that law. Related concerns include copyright, confidentiality in news gathering, freedom of information, and ownership of the media.

10
Sex and Violence

Introduction

Sex and violence are basic items of mass media content. Newspaper headlines scream almost with glee at a particularly bloody murder, rape is usually good copy, and armed robberies get bigger stories if shooting is involved. Sex appeal, clinical sex advice, romance, and vicarious sex have long been staples of magazines. Television thrives on the same diet, though in live news usually only a pool of blood can be filmed. Entertainment programming, however, can be tailor-made with violent action and increasingly suggestive sexuality. Now that the family movie has gone, movies also rely heavily on sex and violence to draw audiences. The questions addressed in this chapter are, how are the media implicated in sex and violence, and what effect does such content have on their audiences?

Pornography is currently more controversial than violence in the media. It is, perhaps, one of the mysteries of our culture that we deplore violence, yet horror films are often rated PG—and we enjoy sex, but the explicit treatment of sex is rated X.

In the first reading, Barry Sapolsky gives an overview of the subject. In the last decade or so, pornography has not only grown but has changed; today there is more violent and dehumanizing pornography than ever before. The subject is now a public issue. While consumers buy and rent home video porn, large interest groups are mobilized to put porn out of business. Although the report of the 1968 Commission on Obscenity and Pornography found that erotic materials do not cause sex crime, the issue was not resolved.[1] Sapolsky reviews the research on pornography and aggressive behavior. Nonviolent pornography has varying effects on aggression depending on its context. Violent pornography, however, appears to encourage aggressive behavior toward women. The recently issued Meese report stresses the latter finding and urges strong legal action to suppress every type of material it finds pornographic. While most people would agree to a ban on child pornography and violence, it will be interesting to note how much of the current antipornography movement is directed not only to these but to suppressing sexuality in general.[2]

The next reading reports in more detail on some of the findings discussed by Sapolsky. Edward Donnerstein and Daniel Linz report that their research indicates that violent pornography is indeed harmful, as are materials that "perpetuate ideas of women as sexual objects."

Academic researchers have investigated the effects of violent television programs on children. Albert Bandura's laboratory research, for example, has shown that viewing violence reduces inhibitions on aggressive behavior and teaches children aggression. This apparently holds true for adults, too, for most TV viewers know how to commit murder, elementary forms of torture, and other crimes, even if they do not practice them. The mass media effects, together with novels and handed-down nursery tales and folklore, are perhaps more important in the formation of a climate of violence than in triggering it directly. The networks claim that their programming is not harmful, and both NBC and ABC have sponsored research, presumably in the hope of supporting their position.[3] Other researchers also have refuted the argument that violent programming directly affects behavior.[4]

Like movie violence, the TV variety is profitable. Violent programs often get good ratings, and the ratings attract sponsors. Some leading corporations, among them McDonald's, Golden Grain, Magnavox, Pepsico, Quaker Oats, and Kellogg, have sponsored programs with a high incidence of violent episodes. Other heavy advertising corporations—Johnson and Johnson, Alberto-Culver, Safeway Stores, General Motors, and Bristol-Meyers—have sponsored relatively violence-free programming.[5] Support for violent programming, then, is in part the sponsor's choice.

The most prominent investigator of TV violence today, the person credited with putting the networks under fire as never before, is George Gerbner.[6] Using methods contested by the networks, he and his associates have devised a TV violence profile of the year's programming. During the 1970s, there was no significant lessening in network violence.[7] Gerbner claims that high audience consumption leads to the development of a "mean world" view; that is, heavy viewers "see the real world as more dangerous and frightening than those who watch very little." They "are less trustful of their fellow citizens and more fearful of the real world."[8] Gerbner adds that the antiviolence movement has often missed the main point: TV violence is probably presented by corporate America not to stimulate off-screen violence but to use symbolic violence for social control. TV violence is the precursor not of more violence but of ultimate oppression.

In the last reading of the chapter, Kenneth Hirsch summarizes the research on media violence and audience behavior. We live in a society that seems to be amazingly tolerant of violence. As the surgeon general claimed some years ago, television violence is harmful, and the evidence mounts to support his claim.[9]

Notes

1. *Report of the Commission on Obscenity and Pornography* (New York: Bantam, 1970). The Violence Commission reached a different conclusion on its subject matter. This contradiction in the interpretation of media effects is dealt with by Richard A. Dienstbier, "Sex and Violence: Can Research Have It Both Ways?" *Journal of Communication* (Summer 1977).

2. Helen Dudar, "America Discovers Child Pornography," *Ms. Magazine* (August 1977): 237–240; Dolf Zillmann and Jennings Bryant, "Pornography, Sexual Callousness and the Trivialization of Rape," *Journal of Communication* (Autumn 1982).

3. For a critique of the NBC study, see Rose K. Goldsen, "NBC's Make-Believe Research on TV Violence," *Trans-action* (October 1971): 28–35. J. Ronald Milavsky and Allen H. Barton responded with "In Defense of NBC Violence," *Trans-action* (January 1972): 30-31.

4. This seems to be the case presented by Seymour Feshback and Robert D. Singer in their book, *Television and Aggression* (San Francisco: Jossey-Bass, 1971). See also Robert M. Kaplan and Robert D. Singer, "Television Violence and Viewer Aggression: A Reexamination of the Evidence," *Journal of Social Issues* 32 (1976).

5. See Ronald G. Slaby, Gary R. Quarfoth, and Gene A. McConnachie, "Television Violence and Its Sponsors," *Journal of Communication* (Winter 1976).

6. See Anthony Haden-Guest, "The Man Who's Killing TV Violence," *New York*, July 11, 1977.

7. George Gerbner, Larry Gross, Michael Morgan, and Nancy Signorielli, "The Mainstreaming of America: Violence Profile No. 11," *Journal of Communication* (Summer 1980): 10–29.

8. George Gerbner and Larry Gross, "The Scary World of TV's Heavy Viewer," *Psychology Today* (April 1976): 41.

9. See Eugene H. Methvin, "TV Violence: The Shocking New Evidence," *Reader's Digest* (January 1983): 49–53.

PORNOGRAPHY TODAY

Barry Sapolsky

Barry Sapolsky is an associate professor of communication and director of the Communication Research Center at Florida State University, Tallahassee.

A 1985 survey by *USA Today* reveals that X-rated movie houses are closing down at the rate of fifteen a month. Simultaneously, hard-core videocassette sales increased from $220 million in 1983 to nearly $400 million in 1985.

The Parents Music Resource Center, concerned about pornographic and sexually explicit rock music, calls for record companies to put a rating system in place so parents can protect younger children from mature themes.

Playboy magazine's monthly circulation declines to 3.4 million readers, down from an all-time high of 7.2 million in 1972.

An alliance of feminists and religious fundamentalists prompts Indianapolis, Los Angeles, Minneapolis, and the state of Maine to consider antipornography measures. Some of the proposed ordinances would allow women to sue porn purveyors for sex discrimination.

A Christian publishing house in Waco, Texas, announces plans to distribute the report of the Meese commission on pornography, including hundreds of pages of excerpts from highly explicit sexual materials, to Christian bookstores to alert communities to the graphic nature of widely available pornography.

In response to the Meese commission, 10,000 convenience stores throughout the United States discontinue sales of *Playboy, Penthouse,* and other adult magazines.

One of the most controversial, emotion-laden issues in mass media is that of pornography.[1] The debate over pornography's antisocial effects has been reignited during the year-long study by the Attorney General's Commission on Pornography.[2] Actually, renewed attention to the social impact of pornographic materials can be traced to three developments beginning in the 1970s. First, the nature of hard-core pornography has evolved from nonviolent depictions of intercourse and oral sex prevalent in the 1960s to the violent and degrading images of sexual conduct found in the 1970s and 1980s. Included in the current wave of pornography are portrayals of rape, sadomasochism, and other acts generally demeaning to women. It is the coercive, antifemale tone in recent pornography that is most disturbing to feminists, social scientists, and lawmakers.

What is the reason for this change in pornographic content? One explanation is that habitual users of pornography become immune to the shocking and disturbing qualities of available films and photographs. Satiation with milder forms of pornography leads these individuals to seek out newer, stronger materials. The pornography industry, aware of the potential for dulling the consumer's arousal and emotional responses, serves up ever more novel sexual behaviors. This tendency may explain in part the abundance of violent pornography prevalent today.

The fusion of sex and violence has permeated more widely available and tamer entertainment media as well. The depiction of sexual violence directed at women is a prominent theme in R-rated "slasher" films, such as *I Spit on Your Grave, Prom Night,* and *When a Stranger Calls.* MTV (Music Television), which reaches more than 28 million cable subscribers, frequently plays music videos featuring violence with sexual overtones. The incidence of sexually violent pictorials in *Playboy* and *Penthouse* has been shown to be on the increase since the 1970s.[3] Photographs suggesting themes of bondage and sadomasochism have even been found in popular women's fashion magazines.

A second development in the pornography controversy is the role new technologies have played in making sexually explicit materials more accessible. So-called home porn has been made possible through the tremendous growth in cable television. Specialized pay cable services such as the "Playboy Channel," "American Extasy," and "Bravo" offer an array of explicit movies. Even mainstream services such as Cinemax and Showtime run adult sex films late at night.

Another technology allowing greater access to pornography is the videocassette recorder (VCR). With the advent of home video, pornographic films are no longer the exclusive domain of adult movie theaters. Middle-class Americans can now buy or rent X-rated materials from video stores. Video retailers report that adult videocassettes represent from 15 to 25 percent of their total sales.[4]

The new technologies allow today's consumers previously unheard of ease in gaining access to pornography. Most recently, the telephone ("Dial-a-Porn") and the computer have been added to the available channels for disseminating explicit sexual words and images. The new communication technologies (in the case of Dial-a-Porn, a new use for an old technology) have fostered increasing privatization of pornography consumption. More will be said later about the efforts to control these new technologies.

Finally, renewed interest in pornography has been stirred by widely divergent groups—feminists, religious fundamentalists, and political conservatives—that have joined forces in an effort to eradicate violent pornography.

Susan Brownmiller, an outspoken critic of pornography, labels it "antifemale propaganda" intended to ridicule and humiliate women so that acts of aggression against them are viewed less seriously.[5] Right-wing religious fundamentalists (Moral Majority, National Federation for Decency, and Morality in Media, among others) seek nothing less than the elimination of pornography. Less extreme groups such as the National Coalition on Television Violence and the Parents Music Resource Center have called attention to the explicit, violent sexual words and images in rock lyrics and music videos. The efforts of the antipornography forces may be paying off: a 1985 Gallup poll revealed that two-thirds of Americans support a ban on magazines, movies, and videocassettes featuring sexual violence.

In this reading, I review the evidence amassed by social scientists on the antisocial effects of pornography. Two government-sponsored commissions, charged with the task of assessing the impact of pornography on society, frame the examination of the research literature.

President Lyndon Johnson appointed the Commission on Obscenity and Pornography in 1968 to study, among other things, "the effect of obscenity and pornography upon the public, and particularly minors, and its relationship to crime and other antisocial behavior."[6] In order to determine the effects of sexually explicit materials, the commission funded experiments, surveys, and studies of rates of sex crime offenses. In September 1970, the commission issued its report containing the controversial conclusion: there is "no evidence to date that exposure to explicit sexual materials plays a significant role in the causation of delinquent or criminal behavior among youths or adults. The commission cannot conclude that exposure to erotic materials is a factor in the causation of sex crime or sex delinquency."[7]

The controversial no harm conclusion of the commission was subsequently strongly criticized. A majority of the commission members were said to hold liberal, anticensorship attitudes. The liberal bias of the panelists and their staff was believed to influence the commission's recommendations. Furthermore, a number of research studies on which the commission based its conclusions suffered from serious limitations. A minority report critical of the commission's findings charged that "the scanty and manipulated evidence . . . is wholly inadequate to support the conclusions and sustain the recommendations."[8] One commissioner, Victor Cline, called the Effects Panel report "seriously flawed, and omitting some critical data on negative effects."[9] The commission report has been criticized as well for its failure to consider the consequences of exposure to violent pornography. It must be remembered, however, that pornography in the 1960s contained less sexual violence than do materials available today. Accordingly, commission-sponsored research on the harmful effects of pornography included little aggressive activity found in today's explicit magazines and movies.

The Report of the Commission on Obscenity and Pornography, along with the recommendation that antipornography laws be relaxed or repealed, was rejected by President Richard Nixon. However, the controversy and shortcomings of the commission report inspired a new round of research on the effects of pornography. Much of the research in the 1970s employed laboratory experiments aimed at developing and testing theories to explain the varied human response to sexual stimuli. In particular, a great many studies focused on the effects of exposure to pornography on aggressive behavior.

In the decade following release of the commission report, researchers explored the pornography-aggression connection. Their investigations were aimed at determining if a person would behave more aggressively toward others after reading or watching sexual materials. The bulk of this research employed nonviolent images of nudity, intercourse, and oral sex. The *Playboy* nude was a popular form of erotica used in the experimentation.

The methodology employed in nearly all of the pornography-aggression research consisted of three phases: provocation, exposure, and retaliation. To begin, the male subject (nearly all of the research in this area has been confined to males) was brought into the laboratory and led to believe that the experiment involved a relatively innocuous topic such as "physiological aspects of learning." Another male, actually a confederate posing as a subject, was also present to participate in the experiment. Within the context of the study, the confederate would provoke the subject. Provocation was typically accomplished by the confederate's delivering mild electric shocks or prepared insults to the subject. The provocation was necessary to create a reason or motivation for the subject to behave aggressively toward the confederate when an opportunity to retaliate was later presented.

Next, the angry subject was exposed to the experimental stimuli—still photographs, slides, or motion pictures containing various sexual postures and acts. A control condition might be included in which subjects viewed nonerotic neutral stimuli. Some investigators would also monitor the subject's physiological response, such as heart rate and blood pressure, during the viewing period. These measures documented the subject's arousal from watching the sexual materials.

Finally, immediately after the exposure phase, subjects were given an opportunity to retaliate against the confederate-annoyer. The retaliation might take the form of electric shocks or some other injurious behavior. The subject was led to believe that the confederate would be on the receiving end of these actions; of course, he was not. In this way, the researcher could measure males' motivated aggression following exposure to pornography.

What do these experiments reveal about the effect of pornography on aggression? One group of studies demonstrated an aggression-enhancing effect; angered subjects exposed to pornography later behaved more aggressively toward their annoyer than did control subjects. A second group established an aggression-reducing effect. What could explain these contradictory findings?

A closer look at the pornography used in these investigations offers a possible explanation. Aggression increased after exposure to highly arousing, explicit films. In contrast, aggression was lower after subjects viewed mildly arousing, less explicit still photographs. Apparently, the more arousing was the sexual imagery, the more likely aggression would be increased. This is due to a phenomenon referred to as *excitation transfer*.[10] For instance, after jogging or riding a bicycle, an individual's heart continued to beat more rapidly than normal for a considerable period of time. During this "recovery" period, residues of excitation or arousal can energize feelings or behaviors. Thus, in the experimental setting, lingering arousal intensifies an angry subject's level of retaliation. The more exciting the pornography, the more arousal is available to boost aggression. *Playboy* nudes and other minimally arousing sexual materials do not excite the individual enough to heighten aggressive behavior.

Why would milder forms of pornography actually reduce aggressive behavior? Here the effect may result from the positive feelings experienced by the viewer of trivially arousing, pleasant sexual images. The provoked individual finds it difficult to maintain feelings of anger when immersed in the pleasing experience of viewing beautiful nudes. The incompatibility of these emotions leads to comparatively less aggressive behavior when the subject is given an opportunity to get back at his annoyer.

When the research on nonviolent pornography and aggression between males is reexamined, we find that two factors explain much of the results: arousal and affective response (whether the viewer responds positively or negatively to the sexual images). The Arousal-Affect Model predicts the impact of exposure to nonviolent sexual materials on aggressive behavior.[11] If a pornographic movie creates both high arousal and a strong negative reaction (feelings compatible with anger), it will increase the degree of retaliation. If still photographs of sexual activity do not arouse the viewer but do foster positive emotions, anger and subsequent efforts to retaliate will be reduced. In sum, under carefully specified conditions, pornography can either promote or reduce antisocial behavior. Arousal and affective response, central to the direction of pornography's impact, will be influenced by a variety of factors, including

the specific type of sexual activity displayed,

the mode of presentation (slides, film, or some other form),

the degree of explicitness of the sexual materials,

the sexual socialization of the viewer,

the sexual experience of the viewer,

the viewer's prior experience with pornography,

the gender of the viewer, and

other personality characteristics of the viewer (such as level of sex guilt, or authoritarianism).

Thus far we have considered the effect of nonviolent pornography on a particular form of antisocial behavior: intermale aggression. We now turn our attention to the kinds of pornography featuring rape, sadomasochism, and other portrayals of coercive sex. In addition, we will look at recent studies of male aggression toward females following exposure to sexually violent materials.

There are a number of reasons for concern about sexually violent pornography. First, violent pornography often makes it appear that women enjoy being overpowered by men and ultimately derive pleasure from physical abuse and rape. The male consumer of this kind of pornography may be led to believe that force is an acceptable means to obtain sexual gratification. The lesson from violent pornography is that women really "want it," even if they initially resist a man's advances. Second, when a male is repeatedly sexually aroused by violent pornography, a subtle form of conditioning can take place. The male gradually finds fantasies, words, and images involving rape and other violent sexual acts arousing. He may then be more likely to seek out sexually violent materials and be less bothered by the degrading treatment of women found in much of today's pornography.

To a large degree, what we know about how violent pornography affects attitudes and beliefs is the result of research by Neil Malamuth.[12] He and his colleagues have shown that exposure to violent pornography can change men's perceptions of rape and rape victims. After viewing pornography in which the female victim responds positively to being raped, males are more likely to be accepting of rape myths and interpersonal violence against women. A measure called the likelihood of rape was created by asking men how likely they would be to rape a woman if they were assured of not being caught and punished. After exposure to violent pornography, men having a stronger likelihood of rape are more likely to believe women enjoy being raped.[13] Malamuth concludes that "mass media can contribute to a cultural climate that is more accepting of aggression toward women."[14] In particular, men who show an inclination to behave aggressively toward women may be most influenced by images of sexual violence in the media.

The impact of violent pornography on aggressive behavior toward women has been a major focus of research in the 1980s. Edward Donnerstein is widely recognized as an authority on this subject. His experiments (using essentially the same methodology described earlier) have shown that men who view violent pornography (such as rape) are subsequently more aggressive toward women than men who view nonviolent pornography (such as consenting intercourse).[15] This is the case whether the depiction of rape culminates in the woman's responding with disgust or with pleasure.[16] Why would violent pornography stimulate aggression toward women? One reason is that it works to reduce normal inhibitions against such actions, particularly when the female victim responds with pleasure. Seeing coercive, harmful acts against females coupled with their favorable responses tells men that it is okay to hurt women. In addition, the fact that a woman is both the victim of violence in pornography and the potential target of a man's aggressive inclinations (in real life) sets up a kind of association that can help to promote acts of sexual violence.

What is the critical component in violent pornography that affects both male aggression toward females and, in a larger sense, attitudes toward women and rape? Donnerstein has suggested that it is the aggressive component and not the sexual component that is essential. He has demonstrated that both nonpornographic and pornographic violence increases male aggression toward women, males' acceptance of rape myths, and males' willingness to rape. This is not the case for pornographic films devoid of any violence.[17] Taken together, this research leads to the conclusion that "there is a direct causal relationship between exposure to aggressive pornography and violence against women . . . and little evidence that nonviolent pornography has any negative effects."[18]

The great wealth of research on pornography effects generated by the mid-1980s in turn has helped to focus the nation's attention on a perceived social ill. Prompted by pressure from special interest groups and the mounting evidence on pornography's antisocial effects, the Attorney General's Commission on Pornography was established in February 1985. In a brief period of time, the commission's methods, conclusions, and recommendations have stirred up a national debate on the impact of pornography on American society.

The commission set about the task of studying the relationship between exposure to pornographic materials and antisocial behavior. The presidential commission sixteen years earlier was given a budget of $2 million and two years to complete its work. The new commission received only $500,000 and one year to produce a report. An important outcome of these limitations was that the commission could not sponsor any new, independent research. Instead, it relied on testimony from public hearings in six major cities and a review of past social and behavioral science research. The commission's conclusions regarding the question of whether pornography is harmful draw heavily upon the social science analysis I have previously summarized. The key findings of the commission include the following:

Sexually violent material: "Substantial exposure to sexually violent materials . . . bears a causal relationship to antisocial acts of sexual violence and, for some subgroups, possibly to unlawful acts of sexual violence. . . . The evidence is also strongly supportive of significant attitudinal changes on the part of those with substantial exposure to violent pornography" (pp. 326–327).

Degrading nonviolent pornography (degrading pornography includes portrayals of the nonviolent domination and humiliation of women): "Substantial exposure to materials of this type bears some causal relationship to the level of sexual violence, sexual coercion, or unwanted sexual aggression in the population so exposed." Moreover, "material of this variety is likely to increase the extent to which those exposed will view rape or other forms of sexual violence as less serious than they otherwise would have" (pp. 332–334).

Nonviolent nondegrading materials (for example, those featuring consenting partners): "There is no persuasive evidence to date supporting the connection between nonviolent and non-degrading materials and acts of sexual violence" (p. 337).

Based on its rejection of previous claims of the harmlessness of pornography, the commission put forth ninety-two recommendations. In the light of the commission's emphasis on the matter of law enforcement, these recommendations are directed at policymakers and law enforcement agencies at the federal, state, and local levels. A number of recommendations relate to the mass media and related communication technologies. Among these recommendations are the following:

1. Congress should amend Title 18 of the U.S. Code to specifically proscribe cable television programming.
2. Congress should enact legislation to prohibit the transmission of obscene material through the telephone or similar common carrier.
3. U.S. attorneys and state and local prosecutors should use all available statutes to prosecute obscenity law violations involving cable and satellite television.
4. The Federal Communication Commission should use its full regulatory powers and impose appropriate sanctions against providers of obscene dial-a-porn telephone services and cable and satellite programmers who transmit obscene programs.

Numerous other recommendations address the matters of child pornography, adults-only pornography outlets, and enforcement of obscenity laws in general. In regard to the last issue, the question of what constitutes obscenity is a complicated one beyond my scope here. Regardless of how it is defined, attempts to regulate obscenity immediately create fear that the First Amendment protection of free speech will be abridged in some way. In the view of the commission, enforcement of existing obscenity laws has been too lax in recent decades. Therefore the commission's recommendations are aimed at giving obscenity violations a higher priority at all levels of law enforcement.

Much like the 1970 presidential commission, the attorney general's commission has provoked substantial criticism and controversy. The eleven-member panel was said to contain too many individuals holding antipornography biases. Its chairman, Henry E. Hudson, has previously served as a county prosecutor who distinguished himself through shutting down adult bookstores and arresting dealers of pornography. Critics contend that the commission was too conservative and too heavily weighted toward law enforcement. Interestingly, the presidential commission formed in the late 1960s was condemned for the opposite reasons: being too liberal and too anticensorship. Obviously prevailing political ideologies can play an important part in the composition of government-appointed commissions.

The American Civil Liberties Union and others claimed that the commission was determined from the outset to find a link between pornography and sexual offenses, censor sexually explicit materials, and curb the distribution of popular magazines, books, and films. According to the ACLU, the commission's procedures were "so intellectually indefensible that they taint the integrity and credibility of any final recommendations."[19] Numerous researchers and even two of the commissioners (Judith Becker and Ellen Levine) charged that the commission too eagerly drew the conclusion that pornography can lead to violence. Such a conclusion, they said, could not be defended from available social science research.

One of the commission's most controversial actions was to release a letter to many major U.S. corporations (including publishers, cable operators, and convenience and drug store chains) informing them that "the commission received testimony alleging that your company is involved in the sale or distribution of pornography." Booksellers, magazine publishers, and others accused the commission of attempting to create a blacklist. Although the commission later withdrew the letter and its plan to publish the names of identified distributors in the final report, the damage was done. Soon after, thousands of 7-Eleven stores announced they would no longer sell *Penthouse*, *Playboy*, and *Forum* magazines.

It remains to be seen whether the commission's findings and recommendations will significantly affect the distribution of pornography in the United States. Clearly, though, opponents of obscenity now have the prestige and force of a federal commission on their side. Lawmakers and the courts will ultimately decide if sexually explicit material is to be censored. Even before release of the commission report, legislative efforts were underway to control the flow of pornography. In 1985, Senator Jesse Helms introduced the cable porn and dial-a-porn control bill. The proposal was also aimed at future technological developments involving radio and television such as satellite transmission. Because cable television is a subscription service carried into the home over privately owned wires, it has received First Amendment protections afforded to the print media. Thus, like books, magazines, and newspapers, cable has been restricted only by the obscenity guidelines in the landmark 1973 Supreme Court ruling, *Miller v. California.* Now Helms would like the same obscenity statutes and content restrictions governing radio and television, which broadcast over the public airwaves, to apply to cable television. His bill would outlaw the transmission of "obscene, indecent or profane" material via cable television. Both the FCC and the ACLU have objected to the Helms bill on constitutional grounds.

Since 1984, California, Utah, Maine, and Florida have introduced legislation to curb the distribution of pornography over cable, telephone, and even the computer. Although these bills have not been passed into law or have been struck down by the courts, the message is clear: states and municipalities will continue to push for stronger controls on the obscene content of communications. Urged on by prodecency groups and the conclusions of a federal commission, state and local leaders may yet succeed in limiting obscene words and images in the mass media. Protectors of the First Amendment fear that what we are seeing is a rebirth of censorship in the United States. How far we go in the direction of censorship will ultimately be decided by the courts, which bear the responsibility of upholding First Amendment rights of free speech.

Notes

1. Throughout this reading, the term *pornography* is used to refer to sexually explicit materials. The term is used in a descriptive and not a pejorative sense.
2. Report of the Attorney General's Commission on Pornography (Washington, D.C.: U.S. Government Printing Office, 1986).
3. Neil Malamuth and Barry Spinner, "A Longitudinal Content Analysis of Sexual Violence in the Best-Selling Erotic Magazines," *Journal of Sex Research* 16, no. 3 (1980): 226–237.
4. Tom McNichol, "Smutbusters Take Aim at Video," *Channels* (September–October 1985): 59.
5. Susan Brownmiller, *Against Our Will: Men, Women, and Rape* (New York: Bantam Books, 1975).
6. Report of the Presidential Commission on Obscenity and Pornography (Washington, D.C.: U.S. Government Printing House, 1970), p. 1.
7. Ibid., p. 27.
8. Ibid., p. 385.
9. Ibid., p. 390.
10. Dolf Zillmann, "Excitation Transfer in Communication-Mediated Aggressive Behavior," *Journal of Experimental Social Psychology* 7 (1971): 419–434.
11. Barry Sapolsky, "Arousal, Affect, and the Aggression-Moderating Effect of Erotica," in Neil Malamuth and Edward Donnerstein, eds., *Pornography and Sexual Aggression* (Orlando, Fla.: Academic Press, 1984), pp. 85–113.
12. Neil Malamuth, "Aggression against Women: Cultural and Individual

Causes," in Malamuth and Donnerstein, *Pornography and Sexual Aggression,* pp. 19–52.

13. Neil Malamuth and J. Check, "The Effects of Exposure to Aggressive Pornography: Rape Proclivity, Sexual Arousal and Beliefs in Rape Myths" (paper presented at the eighty-ninth Annual Meeting of the American Psychological Association, Los Angeles, 1981).

14. Malamuth, "Aggression," p. 40.

15. Edward Donnerstein, "Aggressive Erotica and Violence against Women." *Journal of Personality and Social Psychology* 39 (1980): 269–277.

16. Edward Donnerstein and Leonard Berkowitz, "Victim Reactions in Aggressive Erotic Films as a Factor in Violence against Women," *Journal of Personality and Social Psychology* 41 (1981): 710–724.

17. Edward Donnerstein, "Pornography: Its Effect on Violence against Women," in Malamuth and Donnerstein, *Pornography and Sexual Aggression,* pp. 53–81.

18. Ibid., pp. 78–79.

19. "Draft Pornography Report Puts Cable in'Bad Light," *Cablevision,* February 24, 1986, p. 11.

SEXUAL VIOLENCE IN THE MEDIA: A WARNING

Edward Donnerstein and Daniel Linz

Edward Donnerstein is a psychologist in the Center for Communication Research of the Communication Arts Department, University of Wisconsin. Daniel Linz is in the Psychology Department, University of Wisconsin.

Reprinted with permission from *Psychology Today* magazine. Copyright © 1984 American Psychological Association.

The President's Commission on Obscenity and Pornography concluded in 1970 that there was no relationship between exposure to erotic material and subsequent antisocial behavior. Many liberals and people opposed to censorship of any kind applauded this finding, but some social scientists were more cautious and warned that pornography, might heighten the chances that some viewers would behave in bizarre or antisocial ways. In the light of the increasingly violent nature of pornography and the results of ongoing research that focuses on the fusion of sex and violence, those warnings probably should be taken seriously.

Researchers have shown, for example, that exposure to even a few minutes of sexually violent pornography, such as scenes of rape and other forms of sexual violence against women, can lead to antisocial attitudes and behavior. It can increase the viewer's acceptance of rape myths (for example, that women want to be raped), increase the willingness of a man to say that he would commit a rape, increase aggressive behavior against women in a laboratory setting, and decrease one's sensitivity to rape and the plight of the rape victim. If a brief exposure to sexually violent pornography can have these effects, what are the effects of exposure to hours of such material?

As depictions of sex and violence become more numerous and increasingly graphic, especially in feature-length movies shown in theaters, officials at the National Institute of Mental Health are becoming concerned and note:

"Films had to be made more and more powerful in their arousal effects. Initially strong excitatory reactions [may grow] weak or vanish entirely with repeated exposure to stimuli of a certain kind. This is known as habituation. The possibility of habituation to sex and violence has significant social consequences. . . . If people become inured to violence from seeing much of it, they may be less likely to respond to real violence."

This loss of sensitivity to real violence after repeated exposure to films with sex and violence, or "the dilemma of the detached bystander in the presence of violence" (a topic to which social scientists should be directing more of their efforts, according to the surgeon general, C. Everett Koop), is the major focus of our research program at the University of Wisconsin in Madison. We and our colleague, Stephen Penrod, are investigating how massive exposure to commercially released sexually violent films influences viewer perceptions of violence, judgments about rape and rape victims, and general physiological desensitization to violence and aggressive behavior.

Unlike previous studies in which subjects may have seen only ten to thirty minutes of material, the current studies eventually will examine up to twenty-five hours of exposure and allow us to monitor the process of desensitization in subjects over a long period of time. We will examine not only aggressive behavior but perceptual and judgmental changes regarding violence, and we will look for ways of mitigating potential negative aftereffects of exposure to mass-media violence.

We already have conducted a study to monitor desensitization of males to filmed violence against women and to determine whether this desensitization "spilled over" into other decision making about victims. Male subjects watched nearly ten hours (five commercially released feature-length films, one a day for five days) of R-rated or X-rated movies. They saw either R-rated, sexually violent films such as *Tool Box Murders, Vice Squad, I Spit on Your Grave,* and *Texas Chainsaw Massacre*; X-rated movies that depicted sexual assault; or X-rated movies that showed only consenting sex. The R-rated films were much more explicit with regard to violence than they were with regard to sexual content. After each movie, the men completed a mood questionnaire and evaluated the films in several ways. The films were shown in reverse order to different groups of men so that comparisons could be made of the same films being shown on the first and last day of viewing.

After the week of viewing, the men watched yet another film. This time, however, they saw a reenactment of an actual rape trial. After the trial, they were asked to render judgments about how responsible the victim was for her rape and how much injury she had suffered.

Most interesting were the results from the men who had watched the R-rated films such as *Texas Chainsaw Massacre* or *Maniac*. After the first day of viewing, the men rated themselves as significantly above the norm for depression, anxiety, and annoyance. On each subsequent day of viewing, these scores dropped until, on the fourth day of viewing, their reported levels were back to normal. What had happened to the viewers as they watched more and more violence?

We argue that they were becoming desensitized to violence, particularly against women. But this entailed more than a simple lowering of arousal to the movie violence. The men began to actually perceive the films differently as time went on. On Day 1, for example, on the average, the men estimated that they had seen four "offensive scenes." By the fifth day, they reported only half as many offensive scenes (even though exactly the same movies, but in reverse order, had been shown). Likewise, their ratings of the violence within the films receded from Day 1 to Day 5. By the last day, the men rated the movies as less graphic and less gory and estimated a fewer number of violent scenes than on the first day of viewing. Most startling, by the last day of viewing graphic violence against women, the men were rating the material as significantly less debasing and degrading to women, more humorous and more enjoyable, and they claimed a greater willingness to see this type of film again. This change in perception due to repeated exposure was particularly evident in comparisons of reactions to two films, *I Spit on Your Grave* and *Vice Squad*. Both films contain sexual assault; however, rape is portrayed in a more graphic and detailed manner in *I Spit on Your Grave* and a more ambiguous manner in *Vice Squad*. For men who had been exposed first to *Vice Squad* and then to *I Spit on Your Grave*, the ratings of sexual violence were nearly identical. However, subjects who had seen the more graphic movie first saw much less sexual violence (rape) in the more ambiguous film.

The effects of desensitization were also evident in the subjects' reactions to the reenacted rape trial. The victim of rape was rated as significantly more worthless and her injury as significantly less severe by those men who had been exposed to filmed violence than by a control group who saw only the rape trial and did not view any of our films.

Where does the research go from here? We will continue to investigate desensitization effects in reported mood and anxiety ratings, as well as physiologically. Massive exposure to films portraying violence against women will be used to study aggression against women (in a laboratory setting). And we will look into the effects of movies that do not explicitly portray violence against women but that perpetuate ideas about women as sexual objects (the new wave of teenage sex films such as *Porky's* and *My Tutor*).

Finally, we are searching for ways to counter the negative effects we have been finding. The subjects in all of our studies receive extensive debriefing after seeing the film. These debriefings take the form of sessions with the experimenters and videotaped presentations that dispel certain myths about rape and attempt to "resensitize" subjects to the issue of violence, particularly violence against women. We have found that these debriefings produce a marked decrease in acceptance of rape myths and violence against women. We are also investigating the effects these debriefings have when presented to subjects prior to viewing the films. If this proves to be effective, it might eventually be advisable to package sexually violent films with a warning that would help counter the negative effects of exposure to mass-media sexual violence.

MEDIA VIOLENCE AND AUDIENCE BEHAVIOR

Kenneth W. Hirsch

Kenneth William Hirsch served as research consultant for the California Commission on Crime Control and Violence Prevention, with special responsibility for the analysis of media violence. He has conducted research on children's perceptions of television and film violence in the United States and Sweden. He is professor of communication studies at California State University, Sacramento.

A Norwegian Controversy

In the spring of 1977, Norwegians were concerned about whether to reduce violence on television. The controversy centered on whether to continue showing a popular program. Some thought the program was too likely to nudge edgy, angry people among the viewing audience into actual fights. Others disagreed; they thought the evidence that the program might have harmful effects on its audience was too indirect and uncertain. Some thought that the program would, in fact, have a beneficial effect.

In Norway, television consisted of the programs available from a single channel. Thus, Norwegian viewers were restricted to the material provided by that one network. The network set aside a night for comedy programs, another for variety programs, another for dramas, and another for serious news analysis. The most popular television viewing night was Friday night—mystery night.

The series that caused the controversy was produced in the United States. It was "Ellery Queen," one of the least violent action-adventure program series ever produced by the U.S. television industry. The formula for the "Ellery Queen" series ensured that even the most squeamish among American viewers could watch the programs without being upset by depictions of gory violence. In each hour-long program, the emphasis was on logic, usually expressed in dialogue by the main character, Ellery Queen, as he helped his father and other police officers solve a baffling murder.

Almost always, viewers were made aware of the murder indirectly by overhearing an argument off-screen, often followed by the sound of a shot or a blow, perhaps accompanied by grunts and cries. This would be followed by a statement from a character, on-screen, that so-and-so had been shot with a bullet from a Bombay dueling pistol or such-and-such had been bludgeoned with the green marble giraffe. But we never saw the violence.

The 1977 Norway "Ellery Queen" controversy tells us that it is possible for citizens of another nation, whose standard of living, educational, and technological levels are similar to our own, to hold a very different view of the place to be occupied in their everyday life by media violence. What we accept in the United States as normal in the media may be considered abnormal by non-Americans who are otherwise rather like ourselves.

Unresolved Issues

Norway's concern over "Ellery Queen" seems far removed from the long-running argument about media violence in the United States, where television is likely to serve a diet of terrorist murders on the news, fictional crime-doesn't-pay programs such as "Miami Vice" and "The Equalizer," and "good-ole'-boy" movies such as *Texas Chain Saw Massacre*. Yet the main issue of the argument is the same: whether media violence should be restricted. It remains a difficult issue, for many people feel that violent programs are often entertaining. The scientific evidence that media violence does harm seems remote; moreover, there is a plausible catharsis argument to buttress continuation of particularly violent programs. And federal government intervention could stifle freedom of the press. But many others are concerned that children, particularly, are vulnerable to brutalization from media violence, yet they must be taught to cope with real life, some of which may involve encounters with violence. Another concern is that perhaps too much emphasis is put on being tough and ready to fight, not a good lesson in a world where nuclear confrontation is a possibility.

The real difference between the Norway of 1977 and the United States of today has to do with that part of the two nations' cultures that provides media experience. Norway's was an experience of relative innocence, with little depiction of gory violence. Thus it was possible for Norwegians to be concerned over what would not faze many Americans. In the United States, movies and television have given an experience of ever more bloody, ever more destructive, ever greater amounts of violence. During 1957, when over thirty hours per week of original dramas written and produced for U.S. television broadcast were cancelled in favor of Hollywood-crafted continuing character series, the amount of violence in television prime-time entertainment escalated greatly.

A team of University of Pennsylvania researchers led by George Gerbner has made detailed yearly counts of violence in U.S. television (Gerbner et al. 1976, 1980). Their "violence profile" and other measurements indicate that since 1967, the first year of their examinations, the levels of violence in television have remained high, with no more than slight, temporary drops. Furthermore, the level of violence in children's programs is consistently about 50 percent higher than in adult programs and appears to be increasing.

Now, as more recent movies are run on network television and with the constraint of potential denial of license renewal by the Federal Communications Commission (FCC) removed, the amount and bloodiness of television violence is unrestrained. Furthermore, videotape rentals of action-adventure movies, which tend to be more violent than their television program counterparts, are displacing an increasing amount of television viewing.

Thus, we should expect people born and raised during the television era to have a much higher level of experience with depictions of violence than those born and raised in any previous historical era. How high? Let us construct a typical American college student, using conservative numbers. We will name her Jane Strongheart and discuss her reactions to media violence.

Jane Strongheart. Born in 1965 and now completing her last year of a degree in nursing and soon to enter the work force, Jane Strongheart has been watching television regularly since the age of two. At that time, her mother, a part-time university student, found TV viewing one of the better ways to keep Jane occupied while she studied and prepared meals. Jane watched from two to five hours of television per day, often while playing in other ways. She shared with other small children a belief that there were small, real people inside the television set who were talking directly to her, and so she often talked to them. Although she could understand what she was watching, she could not follow the more complex, scene-to-scene story lines. Because she was too young to make sense of story connections, Jane learned two lessons from watching the typical Westerns and action-adventure programs in which the story followed a pattern:

1. Bad guy uses a gun to rob people.
2. Good guy chases, fights, and defeats bad guy.
3. Good guy uses gun to compel bad guy to go to jail.
4. Jail and prison will (presumably) punish bad guy.

Lesson 1 is that the use of violence, and especially the use of a gun, to get something is effective. (The bad guy got the money.) Lesson 2 is that the threat of violence by means of a powerful weapon is an effective way to compel others to do your bidding. (The good guy compelled the bad guy to surrender and go to jail.)

By the time she was in preschool, Jane was selecting her own TV programs. When she entered the first grade, she had already spent more time watching television than she would later spend attending classes for her nursing degree. At age eight, in the third grade, her viewing patterns were indistinguishable from those of her parents who, like most other adults, spend about 40 percent of their leisure time watching television (now including video recordings). This became a regular pattern; from age two through high school graduation, Jane has spent more time watching television than attending classes.

In her teens, Jane dropped off a bit on television viewing but made up for it with movie going. She went to movies with girlfriends and on boy-girl dates. She and her friends especially liked to laugh at monster movies and scream at slasher movies.

Although she had never seen anyone killed and had only witnessed one real fight between adults, in which her uncle Joe had been punched on the shoulder and neck by an angry client (Joe sold used cars), by the time she entered college she had witnessed over 18,000 killings in fictional movies and television programs and one real killing in a news program story of a shoot-out between police and terrorists where the camera caught the moment in which a man was hit and killed by a bullet.

Jane is typical of many young adults today. Living in a large city while studying nursing, she feels particularly vulnerable to attack while outside the apartment she shares with fellow students. Thus, she has purchased a Saturday night special cheap revolver and keeps it in her purse on nights when she studies late at the library, must work a hospital graveyard shift, or has evening classes. It is Jane's perception of the danger of her urban world that distinguishes her and many like her from others who watch little television containing violence. The perception of increased danger and the need to purchase guns for home and personal protection is a factor contributing to the high level of murders per capita in the United States, where guns are so easily available. Far more guns in homes end up being used in deaths arising out of disputes among family and friends than ever are used to frighten off burglars, would-be rapists, and street muggers.

Also indicative of the relationship between high consumption of television and film violence and increased belief in danger are several research studies indicating that those who tend to watch the most TV and the most violent television (younger adults and teenagers), who come from less affluent backgrounds, and tend to rely more on television for their news and less on newspapers also consistently overestimate the likelihood that someone like themselves will be murdered, raped, or otherwise assaulted. The danger of these distorted perceptions to society is that trust and willingness to help strangers decline while the probability of becoming innocent victims of trigger-happy, honest but scared, overreacting, others increases.

The Growth of Media Violence

There has been a huge increase of violence in twentieth-century media. Perhaps literature has always been bloody, but even the fastest and most dedicated reader cannot make it through a printed description of more than a few murders a day by reading Shakespeare, Mickey Spillane, and Norman Mailer. In contrast, the viewing of four hours of prime-time TV or a couple of rental videotape movies can easily present several times as many deaths, maimings, rapes, and beatings as could be encountered in the same amount of time spent reading periodicals and books. The amount of violence is not the only factor of importance in the impact of television and movies. These moving-image media, with their close depictions of what we can see and hear, are much more engaging of our sensory attention than is the reading of abstract symbols on paper, which must be translated and reconstructed into an approximation of sensory experience.

We must examine whether the large volume and sensory increase of media violence, especially movies and television, has caused people to do more violence than they otherwise might have done.

Social Effects of Media Violence

Prosocial Effects

Media violence does have prosocial effects—that is, outcomes of benefit to society. The primary prosocial effect is entertainment. U.S. action-adventure television programs and movies are in demand throughout the world.

A second prosocial effect is informational. Television and film documentary and news presentations present information on the actualities of violence in the world. The degree to which people obtain their perceptions of the presence of violence in their communities was made clear to me by research my colleague John Hwang and I conducted in 1974 to determine how much problems commonly dealt with in the news are actually present in the lives of Sacramento residents. We were able to determine that, apart from what they learned from the media, Sacramento residents' collective experience of danger from violence and violent crime was one of the least prevalent problems in their lives.

A third prosocial effect of media violence, especially that contained in police action-adventure programs and movies, is asserted to be moral teaching. This assertion is strongly supported by the writers, producers, directors, advertising agencies, and sponsors of such programs, the banks involved as financial partners in violent movie ventures, law enforcement officers, and many other ordinary people who sincerely believe that the media can teach strong moral lessons. They assert that violence used by persons legitimized by society to catch and punish crooks and to fight for morally admirable causes helps teach viewers the lesson that crime does not pay.

The available research, however, calls into question the consistency of this asserted prosocial effect. Although humans have used violence in cautionary tales to teach the lessons of morality in almost every culture and historical era, the teaching has usually been closely tied to the tale. Active discussion of the moral points seems to be necessary for the lesson to take. Thus, adults and children who watch the large number of cautionary violence television programs alone may in fact be failing to make the desired moral connection. They may instead be learning the lesson of instrumentality, the lesson of violence used as an instrument to get something of value or to compel others to do one's bidding.

The presence of prosocial effects is undeniable. Few people who enjoy television and movies containing violence feel that they are endangered by it and appear willing to take any risks. But it would be incorrect to conclude that violence needs to be present in entertainment in order to be of interest to people. The television and film industry has used violent action as a reliable means of attracting a certain level of viewer interest in otherwise repetitive stories. Violent action is regularly added to scripts to make them more attractive. Nevertheless, some research on college students indicates that the violence itself is not what viewers are interested in so much as the quality of action and story associated with the violence.

One of the reasons media management include violence is the high cost of producing scripts that are strong enough to stand on their own without the addition of violence. Moreover, there are only a limited number of writers whose skill is great enough to provide consistently attractive nonviolent stories. Station and network program decision makers generally take what they consider to be the safe path of plenty of action to ensure that their programs will attract the teen-age and young adult audiences greatly desired by advertisers of consumer products.

Antisocial Effects

If the prosocial effects of media violence were all there was to be concerned about, we should have no controversy on media violence. There are also antisocial effects, defined as outcomes of television violence that cause harm to society.

Antisocial effects are harmful to viewers and to those with whom viewers interact. Thus, antisocial effects of media violence have been found to include the production of nightmares and anxiety among young Swedish children, confusion of reality with fantasy among U.S. and Swedish children, and fear increases during time of war among Israeli children. The antisocial effects on which we will focus are those having to do with the reproduction and tolerance of violence by audience members of movie and television presentations containing violence.

Arousal and Justified Violence. Strongly felt feelings, such as anger, fear, and excitement, present physiological indications of their presence. Sweating, breathing fast, fast pulse, elevated blood pressure, eye pupil dilation, higher voice pitch, and tightened muscles are physiological indicators of arousal. Fear, excitement, and anger are specific types of arousal. They serve to ready the body for action—perhaps fighting or running away—in response to danger.

There is a type of controlled experiment in which participants, usually young men, are aroused to anger or humiliation by another person, given an experience whose influence is of interest, and then given an opportunity to act violently against the person who angered or humiliated them. Experiments by Leonard Berkowitz of the University of Wisconsin used this basic design. Berkowitz and his associates explored the role of arousal as a facilitator of violent acts by viewers of film and television violence.

In one of their experiments (Berkowitz and Powers 1979), a group of previously aroused participants were led to believe the person getting a vicious beating in a film scene was a bad person for whom the beating was justified. Another group of participants saw the same scene, but it was explained as depicting a nice guy who was being wrongly punished. The participants who saw the justified violence did far more violence to the people who had angered them than the participants who saw the unjustified violence. Thus, portrayals of justified violence, such as occurs when police fight crooks, are actually more potent elicitors of violent acts by viewers than portrayals of unjustified violence, such as occurs when vicious crooks mug the elderly.

The explanation appears to be that when viewers of TV violence later find themselves in high-stress situations where violence would seem to offer a quick and easy solution, the normal inhibitions that work to prevent the commission of violence may be undermined by the TV violence. The viewer who sees socially sanctioned, justified violence releases inhibitions against acting violently, inhibitions that would otherwise prevent violence and lead him or her to undertake the difficult and time-consuming path of negotiation, cooperation, and compromise.

Percy Tannenbaum and Dolph Zillman (1975) of the University of California at Berkeley demonstrated that nonspecific nature of arousal in a dramatic way. After arousing college males by showing them sexy pictures, they found that whether the men subsequently tried to accomplish sexual or violent behavior depended on the cues presented to them. In other words, a person might be aroused by something sexual, watch a murder on television, and become violent instead of erotic. Thus, there is a potential link between sex and subsequent violence that may be activated by violence cues.

Social Learning and Modeling Violence. In the early 1960s, Albert Bandura began experiments at Stanford University with preschool children. A great deal of evidence indicates that children learn about how to deal with others (social learning) primarily from observation of their parents and other people important to them. They model their behavior on the behavior of persons who are central in their lives. During early childhood, boys are particularly urged by their parents to be tough, competitive, assertive, and independent; girls are encouraged to be more demure, accepting, and concerned with love and nurturing. Children who act in accepted ways are rewarded with affection and praise. Thus, modeling is reinforced.

Bandura and his associates investigated many aspects of modeling. They found that preschool children will model the display of violence by an adult. In one experiment, preschoolers were divided into four groups. One group saw an adult beat a human sized inflated "Bobo Doll." Another group saw the same activity on a film presentation. A third group also saw a film presentation, but the adult was dressed and made up as a cartoon cat character. The fourth group saw no demonstration of beating the doll.

After the show, the children were allowed to play in a room in which were various toys, including a Bobo Doll. Children from the three groups that saw the doll beaten by an adult also beat the doll themselves when they had the opportunity. The fourth, control, group of children were much less inclined to beat the doll. Thus, the depiction of violence on film was as potent for social learning as a live model.

Social learning explains a great deal of television's influence on children and adults. For example, considerable prestige and approval may be transferred to violence when a television drama is shown whose hero uses violence to save a lovely, honest, deserving woman. It explains how long-term build-ups of violent behavior among viewers may occur as a consequence of seeing violence succeed repeatedly. Carrying the concept a bit further indicates how persons may learn cool violence, such as that carried out by hired assassins. The explanation is that repeated use of violence and the threat of violence that are reinforced by success and approval of others may lead to violence being used unemotionally as a tool to obtain desired goals.

Tolerance of Violence Used by Others. A vicious effect of media violence leads to the tolerance of violence by others and the acceptance of it as a simple, fast way to solve otherwise complex and difficult social problems. Ronald Drabman and Margaret Thomas (1974) have conducted several laboratory experiments demonstrating that children who watch violent films are more likely not to intervene when others are fighting. They randomly assigned school-age children to two groups, one of which watched benign films and the other of which watched violence typically seen in prime-time television programs. The children in both groups were made to understand that other, younger children were playing in an adjacent room, that no adult was present, and that they were to keep track of those younger children. After starting the film and leaving the room, Drabman and Thomas turned on a tape recorder in the adjacent room, where the little children were supposed to be playing.

Soon, sounds were heard coming from that room indicating that the little children were fighting and that some were being hurt. The outcome was that the older children who watched the film violence were much less likely to intervene by going into the next room to calm down the little children than were the older children who watched the benign films. This work, which has been replicated under a variety of conditions, demonstrates the existence of a desensitizing effect in which the consumption of media violence leads to tolerance of violence done by others. Whether this effect extends in time is unclear. If it does, adults who watch a great deal of stories in which police use justified violence against bad guys would tend toward an increased tolerance of war to solve difficult social problems and to maintain self-respect. And desensitization to the use of violence by others can manifest itself as tolerance of the violent persecution of others and lead to the tragedy of genocide.

Long-term Effects

The research described tends to examine what happens to viewers and their contacts within a short time of being exposed to television and movie violence. Most of the controlled experiments measure the violence done by viewers within minutes following their having viewed the violent material. But television and movie violence are not viewed in that manner. They are viewed repeatedly, over a period of years. Whatever effects they may cause need not be caused suddenly. In the same way, we should expect their effects to persist.

Although the vast majority of research studies on television and film violence are short term, four long-term studies exist.

Aletha Huston-Stein and Lynette Friedrich ran a controlled field experiment with preschool children who attended a special summer school session nine weeks long. During that time, the children, divided into three groups, saw daily sets of TV programs for two weeks. The aggressive group saw Batman and Superman cartoons. The neutral group saw ordinary children's films. The prosocial group saw "Mister Rogers' Neighborhood." The children were observed systematically every day so that changes in their behavior, obvious and subtle, could be noticed. The outcome was that the aggressive cartoons caused the boys who started out pushier and more aggressive than the other boys to become much more so than their peers. Children who watched the neutral programs and especially those who saw the prosocial programs, boys and girls alike, became gradually more cooperative and self-controlled, as one would expect they should from experience in a preschool. Apparently the more benign television and film material facilitated the social learning they were engaged in at the preschool.

In the longest-running study of all, Leonard Eron and Ronald Huesmann and their associates (1972) began studying over 300 eight-year-old boys. The boys were rated as to their tendency to be violent by their teachers and peers. They were then followed up for ten years, to age eighteen. The boys who were a bit more violent at the start were no more likely to increase their viewing of television violence by age eighteen. The boys who, though no more violent than the average, started out with a greater than normal consumption of violent television by age eighteen exhibited a level of behavioral violence above that of their peers. This cross-lagged correlation finding, though not as strong an indicator of causality as a controlled experiment would be, presents the longest-term set of evidence that violent television can influence real-life behavior in an antisocial manner.

An older group of 1,500 boys, ages twelve through seventeen, was studied systematically during a six-month period in London by William Belson (1978). Those who watched a larger amount of television violence became more violent during the six months; those who were initially more violent did not necessarily watch more violent TV as time went on. In other words, as with the younger boys studied by the Eron and Huesmann research team, it was more the case of television violence leading to human violence than human violence leading to a preference for violent television.

Tannis MacBeth Williams (1986) of the University of British Columbia has just published the long-awaited results of a remarkable research project. Her research team found an isolated community in northern Canada before it got television and studied it, along with similar comparison communities, during the two-year period in which television first came into the homes of its residents. Among the many findings is that since the advent of television, boys and girls have become more violent than had boys and girls at similar ages before the advent of television. This controlled field experiment presents the most valid, naturalistic, and solidly based evidence of media violence causation of audience antisocial effects that it is possible to acquire in the present stage of communication research.

Together, these long-term research studies confirm what the wealth of short-term studies have been telling us for many years: media violence is harmful to viewers.

Surgeon General's Report

The Surgeon General's Scientific Advisory Committee report on television and social behavior was presented in 1972. Between the 1972 report and the 1982 follow-up report, the news media generally misinformed the public about its conclusion. The well-respected television critic of the *New York Times* saw an early copy of the summary report and misinterpreted the main finding, which was written cautiously and obscurely, in scientific jargon. The critic reported the outcome as meaning TV violence could harm children who were predisposed to do violence because of some abnormal adjustment, implying that the vast majority of children were safe from any harmful influence. Although the Congressional Subcommittee on Communications held immediate hearings to clarify the findings, these were too late. The story was picked up and distributed and seems to have been influential.

Media Opposition

Each of the three networks has done its own research. In nearly all instances, the work has been methodologically shoddy and biased. Although the surgeon general's report stated that television and film violence does contribute to the causation of violence among viewers, the three networks continued to oppose any restraints on their freedom. They have succeeded. Since the election of President Reagan, the Congress has relieved the FCC of its responsibilities to hold broadcasters to criteria designed to ensure compliance with the "public convenience, interest and necessity" requirement of the Communication Act of 1934 and its successors, which is supposed to govern broadcasting.

Catharsis

Although catharsis has been considered a viable theory of violence, it has been strongly discredited by the scientific research. Yet many people believe in catharsis, as do the vast majority of working television and filmmakers. *Catharsis* was the term Aristotle gave to the process in which Greek theater goers would become involved in a tragedy and then feel drained of emotion on leaving the theater. The notion was extended to claim that watching television and movie violence would actually drain viewers of their "need" to do violence.

Only one research study has found evidence that catharsis exists, a study in 1961, which used weak measures. Subsequently its inadequacies were well documented in the scientific literature. Dozens of other research studies have tried and failed to repeat those findings and find any other evidence of catharsis. But catharsis continues to stay alive, possibly because it seems such a good rationalization and surely because it is in widespread use as a theory underlying the clinical treatment of many people undergoing mental therapy and counseling.

Possibilities for Change

It seems likely that we should not expect any relief from television violence in the near future unless a political coalition of people concerned about violent pornography becomes powerful and spills over into the regulation of television broadcasting. If, as a result, interest and concern are generated about violence in TV broadcasting, perhaps restrictions similar to those present in Sweden will begin. In Sweden, violence in television program broadcasts is restricted, and a rating system similar to that in use in American movie theaters is enforced. Instead of restricting children from attending movies containing sexually explicit scenes, however, they are restricted from attending particularly violent movies.

There is another possibility, suggested by FCC commissioner Nicholas Johnson at the Congressional Subcommittee hearings on the surgeon general's report in 1972. Johnson suggested that victims of violence sue the stations and networks that put out media violence for harm done, much as victims sue manufacturers whose products fail and cause them harm. This suggestion, along with others for forcing media violence producers to pay for part of the hospitalization costs of violence victims and requiring them to demonstrate that their programs do not harm viewers before being allowed to put them on the air (much as the drug industry must demonstrate that new drugs are not harmful before being allowed to sell them), were proposed to the California Commission on Crime Control and Violence Prevention in 1981. So far, the commission has not proposed action based on the suggestions.

In the absence of any restrictions on media violence, the best protection against its antisocial effects is knowledge that viewers are susceptible. That knowledge can strengthen our resolve to avoid the easy, violent solution to difficult and complex social problems.

References

Attorney General's Commission on Pornography. 1986. *Final Report.* 2 vols. Washington, D.C.: U.S. Department of Justice.

Bandura, Albert. 1978. "Social Learning Theory of Aggression." *Journal of Communication* 28:12–29.

Bandura, Albert, Dorothea Ross, and Sheila Ross. 1961. "Transmission of Aggression through Imitation of Aggressive Models." *Journal of Abnormal and Social Psychology* 63:575–582.

———. 1963. "Vicarious Reinforcement and Imitative Learning." *Journal of Abnormal and Social Psychology* 67:601–607.

Belson, William A. 1978. *Television Violence and the Adolescent Boy.* Lexington, Mass.: Lexington Books.

Berkowitz, Leonard. 1962. *Aggression: A Social Psychological Analysis.* New York: McGraw-Hill.

———. 1965. "Some Aspects of Observed Aggression." *Journal of Personality and Social Psychology* 2:359–369.

———. 1973. "Studies of the Contagion of Violence." In Herbert Hirsch and David C. Perry, eds., *Violence as Politics: A Series of Original Essays*, pp. 41–51. New York: Harper and Row.

Berkowitz, Leonard, and E. Rawlings. 1963. "Effects of Film Violence on Inhibitions against Subsequent Aggression." *Journal of Abnormal and Social Psychology* 66:405–512.

Berkowitz, Leonard, and Patrick Powers. 1979. "Effects of Timing and Justification of Witnessed Aggression on the Observers' Punitiveness." *Journal of Research in Personality* 13:71–80.

Drabman, Ronald S. and Margaret H. Thomas. 1974. "Exposure to Filmed Violence and Children's Tolerance of Real Life Aggression." *Personality and Social Psychology Bulletin* 1:198–199.

Eron, L. D., L. R. Huesmann, M. M. Leftkowitz, and L. O. Walder. 1972. "Does Television Violence Cause Aggression?" *American Psychologist* 27:253–263.

Gerbner, George, and Larry Gross. 1976. "Living with Television: The Violence Profile." *Journal of Communication* 26:172–199.

Gerbner, George, Larry Gross, Michelle Morgan, and Nancy Signorelli. 1980. "The 'Mainstreaming' of America: Violence Profile No. 11." *Journal of Communication* 30:10–29.

Leftkowitz, Monroe M., Leonard D. Eron, L. O. Walder, and L. R. Huesmann. 1972. "Television Violence and Child Aggression: A Follow-up Study." In *Surgeon General's Report,* 3:35–135.

Pearl, David, and Update Project Staff. 1982. *Television and Behavior: Ten Years of Scientific Progress and Implications for the Eighties.* Vol. 1: *Summary Report.* Washington, D.C.: National Institutes of Mental Health.

Stein, Aletha Huston, and Lynnette K. Friedrich. 1972. "Television Content and Young Children's Behavior." In *Surgeon General's Report,* 2:202–317.

Surgeon General of the United States Scientific Advisory Committee. 1972. *Surgeon General's Report: Television and Social Behavior.* 5 vols.

Tannenbaum, Percy H., and Dolph Zillman. 1975. "Emotional Arousal in the Facilitation of Aggression through Communication." In L. Berkowitz, *Advances in Experimental Social Psychology.*

U.S. Congress. Senate Committee on Commerce. 1972. *Hearings before the Subcommittee on Communications regarding the Surgeon General's Report.* 92d Cong., 2d sess., March 21–24.

Williams, Tannis MacBeth, ed. 1986. *The Impact of Television: A Natural Experiment in Three Communities.* San Diego: Academic Press.

11
Women and Minorities

Introduction

The relation of mass media to sexism and racism in American society is a complex issue. It can be approached by asking, first, how the media cover different racial and ethnic minorities and the sexes, and, second, how these groups should be treated if the media are to help build a less discriminatory society. Media coverage involves quantitative and qualitative aspects. How much time is given to the various groups, and what type of coverage are they given? A related question is whether the media employ and promote women and minorities on the same basis as white males.

Much research has been done on the treatment of women and blacks on television. Charlotte O'Kelly and Linda Bloomquist[1] did a content analysis of network programming and found both groups stereotyped and underrepresented.[2] More exposure therefore would not necessarily change people's attitudes on racism and sexism.

Dorothy Gilliam, writing about black journalists, claims that the black community and black journalists are "excluded, mishandled, and exploited by the media."[3] Black journalists are generally unwanted by newspaper management, frustrated (even at the *Washington Post*), and distrusted by other blacks. Newspapers should "make hiring and promotion of blacks a top-priority objective" and give them sufficient autonomy to cover the black community realistically. More recently, Michael Massing has shown that despite gains in employment by blacks, power in television news is still a white monopoly.[4] Meanwhile, the alternative news provided by the black press struggles to survive.[5]

When the media attempt to reduce racism, their attempt can backfire. "All in the Family," the highly popular TV program, was supposed to reduce racism, and it won an NAACP award for its contribution to race relations. But research on the effects of Archie Bunker's bigotry suggests a negative outcome: lovable Archie wins supporters and reinforces the racism of the bigots in his audience.[6]

Dan Georgakas has shown that native Americans are also given sorry treatment in film. Georgakas is not concerned with the old TV rerun movies in which the Indians were blatantly the bad guys but with the modern genre, the supposedly authentic Indian movies: *A Man Called Horse, Soldier Blue, Little Big Man,* and *Tell Them Willie Boy Is Here.* He finds that authentic headdresses, dwellings, and artifacts provide an incongruous background for plots that distort the Indian life-style and preserve "the standard myth that the white man can do everything better than the Indian."[7]

On sexism in the media, Helen Franzwa has analyzed women's magazine fiction and concludes that despite an increase of women in the work force, they are usually portrayed as docile homebodies, housewives, and mothers.[8] Alternatively they play negative sex roles, their lives centered around the absence of men; they are presented as sad or comic husband-seeking singles, widows, and divorcees or as aging spinsters. Women are seldom portrayed as individuals with independent lives and careers. Above all, perhaps, the media treat women as sex objects, typified by the illustrations, if not always the text, of *Playboy.*

Much attention has been given to the gains of women in the newsroom. Terri Schultz-Brooks, for example, finds that newspapers have been reluctant to promote women, and gains have come at great cost.[9] Women have experienced similar problems in television news, particularly at the network level.[10]

Muriel Cantor has claimed that although the treatment of women in public broadcasting is better than on commercial television, there is much room for improvement.[11] This holds true for programs aimed at adults and even in an area where public television is often thought to be uniquely enlightened, children's programming. The Task Force on Women in Public Broadcasting, in which Cantor was an active member, also found evidence of discriminatory employment practices in public broadcasting.[12] Cantor concludes that women are still seen as a special interest group rather than an integral part of the population involved in all social and political issues.

Bruce Johansen, in the first reading, gives an overview of the issue of race and ethnicity in the media. He begins by explaining the concept of stereotyping. We should be concerned with these "mental images that demean and degrade" people. One set of stereotypes has long been cultured by the media, "Cowboys and Indians," which seriously distort Indian history and character. The Frito Bandito similarly distorts our picture of Mexican-Americans. Johansen then looks at minority employment in the media and finds blacks, Asians, Native Americans, and Hispanics still underrepresented. Recent attempts to hire and train minorities need to be continued. He concludes by describing the numerous forms of minority media.

Jannette Dates next examines how African-American women are portrayed on television. Are they also stereotyped? In prime-time programming in the 1980s, she finds less stereotyping than in the earlier years of television. In the 1950s, African-Americans either portrayed images that whites believed, or like Pearl Bailey were nonthreatening. Cicely Tyson played a much more authentic role in the 1963–1964 season, and others were to follow. The all-black programs of the 1970s, while a breakthrough, still displayed stereotypes. "Roots," however, was not only hugely successful, it gave an admirable view of black history and the struggle for survival. "Fame" and "The Cosby Show" exhibit strong characters, but "Gimme a Break" shows a dismal return to earlier stereotypes.

Do black (and other) journalists have a responsibility to promote black progress in society? Yes, says Trace Regan in the third reading. Making some attempt to show blacks in a favorable light—for example, getting a black expert witness—is perfectly legitimate. But the news should not be distorted, just colored accurately. Above all, this means abolishing harmful stereotypes of minorities.

How much do the media discriminate against women? Tina Pieraccini provides some answers in the next reading. Like the racial and ethnic minorities dealt with in this chapter, women's images have changed over time, but all too often they are still harmful. And they too are underrepresented. In TV entertainment, only a few recent shows like "Kate and Allie" and "The Golden Girls" have portrayed women favorably. Current signs, however, show a return to women as "invisible, irrelevant, or victimized." In television news, women have made gains in recent years, but they still often are assigned to women's stories and for on-camera jobs must be beautiful and young. Finally, studies of advertising indicate that it is the biggest offender in perpetuating sexism. Women in ads are still primarily shown as stupid consumers or sex objects.

Caryl Rivers, in the last reading, provides more detail on myths that the media spread about women. Many of these myths have been around for centuries but are still with us today, often in modernized form. The press has been promoting the idea that women are genetically different (usually inferior in some quality) from men, despite dubious scientific evidence. Many of the myths clearly serve to keep women "in their place."

Notes

1. Charlotte O'Kelly and Linda Bloomquist, "Women and Blacks on TV," *Journal of Communication* 26 (Autumn 1976).

2. This seems to be the case even in advertising. See J. David Colfax and Susan Frenkel Sternberg, "The Perpetuation of Racial Stereotypes: Blacks in Mass Circula-

tion Magazine Advertisements," *Public Opinion Quarterly* (Spring 1972): 8–18. See also James D. Culley and Rex Bennet, "Selling Women, Selling Blacks," *Journal of Communication* (Autumn 1976), and Judith Hennesse and Joan Nicholson, "NOW Says: TV Commercials Insult Women," *New York Times Magazine,* May 28, 1972. An *Ebony* editorial (May 1973) notes that although more blacks are on TV now than in the past, the content serves neither whites nor blacks. Readers were urged to complain to the FCC.

3. Dorothy Gilliam, "What do Black Journalists Want," *Columbia Journalism Review* (May–June 1972).

4. Michael Massing, "Blackout in Television," *Columbia Journalism Review* (November–December 1982): 38–44.

5. Phyl Garland, "The Black Press: Down But Not Out," *Columbia Journalism Review* (September–October 1982): 43–50.

6. Neil Vidmar and Milton Rokeach, "Archie Bunker's Bigotry," *Journal of Communication* 24 (Winter 1974). See also Stuart H. Surlin, "Five Years of 'All in the Family': A Summary of Empirical Research Generated by the Program," *Mass Comm Review* 3 (Summer 1976).

7. Dan Georgakas, "They Have Not Spoken: American Indians in Film," *Film Quarterly* 25 (Spring 1972).

8. Helen Franzwa, "Working Women in Fact and Fiction," *Journal of Communication* 24 (Spring 1974).

9. Terri Schultz-Brooks, "Getting There: Women in the Newsroom," *Columbia Journalism Review* (March–April 1984): 25–31.

10. See Joan Barthel, "Why There Are Still No Female Dan Rathers," *TV Guide,* August 6, 1983, pp. 4–10; and Judy Flander, "Women in Network News: Have They Arrived or Is Their Prime Time Past?" *Washington Journalism Review* (March 1985): 39–43.

11. Muriel Cantor, "Women and Public Broadcasting," *Journal of Communication* 27 (Winter 1977).

12. For a fuller account, see Caroline Isher and Muriel Cantor, *Report of the Task Force on Women in Public Broadcasting* (Washington, D.C.: Corporation for Public Broadcasting, 1975).

RACE, ETHNICITY, AND THE MEDIA

Bruce E. Johansen

Bruce Johansen holds a Ph.D. and B.A. from the University of Washington and an M.A. degree from the University of Minnesota. He is an associate professor of journalism at the University of Nebraska at Omaha. He has also served as associate editor of *La Voz*, a bilingual newsmagazine based in Seattle, and as education/program coordinator for the Concilio for the Spanish Speaking of Seattle. He has published four books, and has worked as a reporter for the *Seattle Times*.

What is a racial stereotype? Does society have an interest in understanding and trying to eliminate such mental images? How many blacks, Latinos, American Indians, and Asians are employed in the United States' "mainstream" broadcast and print media? Why are media professional organizations making a concerted effort to increase their numbers? These are the questions that this reading will discuss.

The Concept of Stereotyping

The concept of stereotyping as it is used today did not exist before World War I. And for nearly a half-century after that, it was used mainly in academic discourse. With the stirrings of the civil rights movement beginning in the 1950s and the social unrest of the 1960s, the term was propelled into popular usage.

The concept of stereotyping as a mental image was constructed by Walter Lippmann, the distinguished columnist, author, and diplomat. In his book *Public Opinion*, Lippmann wrote that people create stereotypes to help them deal with the "great, blooming, buzzing confusion" of everyday reality. (Lippmann 1922, p. 80). Since no single person can directly observe more than a tiny fraction of events in the world, we rely on the reports of others and then fit them into our own perceptual framework. Since we rely on the mass media to act as our eyes and ears for the larger reality we cannot directly observe, it is especially important for media professionals to understand the differences between stereotypes and reality.

Lippmann found psychological economy in stereotyping: "For the attempt to see all things freshly and in detail, rather than as types and generalities, is exhausting. . . . We notice a trait which marks a well-known type, and fill in the rest of the picture by means of the stereotypes we carry around in our heads." (Lippmann 1922, pp. 88, 89).

According to Lippmann, "A great deal of confusion arises when people decline to classify themselves as we have classified them" (Lippmann 1922, p. 151). Yet whenever social change takes place, stereotypes are challenged and altered. As recently as the 1950s, *Little Black Sambo* was an acceptable children's cartoon, Stepin Fetchit was a well-regarded black image in some circles, Tonto rode alongside the Lone Ranger, and the Frito Bandito, created to advertise corn chips, was filching snacks coast to coast. Stereotypes of slant-eyed Asians ran through popular literature during World War II. Each stereotype, in its turn, was challenged and found to be at odds with the broader, more complex reality.

It is in society's interests to challenge and eradicate erroneous racial stereotypes. The United States is a racially and culturally pluralistic country and one that is becoming more so every day. By the mid-1980s, between 20 and 25 percent of the nation's population was of non-European descent. It is clear that a racially and culturally pluralistic society cannot function well if a large number of its citizens are unfairly restricted by mental images that demean and degrade them. In large measure, attitudes must change before actions, including attempts at remedying past injustice. Changes in stereotypes are basic to changes in attitudes, and the media, print and electronic, are powerful shapers of popular images and attitudes.

Media Stereotypes

Cowboys and Indians

As a result of the spread of United States media culture around the world, one can find children playing Cowboys and Indians in the streets of Manila, London, Johannesburg, and São Paulo. From the time that Lippmann invented the concept of stereotyping, Hollywood has been illustrating it with thousands of films that stereotype American Indians.

According to Phil Lucas, a Choctaw filmmaker, the cowboy movie genre has also spawned "dime novels, poems, books, essays, journals, plays and, more recently, television [shows] and advertising that has erased the varied cultural and ethnic identities of over 400 distinct tribes and nations . . . and replaced them with a permanent fictional identity . . . the Hollywood Indian" (Lucas 1980, p. 69). He adds that "The movies have nurtured and consistently perpetuated the idea that Indians are quaint and strange but not quite human, portraying them as savages and renegades, killers of innocent pioneer women and children, and merciless scalpers" (p. 69).

Lucas dissected the movie image of the Indian as what he calls a "one-dimensional caricature" in his Public Broadcasting series "Images of Indians." Comedian Charlie Hill, an Oneida, reversed the stereotype when he looked at the propensity to use Indians as mascots for sports teams: "We're the Bucks, the Braves, the Washington Redskins, the Cleveland Indians. They wouldn't ever have the Washington Whiteboys, the Cleveland Caucasians, or the Negroes. Nobody would stand for it" (Lucas 1980, p. 70).

Some films traffic in historical inaccuracy as well. Lucas cites *Apache* (1949), in which Masai, an Apache played by Burt Lancaster, escapes a prison train headed for Florida. In his long trek home, Masai encounters an Indian farmer in Oklahoma who advises him to take up the hoe, saying that the white man has taught him to grow corn. In fact, it was the Native Americans who taught the immigrants from Europe how to grow corn, as well as a number of other crops indigenous to the New World. "Geronimo" (1962) was cast as blue-eyed Chuck Conners, who created a macho character completely at odds with the Apaches' matriarchial traditions.

In the 1970s, some attempts were made to create more realistic portrayals of Native Americans in commercial films, but many of these fell short. For example, *A Man Called Horse* (1970) attributed to the Lakota (Sioux) the practice of abandoning elders to die in the snow. Commented Lucas, "Nothing could be farther from the truth" (Lucas 1980, p. 75). *Little Big Man* (1970) cast its main character as a white, while in history he was a Lakota. In history, Little Big Man was no hero to the Indians. He was the man who held Crazy Horse down while soldiers of the U.S. Army stabbed him to death with bayonets.

Advertising: The Frito Bandito and Other Stereotypes

One of the Frito-Lay Corporation's most successful television pitchmen was a racial stereotype. In the late 1960s, the Frito Bandito rode into living rooms coast to coast, threatening to steal children's corn chips. Children lucky enough to eat their corn chips before the "Bandito" snatched them found "Mexican"-style mustaches sprouting from their upper lips. "He's cunning, clever—and sneaky!" the ads proclaimed.

The company said that the character was meant as a humorous attempt to "leave our trademark implanted on your memory" (Wilson and Gutiérrez 1985, p. 109), but many chicanos did not see it that way. They told the company that the Frito Bandito was a warmed-over stereotype of a Mexican bandit. By 1970, after a boycott was organized against the company and television stations airing the commercial, Frito-Lay cancelled what had been, for it, a very successful advertising campaign.

A decade later, Frito-Lay showed it had learned from its mistakes by advertising Tostito corn chips with a distinguished-looking (and sounding) Latino recalling his boyhood in Latin America by eating the company's chips. The new image was still a stereotype, not unlike that of the Latin lover popularized in many movies but a less offensive one than the Bandito. This time, the company also placed its advertising in media aimed at Latino communities, another change, in line with increased emphasis nationwide on ethnic and minority marketing.

"The portrayal of racial minorities . . . [has] been, to a large extent, supported by a system of advertising which requires the media to cater to the perceived attitudes and prejudices of the white majority and that also reinforces such images in its own commercial messages. . . . Over the years, advertisers have employed Latin spitfires such as Chiquita Banana, black mammies such as Aunt Jemima, and noble savages such as the Santa Fe Railroad's Super Chief to pitch their products to a predominantly white audience" (Wilson and Gutiérrez 1985, pp. 113–114). In the late 1960s and early 1970s, black, Latino, American Indian, and Asian civic organizations challenged one stereotypical advertising campaign after another, until agencies and companies got the message.

Advertising is, by definition, the business of creating images, including stereotypes, to sell products, tendency reinforced by the messages' brevity. After community pressure forced many advertising agencies to abandon stereotypes of domestic minorities for this purpose, many capitalized on the "new patriotism" of the 1980s to lampoon Russians and the Soviet Union. One beer commercial, for example, featured a smiling Russian saying he enjoyed his new home because "Here I can always find a party. In Russia, [the] party always finds you." Wendy's, the hamburger chain, contrasted its devotion to customer choice with an imagined Russian fashion show that showed a fat Slavic woman in what looked like a potato sack ("daywear"), the same sack with a beach ball ("swimwear"), and the same sack again, waving a flashlight ("evening wear"). These ads used the same elements that the Frito Bandito and other commercials had combined earlier when racial stereotypes were in fashion: humor, a simple pitch, and a stereotype reinforcing prevailing assumptions.

Stereotypes do not change easily. On the contrary, they must be challenged, not only by people who consume media but by those who create the images by which we define our assumptions. Increasing minority employment in all types of media is one way to do this.

Minority Employment in the Media

In 1955, *Ebony* reported that only thirty-one blacks worked on white-owned newspapers in the United States. So few blacks worked in broadcasting outlets that the magazine did not even bother to count them (Marzolf and Tolliver 1977, p. 18). Judged against such a beginning, impressive strides have been made in the last three decades. Nevertheless, minority employment, especially in newspapers, is nowhere near nonwhites' proportion of the general population, despite concerted efforts by journalism educators and professional organizations.

Broadcasting stations have made the most dramatic gains. In 1976, the Federal Communications Commission reported that at 665 commercial television stations in the United States, 14 percent of the employees were members of minority groups. One hundred fifty-eight noncommercial stations reported 13 percent minorities in their work force (Marzolf and Tolliver 1977, p. 25). By 1982, minority employment in television had risen to 17 percent in broadcasting stations and 14 percent in cable television (Wilson and Gutiérrez 1985, p. 159).

For newspapers, the record has been dismal. The American Society of Newspaper Editors (ASNE) has set a goal of reaching parity with the general population by the year 2000. In 1986, the ASNE said that 6.3 percent of daily newspaper employees were minorities, up from 5.76 percent in 1985, and 3.95 percent in 1978. This is a broad measure, including categories other than newsroom employees. In the newsrooms of the nation, the situation is even worse. According to the U.S. Bureau of Labor Statistics, in 1983 2.9 percent of newspaper editors and reporters in the United States were black and 2.1 percent Latino (Baum 1986, p. 4). Another study, released in 1986, showed that the minorities' share of newsroom employment was shrinking. This study reported that about 3 percent of U.S. journalists were black, down from 4 percent in 1971. Latino employment stood at 0.5 percent, down from 1 percent in 1971 (*Wall Street Journal* 1986, p. 1).

Defining Minorities

The statistics cited on minorities should not be taken too literally because there exist a number of definitional problems in accurately measuring minority employment in the media, or any other field. What makes a person a member of a minority group? The simplest answer would be, "He or she is nonwhite." But what about a child of a mixed marriage or the offspring of a marriage between two members of different minority groups? Should members of groups with high academic and professional achievement (such as Japanese and Chinese) be counted in programs meant to address problems of economic and social inequity? And what about impoverished whites? They are not minorities in a racial sense, but they are in an economic sense.

How much "minority" blood should a person have to fall within a given category? Each American Indian tribe or nation sets its own rules for membership on a tribal roll. Some tribes require a ¼ (25 percent) "blood quantum," while others enroll members with as little as ¹⁄₃₂ (3 percent) Indian blood. For purposes of the U.S. Census, anyone may classify him- or herself as he or she pleases. In some trades and professions with affirmative action programs, employees are allowed to change their ethnic or racial classification at least once a year.

Keeping in mind problems of definition in measurement, the 1980 U.S. Census reported that roughly 20 percent of the country's population was black, Latino, Asian, Native American, or of Pacific Island origin. Of 226 million total residents, the census counted 26.5 million blacks (11.7 percent), 14.6 million Latinos (6.5 percent), 3.5 million Asians and Pacific Islanders (1.5 percent), and 1.4 million Native Americans (0.6 percent).

The percentage of the population identified as minority is steadily increasing.

Put another way, between 1970 and 1980, blacks' proportion of the United States population increased 5.4 percent (0.6 divided into 11.1 percent). Latinos' proportion increased 42.2 percent. Asians and Pacific Islanders increased 87.5 percent, and Native Americans increased 50.0 percent. The increase in actual numbers was even greater, in line with the rise in the general population. The percentages cited here indicate only *proportional* increases.

Presenting the Minority Viewpoint

The census data tells a story of a nation that is rapidly becoming multicultural and multilingual and one where the mass media will have to include substantial numbers of minority employees if they are to report events in society with any degree of reality. When many cities exploded in violence during the 1960s, the news media were caught flat-footed.

The Kerner Commission sought to address the causes of the violence and suggested solutions. Among recommendations affecting the news media, the commission advised:

That the news media portray blacks as a matter of routine and in the context of the total society.

That editors and reporters recognize the significance of the urban story and develop resources to cover it, including assignment of reporters on regular beats.

That the mainstream press and black-owned press establish better lines of communication.

That the white-owned media reverse the "shockingly backward" efforts to recruit, hire, and promote black journalists and to get them into positions that not only report the news but define it as well.

Ten years after the Kerner Report, a conference met at the University of Michigan's Howard R. Marsh Center for the Study of Journalistic Performance to assess the record. The conference, titled "Kerner Plus 10," found some improvement but not nearly enough. Robert C. Maynard, an outstanding black journalist said this in his keynote address:

> Long before Kerner, Walter Lippmann said it was the responsibility of the daily newspaper to see to it that its readers were not surprised by events. Few newspaper readers could say that the urban events of the 1960s came as anything but a sudden and searing shock. We all remember the story told of James M. Roche, the head of General Motors, standing on the roof of the G.M. building above Detroit in summer, 1967, watching the flames in utter dismay that such savage forces were at work in his city. (Marzolf and Tolliver 1977, p. 2)

At another time, Maynard said:

> So we have a case of double-barreled misconceptions. The whites have no notion of what it is like to live in today's inner city because our newspapers do so little to bring that fact alive. On the other hand, the positive aspects of black American history and culture are obscured for much the same reasons—because in all too many instances there is no black in a position to help shape a product so that it reflects accurately all the disparate elements that make up our society. (Marzolf and Tolliver 1977, p. 3)

Why the Effort

In the nearly two decades since the Kerner Commission report, media educators and professional groups have expended considerable effort to train, recruit, and hire minorities. After all that effort, however, 86.7 percent of all United States newspapers in 1986 had no minorities in managerial positions (ASNE 1986, p. 12).

Minorities must be trained, recruited, and hired into the mass media. First, there is the matter of economic justice. Without social and economic mobility, the American dream becomes just another stereotype, a myth, in the eyes of large and growing segments of the U.S. population. Second, there is the matter of perceptual accuracy. The media need minority perspectives to present a full, accurate, and timely picture of national life.

Realizing this, many programs were established following the Kerner Report to train minority group members for media work. One of the best known was the Columbia Program for Minority Journalists, which trained more than 230 men and women before it lost its funding in 1974. In 1976, the program was revived at the University of California, Berkeley, as the Summer Program for Minority Journalists. The Dow Jones Newspaper Fund has trained more than 3,000 high school students at its summer Urban Journalism Workshops sponsored by journalism schools and newspapers across the country. The same fund also publishes *Minority Journalism Career Guide,* which provides information on scholarships, salaries, course of study, and other advice. And nine universities have banded together to recruit minorities for graduate study in journalism. Many individual journalism schools and departments also produce programs.

Minority journalists also have formed their own national organizations and scores of local groups. Membership in the National Association of Black Journalists topped 1,000 by 1985, and 1,100 people attended the 1986 convention of the National Association of Hispanic Journalists in Washington, D.C. The convention program listed 22 national, regional and local Hispanic media organizations. Asian Americans and Native Americans also now maintain national media organizations.

Minority Media

Publications and broadcasting media aimed at specific minority groups have increased in numbers and audience as well. The *Editor & Publisher Yearbook* (1984) lists 2 daily and 159 weekly newspapers aimed at black audiences, 5 dailies and 24 weeklies in Spanish, 10 dailies and 2 weeklies in Chinese, 6 dailies and 4 weeklies in Japanese, and 1 Filipino weekly. The lists published in *E & P* are not complete, since they fail to include many Native American papers published on reservations and small publications for other minority groups.

At least 275 radio stations in the United States broadcast black-oriented programming, and many of them draw substantial white audiences as well; 130 are broadcast in Spanish and 2 in Japanese. Four other stations aim at Native American audiences. These statistics are for full-time formats. Many other radio stations include specialized ethnic programming within formats geared for broader audiences (*Broadcasting/Cablecasting* 1983, p. F-55; Wilson and Gutiérrez 1985, p. 230).

Within the last few years, cable networks have been established for minority audiences, including Black Entertainment Television (BET) and the Spanish International Network (SIN).

Summary

The concept of stereotyping as a mental image was developed by Walter Lippmann shortly after World War I. With the civil rights movement, beginning in the 1950s, the concept was increasingly applied to mistaken notions based on race and ethnicity. Blacks, Latinos, Asians, and American Indian individuals and organizations have fought hard, with some success, to remove degrading stereotypes from print and broadcast media, both in news and advertising, as well as in motion pictures.

At the same time, minority groups have sought better representation in mainstream media. Although the number of minority editors, reporters, and broadcasters has increased dramatically since the 1950s, it still lags behind their proportion of the population. Many educational institutions and professional organizations have joined the effort to desegregate the mass media in the United States.

The United States is rapidly becoming a multilingual, multicultural nation, and increased minority employment in the media reflects this trend. At the same time, newspapers, magazines, and broadcasting aimed at minority audiences also have grown, continuing a long tradition of publishing service to individual communities.

References

American Society of Newspaper Editors. 1986. "1985–86 Committee Reports." Washington, D.C.: ASNE.

Baum, Mary. 1986. "We Define First, Then See." *University of Nebraska at Omaha Gateway,* April 11, p. 4.

Broadcasting/Cablecasting Yearbook. 1983. Washington, D.C.: Broadcasting Publications.

Editor & Publisher Yearbook. 1984. New York: Editor & Publisher.

Lippmann, Walter. 1922. *Public Opinion.* New York: Macmillan.

Lucas, Phil. 1980. "Images of Indians." *Four Winds* (Fall): 69–77.

Martínez, Tomás. 1969. "How Advertising Promotes Racism." *Civil Rights Digest* (Fall): 8–9.

Marzolf, Marion, and Melba Tolliver. 1977. *Kerner Plus 10: Minorities and the Media, a Conference Report.* Ann Arbor, Mich.: University of Michigan Department of Journalism.

U.S. Population Reports. 1970, 1980. U.S. Department of the Census.

Wall Street Journal. 1986. April 1, p. 1.

Wilson, Clint C. II, and Felix Gutiérrez. 1985. *Minorities and Media: Diversity and the End of Mass Communication.* Beverly Hills, Calif.: Sage.

GIMME A BREAK: AFRICAN-AMERICAN WOMEN ON PRIME-TIME TELEVISION

Jannette L. Dates

Jannette Dates is an associate professor at Coppin State College, Baltimore. She received her Ph.D. from the University of Maryland and is active in communications research. She has published articles in *Journal of Broadcasting* and *Journalism Quarterly* and is coauthor of *Split Image,* a book about African-Americans in mass media, to be published in 1987.

Since the 1950s when television emerged as the dominant medium for the entertainment of mass audiences, professional critics and average consumers alike have debated the accuracy and tone of African-American images on the small screen. Some argue that the few black images allowed airplay were severe distortions that comforted white viewers at the expense of black culture (Fife 1974). Some contend that television networks merely picked up the threads of an already established pattern, begun in minstrelsy and carried forward through the film and radio industries whole-cloth into television (Bogle 1973).

This reading examines and analyzes the black female presence on network television, concluding that the period of the 1980s was the watershed when the African-American woman was more consistently seen in nonstereotypic roles on television.

In early television, African-Americans were essentially excluded from drama because of racial quotas used by some producers, whereby only a prescribed number of black performers could appear on the screen at one time (MacDonald 1983). Some producers ignored African-Americans in drama in order to avoid disputes over racial quotas and sensitive story lines (Cripps 1975). Some scholars (Gitlin 1982) argue that early television generally ignored divisive social issues and featured people with happy problems. Within this context, shows with numerous black characters or themes about black people's concerns were not considered appropriate. As a result, African-American participation in dramatic television, occurring with any frequency on the networks, began only during the germination of the civil rights era. Then, some half-hour dramatic shows included African-Americans as guest performers, such as Diahann Carroll on the "Peter Gunn" series (1958–1961).

In early television, black women were represented in situation comedies by Ethel Waters, Louise Beavers, Ruby Dandridge, and Butterfly McQueen; they appeared at various times on "The Beulah Show" (1950–1953). The Beulah character originated as a supporting role on radio's "Fibber McGee and Molly Show" (Brooks and Marsh 1979). The series featured Beulah, a shiftless boyfriend, and her girlfriend juxtaposed to the white, middle-class family whose problems were the focus of Beulah's life. An example of the strength of Beulah's involvement with her white employers (the Hendersons) is demonstrated in the television show in which Beulah attempted to make the Hendersons' marriage stronger. She manipulated, fretted, and counseled because she sensed that the Hendersons were taking each other for granted, and she set out to revive their "failing" relationship. She talked about the Hendersons' problems with her girlfriend (Oriole) and her boyfriend (Bill). Her friends were as serious about helping Beulah with the problem as she was. The Aunt Jemima image that Bogle discussed in *Toms, Coons, Mulattoes, Mammies and Bucks* is strongly evident here. Unlike the mammy, who was domineering, strong-willed, and bossy, according to Bogle the Aunt Jemima was kind, generous, caring, and sincere (Bogle 1973). These qualities were typical of the performances of the maids on this show.

Beulah brought comfort to white television viewers, as other African-American women were to do throughout the following decades. Here was a black person who was not a threat: not sexy, not attractive in the European-oriented sense of American television, and who did not question the system that relegated her to the servant's position. She put her own life on hold as she fretted about the lives of the whites whom she so faithfully served. White viewers could not conceive of Beulah wanting to be anything but a maid or of her fighting for her children to have a life that was better than her own.

"The Amos 'n Andy Show" (1951–1954), another situation comedy, also featured black women: Ernestine Wade played Sapphire, Amanda Randolph played Sapphire's mother, and Lillian Randolph played Madame Queen. In the "Amos 'n Andy Show," the characters usually spoke in dialect, showed lack of control of events surrounding their lives, and demonstrated a general lack of knowledge and education. When a more educated person appeared in the program (Sapphire's sister, Hortense, in a 1951 program), the character was developed lacking common sense, odd, sexless, and unable to attract male companionship. The Sapphire character was developed as a shrew who manipulated and dominated her husband (Kingfish) and as one whose shrill voice made the males in her environment tense and apprehensive.

The black female presence was evident on network television in the early years in one other genre: variety shows. African-Americans had always been accepted as entertainers (comics, dancers, and singers) for white America. Television followed the pattern.

In many ways, singer Pearl Bailey typified African-American female participation in early network television variety programs. A look at *Jet* magazine listings for the decade reveals that Bailey appeared on network variety shows more than forty times. Bailey had numerous Broadway shows, a few Hollywood films, and many night club appearances to her credit when she began appearing on network television. She quickly became a favorite with variety show hosts such as Milton Berle and Ed Sullivan. Sassy, sarcastic, and witty, Bailey had a knack for pleasing viewers of both races with her unique showmanship. Her style was to talk and sing about men and the problems women had handling relationships. Her wry comments made men laugh at themselves and women laugh in recognition of evoked feelings. A warm, loving person, Bailey was no threat to white viewers, and she pleased black viewers as well. Although she had experienced race-related problems and solved them in public in some instances, Bailey brought no social issues to television viewers. Thus, in the 1950s viewers were entertained by African-American stars who they probably assumed were happy to appear so frequently on other people's shows.

During the 1960s, the networks continued their use of African-Americans as guests on variety shows as the dominant genre for black artistic exposure. There were gradual inroads into other categories, however. During the 1963–1964 season, for example, CBS aired a weekly drama, "Eastside/Westside," a series about a young social worker in the New York slums. Cicely Tyson, who portrayed the office secretary, was the first black woman on network television to play a dramatic leading role in a continuing series; she sported a short-cropped natural hair style, also a first for the networks. In this role, Tyson made a statement about her lack of interest in American conventions and her desire to demonstrate independence (Tyson 1973). Although most critics appreciated the realism of the series, viewers were uninterested in such topics as child abuse, welfare, problems of aging, drug addiction, and crime. Happy, easily solved problems were still dominant. Loyal viewers flocked to watch "The Lucy Show" and "The Adventures of Ozzie and Harriet." Airing the stark reality of "Eastside/Westside" was an exercise in futility. The critically acclaimed series lasted one season.

The action-adventure genre had few African-American women in evidence in the 1960s. "I Spy," starring Robert Culp and Bill Cosby, launched in 1965, offered viewers no black female star, but many women were romantically linked with or rescued by Cosby during the three years of the show's run in prime time. Nancy Wilson and Diana Sands were among that group. Later the situation comedy "The Bill Cosby Show" (1969–1971) featured talented black women, including Lillian Randolph, Beah Richards, and Olga James, who were regular members of the cast (Brooks and Marsh 1979).

The civil rights movement, coupled with other pressures, helped push the networks toward airing more series with black stars. "Julia," starring Diahann Carroll, premiered in 1968. In the series, Carroll played a widowed mother who was a nurse with a gruff but liberal boss. Carroll wore designer clothes and had few problems that were typical of African-American women. The show, criticized as too middle class in orientation, lasted three seasons.

The school drama "Room 222" (1969–1974) tackled current social issues and problems of relevance to young people, including racial prejudice, with careful, slick production techniques and believable story lines. It featured Denise Nicholas, who provided professionalism and romantic interludes with costar Lloyd Haynes, who played a black history teacher in an integrated high school. The program received numerous awards, critical acclaim, and good ratings.

In many ways, Lena Horne was typical of the African-American female presence on the networks during the 1960s. She was a frequent entertainer on other people's shows; she was treated with great respect, carried herself with dignity, and was a creative artist who fiercely controlled her performances according to her own interpretations. Black viewers were justifiably proud to see her on the occasional specials in which she starred. Horne came across as aloof, controlled, lady-like, and lovely. Viewers enjoyed her appearances because of the distance she put between herself and her audience; black viewers saw her as cool, just like middle-class white women, and whites found her protestant reserve and control appealing. However, when Horne sang songs such as "The Lady is a Tramp," she insinuated that viewers might not believe merely what they were allowed to see (Horne 1965).

The 1960s therefore allowed for a new kind of black presence on television. African-American men and women appeared in variety shows, a few specials, and a few dramatic series. They were gradually emerging from the entertainer genre as the only avenue for black talents. The few shows that had black stars, however, generally skirted around divisive social issues.

The conservative mood of the 1970s brought an end to the few thrusts toward social-issue-oriented drama. Thus, comedy and variety programming continued to offer the most opportunities for black women during this era.

In the 1972–1973 season, "The New Bill Cosby Show," a comedy-variety series, provided national exposure for a number of talented, creative black artists, including Moms Mabley, Lola Falana, and Roberta Flack, who were well known in black communities but relatively obscure in the larger arena.

"Sanford and Son" (1972–1977), "That's My Mama" (1974–1975), "Good Times" (1974–1979), "What's Happening?" (1976–1979), and "The Jeffersons" (1975–1985) were part of the crop of black situation comedies that emerged in the 1970s. Except for "The Jeffersons," they featured almost all-black casts and focused more realistically on problems faced by blacks instead of the middle-class-oriented fantasy worlds of shows like "Julia" and "I Spy." Nonetheless, the images presented were still often negative ones. The comedy "Sanford and Son" was a modern version of "Amos 'n' Andy," featuring outlandish (though often funny) plots and one-dimensional characters portrayed as lacking intelligence. In "That's My Mama," the character Mama was typical of black matriarchal roles, and the male lead was portrayed as shiftless and immoral. "Good Times," another situation comedy, also reinforced the myth of the black matriarch (Moore, 1980).

African-American television images of the 1970s were largely controlled by producers Norman Lear and Bud Yorkin. Many of the characters, though lacking in depth and dimensionality, rang true as authentic types within the black community and the rest of society. Additionally, Lear and Yorkin brought wrenching social issues into the heart of prime-time television. They sensed what the public would accept and what it wanted. They would accept these wrenching social issues but only within the context of quick, comforting laughter and easily obtained solutions. Michael Arlen (1976), media critic for the *New York Times*, argued that the dependence of these shows on gags, grimaces, and the steady presence of anger (with a barrage of insults and vituperation) often had only the sound track and vaudeville-type mugging to let viewers know that the show was supposed to be funny (Arlen 1976). No serious look at issues was permissible in these contexts. While white viewers could feel liberal because they watched black actors in network comedies, usually they were merely comforted by the images because the characters did not make them feel a need to face problems and take a stand on moral or ethical issues. As viewers perceived it, the problems raised in these comedies, except for "Good Times," were brought about because of the ineptness, corruptibility, or short-sightedness of the black characters and not because of social forces the viewers might perceive as being within their (the viewers') control.

During the last week in January 1977, ABC-TV telecasted one of the first made-for-television movie mini-series. "Roots I" and later "Roots II" (1977 and 1978) broke all previous records for high ratings and for national attention paid to the subject of African-Americans. Most critics agreed that the overall impact of the two series was beneficial to African-Americans; they projected sympathetic portrayals of positive protagonists with indomitable spirit in admirable struggles with the problems of life, where racism constrained most facets of their existence. But some critics argued that "Roots" on television failed to reflect how the use of Afro-Americans as human capital literally built America and how they received minimal rewards for their efforts (Staples 1977). Critics believed this major flaw reflected reality, particularly because African-Americans typically had negative self-perceptions and were usually unaware of the vast contributions blacks had made to the nation's successes.

"Roots" and "Roots: The Next Generation" provided numerous roles for black women. The impressive cast included Cicely Tyson, Maya Angelou,

Beverly Todd, Madge Sinclair, Leslie Uggams, Olivia Cole, Lillian Randolph, Lynn Moody, and Debbie Allen.

After the success of "Roots" and "Roots II," many believed that the brilliant talents of the participants from the two series would be in high demand. However, roles for African-Americans in drama on commercial television were almost as scarce after "Roots" as they had been before. Many began to believe that white America could not take a consistent, serious look at African-Americans, or allow black people to share their view of their culture and partially define their own image. As a result, success with a dramatic commercial television series featuring African-Americans continued to elude black creative talents. No long-lasting dramatic series focusing on black life in the United States was tried, except for "Harris and Company," which aired briefly in 1979, and "Palmerstown U.S.A.," which aired in 1980 (Watkins 1981). Neither series was allowed to build an audience, as other series had sometimes been allowed to do.

Isabel Sanford, Louise of "The Jeffersons," is a good example of the female African-American presence on television in the 1970s. She starred in a prime-time series, which in the original years made strong note of African-American heritage and focused on aspects of that culture. She experienced great success with her series. Though she was submissive to her husband, George, to a degree, she exercised great influence on him because no matter what the conflict in the series, George was never correct. Therefore Louise was the pivotal character around whom most conflicts were resolved.

Although blacks were still entertainers, playing in comedies, they were now the stars in the series. They could use their influence to help open doors for other blacks. By their presence in prime time and because of their use of black cultural elements that became part of American mainstream culture, they represented a new force in American mass media. In the 1970s, there was a change in typing for black shows and a minor step toward reality; basically, however, the majority group, whites, invented black minority television persona so that the majority could more easily cope with a group it did not care to learn about and understand. There was an African American female presence during this era, though it was usually one-dimensional. The majority culture had "The Mary Tyler Moore Show," "M*A*S*H," and "Lou Grant"; African-American women had to wait for another decade to have multidimensional stars.

The ensemble television series gained popularity in the late 1970s and 1980s. Series of this type featured a multiracial, multiethnic, male and female cast of characters who produced weekly drama, or comedy, or a mixture of both. To many viewers and critics of television, these ensemble groups represented a more realistic approach to a reflection of American culture than had previous series. One such show, "Fame," premiered as a television series in 1981 and lasted two seasons on NBC. Based on the successful 1980 movie of the same name, it probed the interactions of a cast, studying or teaching music, dance, theater, and academics at a high school whose prototype was the New York City School of Performing Arts. Critics and some loyal fans gave the series high marks. In Europe, the series was a phenomenal success because of its youthful exuberance, big city atmosphere, and inspirational dancing and music. There were strong roles for black women in the series during its first few years. Debbie Allen, the star (teacher), also choreographed the show's dances. It stayed on the air, despite mediocre ratings, until the end of the 1982–1983 season. Metromedia picked up its option and agreed to air the series, which survived for at least three more seasons in off-network programming.

In the fall of the 1984–1985 season, Bill Cosby's NBC entry, "The Cosby Show," featured Cosby as Cliff Huxtable, an obstetrician living with his wife and four children in a New York brownstone. Their fifth child, away at college most of the time, appeared sporadically in featured parts. The show put African-American images on the screen whom people could admire. Of the seven regular members of the cast, five were female. Phylicia Ayers-Allen (later Phylicia Rashad) played his wife, Clair, an attorney. Lisa Bonet, Keshia Knight Pulliam, and Tempsett Bledsoe played Denise, Rudy, and Vanessa, while Sabrina Le Beuf played Sondra.

With the paucity of black stars on prime-time network television in the early 1980s, it was coincidental that Cosby's return paralleled the return of Diahann Carroll to network television during the same season. They had broken television's color barrier nearly twenty years earlier with Cosby's "I Spy" and Carroll's "Julia." Carroll's feisty role in the nighttime serial "Dynasty," beginning with the 1984 season, became increasingly important in that series. Carroll seemed made for the part; she was glamorous, exquisitely groomed and coiffed, and unintimidated by the wealth or mean spirits of the white family she so recently joined.

In 1985–1986, "227," starring Marla Gibbs (formerly "The Jeffersons" maid, Florence), was among the most well-rounded shows on the air that focused on the black female presence. Gibbs played Mary, a tenant in an apartment house in an urban neighborhood, whose husband and children formed a background for many of the show's plots. Gibbs and her female neighbors interacted in story lines that followed themes of concern and interest to women in the 1980s. They faced problems similar to those faced by the general populace, blended smoothly with ones unique to black women. The writers attempted to maintain credibility as they showed how some women handle problems.

Debbie Allen and Phylicia Rashad, who are sisters, typified the black female presence on network television in the 1980s. Allen, an indefatigable actress-dancer, was well liked by many for her pithy, brief role in the movie

Fame. She had played roles on television in shows such as "Good Times" and in commercials; she also had appeared on Broadway and in road shows. Her versatility and skills were demonstrated again and again as she danced and sang in some television programs and played brilliant dramatic parts. When she burst into American homes in the key role as Lydia in the television series "Fame," audiences immediately responded to her strong-willed, no-nonsense but sensitive, caring character.

Rashad (formerly Ayers-Allen) had starred in off-Broadway productions and then landed roles in Broadway productions. She also performed in the long-running daytime television serial "One Life to Live." Tapped by Bill Cosby to play his wife in "The Cosby Show," Rashad brought to prime-time television viewers a woman who was beautiful, feminine, smart, strong, professionally competent, and self-confident.

Allen and Rashad were different in many respects from other African-American female stars in previous eras. The women before Allen and Rashad were nurturing care givers or supporters, making few demands. Although Rashad and Allen's characters were sympathetic and nurturing, they usually demonstrated a quiet, firm understanding of their own needs and desires and a willingness to make demands of others.

Nonetheless the nurturing, subservient care-giver roles African-American women have played through the decades have not disappeared. Many critics found the mammy-like image evoked by Nel Carter's character on "Gimme a Break," which premiered in 1981, a return to the proud but servile, cocky but nurturing, loyal mammies. On "Gimme a Break," Carter seemed cognizant of the parallels between her character and other demeaning roles black women had played when there were few options for them if they wanted to practice their craft. She parodied Butterfly McQueen's scene in the 1939 film classic *Gone With the Wind* in one episode and defended her mammy-like role to a visiting friend in another. Nonetheless, she continued in the role because it was a hit with crossover markets and because roles for African-American women, scarce in all forms of mass entertainment, were hard to find in network television in the early 1980s.

Many critics tried to be positive about the show, knowing that it was a small breakthrough for an African-American woman to land the lead role in a hit series. A number of factors, however, prevented reviewers from feeling comfortable with the series. First, the opening song laid bare the show's theme; its lyrics, sung by the star, were "Gimme a break. I sure could use it. I finally found where I belong!!" Some questioned whether this meant that African-American women belonged in someone else's home caring for white offspring and neglecting lives of their own.

Second, in the series, Carter played an ill-tempered mammy to the white children. Since she was so ill tempered and white viewers might have been offended by her physical abuse of the white youngsters on the show, the writers included the character Addie as a foil for Nel's temper. On numerous occasions, Nel insulted Addie, yelled at her, and slapped her around. Addie often ducked when no punch was thrown because she was so used to the abuse. Moreover, Nel demonstrated lack of respect for her African-American heritage. In one program, Nel went to court to beg the judge not to take "her babies"; she had promised their dead mother that she would raise them. The judge decided against the children's aunt and in Carter's favor when Nel fell to her knees, crying and beseeching the judge to let her keep "her" children. For a young, African-American woman to carry on in this manner, passionately seeking to continue in a servant's role, on network television in the 1980s was astounding. In another example of her insensitivity to her own history and culture, Nel noted in one episode that one of the characters had broken an irreplaceable knickknack that had been handed down to Nel by her grandmother, who had immigrated to this country on a slave ship. There are two issues here. First, Africans did not immigrate to the New World; they were forcibly brought in. Second, usually African slaves did not have clothes on their backs when they landed, let alone trinkets and knickknacks.

Like "Beulah" from the 1950s, the mammy in "Gimme a Break" lacked sex appeal, was unquestioning of her servant's role, put her own life on hold as she fretted about the problems of her white employers, and was inconceivable as a system fighter who would want more for African-American children than she had. Despite the fact that "Gimme a Break" continued the tradition for black females in the mass media, the 1980s saw a major advance for the African-American female presence on prime-time network television. The question arises, Would Cosby's show, and the spinoffs and imitations that followed, free white, male decisionmakers, making them more inclined toward inclusion of African-American women in network programming? Extraordinarily talented black women could help develop realistic portrayals of black culture in entertaining, creative ways. Moreover, most Americans would not be content with more of "Gimme a Break," as much as they recognized the multitalents of the star in the series. After seeing Allen and Rashad, they could justifiably sense that others like these talented African-American women waited in the wings for an opportunity to perform with equal skill and vigor.

References

Allen, Richard L., and David E. Clark. 1980. "Ethnicity and Mass Media Behavior: A Study of Blacks and Latinos." *Journal of Broadcasting* 24 (Winter).
Arlen, Michael J. 1976. *The View from Highway 1: Essays on Television.* New York: Farrar, Strauss, & Giroux.

Block, Carl E. 1970. "Communicating with the Urban Poor: An Exploratory Inquiry." *Journalism Quarterly* 47 (Spring).

Bogle, Donald. 1973. *Toms, Coons, Mulattoes, Mammies, and Bucks: An Interpretive History of Blacks in American Film*. New York: Viking.

Brooks, Tim, and Earle Marsh. 1979. *The Directory to Primetime Network T.V. Shows: 1946 to Present*. New York: Ballantine Books.

Cripps, Thomas. 1975. "The Noble Black Savage." *Journal of Popular Culture* 8 (Spring).

Fife, Marilyn. 1974. "Black Images in American T.V.: The First Two Decades." *Black Scholar* 6 (November).

Gitlin, Todd. 1982. "Prime Time Ideology: The Hegemonic Process in Television Entertainment." In Horace Newcomb, ed., *Television: The Critical View*. 3d ed. New York: Oxford University Press.

MacDonald, Fred J. 1983. *Blacks and White T.V.* Chicago: Nelson Hall.

Moore, Melvin. 1980. "Black Face in Prime Time." In Bernard Rubin, ed., *Small Voices and Great Trumpets: Minorities and the Media*. New York: Praeger.

Staples, Robert. 1977. "Roots: Melodrama of the Black Experience—Forum: A Symposium on Roots." *Black Scholar* 88 (May).

Stroman, Carolyn A., and Lee B. Becker. 1978. "Racial Differences in Gratification." *Journalism Quarterly* 55 (Autumn).

Tyson, Cicely. 1973. Interview. "North Star" Television Series, WBAL-TV. February.

Watkins, Mel. 1981. "Beyond the Pale." *Channels* (April–May).

COLOR THE NEWS ACCURATELY

Trace Regan

Trace Regan teaches journalism at Ohio Wesleyan University.

Reprinted from *The Quill*, 72:11, December, 1984. Used by permission.

Can black reporters make a conscious attempt to enhance or protect the image of the black community without compromising their integrity as journalists? The question has dominated recent meetings of black journalists. At one such event, a Chicago regional meeting of the National Association of Black Journalists, a lawyer, making an analogy to his relationship with his clients, asked if black journalists couldn't ignore unfavorable news about blacks and go only with news that aided black "liberation." An advertising executive wanted to know if black journalists could "doctor" the news to create positive black images.

Much of the sentiment expressed by the nonjournalists at this conference reflects the thinking of many blacks in general. Some believe that black reporters should never report anything negative about black people. They say that would be disharmonious for a group fighting pervasive racism. For them, the question about journalistic integrity is irrelevant. Ethnic loyalty is the only thing that matters. And any black-on-black reporting that fails to promote such loyalty may even be seen by a few as traitorous.

I am black, and I was a broadcast journalist for nine years. I have argued frequently that, for several reasons, it would hurt the black community if black journalists refused to report stories critical of black leaders.

My point is that black journalists can do stories that are critical of black leaders or aspects of black life and still serve as guardians of the image of the black community. What's more, black journalists—indeed, all journalists—can do this without compromising their integrity as journalists.

By protecting the image of blacks in the news media, I mean making a conscious attempt to avoid unnecessary negative portrayals of blacks and to oppose such portrayals in the work of colleagues. And, consistent with journalistic principles, I also mean making an attempt to enhance the image of blacks.

Say you're doing a TV story that calls for interviewing a doctor. You deliberately select a black doctor whose expertise matches that of any white doctor who would have been randomly selected. So *who* the doctor is, is a nonsubstantive element in your story. You will report the story as you would have had the doctor been white. No difference in substance. But now, you can also project a positive black image at the same time.

In fact, working black experts into stories like this serves the *whole* community. The cumulative effect can help fight stereotypes, help impressionable youngsters to see people as individuals, not as racial groups.

I'm not talking about employing a heavy journalistic hand—one that advocates. That's not the balanced journalism that reporters should strive for.

Finding positive and newsworthy stories about blacks is, of course, another way of portraying blacks favorably. And black TV reporters can also serve as positive role models by comporting themselves well, on and off the air.

Black journalists could also be just as effective in serving the black community by avoiding unnecessary negative depictions of blacks, particularly when these portraits provide fodder for racists.

Say you're doing a story about a cutback in a welfare program, and you want to humanize it. So you decide to profile a family that would be hurt by the cutback. I would suggest selecting a white family more often than not. This would not be a sinister decision (there are more whites than blacks on welfare). It would not hurt whites. You would not be reinforcing a racist notion that whites are, say, lazy. That stereotype doesn't exist about whites.

But unfortunately, it does exist about blacks. And profiling black families in story after story like this would nourish that stereotype about blacks.

I'm not suggesting that reporters, as a general policy, should ignore the fact that blacks are on welfare (or, when relevant, that blacks are disproportionately represented on welfare rolls). That would foster an inaccurate perception of who welfare clients are. And accuracy is essential to a reporter's credibility. But reporters shouldn't fly off in the other direction either. They should resist any knee-jerk tendency always to run to minorities who are poor for soundbites in stories like this.

Black journalists, particularly those in positions of some authority, should check the work of white colleagues (black colleagues, too, for that matter) to see that stories about blacks don't inadvertently insult the black community.

For example, reporters should not write about blacks in a stereotypical way. A reporter shouldn't point out that a black newsmaker drives a Cadillac when the reporter wouldn't do that if that newsmaker were white.

Screen the artwork and pictures of blacks. Unnecessarily offensive images ought to be rejected.

Also, broadcast journalists should consider carefully the use of file tape that shows blacks in an unfavorable light. In selecting generic video for a story on the latest crime statistics, don't always show, for example, blacks in prison. Make an effort to find appropriate video of whites, too. *Think* about the images that are projected.

Undoubtedly, some will disagree with my position and may even dismiss me as a "booster journalist." They will argue that I favor "orchestrating" the news and point out that the very idea of trying to aid some particular group is bad journalism. That good journalism is about serving the public good, period, and not some segment of the public.

I think the violation of journalistic principles that some may see in these recommendations is conceptually attractive but pragmatically false.

I don't believe that journalists should duck newsworthy issues or in any way alter the substance of the stories they report or "tone down" relevant information, no matter whom it embarrasses. What I have suggested embraces the ideals of journalism and, I think, simply allows a reporter to make changes in the non-substantive elements of a story to minimize any effect that might sustain racism.

I do agree, however, that if journalists aren't careful in serving in the guardianship role I recommend, they can come dangerously close to transforming themselves from reporters into publicists, which would not help the black community or the general public. But I don't think anything I've suggested crosses that fine line.

The task for journalists, then, is to be conscious of their obligation to serve the public good; and in doing that, to know what a news story is, what its focus ought to be, what it should include, and how it should be presented. That's what good news judgment is all about. If reporters assumed this guardianship role and exercised good news judgment, their integrity as journalists would always remain intact. And they would serve the public good in more ways than one.

SEXISM AND THE MEDIA

Tina Pieraccini

Tina Pieraccini is an associate professor of communication studies at the State University of New York College at Oswego, where she has taught courses in broadcasting, public relations, and communication since 1976. Prior to that she taught public speaking at the University of Rhode Island. Pieraccini earned her B.A. in speech from the University of Rhode Island and her M.A. in mass communication from the University of Massachusetts at Amherst.

> The portrayal of women in the media has often been one of exaggeration, distortion and intended ambiguities.
> —Dal Dearmin, 1986

Because of its pervasiveness in our society, the media exerts an important influence on our attitudes, values, and behaviors. The image of women as portrayed in the media deserves serious consideration, then, because the way women are presented in the media can be an important factor in shaping the next generation's attitudes and behavior toward women.

The image of women in the media has changed over the last thirty years. In the 1950s, when most women stayed home, the media showed them searching for better ways to do laundry and seeking improved formulas for shiny hair. Women's roles were limited to that of wife and mother, and women were seen almost exclusively in domestic settings.

In the 1960s women began to emerge from the home. A popular cigarette ad campaign observed that women had "come a long way." Critics questioned just how far women had really come, though, since the ads also referred to them as "baby." Throughout the 1960s, the image of the new woman shifted from homemaker to sex object. In addition, women in the role of victims of crime and violence increased as the decade progressed.

In the 1970s the media portrayed women who could do it all. They were depicted as juggling career and home and succeeding at every challenge as the Superwoman hit the airwaves and magazine pages. In actuality, career women with families were struggling with difficult conflicts between home and career. The media sold guilt as effectively as it sold perfume.

The 1980s have given birth to the Media Professional Woman. In the beginning of the decade, she was the competitive, aggressive, independent executive. But by the mid-1980s, she has begun to soften. Now she is the Feminine Feminist. She has career, family, and friends, and, like the super-woman of the 1970s, she can do it all.

Whatever the image, women continue to be seen in stereotypical roles in the media. An understanding of this is important, because media images are important sources of behavior to be modeled. In fact, to a certain degree, the media establish the standards for social behavior. George Gerbner has developed an index used to determine television's effect on the perception of women by viewers. He concluded that viewers' degree of sexism increased with the amount of time spent watching television. His studies determined that there is a strong correlation between the image of women on television and their position in the minds of viewers. Further, studies involving children have concluded that the more television a child watches, the more sex typed he or she becomes (Liebert 1982). While there is no certain way to determine exactly how much of what one sees, reads, or hears via the media is transferred into measurable behavior, it is important for us to realize that the media shape and reinforce values and perspectives.

Two particular criticisms have been levelled against the media for their portrayal of women. The first concerns the *underrepresentation* of women in the media: that is, women are frequently omitted from media depictions. The second concerns the *misrepresentation* of women in the media: that is, a distorted view of women is often presented. To illustrate these and other concerns about women in the media, I will analyze three areas: television entertainment, television news, and advertising in order to determine which images are projected and what messages we receive from the media about women.

TV Entertainment

> Marriage, romance, and family are women's concerns in the world
> of television.
> —Gerbner and Signorelli, 1979

In programs first seen in the 1950s (and then in syndication for later generations), the most prevalent image of women was that of wife, mother, and homemaker. The variation was seen in the effective, skilled, competent wife, mother, and homemaker versus the ineffective, unskilled, incompetent wife, mother, and homemaker.

First consider the effective wives. The dutiful homemakers were always perfectly groomed, wearing perfectly ironed aprons, showing no signs of stress and no aspirations to escape life in the kitchen. Their dust-free homes were the center of their self-concepts, while strong, omnipotent partriarchs ruled the family.

"The Adventures of Ozzie and Harriet," for example, brought this image of the typical middle-class family into television homes from 1952 to 1966. The nuclear family was the focal point of the plots, as the two sons, and their parents, experienced the vicissitudes of growing up.

In 1954 "Father Knows Best" joined the lineup, presenting the classic wholesome family, the Andersons: Mom, Dad, and three children. They, too, experienced the problems of growing up with everything working out in thirty minutes and, as the title suggested, with Dad's advice and wisdom.

"Leave It to Beaver" introduced the Cleaver family in 1957, bringing family comedy to the screen through the pranks of two siblings, Wally and Beaver. Their parents were typical, nice, and middle class. Mom was seen most often in the kitchen, while Dad assumed the familiar role of helping his sons grow up by providing wise advice and counseling.

In "The Donna Reed Show," introduced in 1958, the typical all-American family was personified by the Stone family, featuring Mom, Dad, and two teenagers. The plots and adventures were similar to those of the Nelsons, the Cleavers, and the Andersons, and Mom was always there—usually in the kitchen.

In contrast, consider the ineffective, unskilled wives. They were portrayed as silly, dizzy, often stupid, and always getting into trouble. "I Love Lucy" led the parade of scatterbrain housewives when it first aired in 1951. Unlike the dutiful wives, Lucy longed for a career in show business, much to the dismay of husband bandleader Ricky Ricardo. Most plots saw Lucy devise a scheme, get into trouble, and return home after being rescued by Ricky. The program ran until 1957 in original episodes, but has continued in syndication throughout the world. Another example of this stereotype was "The George Burns and Gracie Allen Show," which ran for eight years perpetuating the myth that women are simpleminded and unable to think or handle everyday situations without the aid of a husband.

Prime time in the 1960s saw a gradual emergence of women from the kitchen to the bedroom. By today's television standards, the sexual emphasis was mild, but the implications and stereotypes were abundant, and set the basis of sexual overtones and sexist undertones that continue to this day. "The Dick Van Dyke Show," which premiered in 1961, featured Mary Tyler Moore as Laura Petrie, the devoted wife and mother who had given up her career as a dancer when she married Rob, the head writer for a TV comedy show. Most episodes revolved around Rob's work setting. Laura was a dutiful wife and loving mother.

The unique family the Clampetts were introduced in 1962 on "The Beverly Hillbillies." The story revolved around a family from the hills of Tennessee who strike oil and head to Beverly Hills. The only sane, clear-thinking member of the clan was the strong patriarch, Jed. Elly May, the daughter, was scantily clad each week as the program soared in the ratings.

Fantasy emerged as the basis for comedy in two shows of the decade. "Bewitched," which aired in 1964, starred Elizabeth Montgomery as a good witch named Samantha who was married to a mortal who did not condone his wife's use of witchcraft, the basis of the plots. As a dutiful wife, Samantha denied who she was to please her husband. And in another fantasy-based situation comedy, Barbara Eden perpetuated the myth of woman as slave to her male master in "I Dream of Jeannie," which aired from 1965 to 1970. In the pilot episode, Major Tony Nelson, played by Larry Hagman, finds an antique bottle, which houses a genie (Eden), who pledges to please her master forever. But her magical powers, like Samantha's, were a constant source of disagreement to her master. It is interesting to note that her rather skimpy genie outfit, mild by today's standards, was quite a concern of network programmers at the time.

In 1966 Marlo Thomas was introduced as "That Girl," who, like Lucy before her, dreamed of a career in show business. But unlike Lucy and most other women on television to this point, she was single. The depiction of her relationship with boyfriend Donald was guarded—they were in a permanent state of abstention, and kissing took place at the front door only.

The late 1960s saw a wave of crime and police action-adventure programs, including "Hawaii Five O," "It Takes a Thief," and "Felony Squad," which presented women as victims of violent crimes, a theme that would continue throughout the 1970s with such programs as "Starsky & Hutch," "Baretta," and "Police Story."

Television entertainment in the 1970s felt the influence of the women's movement, and of producer Norman Lear, who set the tone for realistic programs. Although most of the depictions of women throughout the 1970s were stereotypical, some situations were reflective, if not accepting, of women's changing roles. Consider Lear's classic, "All in the Family." Archie Bunker was clearly and blatantly a bigot. Some identified with him, while others perceived his discriminatory remarks as exaggeration to exemplify absurdity. While wife Edith represented the submissive, subservient wife of earlier decades, her daughter Gloria represented the new woman, who could think for herself, often disagreed with her husband on issues, and wanted more for herself than home and kitchen.

The number of single, professional women increased in television programming during the 1970s. The most memorable representation was by Mary Tyler Moore as Mary Richards on "The Mary Tyler Moore Show." Mary was an independent career woman whose life did not revolve around men, though the supporting cast shouted stereotype from the egomaniac anchorman to his dizzy blonde wife. And note should be made that while everyone else in the newsroom called the boss "Lou," Mary always referred to him as "Mr. Grant."

Other single women represented on the airwaves included "Rhoda," a Mary Tyler Moore spinoff, and Ann Romano on "One Day at a Time" as a divorcee, a first for network television in 1975. Ms. Romano, as she preferred to be addressed on the show, was the first of a series of displaced homemakers—perhaps a stereotype but nonetheless reflective of a rise in divorce and changing norms of family life.

Following the lead of Ann Romano was Alice Hyatt, a widow with a son to raise on her own on "Alice." The program showed the problems of single parenting amid a comical array of stereotypical characters at Mel's Diner. Alice was the most common depiction of the displaced homemaker. She survives despite lack of skills, education, or training as a waitress, but remains trapped in a job with no future for the rest of her life.

Sex continued to dominate TV programs into the late 1970s, and also began to replace the violence more prevalent in the 1960s. Programs such as "Three's Company," "Laverne and Shirley," and "Charlie's Angels" played on the singles theme and life-style. The adage that "sex sells" was evident: cleavage became commonplace on prime time as women were seen in a perpetual state of half-dress.

One highlight of the 1970s was the critically acclaimed "M*A*S*H". The program featured a woman as a total person in the character of Margaret Hullahan. She was seen as head nurse, friend, and lover, as strong, vulnerable, caring, and tough. And although in early episodes she was seen in her "Hot Lips" role, the character seemed to grow parallel to and reflect the women's movement of the decade.

The 1980s witnessed the rise of prime-time soap operas. "Dallas" led the parade when it premiered in 1978. Women were exploited on "Dallas" and on those that followed—"Dynasty," "Knots Landing," and "The Colbys." The evening soaps featured scene after scene in the bedroom and depicted women as scheming, manipulative, and submissive to men—especially rich, powerful men. The plots were as trite as the values of the characters. Women seemed to value clothes, jewelry, and furs above all else. There was one positive note, however—the trend to feature a strong matriarch as family head rather than the traditional patriarch.

The 1980s did see some improvements in network programming. In 1984 the National Commission on Working Women applauded that television season for increasing leading roles for women and cited more diverse roles as well. With one exception, every new program introduced to the television viewing audience in 1984 featured female characters. "Kate and Allie," a situation comedy about two displaced homemakers with three children between them all living under one roof, dealt with the problems and issues of single parenting with sensitivity and without sexual overtones. And rather than depicting women in competition with each other, they were shown as two caring friends who existed in cooperation with each other. Other highlights of the early 1980s included the return of "Cagney and Lacey," a well-done police action drama by women, starring women, and dealing with women's issues. Sharon Gless and Tyne Daley were convincing as two tough New York City cops who solve crimes with their instincts and clear-thinking minds, not with their bodies.

Another critically acclaimed program introduced in 1981 was "Hill Street Blues." Major female characters—including Veronica Hamel as lawyer Joyce Davenport—were depicted as competent and intelligent. While in the first few years of the program the character of Faye Furillo, ex-wife of central character Captain Furillo, was depicted as a displaced homemaker who could not survive without help from her former spouse, this character grew and developed as the program progressed into the mid-1980s by which time she had a job and had learned to think for herself.

Other highlights occurred in the form of made-for-TV movies and specials that presented realistic depictions of problems facing women, including abuse, divorce, and abortion. In 1983 Farrah Fawcett starred in a made-for-TV movie, "The Burning Bed," based on an actual story of an abused wife who doused her husband with gasoline and set him afire while he slept. The program not only handled the issue realistically, but many local stations ran abuse hot line numbers for women in need of counseling or other help. The response was significant.

Many of the gains of the early 1980s, unfortunately, were lost by mid-decade. The 1985 season was met with criticism from the National Commission on Working Women (NCWW), which described that year on television as "the return of the woman as victim theme in action/adventure and cop/detective shows." One especially disturbing trend that season was the lead-female-character-as-rape-victim syndrome. This season, said the NCWW, women were either "invisible, irrelevant or victimized."

One delightful highlight of the 1985 season, on a more positive note, was the introduction of "The Golden Girls," a situation comedy on NBC starring women over the age of fifty.

Current figures do point to a victory in terms of representation. For the first time in television history, the male-female ratio is fifty-fifty, and only 8 percent of women on TV entertainment programs limit themselves to traditional roles. This is more representative of the society in general, since 76 percent of women held jobs outside the home in the 1980s.

Women in Television News

> In recent years about half the contestants and several winners of the
> Miss America Pageant, when asked what they wanted to be when
> they grew up, answered, "a television anchorwoman." It's also in-
> teresting to note the great number who have gotten their wish.
> —Linda Ellerbee, 1986

From 1948 when Pauline Frederick made her television debut as the first
woman newscaster, to the late Jessica Savitch being told in 1969 by her college professor, "There's no room for broads in broadcasting," to the 1986
presentation by the International Radio and Television Society of Broadcaster
of the year to NBC's Jane Pauley, women in TV journalism have struggled to
enter the traditionally male-dominated territory of television news.

Throughout the 1950s when the women pioneers in television journalism
joined Pauline Frederick, they found themselves trapped in the soft news
camp. Frederick was assigned to interview the wives of presidential hopefuls,
and most other women in the field covered fashion, food, weather, and other
light fare. In her autobiography, *Anchorwoman,* Jessica Savitch commented
on the lack of women in the business as she grew up: "I had no role models
because there were none." The inclusion of women into television journalism
would be a slow journey.

With the exception of a succession of "Today" "girls," few women entered the field in the 1960s. The turning point would not come until 1971—
when the Federal Communications Commission announced it would require
stations to include affirmative action plans for women in their license renewal
applications. As a result, jobs for women in television journalism experienced
the largest increase of any job category from 1971 to 1977 (Singleton and
Cook 1982).

Although women were entering the field in unprecedented numbers, the
treatment they received—and their salaries—was far from equal to their male
counterparts. In 1974 when Leslie Stahl proceeded to find her place for election night coverage, she found the anchors' desks labeled "Cronkite,"
"Rather," "Wallace," and "Female." Judy Woodruff entered the field in the
early 1970s; her job required her to change the color of her hair as well as
her eyes. In 1976, Barbara Walters, after fifteen years on "Today" received
not only a coanchor offer from ABC but a million-dollar-a-year contract.
Cartoons, however, pictured her reading news in a low-cut evening gown.
Sexism was abundant in television journalism throughout the 1970s. Gains
were not achieved easily or without opposition from male colleagues.

The networks wanted female employees to be visible, and so promoted
them. They frequently appeared in magazines, on talk shows, and in commercial spots. Not surprisingly, these promotional efforts invariably focused

on beauty routines, wardrobe decisions, and personal lives rather than job-related issues. Attractiveness seemed to be the condition for employment. Linda Ellerbee, who entered the field in 1973, said in her book *And So It Goes,* "There are no ugly women in television news." Women were held back due to the common belief that a female voice had less credibility than a male voice. Studies dispelled this myth by finding no difference in the credibility of males versus females (Stone 1974), but new management did not agree.

The female journalists of the 1970s continued to cover soft news. The U.S. Commission on Civil Rights studied network news in 1974–1975 and concluded that female journalists were limited to covering stories labeled "women's interest." In 1977 a follow-up study confirmed previous findings. Another study, in 1982, found some gains, but generally women journalists reported fewer stories than males on foreign affairs, economy, and disaster. News assignments to female journalists were most often in the areas of U.S. government, the environment, and social problems. The study concluded that sexual stereotyping exists in the assignment of TV network news stories (Singleton and Cook 1982).

While the 1970s were years of adjustment for women in TV news, the 1980s have seen some positive advances for women in the field. For instance, Diane Sawyer has joined the ranks of the highly respected team of "60 Minutes" journalists. Connie Chung anchors a weekend network newscast. Barbara Walters hosts ABC's news magazine "20/20" and the White House beat is no longer male dominated. Each of the three networks has a coanchor situation on the morning news, and gone are the days of exclusive soft news assignments for women. In fact, by 1982 97 percent of all local television newsrooms had at least one woman, as compared to 57 percent in 1972 (Schultz-Brooks 1984).

There have been increases in women in management positions as well. In the mid-1970s, there were almost no female news directors. Today, *Broadcasting Magazine* reports that women are in charge of 10 percent of the television newsrooms and 18 percent of the radio newsrooms. And *TV Guide* reports that more than one-third of all news anchors and 20 percent of network reporters are women.

Issues regarding sexism in the newsroom have not disappeared; they have shifted. Looks and age have replaced hiring quotas and assignments as the most crucial areas of concern. Linda Ellerbee (1986) commented on the hiring of female journalists based on looks: "In 1985, the British Broadcasting Corporation announced it would no longer televise beauty pageants because they were demeaning to women. If that were to happen here, some future anchorwomen would have to find other ways to audition."

The issue of attractiveness became national news in 1981 when KMBC in Kansas City, on the advice of news consultants, demoted anchor Christine Craft because she was, according to the consulting firm's report, "too unattractive, too old [she was thirty-eight] and not deferential enough to men." Craft filed a sex discrimination charge and was awarded $500,000. Looks over ability was national news after the much-publicized trial. Women celebrated her victory, and the decision was seen as a turning point for female journalists; however, when Metromedia, owners of KMBC, filed an appeal, the decision was reversed. Craft appealed, and the case remains unresolved.

Ageism is another factor for females in TV news, although it does not seem to affect males. Dan Rather is considered young. Barbara Walters is not. Yet they are the same age. There have been some notable female survivors in the television news business, including Barbara Walters and Marlene Sanders, both over fifty; Pauline Frederick, who in 1974 retired at age sixty-five; and Dorothy Fuldheim, the first television anchorwoman, who began in 1947 and still did commentary on the air at WEWS in Cleveland past the age of ninety.

Thus, sexism in the newsroom certainly has not disappeared in the 1980s, but there have been some significant gains.

Women in Advertising

Advertisers have been attempting to win the female consumer decade after decade while perpetuating stereotype after stereotype in the process. Over the years, advertising practitioners have received much criticism from consumers, consumer groups and advocates, and feminists regarding their treatment of women.

A comparison of ads from 1958 with those in 1970 and 1972 concluded that the home and hearth stereotypes of the 1950s advertising continued into the 1970s. (Belkaovi and Belkaovi 1976). A glance at television commercials or women's magazines suggests those stereotypes continue to be reinforced, along with a few additional distortions of women's changing roles.

By now the scenario is familiar: the 1950s homemaker, the 1960s sex object, the 1970s superwoman, the 1980s career woman. It is in advertising that the stereotypes are most clear, most blatant, most exploitive. Perhaps because the advertiser has only seconds of airtime or limited print space, the image is most exaggerated and consequently most exploitive.

Throughout the 1950s and into the 1960s, the message was clear: women belonged in the home. Most advertisers portrayed women in the kitchen, cooking, cleaning and doing laundry. They also used sex to sell products. Ads of the decade treated women as sex objects. Cheesecake and nudity were frequently used techniques in the 1950s. It was not uncommon, for example, to see a sultry woman in a suggestive pose stretched across the hood of an automobile or Esther Williams selling soap in a bathing suit.

The 1960s continued with the theme that sex sells. In 1962, Cole swimsuits featured attractive models wearing the product with the slogan "Girls were made for playthings," and by 1968 even milk was being sold with a blonde wearing a bikini with the slogan, "Every Body needs milk."

The women's movement of the 1970s saw increased critical interest in these demeaning depictions of women, as the first comprehensive studies emerged. In 1970, Courtney and Lockeretz (1971) analyzed 729 advertisements that appeared in general interest magazines during one week. Their four conclusions were that: 1) women were almost always pictured in the home, 2) women do not make decisions, 3) women are dependent on men, and, 4) women are sex objects. The study, entitled "A Women's Place," also reported that 45 percent of the males in the ads were seen working outside the home, while only 9 percent of the females were. Further, of those 9 percent, 58 percent were entertainers.

In their follow-up study of ads in print publication in 1972, Belkaovi and Belkaovi found only a slight variation, with more working women being depicted. Their jobs, however, were limited in scope to traditional female jobs, including secretary and clerical positions. Also in 1972, Hennesee and Nicholson reported that, of the advertisements they had analyzed, only 3 percent of women were depicted as antonomous individuals and 40 percent of all women were seen in the home. And in 1974 Sexton and Haberman analyzed 2,000 ads from *Good Housekeeping, Look, Newsweek, Sports Illustrated,* and *TV Guide.* The results were predictable: only 16 percent of females were seen in nontraditional roles. They concluded that women were portrayed in traditional roles as seductive and ornamental.

The first organized protests aimed at specific advertisers took place in the 1970s. Many of the protests were organized by the National Organization for Women (NOW). NOW's Barefoot and Pregnant Award of the Week for Advertising Degrading to Women brought attention to some of the most offensive and sexist advertising campaigns of the decade, including the National Airlines campaign that featured attractive stewardesses saying, "I'm Karen, fly me," and all the ads for feminine hygiene sprays, which were blatantly degrading to women. *Ms. Magazine* also began to run its "No Comment" page, featuring ads considered sexist. The intent was to encourage feminists to boycott the products being pitched. One such attempt focused on the "Hit me with a Club" campaign for Heublein Club Cocktails. The implication of the women in the ads inviting physical abuse was offensive to many.

By 1979, nudity in advertising was becoming commonplace. Lily of France lingerie featured close-to-nude models in a police lineup with the slogan, "Once you've worn it, you can never plead innocent," and Cotler jean ads featured a couple embracing—she naked, he in jeans only—with the headline, "Everybody's Getting into Cotler's Pants."

In the 1980s there have been some minor improvements, but in general the stereotypes of previous decades continue, and women still are most often seen in subservient positions to men (Courtney and Whipple 1983). Certainly reflective of the tenor of advertising in the 1980s are the designer jean advertising campaigns. Almost all the ads for designer jeans play on sexual fantasy. Howard Goldstein, creator of "The Jordache Look" campaign, put it this way in the October 6, 1980, issue of *Newsweek*: "People don't buy clothes because of how they look in them, but because of how they think they look. We're selling the image." And the image shouts sex. The Jordache Look campaign, which featured models—male, female, and even children—wearing only their tight Jordache jeans, received much criticism; and those depicting children naked from the waist up were banned by several television stations.

Another designer jean advertiser who has experienced the self-censorship of television stations of some of his more suggestive ads is Calvin Klein. In 1980, when fifteen-year-old Brooke Shields suggestively sold her "Calvins," feminist groups protested. "Nothing," Shields proclaimed, "comes between me and my Calvins." Although that campaign, too, was short-lived as a result of criticism, ads for Calvin Klein jeans and other products continue to get sexier and, some claim, border on pornographic. Klein's 1985 campaign for Obsession perfume depicting nude models in a variety of lovemaking situations with multiple partners was criticized by many. Television stations refused to air the spots, but they appeared frequently in women's magazines.

Another familiar advertiser presented a fantasy theme for more than twenty years featuring women dreaming of a myriad of adventures while dressed in a Maidenform bra. One of the ads from 1963 featured a model posed on a fire truck dressed in high black boots, fire hat, and her bra, stating, "I dreamed I went to blazes in my Maidenform bra." In 1969 the fantasy theme was dropped. In the 1970s the new Maidenform woman was portrayed as a doctor, a lawyer, a stockbroker, or even a basketball referee, with a new slogan—"The Maidenform woman; you never know where she'll turn up." Since the company wanted to display its product, the models were showing up in hospitals, in courtrooms, on Wall Street, and even on the basketball court in their underwear. Women's groups were outraged. Women against Pornography gave the ad campaign its ZAP Award for sexist advertising. Since then, the Maidenform campaign has softened. The ads still display the product on models but generally in the privacy of their bedrooms.

Advertisements in the 1980s are full of psychological and sexual themes. The use of lurid dialogue, phallic symbols, and cheesecake photography is abundant. Sexual fantasies sell products. Research suggests that the use of a "sexual theme" as fantasy fulfillment is highly successful in aiding brand recall (*Advertising Age* 1983).

The attractive, alluring women in shampoo and diet soda ads, the happy couples in car and liquor ads, and the available partners in perfume and cologne ads are portrayals of consumers' fantasies and dreams. These myths regarding women are sold as effectively as the products. The consumer buys the perfume along with the advertiser's concepts of love, success, popularity, and sexuality. Consider the following myths perpetuated in advertising.

Myth Number One: Certain Product Use Will Result in a Happy and Fulfilling Love Life. Subtle promises are made through advertising that certain products increase sexuality—that is, increase our attractiveness to the opposite sex. Such sexual overtones are pervasive in advertising, and the images projected are demeaning to women. Ads for perfume use sex blatantly to sell, while less blatantly suggestive ads for low-calorie foods and diet drinks still make romantic promises to consumers. The message is clear: buy the product, and romance will follow. The myth presents glittering images in relation to product use.

Myth Number Two: Blondes Have More Fun. Media sex symbols are abundant, and it is no coincidence that so many of the top stars and models, and even newswomen, are blondes. Advertisers have been selling American women the blonde myth for decades, from the 1960 Clairol campaign, "If I've only one life to live, let me live it as a blonde," to later campaigns such as the "Is it true blondes have more fun?" series. Loreal ads featuring blonde models are frequently seen today, claiming "I'm worth it." Again the message is clear: Become a blonde, and your dreams will come true.

Myth Number Three: Women Must Be Thin. The media have sold us the concept that thin is in. In the process, ads are teaching adolescents and younger children that they must be thin—at any cost. The result is that anorexia nervosa has become all too common among teenage women. Ads for diet sodas, diet meals, diet plans, diet books, and even diet candy are seen throughout magazines amid the pencil-thin models. It is no wonder we have become so weight conscious. One diet candy ad summed up the myth: "Lose weight and be happy by eating candy."

Myth Number Four: Women Must Remain Youthful. Advertisers have sold us the myth that women must not age. When they do use a model over the age of forty, she looks younger. Ads for skin care products continue to sell claims such as "look younger, control the signs of aging, hide the wrinkles." The message is clear: youth is of utmost importance.

Myth Number Five: Women Are Submissive and Accept Violence. Often men are depicted in positions of dominance and control over women in ads. A particularly disturbing area in the juxtapositioning of sex and violence in the media, creating sexual confusion. A recent Calvin Klein ad depicted a woman in ripped jeans and a blouse torn open. She is positioned against a tree, with legs and arms spread as though she has been tied up. The scene suggests rape, but her face suggests enjoyment. Rape is made to look like sensual fantasy, not sexual violence. Research indicates that men are desensitized to violence against women in a sexual context (Donnerstein 1980). The media contribute to the confusion and support the myth that women accept violence. This new brand of advertising combines sadomasochism with violence. The themes of bondage often projected in advertising are disturbing. *Advertising Age* in October 1983 admonished many of the jeans advertisers for their use of the bondage theme.

Myth Number Six: Sex Sells.   Sex sells, but David Ogilvy suggests not always (Ogilvy 1985). Ogilvy says the ads must show some relevance to sex if sex is used to sell. For example, he claims sex will sell perfume or lingerie, but not floor wax or cat food.

Sex will almost always get attention but will not always result in brand recall or purchase completion. "You will get the consumer to look at the ad but not necessarily to buy it," says Dal Dearmin, a vice-president with the advertising firm of Ingalls, Quinn & Johnson. In fact, some practitioners feel too much sex will distract the consumer so much that he or she will forget what is being advertised. Alexander and Judd (1978) concur that nudity in advertising does not improve brand recall. For male subjects in particular, nudity can be too distracting to be successful.

In general, a sexual strategy will be successful when it is relevant to the product being pitched. In 1981, Paco Rabonne cologne launched its rather risqué campaign featuring a man in a bed who gets up to answer the telephone. Suggestive dialogue follows. She says, "You snore." He says, "And you steal all the covers; what time did you leave?" Sales for the cologne went up 25 percent.

Some advertisers are showing signs of softening. Attention to wording and gender is becoming apparent. Women in prestigious jobs are depicted. Men are seen in the kitchen caring for families. But these positive depictions are not the norm. Sexism has not disappeared from the media, nor are there any signs that it will during the remainder of this decade. Indeed, it appears that the mirror being held up in the media through television entertainment, through television news, and through advertising is distorting the images of women it claims to represent.

References

Advertising Age. 1983. May 5.

Alexander, W., and B. Judd. 1978. "Do Nudes for Ads Enhance Brand Recall?" *Journal of Advertising Research* 18 (February): 47–50.

Alter, J. 1985. "TV Women: Give Us Some Time." *Newsweek*, July 22.

Anderson, D. 1981. "My Side." *Working Women* (April).

Bartos, Rena. 1982. *The Moving Target.* New York: Free Press.

Belkaovi A., and J. Belkaovi. 1976. "A Comparative Analysis of the Roles Portrayed by Women in Print Ads." *Journal of Marketing Research* 13 (May): 168–172.

Bosworth, P. 1985. "Diane Sawyer Makes News." *Ladies Home Journal* (February).

Brooks, Tim, and Earle Marsh. 1981. *The Complete Directory to Prime Time Network TV Shows, 1946–Present.* New York: Ballantine Books.

Courtney, Alice, and Thomas Whipple. 1983. *Sex Stereotyping in Advertising.* Lexington, Mass.: Lexington Books.

Courtney A., and S. Lockeretz. 1971. "A Woman's Place: An Analysis of the Roles Portrayed by Women in Magazine Advertising," *Journal of Marketing Research* 8 (February): 92–95.

Craft, C. 1983. "The Marketing of Television News." *Ms Magazine* (November).

Dearmin, Dal. 1986. Interview, Boston, Massachusetts, July 12.

Donnerstein, E. 1980. "Aggressive Erotica and Violence against Women." *Journal of Personality and Social Psychology* 39:269–277.

Ellerbee, Linda. 1986. *And So It Goes—Adventures in Television.* New York: Putnam Sons.

Entan, Robert, and David Paletz. 1981. *Media Power Politics.* New York: Macmillan.

Foltz, K. 1985. "A Kinky New Calvinism." *Newsweek,* March 11.

Frons, M. 1980. "The Jeaning of America." *Newsweek,* October 6.

Gerbner, George, and N. Signorelli. 1979. "Women and Minorities in Television Drama, 1968—1978." Research report. Annenberg School of Communication, University of Pennsylvania.

Gross, M. 1985. "Sex Sells." *Saturday Review* (July–August).

Harrison, B. 1985. "Barbara Walters, Survivor." *McCalls* (January).

Hartman, T., and D. Richmond. 1982. "Sex Appeal in Advertising." *Journal of Advertising Research* 22 (October–November):53–61.

Hennessee, J., and J. Nicholson. 1972. "NOW Says: Commercials Insult Women." *New York Times Magazine* (May 28).

Liebert, Robet, et al. 1982. *The Early Window.* New York: Pergamon Press.

Marin, Alan. 1980. *50 Years of Advertising as Seen Through the Eyes of Advertising Age.* Illinois: Crain Communications.

Matusow, Barbara. 1983. *The Evening Stars.* New York: Ballantine Books.

Meehan, Diana. 1983. *Ladies of the Evening.* New Jersey: Scarecrow Press.

Metz, Robert. 1977. *The Today Show: An Inside Look at 25 Tumultuous Years.* Chicago: Playhouse Press.

Millum, Trevor. 1975. *Images of Women.* New Jersey: Rowman and Littlefield.

Moyer, D. 1983. "Breaches of Bad Taste Label Some Overseas Jeans Ads." *Advertising Age,* October 3, p. M40.

Ogilvy, David. 1983. *Ogilvy on Advertising.* New York: Crown Publishers.

Quinn, Sally. 1975. *We're Going to Make You a Star.* New York: Simon and Schuster.

Savitch, Jessica. 1982. *Anchorwoman.* New York: Putnam Sons.

Schultz-Brooks, T. 1984. "Is the News Business Being Fair to Women?" *Working Women* 9 (December):119–122.

Schwartz, Tony. 1974. *The Responsive Chord.* Garden City, N.Y.: Doubleday.

Sexton, Donald, and P. Haberman. 1974. "Women in Magazine Advertisements." *Journal of Advertising Research* 14 (August):41–46.

Singleton, L., and S. Cook. 1982. "Television Network News Reporting by Female Correspondents: An Update." *Journal of Broadcasting* 26:1 (Winter).

Stone, V. 1974. "Attitudes toward Television Newswomen." *Journal of Broadcasting* 18 (Winter).

Thomas, M. 1984. "Changing Sexual Attitudes towards Women Reflect Themselves in TV." *TV Guide*, May 2.

U.S. Commission on Civil Rights. 1977. *Window Dressing on the Set: Women and Minorities in Television.*

———. 1979. *Window Dressing on the Set: An Update.*

Wilson, J. 1984. "Are Newswomen Changing the News?" *Ms Magazine* (December).

Yovovich, B. 1983. "Sex in Advertising—The Power and the Perils." *Advertising Age* 54 (May 2):M4–5.

MYTHOGYNY

Caryl Rivers

Caryl Rivers is professor of journalism and director of the science communication program at Boston University. She is a novelist and coauthor of *Lifeprints: New Patterns of Love and Work for Today's Women.*

The Quill 73:5 (May 1985). Reprinted by permission of the publisher, from *When Information Counts,* edited by Bernard Rubin (Lexington, Mass.: Lexington Books, D.C. Heath and Company, Copyright 1985, D.C. Heath and Company).

The image of women in the media is more often than not strangely contorted. Much of what the media present as "objective fact" about women is in truth a mishmash of myth and misinformation. This is little changed from the days before the women's movement. Behind the headlines on such contemporary staple stories as sex and the brain, premenstrual syndrome, math genes, and stress and "superwomen" boils a steaming cauldron of mythology, of which few of the journalists who write these stories are aware.

As Elizabeth Janeway points out so incisively in *Man's World, Woman's Place,* every society invents myths about itself and then proceeds to act on those myths as if they were fact. Mythmakers are usually small, powerful, elite groups—referendums are not held on popular mythology. In time, myth becomes indistinguishable from truth. Plato's cave dwellers, inhabiting a world of darkness, saw their shadows dancing on the wall in the firelight and thought it was the shadows that were real.

The people who can learn to manipulate social mythology are powerful indeed. One of the great inventions of the twentieth century was the studied, methodical engineering of myth for political ends. Aryan supremacy is an absurdity, but it still managed to plunge the entire world into war and madness.

More often than not, the mythology that operates where women are concerned is of the unconscious rather than the programmed variety. One of these myths with roots deep in history is the myth of feminine weakness. Women are not as rational, as stable, as competent, as logical as men. (Thus, they are not to be trusted.)

In the nineteenth century, the conventional wisdom of the medical profession was that the brain and the reproductive organs could not develop at the same time. Women were to be kept away from rigorous intellectual activity to protect their ability to function as wives and mothers. Does this sound dated, old hat? Indeed. But its residue can be found in intriguing places.

For example, Theodore H. White, writing in 1984 in the *New York Times Magazine* about the election campaign, looks askance at the women's movement, fearing it will lead to the "balkanization" of American politics. (Translation: When anybody other than white males gets power, it's balkanization.) White says that laws are necessary to protect women against "the hazards visited upon them by nature."

Is he speaking, perchance, of the vapors? Men die, on the average, some eight years earlier than women; they are much more likely to drop dead in the prime of life with a heart attack, to die of lung cancer, to get ulcers, to drink themselves to death. But would any journalists *ever* write of "the hazards visited upon men by nature"? When it comes to hazards, both women and men have their share, though women come off a little better. But the only weakness that is perceived is the female one.

It intrigues me that any piece of "news" that seems to document female instability vaults right into the headlines. Premenstrual syndrome is a classic example. Here is a condition that, in its extreme form, affects only a tiny minority of women. Indeed, many women do experience physical symptoms before the onset of their periods, changes in mood among them. For most, it's a minor inconvenience. Most women do not go berserk, cause mayhem, or go after their lovers with butcher knives. Why, then, did this syndrome get headlines all over the globe and its own thirty minutes on "Nightline" while more devastating medical problems get barely a mention?

Because the story validates a long-cherished myth about women—they are unpredictable, crazy creatures who are prisoners of their hormones. Men, of course, never go berserk or hack up their families, pick off pedestrians from a twenty-second-story window with a rifle, abuse children, or beat up little old ladies. Will "Nightline" ever do a story on testosterone poisoning?

The myth of female weakness also lurks behind much of what passes for "objective" reporting on scientific theory. In recent years, theories of biological determinism have become chic, especially sociobiology and "genes-and-gender" science.

Sociobiologists, many of them, dismiss culture with a nod and insist that just about everything we do is programmed into our genetic structure. Harvard's E. O. Wilson suggests there may even be a gene for religion. (Different genes, one wonders, for Orthodox and Reform Jews, and for Baptists and Unitarians?)

Sociobiology's critics point out that much of this stuff is highly theoretical and simplistic; sociobiologists tend to take wild leaps in their search for a theory that wraps everything up in a neat little package. But it is not the least bit surprising, and not at all accidental, that sociobiology became so trendy.

In a time of diminishing resources, how comforting it is to have a theory that says things are the way they are because of inevitable genetic forces. Forget Head Start. Forget the ERA. Forget affirmative action. Social justice is expensive—and painful. Articles in the popular media in recent years have suggested that there are people with "criminal" genes. Don't waste money on rehabilitation. Rape and wife beating and child abuse are natural genetic adaptations—so women and children just have to relax and enjoy it.

"Genes-and-gender" science and the game I call "musical hormones" are very much in vogue these days. Take, for example, the flap over "math genes."

Two scientists at Johns Hopkins University, looking at national math testing data, found that boys did very much better than girls. This was nothing new; such results have been popping up for years. What was new was the scientists' interpretation of the data. They said that the gap was so large that it has to be due to some genetic differences, not just to culture. Headlines all around the country trumpeted that boys have better "math genes" than girls.

Critics, of course, attacked this interpretation. They found little solid evidence for such a statement, given the intense social pressure on girls to avoid math and the sciences. The Hopkins researchers cited special programs set up to help girls in math. But it is not a bit naive to expect that the existence of special programs over a relatively short time span would undo a deep cultural bias? The critics, of course, didn't get the same play in the press that the original story did. And the reference to "math genes"—as if they were fact, not disputed theory—keeps cropping up in the media. Its very persistence could mean that slowly and quietly programs to seek out and encourage talented young women in math and science will quietly choke and die, the victims of another bit of media mythology.

Sex differences sell. We are seeing a whole spate of stories about differences between male and female hormones and behavior. This is new, very complex research, and there is great debate among scientists about the findings. But in the headlines, speculation becomes fact, theory becomes gee-whiz prose. As science writer Barbara Beckwith points out in her research on genes-and-gender science, this genre has been grist for the mill of a whole range of magazines, from *Science* to *Cosmopolitan*. (Pack journalism being what it is, one cover story begets another faster than two bunnies in heat.) Most of the stories give short shrift to critics who say that connections between hormones and genes and behavior are tentative, and much of the speculation may turn out to be eyewash—just like the "science" of measuring the brain to discover which ethnic and racial groups are smarter.

Oversimplification abounds in much of the coverage. One newspaper headline announced that brain differences were the reason there were few female geniuses. The article, about left-brain/right-brain differences, never gave the reader the notion that there might be some other historical reason for the dearth of female genius. The fact that in the first two centuries of the Republic women were not permitted through the doors of universities might have had some slight impact on their intellectual accomplishments.

Gee-whiz science stories tend to accept uncritically the latest—and most chic—authority the reporter has interviewed. An example comes from the *Playboy* series on sex differences by Jo Durden Smith and Diane de Simone. The writers detail an interview with a scientist who speculates that females, because of brain function, may be better than males in integrating verbal and nonverbal function. She says that this may be at the root of what we call female intuition.

The writers describe leaving the interview convinced that she is right:

"'Female intuition!' says one of us as we walk outside into a bustle of students.

"'Men's difficulty with emotions!' says another. 'In the brain!'"

If these writers had been a bit more critical, they might have examined other explanations of the same phenomenon. Let's take a look at one, from another scientific discipline. Psychiatrist Jean Baker Miller (*Towards a New Psychology of Women*) suggests that societies have two categories of people, the dominants and the subordinates, who behave in different ways. Dominants are powerful, and they assign to themselves the jobs that are high in status and material rewards. The less valued jobs are assigned to subordinates, who are encouraged to develop a certain cluster of traits—submissiveness, dependency, passivity. Subordinates quickly learn how to use this behavior for protective cover. Blacks often had to learn the shuffle and the "Yassuh, Boss" to survive. Women got very good at the Dumb Blonde and Clinging Vine routines. Subordinate groups, unable to make demands or reach openly for power, become experts at manipulation. They know much more about the dominants than vice-versa, because their survival depends on it. They become highly attuned to dominants, able to predict reactions of pleasure or displeasure.

Miller writes: "Here, I think, is where the long story of 'feminine intuition' and 'feminine wiles' begins. It seems clear that these mysterious gifts are in fact skills, developed through long practice, in reading many signals, both verbal and nonverbal."

Women, says Miller, are aware early on that they have a duty to nurture: "I must care for those who are not me." Female socialization is akin to a Ph.D. in caring. I have two teenagers—a son and a daughter. My daughter is deluged with teen magazines that tell her how to handle jealousy, friendships, her friend's feelings, her boyfriend's feeling, breaking up, making up—she is being schooled to manage emotions. My son gets absolutely no such advice from society. Boys grow up expecting women will manage emotions for them. No wonder they aren't very good at it.

So—it is hormones or training that accounts for behavior? The truth of the matter is that human behavior is a very complex affair, a tangle of biology and environment that is extremely difficult to sort out. To understand it, one must be able to examine elaborate sets of forces, acting in concert. The "reductionism" that often operates in the sciences makes this nearly impossible. It's like saying a car runs because of the spark plugs, and then looking very intently at the spark plugs. You wind up knowing a lot about plugs, but not a lot about the engine. And gee-whiz science writing often falls prey to this fallacy.

It's important for women to understand all this, because of the absolutely dismal history of the interaction between biological determinism and politics. It's a truism that biological theories of differences between the sexes and races are inevitably used against the group that doesn't have political power. Harvard biologist Jon Beckwith sees a chilling parallel between today's "genes-and-gender" fad and the popularization of the "science" of eugenics early in the century. Popular science journals then ran such articles as "A Study of Jewish Psychopathy" and "The Racial Element in National Vitality," promoting the idea that social behavior was inherited. The *Saturday Evening Post* took up the cudgel as well, with the result that there developed popular support for sterilization and miscegenation laws, and immigration laws that discriminated against Slavs, Jews, Southern Europeans, and other groups.

The "genes-and-gender" stories of today often are very slick; the bias is buried in jargon and pseudo-science. But they can indeed build popular support for slowing the drive for equality between the races and the sexes. For example, an *Education Digest* article, citing brain research, proposes setting up different learning sequences for boys and girls to "allow for their separate predispositions." If that happens, guess who's going to get the good stuff and who's going to get the *drek*. Separate but equal? Ho, ho, ho!

Many of the genes-and-gender articles appear, on the surface, to be somewhat even-handed, since they seem to be saying that both boys and girls get a share of "good genes." Boys are good at math; girls are good at verbal skills and communication. This, they say, is the decree of nature, and will always remain so.

Well, then, shouldn't we expect some action? Certainly, women, with their marvelous intuition and their ability to communicate, will immediately be appointed to most ambassadorial posts. Surely they will get the lion's share of editing and writing jobs. They will be made tenured professors of literature. They will be made managers in major corporations, where their ability to communicate will doubtless boost productivity.

Don't hold your breath. Women will keep on getting the low-paid jobs in the day-care center, in the elementary school and the typing pool—unless the drive for equal opportunity is kept in high gear. Remember, this is a society that hasn't even been able to pass the ERA. Women had better be on guard; they could be talked out of the rights they've won the hard way by people who say they haven't got the right genes, or hormones, or the right structure in the brain.

One thing we do know is that social change *does* change behavior. It didn't take thousands of years of genetic change to end slavery. It took an act of law. The quantum leap in performance displayed by American women in the 1984 Olympics came not as a result of any change in hormones, but from Title IX of the Elementary and Secondary Education Act, which insisted that money and resources be allocated to women's athletic programs. In the early 1900s, the "criminal class" was overwhelmingly white, often Irish, Jewish, Slavic. Now it's largely black, Hispanic, or other minority. Was there a sudden genetic change among Jews, Irishmen, and Slavs? No. They just moved up and out of poverty, to be replaced by newer groups at the low end of the totem pole. Social justice doesn't have to wait for evolution.

The myth of female weakness, as we've seen, can be a powerful force in the distortion of reality. There's another, nearly as potent: the myth of female strength. (Illogical? Mythology doesn't operate by the rules of logic.)

Rooted deep in our culture is the notion that if women obtain political power, the world will go to hell in a handcart. Not only will the world go awry if women have power, says the myth, but women themselves will suffer. This bogeyman runs through the women-and-stress stories that are popping up in the media like mushrooms these days. The advice in them is seductive, because it seems so sympathetic: "You poor dear, we don't want to see you harmed!" The scent of crocodile tears is overwhelming.

The message being beamed to women is that if they set their sights too high, they will start having heart attacks, develop ulcers, and hound themselves into early graves.

It's interesting to see that these warnings are almost always aimed at women heading for high-prestige jobs. How often do you see a headline that says "Watch Out for the Typing Pool! It's a Killer!" Not often. But it may be the truth.

The Framingham Heart Study shows that working women do not show increasing coronary symptoms, with one exception: women in low-level clerical and secretarial jobs. And a major study by Columbia University's Robert Karasek, an industrial engineer, shows that lack of decision-making power is a factor in coronary risk. The truly lethal combination, his study shows, is high psychological demand and little decision-making power.

Karasek and his colleagues indexed jobs according to the demand-control index. Many of the jobs in the high-demand/low-control quadrant were "female ghetto" jobs—sales clerk, telephone operator, waitress, mall worker, garment stitcher. Why aren't women being warned away from these jobs? Because society needs drones, that's why. Disturbing projections on the future of the work force show that it's not in the glamor fields of high tech that the greatest number of jobs will be created but the low-paid service sector of the economy.

Another bogeyman to emerge from the myth of female strength is the new darling of the feature pages: Superwoman. She's chairman of the board, a dazzling dresser and party-giver, but she always has time to dash home and read *Winnie the Pooh* to the kiddies and whip up a batch of nutritious, non-carcinogenic Toll House cookies. It's an image that, on the surface, seems flattering. In reality, it's designed to scare "ordinary" women right down to their toes. The message underlying Superwoman stories is that a woman has to be more than a mere mortal to manage having both a career and a family. If you can't scare women away from achievement by saying it's going to make them sick, try another tack: Imply that only exceptional women can do it. And Superwoman does scare women off. When a student newspaper at Boston University did an informal poll of women students, asking whether they could manage career and family, most expressed serious doubts. These young women were ignoring the experiences of millions of real women around them—women who manage job and family but are not Superwoman—and listening to the siren song of myth.

The media inadvertently foster the Superwoman myth in stories about women with good jobs, because the emphasis is always on what such women accomplish, but not the ways they manage or the trade-offs they make. As an author, I am interviewed fairly often, and there are times when I do not recognize the disciplined, dynamic, supercharged woman on the printed page. The stories do not mention that I never remember my dentist appointments, that my office looks like the town dump, or that my children say my home-cooked meals could inspire a TV show: "That's Inedible."

But the Superwoman image just seems too sexy for the media to let go of. Recently, I was interviewed by a reporter who did an excellent story about how working women aren't Superwoman and the image is harmful to women. But what headline was stuck on the story? This one: "Those Superwomen Are Real—and Happiest!"

The myth of female strength also means that when things go wrong, women will get blamed—mothers in particular. When a woman has a child, perhaps the best thing she can do is absolutely refuse to read any newspaper or magazine article with the word *mother* in it. You can bet she's going to catch hell for something.

In the 1950s, when women stayed home dutifully and lavished their time on their children, they were blamed for destroying their kids' character. "Momism" became a national buzzword. Critics said that American POWs broke under torture in Korea because their mothers had spoiled them. (Maybe their mothers should have locked them in the closet for days on end, blindfolded, to prepare them for brainwashing.) When mothers went out to work, they were blamed for alienation, latchkey children, low SAT scores, drug abuse, teenage pregnancy, cavities, and the decline of American civilization. Mothers are the favorite scapegoats of the media. There is *no way* they can win.

We are going to see, I think, more and more in the media of biological determinism and myth-as-science. The economic picture does not seem rosy; already a mean-spiritedness seems to be rolling across the land. Many Americans want to believe that people go to soup kitchens to save money, or sleep on sidewalk grates for kicks. The time is ripe—perhaps overripe—for theories that buttress the status quo.

At the same time, information is increasingly becoming a commodity to be sold to the affluent. Magazines desperately try to purge their subscription lists of readers who are not the Yuppies advertisers adore. Best-bagel and boutique journalism spreads like a malevolent weed. Editors grow increasingly impatient with the notion of giving their upscale readers information that will make them uncomfortable. Stories about affirmative action, poverty, the mentally ill, the homeless are just not "sexy."

It's not only women, of course, who need to beware such trends—but also men who are committed to the idea of a society where social justice is not a hollow phrase. Blacks, Hispanics, gays, Orientals—all will be affected directly by social mythology. As our society becomes increasingly Hispanic and Oriental, I await the new scientific findings about these groups. Will Hispanics be found to be overly "right-brained"—perfect for playing guitars and doing the tango, but for God's sake keep them out of Harvard? Do Orientals lack "originality" genes? Maybe their SAT scores go off the scale, but everybody knows they're just great copiers.

The media are an enormously powerful force—for good or ill—in all of this. They can shift the rudder that steers us in one direction or another. But if neither the practitioners nor the consumers of journalism understand the forces to which they are subject, we are all in trouble. If they continue to believe in the illusion of "objective," value-free "news," if they can't detect the strong distorting current of mythology, we may sail our ship in directions that many of us do not wish to travel.

Index